LISTENING TO THE MUSIC THE MACHINES MAKE

LISTENING TO THE MUSIC THE MACHINES MAKE

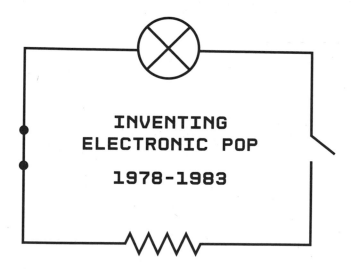

**INVENTING
ELECTRONIC POP**

1978-1983

RICHARD EVANS

OMNIBUS PRESS

London / New York / Paris / Sydney / Copenhagen / Berlin / Madrid / Tokyo

Dedicated to the memory of John Evans
1940–2002

My Dad. He introduced me to books and films and comedy but had no great interest in music. Discovering music was entirely my own adventure. Dad was always bemused by my various musical obsessions and was amazed that there was a music industry in which I was able to make a living. He would never have read this book but would have been proud that I wrote it.

ACKNOWLEDGEMENTS

In the same way that it takes a village to raise a child, it takes an army to publish a book, and I am incredibly lucky to have had an amazing cast of characters on my side throughout the writing and publication of mine.

First, I would like to thank Charlotte Robertson who introduced me to the Hamilton Agency's Matthew Hamilton, who agreed to become my agent. In turn Matthew brokered a deal with David Barraclough for Omnibus Press to become my publisher. David then introduced me to Nick Jones who so patiently edited the manuscript with an amazing eye for detail and an enviable knack for joining the dots. The team at Omnibus Press then stepped up to not only turn my words into the book you are holding right now, but also to send it into the world: David Barraclough, Claire Browne, Debra Geddes, Greg Morton, Sam Nikdel, Neal Price, Giulia Senesi and David Stock, thank you for everything.

It was important to me while writing *Listening to the Music the Machines Make* that, instead of relying on asking this cast of extraordinary characters for new recollections of events from forty years ago, I would instead revert to original source material wherever possible. That decision led to my investing a huge amount of time at the British Library, where I spent countless hours scouring the music press of the late seventies and early eighties to extract the original interviews, reviews and information which form the backbone of this book. It was largely researched and written during the pandemic of 2020 and 2021 and I am extremely grateful to the British Library for their diligence in not only re-opening their doors as soon as they were able, but also for providing such a safe and welcoming environment to work in during such difficult times.

In the cases where my research was lacking, or where I was keen to get some additional clarification on events, I was extraordinarily lucky to have access to a number of the key figures who feature in the text. In alphabetical order I am extremely grateful to Neil Arthur, Dave Ball, Andy Bell, Vince Clarke, Rusty Egan, John Foxx, Gareth Jones, Daniel Miller and Martyn Ware for making themselves available while I was writing, as well as to the many artists I have previously interviewed for This Is Not Retro, some of whom very kindly allowed me to use my time with them to answer additional questions back when this book was little more than a glimmer of an idea.

'Listening to the music the machines make' is a line from the track 'Just For A Moment' from Ultravox's 1978 album *Systems Of Romance* and I am hugely indebted to the band's John Foxx for allowing me to use his words as the title, and for his encouragement while I was getting the project off the ground. Thank you also to Steve Malins for connecting us. I am also grateful to Warren Cann and Jonas Wårstad for allowing me to quote from their conversations, and to David Buckley for his various clarifications.

I have been fortunate to work with Erasure for many years, but nevertheless I am deeply touched by Andy Bell and Vince Clarke's support of this project. A huge thank you to both of them for answering my questions; to Vince for so generously agreeing to write the foreword and to Andy for so readily agreeing to help me launch it. Thank you also to the subscribers to the Erasure Information Service for their brilliant, enthusiastic and generous support.

Writing wisdom decrees that when you're writing something it's useful to have someone in mind as the person you're writing for. For me that was Clayton Wehrle, my closest friend and partner in crime for many decades, who was the first person to read my early drafts and whose feedback and encouragement was crucial in turning this book into a reality.

And finally, there aren't really enough words to sufficiently thank my wife, Beverly, and my daughter, Arianne, for their love, patience and support. Not only did they lose me to writing for many days, weeks and months, but they were also forced to nod and smile politely when I talked about what I was doing. Thank you, I love you both. You don't have to read it, but this is for you.

INTRODUCTION

When Richard first asked me to write the forward for this book, I was well and truly chuffed. This is a fascinating, in-depth look at the music changes and innovations that occurred between 1978 and 1983, a period that – without a doubt – transformed my own personal musical beginnings and direction.

Instead of relying on the dodgy memories of the artists who were making electronic music in the late seventies and early eighties, he has largely gone back to the music press of that period, building the narrative from the original reports, reviews and interviews that we all gave back then. When Richard has needed a bit of clarification, I've tried to supply some extra information and I know that many other artists and musicians featured in this book have done the same.

Although my memories of those early days are often hazy, I do remember how it all started for me. The first single I ever bought was Sparks' 'This Town Ain't Big Enough for Both of Us', which I played until I wore it out. Music had me hooked. I loved that record and still do, and although Sparks weren't electronic as such, they did comprise of a miserable-looking bloke behind a keyboard and a flamboyant, operatic singer out front – a spectacle I'd never witnessed before.

Then I saw *The Graduate* and that got me into the music of Paul Simon. I bought the soundtrack album and the songbook and I learned to play those songs. I realised that making music, writing songs and even performing was something I could do myself. I didn't need a fancy recording studio or a major record deal to do the thing that I loved doing the most.

Finally, it was OMD who got me interested in the possibilities of electronic music. Their single 'Electricity' and particularly its B-side, 'Almost' was like the 'folky' music I'd been listening to, but created with a completely new and original sound palette. Here was something that I could relate to, a style I could explore, a world with endless possibilities.

These were some of my personal influences, but everyone brought their own thing into their music then. Punk, glam rock, disco… you can hear all of those things in the sound of lots of the bands in this book. We all started influencing each other, we all got better at what we were doing, and the technology kept developing. These were transformational times and what made it exciting was that a lot of artists, like myself, were just making it all up as we went along.

Vince Clarke, New York, 2022

CONTENTS

INSPIRATION

1977

'We certainly didn't design the instrument with the idea that a guy with no musical training would use it. We always hoped and planned that it would be used by decent musicians. The keyboard was an afterthought. That was one convenient way of controlling it, switching it on and off and changing the pitch. The Minimoog was conceived originally as a session musician's axe, something a guy could carry to the studio, do a gig and walk out. We thought we'd sell maybe 100 of them.'

Robert Moog

IT'S AN INESCAPABLE IRONY that this tale of electronic revolution begins, if it can be said to begin anywhere, with a blue acoustic guitar. The blue acoustic guitar that filled the screens of millions of television sets as *Top of the Pops* beamed across the nation on the night of July 6th, 1972. That evening's TV audience had already been treated to performances from The Who and Lulu, and next it was the turn of David Bowie, performing his latest single, 'Starman'. Bowie's elegant hand, starkly white against the blue of the guitar, strummed the song's opening notes and the image crossfaded into mainstream Britain's first glimpse of Bowie's latest creation: Ziggy Stardust & The Spiders from Mars.

'The way he looked was astonishing,' recalled Spandau Ballet's Gary Kemp later. 'It was androgynous yet very sexual.' And there was no part of the performance more charged than the electric moment when Bowie locked eyes with the camera, pointed straight into the lens, uttered the immortal line, 'I had to phone someone so I picked on you,' and, for all the world like some futuristic Pied Piper, reached out across the ether to create a million instant and deeply personal connections. In that moment Bowie kicked open the doors of possibility for a new generation and offered a tantalising glimpse into the bright new future promised to anyone brave enough to follow, Kemp among them. 'I had been chosen,' Kemp confessed in his autobiography, *I Know This Much*, several decades after the Starman had landed. 'That night I planned my future.'

And follow they did. For those members of that evening's audience who, whether they knew it or not, were ready to embrace something new, exciting and dangerous, the three-minute-fifty-second performance offered more than enough time. By the time the *Top of the Pops* studio audience's somewhat self-conscious applause broke Bowie's spell, for many the world had changed completely and irrevocably. 'I think it stands as one of the pivotal moments of modern music,' reflected Gary Numan later. 'To say it stood out is an epic understatement.'

Ziggy Stardust was an alien rock star from another world, come to Earth to warn the planet's population of its imminent demise, a message he delivered – with the support of his band, the Spiders from Mars – through the intergalactic medium of rock'n'roll. Examine the concept now through the prism of half a century and it looks decidedly flimsy and unpromising, but in 1972 the world was still under the thrall of all things space-related, the first man to walk on the the moon having done so less than three years previously.

If you watch the performance today, with the benefit of more than fifty years of liberal hindsight, it's almost impossible to truly appreciate exactly how Bowie's blend of music, lyrics and studied aesthetics made his *Top of the Tops* performance so explosive. On their own, none of the individual elements that combined to make the performance so incendiary were particularly innovative, but Bowie's talent lay in his ability to consider, absorb and combine elements – the dyed hair, the elaborate make-up, the immaculately varnished fingernails, the ambiguous eroticism – in such a way that it seemed they all came from him.

Preceding the release of 'Starman' by just a few weeks, Marc Bolan's T. Rex were already enjoying the success of their second chart-topping single of 1972, 'Metal Guru'. T. Rex's most recent *Top of the Pops* appearance had aired just three weeks previously, Bolan resplendent in make-up and sparkles. Unlike Bowie, Bolan was no stranger to *Top of the Pops*, and T. Rex's previous album, *Electric Warrior*, had been the nation's best-selling album of 1971 alongside two hit singles, 'Get It On' and 'Jeepster', which reached number one and number two, respectively, in the UK singles chart.

As 'Starman' ascended the charts, Alice Cooper was also riding high with his 'School's Out' single and album. *School's Out* was Cooper's third hit album in the UK in eighteen months, and the singer had already introduced the contemporary *Top of the Pops* audience to the idea of a man in make-up, even if the make-up in question did owe more to Hammer horror theatricality than it did to Bolan's hippie whimsy or Bowie's gender-bending space-age androgyny. Nevertheless, Cooper, with his obvious shock-rock rebellious appeal, was a definite influence on the emerging generation of future music makers coming of age in the early seventies, as were the first wave of glam rock acts, including Slade, The Sweet and Gary Glitter, all of whom had achieved significant chart success over the previous six months.

But none of the acts who preceded Bowie would have such an extraordinary and galvanising effect on their young audience. 'When Marc Bolan wore glitter on his face during his performance of 'Hot Love' on *Top of the Pops* in March 1971, he was partly responsible for the flowering of a new musical genre,' mused journalist Dylan Jones in his 2012 book *When Ziggy Played Guitar*, concluding, 'Bowie's 'Starman' appearance was the full garden centre.' Some fans favoured Bolan, others Bowie, but both were important influences in shaping the next generation. 'Later we'd divide the era into "AB" and "BB" – "After Bowie/Bolan" and "Before Bowie/Bolan",' Marc Almond revealed in his 1999 autobiography *Tainted Life*. "BB" it was OK to have what would later be referred to as the old farts – the ELPs, the Yeses and the Tulls – in your collection. "AB", of course, everyone would deny that they'd ever had these bands' albums.'

By 1972, Bolan was in the process of completing a personal transition that had seen him shed his previously earnest, ethereal, flower-child persona – under which he had been responsible for the release of a trio of successful albums under the name Tyrannosaurus Rex over the previous three years – and, in 1971, successfully transform himself into the electric warrior he referenced in the title of the first T. Rex album. Like Bowie, Bolan was acutely aware of the importance of image: 'Ninety-five percent of my success is the way I look,' he admitted to *Creem* magazine's Cameron Crowe. 'That's what people pick up on. The music is secondary. You do have to have good music, though, after the initial physical contact. But initially, it's got nothing to do with music.'

While Bolan's 1972 styling still owed an obvious debt to the 'flower power' aesthetic that linked him to his previous incarnation as a whimsical poet and hippie, Bowie contrived his reinvention as Ziggy to look like it came from the future rather than from the past. Ziggy Stardust appeared from nowhere in a blaze of colour and controversy, despite the fact that, against popular evidence to the contrary, David Bowie wasn't actually a new artist at all.

In fact, in July 1972, David Bowie wasn't even new to *Top of the Pops*. He had appeared on the show just a few months previously, accompanying former Herman's Hermits frontman Peter Noone on his hit 'Oh! You Pretty Things' – a song written and composed by Bowie – in a performance that was also repeated the following week. Prior to that recording, Bowie had appeared on the show in his own right just once (although the performance was repeated), in October 1969, awkwardly clad in a silver jumpsuit, performing his debut hit 'Space Oddity'. 'Space Oddity' was a Top 5 success for Bowie, albeit a serendipitous one, the song having been picked by the BBC as part of the soundtrack to their coverage of the 1969 moon landing, which in turn led to its rush release as a single by Philips Records in the July of that year.

In the immediate wake of the moon landing, and the ensuing appetite for anything space-related or futuristic, 'Space Oddity' had become a hit, the song's novelty status further emphasised by an extensive press advertising campaign around the single. This featured a foil-clad and curly-haired Bowie endorsing the Stylophone – the 'pocket electronic organ' later to become more commonly associated with Rolf Harris – which had been used to create some of the space-age sounds on 'Space Oddity', and which the Stylophone advert breathlessly – and rather optimistically – described as 'The greatest craze since the Yo-Yo'.

While 'Space Oddity' was a significant hit, the album it was taken from, Bowie's second, *David Bowie*, failed to capture the zeitgeist in the same way. Anyone coming across the album on the back of 'Space Oddity' and hoping for more of the same would end up disappointed, because the nine songs across the release were completely different not only to that single, but to each other, instead meandering through a variety of musical styles, reflecting a curious mix of folk, music hall and quirky influences which – although they showcased the various inspirations Bowie had bought to bear on the project – ultimately failed to convey a clear sense of the kind of artist he was. As a result, after 'Space Oddity', Bowie's star rapidly faded to the apparent indignity of a one-hit wonder.

Despite the sci-fi echoes that link 'Space Oddity''s Major Tom to 'Starman''s Ziggy Stardust, the three-year gap between the two songs also marked a crucial division between not just two very different decades, but also between two very different generations. As a result, a significant proportion of the young and impressionable minds to be found amongst 1972's *Top of the Pops* audience had little, if any, prior knowledge of Bowie's work – which by then amounted to four albums and ten singles – and even for those who were able to join the dots between the two releases, 'Starman''s explosive arrival only served to emphasise its distance from Bowie's more tentative debut. For a significant part of this new audience, Ziggy Stardust had simply been beamed into their living rooms fully formed and without precedent.

Bowie's emergence as Ziggy resonated particularly with the generation this book is really about, those in their early teens in 1972, struggling perhaps to make sense of the world and their place in it, and in search of something to call their own. 'At school the next day nobody talked about anything else,' remembered Duran Duran's Nick Rhodes. 'The approach, the look, the sound of him, the excitement that he was singing about aliens… at that time of my life, when I was just discovering music, it was so magnetic, and he was genuinely exciting.'

But being a Bowie fan in 1972, particularly if you were young and male, was a brave statement. Bowie was androgynous, ambiguous, flamboyant and colourful in an era where embracing even one of those concepts could lead to your taking your life in your hands. After Bowie's performance of 'Starman' on *Top of the Pops*, any sort of allegiance to Ziggy Stardust was divisive. You either nailed your colours to Ziggy's mast or you turned against those who did. That Bowie had told *Melody Maker* that he was gay earlier the same year just added fuel to 'Starman''s fire. 'Next day all hell broke loose in the playground,' reflected Marc Almond later. 'Bowie was a queer, and if you liked him you must be queer, too.'

Bowie's androgynous presentation was a dangerous but exciting concept in the early seventies, when the only real gay figures in the mainstream were figures of limp-wristed fun: John Inman's Mr Humphries in the TV sitcom *Are You Being Served?*, for example; or Larry Grayson, who would later present *The Generation Game* but in 1972 was fronting the camp comedy chat show *Shut That Door!*. But Bowie's appeal was broader and more dangerous: 'Bowie came from a planet I wanted to go to and he set the benchmark for me of what all performance in pop music should be about,' remembered Gary Kemp. "Starman' seemed like a camp theatrical folk song set in the future. I fell in love with it, and with him, even as a young straight boy.'

That so many of those who had fallen under the spell of Bowie's colourful 'Starman' had also done so in the knowledge that their parents thoroughly disapproved of Bowie's ambiguous but flamboyant sexuality only added to the rebellious thrill. 'You didn't just buy into how great the songs were, or how strange the lyrics were, you bought into him being different,' asserted Nick Rhodes with satisfaction, 'and it rubber-stamped you as being someone who thought about life in a different way.'

In the direct wake of 'Starman', another single, 'Popcorn' by Hot Butter (named not for the popping electronic noises the track contained, but because the composition was both 'pop' and 'corny'), was rushing up the chart. Capturing some of the same spirit of futurism as 'Starman', but in an entirely different way, 'Popcorn' would quickly overtake and outsell Bowie – 'Starman' reached number ten in the UK singles chart at the end of July – on its way to reaching its number five peak in the second half of August.

'Popcorn' was written by composer Gershon Kingsley, who had originally released the track in 1969 as part of an album entitled *Music To Moog By*, which featured primitive electronic versions of popular songs – including 'Twinkle, Twinkle, Little Star', The Beatles' 'Paperback Writer' and the folk song 'Scarborough Fair' – designed to capitalise on the success of Walter Carlos's *Switched On Bach*, which had performed a similar task for classical music the previous year. Released over the course of Carlos's pioneering transgender journey, subsequent editions of *Switched On Bach* were released under the name Wendy Carlos, but combined sales of the album were astonishing and the album remained at the top of the *Billboard* classical albums chart for three years on its way to selling over one million copies in the USA alone.

Kingsley subsequently put together The First Moog Quartet in order to be able to tour the album in the USA at the start of the seventies, and recruited Stan Free to play in the band, and it was Free who then recorded 'Popcorn' under the name Hot Butter. In addition to its success in the UK, Hot Butter's version of the track was a multimillion-selling international hit which topped the charts in Australia, Germany, Holland and Switzerland, and reached the Top 10 of the *Billboard* pop singles chart in the USA.

While Hot Butter's 1972 eponymous album failed to capture the public consciousness in the way 'Popcorn' did, it was nevertheless a signpost to an electronic music future. Hot Butter was instrumental in shifting the perception of the synthesiser from a classical music to a popular music context. Since 1972, 'Popcorn' has been covered hundreds of times, including versions recorded by artists as diverse as Jean-Michel Jarre – who covered 'Popcorn' in 1973 under the name Pop Corn Orchestra and then used the song as an influence to shape the sound of 'Oxygène (Part IV)' on his *Oxygène* album in 1976 – James Last, Muse, Aphex Twin (working under the name Caustic Window), Herb Alpert, Crazy Frog (whose version reached number twelve in the UK singles chart in 2015), and Dan Lacksman prior to his joining Telex.

In addition to providing 1972's generation of music fans with a glimpse of the future, the *Hot Butter* album also provided a nod to the past by including a cover of an earlier hit, The Tornados' 1962 instrumental 'Telstar'. Sounding for all the world like something from a 1950s movie soundtrack, the original 'Telstar' was such a success, and for so long, that even a decade after release it was still providing radio listeners and music fans with a route into electronic music.

Written and produced by the eccentric British sound engineer Joe Meek, 'Telstar' predominantly featured the sound of a clavioline – an electronic keyboard, invented in 1947, which was a forerunner to the earliest analogue synthesisers – and quickly topped the singles charts in both the UK and the USA. 'The collage of buzzes and zaps that open the record remains a stunning and precise exercise in the art of recording electronic sounds,' the *San Francisco Chronicle* enthused in 1978. 'Meek employed all sorts of techniques to get the sounds he wanted – such as the phasing and echo of an amplifier being short-circuited, scraping a screwdriver against a glass ashtray, banging the studio door shut in time, or recording a flushing toilet.'

Doctor Who producer Verity Lambert at the BBC Radiophonic Workshop, 1963.

In a 2012 feature, *Mojo* magazine placed 'Telstar' at number two in a ranking of the fifty greatest electronic records of all time, where it sat between Louis and Bebe Barron's 1956 film score for *Forbidden Planet*, which topped the list, and the Radiophonic Workshop's theme music for *Doctor Who* at number three. As important as 'Telstar' in introducing the power and potential of electronic music to a mainstream audience, that theme soundtracked the first episode of *Doctor Who* when it debuted the year after 'Telstar', in November 1963. In 2010, *Doctor Who* was awarded a Guinness World Record as the world's most successful TV sci-fi show, and in 2019 *Electronic Sound* magazine, without a trace of hyperbole, declared the track 'possibly the most important piece of British electronic music ever'.

Although the *Doctor Who* theme was composed by Ron Grainer, it became an electronic track through the efforts of Delia Derbyshire, who had been assigned the task in the course of her work at the BBC's Radiophonic Workshop, set up in 1957 to produce theme and incidental music, and sound effects, in support of the BBC's radio and television programming. As the project pre-dated commercial synthesisers, the *Doctor Who* theme was created using manipulated sounds and physical tape-editing techniques. 'Oscillators were manhandled into creating a melody; whooshes and hisses would be carved from white noise. And it was all done on tape,' marvelled writer Dave Thompson in his book *I Feel Love*. 'There were no computers on which to compose, no samplers to store a universe of noises, no programs with which to 'see' the sounds. Every single note was created manually; every piece of tape was marked with a china marker, then spliced with razor blades and sticky tape.'

The results were startling, even to Ron Grainer, who had provided the original score. According to the biography on Delia Derbyshire's website, 'On first hearing it Grainer was tickled pink: 'Did I really write this?' he asked. 'Most of it,' replied Derbyshire.' *Doctor Who* was an instant hit and became a cornerstone of BBC programming for the next twenty-five years until 1989, when the show went on a fifteen-year hiatus. Something of a rite of passage for each successive generation who fell under its sci-fi spell, the impact and multiple influences of *Doctor Who* cannot be overstated. For many, the show was the first step in a journey into science fiction, a genre which in itself provided another rich seam of influence on our emerging generation of electronic music artists.

'Was science fiction an influence on The Human League?' Phil Oakey later deadpanned in an interview for Scotland's *The Herald*. 'I'm afraid it was.' In fact Oakey was unashamed of his love of sci-fi. 'More than anything, I was a sci-fi buff,' he told Simon Reynolds in 2005. 'I had every science-fiction paperback you could get.' In the same interview, Oakey also singled out science fiction authors J. G. Ballard and Philip K. Dick as particular influences. Considered part of the New Wave of science fiction for their work's frequently experimental nature and dystopian themes, both authors were extremely influential on Oakey and his peers.

Gary Numan freely admits to having been hugely influenced by Philip K. Dick's writing, to the extent that not only do Dick's themes frequently seep into Numan's songwriting, but the American writer was also instrumental in inspiring Numan to write science fiction of his own, stories which would provide the framework for his subsequent song lyrics. 'The bulk of the songs on the *Tubeway Army* album were based on science fiction stories I'd been writing,' Numan would admit later. 'I'd been trying to write a book, a collection of short stories that together described a particular world: a London of the future.'

J. G. Ballard's writing was even more inspirational, and artists as diverse as The Normal, Buggles, John Foxx, Cabaret Voltaire, Joy Division and Throbbing Gristle would freely admit to his influence. John Foxx, a science fiction fan for most of his life, was such an admirer of Ballard that he was invited to discuss the writer and his work for the influential website Ballardian, in which Foxx was asked what it was about Ballard's work that gave it such resonance for the post-punk generation. 'I think some of this may have been an attraction to the new modes of physical and intellectual violence on offer and to the uncompromising outer edge stance,' Foxx explained. 'He was the first radical and relevant novelist of this technological age in Britain.'

'I still think J. G. Ballard is the greatest British writer of the last century,' Phil Oakey proclaimed to the *Scottish Herald* in 2012. 'We did a tribute song to J. G. Ballard very early on. Because Roxy Music had done '2HB' for Humphrey Bogart, we did '4JG'.' And Ballard wasn't the only science fiction influence on The Human League. 'I was really into Kubrick,' Martyn Ware recalled, adding Anthony Burgess to the band's list of influences: 'We'd seen *2001: A Space Odyssey*, of course, so when news came out that the next film he was working on was *A Clockwork Orange*, we rushed out and bought the book. When we read the section where the bands are mentioned, we were always wondering, 'What do the Heaven Seventeen look like? What do they sound like? Are they a gospel band?''

Stanley Kubrick's film adaptation of Burgess's *A Clockwork Orange* premiered in the UK in January 1972 to immediate controversy over the movie's 'pornographic' and extraordinarily violent scenes, all of which played out to a compelling electronic soundtrack courtesy of Wendy Carlos. A mixture of electronic interpretations of classical pieces and original music, Carlos's muse on *A Clockwork Orange* was decidedly darker and more disturbing than her work on *Switched On Bach*, and both were thrilling to the hearts and minds of the emerging generation. 'The music was a massive influence on us,' Martyn Ware admitted to *Electronic Sound*. 'Electronic music, futuristic imagery: it was a perfect storm for us... Looking back a lot of it is misogynistic and wrong, but that sense of teens against the world, its transgressive nature, the dysfunctional gang culture, it was very exciting, but it had intellectual depth and was designed to make you think.'

David Bowie had also been impressed by *A Clockwork Orange* and is said to have watched the film several times while he laid down the blueprints for the Ziggy Stardust project. 'The idea was taking the recent past and restructuring it in a way we felt we had authorship of,' Bowie told *Mojo* in 2002. 'My key 'in' was things like *Clockwork Orange*: that was our world, not the bloody hippie thing. It all made sense to me. The idea of taking a present situation and doing a futuristic forecast, and dressing it to suit: it was a uniform for an army that didn't exist.'

'Starman', and subsequently *The Rise And Fall of Ziggy Stardust And The Spiders From Mars*, the album from which the single was taken, was a huge hit for Bowie and positioned him as one of the most exciting and innovative artists of his generation. Within a year of 'Starman''s *Top of the Pops* debut however, Bowie killed off the Ziggy Stardust persona in favour of reinventing himself once again, this time as Aladdin Sane, complete with the iconic zigzag of lightning painted across his face, in time for his his next album project. 'This is not only the last show of the tour but this is also the last show that we'll ever do,' he would announce before launching into Ziggy's blistering swansong in the shape of an extended rendition of 'Rock 'N' Roll Suicide', a highly appropriate track to serve as Ziggy's epitaph.

But Ziggy's work was done and the audience Bowie had attracted with The Spiders From Mars stuck with him through *Aladdin Sane* and then through the subsequent albums *Pin Ups*, *Diamond Dogs* and *Young Americans*, with more and more fans pledging their allegiance from project to project. 'In my school there were hardcore T. Rex fans and then there were hardcore Bowie fans, and I was loyal to Bolan,' Gary Numan told *Mojo* magazine in 2016. 'But then I heard *Aladdin Sane* and I just thought, 'Oh God this is insane!' Then you start going back, and I bought everything.'

Although he had enjoyed an enviable level of commercial and critical success since the 1972 release of 'Starman', starting with the release of his album *Station To Station* in January 1976, Bowie had begun to explore the possibilities of electronic music, and he took his followers with him: 'My attention had been swung back to Europe with the release of Kraftwerk's 'Autobahn' in 1974,' the singer told *Uncut* magazine later. 'The preponderance of electronic instruments convinced me that this was an area that I had to investigate a little further.'

'Autobahn' had been an unlikely hit for Kraftwerk in 1975 when it had reached number eleven on the UK singles chart in June, the same week that their album of the same name, which had been released at the end of 1974, peaked at number four in the UK albums chart. Kraftwerk didn't perform 'Autobahn' on *Top of the Pops*, but they did perform it on *Tomorrow's World*, which is where they caught the attention of future Joy Division and New Order drummer Stephen Morris: 'It was the most un-rock-and-roll thing I'd ever seen and all the more enticing because of that,' Morris recalled in his autobiography *Record Play Pause* in 2019. 'Electronic drums played with knitting needles, that got my attention. I might never be Keith Moon, but I could see myself doing something like that.'

Morris wasn't alone finding himself in thrall to Kraftwerk. 'It was 'Autobahn' that was like the birth certificate of electronic music,' Martyn Ware told Rudi Esch for the latter's *Electri_City* book in 2016. ''Autobahn' was a key moment, all teenagers are looking for something new that they could make their own. I was absolutely hooked,' OMD's Andy McCluskey enthused in the same book, further adding that he also saw Kraftwerk play in Liverpool in September the same year: 'It was as if I was watching the moon landing; the whole presentation was so radically different and new, as if it was from another planet.'

Frequently dismissed at the time as a novelty hit constructed around the sounds made by a car, Kraftwerk were actually extremely serious about their work. ''Autobahn' was about finding our artistic situation: where are we? What is the sound of the German Bundesrepublik?' the band's Ralf Hütter would tell *Uncut* in 2009. 'It's not about cars, it's about the Autobahn. People forget that. It's a road where we were travelling all the time: hundreds of thousands of kilometres from university to art galleries, from club to home.'

By actively seeking to lay new cultural foundations, ones that deliberately sidelined Anglo-American influence in favour of establishing a cultural landscape that was unique to post-war Germany, this new generation was one determined to look to the future rather than to the past. 'Krautrock' – a troubling and unintentionally disrespectful term coined by the English rock press anxious to label the disparate, and frequently unconnected, collection of German musicians operating at that time – was one result of such utopian thinking, alongside equally significant and exciting breakthroughs in art, design, architecture and the creative arts. 'Being members of a younger generation of German people, we feel somewhat cut off from the old culture of the country,' Ralf Hütter told *Sounds*' Geoff Barton in 1976. 'Many people of our age and also younger have been Americanised and Anglicised. They have turned to Anglo-American music. This is because, after the war, there did not exist any German culture within a respectable level of consciousness.'

In his excellent history of the movement, *Future Days*, David Stubbs reassessed the problems associated with the use of 'krautrock' as a catch-all term for what is an extraordinarily diverse scene. 'Over the years the word 'Krautrock' has lost the accidentally pejorative connotation it once had: It's become semantically cleansed with the wash of time. It's used unselfconsciously by a generation who would no more dream of calling Germans 'Krauts' than they would call them 'Jerries', 'Fritz' or 'the Boche'. There is, quite simply, something jaggedly appealing about the very way in which the word sits on the page or rolls off the tongue. It's certainly preferable to other options that never really stuck, such as 'Teutonic Railroad Rock 'n' Roll'.'

While Kraftwerk's influence on David Bowie wasn't overtly obvious in the way the *Station To Station* album sounded in 1976, Bowie nevertheless paid the Düsseldorf act the compliment of playing the first side of the *Autobahn* album over the PA before taking to the stage each night on his subsequent *Station To Station* tour. Bowie also enthusiastically talked up Kraftwerk, and the various Teutonic influences that had informed the making of the record, in interviews in support of *Station To Station*. 'I was a big fan of Kraftwerk, Cluster and Harmonia, and I thought the first Neu! album was gigantically wonderful,' Bowie told *Mojo* in 1991. 'Having the choice of what the future was going to bring, looking at that against punk, I had no doubt where the future of music was going, and it was coming out of Germany.'

Bowie's patronage would prove important not just to Kraftwerk's story but also to the popularisation of krautrock as a whole. In an interview for *Mojo* in 2005, Kraftwerk's Ralf Hütter would acknowledge the power of Bowie's support: 'That was very important for us, because it linked what we were doing with the rock mainstream. Bowie used to tell everyone that we were his favourite group, and in the mid seventies the rock press used to hang on every word from his mouth like tablets of stone.'

Crucially, as a result of Bowie's evangelising of all things German and electronic, the more curious members of his fanbase, particularly those who had grown up in thrall to his influence and were now starting to make music of their own, were introduced to a new world of sounds, technology and sonic possibility. Rusty Egan – who would soon go on to become a leading light in the formation of the Blitz club, and again in the creation of Visage – is quick to acknowledge Bowie's influence on his own musical tastes: 'Via Bowie I found Kraftwerk, and that lead to Neu!, Can, Cluster and krautrock as it was called.'

At a time when the mainstream music industry was obsessed with the punk scene, Bowie had bypassed that movement and had instead stepped outside prevailing musical fashions for his next musical move. 'In a way it was great that I found these bands, because I didn't feel any of the essence of punk at all in that period, I just totally bypassed it,' Bowie told *Mojo* later.

In 1976, in collaboration with former Roxy Music synthesist Brian Eno, Bowie was building on the electronic influences which had started to bleed into the sound of *Station To Station*, and had recorded two albums for release in 1977. *Low* and *"Heroes"* (the double inverted commas are part of Bowie's title, to indicate the irony that loads the word) were the first two instalments in what would become known as Bowie's Berlin Trilogy, with 1979's *Lodger* later completing the set. (Ironically, of the three, only *"Heroes"* was actually recorded in Germany, at the legendary Hansa Studio which overlooked the Berlin Wall. The previous album in the trilogy, *Low*, had been mixed at Hansa but the actual recording had taken place in France, at the Château d'Hérouville studios near Paris, while the creation of *Lodger* was later divided between Montreux's Mountain Studios and New York's Record Plant Studio between periods of touring in support of the first two records.)

Bowie's enthusiasm for Neu! – whom he would later describe as 'Kraftwerk's wayward, anarchistic brothers' – is thought to be responsible for the concept of dividing both *Low* and *"Heroes"* into two distinct and sonically separate sides, the German act having adopted a similar structure of 'night' and 'day' sides in 1975 on their final album, *Neu! '75*, and in fact *New Music: Night And Day* had been Bowie's working title for *Low*. In addition, the *"Heroes"* album

14

and single are both thought to have been named, in part, after Neu!'s track 'Hero', which also featured on that same swansong release.

Acceptance of the startling new sounds that permeated Bowie's Berlin albums – particularly at the start of the trilogy with the release of *Low* – was not always immediate. In his autobiography, *Take It Like a Man*, Boy George, then as now a dedicated Bowie fanatic, recalls how his first exposure to *Low* had been a shock: 'When I first heard *Low*, I remember thinking, 'What's he done? What is this record?'' It was only after further exploration that *Low* started to attract the kind of plaudits – from the media and from Bowie's ever curious fanbase – that now firmly position it as a modern classic. Boy George was among those who recovered from their initial shock: 'Momentarily I was horrified, but then, literally overnight, I realised that it was an amazing record.'

New Order frontman Bernard Sumner, then just a few months away from making his own recording debut with his first band, Warsaw, was another of the legions of music fans to be startled by Bowie's latest departure, later recalling, 'It was a whole new kind of music to me, one that was moving things on, looking to the future, not the past.' Such was Bowie's influence that Warsaw adopted their name in direct response to the track 'Warszawa' from *Low*, although they would famously rechristen themselves Joy Division shortly before the release of their first recordings in 1978.

American music magazine *Phonograph Record* was equally quick to accept and embrace the gauntlet thrown down by Bowie's new direction, describing *Low* as 'the inner document of someone either on the edge of psychosis or obsessed right down to the bone. Nothing fits or holds firm, nothing makes rational sense, nothing follows the formal or practical rules of the game'. Given Bowie's precarious physical and mental state during the making of the first two Berlin albums, this was a shrewd assessment.

Ostensibly travelling to Germany in search of a new muse in the guise of electronic experimentation, Bowie was also running away from America and the previous chapter of his life, which had seen him enjoy huge professional success while simultaneously struggling with deep personal lows, less than obliquely referenced in the choice of *Low* as the title of the first album of the trilogy. Commercial success had provided Bowie with both the financial means and the unscrupulous connections to descend into a cocaine-fuelled paranoia of his own making. Before leaving the USA for Europe, Bowie had finished filming the 1976 movie *The Man Who Fell to Earth* and was in a very dark place indeed. Biographer David Stubbs would later sum up the singer's state of mind as 'paranoid, convinced that every passing light in the sky was a visiting UFO, storing his urine in the fridge, waiving the usual mortal cravings such as the need to eat food regularly, developing an obsessive interest in the occult'.

Under such circumstances it was perhaps inevitable that *Low* – which features songs originally conceived as a soundtrack to accompany *The Man Who Fell to Earth*, and sports a still photograph of Bowie in character as the alien Thomas Jerome Newton from the film on its sleeve – would be a record that explored dark moods and atmospheres. In contrast to Bowie's previous work, which had broadly followed more traditional narrative structures, *Low* is musically and lyrically – where there are lyrics at all – fragmented, complex, and introverted.

Testament to the unwavering support of the David Bowie audience, *Low* peaked at number two in the UK albums chart at the start of February 1977, bolstered by a hit single, 'Sound And Vision', which reached number three in March. A further single, 'Be My Wife', subsequently failed to chart upon its release in June. By September, Bowie's attention had switched to the release of his second album project of the year, *"Heroes"*, and the single of the same name, which peaked at twenty-four at the start of November. Released in October, the *"Heroes"* album peaked at number three as part of a respectable eighteen-week chart run which included seven weeks in the Top 10.

Although stylistically similar to *Low*, *"Heroes"* is the sound of Bowie starting to emerge from his own nightmares and, despite a continuation of the electronic soundscapes that so unnerved listeners to the first part of the trilogy, is a warmer and less fragmented record, with elements that are not only more commercial, but which even touch on the romantic. The sound of *'Heroes'* was a distinct relief, not only for those fans unconvinced by *Low* but also for RCA Records, Bowie's label at that time, who launched a campaign designed to emphasise Bowie's domination of the recent past while celebrating his unique vision and his vast influence by ushering in the new album with the advertising copy line 'There's Old Wave, There's New Wave and there's David Bowie'.

Vincent Martin – then playing guitar in the Basildon band No Romance In China, but shortly to go on to rechristen himself Vince Clarke and form Depeche Mode – still considers *"Heroes"*, and Bowie's Berlin Trilogy, to be among his favourite albums ever. Identifying the title track in particular as a song that resonated with him at the time of its release, Clarke cites the record's palpable sense of darkness and disquiet as part of the reason for his affection, alongside the sense that the album was 'very anti-establishment, and something your parents wouldn't approve of'.

Andy McCluskey also considers the *"Heroes"* album and single to be among Bowie's finest moments, and remembers having a similar reaction to the record as Clarke, later noting the album's 'severe melancholy and sombre attitude', praising the title track as 'one of the greatest songs ever', and acknowledging it as an unconscious blueprint for the distinctive vocal style he would himself develop as frontman of his own group, Orchestral Manoeuvres In The Dark, who would start releasing music of their own just a year later.

Punk had established the crucial DIY attitude which underpinned much of the music that came in its wake, but the anarchic energy that showcased the movement's greatest moments in response to *Sideburns* fanzine's now legendary call to arms – 'This is a chord. This is another. This is a third. Now form a band' – had quickly dissipated, leaving behind a vacuum that a new musical generation were anxious to fill with a brand new sound that they could call their own. 'All that anger and revolutionary spirit didn't go away, it simply became repurposed – transmuted into a defiant icy cool, much more energy-efficient than all that shouting,' John Foxx told The Quietus.

Writing about the influence of this period of Bowie's career on the emerging generation in his book *Strange Fascination*, Bowie biographer David Buckley also paid tribute to the impact of *"Heroes"* on post-punk's immediate landscape, noting that 'The synth overtook the guitar as the instrument par excellence for the man or woman with big ideas and great tunes but minimal conventional musical wisdom or proficiency.'

Crucially this restless rejection of everything that had come before came at exactly the same time as a technological watershed which saw the synthesiser, an instrument previously associated with virtuoso musicians with deep pockets and a weakness for the worst musical excesses of progressive rock, start to appear on the domestic market. Suddenly the kind of technology that powered Kraftwerk was available to anyone for the price of a decent electric guitar.

Kraftwerk, Bowie's gateway to the krautrock world, paid Bowie the compliment of namechecking him, and his Berlin companion Iggy Pop, in the lyrics to *Trans-Europe Express*, another classic album to emerge in 1977, whose release dropped neatly between Bowie's *Low* and *"Heroes"*. In turn

Bowie returned the compliment on the *"Heroes"* album with the track 'V-2 Schneider', named in tribute to the Düsseldorf act's Florian Schneider. That track was in turn exposed to an even greater audience – hundreds of thousands of record buyers in fact – when it preceded the release of the album and appeared as the B-side to Bowie's "Heroes" single.

Released in May, *Trans-Europe Express* was in itself another crucial release in bringing the notion of the possibilities of electronic music to a new generation. '*Trans-Europe Express* had everything, it was retro yet futuristic, melancholic yet timeless, technical, modern and future-looking yet also traditional. You name it, it had it all,' Martyn Ware later recalled for Rudi Esch. The *Trans-Europe Express* album and its associated singles, the title track and 'Showroom Dummies', all failed to chart in 1977, a repeat of the fate of Kraftwerk's previous album, 1976's *Radio-Activity*, and its sole single, 'Radioactivity'. 'It was through *Radio-Activity* that we were inspired to make electronic, futuristic music,' OMD's Paul Humphreys told Esch. 'We listened to that one album every day.'

Brian Eno's role in creating interest in the possibilities of electronic music should also not be overlooked. Like Bowie, Eno, through his involvement in the early Roxy Music albums, and through his onstage eccentricity and scant regard for any prevailing sartorial or musical conventions, was already a significant figure in the eyes of the fledgeling generation of music makers who were searching for something new to make their own. OMD's Andy McCluskey would later confess that while his interest in David Bowie had generally declined since 1972's Ziggy Stardust releases, his interest in Brian Eno's work had steadily increased over the same period: 'I remember one of our great mantras was something Brian Eno had said, 'If you've got a collection of rubbish instruments, then you're the only person who has got those rubbish instruments, so that's your sound. Celebrate it.''

'Eno is a gaunt, pale gentleman who's deeply into electronics and overlays the band's sound with an aural frieze of squeals, squirts, screams and sirens,' reported *Melody Maker*'s Richard Williams in February 1972 in a very early Roxy Music live review, further noting that Eno made his contributions to the performance from the sound desk at the back of the hall rather than from the stage. An accidental musician in all senses, Brian Eno had started out as Roxy Music's sound-man, and recalled his elevation to musician and band member for Djuna Parnes in 2001: 'I started off mixing the band at the back of the auditoriums. I would mix, and I had a synthesiser there. And then I started doing backing vocals as well, and it started getting a bit weird. The audience would wheel round to look at me. I don't remember it being a big decision, me joining the rest of the band on stage.'

Roxy Music released their first single, 'Virginia Plain', at the beginning of August 1972, and by the end of the month, just weeks after David Bowie's debut of 'Starman' on the same show, they were on *Top of the Pops*, where they received a similarly enthusiastic response. Although Bryan Ferry's twinkling outfit and debonaire good looks dominated the performance, and while most of Roxy Music sported the kind of glam rock sparkles and animal prints that sat comfortably alongside Slade, Mott The Hoople and Alice Cooper – all of whom had featured on the same show – it was Eno who cut the strangest dash of all. The *Top of the Pops* performance offered little more than fragmented glimpses of an extraordinary figure, apparently dressed entirely in black feathers with the exception of sparkly silver gloves and a fetching black glittery bracelet, operating a compact bank of synthesisers. But those glimpses were enough. 'Much of 'Virginia Plain''s weirdness emanated from a small wooden box with dials played by an androgynous character wearing silver gloves. Thus, Brian Eno introduced electronic music to the mainstream,' enthused *Guardian* journalist Caroline Sullivan in 2011 when she nominated the performance as one of the fifty key events in the history of rock music.

'The image put over both by their stage appearance and their music is one of the future. Sci-fi rock'n'roll. Bryan Ferry, Roxy's lead singer and songwriter, sees their music as drawing both from the landmarks of rock'n'roll and the best of ultramodern electronics,' reported *Beat Instrumental*'s Steve Turner a few weeks after Roxy Music's *Top of the Pops* debut, by which time 'Virginia Plain' had already spent a month in the UK Top 10 and had peaked at an impressive number four. One single into their career and Roxy Music's mannered art-school channelling of glam rock, in combination with Brian Eno's status as a non-musician who nevertheless managed to create startling, interesting and challenging sounds, was already enough to endear the band to the next generation of artists who found much to admire in Roxy Music's studied erudite aesthetic.

'I realised that there were certain areas of music you could enter without actually learning an instrument which at my age I certainly wasn't about

Ultravox! (Warren Cann and John Foxx), circa 1978.

to do,' Eno told *Melody Maker* in 1972 shortly before Roxy Music released 'Virginia Plain', and the new generation pricked up their ears. 'As Ultravox! we were immensely inspired by the art-school aspect of glam rock,' Chris Cross told Rudi Esch. 'Musically speaking, Ultravox! were the sons of Roxy Music, New York Dolls, David Bowie, and later of Kraftwerk too,' which is ironic as Ultravox! would spend much of the next five years defending themselves against allegations that they were little more than art-school, glam-rock, Roxy Music copyists.

Cabaret Voltaire even went as far as to cite Eno's influence as a primary reasons for their very existence: 'Just listening to Eno talk in interviews about how anyone can make music because you don't need to learn an instrument, you can make music with a tape recorder or with a synth. That was the inspiration that really got us started,' Richard H. Kirk told Simon Reynolds, while Kirk's bandmate Stephen Mallinder was even more definite: 'If there hadn't have been Roxy Music, well Eno specifically, there wouldn't have been Cabaret Voltaire, at least not in the form it took,' he declared in 2014.

Although he cites Eno as the one who put Giorgio Moroder's 'Munich Sound' onto his radar – 'Eno and I exchanged sounds that we loved. Eno offered, among others, Giorgio Moroder and Donna [Summer]'s military R&B and I played him Neu! and the rest of the Düsseldorf sound. They sort of became our soundtrack for the year 1976' – Bowie was no stranger to disco.

Although he claimed not to be a fan of the genre as such, he was nevertheless able to acknowledge the success he had enjoyed with the disco-influenced sounds that ran through his *Young Americans* and *Station To Station* albums. Bowie famously described *Young Americans* as 'plastic soul' and defended the release in 1978 saying, 'It was seriously a plastic soul album. It was definitely me portraying, as a white Englishman, my view of American black music, somebody who watches more from outside than actually getting involved with it inside.'

What is certain is that Donna Summer and Giorgio Moroder's 'Love To Love You Baby' in 1976, and 'I Feel Love' in 1977, had a tangible influence on both Eno and Bowie, as the latter revealed in a 1989 interview with Kurt Loder for the sleeve notes to accompany the compilation *Sound + Vision*: 'One day in Berlin, Eno came running in and said, 'I have heard the sound of the future.' He puts on 'I Feel Love' by Donna Summer. He said, 'This is it, look no further. This single is going to change the sound of club music for the next fifteen years.' Which was more or less right.' 'I didn't realise that Bowie was so impressed by this song,' Moroder reported later, having met Bowie when the pair worked together in 1982 on the title track to the movie *Cat People* and hearing first-hand how, after their first exposure to 'I Feel Love', Bowie and Eno spent several days in a state of severe depression following the realisation that Moroder had stolen a march on their search for a brand new sound.

And it wasn't only David Bowie and Brian Eno who were in thrall to Moroder's new sound; 'I Feel Love' had an equally instant effect on an entire generation of electronic music-makers. ''I Feel Love' was the turning point for me,' Martyn Ware confessed later. 'It was a neon sign of what was possible, a pure crystalline beauty in pop music, and an amazing hybrid of black and white music.' 'The day I joined the band [The Human League] Martyn came round to my house and he had two records under his arm. One was 'Trans-Europe Express' and one was 'I Feel Love' and he said, 'Look, we can do this,'' Phil Oakey recalled in the BBC television documentary *Synth Britannia* in 2009, adding, ''I Feel Love' just didn't sound like any record that had been before. It came on the radio and you couldn't quite believe what you were hearing. We were in fact much more influenced by Moroder than we were by Kraftwerk.'

In Scotland, 'I Feel Love' was having a similarly galvanising effect on another pair of musicians who were about to embark on an electronic journey of their own as Simple Minds: Jim Kerr and Charlie Burchill of Glasgow punk act Johnny & The Self Abusers, who first heard Donna Summer and Giorgio Moroder's epic blasting through the PA before their band took the stage for what would be one of their last ever concerts. 'This thing came out of the speakers and I just thought, "Oh my God, what is that?" This wailing voice and the rhythm and all that,' Kerr recalled in an interview for BBC Scotland. 'I said to Charlie, "How do we get a sound like that?" He said, "We need a synthesiser," and I said, "Who in Glasgow has got a synthesiser?" To which he replied, "No one."'

But the influence of disco on the emerging generation didn't begin and end with 'I Feel Love'; the genre's impact was far broader and much less discriminate. 'ABBA are seen in a very different light today,' Blancmange's Neil Arthur muses today. 'But we loved ABBA too, absolutely bloody loved them.' And The Human League's Phil Oakey frequently spoke of his disco ambitions for the group: 'We want to be like ABBA or Donna Summer or someone like that,' he confessed to *Record Mirror* in 1981. 'Disco music is cool,' Martyn Ware later told the Red Bull Music Academy. 'Some of it was shit but we [The Human League] thought it was cool and it gave us more of a maverick attitude because everybody was going: "Disco is finished!" So we would go: "Fine, we love it."'

In Birmingham, a band called Dada was a stepping stone towards the group who would eventually become household names as Duran Duran, and would declare their intention to combine Chic with the Sex Pistols, although the band's Nick Rhodes would later add Giorgio Moroder to that list. 'We wanted to mix glam rock and punk rock with a little bit of disco, although the prime motivation for forming in the first place was David Bowie. It always was,' Rhodes declared in Dylan Jones' *When Ziggy Played Guitar*. 'An entire generation of groups who formed in the late seventies or early eighties only happened because of David. He is basically responsible for British music in the first half of the eighties. There was a decadence about him that was very appealing, something dark, something German, but something very exciting.'

And so it is against this transformative backdrop that we find a generation of musical pioneers gather those musical and cultural influences and start to mould them into startling new shapes. Armed with the two most powerful and influential tenets to emerge from punk rock – the belief that musical education, knowledge and virtuosity was no longer a prerequisite in the making of music; and a willingness to embrace the DIY spirit that facilitated some of punk's greatest moments – while sidestepping the movement's increasingly dated sonic qualities, they managed to couple the essence of punk with the best the previous generation had to offer: specifically the serious electronic experimentation of Krautrock, the glitter of glam rock, and the decadent pop sheen of disco.

REVOLUTION

1978 & 1979

'All over the country, in oddball studios and on oddball labels, new music is being made – electronic, self-conscious, simple, stark, pretentious, anti-commercial. I don't expect many of these groups to amount to much... but they're true rock eclectics, pulling elements from here and there and something must come good some time.'

Melody Maker, December 30th, 1978

Sex Pistols, 1977.

1978

1978.1 Sex Pistols / The Future / The Human League / The New Musick / Devo / David Bowie / Tubeway Army / Ultravox!

ON JANUARY 14TH, 1978, the Sex Pistols arrived in San Francisco to play the seventh concert of their debut tour of the USA where, at the city's Winterland Ballroom, they famously disintegrated on stage before splitting up and cancelling all future shows and commitments. The band's single-song encore – 'You'll get one number, and one number only' – had, appropriately, been a shambolic cover of The Stooges' 'No Fun', Paul Cook and Steve Jones desperately trying to hold the song together while Johnny Rotten lost interest and Sid Vicious lost the plot. As the band left the stage in a squeal of feedback, Rotten uttered the immortal line 'Ever get the feeling you've been cheated?' and one of the most important chapters in the history of rock slammed shut. The Sex Pistols' Winterland Ballroom show may not have provided the actual moment of punk rock's demise, but it certainly dealt the movement a devastating, and highly symbolic, blow.

Punk would, of course, continue in one form or another for some years to come – in fact there are those who would go so far as to say that it never really died at all – but by 1978 much of the original spirit of revolution was already spent, and a myriad of commercial punk bands had swept in to fill the vacuum the movement had unexpectedly left behind. Midge Ure, speaking as one who had fallen for punk's early promise, but by 1978 was eager to move on to new things, would later note, 'Punk had become high-street fashion, so the ones who had instigated the look, who were in at its very conception, didn't want to be punks any more. Their little sisters were doing that now.'

Arguably, punk's decline would have been even more rapid if it hadn't been for the frantic mechanisations of the music business itself, an industry now hungry to harness some of the commercial possibility those legions of little sisters represented. With few exceptions the mainstream music industry had arrived late to punk's joyous, irreverent party, and had then over-invested in the signing, recording and promotion of a miscellany of acts, sporting safety pins and clad in uniform leather and studs, most of whom had cynically jumped on punk's bandwagon, and whose very existence underlined the end of a glorious golden age.

Despite the rapid and blatant commercialisation of punk, its energy would resonate through musical culture for decades to come and, as the seventies accelerated towards an end, it was this spirit and influence that was seized upon by the next generation of artists, each desperate to subvert the immediate post-punk landscape. Consequently punk's energy, aesthetic and attitude continued to underpin much of the more interesting music that was being released at the time, despite the rapid migration away from the movement by those in the know who were already moving on to explore new sounds and new styles.

Martyn Ware – previously of Sheffield experimental electronic act The Future, but by 1978 one of the founding members of The Human League – had already outgrown a series of punk-influenced acts, amongst them the dubiously named, and thankfully short-lived, Musical Vomit and The Dead Daughters. Ware was among the first wave of musicians and non-musicians alike who had come to recognise punk's limitations while simultaneously embracing and celebrating the new possibilities and opportunities the genre had opened up for them: 'All the infrastructure around punk we absolutely loved,' he explained later, 'it's just that the actual music we saw as being quite old-fashioned.'

And in 1978 there was no worse crime than being old-fashioned. The bright new technology that had long been promised by science and science fiction alike was suddenly becoming tangible. To our emerging generation – who had already borne witness to extraordinary moments of scientific triumph while still at an impressionable age – startling advancements in technology were not only promised, they were expected. In short, it must have seemed like some of the futuristic glimpses offered by the books and films of the day, and the real-life scientific revelations previously only glimpsed through the window of *Tomorrow's World*, were being honoured simultaneously: space travel, home computers, pocket calculators, microprocessors, video games and – most crucially of all, for the purposes of this story – the sudden availability of affordable synthesisers, the creative weapon of choice for many of this first post-punk generation.

Synthesisers were not new at the end of the seventies – indeed by the time of the Sex Pistols' demise they had been around in one form or another for decades – but their sudden affordability meant that the instrument was no longer the preserve of the wealthy and the privileged, and could now be purchased at a price similar to that of an electric guitar. As a result, a new wave of sonic experimenters, many of them without any conventional musical training, were repurposing the synthesiser as a punk instrument, making noises that were light years away from the highbrow sounds of the progressive rock acts of the previous generation: the swirling, rushing space-sounds popularised by artists like Jean-Michel Jarre; the avant-garde psychedelic and experimental soundscapes of the so-called 'krautrock' bands; or the quirky bubbling bleeps that had fuelled novelty records such as Space's 'Magic Fly' or Hot Butter's 'Popcorn'.

Further inspirational cornerstones came from the dancefloor, and were rooted in the precision electronic sounds coming out of Germany: from Düsseldorf the stark electronic purity of Kraftwerk, and in particular their 1977 album *Trans-Europe Express*; and from Munich the dance-floor sheen of disco, courtesy of Giorgio Moroder, whose pulsing beats underpinned Donna Summer's epic 'I Feel Love' among others.

Martyn Ware's introduction to *Trans-Europe Express* came courtesy of Richard H. Kirk, whose band Cabaret Voltaire had been tinkering in the electronic arena from as early as 1973, and who were a huge influence on The Human League and their Sheffield peers. Ware would later remember being transfixed by that introduction to *Trans-Europe Express*, played over a PA system at a party, and would also acknowledge disco's influence on The Human League while simultaneously distancing the band from it, telling *ZigZag*'s Chris Westwood, 'I'd say we were dance biased. Disco's a bit of an evocative word isn't it?'

In a very real sense, Martyn Ware and his musical peers were among the first post-punks to reinterpret and reshape punk's stance and DIY attitude for their own purposes. The Human League was just one of an emerging wave of artists rejecting punk's one-dimensional guitar legacy in favour of replacing traditional instruments with electronic ones in pursuit of creating something entirely new, as Ware would later summarise: 'What we did is we took the attitude of punk and gave it a different context, i.e. let's make music that nobody's heard before.'

Overcoming any musical shortcomings through their use of new technology, in January 1978 The Human League demoed their first electronic experimentations. The band that entered their Devonshire Lane rehearsal space in Sheffield to commit those first recordings to tape was a trio of rather earnest young men – Martyn Ware (synthesisers), Ian Craig Marsh (synthesisers) and Philip Oakey (vocals, and owner of a saxophone he had conspicuously failed to learn how to play) – who had come together to realise a musical vision that was entirely their own, and which was in part dictated by a musical proclamation displayed on the wall of their workspace. With the exception of the human voice, only electronic instruments were to be used in the band's compositions, and 'bland' words – and in particular the word 'love' – were to be avoided at all costs.

Ware now laughs about the band's uncompromising early attitude: 'It was the arrogance of youth that said that guitars were just so last week, and the future was electronic, pure electronic, and we were never going to use anything other than electronic instruments.' But the fact remains that the manifesto would not only dictate the musical direction on those original demos – which notably included early versions of the tracks 'Being Boiled', 'Circus Of Death' and 'Toyota City', each painstakingly recorded in mono using the primitive two-track technology available to the band at that time – but would remain rigidly in place for the duration of the band's first two album projects.

It wasn't just the music makers who were turning away from the punk movement that had galvanised them into entertaining musical ambitions of their own, however. As the clock ticked into 1978, the UK music scene as a whole sank into something of a stupor after the adrenaline shot of the previous eighteen months. Recently rejuvenated by the role they had played in punk's success over the previous couple of years, the music press were also sensing the shift away from that movement and were casting their critical nets far and wide in search of the next big thing. As a result, pretty much any band sporting even the most tenuous of post-punk credentials was suddenly under the microscope, as the media, the music industry and even the fans struggled to identify which of the fledgling efforts emerging from punk's shadow would be the ones worth watching.

Recognising the escalating demise of punk, *Sounds* writer Jon Savage, one of punk's most public champions, was admirably quick to look towards the future possibilities offered by electronic music, and had already identified US act Devo as one name to watch in 1978. The Akron, Ohio band had appeared on Savage's radar the previous year when the journalist discovered a pair of eccentric DIY singles that Devo had released in North America on their own Booji Boy label. Savage was sufficiently enamoured to place the first of those releases, the double A-side single 'Jocko Homo'/'Mongoloid', among his favourite singles of 1977.

Subsequently, Savage provided Devo with some of their earliest UK press exposure at the tail end of 1977 when, already looking towards music's immediate future, he included them in an odd, oblique, and rather pretentious, collection of features that he and various *Sounds* colleagues had penned under the banner 'The New Musick', which had run across two consecutive issues of the paper spanning the end of November and the beginning of December 1977. In addition to Devo, *Sounds* also identified Kraftwerk (who appeared on the cover of the first of The New Musick issues), Siouxsie & The Banshees (who were on the cover of the second, and who, despite their influence and status at the time, were yet to release their first record), Brian Eno, Throbbing Gristle and, more broadly, the disco and dub genres.

Despite having exercised a massive influence over music since 1973, and having recently released two of his most revolutionary and influential albums – *Low* and *"Heroes"* – over the course of 1977, David Bowie was conspicuously absent from *Sounds'* list, possibly because he had stolen a march on the paper and had already identified and championed several of the influences their list contained. With his cultural radar constantly tuned into the musical zeitgeist in search of new inspirations and interests, a number of up-and-coming acts exploring music's new experimental and electronic possibilities had already caught Bowie's eye, in particular Kraftwerk and the robotic 'motorik' disco sounds of Giorgio Moroder's work with Donna Summer.

Additionally, Bowie had already positioned himself as one of Devo's earliest champions. Having received Devo's demo tape in March 1977 whilst on tour in America with Iggy Pop, and having been quick to recognise something interesting in Devo's innovative and conceptual approach, Bowie had assumed an almost paternal role in the act's early career, and had publicly stated his intention to produce their debut album while introducing the band to the stage at an early Devo show at New York club Max's Kansas City in November of the same year.

By the start of 1978, the first domestic British releases for Devo were still some months off. January would instead see Bowie himself become one of the first artists to place a musical mark on the new year with the January 6th single release of 'Beauty And The Beast', the final single to be taken from the *"Heroes"* album, which had been released just a few months previously, but which had already left an indelible impression on an entire generation of musicians and music fans.

Amongst that generation was a nineteen-year old Bowie fan who considered 'Beauty And The Beast' 'The best thing Bowie's written' and who was about to embark on a musical journey all of his own. That young Bowie fan was just a couple of weeks away from the release of 'That's Too Bad', the debut single from his band Tubeway Army, an act which would very quickly go on to have an immeasurable impact on the development of electronic music.

Tubeway Army had recently signed to the fledgling independent label Beggars Banquet on the strength of the punk credentials evident across their demos and in their live performances. At that time, Beggars Banquet – one of a rash of new labels springing up to create an alternative infrastructure around the explosion of new punk acts – was primarily a punk label, and prior to 'That's Too Bad' had issued just a handful of releases: early singles from The Lurkers and The Doll – each notable now for being co-produced by Steve Lillywhite, one of the most successful producers working today – and an album, *Streets*, which was a compilation of contemporary punk acts, vaguely interesting for The Members' first appearance on vinyl and for the inclusion of 'Talk Talk Talk Talk' by The Reaction, a later version of which would give

The Reaction's lead singer, Mark Hollis, a significant hit in 1983 when he revisited the song with his next band, Talk Talk.

Deliberately – some might say cynically – recorded in a punk rock style, as that was the genre Tubeway Army had calculated was most likely to get them signed, and recorded at Spaceward Studios in Cambridge in late 1977 at the expense of their frontman's unusually supportive parents, the audio quality of the band's three-track demo was sufficiently high that – notwithstanding a quick remix session – the single version of 'That's Too Bad', and of its B-side, 'Oh! Didn't I Say', were the same recordings that the band had originally submitted to Beggars Banquet in the process of securing their deal, and both were credited entirely to Valeriun (variously also spelled Valerian and Valerium), the stage name adopted by Tubeway Army frontman Gary Webb.

Look back on 'That's Too Bad' today, with the benefit of over forty years of perspective, and the single still retains a certain charm. Even now it's not difficult to recognise the potential of Tubeway Army as Beggars Banquet must have seen it: Webb's vocal delivery, replete with the requisite punk rock sneer demanded by the period, is unusual and distinctive, already hinting at life beyond punk's narrow format, and the song's structure and performance are more than competent, notable traits at a time when striking a suitably anarchic pose was frequently valued over musical ability. That the band – and Webb in particular – also looked good and presented themselves well on stage was another important factor.

Despite having arrived on the scene while punk was still alive and kicking, and having positioned Tubeway Army as a punk band, Webb had already anticipated a change in the prevailing tide and was determined not to be caught up in a movement he considered to be in terminal decline, as he would later clarify: 'I didn't know at that point that the move was going to be into electronic music, I just knew I had to move somewhere. I became very frightened that the next big thing was going to come along soon and wipe away the remnants of punk. To me punk was dying on its feet. I didn't want to be associated with it any more, I wanted to be the next big thing.'

And becoming the next big thing was an ambition Webb embarked upon with an almost fanatical intensity, resigning from his job as a forklift driver on the same day 'That's Too Bad' was released in order to concentrate all his energies on his musical career. 'I had nothing to lose,' he admitted later, 'I'd made a mess of school, had no conventional career to fall back on, nothing to stop me devoting myself to it absolutely.'

Upon its release on February 10th, sales of 'That's Too Bad' were quietly encouraging: the single shifted a few thousand copies relatively quickly despite attracting only lukewarm attention in the music press. *Melody Maker* in particular was less than encouraging about Tubeway Army's debut, summing up the release as 'Feeble Johnny Rotten imitator gabbles indistinctly over 'Day Tripper' riff.' Equally tepid in their support of the single, *Sounds* also dismissed the release, describing it a 'recycler-ready turkey' while providing a glimmer of grudging support for the band by conceding that 'John Peel'll probably love it'.

Sounds were correct. John Peel liked and played 'That's Too Bad', and in the process became one of Tubeway Army's earliest and most influential supporters, making a major contribution to the single's modest success, which otherwise amounted to little more than some lacklustre reviews, a developing profile on London's live circuit, and an element of good timing which allowed Tubeway Army to benefit from the word of mouth power of the punk rock grapevine, something Beggars Banquet's Martin Mills would later acknowledge: 'Those were the days when there were so few punk/new wave records coming out on small labels that people following that sound would buy anything that was remotely punk or on a small label. They'd buy them almost without knowing whether they liked them or not.'

Any savings in recording expenses that Beggars Banquet were able to make from releasing the already-recorded demo version of 'That's Too Bad' were quickly wiped out when Tubeway Army went into a more sophisticated studio, The Music Centre in Wembley, to record their second single. Intrigued and excited by all the technology suddenly at their disposal, the band proceeded to lose themselves down a rabbit hole of sonic possibilities. Having run up a significant bill for extra studio time, the band finally delivered the single, 'Bombers', to the palpable disappointment of the label, as Martin Mills would recall: 'It was recorded a bit too cleanly for the type of music it was. It ended up as a studio-produced sound, which it wasn't in essence. It was smoother than 'That's Too Bad' but not far enough in another direction to make it worth going in another direction.'

More importantly, the process had allowed Tubeway Army, and Valeriun in particular, to open up to the idea of embracing a wider palate of opportunities, and 'Bombers' nevertheless represents an important step along the band's journey. Tubeway Army were growing up in public and, while they didn't yet know where they wanted that growth to take them, there was one thing they were sure of: they had no interest in being another of the one-dimensional punk act that were starting to crowd 1978's release schedules.

In their review of the 'Bombers' single upon its July 1978 release, *Melody Maker* were cautiously supportive, describing the song as 'interesting if flawed' and praising Tubeway Army's new musical trajectory, noting, with something akin to approval, that 'the treatment shows they're beginning to scour the studio for possibilities'. *Record Mirror*, meanwhile, were less objective, singularly failing to identify any redeeming features in the song at all and simply imploring the band to 'please give up gracefully'. While music fans will be forever grateful that Tubeway Army chose not to heed *Record Mirror*'s advice, 'Bombers' ultimately did little to further the band's cause. The single sold roughly the same number of copies as 'That's Too Bad', but nevertheless, as the first tangible step towards the band's reinvention, it does illustrate an important move away from the increasingly stale punk stylings of the day.

Sitting side by side with 'That's Too Bad' on the release schedules and review pages in February 1978 was *Retro*, a four-track EP from London five-piece Ultravox!, another group of earnest young men in the process of sidelining punk in order to reinvent themselves as something considerably more musically fulfilling, creatively satisfying and current. Significantly more established than Tubeway Army, Ultravox! – who had been around in one form or another since 1974 – had kicked off 1978 by announcing the *Retro* EP as an interim release to bridge the gap between their second and third album releases.

Retro was a live release which neatly encapsulated the sound of a band at a musical crossroads by showcasing live versions of four key tracks from their career to date. Alongside the broadly conventional rock sounds of 'The Wild, The Beautiful And The Damned' and 'Young Savage' sat a pair of tracks which provided important clues towards the increasingly electronic direction that Ultravox! were now exploring. 'My Sex' had first appeared on Ultravox!'s eponymous debut album at the start of 1977, the band's first real step on a journey towards an electronic sound; and 'The Man Who Dies Every Day' had appeared on the second Ultravox! album *Ha! Ha! Ha!*. Each represented an important step towards the band rejecting their previous glam, punk and art-rock stylings in favour of capturing some of the spirit of the changing times. 'There was a great need for something far more capable of conveying all the wonder, fear, beauty, romance, bravado, hope and inadequacy that everyone felt,' frontman John Foxx would later acknowledge.

Formed in London some four years previously, Ultravox!'s first stable line-up – John Foxx, Billy Currie, Warren Cann, Chris Cross and Stevie Shears – spent their first two years together working variously under the names The Zips, The Innocents, The Damned, London Soundtrack, Fire Of London and Tiger Lily before eventually settling on Ultravox!. According to Foxx, talking to the *NME* in 1977, the final choice of name was decided because 'It sounds like an electrical device, and that's what we are', although he would later add the further, and rather more mischievous, qualification that 'everyone disliked it, so we thought it must have some virtue'. The exclamation mark was sometimes explained by the band as a deliberate nod to the influence of Neu! although Foxx, with a touch of embarrassment, told *ZigZag* in 1978 that the truth was more prosaic and the exclamation mark was a considered publicity stunt: 'I thought that if we had it in headlines, it would mean that we were extraordinary by an exclamation mark. It was a stupid idea.'

Prior to becoming Ultravox! the band released one single as Tiger Lily: a cover version of the Fats Waller standard 'Ain't Misbehavin'', which they had been commissioned to record for the soundtrack to a 1974 movie of the same name. As it happens, the makers of the film – which was a dubious compilation of vintage soft porn clips from the 1930s and 1940s overlaid with music and intercut with footage of dancing – would eventually ditch the Tiger Lily version of the track in favour of the Fats Waller original, but the new version was nonetheless released as a single on the Gull label in March 1975 with an original composition, 'Monkey Jive', on its B-side.

Ultravox!'s next venture into recorded music would come shortly after signing to the Island Records label in 1976. *Rock & Reggae & Derek & Clive* was an album compilation designed to showcase Island Records' roster at that time and was released in October of that year. Ultravox!'s contribution to the album, an early version of the song 'The Wild, The Beautiful And The Damned', was credited on the album sleeve to '?' as the band had been unable to settle on a satisfactory name in time for the release's production deadline. Island Records tried to turn the situation to their advantage by playing up the 'mystery band' angle in the album's sleeve notes, which read – slightly inaccurately given the band's recent foray into soft porn soundtracks – 'The first time the band have been heard on record. They are a brand-new British group whose debut album, from which this track has been taken, is currently being produced by Brian Eno,' which only served to surround the band's introduction to the public and, perhaps more importantly, to the media with an unwelcome aura of record company manipulation at such a crucial point in their nascent career.

The perception that the steering hand of Island Records was somehow manipulating Ultravox! to the label's own ends would feed the media's perceptions of what the band were trying to achieve for quite some time. Their earnest pretentiousness and studied art-school aesthetic certainly set Ultravox! apart from most of the acts around them at that time, and it wasn't until the emergence of punk, which finally gave them a context in which their alternative sounds and approach could be fully accepted on their own merit, that Ultravox! could start to find their feet and emerge as the pioneering entity they most certainly were.

At that time Roxy Music provided an easy and convenient point of comparison for any journalist who might want to reference an example of an art-school band. An *NME* live review from February 1978 declared that Ultravox! 'positively reek of art school', and the timing of Ultravox!'s signing with Island Records, hot on the heels of Roxy Music's split and subsequent withdrawal from the same roster, meant that, over the course of the three albums they recorded for the label, Ultravox! would be dogged by media assumptions that they had somehow been groomed to step into Roxy's glittery art-rock shoes. A 1977 *NME* feature on Ultravox! noted 'uncomfortable similarities to Roxy Music – the lack of musical history, the high stylisation content both in music and appearance, and the comparatively lavish sleeve on their debut album – which have led to rumours of the group being no more than a bunch of session musicians put together by Island to fill the Roxy gap.'

The decision to then bring in Brian Eno to co-produce Ultravox!'s debut album only served to compound those media assumptions, even though the choice of producer had come from the band and not from the label. Foxx had actually approached Eno at Island Records' creative hub of offices, studios and rehearsal rooms in West London during the negotiations with the label that led to Ultravox!'s signing and, on behalf of his band, had asked Eno to produce their album on the very straightforward grounds that 'We liked the things he did, because they were unorthodox, and we were very enamoured of things that were unorthodox at the time,' to which Foxx added, 'Eno seemed the only salvation – plus the fact that no one else could make head or tail of what we were doing.' The match was subsequently approved by Island who were keen to have their new signings work with a 'name' producer in addition to the then-unknown Steve Lillywhite, who had previously befriended the band and who – using downtime at Phonogram Studios in Marble Arch where he was working as a tape operator – had produced the demos that had contributed to Ultravox! securing their Island deal.

Looking back on the making of that first album – and noting that the Ultravox! who recorded it were a fairly straightforward rock act who were only just starting to experiment with electronic sounds – John Foxx recalled that Eno's involvement was somewhat divisive within the group. In particular, drummer Warren Cann was less than impressed by Eno's lack of technical prowess in the studio, while Billy Currie, Chris Cross, Stevie Shears and Foxx himself had enjoyed the process much more. Cann later told Jonas Wårstad that the resulting album 'was absolutely not what we had actually envisaged', a statement which Foxx doesn't necessarily disagree with, although he has since countered that Eno's lack of studio skills paled in comparison to what he brought to the table in other ways: 'Brian encouraged use of the studio as a means of communal transport. Can do. Just drive the damn thing. Let's see what this does. The fact that he may not have been so technical wasn't the issue. What mattered was the view of the craft we were operating.'

In a technical sense, Eno was, at that time, working in a similar DIY spirit to the one that underpinned punk, but was approaching his work in a more cerebral and studied way that betrayed his own art-school background, and which any true punk devotee might consider the antithesis of their movement. Eno did consider the Ultravox! of 1976 to have been born from punk rock roots but noted that they were in the process of making an important transition to something less derivative and more substantial: 'They were a very early punk rock band. They started two years ago and they were into that thing and gradually they matured. This album sounds very much like the early Roxy ones – not in terms of sound, but in terms of juxtaposition of things that are definitely going somewhere very interesting with things that are the remains of something else.'

Eno's impact on Ultravox! was also felt in other, more practical ways. It was he who introduced the band to their first proper synthesiser, bringing a Minimoog into the studio for the band's perusal and experimentation. Eno was not, however, the ideal person to instruct the newcomers in the Moog's usage, as Ultravox! drummer and percussionist Warren Cann would later recall for Jonas Wårstad, underlining his concern at Eno's lack of technical prowess at that time: 'He had all these little pieces of tape stuck by the keys with the names of the notes written on them, plus little pictures stuck on adjacent to some of the control knobs. I pointed to a cute picture of a sheep and asked, 'What's that mean?' He replied, 'Well, I don't know what that knob does but, when I turn it, it makes the sound 'woolly', so the picture of the sheep."

In turn, Billy Currie – who would go on to become Ultravox!'s own synthesiser expert, but at that time was providing the band's viola, violin and electric violin sounds – recalls Eno as having been 'very patient and helpful' during those album sessions, while admitting that, although he was theoretically open to Eno's ideas of experimentation, the reality was that he found it difficult to let go of what he now describes as his own black-and-white approach. Some of this difficulty can be attributed to the fact that most of the songs that make up the Ultravox! album were written well before the band went into the studio with Eno to record them – in the case of 'The Wild, The Beautiful And The Damned' and 'I Want To Be A Machine' that period was several years – and they had been honed and polished in rehearsal and onstage over that period of time and the band were reluctant to let such creative investment go to waste.

A notable exception to this process was the genesis of the one track created in collaboration between band and producer. In addition to the impact Eno had on Ultravox! by introducing them to the cutting-edge technology of the time, he also contributed hugely to a second pivotal moment in the band's history: the creation in the studio of the track 'My Sex', which represented an important step towards the material that would come to inform the direction of the band's second album, something Foxx would later acknowledge in an interview for David Sheppard's biography of Brian Eno, *On Some Faraway Beach*: 'For me, it was the best thing on the record – synths, drum machine; the way forward.'

It was during the final sessions with Ultravox! that Eno received the call from David Bowie to become a prime collaborator and co-conspirator in the creation of *Low*, as John Foxx told Sheppard later: 'It was quite funny really, because Brian went all coy; wasn't sure if he should really do it and so on. We all howled 'Go on Brian, you have to.' Of course he was just showing off by playing hard to get. It was endearing really.' Presumably it was a more buoyant and confident Eno who then rendezvoused with Bowie in France, having successfully tested some of his creative strategies and techniques on Ultravox!.

Such was the band's enthusiasm for 'My Sex' that they used it as the B-side on the debut Ultravox! single 'Dangerous Rhythm' when it was released in February 1977 to a broadly enthusiastic critical reception. *Sounds* archly proclaimed the release as their 'Debut Single & Eno Production of the Week', noting that the 'Rich emetic bass, precise Ringo drums, synthesiser cascades and Eno's hand in the production make this the best and most confident debut single since 'Anarchy'.' The media's insistence on allocating swathes of praise to Eno, however, was a situation which would increasingly irritate the band over the course of the *Ultravox!* album project, given that they had decided against using the bulk of their co-producer's work on the finished record. That said, even Warren Cann would later concede that Eno's name 'did help bring about some attention that might not otherwise have been paid to us concerning that first album, but it had never been our intention to do that'.

Just three months after the release of *Ultravox!*, and following an intense period of promotion and touring to support the release, Ultravox! had already started work on a second album which they preceded with the May 1977 release of a brand new single, 'Young Savage'. A glorious explosion of a song, 'Young Savage''s exhilarating punk exuberance, all glam-rock stomp and fuck-you attitude, coupled with the DIY stylings of the newsprint collage on its sleeve and its enthusiastic reception live, ensured that the song quickly connected with the largely punk audience the band were attracting at the time. *Sounds* were once again enthusiastic in their review, describing the song as a 'cocaine brain speed cocktail', although the *NME*, while praising Stevie Shears' guitar work and noting 'Young Savage''s speed and ferocity with something like approval, were less enamoured, dismissing the track as sounding 'like one that didn't make the first album'.

Ultimately 'Young Savage' did fail to make an appearance on Ultravox!'s second album, *Ha! Ha! Ha!*, when it appeared in the autumn of 1977, leaving the single forever destined to occupy an uneasy space between the band's first two album releases. But the single release wasn't wasted, and 'Young Savage' aimed a spirited message of defiance at the band's increasingly vocal detractors, while incinerating the band's earlier releases in a blast of defiance that would see Ultravox! replace any last vestiges of naivety that might have been lingering since releasing their album debut with the frustration, anger and aggression that fuelled their second.

Taking inspiration and momentum from the positive experiences they shared with Brian Eno in the creation of 'My Sex', and setting that alongside the negative experiences they suffered at the hands of the media, *Ha! Ha! Ha!* was conceived and recorded very quickly in the wake of 'Young Savage', and finally hit the shops on October 14th, 1977, just eight months after the release of *Ultravox!*.

Ha! Ha! Ha! was recorded in Phonogram Studios in London, with Steve Lillywhite stepping up to produce the record with the band. Phonogram was the studio where Ultravox! had recorded the Steve Lillywhite demos that had led to their signing with Island, but it was an altogether more confident band that returned to the scene of those early works. The demo sessions there had been recorded out of hours and off the books, so not only were Ultravox! now allowed the luxury of working there officially, but the relative security of their record deal also meant that the band had been able to invest some of their advance in new equipment for the sessions.

The decision to further embrace the potential of technology was crucial in dictating the trajectory of the band's developing sound and the sonic shape of *Ha! Ha! Ha!*. The haul of new equipment included the acquisition of the band's first synthesisers, amongst them an ARP Odyssey for Billy Currie and a Roland TR-77 drum machine which was operated by Warren Cann, who was unfazed by the new technology threatening to unseat him from the drum stool, and was instead actively mesmerised by the device's perfect rhythm and tempo. Cann would later describe the TR-77 as 'entirely unprogrammable', although through a convoluted system of trial, error, patience and bloody-mindedness he eventually managed to tame the technology 'By popping the buttons in and out like station surfing on an old car radio'.

Foxx would later explain that Ultravox!'s plan for the second album was to 'refine and distill' the immediate, experimental and stripped-down creative process they had enjoyed with Brian Eno, while redirecting and reinterpreting the music through drum machines, synthesisers and technology. While tracks like 'ROckWrok', 'The Man Who Dies Every Day' and 'Artificial Life' are telling indicators of Ultravox!'s increasing interest in electronic possibilities, it is 'Hiroshima Mon Amour' that most successfully showcases the band's new direction.

In the same way that 'My Sex' sat at odds with the other tracks on the *Ultravox!* album, 'Hiroshima Mon Amour' was the cuckoo in the nest of *Ha! Ha! Ha!*. Having recorded an initial version of the track in the same art-glam-punk style that characterised the majority of the new record, the band, and Billy Currie and John Foxx in particular, continued to tinker with the song, specifically feeling that 'Hiroshima Mon Amour' 'would be more effective played with a more detached feel', to which end the band introduced the use of the TR-77 operated, with some difficulty, by Warren Cann, a process Billy Currie now drily recalls as 'a bit of a drama'. Currie also remembers being immediately interested in further pushing the possibilities of the track, and contributed electric violin, and then an Elka String Machine part to lead the track and also to underpin its understated appeal. A saxophone part, courtesy of saxophonist CC from the band Gloria Mundi, was finally added to provide a warm analogue layer to counterpoint the detached, mechanical vocals and drum patterns that now underpinned the track.

Ultravox! were delighted by the new version of 'Hiroshima Mon Amour', and the original version of the song – the sound of which Warren Cann would describe in an August 1978 interview with *Sounds* as 'like getting your face slowly dragged across some concrete' – was subsequently dubbed the 'Alternative Version' and relegated to the B-side of the 'ROckWrok' single in early October 1977. Meanwhile the futuristic electronic version was the one to appear on the *Ha! Ha! Ha!* album. If 'My Sex' represented a pivotal groundbreaking moment for the band on Ultravox!'s eponymous first album, then 'Hiroshima Mon Amour' represented an equivalent moment on *Ha! Ha! Ha!*.

Julie Burchill reviewed *Ha! Ha! Ha!* for the *NME* upon the album's release in October 1977, and while she recognised the validity of Ultravox!'s aim of overlaying punk's stripped-back energy with strands of glam rock's twinkly DNA, she was equally quick to dismiss the band as 'too old' (John Foxx, the band's oldest member, was just twenty-nine at the time, an apparently impossible age to the then-eighteen-year-old Burchill), and appeared to instantly lose interest in the record as a result. While her comments were certainly valid on the evidence of the album opener, 'ROckWrok', it does seem entirely plausible that Burchill didn't even listen to the record for long enough to discover the other facets of the band which sat at odds to the rest of the album and switched the prevailing sonic mood (Roxy Music, The Stranglers, John Lydon) to something altogether sparser, cooler and noticeably more electronic.

Reviewing *Ha! Ha! Ha!* for *Sounds* the week following Burchill's *NME* review, Pete Silverton noted the record's 'unrelenting seriousness' as well as its art-school overtones, and its distinct lack of humanity. Describing the songs as a mixture of the adventurous, the orthodox and the 'wilfully different', Silverton also opined that the record could be considered an effective case study of 'the bad effects the mere acquisition of a synthesiser can have'. Listen to the record today and the use of synthesisers, while prevalent throughout the album, is hugely conservative by later standards, and the Ultravox! that made *Ha! Ha! Ha!* would still be more accurately classified as a rock group using electronics rather than an electronic group playing rock.

Such lukewarm reactions from the music press would become the norm for Ultravox!, whose long-running battle with the way the media portrayed them was then still in its infancy. Nevertheless, when it came to *Ha! Ha! Ha!*, the band themselves could understand some of the negativity that was thrown their way. The album had been made during a difficult time for Ultravox!, whose debut had failed to live up to their own expectations and who, as a result, had channelled the anger and frustration they were experiencing into the new songs. While the speedy writing and recording process added an urgency and a spontaneity to the finished record, by the time it hit the record shops Ultravox! were already impatient to be developing their sound further.

In the wake of the release of *Ha! Ha! Ha!*, Ultravox! found themselves at something of a career crossroads. The band's musical output to date had allowed them to work broadly within the traditional parameters of rock, while at the same time allowing them both the space to step outside the constraints of those expectations, and the freedom to explore the emerging possibilities of the new electronic ideas that were becoming their obsession. Additionally, such a rapid shift in Ultravox!'s sound, style and approach shone a light onto the limitations of the band's line-up, which was starting to fracture under the weight of progress. As positive and interesting as this creatively schizophrenic state had been to the band over the course of their first two albums, the situation had now started to cause conflict within the group, or more accurately between the majority of the group – those anxious to explore the new sonic landscapes their increasingly futuristic vision promised – and guitarist Stevie Shears, who was keen to continue channelling the stripped-back aggression and energy that punk had brought to the Ultravox! sound.

Not that Ultravox! had ever consciously aligned themselves with punk, but the movement had importantly provided them with a context in which they – and other bands and artists with similar ambitions determined to plough a less than conventional furrow – could catch some of the momentum of those transitional times for their own purposes. In fact Ultravox! would have been hard pressed to identify acts they might consider true peers from among those responsible for the punk and post-punk soundscapes into which they had released their first two albums. As John Foxx would later recall, 'We decided to let the whole thing rush by us while we made a still place to conduct our own experiments.'

Stevie Shears aside, for the rest of Ultravox! the opportunity to put the increasingly anachronistic punk scene behind them couldn't come soon enough. While they had built up a decent following from among the punk curious, their use of synthesisers was anathema to the punk purists, who still associated the instrument with the type of indulgent, old-school progressive rock that punk was supposed to have swept away. To challenge the punk orthodoxy even further, Ultravox! also had the audacity to use 'classical' instruments on stage and that, as the band's violin and viola player Billy Currie would later recollect – and with a great deal of feeling – took the potential for confrontation and trouble to a whole new level.

Any subtleties in the layered electronic sounds that underpinned the original studio versions of the songs that featured on the *Retro* EP are largely lost amid the frenetic, turbo-charged sounds that characterised Ultravox!'s 1977 live show. Despite being dogged by a media quick to dismiss the band as mere glam-rock copyists, forever destined to be a step or two behind the times, the EP actually serves as an excellent document of the transition the band was making as they moved from their punk, glam and rock beginnings into a new creative space of their own design.

Retro was released on February 10th, 1978 and coincided with the band completing a seventeen-date UK tour which ended with three shows at London's Marquee. The *NME* were cautiously enthusiastic about the live show, summing up the band as 'some futurism here, a threat of cybernetics there, a hint of asexuality, a suggestion of languid decadence, a whiff of narcotics, a je-ne-sais-quois of French for that certain chicness', but were far less enthusiastic in their review of the EP, quickly affecting a bored tone and describing Ultravox!'s urban and technological themes as 'very tiresome'.

Around the time of *Retro*'s release, Ultravox! distanced themselves further from the rapidly cooling embers of punk by parting company with Stevie Shears and recruiting a new guitarist, Robin Simon, to take his place. Simon joined the band from Neo, a London-based punk-influenced act whose recorded output at that point had amounted to two live tracks on the 1977 punk compilation *Live From The Vortex*, but who had come to Ultravox!'s attention through sharing the bill with them at various London shows.

At the same time, the band also quietly dropped the superfluous exclamation mark from the end of their name and prepared themselves for the next step along a career path that would ensure their place among the true pioneers of electronic pop. By the spring of 1978 the impressive work ethic that had fuelled the rapid recording and release of their first two albums was kicking in once again as Ultravox started to plot the direction of their third – and Germany featured prominently in those plans.

Keen to explore more of the possibilities suggested by the moments of electronic experimentation that had led to the creation of 'Hiroshima Mon Amour', 'My Sex', 'The Man Who Dies Every Day' and 'I Want To Be A Machine', Ultravox wanted to follow in the footsteps of the original electronic innovators, and decided to approach the influential German producer Conny Plank – who had already worked on records for Kraftwerk, Brian Eno, Neu! and Cluster, among others – to produce their next record.

On tour in Germany in March 1978, on a day off between shows, Ultravox took the opportunity to set up a preliminary meeting with Plank at his studio near Cologne. Upon arriving at the rural studios they were immediately, and happily, reacquainted with Brian Eno, who was working with Plank on the former's latest project, producing the debut album for Devo, who, after David Bowie and Jon Savage's enthusiastic patronage the previous year, were already starting to attract considerable attention across 1978's post-punk media landscape. Aided by Eno, Ultravox's meeting with Plank was declared a success, a deal was struck, and the band arranged an imminent return to Wolperath to start work on their third album.

DYLAN U.K. CONCERTS

Page 3

new MUSICAL EXPRESS

BOB
MARLEY
STEVENS
C.I.A.
American concert report P11

KRAFTWERK
THE MUSIC
MACHINE
Album review P29, Thrills P12

'NEW
PISTOLS'
DELIGHT
Cook, Jones interview P7

1978.2 Kraftwerk / Devo / Brian Eno / Japan

MEANWHILE, IN DÜSSELDORF, LESS than forty miles to the north of Conny Plank's studio, Kraftwerk were preparing to emerge from their own studio, Kling Klang, to launch their new album *The Man-Machine*. Released just over a year after their influential *Trans-Europe Express* album, Kraftwerk's new record was produced by the band's founding members Ralf Hütter and Florian Schneider and, upon its release in May, easily asserted Kraftwerk's dominance of the electronic music arena.

At the end of April the *NME* put Kraftwerk on their cover and accompanied that honour with a one-and-a-half-page review from Andy Gill which – while using a great deal of column inches to debate the album's perceived links to fascism, totalitarianism and constructivism – justly hailed *The Man-Machine* as 'one of the pinnacles of '70s rock music... Devo can doddle around in the silly suits and give evasive answers to questions about their "philosophy" for all they're worth,' mused Gill, 'the fact remains that Kraftwerk are the only completely successful visual/aural fusion rock has produced so far.'

The same week saw Jon Savage tackle *The Man-Machine* for the review section of *Sounds*. Awarding the album four and a half stars, Savage heaped praise upon the release, hailing *The Man-Machine*'s 'conception, production, technique and execution' as 'impeccable and near brilliant'. Contemplating whether the album was a masterpiece of self-conscious kitsch German humour or simply 'flawlessly, preciously empty', Savage nevertheless paid tribute to the 'very precise, very beautiful, and very stylised' nature of the album, concluding that 'as a consumer package, as sound, this album is nigh irresistible'.

The following week, *The Man-Machine* was *Melody Maker*'s lead album review, although writer Karl Dallas was not entirely convinced by the record, acknowledging that while *The Man-Machine* contained 'considerably more musical appeal' than either *Radio-Activity* or *Trans-Europe Express*, for him there was a lack of the coherence that had made *Autobahn* a stand-out release. In fact much of the review was given over to comparing and contrasting Kraftwerk's 'hard-edged, mechanised to the ultimate, de-humanised, even inhuman' sounds with Tangerine Dream's 'great sprawling romanticism'. Ultimately Dallas did manage to concede that 'on its own terms, this is really a rather good album'.

'It was really *The Man-Machine* that brought me into Kraftwerk properly,' Gary Numan told David Buckley in *Publikation*, Buckley's 2012 biography of Kraftwerk. 'Kraftwerk seemed to be totally technology-driven. It had to be machine made. I was much, much less of a pioneer than they ever were. They were streets ahead of pretty much everybody. And most of the people that followed, me included, just took elements of it, really, and added it to something else. They were genuinely pioneering.' For Duran Duran, the timing of the release of *The Man-Machine* couldn't have been more perfect, as John Taylor recalled in the same publication: 'It was 1978 when we decided we were going to form a band together. We decided to get a synthesiser, because we liked the way things were going, we liked the rhythmic things that were happening in the synthesiser world. I'd have to say that Kraftwerk were part of that.'

While *The Man-Machine* failed to translate such enthusiastic journalism and musical influence into commercial success – at the time the album managed to peak at number fifty-three in the UK charts – it was followed by a single release of 'The Robots'. Limited to 10,000 copies, each single was packaged in a 'unique dimensional construction' sleeve and was available at a recommended retail price of 80p. Calling it a 'nice way to start the day', *Sounds* made 'The Robots' their Single of the Week, assigning Kraftwerk the dubious label of 'fun huns' and recognising the band's position as 'way out ahead of their even more numerous imitators'. In *Melody Maker*, Ian Birch described the release as 'rinky-dink disko for all aesthetic androids everywhere' and extolled the single for being 'hypnotic and stimulating' and 'sharp, stainless, and always in motion'.

Meanwhile the *NME* – hailing Kraftwerk as 'the only engineers extant working in this maligned field who can make the machines speak' – were on more mischievous form, describing the single's special sleeve as foolish on the grounds that it was 'impossible for stupid people like me to put back together again' and noting that playing the single at 33 1/3 rpm still sounded great, 'though you have to dance in slow-motion, like a drunk'.

'The Robots' was not a UK hit but EMI were undeterred and in the middle of October released another single from *The Man-Machine*, 'Neon Lights' (on luminous vinyl), which received similarly enthusiastic reviews from the music press and even nudged the lower reaches of the UK singles chart, when it peaked at fifty-three at the end of the month. 'Quite perfect in every way,' enthused *Sounds*. 'Being a bigot, I used to dismiss Kraftwerk for being German and Weather Report for being jazzy. I've made worse mistakes, but in certain moods I find this kind of aural hypnosis more powerful than my prejudices,' declared *Melody Maker*.

While *The Man-Machine* project revolved around Kraftwerk's assertion that the future relationship between man and machine was becoming increasingly inseparable, Devo were simultaneously approaching their work from an opposite standpoint, and were instead exploring de-evolution, the notion of a future where mankind would devolve over time and return to a simpler state, a guiding principle that underpinned much of Devo's work, and which also gave the band their name.

Eccentric, driven, and unorthodox in their approach, Devo had publicly asserted that the only people they would consider producing their debut album would be David Bowie or Brian Eno, and were fortunate indeed when Iggy Pop professed to be much taken by the Ohio act's avant-garde, experimental sounds after they managed to get a demo tape to him during the March 1977 US tour for *The Idiot*. Pop listened to the tape and loved it, something he would later recall for Jeff Winner's documentary film *Are We Not Devo?*: 'I felt like Columbus, I felt like I just discovered America, and it was Devo.'

After listening to the demos, Pop reacted in exactly the way that Devo had hoped and shared the tracks with his friend David Bowie, producer of *The Idiot* and Pop's keyboard player on the tour to promote that album. Bowie was equally enthusiastic about Devo's innovative portfolio of sounds and, in turn, pronounced them 'the band of the future', encouraging Brian Eno to listen to their work and to experience their live show.

As it would turn out, Bowie's commitment to act in the film *Just a Gigolo* meant that he was not able to schedule a suitable block of time to produce Devo's debut album and, after apparent interest in the task from both Iggy

Pop and Robert Fripp (who had accompanied Brian Eno to the Devo show at Max's Kansas City), that duty eventually fell to Eno, who also financed the recording sessions which took place at Conny Plank's studios in Germany in early 1978.

In the event, the relationship between Devo and Brian Eno turned out to be less than satisfactory on both sides, as Devo struggled to see beyond the scope of their own original demo concepts and stubbornly refused to adopt Eno's trademark studio spontaneity in favour of following more regimented processes of their own, an impasse that left Eno perplexed. 'They were a terrifying group of people to work with because they were so unable to experiment,' Eno confessed to *Mojo* in 1995.

Bowie was at least present for some of the making of the album – which would become *Q: Are We Not Men? A: We Are Devo!* – and although he wasn't particularly hands-on in the process, he was – between squabbles with Brian Eno over appropriate credit for Eno's input into the *Low* and *"Heroes"* albums – able to offer feedback on the recordings and to jam with Devo during such time he was able to spend at the studio. After Bowie's death in 2016, Devo's Gerald Casale mused on what might have happened to the sound of the album had Bowie assumed production duties, and guessed that it would, in all likelihood, have been very different, particularly if Devo had been able to take direction from Bowie in a way that they hadn't been able to with Eno.

Recalling the brief time he had been present during Devo's recording sessions in Germany, Ultravox's Billy Currie would later recollect, 'It wasn't a great atmosphere. It was peculiar. I mean the singer was on the floor playing with cards, he looked like he was in his own unreal world.' Although Currie did qualify that opinion with the generous observation that 'We were in the middle of a tour, so we probably looked pretty strange too.'

Devo's Mark Mothersbaugh would later come to view the lost potential of the Eno sessions with something approaching regret, admitting 'we were overtly resistant to Eno's ideas. He made up synth parts and really cool sounds for almost every part of the album, but we [only] used them on three or four songs.' The band's Jerry Casale voiced similar feelings to *The Times* in 2010, saying, 'Brian kept trying to add beauty to our songs, because he was a little appalled at how brutal and industrial our aesthetic was. He thought maybe he could fix that for us, but we didn't want fixing back then.'

Regardless of whether the relationship was ultimately successful or satisfying for the parties involved, as a result of the high-profile attention of

Bowie and Eno, coupled with Jon Savage's initial support, Devo – whom Bowie would describe to *ZigZag* as 'Three Enos and a couple of Edgar Froeses in one band' – would enjoy extensive coverage in the UK music press throughout 1978, including front covers and significant features for both *Sounds* and *NME* over the course of the year. The combination of the hype that surrounded them as one of 1978's next big things, alongside a packed release and tour schedule, ensured that Devo's cerebral, unorthodox practices placed them very firmly on that year's musical map as electronic music trailblazers.

Meanwhile, Devo's first domestic single release in the UK had been the February 1978 release of 'Mongoloid' and 'Jocko Homo' on the Stiff label. The single was well received upon its UK release with the *NME* dubbing it 'catchy', to the extent that they predicted it would be sung on football terraces around the country. Peaking at a very respectable sixty-two in the UK charts, the success of the single paved the way for the release of a second, Devo's unique take on The Rolling Stones' '(I Can't Get No) Satisfaction', which Stiff released under the typographically demanding, but altogether more 'Devo' title '(I Căn't Gèt Mé Nö) Såtisfactiön'.

Upon its release in April 1978, *Sounds* made '(I Căn't Gèt Mé Nö) Såtisfactiön' their 'Nice One of the Week', and the *NME* awarded it Single of the Week, holding the track up as justification for 'all the media knicker-twisting' the band were attracting at the time, and describing the single as a 'singularly brilliant little manoeuvre'. Equally excitingly for the band, upon hearing Devo's jerky, mechanical take on his song while they were seeking permission to release their version of the track, Rolling Stones frontman Mick Jagger declared it his favourite cover of the song ever, and was presumably also delighted by the extra royalties heading his way after Devo's version reached number forty-one in the UK singles chart.

When two different record labels subsequently claimed to be releasing Devo's debut album – the fruits of their German adventures with Brian Eno – with announcements to that effect appearing in the music press from Warner Bros and then from Virgin Records in early 1978, the band's cachet, and the hype that surrounded them, rose even further. The truth is altogether more prosaic: Virgin Records had signed the band for the UK and Europe, while Warner Bros had signed them for North America, although there is a strong suggestion that Warners were under the impression that their deal with the band was an exclusive one which covered the world.

A press release was subsequently circulated to announce that Devo's debut album, despite announcements to the contrary from Warner Bros, would be released by Virgin Records on August 25th alongside a new single – erroneously reported as 'Come Back Johnny' – on the same date, with the promise of a full UK tour to take place in the autumn. Additionally the release reported that the album would be issued in five different coloured-vinyl editions (grey, white, blue, yellow and red) and would be supported by a vast array of promotional merchandise to include badges, T-shirts, armbands, posters and shop-window displays.

'Come Back Johnny' turned out to be a misprint, and 'Come Back Jonee' and was subsequently released as a single with a level of commercial support similar to that behind to the album, the *NME* reporting that the first 25,000 copies of the single would be pressed in 'industrial grey' vinyl. In a case of odd scheduling, 'Come Back Jonee' was released just three weeks after the final Devo release on Stiff, a single cannily entitled 'Be Stiff', which was itself available in a choice of black, transparent or yellow vinyl editions upon its August 4th release.

'Be Stiff' was the first of the band's releases to really feel the cold indifference of the UK music press. *NME* designated 'Be Stiff' crass, dismissing the single as 'The best Rolling Stones record that Bad Company never made.' *Melody Maker* were similarly quick to express their own disappointment, describing the release as 'music for constipation' and ending their lukewarm review with the damning sign-off, 'No, we are not the backlash. We're just let down.'

Once again it was left to *Sounds* to deliver a less polarised review of the release, which they duly delivered under the heading 'Other Interesting Singles', but even *Sounds* was forced to admit that despite 'Be Stiff' being an 'extremely commercial, highly eccentric little single' it nonetheless lacked some of the ingenuity and charm so evident on 'Jocko Homo' and the band's other previous efforts. 'Quirky with strangled guitar but more straightforward rock than usual,' was *ZigZag*'s take on 'Be Stiff', to which they added, 'Are we not men? We are SUPERSTARS!'

'Be Stiff' nevertheless charted at seventy-one in the UK singles chart, in the process becoming an unsurprising anthem for the Stiff label who had released it and who, in 1979, even went so far as to release a rough and ready album containing six cover versions of the song courtesy of the artists involved in the label's *Be Stiff '78* tour – Mickey Jupp, Rachel Sweet, Wreckless Eric, Jona Lewie, and Lene Lovich – each of whom delivered their take on the single alongside a final version, credited to the Be Stiff Ensemble, which featured all the artists performing together.

Given the decidedly tepid reaction to the 'Be Stiff' single just three weeks previously, it's perhaps unsurprising that 'Come Back Jonee', Devo's first release on Virgin and the first glimpse at the band's new material, was given similarly short shrift. *Melody Maker* opened their review with 'Are we not a con? We will be rich now,' before judging the A-side a 'turgid wedge of banality' and the B-side – 'Social Fools' – 'absurd and empty pseudo-intellectual posturing'. The *NME*'s Danny Baker found 'Come Back Jonee' to be the sound of a band with 'their trousers well and truly jammed around their ankles' and summarily dismissed the release for sounding 'as thin as a British Rail sandwich'.

Once again *Sounds* were on hand to add some positivity to the mix, predicting another hit single for Devo while noting how 'Come Back Jonee' 'rips along in jolly exciting fashion'. But even the ever-supportive *Sounds* were confused by the choice of 'Social Fools' as the single's B-side, having already reviewed that track less than a month previously when it made a prior, and now confusing, appearance as the B-side to the 'Be Stiff' single.

Devo's debut album *Q: Are We Not Men? A: We Are Devo!* – hereafter simplified to *Are We Not Men?* – followed in September. Named in part after a phrase from H. G. Wells' 1896 sci-fi classic *The Island of Doctor Moreau*, the album was the result of the band's alliance with Brian Eno, and saw Devo retain their status as music press darlings after the recent negativity they had attracted around the releases of 'Be Stiff' and 'Come Back Jonee'.

Having stated their intention to give an unbiased review, with a promise that they would try to forget the avalanche of hype that had already been showered upon Devo, *Melody Maker* were extremely complimentary about the *Are We Not Men?* album, which they summed up as 'one helluva fine debut'. *Melody Maker* also found much to admire in the sonic qualities the band had achieved, and offered particular praise for the remade and remodelled versions of those tracks – '(I Can't Get No) Satisfaction' (on the album the typographic embellishments that accompanied the single version had been quietly dropped), 'Mongoloid', 'Sloppy (I Saw My Baby Gettin')' and 'Jocko Homo' – that had already appeared in earlier, more rudimentary versions across the early Devo singles.

Over at the *NME*, Julie Burchill was less enthusiastic about the virtues of *Are We Not Men?* and – exactly as she had done in her review of Ultravox!'s *Ha! Ha! Ha!* earlier that year – presented the band's advanced age (Devo's average age in 1978 was twenty-six) as part of the rationale for her complete rejection of the album and the band, before adding several more reasons to her list of objections: 'Devo are old, ugly and boring. Their record won't sell. Their gigs won't do well. They will never be a household name.'

Given *Sounds'* key role in building up the myth of Devo in the approach to the release of their debut album, it was perhaps inevitable that the paper would take considerable glee in starting the process of tearing the band back down. Rather than deferring to Jon Savage, the band's champion in the *Sounds* office, Peter Silverton was instead drafted in to review *Are We Not Men?*, and while he was able to praise the humour in the record, as well as its thoughtful lyrics, he questioned how groundbreaking the album actually was, writing, 'I can't understand why no-one's yet stood up and screamed "The King has no clothes; long live the King". For all its quality, this album breaks about as much new ground as Darts' 'It's Raining'.'

For Silverton, the problem with *Are We Not Men?* was more about the production of the album than the songs, as he would explain: 'Eno has pasteurised their idiosyncracies into a Notting Hill Gate intellectual's conception of what a garage band should sound like.' He did nevertheless acknowledge that the record would go on to sell 'by the sack' and he was right. *Are We Not Men?* was a UK hit, reaching number twelve in the UK album charts and achieving respectable sales of over 60,000 copies by the following January on the back of a UK tour and a high-profile PR campaign which, in addition to the myriad of merchandise options the *NME* had reported in July, saw multiple full-page and half-page adverts for the album placed across the UK music press.

Devo's first UK concert since the release of *Are We Not Men?* took place at the Edinburgh Odeon on November 26th, by which time the band had already had the opportunity to hone their show with a run of dates across North America. Those shows, to support the US release of *Are We Not Men?*, were well rehearsed, polished affairs which included costume-changes and choreography, and saw Devo open their set each night with the screening of three short films about the band. The *NME* attended one of the four shows Devo played over two dates at The Bottom Line in New York City in October and found the films a useful way to put Devo in some sort of context, prior to the band taking to the stage: 'These movies are the key to appreciating the band. You can ignore the philosophising and get off on the sheer outrageous absurdity and humour of Devo's vision of our universal pin-headedness.'

Sounds were at the band's first two UK shows, in Edinburgh and Glasgow respectively, where, under the headline 'The Sound of Things Falling Apart' – taken from a quote in the accompanying piece in which the band's Mark Mothersbaugh described Devo as 'the sound of things falling apart' – writer Tony Mitchell delivered a two-page feature which reported on a pair of shows similar in content and structure to the ones Devo had been playing in the USA. 'Mouths were agape, eyes agog in disbelief or simply in resolute determination to consume every last fragment of a precious new experience,' Mitchell wrote of the Edinburgh audience.

As the tour rolled into Newcastle for its third UK date, the *NME*'s Andy Gill was on hand to cover Devo's shows there and in Sheffield for another double-page feature on the band, and pulled no punches in confessing to not going into the experience as the biggest fan of the *Are We Not Men?* album. 'Only a fanatic with seriously-impaired hearing facilities would say that the Devo album was anything other than weak, insubstantial and insipid, and I'm no exception. Like an almost-finished bowl of cornflakes, all it contained was a few soggy bits of indeterminate something sinking in milk-dregs.' Given the extremity of his feelings on the subject of *Are We Not Men?*, Gill was generous enough to reassess his opinion of those same songs after seeing them presented in the 'short, sharp, humorous context' of Devo's Newcastle show, an experience which, for Gill, provided the songs with the 'power and dynamism' he felt they lacked on the record.

While the music press spent much of 1978 heaping praise upon Devo, at the same time a hype of a different kind was swirling around a very different new band, equally intent on making an impression. But where Devo's presence in the pages of the weeklies was initially born of enthusiastic journalism, Japan's came courtesy of their record label, Hansa, intent on launching their latest signings in style by delivering a veritable tsunami of advertising, including full-page advertisements in *Sounds*, the *NME* and *Melody Maker*.

In fact, alongside their enthusiastic reviews of Devo's '(I Cån't Gèt Mé Nö) Såtisfactiön', the April 8th editions of *Sounds*, *NME* and *Melody Maker* all carried full-page adverts celebrating the release of Japan's debut album, *Adolescent Sex*. The *NME* and *Melody Maker* also reviewed Japan's debut single, an unlikely cover of Barbra Streisand's 'Don't Rain On My Parade', which had been released the previous week. *Melody Maker* suspended judgement on the release and used their review to simply note that the track was a cover of the Streisand classic 'for the sweet young things in the Hollywood choreography of today'; while *NME* described it as a 'fairly clever Tubes-like overkill job' before swiftly rejecting it as 'some gimmick merchant's idea of the easiest route to a fast buck'. *Sounds* had reviewed the release the previous week and described the track as being a 'heavy metal version of the Broadway showstopper' while dismissing it as 'a nice joke'.

At the same time, Japan announced that they were about to head out on the road as support act to US rock behemoths Blue Öyster Cult, then riding high on the success of '(Don't Fear) The Reaper', on the UK leg of the latter's tour in April, May and June 1978, fuelling the misconception that Japan – who had previously experimented with the names Hype and Future Rock – were little more than a regular rock act, a belief which would dog the band's efforts for some time to come. In the band's first ever interview for the *NME* a year or so later, the ever-acerbic Julie Burchill would describe Japan as 'A quintet of Miss Havershams who stopped their clocks in 1972', and the quintet in question – David Sylvian, Mick Karn, Steve Jansen, Richard Barbieri and Rob Dean, each sporting make-up and coloured hair – certainly looked as if they were wearing their glam-rock hearts on their crushed-velvet sleeves, but the reality was that Japan were actually a considerably more challenging proposition, and one that was significantly less easy to categorise.

As in the cases of Tubeway Army and Ultravox!, Japan were yet to settle into the musical style they would later become synonymous with, and were exploring the possibilities that punk had opened up for them. Enter German pop label Hansa – the record label arm of the famous Hansa Studio business in Berlin – on the hunt for fresh talent and who, as a result of recent stellar success with Donna Summer, Amii Stewart and Boney M, had recently arrived in London with their pockets stuffed with disco cash, which they were anxious to invest in the next big thing, whatever that may be.

Noisily heralding their arrival, Hansa promptly launched an open call for new artists to get in touch, an initiative they advertised with full-page advertisements in the music press alongside a high-profile poster campaign featuring two provocatively posed and scantily clad women, each awkwardly straddling a selection of musical instruments, paired with the equally unsophisticated slogan 'Wanna be a recording star? Get your ass up. Take your chance.'

Hansa's poster had subsequently been spotted by Simon Napier-Bell, a music industry veteran who had previously worked with Marc Bolan and The Yardbirds among others, who had recently stepped in to become Japan's manager. Napier-Bell would later recall the poster as being 'so amazingly non-credible that I was embarrassed even to notice it', but he was desperate. Having conspicuously failed to catch the eye of any label for his new signings, despite his extensive industry connections and experience, Napier-Bell now found himself under mounting pressure from Japan to deliver the record contract he had promised them. A demo tape and a photograph of the band were duly sent to Hansa.

As unsubtle as Hansa's campaign was, it worked, reportedly attracting well over a thousand responses from up-and-coming pop hopefuls across the country, from which the label identified the twenty acts – Japan among them – they felt had the most pop potential, and invited them all to audition at North London's Morgan Studios in May 1977. Each audition lasted just fifteen minutes and was audio-recorded and videotaped for Hansa's consideration, and ultimately led to the promised recording contract being awarded to Crawley act Easy Cure, although Japan had impressed the German executives sufficiently that they too were offered a contract.

Incidentally, Easy Cure turned out to be less malleable than Hansa had hoped and, having recorded a succession of Beatles and Bowie cover versions at the ominous urging of the label, all of which the band hated, would prove to be too challenging a proposition, rapidly parting ways with the label before any of their recordings made it onto Hansa's release schedule. Having left the label with some studio experience, and several promising demo recordings, without having to part with the commercial rights to any of their songs – which included early versions of 'Killing An Arab' and '10:15 Saturday Night', both of which had appeared on the original demo the band had sent Hansa as their entry into the talent competition – Easy Cure would shortly rechristen themselves The Cure on the way to becoming one of the most important and influential bands of their generation.

To the excitement of the band, and presumably to the great relief of Simon Napier-Bell, Japan signed to Hansa in June 1977 and, equipped with a raft of new equipment purchased with the money from their advance from the label, spent the latter part of that year recording their first album and playing sporadic live shows. Hansa's perceived lack of credibility must also have weighed upon Japan, because in early 1978, in an interview for the first Japan fan club newsletter, the band were swift to distance themselves from the undignified circus of their label's audition process, and claimed that, entirely without connection to the commercial circus that was their talent competition, Hansa had somehow seen promotional pictures of the band

and had been suitably impressed to contact Japan directly to offer them a deal. Eventually, of course, the truth would out, causing bassist Mick Karn, revisiting the subject for his memoir in 2009, to ponder the point: 'There were posters all over London, boldly asking: "Do you want to be rock stars?" Well, yes, I suppose we did.'

Importantly, Japan's studio experience was more successful than Easy Cure's and Japan's debut album consisted entirely of their own material, with the exception of one cover song, the same version of 'Don't Rain On My Parade' that had been their first single, which the band had been playing at their occasional live dates around London at the suggestion of guitarist Rob Dean, a self-confessed lover of musicals.

'Don't Rain On My Parade' had been included in their live set because, displaying a contrariness that would dominate their entire career, Japan felt it was a track that no other band would ever think of covering. Having subsequently recorded a 'very rough' version of the song over the course of the initial sessions for the first album, thinking that it could perhaps be used as a B-side, frontman David Sylvian would later recollect that Hansa then 'went overboard' about the track, which they promptly nominated to become Japan's debut single in March 1978.

The idea that putting out a cover version instead of an original track would offer a better insight into what the band was all about was a sign, if one was needed, of Hansa's commercial intentions, the same intentions that had already alienated Easy Cure: Hansa were looking for good-looking bands they could mould into the kind of commercial pop acts with which they had made their name and earned their fortune, something Mick Karn would later acknowledge: 'They'd only chosen us on the strength of our image: now fully made-up, hair dyed, and dressed in the second-hand ladies clothes we'd grown accustomed to to hunting down.'

The release of *Adolescent Sex*, a week after the release of the 'Don't Rain On My Parade' single, triggered a flurry of advertising and promotional activity across the music press, and the level of spending was conspicuous: full-page and half-page advertisements appeared in the *NME*, *Sounds* and *Melody Maker* before, during and after the album's release, an expensive campaign presumably financed by Hansa's recent disco success, and a luxury not many of the emerging artists at the time were able to afford.

Sounds' Jane Suck provided the band with their most enthusiastic album review, offering odds of five-to-one that the 'David Sylvain' (erroneously) credited on the album sleeve was, in fact, New York Dolls' Sylvain Sylvain, and describing the album as 'Filthy rock'n'roll' while noting its 'sophisticated keyboard things and clever clever production work'. In an interview feature for the same publication a few weeks later, Geoff Barton was equally positive, declaring that *Adolescent Sex* was 'By far the most interesting debut release from a British band so far this year'. *Melody Maker* were less certain, describing the album as bordering on 'the lethally boring' despite its 'sharp and modern disco funk rhythms', and finishing with the more promising proclamation that, if Japan were to 'hold on in there and weather the inevitable abuse, in a couple of years they might be in the double platinum bracket'.

Japan's second single, 'The Unconventional', was released in the UK in August 1978, several months after an international release which had seen the seven-inch achieving some minor chart success in both Germany and the Netherlands. Media reaction to the single was mixed. *Sounds* described 'The Unconventional' as 'The freshest sound this week, synthetic but funky, with a dehumanised vocal over spluttering Stevie Wonderish rhythms and chunkachunka guitars' but felt that the 'trite and poppy' lyric let the release down. *Melody Maker* offered a glimpse of positivity, suggesting that 'Japan's problem is that they know what should be done to make it but they haven't quite got the technique yet,' and remained unconvinced by the 'surrogate techno-flash rock' in evidence on the single, predicting – correctly, as it would turn out – that the release had as much chance of being a hit 'as Ian Paisley has of being Pope'.

1978.3 The Normal / Cabaret Voltaire / Throbbing Gristle / Orchestral Manoeuvres In The Dark / The Human League / Suicide / Joy Division / Robert Rental / Thomas Leer

JUST WEEKS AFTER THE release of Japan's *Adolescent Sex* album, another new project was launched with significantly less dazzle and considerably less conspicuous marketing spend. The Normal was a one-man project, released on a one-man label, whose debut single, 'T.V.O.D.', was released in April. The one man in both instances was Daniel Miller, a young film editor working with a tiny home studio he had set up in his mother's house in London's Golders Green.

With a passion for the krautrock sounds coming out of Germany, and with a particular respect for Kraftwerk and Neu!, Miller was delighted by the subversive potential of electronic music at that time. 'I was very influenced by punk,' Miller would later explain, 'but musically it didn't excite me.' For Miller the potential offered by the first wave of affordable synthesisers hitting the UK market at the time was much more exciting: 'I thought electronic music was the next logical step. A synth was no longer an elitist instrument, and that was an important point. You didn't have to be a musician; if you had good ideas, you could make music out of electronics.'

In early 1978, Miller started his electronic experimentation with the ambition to record and release just one single and, at the time, was mostly unaware of the other artists operating in a similar space who were yet to emerge as his peers: 'I was doing it in a vacuum, it was all my world in my own head, as far as I was concerned,' he admitted to The Quietus later. Selecting the two tracks required for the release, Miller decided upon The Normal as the name of the act, and Mute as the name for his label, and, inspired by punk act The Desperate Bicycles' recent demystification of the process, set about making and releasing his record.

The double A-side single – featuring the tracks 'T.V.O.D.' and 'Warm Leatherette' and lyrics inspired by J. G. Ballard's dystopian novel *Crash*, a book Miller had recently received from a friend as a distraction from a recent romantic break-up – was recorded in a single day, the tracks painstakingly assembled on Miller's four-track home set-up, which he had supplemented for the day with the addition of a rented Roland Space Echo, which he ended up barely using.

According to Boyd Rice, who would later release several albums on Mute under the name NON, it was actually early considerations over the sleeve design that informed Miller's choice of which songs to record for the single: 'The reason he chose those two songs he did was because he was making the cover with Letraset and they have these generic images, and there was the one of the man helping the woman out of the car, and then there was the one of the guy watching TV. He liked those images and he used those songs because those were the songs that went with those images.'

Simone Grant, a friend of Daniel Miller's, was persuaded to take care of artwork for the single, which sported a stock photograph of a pair of car-crash test dummies. A further Letraset image, this one a stylised aerial view of a man walking, intended for use on architectural drawings, was pressed into service as the Mute logo, an image which, notwithstanding a tweak or two over the years, remains in use as the label's logo to this day. On a whim, Miller added his home address to the single sleeve – 'I thought it was something you just did' – and Mute 001 was ready to go out into the world.

With the test pressings of the seven-inch in his hand, Miller visited London's Rough Trade shop, where he was given the opportunity to play the record to Rough Trade bosses Geoff Travis and Richard Scott, who liked the single enough to not only take on distribution for the release, but also to advance Miller the money to increase the record's first pressing from 500 to 2,000 copies. 'The idea of the independent movement was so new and exciting then,' Travis told Simon Reynolds for an *Uncut* feature in 2001. 'People would rush out and buy anything that was part of it. This is what people forget: the records used to sell. Anything halfway decent shifted from 6,000 to 10,000. The Normal's single sold over 30,000.'

Another of the seven-inch test pressings made it into the hands of notoriously caustic journalist Jane Suck, who promptly reviewed the single for *Sounds*, several weeks before release, gleefully proclaiming it her 'Single of the Century' and applauding 'T.V.O.D.''s 'Kraftwerk style disco psycho moon stomp' and Lou Reed leanings. Miller was dumbfounded: 'I couldn't fucking believe it. It then got other good reviews and John Peel played it.' Six weeks after Jane Suck's review, *Sounds* followed up with a full-page feature on The Normal, and Daniel Miller's music business career was launched.

Upon the single's actual release, *Melody Maker* were also enthusiastic and their review closely echoed Jane Suck's enthusiasm, stating that 'all that is currently en vogue is here' and describing 'T.V.O.D.' as an interesting but contrived 'intelligent, space-styled, disco stomp for darling androids'. The review marked out the single's second track, 'Warm Leatherette', for particular praise, calling it 'a robotic tale of weird sex' and noting that the song was 'pure Kraftwerk in construction', a comparison which particularly delighted Daniel Miller.

The *NME* contented themselves with simply describing the two songs featured on the single – "T.V.O.D.' is about sticking the aerial into your skin and mainlining the transmission. 'Warm Leatherette', the flip, deals with sex, cars and crashes, and suggests a liking for J. G. Ballard's 'Crash" – and drew parallels between the sound of The Normal and a similarly pioneering electronic act who were also starting to attract the attention of the music press: Cabaret Voltaire.

Cabaret Voltaire – Richard H. Kirk, Stephen Mallinder and Chris Watson – had been the subject of their own feature in *Sounds* just a few weeks before The Normal were given the same opportunity, Jon Savage having headed north to interview the Sheffield three-piece in the studio they had set up in an attic, where they had been conducting their own electronic experiments since 1974. Savage – emerging as a key figure in the development of the post-punk electronic music scene – found Cabaret Voltaire to be a challenging trio and his piece riffed on the flickering badly tuned television set and the distant – 'dull, percussive, hypnotic' – sounds from Sheffield's factories which formed the backdrop for his interview, as it moved restlessly from subject to subject.

Although Cabaret Voltaire were still some six months away from their first commercial release, Savage talked about the band's most recent demos, eight tracks recorded in October 1977, noting with approval that the synthesisers 'are used as instruments with tonal qualities of their own rather than to reproduce the sound of another', and outlining his immediate impressions as 'haziness and blandness: the songs are short, remote and synthetic. A cool yet harsh throb, slivers of sound slowly edging their way under your skin. Itchy. Few melodies, more a concern with sound as texture, with the possibilities of sound within the instruments themselves.'

Prior to the *Sounds* profile, Cabaret Voltaire's only national press attention of note had come courtesy of the *NME*'s Andy Gill the previous January when, in a live review, he described them as an 'experimental pop band', which he was quick to qualify with 'although the average rock fan could be excused for wondering where the 'pop' part had gone'. Gill's review did, however, provide an insight into the band's sound at that time: 'To generalise, their songs start with a basic rhythm-generator pulse, treated electronically (and taped for live use), to which Mallinder adds an insistent bass throb. Into this, Watson stabs organ notes to pick out the melody line, over which Kirk spreads viciously-treated guitar distortion. And on top of everything, there's Mallinder's treated vocals echoing in and out.'

In June 1978, *Sounds* sent Jon Savage to interview another act working at the vanguard of electronic music. London-based Throbbing Gristle – Chris Carter (keyboards), Peter 'Sleazy' Christopherson (tapes and machines), Cosey Fanni Tutti (guitar) and Genesis P-Orridge (bass, vocals) – had recently released their first single, 'United', which, despite sounding as though it had been recorded in a biscuit tin, shared some broad musical characteristics with both The Normal and Cabaret Voltaire: the synthetic pop sensibilities and deadpan vocal styling of the former, combined with the more challenging and experimental sonic textures and layers of the latter. In fact in the *NME* in July 1978, Throbbing Gristle's electronics expert Chris Carter would name Cabaret Voltaire as an act he considered to be working in a similar sphere.

While Cabaret Voltaire had been, in Jon Savage's words, 'treading water' in Sheffield since 1975, Throbbing Gristle had moved more quickly. Although 'United' was their first single, the band had already released their debut album, *The Second Annual Report*, on their own Industrial Records independent label in November 1977, and had been weaving a web of notoriety around themselves for a number of years before that.

Throbbing Gristle was born from the COUM Transmissions music and performance art collective (funded by The Arts Council of Great Britain), who had been the cause of great controversy in 1976 after staging a confrontational art show, entitled 'Prostitution', at London's ICA. Exhibits at the show, which included 'explicit photographs of lesbians, assemblages of rusty knives, syringes, bloodied hair, used sanitary towels', so outraged the Conservative

MP Nicholas Fairbairn that he notoriously pronounced the maverick group 'wreckers of civilization'.

The Second Annual Report could accurately be described as a difficult album, and upon its release the music press didn't disagree. *Melody Maker* were admirably restrained and politely noted that the 'rather daunting music' contained on the record 'defies convenient categorisation'. *ZigZag*'s Kris Needs described the record's sonic assault as having the power 'to induce anything including nausea, tears, terror, anger, irritation, delight or boredom', while *Sounds'* assessment was that the album lacked 'tunes to hum in the shower'. *The Second Annual Report* – which was initially released in a run of just 785 copies, all the band could afford to press at the time – was in fact less an album than a collection of live recordings alongside a couple of new tracks and the soundtrack for a film the band had made entitled *After Cease To Exist*.

The original recordings for *The Second Annual Report*, and subsequently for the 'United' single, were made on cassette and were then transferred to vinyl – a process which explains at least some of the album's challenging acoustics – and the record was packaged in a plain white sleeve, the cheapest packaging option available to Throbbing Gristle, and one that dovetailed perfectly with their industrial aesthetic and their slogan 'Industrial Music for Industrial People'. Although the album title might suggest otherwise, there was no 'First Annual Report', although the band had produced an earlier cassette which covered their earliest musical experimentation, which they distributed amongst their own circle under the mischievous title *The Best Of (Volume 12)*.

Despite the challenging music contained on *The Second Annual Report*, the press were broadly supportive of the record: slightly baffled, but cautiously sympathetic to what they saw as a first step towards a brave new musical world, as cutting edge as it was possible to get at that moment in time. *ZigZag* recognised that Throbbing Gristle were pulling in little influence from mainstream rock, and praised the band for pursuing such a non-traditional musical pathway: 'There's straight, commercial music and there's the area of people who are trying to produce music which is actually contemporary, actually about this year.' *NME* would be more direct in a later piece, observing that 'Most of the tracks aren't songs as such, but electronic screams of anguish.'

Perversely and subversively, in the manner of all Throbbing Gristle activity, in May 1978, when the band followed up *The Second Annual Report* with 'United', their first single, the new release represented a turnaround in style so complete that it led *Sounds'* Jon Savage to describe the single as 'a simple electronic disco love song'. The positivity continued and Savage further described 'United' as 'a pure and potent spell... a near perfect synthetic mantra to dance at dawn or to chant on the terraces'. The single's B-side, 'Zyklon B Zombie', also came in for praise from Savage, who approved that the track demonstrated the other, wilfully uncommercial side of Throbbing Gristle with its 'thrashing and throbbing subterranean drone' and the 'snotty, irritating chorus that stays in your head unwanted, bugging you like the kid who follows you all the way home pestering you with a nasal whine'.

More surprising again was the *NME*'s decision to make 'United' their Single of the Week in June, applauding the release as 'A simpleminded dance tune, with a hook that's hard to fight off' and noting, with approval, that the maverick four-piece had managed to not only deliver a single with such commercial potential, but that the ploy came with 'no loss of integrity involved'. *Melody Maker* also approved of the release for similar reasons, reporting that with the greater accessibility and 'hummable melodies' a commercial platform could provide Throbbing Gristle with the opportunity to be even more subversive.

Meanwhile on the Wirral, The Normal's 'Warm Leatherette' was having a galvanising effect on two members of another band who heard it playing over the speakers of the now legendary Eric's club in Liverpool, the record immediately providing a moment of musical revelation and clarification that would change both their lives forever. Andy McCluskey and Paul Humphreys, school friends united in their love of Kraftwerk, krautrock and Eno, formed the musical and lyrical core of The Id, a seven-piece band that was their latest musical project, following recent experiments under the less-promising names Equinox and Pegasus. As the duo were questioning their next move, McCluskey would later recall that 'Warm Leatherette' came along at exactly the right moment: 'Someone English had been listening to the music that we loved, and he had made a record. We had to act.'

And act they did. The discovery that 'Warm Leatherette' was made by an English artist drawing on similar influences to McCluskey and Humphreys was one of the final nails in the coffin for The Id. Analysing the situation later, McCluskey would acknowledge that 'The line-up wasn't right for the sound that we wanted. The more we listened to Kraftwerk, the more The Id wasn't quite what we wanted to write.' Paul Humphreys concurred, adding, 'We'd wanted to be conventional, but ended up too conventional. We had felt obliged to write bits in for the guitarists in the band, to make arrangements with them to fit in with what we'd written. We had to have something for them to play – otherwise they just stood around all night. Sometimes our material just didn't suit that set-up.'

Eric's club provided more inspiration, and further evidence that a new musical path was required, when McCluskey and Humphreys witnessed Liverpool post-punk act Dalek I Love You, whose musical trajectory was a better fit for the former's vision of the future. McCluskey: 'They'd go on stage in Eric's with just the four of them, no drummer, just a drum machine, cover the whole stage in newspaper – the stage, the back wall, the ceiling – and do these great songs, but with a drum machine, bass, a keyboard and guitar. It was much more like a new wave pop version of Kraftwerk, though they weren't as electronic sounding because they had the guitar and bass.' Fortunately for Andy McCluskey, although less fortunately for The Id, Dalek I Love You happened to be looking for a new singer and McCluskey's interest in what they were doing led to his being recruited as their frontman.

The new Dalek I Love You line-up played a handful of shows during the summer of 1978 but a lack of involvement in the band's songwriting left McClusky dissatisfied with his position in the band. 'I loved Dalek's strange pop songs, but ultimately I was frustrated at not being involved with my own songs,' he explained later. The band and their new singer parted company and McCluskey went back to the tried and tested partnership he'd always enjoyed with Paul Humphreys. This time, instead of building a conventional line-up around themselves, McCluskey and Humphreys returned to work as a duo under the name VCL11, the name taken from the number printed on a valve pictured in a circuit diagram on the reverse of Kraftwerk's *Radio-Activity* album.

At the core of this new stripped-down electronic approach were the songs The Id had recorded at Liverpool's Open Eye studios earlier that year – 'Electricity', 'Julia's Song' and 'The Misunderstanding' – repurposed to fit McCluskey and Humphreys' new musical vision and supplemented by other McCluskey and Humphreys compositions that The Id had performed live, including 'Red Frame/White Light' and 'Radio Waves'.

This time, and more as a result of good fortune than of good planning, the duo found themselves in better step with an emerging wave of other electronic acts, a situation that was both a comfort and a pressure. 'That summer of '78 really shocked us because we'd been into all this electronic music for a couple of years and we thought we were the only people in the whole of

Britain who were interested in this kind of music,' recalled Andy McCluskey in Mike Humphreys and Johnny Wallers' book *Messages* later. 'Then we heard 'Warm Leatherette' by The Normal, then we heard Cabaret Voltaire, then we bought 'Being Boiled' by The Human League and we thought, 'Jesus, there's loads of other people out there!''

'Being Boiled' was the debut single release from The Human League and held the peculiar honour of being reviewed for the *NME* by former Sex Pistol John Lydon, whose vehement two-word verdict on the release simply read 'Trendy Hippies'. To put his review into perspective, Lydon was equally scathing of all the records he was given to listen to, including his Single of the Day, Captain Sensible & The Softies' 'Jet Boy, Jet Girl', which was duly described as 'a right load of nonsense'.

Melody Maker, at least, was initially willing to give 'Being Boiled' slightly more attention, and managed to note the 'heavy-heavy sinister overtones' of the release and describe the B-side, 'Circus Of Death', as 'GRIM' before, to all intents and purposes, shrugging it's shoulders and abstaining itself of all further critical responsibility – 'Haven't a clue what the other side's about, but it mentions Buddha a lot if that's any help' – then signing off with the slightly hysterical proclamation that 'The machines are taking over'.

It seems entirely likely that The Human League would have been delighted that the task of unpicking their work was seen as challenging – in fact the way the band had introduced themselves to the media was equally opaque and uncompromising. An early press release put out by the band's original label, Edinburgh's Fast Product, proclaimed that The Human League was formed in 1977 'due to the members finding no conventional channels for their immense talents', and outlined their manifesto as 'Interested in combining the best of all worlds, the League would like to positively affect the future by close attention to the present, allying technology with humanity and humour.'

To give them their due, the *NME* took a second stab at decoding both 'Being Boiled' and 'Circus Of Death' a couple of weeks later, as part of a review of The Human League's first ever live show (promoted by Sheffield University's NowSoc at the Psalter Lane Art College on June 12th, 1978, an event that was later commemorated by the installation of a blue plaque at the site of the former venue), and were quick to recognise such humanity and humour, describing the band as 'a fine, fun little outfit whose humour doesn't stoop to facile punchlines and sleazy innuendo, but relies more on undercurrents of eccentricity and parody'. 'Being Boiled' itself was described as 'a funky little number dealing variously with silk manufacture and the generation gap', while 'Circus Of Death' was subject to the following analysis: 'The story deals with a clown who takes a drug which gives him unlimited power. Things get out of hand, and McGarrett of *Hawaii Five-O* is called in to sort out the problem. More than that, I can't say.'

Sounds chose to be less speculative in their assessment of the single and instead sent John Gill to interview the band about the release at the suburban Sheffield home of the band's Ian Marsh ('synthesiser, devices'). The aesthetic of the room where the interview took place – featuring the plaster ducks so beloved of parlour rooms of the period, juxtaposed with 'broken clockwork tin cars and spaceships, battered sci-fi annuals, strange funfair-cum-laboratory "sculptures" and pieces of seventies technology' – provided an insight into the various influences and personalities of The Human League.

In response to *Sounds'* inevitable question as to what 'Being Boiled' was actually about, Phil Oakey, The Human League's lyricist and frontman ('vocals, occasional electronix and asymmetrical hairdo'), explained that the song was inspired by the moral irresponsibility of sericulture (the culture of silkworms, who are dropped in boiling water to remove their skins) and its connection with Buddhism. Or possibly its connection with Hinduism, Oakey having borrowed a book on the former, which pointed him towards the latter: 'I read it and realised I was actually interested in Hinduism. I didn't like Buddhism after that.'

A similar analysis of the meaning of 'Circus Of Death' confirmed *NME*'s speculation that it was about drug-fuelled clowns trying to take over the world, while providing the additional information that the track had been written in response to a film entitled *Circus of Horrors*. 'It's like a subliminal trip through all the very trashiest films,' Martin Ware ('synthesiser, devices and infrequent voice') would explain helpfully. And, according to Phil Oakey, *Hawaii Five-O* detective Steve McGarrett makes an appearance simply because 'I happen to think Steve McGarrett's a very good-looking guy. I wish I looked like him.'

Unsurprisingly, Oakey's own sartorial style in 1978 sat some considerable distance from the suave and conventional good looks required of television heartthrobs of the sixties and seventies, and delivered in the *Hawaii Five-O* character of McGarrett by actor Jack Lord. In fact Oakey was already notorious around Sheffield for his unusual and eccentric appearance, and was even then sporting an early version of what would become his trademark asymmetric hairstyle. 'I thought, "What have all big pop stars got that sets them apart?" And the only thing that I could think of that made them all different was a hairstyle. David Bowie, Rod Stewart, Marc Bolan, The Beatles – they all had odd hairstyles, so I thought that I had better find one.'

In the 1982 biography *The Story of a Band Called The Human League*, writer Alaska Ross went so far as to describe Oakey's decision as a 'masterstroke', and praised the 'innate sense of style and grasp of what gets you noticed' which led to one of the most recognisable hairstyles of the eighties, while enthusiastically celebrating the frontman's 'acute understanding of the way that the pop business works'. The book also reports Oakey's own – considerably more prosaic – recollection of that creative process: 'One day, I saw a hair model on a bus, a girl called Penny, and I went over and said, "Where did you get your haircut, I want one of those." It was as simple as that.'

'Being Boiled' wasn't alone in falling victim to John Lydon's uncompromising dissection in the July 22nd, 1978 edition of the *NME*. New York electronic duo Suicide's debut UK single, 'Cheree', was among the other new releases to come under the former Sex Pistol's caustic gaze, only to find itself filed under 'Cheek of the Week' and duly dismissed as 'Complete rubbish, a combination of 'J'Taime' [sic], taped hiss and something awful.'

In a slightly more objective review just one week earlier, the *NME* had in fact already declared the single their 'Creepy Experience of the Week', writing, with a touch of petulance: 'One man singing, one man playing a whole gang of unpleasant objects wiv keyboards attached, quiet, hissing and so impossible [sic] evil it'd scare you to death if it wasn't all so/so/so studied.' *Melody Maker* was also unimpressed by 'Cheree', speculating that the single might be a love song of sorts, before ultimately dismissing it as 'a poor attempt at ambiguous lyrics, set to monotonous backing'.

Melody Maker's latest thoughts on the band were a dramatic about-turn in comparison to those of their writer Richard Williams, who had enthusiastically reviewed an import copy of Suicide's eponymous debut album back in January of 1978, a full six months before the domestic release of the album in the UK in July. Lamenting the lack of new directions across 1978's immediate post-punk landscape, Williams had made much of the fact that Suicide's debut – as well as similarly pioneering releases from Devo, Talking Heads and Television – contained something genuinely new and exciting to kick-start the new year, while pointing out how 'The Sex Pistols and the Tom Robinson Band are, for all their virtues, very old-fashioned groups; in no sense do they represent a New Music.'

Encouraged by the freshness of sound contained in the seven tracks that made up the Suicide album, Williams had been admirably quick to recognise something important in the band's output, and hailed the release as 'an album which proposes yet another way out of the much-publicised new wave impasse', while focusing in particular on the fine detail of the album's sonic landscapes: 'Martin Rev uses his limited means to create fascinating landscapes, equally notable for their attention to details. Listen closely, and beyond the foreground figures appear tiny details placed around the deep horizon.'

Reviewing the imported *Suicide* album for the *NME* in January 1978, American journalist Lester Bangs, a self-confessed fan of the band and one of Suicide's earliest champions, declared the album 'historically significant' and celebrated the duo – credited on the album sleeve as Alan Vega ('vocals and assorted shouting') and Martin Rev ('synthesizer, percussion box and assorted effects') – for their longevity and singular creative integrity, and for refusing to compromise on their creative vision despite the various distractions around them: 'Definitively these guys have been around for a long time, you know; they're no punk rock bandwagon hoppers.' Like Williams, Bangs singled out the album's epic ten-minute 'Frankie Teardrop' for particular attention, calling the track a masterpiece and drawing attention to the fact that it contained 'the best screams ever heard on any rock'n'roll record', while Richard Williams called it 'the most disturbing creation' since The Velvet Underground's 1967 release of 'Heroin', hailing the track as 'fit to stand in the catalogue of post-psychedelic classics'.

Despite his emerging role as an advocate for all things electronic and experimental, Jon Savage, reviewing *Suicide* for *Sounds* at the start of February 1978, was less sure of the brave new world the album promised, and struggled particularly with the album's distorted and disorientating vocals, a sound he described as similar to 'waking sleep', which led him to speculate that the record might have been more successful as an instrumental album. Nonetheless, Savage also found much to admire in the project, describing the record as 'hypnotic in insistent, caressingly synthetic rhythms and tones', noting 'the screams and drift of the instrument into landscapes of blankness' with approval, while pinpointing Vega and Rev's general aesthetic as 'glacially cool, facing their waking nightmares through deepest black shades. Anonymous, alienated. Beat.'

The level of press interest focused on the album was sufficient to not only catch the attention of the Bronze label in the UK, who would put out a domestic UK release of *Suicide* in July, but also to catch the eye and interest of contemporary UK live agents looking for acts to fill potential support slots. Suicide were quickly booked to open for Elvis Costello at twelve shows across Europe, followed by a further seventeen shows with The Clash in the UK in June and July.

The first show on the Elvis Costello tour – the band's third show outside the USA – took place at the Ancienne Belgique in Brussels on June 16th, 1978. Suicide's set was recorded on a handheld cassette recorder from the crowd by Bronze Records' Howard Thompson, and the recording was eventually released as a live bootleg under the title *23 Minutes In Brussels*. Listen to it today and the simmering hostility that greeted the band from the majority of the Belgian crowd is hard to ignore. Not that things were appreciably better on the dates with The Clash, which seemed to bother Suicide not one bit, *Sounds* reporting how the duo 'showed an enviable, if probably pig-headed, amount of bottle when confronted by the, er, robustness of some of the Clash fans'.

Following those tricky shows with Elvis Costello and The Clash, Suicide subsequently embarked on a series of UK headlining shows which saw them arrive in Manchester on July 28th, 1978 to perform at the city's newest live venue, The Factory. Suicide brought their own support, The Actors, who appeared at several of their dates, but the bill was also supplemented by an up-and-coming Manchester band that was starting to attract the attention of music fans and the media alike. Playing their second show at the venue, Joy Division were riding high on a wave of critical approval after having put out their debut release, an EP entitled *An Ideal For Living*, just a few weeks previously.

An Ideal For Living had been recorded by Joy Division – Ian Curtis (vocals) Peter Hook (bass), Stephen Morris (drums) and Bernard Sumner (guitar and keyboards) – at Oldham's Pennine Sound Studios at the end of 1977 and originally released as a single on the band's own Enigma label (not to be confused with the classical music label of the same name). Featuring four tracks – 'Warsaw', 'No Love Lost', 'Leaders Of Men' and 'Failures' – the EP had been created while the band were still working under their previous name, Warsaw, which they changed to avoid being confused with London group Warsaw Pakt, the title of the first track was changed from '31G' to 'Warsaw' in recognition of the band's previous incarnation.

The name Joy Division had been chosen by the band's singer, Ian Curtis, who had taken it from a 1953 Nazi exploitation novella entitled *House of Dolls*, written by the Jewish writer and Holocaust survivor Yehiel Feiner under the pen name Ka-tzetnik 135633. In the book, 'Joy Divisions' were Jewish women incarcerated in World War II concentration camps and kept for the sexual gratification of the Nazi military.

An Ideal For Living's cover artwork, featuring a young boy dressed in the uniform of the Hitler Youth, banging a drum, had been designed by Bernard Sumner, the band's guitarist – then calling himself Bernard Albrecht – who had found it in a book in the Manchester Central Library and chosen it as 'a powerful image that blended perfectly with our new name'. Each of the 1,000 seven-inch copies came wrapped in a DIY sleeve laboriously hand-folded from a single sheet of paper by the band themselves – to the reported soundtrack of Neil Young's album *Zuma*. Dubious Nazi references and imagery firmly in place, *An Ideal For Living* was released on June 3rd, 1978.

Reviews of the EP were largely positive, although the media was quick to seize upon the Nazi imagery and references. In their review, *Sounds* noted the Hitler Youth imagery and Germanic typography and declared Joy Division 'Another Fascism For Fun And Profit Mob' before conceding that the release's 'grinding riff gloom and industrial bleakness' made it 'interesting, and definitely worth investigation'. In the *NME*, Paul Morley wrote about the EP as part of a wider live review, applauding Joy Division's 'ambiguous appeal' and calling them 'a dry, doomy group who depend promisingly on the possibilities of repetition, sudden stripping away, with deceptive dynamics'.

Morley was also moved to call out the record's underwhelming sonic qualities, and described *An Ideal For Living* as 'structurally good, though soundwise poor, a reason it may not be widely released', a comment that came as no surprise to Joy Division themselves, who were bitterly disappointed with the way their debut release sounded. Confusion over the speed that the record should be cut in order to accommodate four tracks was to blame. Instead of being manufactured to play at 45 rpm like a regular seven-inch single, an EP should in fact be cut at 33 1/3 to avoid it sounding, in the words of drummer Stephen Morris, 'really tinny and quiet', and in the words of bassist Peter Hook, 'fucking shit… really muffled and horrible'.

Nevertheless the EP's sound qualities did at least score over the demo tape that Joy Division had recorded to circulate to record companies in the hope of attracting their interest and support. When one of those tapes was returned to them by one of the labels they had set their sights set on, and someone happened to actually listen to it, the band were bemused to find that the friend who had been given the task of duplicating the cassettes had done so using the external microphone on one tape recorder set in front of the speaker of another, as Stephen Morris later remembered in his memoir *Record Play Pause*: 'The music on the tape was was virtually inaudible, being drowned out by the clatter of knives and forks, snippets of conversation and dialogue from an episode of *Coronation Street*.'

A second release of *An Ideal For Living* would follow in October 1978 – pressed on twelve-inch vinyl to allow the four tracks the necessary space to capture the sound properly, and packaged in a sleeve featuring an entirely uncontroversial black-and-white photograph of some scaffolding – but not before Virgin Records released the compilation *Short Circuit: Live At The Electric Circus*, featuring the band, in June. The *Short Circuit* album was released in response to the closing of Manchester's Electric Circus venue in October 1977 and Joy Division were included with a live version of 'At A Later Date', recorded under the name Warsaw but credited on the album under their new name.

An Ideal For Living was subsequently featured again in the *NME*'s last issue of 1978 in a feature entitled 'The Ones That Got Away', dedicated to celebrating the year's best singles which had been 'released on small labels with little chance of airplay, erratic distribution, and zilch promotion'. 'The Ones That Got Away' also included The Normal's 'T.V.O.D.', The Human League's 'Being Boiled' and a pair of interrelated electronic curiosities in the shape of Thomas Leer's 'Private Plane' and Robert Rental's 'Paralysis'.

Robert Rental (Robert Donnachie) and Thomas Leer (Thomas Wishart) first met as children and had been in different years at the same Port Glasgow school, although they didn't become friends until they embarked on apprenticeships with the same gardening company at the same time, and the seeds of their collaboration were born after hours of 'standing in a potting shed talking about the John Peel show and music'. At that time Leer already had some musical skills but Rental had none and started to learn guitar while acting as roadie for Leer's early bands.

Punk provided the impetus for the friends to work together and the duo, who had moved out of Scotland and were now living in London, formed a punk band called Pressure. Following a brief flirtation with punk, Leer and Rental started to look for a more interesting musical direction as an alternative to 'thrashing out two-chord songs', and Pressure split after the two decided to draw upon Germany as an influence, and – unaware of new artists such as The Normal, The Human League and Cabaret Voltaire – turned to 'Kraftwerk and Can and all that' to provide inspiration.

Thomas Leer recorded 'Private Plane' and its B-side, 'International', in his North London flat using the rudimentary assortment of electronic devices he had pooled with Rental, and then set up the same motley collection in Rental's home in Battersea to record two tracks – 'Paralysis' and 'A.C.C.' – for the latter's single, recorded with assistance from Leer, who is credited on the release as co-producer. Each artist pressed 650 copies of their singles – as many as they were able to afford at the time – which they credited to their own labels: Oblique Records in the case of Leer; and Regular Records for Rental.

Once the singles were pressed, the labels on each single were hand-stamped by the duo using a John Bull printing kit, and both sleeves were photocopied from Leer and Rental's original artwork which, in time-honoured DIY tradition, utilised cut-out and cut-up black-and-white images and a combination of newspaper 'ransom note' titles and hand-lettering, Rental also adding occasional splashes of colour to his sleeves using felt-tip pen. Each sleeve was then hand-folded by its respective artist before it was deemed ready to go out into the world courtesy of Rough Trade, who undertook distribution of both.

Reviews for both singles ran across the final months of 1978, although the more sonically accessible Thomas Leer release tended to overshadow Rental's more challenging and less conventional offerings. *Melody Maker* kicked off by reviewing both singles together at the end of September, spotting the emerging trend for the kind of DIY electronic experimentation ('the sound is frequently on the shambolic side') already evidenced by similar 'Electronic garage bands' Cabaret Voltaire and The Human League, and praising both singles for their 'strong ideas' and shifts 'between textures and moods'.

NME awarded Thomas Leer 'Single of Next Week' but distanced themselves from 'Private Plane' – 'blighted by more electronic farts, burps and belches than Brian Eno digesting with difficulty' – in favour of 'International', which they hailed 'a revelation' for the 'huge-slabs of utilitarian powdered-chords, a haunting organ motif that appears to be emanating from one of those Rolf Harris toys, that sad siren Nico-drone anti-vocal, and it all climaxes into disconcerting epileptic morse-code before fading out then fading back in again.' The *NME* might have underestimated the quiet power of 'Private Plane', but they were right in spotting the use of the Stylophone which powered the electronic feel of the songs, and which Leer would remember as a 350S. 'It was a big one. It had two styluses and a wah-wah pedal, so it was a pretty elaborate kind of Stylophone.' Not one review identified that, despite the use of a Roland drum machine, the Stylophone and a small selection of effects units, neither single – both of which have since been hailed as true electronic music classics – actually featured a synthesiser.

Sounds were equally enamoured with 'International' in their November review, writing "International' is a beautifully and wilfully simple piece of homegrown record making' while spotting the 'heavy Germanic tones and screeches, squelches and all the other sounds that go snap, crackle, pop in the studio', before ending their piece with the simple plea that the record-buying public 'Make this man a star.' But stardom was never the game plan for Leer or Rental, whose ambitions at that moment extended no further then each selling their 650 singles.

On that basis, both releases were a resounding success, and both were entirely sold out by the end of the year, triggering re-pressings by Company Records – who dispensed with much of the DIY charm of the original packaging and repackaged each single in more conventional and professionally printed sleeves – and seeing 'Private Plane' and 'A.C.C.' included on a Cherry Red compilation album entitled *Business Unusual*. Designed to showcase a diverse selection of independent acts working outside the mainstream at that time – it also featured Throbbing Gristle's 'United' and Cabaret Voltaire's 'Do The Mussolini (Headkick)' – the compilation was released in conjunction with *ZigZag* magazine in February 1979.

Thomas Leer's career ambitions at the time didn't even extend as far as playing live, as he would later tell *Electronic Sound* magazine: 'The last thing I wanted to do at that time was a live performance.' Robert Rental, however, was considerably more interested in adding a live element to his project, and on November 11th joined forces with The Normal's Daniel Miller for a special one-off show at the Cryptic One Club – located in the crypt of Trinity Church in London's Paddington – alongside Throbbing Gristle, Cabaret Voltaire and Metabolist.

The show was significant for a number of reasons, but most importantly it represented one of the earliest rendezvous of like-minded electronic experimenters, most of whom were only just realising that there were others like them, and that a nascent scene was starting to develop. For Throbbing Gristle's Genesis P-Orridge the night was significant as the evening in which he accidentally overdosed backstage, and for all the bands concerned the night was significant because journalist Paul Morley was on hand to document the evening for the *NME* and, as a result, to start making important connections between the sounds being produced by the various artists on the bill.

Headliners Throbbing Gristle, just weeks away from the release of their second album, were first to take to the stage and, according to Morley, used 'tapes, guitars, radios, tv's, voices, fingers, rings, a bass, eyes, intensity, a violin, stupidity, gullibility, electronics and stimulants to spew up a rotting, decaying noise'. Lukewarm in his treatment of their performance, Morley also described Throbbing Gristle's set as a 'remote parody of a rock (or whatever) group seriously performing bleached, blank, carefully composed junk', noting that parts of the show would sound good on record, before qualifying that claim with a dismissive 'This doesn't mean that they succeeded or failed; just that they functioned.' In fact, a live recording of this show was released, firstly as a cassette on Throbbing Gristle's own Industrial Records in 1979 as *At The Crypt, London*, and again in 1984 as a 're-processed' vinyl LP mixed by the band's Chris Carter and released under the title *Special Treatment: Live At The Cryptic One London 1978*.

Metabolist were next to play, the four-piece apparently most notable to Morley for being covered in hair, frowning a lot, and fiddling around for 'a very long time' before playing a set of beats and burps he considered to be influenced by the schools of Stockhausen and Gong. People clapped, Morley acknowledged, 'But only barely.' Daniel Miller and Robert Rental's joint performance came next – 'Daniel bowed over a tape/keyboard playkit, Robert, looking endearingly confused, twiddled knobs and sang gently' – and was received with considerably more warmth and enthusiasm, Morley concluding that the music 'was fast, poppy, pulsing and only occasionally messy. It wasn't soppy cosmic, it was brisk fun.'

Before everyone 'departed, smiling into the misty night' the evening was brought to a close by Cabaret Voltaire. Earlier that year *Sounds'* Jon Savage had expressed a concern that the Sheffield three-piece might already be treading water creatively, a sentiment echoed by Morley in his live review, though he added that Cabaret Voltaire were in fact 'an extremely seductive electronic pop group', and showered them with the faint praise that they could almost be 'next year's thing'.

Cabaret Voltaire's appearance in London was in support of their debut release, a four-track seven-inch EP entitled *Extended Play* which they had recorded using a rudimentary two-track recorder at their own Western Works studio in

Sheffield. *Extended Play* had already started to pick up reviews in the music press, including an *NME* review published in the same week as the show which consisted of just seven words, summing up the release as 'Casual Kraftwerk bootlegged in the bath. Meaningful.' Surprisingly, the *NME*'s take wasn't the release's worst review. November's *ZigZag* offered two singularly unenthusiastic sentences about the release, their unpromisingly named reviewer, Hugh Jarse, achieving little more in his review than comparing the EP's 'gauzy, muffled menace' to 'being jabbed in the rectum by a psychotic Smurf'.

At *Sounds*, Jon Savage, who had already been a key champion of Cabaret Voltaire in the media, stepped in to deliver one of the best reviews for *Extended Play*, which he proceeded to hail as a classic, praising the four electronic pieces it contained for their rhythm and repetition, as well as for the 'cool distanced vocals shattered by echo and distortion'. Savage also set the band's music against that of their Sheffield peers The Human League, and concluded that the former's dirtier sound made them the less pretty option. Nonetheless Savage found plenty to celebrate in the fragile beauty evidenced in Cabaret Voltaire's dismantling of The Velvet Underground's 'Here She Comes Now', as well as the chilling grandeur of 'The Set Up'.

In Liverpool the wave of media attention focused on the emerging wave of electronic experimenters was only serving to increase the pressure that Andy McCluskey and Paul Humphreys were already feeling to claim their place among the first acts operating in the electronic arena. The rapid appearance of Devo, The Normal, Cabaret Voltaire and The Human League on the duo's musical radar provided the wake-up call they needed to galvanise them into urgent action. McCluskey and Humphreys duly booked themselves a show at Eric's in Liverpool on October 12th, 1978, playing support to alternative comedian John Dowie.

Although the concert was only intended as a one-off performance it was decided that VCL11 didn't really work as a name and that a new one would need to be chosen for the occasion. Paul Humphreys: 'Since we were only planning to play one gig, the name didn't really matter, but we wanted something unusual and evocative.' Among the 'unusual and evocative' names that were considered and then rejected by the duo were Queen Victoria's Funeral and Margaret Thatcher's Afterbirth. Subsequently a similarly absurd name was chosen from the 'graffiti, discarded lyric ideas and general artistic chaos' that covered Andy McCluskey's bedroom wall and the duo had a new name: Orchestral Manoeuvres In The Dark.

1978.4 Ultravox / Tubeway Army / Japan / Throbbing Gristle

REMOVING THE EXCLAMATION MARK that had previously been part of their name wasn't a radical reinvention, but the release of Ultravox's new single, 'Slow Motion', in August 1978 was a bold one. The first new tracks to emerge from the band's sessions with Conny Plank in Germany, 'Slow Motion' and the single's B-side, 'Dislocation', are underpinned by the same post-punk urgency that categorised much of Ultravox's previous output, but courtesy of the band's classically trained Billy Currie and the input of Plank, both tracks lean unmistakably towards the electronic. A Trojan-horse of a single, 'Slow Motion' smuggled the single's brooding darkness into the mainstream courtesy of Currie's broad synthesiser strokes which, alongside John Foxx's restrained vocals, belied some of the band's previous jagged attitude.

On August 19th, reviews of 'Slow Motion' appeared in all the main music papers. If 'Slow Motion' hadn't been released at the same time as 'Hong Kong Garden', the debut Siouxsie & The Banshees single, *Sounds* would have made Ultravox their Single of the Week, but instead their review was headlined 'There but for Siouxsie' and started with the proclamation that 'If the rest of their new album is this good, these lads may yet live up to all the trumpeting that Island came out with when they first signed.' The *Sounds* review also praised the song's 'intrusively eerie sound' as well as its 'rumbling synthesised backdrop and vocal reverb,' while *Melody Maker* also approved of the 'more natural approach' the single had taken, describing the overall effect as 'more easeful and assured' and applauding the 'power and intricacy' of the song's musical build-up.

In the same issue as their 'Slow Motion' review, *Sounds* also ran a two-page interview feature on the band, the first opportunity Ultravox had been given to discuss their forthcoming album, *Systems Of Romance*. Starting at a disadvantage, the writer of the piece, John Gill, was sent the wrong tape by the Island Records press department and had bizarrely received a recording of a church sermon instead of the album. Gill was therefore forced to experience *Systems Of Romance* for the first time through the 'minuscule speaker' of his cheap cassette recorder just moments before starting his interview with the band, which allowed him to experience little of the album's complexities in advance of the interview.

Perhaps as a result of the mishap with the tape the interview came across as stilted and awkward, as Gill continually and doggedly tried to steer the politely reluctant band into admitting to Germanic influences beyond their choice of Conny Plank as producer. In closing that line of questioning, Foxx unwittingly revealed more about the musical landscape that Ultravox then occupied than he did about the band's affinity with the krautrock acts: 'The reason we like and were interested in those things is because in England things seem very stale. Things seem to be imitating American styles at the time we started. We decided to make something English, related to the other side of the world, like Europe. Somewhere we knew.'

Interestingly, while the entire band, including new guitarist Robin Simon (described by Gill as a 'cherubic blonde'), was present for the *Sounds* interview, John Gill's questions were generally handled by John Foxx ('hawkish') and Warren Cann ('voluptuous-featured'), who identified 'My Sex' and 'Hiroshima Mon Amour' as pivotal moments on their previous two albums and proceeded to equate the 'Slow Motion' single B-side 'Dislocation' – 'a glacial, gothic, nightmarish wall of noise' written spontaneously in the studio 'after a strange rhythm pattern spluttered out of the machines during the recording of 'Just For A Moment'' – as the equivalent moment for *Systems Of Romance*. 'When we work in the studio, we always reach a point where things begin to happen that we don't recognise, so we chase two things to see what'll happen. And that's what happened on the first album with 'My Sex', on 'Hiroshima' and on the new one with 'Dislocation',' explained Foxx.

Despite the relative positivity of the reviews for 'Slow Motion', plus radio play from John Peel (who liked the single the first time he heard it, hated it on second listen, liked it again on his third hearing, and was undecided after that), the single wasn't a commercial success, at least not at the level that Island Records were hoping for. In support of the release, and of their new album, Ultravox played a five-night residency at London's Marquee Club at the end of August as warm-up shows in advance of a 'Special Guest' appearance at the 1978 Reading Rock Festival on August 25th, which saw the band play second on the bill to headliners The Jam.

Sounds were present for one of the Marquee shows, with writer Hugh Fielder reporting that not only were the shows completely sold out, but also that 'almost all their better songs came from the soon-to-be-released third album' (identifying the tracks 'Slow Motion', 'Just For A Moment' and 'I Can't Stay Long' for special mentions), while concluding that Ultravox's work with Conny Plank appeared to have left the band sounding 'slightly less austere and considerably more fluid'.

Ultravox released *Systems Of Romance* on September 8th and – as ever – the media reaction was broadly underwhelming. The *NME* in particular was swift in its assassination of the album, which was carried out by the paper's Ian Penman under the cutting headline 'The Further Decline And Fall Of The Western World'. Penman did manage to inject a small amount of positivity when he described 'Slow Motion' as 'a pretty electronic pop song' but was all too swift to reject the rest of the album as 'weedy, idealistic, pessimistic verbiage'. In an echo of that brief moment of positivity, *Melody Maker*'s Chris Brazier also found something to admire in the album's closing track, 'Just For A Moment', which he enthusiastically described as 'an intriguing mixture of the ghostly and the mechanical, the melodic and the metallic'.

John Gill at *Sounds*, having finally had the opportunity to experience *Systems Of Romance* on a proper audio system, was also impressed by 'Just For A Moment', describing the track as 'a slow, dreamily cinematic song' in a positive four-star review for the paper. 'Slow Motion' also attracted Gill's attention and favour, leading him to describe the track in enthusiastic detail: 'The peaking synth runs and gouging guitar opening give it an air of an overture. The mutant Glitter-beat is quickly established beneath the sharp guitar. The wild, glottal guitar stretches out over the simplistic beat, jarring beneath Foxx's melodic voice.' The review also admired the album's myriad synthesiser sounds (variously described as 'sharp and violent', 'threatening', 'fluttering' and 'whiplash'), although ultimately Gill would conclude that his personal preference lay with the more musically varied tracklisting evident on the *Ha! Ha! Ha!* album, while acknowledging that *Systems Of Romance*'s 'subtle use of electronics and treated sounds' were certainly sufficient to overcome that shortcoming.

As 1978 headed towards its end, Ultravox made their first TV appearance on BBC2's late night music show *The Old Grey Whistle Test* on December 5th. Introduced by the show's Annie Nightingale, the band delivered curiously static performances of 'Slow Motion' and 'Hiroshima Mon Amour', the cameras mostly alternating between close-ups of an impassive John Foxx and glimpses of the inscrutable Billy Currie and Chris Cross each working behind impressive banks of synthesisers and keyboards.

Watching at home, Gary Numan – whose Tubeway Army had released their eponymous debut album the previous week – was making notes of his own. 'I'm a huge John Foxx fan, but I remember seeing Ultravox on TV and feeling that the music was really cool, but the overall look of the band didn't fit,' Numan mused later. 'You shouldn't look like that if you sound like that.' Although disappointed by their *Old Grey Whistle Test* stage aesthetic and presentation, Numan was nonetheless a huge fan of *Systems Of Romance*; in fact in the sleeve notes to accompany the remastered 2006 edition of the album, Numan would tell writer Steve Malins how that album was 'probably the most important album to me in terms of how I wanted to approach electronic music. It was exactly where I wanted to go with my own music.'

During the recording of the debut Tubeway Army album in the autumn of 1978, Numan had set himself a new course, one that would see the frontman reinvent himself yet again, this time wryly shedding his Valeriun identity – 'I wanted to be spacey and mysterious, so I called myself Gary Valeriun. It was a notable mistake' – in favour of becoming Gary Numan, the name under which he would pioneer a charge towards something entirely new: 'I didn't know at that point that the move was going to be into electronic music, I just knew I had to move somewhere. I became very frightened that the next big thing was going to come along soon and wipe away the remnants of punk. To me punk was dying on its feet. I didn't want to be associated with it any more, I wanted to be the next big thing.'

With this indistinct idea of an alternative musical future occupying his thoughts, Numan – reunited with the Tubeway Army line-up who had made the 'That's Too Bad' single: Scarlett on bass, and Rael on drums, although for this release both players would drop those early monikers in favour of their own names, Paul Gardiner and Jess Lidyard – returned to Spaceward Studios in Cambridge, where Tubeway Army had cut their first demos a year earlier.

Keen to ensure that every second in the studio counted, the trio arrived at Spaceward with more than an album's worth of material rehearsed and prepared, and worked through the night to lay down the basic parts for around fifteen new tracks. The band's increasing confidence in their developing musical trajectory was reflected in the fact that neither 'That's Too Bad' or 'Bombers' would be considered contemporary enough for inclusion on the resulting album, although the punk-influenced rock style that had underpinned both singles continued to shape the sound of the new recordings throughout the writing process and into that initial recording session.

Crucially it was over the course of that first album session that Numan came across a Minimoog synthesiser that had been left behind by the studio's previous occupants, and found himself unable to resist pressing a key or two, a moment of idle curiosity which would have a seismic effect on the young frontman: 'Pressing that first key changed my life. Luckily for me it had been left on a heavy setting, which produced the most powerful, ground-shaking sound I had ever heard,' Numan reported later. 'I realised immediately that this was what I had been looking for.'

Having left Spaceward after that first album session with the power and potential of his chance encounter with the Minimoog still resonating through his imagination, Numan found himself more and more dissatisfied with the latest recordings and was eager to find a way of incorporating this powerful new technology into his songs. Beggars Banquet were duly persuaded to book a second recording session and, in the weeks leading up to that return session, Numan set about upgrading Tubeway Army's existing songs to include synthesiser parts, plotting the electronic sounds that he wanted to add to the record on a battered piano in his parents' home.

Inspired and invigorated by the creative process, Numan returned to Spaceward on August 23rd, 1978. Beggars Banquet had been coerced into hiring a Minimoog for the session and, literally overnight, everything changed for Numan and for the label. 'This time, I was allowed to hire a Minimoog for the entire session, and when I returned to their offices, I was an electronic act,' Numan declared. The shift in musical direction took Beggars Banquet by surprise and Numan would later recall, with considerable understatement, that the label's Martin Mills was 'not entirely happy' about the updated sound, before adding, 'I think Martin agreed to release it because they couldn't afford to send me back to the studio to make the punk album, but I could be wrong. It all worked out very well for everyone though.'

In fact the transition from punk to electronic was so rapid that it also took the rest of the band by surprise. Jess Lidyard had laid down his drum parts during the first recording session and therefore wasn't required to be in the studio for the second, and consequently didn't hear the album again until after Numan had added the newly conceived layer of synthesiser: 'When I heard it next, Gary had added keyboards to the songs. I was surprised but a lot of the material was still quite familiar.'

Despite Numan's confident assertion that Tubeway Army was now an electronic act, the band's eponymous debut album isn't a particularly electronic release by modern standards. As Lidyard pointed out, the tracks on the record had been conceived and initially recorded without synthesisers, and the wash of electronic sounds was added fairly sparsely, providing texture, mood and a fresh new dynamic without dramatically altering the basic song structures.

The result is an interesting one. *Tubeway Army* is a schizophrenic album which captures the sound of a band with one foot in their recent punk rock past and the other in an electronic future and the raw rock tracks are certainly made more interesting by the wash of electronic effects that Numan added. Listen to the album today and – notwithstanding Numan's now-familiar jagged, robotic and dispassionate vocal style, and the science fiction nature of his lyrics – *Tubeway Army* reflects an important period in musical history where post-punk's rock sounds were already straining to follow new, and more contemporary pathways.

Released at the end of 1978 in a limited edition of just 5,000 blue vinyl copies intended to satisfy the demand from the modest fanbase the band had built up so far, the album received a launch that was so low-key that *NME*, *Sounds* and *Melody Maker* all failed to run reviews, though *Record Mirror*'s Kelly Pike stepped forward as an early supporter, boldly proclaiming that '*Tubeway Army* is an album which 98 per cent of the population would take an instant and furious dislike to. Being a perverse creature, I have taken quite a fancy to it.' Describing the release as a 'strange, cold album', the review continued in a cautiously enthusiastic manner, Pike noting the 'chilling calculated music structures' that pervaded the album as a result of Tubeway Army's liberal use of synthesised sounds.

Fledgling music industry trade magazine *Record Business* were similarly seduced by the album's prevalent electronic leanings and turned in a particularly prescient review in December: 'Interesting exponents of the "I am a machine" syndrome currently popular in what used to be called the new wave. Tubeway Army proves to be an inventive threesome specialising in doomy words intoned over quirky, interesting riffs of the clockwork variety with occasional sorties into guitar or synthesiser solo territory which prove the band has the ability to take its ideas a step further. Gary Numan, lead vocals, guitars and keyboards also produced the LP and sounds quite a talent.'

As Numan's star ascended, things were looking trickier for his heroes, Ultravox. On December 9th, a fortnight after the release of *Tubeway Army*, and just a few days after Ultravox's *Old Grey Whistle Test* appearance, the music press ran stories to announce that the band was parting company with their label, Island Records. *Melody Maker*'s piece stated that 'The contract with the band will not be renewed when it runs out at the end of the year, and the group is looking at ideas for the release of their next album,' while *Sounds*' report added that the split was 'by mutual agreement and with no recriminations' and that Ultravox were already 'currently considering a number of offers before making their next move'.

Ultravox's final release on the Island label had been 'Quiet Men', the second single from *Systems Of Romance*, released at the end of October to general indifference. *Record Mirror*'s Tim Lott described the single as 'English pop with Germanic synthetic discipline. Insistent repeat pulse, electric percussion', and summarily dismissed the release as 'Good enough to avoid the charts.' *Sounds* were even less supportive, rejecting the single on the grounds that 'if this is disco rhythms with an intelligent face, gimme disco produced by runaways from a home for the mentally retarded'.

The day after the news of Ultravox's split from Island Records was announced, the band headlined a sold-out show at The Lyceum in London, their biggest headline concert in the capital to date. The show was attended by journalist Adrian Thrills, whose review appeared in the *NME* on December 23rd. Broadly supportive of support acts Angletrax, Snips and The Skids, the tone of the review took a very different turn when it came to Ultravox, whom Thrills roundly rejected for their 'abject futuristic baloney' and dismissed overall as 'wretched, strobe-bathed neu Europeans; humourless, plastic and musically dire'. Fortunately for Ultravox, *Record Mirror*'s Tim Lott was also on hand to provide a rather different perspective on the same show. Frustrated by a schizophrenic setlist that saw the band shuttle between the glam-fuelled, punk fury of 'Young Savage' and 'ROckWrok' and the cool Teutonic romanticism of 'Just For A Moment' and 'Quiet Men', Lott urged the band to 'put the things of their childhood behind them and look into the mekkanik [sic] future with all of their metal heart', and recognised something special in the band, noting that 'when they're good, they're very good'.

As Ultravox contemplated their new future from the stage of The Lyceum, Japan were also on tour, this time in support of their second album release of 1978. *Obscure Alternatives* had been released on October 27th, preceded by Japan's third single, 'Sometimes I Feel So Low', in a limited blue vinyl edition at the start of the month to a mostly underwhelming reaction. *Sounds* called the single 'a memorable little number' while comparing the vocals to 'Freddie of "and the Dreamers" fame' before rejecting the band's aesthetic as 'datedly glam'. Meanwhile *Melody Maker* offered no actual opinion on 'Sometimes I Feel So Low', preferring to simply describe the release as 'The Avon ladies of the scene strut out with a discofied boogie thing, complete with moogy drums and keef guitars.'

Praising 'Sometimes I Feel So Low' for its 'barking under-riff, catchy hookline and a lyric that makes sense even in your darkest hours', *Record Mirror*'s Tim Lott was delighted to find a rock record among that week's pop releases, and Tony Parsons in the *NME* – while admitting to having previously been 'tantalized' by some of Japan's earlier output – fell back on unfavourably bracketing the band with the New York Dolls but, despite comparing David Sylvian's vocals to those of 'a maniacally depressed blubbering hausfrau', nonetheless wondered if 'Sometimes I Feel So Low' might be a hit. It wasn't, although the single did pick up some tentative chart activity in some parts of Europe.

The *NME* failed to find much of merit when the release of *Obscure Alternatives* followed the single, although journalist Bob Edmands did identify something positive in Sylvian's vocal performance. 'Singer David Sylvain [sic] sneers with a certain panache,' he wrote, before dismissing Japan for their failure to 'strive towards sleazy menace' on the record, and ultimately for being out of date in delivering songs that 'adopt poses that were fashionable five or six years ago'. Rosalind Russell was more enthusiastic in her review for *Record Mirror*, in which she singled out Richard Barbieri's 'neat' keyboard work for particular praise, calling the band clever ('just not too clever I hope'), and predicting success for the album in Japan.

Fortunately for Japan, it was Geoff Barton, an ardent supporter of the band, who provided *Sounds*' more thoughtful, and certainly more enthusiastic, review. Noting how Japan had 'analysed and improved upon the most exciting elements of their first LP', Barton broke down the album title and offered examples of the obscure ('infectious funkescent rhythm laced with HM guitar snatches, swirling, straining synth and aggressive, vicious, vocals') and the alternative ('since when has a band looked so good and sounded so different?') before summing the release up as 'sounding altogether much more together and concisely confident' while urging his readers to embrace the band with open arms. 'But be careful not to smudge the lipstick.'

Named to reflect Japan's belief in steering their own course, Sylvian would clarify that the *Obscure Alternatives* album title was inspired by 'not accepting what's been given to you, you shouldn't just follow a pattern that's been laid down for you, you should choose for yourself what you want to do and adapt a certain way of thinking' – a sentiment close to the hearts of Japan at a time when it seemed they were unable to make significant headway in a largely indifferent music scene. That said, the band earned their first front cover when *Record Mirror* published a feature by Kelly Pike, who had interviewed Japan in New York, under the title 'Samurai of 42nd Street' at the end of November.

Interestingly, the *Record Mirror* cover featured an image of just David Sylvian rather the entire group, a move which echoed the *Obscure Alternatives* album sleeve, which sported a striking photograph of Japan – taken at an early test shoot by Fin Costello, then at the very start of his journey towards becoming a noted music photographer – but with the focus firmly on David Sylvian at the expense of the rest of the group, who appeared only as shadowy background figures. *Obscure Alternatives* was the first piece of album artwork to shift the visual focus of the band in this way, and would turn out to be the last of the band's studio albums to feature any of the other band members on the sleeves at all.

Although commercial success continued to elude them in the UK, Japan were nevertheless starting to make inroads into international markets and, before their first UK tour in support of *Obscure Alternatives*, had recently returned from playing their first shows in the USA, which saw them play six shows across the country, including two dates at New York's noted new wave venue, Hurrah. Courtesy of Japan's impressive PR machine, much was subsequently made of the band's US and international success in the UK press, although most of that attention was focused East, towards the land the band were named for, Japan.

The band's success in Japan initially stemmed from their image, as Japan biographer Anthony Reynolds would later observe: 'To be blonde, pale and thin in Japan was to be exotic, seductive and mystical.' In fact, when Hansa first approached potential label partners for the Japanese release of *Adolescent Sex* back in spring 1978, it was the photographs of the band, rather than the sound of their music, that most caught the attention of Victor Records' A&R man Akira Yokota. Within weeks of learning about the band, Victor Records had entered into a licensing agreement with Hansa to release Japan's records in their part of the world, by which time photographs of the band attending a Kate Bush album launch party in London had already begun to cause a stir with Japanese pop fans, courtesy of the influential Japanese music magazine *Ongaku Senka*.

In fact such was the impact of Japan's image that a Japanese fan club was formed for the band before they had even released a record, although a Japanese edition of *Adolescent Sex*, featuring the same tracks as the previous UK and international editions but with some changes to the track names ('Transmission' became 'Invitation To Fascination', 'Suburban Love' became 'Carousel Of Love' and 'Television' became 'Temptation Screen'), was eventually released in September 1978.

While a domestic Japanese release of *Obscure Alternatives* wasn't scheduled until March 1979 to coincide with Japan's first tour there, the autumn 1978 edition of Japan's new fan club magazine had already reported 100,000 sales of the band's first album, *Adolescent Sex*, there in its first week of release. While the actual sales total was certainly significantly lower than the fan club's enthusiastic estimate, the band nevertheless sold sufficient quantities of their debut for it to achieve a number two position on the Japanese international artist chart, and a Top 20 spot in the main charts.

The final significant album to come out in 1978 was Throbbing Gristle's *D.o.A: The Third And Final Annual Report*, released on the band's own Industrial Records label on December 4th. Coming out in an initial edition of 3,000 records, *D.o.A* was Throbbing Gristle's second album and featured thirteen tracks, including three live recordings from 1977 and a solo track from each of the band's four members.

John Gill reviewed the album for *Sounds* in the middle of December 1978, noting *D.o.A*'s tendency to present its message without sentiment: 'TG take no sides, leaving pity, shame, disgust and outrage to your decision.' Gill also singled out 'Dead On Arrival' and 'Hamburger Lady' as the two 'most immediately striking tracks' and was further delighted to discover that the band's debut single, 'United', had been dramatically sped up for inclusion on the album, which featured the original four-minute track 'reduced to 16 seconds of accelerating blips and squeaks'.

The *NME* reviewed *D.o.A* in January, by which point the paper had started the new year by rejecting 'Last Year's Things', a list which included 'Being Modern', in favour of 'Next Year's Things', a manifesto for 1979 which included 'Being Contemporary'. Throbbing Gristle, it seemed, were neither. In his *D.o.A* review, Ian Penman roundly rejected the band for wrapping their career in a parcel of 'ropey political cum philosophical claims' which, Penman acknowledged, had subsequently been amplified by the press: 'The murky electronic disembowelments which pass for Throbbing Gristle's "improvised" music have been heard in previous manifestations where there was more sense of purpose and less pretence.'

Fad Gadget, 1980.

1979

1979.1 Simple Minds / Joy Division / Cabaret Voltaire / Billy's / Blitz / Orchestral Manoeuvres In The Dark / Robert Rental & The Normal / Mute Records / Fad Gadget / Silicon Teens / Telex / Tubeway Army / Japan / Sparks / M / Buggles

AT THE START OF 1979 the music press were – briefly – united in their praise for another new band with electronic leanings who were causing a stir beyond their native Glasgow, and had ended 1978 on a high after signing a deal with Scottish label Zoom Records. Courtesy of writer Ian Cranna, the *NME* had already turned in a fervent early review of one of the band's first ever shows in October 1978: 'You know that band everybody's been waiting for?' enthused

Cranna. 'Well here they are. They're called Simple Minds, they come from Glasgow, and they create not just startlingly good rock music, but a whole show, an event, all in their cramped corner of a crowded city pub, the Mars Bar.'

Formed from the ashes of Glasgow punk rockers Johnny & The Self Abusers (who had enjoyed a brief moment of punk notoriety with the November 1977 release of their sole single, 'Saints And Sinners', on the Chiswick label), Simple Minds – 'Here are the names which will soon be familiar,' the *NME*'s Glenn Gibson enthused in a January live review, 'Jim Kerr (vocals); Charlie Burchill (guitar/violin); Michael McNeil [sic] (keyboards); Derek Forbes (bass); Brian McGee (drums). Which songs to watch for? All of them' – were named after a line from David Bowie's song 'Jean Jeanie' and had, in addition to Ian Cranna's enthusiastic accolade, also scored a similarly positive reaction from *Sounds'* Linnet Evans when, in December 1978, she wrote, 'It's only a matter of time before Simple Minds becomes a household name.'

In enthusiastic early features on the band, both the *NME* and *ZigZag* were struck by the fact that Simple Minds appeared to have arrived on their respective radars complete, with songs, art-school aesthetic and stage presence already firmly in place. The recent success of comparable artists such as XTC, Magazine and Talking Heads, and a little more time having passed since punk, meant that by 1979 the negativity and suspicion that had dogged the previous generation of bands perceived to come with art-school pretensions – Ultravox! among them – no longer applied, despite the fact that, like Ultravox!'s Billy Currie, Simple Minds' Charlie Burchill would also sometimes play violin on stage.

'There was always an art thing in us,' Simple Minds' frontman and main spokesman Jim Kerr would muse later. 'We wanted to get a band along those lines of darkness, and a sort of awareness, and put it over in an attractive type of art package. We wanted a band we could project.' And much was made at the time of Simple Minds' considered approach to their music, the *NME* praising the band for their 'rare and persuasive fusion of '70s high-tech rock: their lyrics impressionistic fragments, their music brave exploratory textures'.

In those early features, published before the band had officially released a single note of music, much was also made of Simple Minds' initial demo tape – recorded at Glasgow's Ca Va Sound studio in May 1978 – which had been the catalyst for much of the hyperbole. The *NME* saw that tape as evidence of the band's 'stunning, versatile and adventurous talent', while *ZigZag*'s Lindsay

Hutton – who also described the sound of Simple Minds as 'beautiful, sharp, chilling, rock'n'roll magic' – went so far to describe it as 'one of the greatest demo tapes ever'.

The media furore around the Scottish five-piece even extended as far as the BBC, where BBC2's *Old Grey Whistle Test* duly booked Simple Minds for the band's first ever television appearance. The two-track session, which featured performances of 'Life In A Day' and 'Chelsea Girl', was broadcast nationwide on March 27th, 1979, and also marked the release of Simple Minds' debut single, the aforementioned 'Life In A Day'. Despite playing to what Jim Kerr would describe as 'an otherwise empty room, with nothing but a couple of people sitting on chairs and a handful of bored looking camera operators as an audience for us to feed off', the session was competently and confidently delivered, and the single wore its rather derivative Roxy Music and new wave stylings well enough to score the band a minor hit when it subsequently peaked at a very promising sixty-two in the UK singles chart.

Released on Zoom Records, the tiny Edinburgh-based independent label run by Simple Minds' manager Bruce Findlay, but distributed and promoted by Arista, 'Life In A Day' picked up some cautiously encouraging reviews. In the *NME* Julie Burchill created the category 'Young Literate Punky Late-Comers To Bring Down The Government' under which to file Simple Minds before adding: 'of course, their single is nothing new, everything old, borrowed and blue-eyed-boyish'. Despite finding something of the band's influences in their sound – 'Another lot who'd love to be Roxy Music as they were' – the *Melody Maker*'s Jon Savage was nonetheless able to recognise some of the potential which shone brightly but briefly in the single: 'Very strong synthesised opening, leading into a verse and chorus that immediately loses its way in over-production and the group seem to fall asleep. Inexplicable.'

Simple Minds' debut album, also titled *Life In A Day*, followed in April. *Smash Hits* scored the release eight out of ten and described it as 'A very strong debut album from an exceptionally talented new Scottish band who are certainly destined for the top.' 'They come highly recommended by various scribes, with good street credentials from the Scottish Zoom label, and a flicker of rumour and enigma to spice their arrival,' was the promising opening of John Orme's review of *Life In A Day* for *Melody Maker*, although the tone of the piece took a more ominous turn with the plaintive addition, 'Why, then, do they bore me so substantially?' Further declaring the album to be over-worked and over-reliant on John Leckie's production, as well as being derivative and apologetic, Orme's final lament was that 'Simple Minds content themselves with the echoes of others, and enslave themselves by repetition.'

Deciding to take the musical influences which he felt the band wore so conspicuously on their sleeves – Roxy Music, David Bowie, The Doors, Cockney Rebel – as a positive contributions to Simple Minds' sound, Tony Stewart was more generous in his review of *Life In A Day* for the *NME*: 'It's [Simple Minds'] ability to be selective when embracing these inspirations and to mould them with their own distinctive ideas and visions that creates something that's not essentially innovative but which is certainly rare. But more importantly, there is a distinctive Simple Minds style.' Stewart also praised the contributions Mick MacNeil, Simple Minds' keyboard player, made to the album, while making an important point about the band's sound: 'While Kerr and Burchill form the creative fulcrum, McNeil [sic] is the third member of the sound-triumvirate as he swivels between the keyboards or synthesizer, organ and piano. Strangely enough for a non-writer he has become indispensable to the band: responsible for the textures; an important component to the momentums of the rhythms; and the flexible axis between back and front-lines, contributing an astonishing range of brief but creative solo excursions… Collectively Simple Minds have the talent, resources and uncluttered vision to be one of the most important post-punk bands,' Stewart concluded, adding, 'With their uncontrived commercialism they could also be one of the most successful and hopefully an inspiration to others.'

Life In A Day spent four weeks in the Top 40 of the UK album charts, where it peaked at number thirty, although a second single from the album, 'Chelsea Girl', failed to chart after its release in June. "Chelsea Girl' has little to offer in the way of hard-core content,' wrote *Melody Maker*'s Ian Birch. 'The melody line is thin, the lyrics wistfully insignificant and the sense of innovation almost non-existent.' *Smash Hits*' Red Starr, meanwhile, was more direct in his support: 'A medium paced but urgent ballad, it's a passionate appeal to an empty headed girl from a lonely boy. Simply a classic – acquire immediately if not sooner.'

Simple Minds quickly fell out of love with their album debut which, recognising its derivative nature and limitations, they felt didn't stand up well in comparison to the bolder, more innovative music being made by their peers. Jim Kerr would later talk about how, shortly after delivering *Life In A Day* to the record company, he heard a tape of Joy Division's own debut album, an experience he would later revisit in an interview with *Record Collector* magazine: 'After listening to *Unknown Pleasures* our record sounded like The Boomtown Rats,' Kerr confessed. 'With the greatest of respect, that wasn't what we wanted.'

While the chronology of Kerr's revelation doesn't quite hold up – at the time of the April release of *Life In A Day*, Joy Division had only just finished recording *Unknown Pleasures*, which wasn't released until June – it's entirely possible that Simple Minds had come across recordings from Joy Division who, in addition to their own debut release *An Ideal For Living* the previous year, had recently committed two more songs to vinyl which were getting them, and the newly founded Factory Records label which had released them, a great deal of attention in the music press and across the music industry.

Factory Records was born after Roger Eagles, who ran Liverpool music venue Eric's, approached Granada TV presenter Tony Wilson, then running a Manchester club night called The Factory, with an idea for a collaborative record release designed to showcase some of the new talent emerging from both cities. Allegedly talks stalled after the two parties found themselves unable to agree on a suitable format for their potential joint-venture's debut release, Eagles favouring a straightforward twelve-inch vinyl release, Wilson – apparently influenced by a recent and revelatory acid trip – keen to plough a more unorthodox furrow by putting out the release as a twin-pack of seven-inch EPs.

Ultimately the conversation between Eagles and Wilson came to nothing, but the idea of starting a record label had nevertheless sparked something in Wilson's imagination, and the thought continued to resonate with him until, in spring 1978, he and his business partner Alan Erasmus expanded their Factory club concept to include a label of the same name, and Factory Records was born. Stephen Morris of Joy Division, whose band would be featured on Factory's first ever record release, would later outline the label's business structure in his memoir *Record Play Pause*: 'At the start, Factory wasn't just Tony. It was Tony (the thinking) and Alan Erasmus (the actual doing), to be joined later by Peter Saville (the overall look) and by Martin Hannett (the sound).'

A plan was subsequently struck by the partners for Factory Records' first record, the realisation of Tony Wilson's double-pack seven-inch EP concept, which was to feature two tracks each from the Durutti Column (who were managed by Wilson and Erasmus), Joy Division and Cabaret Voltaire (who had both played shows at The Factory club), alongside three short comedy tracks from John Dowie 'for light relief'. The release, which was entitled *A Factory Sample*, was limited to 5,000 copies and was initially scheduled for release on Christmas Eve 1978, until designer Peter Saville's rather cavalier attitude towards deadlines impacted upon that release date.

If urban myth is to be believed, Factory designer Peter Saville had previously failed to deliver poster artwork he had been commissioned to design to promote the first month of Factory club nights until after two of the four nights the poster was intended to advertise had already run. Similarly, at the end of 1978, production challenges caused by *A Factory Sample*'s ambitiously conceived and unconventional packaging – the two seven-inch singles were packaged in rice-paper sleeves, dyed silver, printed, hand-folded and sealed in a plastic bag – led to the release date being postponed until January 24th, when the first batch of 1,000 copies was finally complete.

As the sleeve for each copy of *A Factory Sample* had to be folded, stuck, and assembled by hand, Joy Division themselves were among those drafted in by Factory Records to complete the work. Earning a reported 50p for every 100 packages assembled, the remaining 4,000 copies of the release were subsequently delivered over the course of the next four weeks, earning Joy Division the princely sum of £20 for their collective work.

Of the four acts who contributed tracks to *A Factory Sample*, Cabaret Voltaire, who had been experimenting with sound since around 1974, were arguably the most established. Hailing from Sheffield, some fifty miles from Manchester, Cabaret Voltaire had already played as part of Factory's series of nights at the Russell Club, often on the same bill as Joy Division, which had put them on Wilson and Erasmus's radar as potentially like-minded souls. The offer to be part of the *A Factory Sample* release came hot on the heels of the release of Cabaret Voltaire's own debut, the *Extended Play* EP, which had emerged on Rough Trade in November 1978, and the Factory release gave the band the opportunity to further showcase their experimental and uncompromising sound with the release of two new tracks: 'Baader Meinhof', which they had recorded for the *Extended Play* EP but which 'didn't really fit', and a new track, 'Sex In Secret', which was recorded specifically for *A Factory Sample*.

In *Melody Maker*, Jon Savage described *A Factory Sample* as an 'intelligent, attractive, surprisingly homogenous sampler', and particularly praised Cabaret Voltaire whose 'dynamism and openendedness [sic] bodes well for the future', and Joy Division for winding their 'claustrophobic, abrasive, yet precise anger even tighter', summing up the release as 'Enterprising, recommended.' Paul Morley submitted a similarly encouraging review for the *NME* which concluded, 'The sampler's sound is often untidy, and in a way the selections seem like left overs – but left overs that invite search. In five years' time rock and pop will be utterly different in form and content to what is foolishly accepted as being rock and pop now. And it'll still be changing. Factory helps it along its way. A game of love. The only way.'

At the start of 1979 things were also beginning to happen for Joy Division. By coincidence the January release of *A Factory Sample* came less than a fortnight after the band's first appearance on the cover of the *NME* – as part of a shared cover which featured a picture of Ian Curtis alongside images of Fast Product's Bob Last, and one of a bus – for a 'New Year New Sounds' feature in the January 13th issue which singled out Joy Division as a band to watch in 1979. 'We'd like to stay on the outside. We'd love it if Tony Wilson said he'd pay us to do an album on Factory. That would be great. We can't afford to do it ourselves, which we'd want,' Joy Division singer Ian Curtis told Paul Morley in the feature. 'But you either stay outside the system or go in totally and try to change it.'

The cover came hot on the heels of the *NME* expressing their approval of the band by including *An Ideal For Living* in their December 1978 'The Ones That Got Away' feature a few weeks previously. That piece was quickly followed by Joy Division's first London show, at the Hope & Anchor in Islington on December 27th, a show which distinguished itself not only for its disappointingly poor turnout – the band's Bernard Sumner would later write in his autobiography that Joy Division played to 'one man and his dog… and I don't think the dog liked us' – or for the decidedly lukewarm *Sounds* review that followed, but as the date the band first witnessed Curtis suffering an epileptic fit.

Formally diagnosed as epileptic in January, Ian Curtis nonetheless joined the rest of Joy Division at The Factory club just three days later, to play alongside Cabaret Voltaire (who headlined the event) and John Dowie at the launch party for the *A Factory Sample* release. The launch, Joy Division's second show of 1979, also served as a warm-up for the band's first live session for BBC Radio 1's John Peel. An early champion of the band, Peel had been quick to air a couple of the tracks from the original first pressing of Joy Division's *An Ideal For Living* EP, and was equally supportive around the release of *A Factory Sample*, giving airtime around release to both Joy Division tracks – 'Digital' and 'Glass' – as well as playing Cabaret Voltaire's 'Sex In Secret' twice, and the Durutti Column's 'No Communication' once.

Perversely, and presumably to the disappointment of the fledgling Factory label, Joy Division failed to include either of the songs they had just released on *A Factory Sample* in their Peel session, or in fact any of the songs that had caused *NME* to single out the *An Ideal For Living* EP for recent praise, and instead chose to record early versions of 'Exercise One', 'Insight', 'Transmission' and 'She's Lost Control'. With hindsight, perhaps it's unsurprising that Joy Division used the Peel session as an opportunity to record four previously unrecorded songs; the band were at a point in their career where they were working productively as a unit and were producing new material quickly. Peter Hook would later estimate that Joy Division were writing two or three complete songs a month at that time, each song honed, rehearsed and ready to be performed live, but existing only in the heads and hearts of the band: 'Everything up to and including *Unknown Pleasures* really existed only when the four of us were in a room together playing it, not written down, not recorded, just from memory.'

With a body of work written and ready to record for their album debut, Joy Division took some time in the early part of 1979 to consider available options for the release of the record. The band's rising profile in the media and across the music industry had been enough to catch the eye of several labels, and the group were sufficiently interested in an offer from a new London-based label, Genetic, that at the beginning of March they travelled south to record some demos with someone at the mixing desk who was about to become another key figure in this story, producer Martin Rushent.

Martin Rushent had been working in recording studios since the early seventies but in 1979 was known for his more recent work producing a number of emerging punk and post-punk acts, The Stranglers, Generation X and the Buzzcocks among them. Rushent had recently founded Genetic Records, a Warner Bros.-financed offshoot of Andrew Lauder's Radar Records which was actively looking for new projects. Turned on to the band by his assistant, Anne Roseberry, who had seen them playing live in Manchester, Rushent arranged for Joy Division to travel to London's Eden Studios, in order to record some speculative demos as a way of exploring the idea of a possible contract.

While the band enjoyed the session – during which they recorded new demo versions of 'Insight', 'Glass', 'Transmission', 'Ice Age' and 'Digital' – and were grateful to Rushent for his interest and enthusiasm, the experience would ultimately come to nothing. On the urging of their manager, Rob Gretton, Joy Division opted instead to remain close to home and chose to trade the Genetic deal (which offered a hefty financial advance, reportedly worth around £40,000, set off by a low royalty rate paid on sales) for a less formal hometown deal with Factory Records which wouldn't pay an advance, but would instead see the band split all profits equally with the label, while fully retaining their independence and staying in control of all aspects of their career. Factory Records' Tony Wilson was less circumspect in his summation of the deal, as he explained later: 'Joy Division and Rob Gretton's attitude was, "Let's do the first album with Tony... we won't have to sign to nobody and we don't have to get on the train and talk to cunts in London".'

History would prove Martin Rushent's instincts about Joy Division to be correct, but the producer was about to meet more artists who would go on to play important roles in this narrative, and he wouldn't have to travel as far as Manchester to find them. By coincidence Genetic Records' London office was located upstairs from what would shortly become the epicentre of a brand new cultural phenomenon.

Today, 4 Great Queen Street in central London is unremarkable. Four-storeys nestling among offices, hotels and coffee shops on the western edge of London's Covent Garden. The upper floors house offices, and perhaps a flat or two, while the ground floor entrance houses a 'gentleman's club' called The Red Room. Without exception everyone passing this shabby blue-painted building with the rather old-fashioned canopy over its front doors fails to give it more than a second glance.

Look more closely, however, and you might locate the low-key black plaque dedicated to reminding passers-by that this was the location of Spandau Ballet's first ever live performance. Rewind the clock to Genetic Records' Great Queen Street base in February 1979, replace the current styling of The Red Room with a World War II-themed wine bar, light that canopy with spotlights and you're at the Blitz: the very heart of what was about to become the hottest new scene in London, and the launchpad for a movement which would become known – whether they liked it or not, and mostly they didn't – as the New Romantics.

Decorated with murals and dramatic historical photographs depicting the bombing of London during the Second World War, the styling of Blitz distanced the club from the daily trials and tribulations of late-seventies Britain: a country which, at the start of 1979, was struggling through what would later become known as the Winter of Discontent. The first night of the Blitz, February 6th, 1979, came just days after a twenty-four-hour Day of Action strike by the public sector unions, the biggest individual day of strike action Britain had experienced for over fifty years and the start of a prolonged period of unrest across the country. Street cleaners were just one of the groups taking industrial action at that time and the rat-infested rubbish that was piled up in the streets and in designated refuse areas, including much of Leicester Square, can only have added to the surreal scenes as a parade of young, extravagantly dressed and immaculately coiffured clubbers descended upon their new spiritual home.

Blitz was the club that put the so-called New Romantics on the map, and is still considered the launchpad for that movement, but the Blitz story really starts some months earlier, in the autumn of 1978, with the launch of a Tuesday night residency at an ailing London venue called Billy's. Located at 69 Dean Street in Soho – downstairs from the home of the infamous Gargoyle Club, which had been frequented since the 1930s by characters including Noël Coward, Tallulah Bankhead, Francis Bacon, Lucien Freud and Henri Matisse, and was said to be haunted by the ghost of Nell Gwyn, King Charles II's mistress – Billy's in 1978 was a decidedly down on its luck Soho dive bar frequented by pimps and off-duty Soho sex workers. 'A sad disco ball pointed its fingers of dissatisfaction at a lonely dance floor and its surrounding empty booths. That is until a fey Welsh boy and his cockney sidekick stepped in.' Enter two more key characters in this story (or three if you include the writer of those words, the soon-to-be Spandau Ballet star Gary Kemp). The fey Welshman was one Steve Harrington, the cockney sidekick Rusty Egan. Both were products of their time, each having fully participated in punk but having become disillusioned by the movement and were now in search of something new.

Harrington had befriended the Sex Pistols when they visited Wales in September 1976 to play a show at Newport's Stowaway Club, and had subsequently moved to London where he took full advantage of what he described as 'punks's social support system', which allowed him to sleep on sofas and work in various unspecified ways for Generation X and the Rich Kids, on the way to reinventing himself as Steve Strange. Rusty Egan – in many ways Strange's opposite – was a musician; he'd drummed with the Rich Kids and The Skids, had an extensive record collection, an even more extensive knowledge of music and an increasing interest in the emerging electronic music scene.

By the autumn of 1978 this unlikely, but surprisingly effective, duo were flatmates, sharing a small flat and big ambitions while looking for something new to fill the space that punk had left in their lives, and in the lives of the people around them. Inspired in part by London's Embassy Club, which had a policy of running different clubs for different scenes on different nights, but which catered to an older and more affluent clientele, starting a club at Billy's was an opportunity for Strange and Egan to do something similar for their own generation.

Having negotiated a deal with Billy's owner which would see the fresh-faced entrepreneurs take the door money and the venue the bar profits, the pair's club career was born, as Strange would later recall in his autobiography, *Blitzed!*: 'We printed up flyers with the tantalising line "Fame, Fame Jump Aboard The Night Train. Fame, Fame, Fame. What's Your Name?" We opened in autumn 1978 and very quickly we were successful. All the punks who were also closet David Bowie fans turned up. Soon it was a regular event known as Bowie Night.'

Inevitably the success of the club brought its own challenges, one being the need to ensure that the crowd were there for the right reasons. With Egan otherwise occupied as the main DJ, Strange was left to police the door to ensure that any potential troublemakers were kept firmly at bay, a role it quickly emerged he was more than eminently suited to. Strange's policy was simple: in order to gain entrance to the club you had to look 'right', a subjective judgement on Strange's part as the Bowie Night palate of styles was a broad one, as *The Face* would later report of its Blitz incarnation: 'It was toy soldiers, cossacks and queens to the outsider, an odd fantasy world down the stairs; to the participants it was a mutual admiration society for budding narcissists, a creative and competitive environment where individualism was stressed and change was vital.' Presumably the effort involved to qualify for entry into what journalist Dave Rimmer would go on to describe as a 'heaving carnival of determined idiosyncrasy' was also an effective deterrent to those potential, and less sartorially adventurous, troublemakers whose presence Strange had originally been sent to deflect.

Legend states that it wasn't unusual for Strange to hold a mirror up to a hapless victim, as if that alone would be enough to persuade them that they simply weren't up to the responsibility of joining this elite circus, and if the mirror alone wasn't enough then a well-aimed, and suitably bitchy, put-down would usually do the trick. Strange would later defend his confrontational tactics, explaining that without strict policing the club would have become something of a tourist attraction, with voyeurs turning up merely to gawp at the freak show it contained rather than participating and celebrating it: 'I was strict on the door because once people were inside I didn't want them to feel like they were in a goldfish bowl. I wanted them to feel that they were in their own place amongst friends, and that anything went.'

Once past Strange's scrutiny, clubbers would follow a staircase down into a dark, less than salubrious basement with a small dance floor, a few booths and a long bar, a space with sticky carpets, memorably served by a 'tiny broken toilet with a door that didn't shut. No toilet paper, no soap and a tap that failed to provide water.' But what Billy's lacked in facilities it more than made up for in providing a safe environment for a misfit crowd of individuals with disparate styles and musical interests, but with nowhere to go after the fragmentation of the punk movement. 'The people who turned up were a bit of a mishmash, but what they all had in common was that they were fed up with punk, and had a love of David Bowie,' recalled Strange. People like the then eighteen-year-old Gary Kemp in fact, who would later recall, 'This was something new, something to do with punk, disco, rock, glam; disparate styles, all of which I loved but until now couldn't bring together.'

Although punk had provided much of the attitude which underpinned Billy's, the club's musical policy was careful to distance itself from that movement, preferring instead to serve up an eclectic mix of music which combined the best of David Bowie with the very latest electronic sounds, delivered alongside unselfconsciously kitsch selections from the recent and distant past: 'Rusty, who DJ'd, tried not to play much punk music, so there was a lot of Bowie on the turntables, along with futuristic German music, 'Being Boiled' by The Human League, 'Warm Leatherette' by The Normal, the theme from *Stingray* and torch songs from Marlene Dietrich,' Gary Kemp would later explain.

Such was the success of the club that by the end of 1978 Steve Strange and Rusty Egan had outgrown Billy's and eventually transported their Bowie Night lock, stock and barrel to the Blitz, where they opened the doors to their new club night in the February of 1979. Legend states that the relocation was of particular relief to Egan, who had temporarily gone into hiding in Germany after a fallout with the owner of Billy's – 'A 300-pound, six-foot-four, black pimp named Vince, who sported a huge black fedora, a long leather coat, and fingers the size of sausages with enough diamond rings to give Liberace cause for concern' – who had taken the news that the duo were planning to take their profitable business elsewhere rather badly.

Strange and Egan had been introduced to Blitz by fashion entrepreneurs – and Steve Strange's sometime employers – Acme Attractions' Steph Raynor and Helen Robinson, who used the bar as a convenient venue for post-work drinks after starting a new shop, PX, in nearby James Street, and who were themselves considering starting their own Tuesday night club at the venue. Robinson: 'I stupidly mentioned it to Steve Strange, and the next thing I knew he'd gone behind our back and was doing a night there. I asked him about it and he said, "Don't worry, I'll let you in for free."' Whether the promised free admission for his daytime employers ever came through or not is a moot point, but one thing was for sure: Blitz on a Tuesday night was a hot ticket.

Blitz was extraordinary not only for its clientele's hair and clothes, their style and their posing, but also for the number of regulars who would go on to become leaders in their chosen fields. Strange's challenging door policy undoubtedly helped to cement Blitz's reputation as an elite hangout, which in turn made passing his muster and getting inside even more essential. But it wasn't just about posing and posturing, although that was, of course, very important; Blitz was also a rallying point for an emerging generation of ambitious young people, a focal point and an incubator. In common with all nightclubs it also fulfilled a more fundamental function as a place to have a good time, a few drinks and a dance, as Spandau Ballet's Tony Hadley was quick to explain: 'There has been so much written about it, and a lot of pretentious stuff as well, when it was basically just a bunch of young girls and guys, all looking the business and having a bloody good time.' A sentiment echoed by Steve Strange: 'People were often either speeding or drunk,' he wrote in his autobiography. 'There was plenty of glamour, but it was also very debauched. There was always someone falling over.'

Gaining admission to the club also offered the opportunity to dive into Rusty Egan's groundbreaking playlist. According to Midge Ure, 'Rusty played the music he liked – mixing up The Only Ones with Bowie, Killing Joke with Roxy Music, Chic with Kraftwerk, Neu and La Düsseldorf. We kept the scene underground. It was a great place to go; style, image and look on a shoestring.' At the start of 1979 Egan was among the very first tastemakers to recognise something vital in the rudimental electronic experimentation emerging from the new wave of electronic artists. 'I went to record companies and listened to the records and picked the tracks,' Egan explained later, when asked about how he always managed to be one step ahead of the mainstream music industry. 'I went to see bands live, I knew lots of musicians and clubs, and I went to record shops, DJ shops and markets. I was always out searching. The record company people went home early, but I was out late.'

Consequently Egan's playlist, which had started with him playing his favourite records at Billy's and had continued into the Blitz, was frequently the first place clubbers would hear the latest electronic sounds, and the DJ booth at Blitz always served up a selection of innovative releases which would include early support for tracks from The Normal, The Human League, Robert Rental, Cabaret Voltaire, Throbbing Gristle, Ultravox!, and Orchestral Manoeuvres In The Dark, alongside other interesting, and largely electronic, releases from previous generations.

Since their debut live show at Eric's in Liverpool in late 1978, Paul Humphreys and Andy McCluskey, whose long hair and indifferent approach to style would have surely seen them left on the pavement had they ever attempted to actually gain admission to Blitz, had been forced to reevaluate their intention to play just one date as Orchestral Manoeuvres In The Dark

Orchestral Manoeuvres In The Dark, 1981.

and then stop. Following their Eric's debut, the venue's owner, the same Roger Eagles who had originally planted the idea of a record label into Tony Wilson's mind, recommended that the duo play another show at The Factory in Manchester as part of the informal reciprocal arrangement which existed between the two venues. 'We played Eric's as a one-off gig, and amazingly they said "We've got these friends in Manchester who have got this club called The Factory, we'll get you a gig there. We do this reciprocation thing; Joy Division came over from The Factory, so we'll send you over there,"' McCluskey marvelled later. 'For three months it carried on like that with us saying "Oh we'd better stay together till next week because someone wants us to do a gig, a record, an interview and by the end of that time we were more or less committed," the singer would tell the *NME* the following year. Further shows followed the one at The Factory, including a December 1978 date at Eric's with Robert Rental & The Normal where OMD stepped in as last-minute replacements for Cabaret Voltaire, who were unable to play. 'They played 'Electricity',' Daniel Miller would recall later. 'And I remember thinking, "My God, that's an amazing pop song." We talked a little bit and they were asking me how to put out a single and stuff.'

With Miller's advice still resonating in their ears at the start of 1979, Orchestral Manoeuvres In The Dark recorded two songs, 'Electricity' and 'Almost', in the garage of their manager Paul Collister in order to enter Liverpool's Radio City 'Battle of the Bands' competition and to use as a demo to distribute to potential promoters and labels. Paul Collister's involvement in the band's career at the time shouldn't be underestimated as not only did Collister handle the band's management duties, but he also had access to the van they used for transporting their equipment and was the owner of Winston, the TEAC reel-to-reel tape player that OMD were then using on stage.

While Orchestral Manoeuvres In The Dark were unsuccessful in the Radio City contest, their efforts in recording the two songs were not in vain. Having been introduced to Factory Records' Tony Wilson while in Manchester for their first show at The Factory club, Humphreys and McCluskey followed up on their meeting by sending Wilson one of the tapes in the hope that it might secure them an appearance on the influential regional TV show *Granada Reports*, which Wilson presented.

Whilst a TV appearance wasn't immediately forthcoming, the Orchestral Manoeuvres In The Dark tape nevertheless made it into a pile of demos languishing in Tony Wilson's car, where it was eventually picked up by Wilson's then wife, Lindsay Reade, who liked the songs enough to recommend to her husband that Factory Records should release 'Electricity' as a single. Prior to Reade's timely intervention Wilson had been unconvinced by the band's potential, something that Andy McCluskey could understand: 'He'd seen us play at The Factory club a few weeks earlier and didn't like the look of these unreconstructed hippie types with a stupid band name.'

A single deal in place, Factory packed Orchestral Manoeuvres In The Dark off to the label's preferred studio, Cargo in Rochdale, to record new versions of the two demo tracks with their producer, Martin Hannett – then working under the punk moniker Martin Zero – to be released as a single. Thrilled to be working in a professional recording studio for the first time, Orchestral Manoeuvres were nonetheless baffled by their producer's eccentricities. 'Hannett was weird and scared the hell out of us,' McCluskey would remember later. 'At one point he just climbed under the desk and went to sleep.'

Orchestral Manoeuvres In The Dark ultimately disliked Hannett's vision for their songs. 'Our original version of 'Almost' was really tight and poppy, but he'd laid it back and covered it in echo. And we thought "This is really boring!" It was a pop song and he'd turned it into this totally lethargic ballad,' McCluskey clarified later. A compromise with Factory was eventually reached, ironically one which would see the band provide their own demo recording of 'Electricity' to be used on the A-side of the single – the production of which was credited to Paul Collister working under the name Chester Valentino – but to keep the Martin Zero production of 'Almost', which Tony Wilson was particularly keen on, for the B-side.

Packaged in a striking black sleeve printed with thermographic black ink – a concept Peter Saville had originally developed for Factory's previous single release, A Certain Ratio's 'All Night Party', but which had been rejected by that band and subsequently reimagined for OMD – 'Electricity' was released as Orchestral Manoeuvres In The Dark's debut single in May 1979. Although the limited-edition pressing is stated as running to 5,000 copies, a persistent rumour around the release holds that the single's challenging packaging kept setting the printing press alight and the run was abandoned after only around 3,000 sleeves were printed.

Despite having to undertake the laborious manual process of packing each single into its striking new sleeve themselves – 'There was a stack of

'Electricity' in white bags and a stack of black bags, and we had to take them all out of the white bags and put them in the black bags. Hand-bagged, every single one' – for Paul Humphreys and Andy McCluskey the effort was entirely justified, as the latter would later recall: 'Once we saw the finished sleeve, we thought "Jesus, this is brilliant!"'

The *NME* were extremely complimentary about 'Electricity', writer Adrian Thrills describing the lead track as 'excellent, melodic, synthesiser pop' and singling out the single's B-side, 'Almost', for particular praise: 'Even better though, is the Martin Zero-produced B-side 'Almost', a doleful, heartsick slab of electronic angst.'

On the back of the media's enthusiasm, plus vigorous support from Radio 1 DJ John Peel, the Factory Records edition of 'Electricity' sold out quickly without anyone quite realising that this pair of pioneering slices of electronic pop actually featured no synthesisers at all, a fact which wouldn't properly emerge until a year later when an *NME* feature reported the surprisingly humble technology involved in the making of the single: 'McCluskey had an old bass, and Paul Humphrey [sic] owned a run-down electric piano and organ that cost in total the princely sum of £75.'

Having dipped their own toes into the waters of live performance the previous November when Robert Rental and The Normal united to play a short run of shows – including the one at Eric's in Liverpool in December 1978 where they had met OMD, and the London show alongside Throbbing Gristle and Cabaret Voltaire at the Cryptic One Club – at the start of 1979 Rental and Miller were persuaded to join the first Rough Trade tour, designed to showcase a diverse selection of the acts associated with Rough Trade's independent label and distribution services, which was booked to play at venues across the UK in February and March.

Headlined by Stiff Little Fingers, the tour also featured the jazz-punk sounds of Essential Logic (advertised at some shows under the name of their singer, former X-Ray Spex saxophonist Lora Logic) as well as Robert Rental and Daniel Miller's collaboration, which was sensibly billed 'Robert Rental & The Normal'. The tour was provocatively designed by Rough Trade to ensure that anyone attending any of the shows would be exposed to radically different types of music over the course of the night, a plan which worked to a degree, but also brought its own challenges as the acts, and particularly those lower down the bill, often played to largely unsympathetic crowds: 'We used to go down really badly on stage, in a violent way. People would throw things at us and jeer,' Miller recalled of the shows later. 'We had some extreme reactions to our music, and I suppose in a way that was what we hoped for, and anyway, the more abusive the audience got, the more musically noisy and difficult we became.'

Not that Rental and Miller made it easy for themselves: 'We were typical difficult artists,' Miller recalls today. 'We decided early on not to play either of our singles but a short section of the backing track was a mash-up of them. The music that Robert and I performed was very much a collaboration. We created a backing track together and improvised over it when playing live so elements of it were different every night but the backing was the same. By the nature of how we performed none of the gigs were the same but also not very different from each other.'

Released at the very start of the Rough Trade tour, the instant success of Stiff Little Fingers' *Inflammable Material* – the Rough Trade label's first album release – which charted at number fourteen on its way to selling over 150,000 records for the band and their label, ensured that the dates were a huge success, attracting the attention of both the media and the record-buying public, a halo effect that also extended as far as Rental and Miller. 'There was always a clutch of people who after the shows were really into it, and that was really encouraging,' Miller enthused. 'You always felt like they were going to go on and spread the word.'

By fortunate synchronicity Melvyn Bragg's highbrow ITV arts programme, *The South Bank Show*, descended upon the tour to report on the rise of the new grassroots independent record label culture which had sprung up in the aftermath of punk. Alongside interviews with various Rough Trade staffers, Lora Logic, and members of Stiff Little Fingers, the show also provided Rental and Miller with national television exposure by broadcasting two performance extracts featuring the duo hunched over their synthesisers in front of a crowd who appeared mostly perplexed by the abrasive pulsating electronic noises, snatches of spoken and musical found recordings, and inaudible lyrics emanating from the tapes and keyboards on stage, sounding for all the world like the soundtrack to a particularly disturbing sci-fi nightmare.

In addition to the *South Bank Show* film footage, one of the Robert Rental & The Normal performances, captured in the unlikely environs of the West Runton Pavilion in Norfolk, was recorded for release as a live album, which was released on the Rough Trade label in 1980. Released in the style of an official bootleg, *Live At West Runton Pavilion* came out as a single-sided vinyl album in a plain red cut-out sleeve. Clocking in at just over twenty-five minutes, no further information, or any sort of tracklisting, is provided other than the name of the artists and the date of the recording which, ironically, was incorrectly stated as 6/3/79, when the show had in fact taken place three days earlier.

Released at the very end of 1980, *Live At West Runton Pavilion, 6/3/79* was reviewed by Ian Pye for *Melody Maker* in January 1981. 'This is the real thing,' Pye declared. 'From the heart of darkest Norfolk comes one side of electronic pastiche, packed with humour, inspiration and wholesome weirdness,' he continued, while warning that while the release was 'not always an easy record to listen to it nevertheless comes across as an imaginative attempt at electronic impressionism. By refusing to take the whole thing seriously the album successfully walks a fine wire between the absurd and the ingenious.'

Robert Rental & The Normal's run of live shows with Stiff Little Fingers and Essential Logic were followed by a clutch of their own dates in Paris, where the stresses and enforced bonhomie of touring had, temporarily, introduced a fractious element into Rental and Miller's relationship, leading to their returning to London to begin work on their next projects separately. For Miller, whose music industry ambitions had at this point extended no further than recording and releasing one single, it was time to consider what, if anything, he wanted to do next.

In a conversation with the *NME*'s Vivien Goldman the following year, Miller would look back on that period with a degree of misgiving, admitting that he had been 'in a very bad way mentally' and had been unable to decide whether he should explore the possibilities of a career in music or simply return to his previous life working as a film editor. Goldman also reported that following the success of 'T.V.O.D.' and 'Warm Leatherette', Miller had fallen into a creative paralysis, spending vast amounts of time 'recording reams of reels at home, disliking everything; still so staggered by the success of 'T.V.O.D.' that it verged on intimidation'.

Despite news to the contrary appearing in *ZigZag* magazine, Daniel Miller had no further release from The Normal up his sleeve. 'Master of his own art, Daniel's been painstakingly piecing a new single together,' Chris Westwood had teased in a feature on The Normal for the magazine's October 1978 issue. 'For all I know, the thing could be on release by the time this reaches the printers, but just now, all I know is that one of the titles is 'First Frame'.' 'I think I got as far as thinking of a song title,' Miller smiles today, 'but that's about as far as it went.'

Having set up Mute Records with the sole intention of releasing just one single, The Normal's 'T.V.O.D.', the underground success of that release forced Miller to revisit the idea of extending the life of the label. Already, aspiring artists, who identified with The Normal's startling new sounds, were using the address printed on the 'T.V.O.D.' sleeve to contact Miller in the hope that he might consider their music for release on the label: 'The single sleeve had my address on it,' Miller would recollect wryly. 'So I was getting sent demo tapes because people thought I was a proper record label.'

Surprised by how few of the acts who had been in touch had managed to catch his attention, and considering the majority of the tapes to be too derivative of other artists to be of interest, it wasn't until a mutual friend – the musician, journalist, illustrator and cartoonist Edwin Pouncey, then better known as Savage Pencil – introduced Miller to his flatmate, Frank Tovey, that Miller finally found a project which would justify his widening the Mute Records remit enough to work with other artists: 'It was the first thing I'd heard that I'd really liked. Then I met Frank, who was Fad Gadget, and we got on really well.'

After an initial exploratory meeting – 'I arranged to meet [Daniel Miller] at a Monochrome Set gig. I got kind of pissed and fell behind the drum kit so we didn't meet that night. I met him at Rough Trade later,' Tovey would recall later – the pair hit it off to the extent that Fad Gadget subsequently became the second artist, after The Normal, to be signed to Mute Records. 'We shared a similar vision,' Miller would later remember in an interview with Medium. 'I said: "Let's make a single." That really was the beginning of Mute Records as a label, as opposed to just my own thing.'

Having returned to his native London after studying fine art at Leeds Polytechnic, Frank Tovey – who later confessed to *The Face* that he had attempted to learn flute, violin and piano as a child but had ultimately abandoned all three: 'As soon as I'd learnt three notes, I'd get bored and give them up' – had started making rudimentary electronic soundtracks at college as accompaniments to the mime-influenced performance pieces which dominated his student output. 'I suppose it was my lack of real musical ability that made me decide to go for synths and the like,' Tovey contemplated in an interview with *Electronics & Music Maker* magazine in 1984. 'It was possible to make some pretty impressive sounds without really being able to play properly, and that was an idea that appealed to me a great deal!'

After graduating from Leeds, Tovey continued his musical experimentations upon his return to the capital, where he swapped the relatively well-equipped Leeds Polytechnic studio for an altogether less promising space: 'I set myself up in this small cupboard within a council flat. A lot of us shared the flat, so the only space I could find was inside the cupboard, where I had a cheap electric piano, a little drum machine and a cassette recorder.' Two of the songs to emerge from those early cupboard sessions were 'Back To Nature' and 'The Box', the latter dealing with the subject of claustrophobia, which is not surprising given the circumstances surrounding its creation. As Frank Tovey would later tell *Smash Hits*: 'The only trouble was I couldn't get enough air in [to the cupboard], so by eleven o'clock at night I was getting really dizzy and realised I was starting to suffocate.'

Although it was originally intended to come out as Mute Records' second single release, and had been awarded the catalogue number MUTE02 accordingly, logistics conspired against the release of the single, and 'Back To Nature' was finally released in September 1979, a couple of months after the July release of MUTE03, the first single from Daniel Miller's most mischievous project, an electronic four-piece from Hornchurch in Essex who called themselves the Silicon Teens.

The debut single from Silicon Teens was an electronic cover of Chuck Berry's rock'n'roll classic 'Memphis Tennessee'. *Smash Hits* described the single as a 'jolly little song', connecting the synthesised cover version with Telex's 'Rock Around The Clock', which had been released a few weeks previously, and revealing Silicon Teens to be Europe's 'first teenage electronic group'. John Peel loved the 'Memphis Tennessee' release so much that, after giving the single its first Radio 1 play at the end of July, he enthused, 'It's been a week or two since I've had a favourite record. I think this could easily be the next.' Incredibly, Peel then went on to give 'Memphis Tennessee' a further seven plays across his radio shows over the next four weeks. Paul Morley also picked up on the potential of 'Memphis Tennessee' in a review for the *NME*: 'That they use synthesizers and electronic percussion to give new vitality and freshness to such ageing pieces is significant. That they could have a hit is no surprise.'

The positive review coverage, coupled with 'Memphis Tennessee''s sudden radio exposure, caught the attention of the media enough that Mute started to receive requests from journalists keen to set up interviews to find out more about Silicon Teens and the band members themselves: Darryl on vocals; and Jacki, Diane and Paul on synthesisers and electronic percussion. Such interest in Silicon Teens caught Daniel Miller somewhat by surprise, and the band's sudden success presented the label owner with a further logistical problem, because Silicon Teens didn't actually exist. In fact, the band were entirely the invention of Miller himself, who had provided all the music and vocals on 'Memphis Tennessee' as well as on the single's B-side, a similarly quirky electronic reworking of Chris Montez's 1962 hit 'Let's Dance'.

Dating back to before the release of The Normal, Daniel Miller had hit upon the idea of reinventing classic rock'n'roll tracks in a fresh, idiosyncratic, electronic fashion as a way of familiarising himself with the workings of his recently acquired first synthesiser, a second-hand Korg 700S which had previously been used on stage by Elton John's live band. Recorded around the same time as the two original compositions that appeared on The Normal's 'T.V.O.D.' single, it wasn't until a chance conversation about cover versions with Rough Trade's Sue Dunne later, after which Miller pulled out those recordings to play her, that it occurred to him that there might be some merit in their release.

Choosing not to release the cover versions under the name The Normal because that would be 'a bit boring', Miller instead came up with the Silicon Teens concept as his vehicle for their release: 'I thought that if I was head of EMI, that's what I'd pay a million pounds for right now, a two-boy two-girl electronic pop group. So I made one up,' he told the *NME* in 1981.

Silicon Teens' take on 'Memphis Tennessee' was released in July 1979, production duties credited to Larry Least – Miller again, working under a spoof identity which echoed that of legendary producer Mickie Most – and packaged in a cheap one-colour graphic sleeve, deliberately designed to look as if it had been drawn by one of the band and which named the imaginary band members but stopped short of picturing them. 'We wanted it to look as if the sleeve had been put together in one of their bedrooms,' Miller explained. 'That's why the logo was hand-drawn on school book graph paper.'

As interest in the band increased, BBC Radio 1 added the single to their A-list – 'John Peel played it and the next day I received a telegram from the BBC saying they wanted to add it to their playlist and could they have some more copies,' Miller marvelled – and a promotional photograph of Silicon

Teens was circulated for media purposes. The press shot consisted of a black-and-white image which compiled the four individual headshots of the teenage quartet, each band member partially obscured behind dark glasses. Upon closer inspection, and with a certain amount of insider knowledge, while the representations of synthesiser players Jacki and Diane remain anonymous, the images of the band's supposedly teenage electronic percussionist, Paul, and vocalist Darryl, bear more than a striking resemblance to, respectively, Daniel Miller (who turned twenty-eight in 1979) and Frank Tovey (who turned twenty-three).

A later request from BBC Radio 1 for Silicon Teens to appear as guests on the station's review show, *Roundtable*, pushed the levels of necessary subterfuge yet further. Frank Tovey was once again pressed into service to play the part of Darryl; another friend, Priscilla, stepped in to fulfil the role of Jacki; and actor Keith Allen adopted the role of the band's manager, Chas Barton. Daniel Miller coached the trio in advance of the interview and also attended the recording as Mute Records' representative. 'It was great, like a performance,' Miller would later tell the *NME*, adding, with just a hint of regret, 'I think [*Roundtable* presenter] Richard Skinner half-sussed it, but he went along with the joke.'

The final piece of deception surrounding the 'Memphis Tennessee' project came in the form of a music video to accompany the single. Featuring the white-suited and formally attired Silicon Teens – including Daniel Miller as Paul and Frank Tovey as Darryl – as the house band on a sinking cruise liner, the video watches as the group's eccentric audience determinedly dances in defiance, or perhaps ignorance, of their imminent watery fate. Looking back on his creation, Miller would later acknowledge, 'It was just a bit of a joke, really, which got a bit carried away.'

While Silicon Teens' version of 'Memphis Tennessee' was catching the attention of the UK media, Sire Records – whose Seymour Stein, an early champion of Daniel Miller's unorthodox approach, had already licensed The Normal's 'T.V.O.D.' for release in the USA – was already enjoying UK success with a similarly quirky electronic cover of another rock'n'roll classic from a Belgian trio called Telex. Their downbeat electronic take on Bill Hayley & The Comets' 'Rock Around The Clock' spent a respectable seven weeks in the UK singles chart, including three weeks in the UK Top 40, where it peaked at a respectable number thirty-four.

Booked to appear on *Top of the Pops* at the end of July 1979, Telex proceeded to deliver a hilariously deadpan performance of 'Rock Around The Clock' in front of a largely baffled studio audience, most of whom failed to grasp the comedy of the performance, which consisted of singer Michel Moers – flanked by his impassive bandmates Marc Moulin and Dan Lacksman, on synthesisers and backing vocals – seated on a chair from which he delivered his dispassionate vocal lines between drinking whisky and reading a magazine.

Treading a line somewhere between the electronic precision of Kraftwerk and the conceptual posturing of Devo, Telex were proving to be a difficult proposition for the mainstream music scene to grasp. Talking to *Smash Hits* for a feature on the band the week following their *Top of the Pops* appearance, Moulin was anxious to make it clear that Telex brought a certain tongue-in-cheek approach to their work, describing their work as 'human music' and stressing that behind the technology, Telex made music with 'a lot of humour in it'.

Taken from Telex's debut album, *Looking For Saint Tropez*, which had been released earlier in the year, 'Rock Around The Clock' was the third single from the album, following 1978's 'Twist A Saint Tropez' release as well as interim single 'Moskow Diskow'. Whilst neither of those singles, nor the album, had enjoyed much in the way of commercial success, Telex nevertheless picked up praise from the media. *Smash Hits* turned in an upbeat album review, praising *Looking For Saint Tropez* as 'a bright, snappy, totally synthesised album' and identifying 'Moskow Diskow' as one of its standout tracks.

Smash Hits' praise for 'Moskow Diskow' would prove hugely prescient. Since its release as a single in 1979, 'Moskow Diskow' – described by *Melody Maker* as a 'stylish, humorous plagiarism of Kraftwerk' – has been increasingly recognised and lauded as a seminal moment in the development of electronic pop, for its proto-techno sound as well as for its influence on successive generations of artists, sometimes in the most unexpected of ways. 'One funny thing about that song: we tend to think it inspired Michael Jackson for 'Billie Jean', using the same chords. In an interview he said he got his idea when hearing a European electronic group on the radio,' recalled Telex's Michel Moers, with some amusement, in 2012. 'We like to believe it was Telex.'

Following the flurry of mainstream interest and exposure that had accompanied Telex and the Silicon Teens' wonky electronic takes on traditional rock'n'roll, the mainstream music industry was swift to identify potential for further profit from such releases. While 'Memphis Tennessee' ultimately failed to echo Telex's chart success, Daniel Miller's next move was to capitalise on that big league interest by signing Silicon Teens to the

Phonogram label group for international release and distribution, and to grant Sire Records' Seymour Stein a similar license to release the imaginary four-piece in North America.

Licensing in place, Mute were able to turn their attention back to Fad Gadget, specifically to the release of his 'Back To Nature' single at the end of September 1979. Although 'Back To Nature' lacked the commercial crossover potential that had ensured Silicon Teens' 'Memphis Tennessee' success, the single enjoyed solid underground support, picking up and consolidating a similar audience to the one Daniel Miller had enjoyed with The Normal the previous year. 'Back To Nature' also picked up some encouraging reactions from the music press. In a November round-up of the latest independent releases worth hearing, *Smash Hits* proclaimed the single a 'clever electronic ditty'.

In advance of the 'Back To Nature' single release, Fad Gadget also began playing live, assisted for a brief period by Daniel Miller, who appeared on stage to free Frank Tovey from his keyboards to allow him to step up as the natural frontman he undoubtedly was: 'On stage, Frank was a very different person: he was then completely transformed in the Fad Gadget character.' Miller's role as a member of the Fad Gadget live band wasn't tenable in the long term due to his various label commitments, but it nonetheless provided Tovey the space to develop his volatile, visceral and provocative Fad Gadget persona until he was in a position to recruit musicians to back him on a more stable basis. Miller's part in the early Fad Gadget live shows may also have been part of the reason that *Time Out* magazine, in their review of 'Back To Nature', mused that perhaps Fad Gadget and The Normal were one and the same thing.

'Back To Nature' and 'The Box' were recorded and mixed for the first Fad Gadget single over the course of just one day at the eight-track RMS Studios in London's South Norwood, marking the first time either Miller or Tovey had worked in a proper studio. Miller, who stepped into the role of producer for the session and adopted some of the DIY techniques he had first started exploring with The Normal, distinctly remembers Tovey taking the creative lead on those early recordings: 'Frank had very clear ideas on what he wanted or didn't want and my task was to help him achieve that. It wasn't easy because we were both untrained musicians and we were learning as it went.'

Deliberately making the decision to resist writing about machines and technology, Tovey explained 'Back To Nature' to Japanese journalist Akiko

Hada the following year: 'I don't like songs about machines, I think that's boring, like Gary Numan and things like that. Just about ordinary situations. 'Back To Nature' is just about people who think they're getting back to the basic way of living, going to the countryside and things like that, but they're still taking along their fly sprays, Ambre Solaire and sunshades, and they're going in their car and staying in a caravan or tent. Not really going back to nature. It's so safe and, you know, they might as well be back in London.'

Despite Frank Tovey's casual dismissal of Gary Numan's lyrical themes, Numan was about to enter an imperial phase, starting in March with the release of a new single, 'Down In The Park', under the name Tubeway Army, the first single from a new album, and a project whose release might have come as a surprise to any fans who had, the previous September, read announcements in both the *NME* and *Sounds* that Tubeway Army had disbanded after the releases of their 'Bombers' single. Citing 'different musical directions' as the reason for the split, both papers also reported that Tubeway Army singer Valerium [sic] would be the only member of the band remaining under contract with Beggars Banquet, *Sounds* further adding that a solo album was expected from the frontman before the end of the year.

This new version of Tubeway Army was to all intents and purposes that solo project, Gary Numan stepping up to orchestrate all aspects of the endeavour, which relegated the rest of the band – Paul Gardiner on bass and Jess Lidyard on drums – to little more than session musician roles. The release of 'Down In The Park' was preceded by Tubeway Army's first ever radio session, which the trio had recorded for BBC Radio 1's John Peel show on January 10th. That session, which broadcast six days later, was the first opportunity for Numan to showcase the transition towards further realising the electronic vision he had hinted at on his *Tubeway Army* album the previous year.

Produced at the BBC's Maida Vale Studios, Tubeway Army recorded three tracks for John Peel, all taken from the band's forthcoming second album which they were making at the time. If you listen to the session now it's striking how the choice of tracks, and their treatments, so perfectly echo the transition from the guitar-orientated sound of the *Tubeway Army* album to the altogether more electronic stylings of what was to come next.

The first of the three session tracks, 'Me I Disconnect From You', has a foot in both camps: the song is underpinned by Numan's jagged rock guitar but overlaid with tentative synthesiser sounds which now sound almost quaint. But by 'I Nearly Married A Human', the third and final track from the session, those ratios are reversed and the track puts the electronic sounds firmly at the front of the song, where it leads both the vocals and the drums. The centrepiece of the session, 'Down In The Park', the first of Numan's songs to be entirely conceived as an electronic track, was shortly to be released as the first single from Tubeway Army's second album, *Replicas*.

More than forty years after its initial release 'Down In The Park' still makes frequent appearances in Numan's live sets, an evergreen classic from his extensive catalogue, which makes it difficult to appreciate today just how startlingly different the song must have sounded at the start of 1979. Numan's session performance is confident and assured and, perhaps as a result of the frontman's own belief in the song, exhibits an admirable understated swagger.

'Down In The Park' was released as Tubeway Army's third single in March 1979 and while it ultimately failed to chart, it nonetheless achieved triple the sales of the band's previous single, 'Bombers', which must have come as a considerable relief to Beggars Banquet, who were still nervous about the unexpected new electronic path their signing – now whittled down to just Numan – had taken. 'Tubeway Army in fact is just one bloke, namely Gary Newman [sic] who likes to look tremendously enigmatic and aesthetic,' wrote *Melody Maker*'s Ian Pye, reviewing 'Down In The Park' at the time. 'Born out of 'The Man Who Sold The World' the song drones along amidst synthesizer washes and a fashionably monochromatic delivery.' Nevertheless Numan remained circumspect. 'The early rise of electronic music, which 'Down In The Park' was part of, was greeted with a mixture of contempt and adoration,' he mused later. 'From the press it was mostly contempt, but the public seemed to go for it in a massive way.'

In addition to showcasing Tubeway Army's new electronic rock sound, 'Down In The Park' was also key in presenting Numan's new aesthetic. Released in a full-colour sleeve, the single artwork features a highly-styled Numan in a bare room, blonde-haired, black clad and awkwardly posed. The result is startlingly detached, alien, and 'other', all qualities which not only reflected Numan's bleak, dystopian, sci-fi lyrics, but also spoke volumes to Tubeway Army's emerging audience of similarly disaffected souls.

Almost certainly by accident rather than by design, Numan's blonde-haired black-clad image was mirrored, just weeks after the release of 'Down In The Park', by bassist Mick Karn in the promotional video made to support Japan's latest release, the first single to be taken from their own forthcoming album. Released in April, the 'Life In Tokyo' single was the UK's first glimpse of a reinvigorated new-look Japan. Still colourful and flamboyant, the band's image had been refined and modernised since the previous year, updating the antiquated glam-rock stylings, which had been so roundly lambasted by the music press, with a tighter, more contemporary aesthetic.

Nor was it just the look of the band that had gone through a transition since the release of the *Obscure Alternatives* album. Japan's music was going through a similar metamorphosis as the band moved away from their glam roots and started pushing in new directions. 'I think the things we were listening to were changing a lot,' Japan's Rob Dean would later acknowledge. 'A lot of electronic music: David Bowie's *Low* and *"Heroes"*, experimental stuff taking it somewhere else, as well as Roxy Music. We listened to a lot of early Ultravox; Eno of course. Got to know a little bit of YMO [Yellow Magic Orchestra]. So it all comes into it.'

Hansa were keen to encourage Japan to evolve further and suggested they work with a more contemporary and commercial producer to help facilitate that transformation. As a result, Giorgio Moroder was drafted in to work with Japan, or more correctly to furnish the band with the hit single that Hansa were so desperately craving. David Sylvian, who had been impressed by Moroder's recent work on the soundtrack to the film *Midnight Express*, was intrigued by the pairing and the song 'Life In Tokyo' subsequently emerged from a one-day session with the band at Moroder's studio in Los Angeles.

'Life In Tokyo' started life as a Giorgio Moroder composition entitled 'Foxes', which had originally been slated as a track for Cher on Moroder's soundtrack to the *Foxes* movie, which would be released the following year. Over the course of the session David Sylvian deftly took the song apart, reassembled it to better suit his band, and provided new lyrics inspired by Japan's recent Japanese experiences. The session with Moroder was reportedly good-natured and professional and, while the band were not overly convinced by the finished track, it nonetheless fulfilled the brief of adding a commercial, accessible patina to Japan's distinctive sound. Sylvian would later describe the session as 'an odd little experience' but would also acknowledge that 'Life In Tokyo' represented another step towards an updated Japan sound.

Released in April, 'Life In Tokyo' came out on the same day as Japan's only UK show of 1979, which took place at The Rainbow in London's Finsbury Park. *Sounds* were in attendance but were mostly negative in their review of the show, writer David Hepworth dismissing the gig as 'barely half full', and Japan themselves as 'weedy' and 'deliberately superficial', although he did briefly touch upon the band's updated image – 'They have worked very hard, particularly on their haircuts' – and updated sound – noting an 'injection of Moroder style keyboards' – before putting his personal feelings to one side for long enough to admit that although he wasn't a fan he could see a bright future for the band nevertheless. *Melody Maker*'s Steve Gett was also at The Rainbow and struck a journalistic balance by reporting that Japan had turned in 'an excellent performance', noting the addition of several interesting new songs which 'strongly suggested Giorgio Moroder' and which added a positive disco element to Japan's funk, reggae and rock stylings, and finally ending his review with the confident prediction: 'When they return to the capital with a third album behind them those empty seats will no doubt be filled.'

Both reviews also mentioned the success the band had recently been enjoying in Japan. Having delayed the Japanese release of *Obscure Alternatives* until the band's tour there in March, Japan played six shows in the country over the course of one week, which included performing in front of over 20,000 people across just two nights at Tokyo's Budokan. The reaction from the Japanese fans thrilled and bewildered the band in equal measure, Mick Karn later remembering the 'hundreds of fans that had been sleeping at Narita airport for three days waiting for our arrival, their screams echoing through the tall terminal, hands grabbing and pulling as we were ushered into a white Cadillac limo by bodyguards, and whisked away.'

Japan's only release of 1979, 'Life In Tokyo' – which had been released as a standard seven-inch single alongside an extended twelve-inch version – failed to attract enough radio, press and audience interest to become a hit, and the band retired to the studio where, after the rapid release of their first two albums, they started work on their third album at a slightly more leisurely pace. *Melody Maker* reviewed the single at the start of May, writing, 'The word is that Japan are going to be very big: they can't fail if they continue to put out stuff as fashionably derivative as this.'

The same week as 'Life In Tokyo' was released, Sparks, in an interview for *Melody Maker*, were reacting to the same paper's review of their new album, *No. 1 In Heaven*, which they had also made in collaboration with Giorgio Moroder, and which had appeared a couple of weeks earlier. 'Some people just don't know when to throw in the towel,' journalist Tony Rayns had sneered. 'Undaunted by nine years of unshakeable public apathy, Ron and Russell Mael, rock's featherweight answer to the Bronte Sisters, have cobbled together yet another album.'

Emerging from a difficult period creatively, Sparks had been keen to explore a more mainstream direction after the relative commercial failure of their previous album, 1977's *Introducing Sparks*. 'We heard 'I Feel Love' by Donna Summer and thought it was an incredible mixture of electronics with a voice that had real warmth to it,' Ron Mael explained to US magazine *Trouser Press* later. 'We wanted to work that way and I wanted to start working with synthesisers, so we approached Moroder – not because he was a disco producer but because he seemed to have the most knowledge of using synthesisers in a commercial way.' And, as far as Sparks were concerned, the collaboration with Giorgio Moroder was a huge success – 'I really like the *No. 1 In Heaven* album,' Ron Mael would confess later – despite Rayns' pessimistic review, and similarly unenthusiastic notices across most of the music press.

'A little bit of glam, a little bit of angst, a little bit of narcissism, a little bit of disco, a little bit of melancholy, a little bit of mystery: a big bit of a perfect pain in the bum,' was Ian Penman's view on the album for the *NME*. Nevertheless, *No. 1 In Heaven* provided Sparks with two significant hit singles in 1979 when 'The Number One Song In Heaven' reached number fourteen in the UK singles chart in June and 'Beat The Clock' peaked at number ten in August, the band's most successful single releases since 1974.

Curiously, the *No. 1 In Heaven* album fared less well, spending a single week at number seventy-three on the UK albums chart in September, but Sparks themselves remained nonplussed, confident that their work with Moroder was a success for both parties. 'We're giving him a bit of musical and, shall I say, hip integrity that he didn't have before because he was just a disco producer. It's him using us and us using him,' Ron Mael pondered in a *Melody Maker* interview later. 'I think the combination of his technological expertise plus our personality is what makes the record so strong.' Sparks were also confident that *No. 1 In Heaven* represented something of a revolution, not just for themselves, but also in a broader sense. 'Just wait six months from now and watch all of the new-wave, synthesiser, disco bands which will be popping up, and disco music becoming very respectable in hip circles,' predicted frontman Russell Mael. 'And then somebody else will capitalise on what we've done.'

Mael was correct. *No. 1 In Heaven*'s lack of commercial success belied its influence across a new generation of music makers. 'It was probably one of the first electro-pop dance records of all time,' Duran Duran's John Taylor enthused in 2021's excellent documentary *The Sparks Brothers*. Taylor's bandmate, keyboardist Nick Rhodes, was equally enthusiastic in the same interview. 'It was a huge influence on our early material,' Rhodes conceded. 'We were already Moroder fans, but this combination was just perfect.'

And Sparks weren't alone in tinkering at the intersection between rock, electronics and disco. In the UK, pop conceptualist Robin Scott was exploring similar territory and, under the name M – 'M wear suits, ID badges and sport a clean shaven, fresh underpants ambience,' *Record Mirror* would declare helpfully later in the year – had recently released what would be one of the most successful singles of 1979, 'Pop Muzik'. 'I decided that new wave and disco could be bridged,' Scott told *Smash Hits* at the beginning of May. 'I admired some disco records but I thought I could maybe make it a bit more interesting… What I wanted was a very impersonal basic backing track with a very individual vocal on top of it,' Scott explained in the same interview, although the irony of what he was trying to achieve wasn't lost on him, as he would admit to *Melody Maker* around the same time: 'The strange thing, of course, is the one thing that new wave was attempting to do was to defeat the purposes of disco and create live music again.'

'Pop Muzik' was a bright, brash pop hybrid – 'a cross between John Lennon (Plastic Ono Band period) and Dutch pop-rock stars, Gruppo Sportivo, with a dash of Devo and Kraftwerk thrown in for good measure,' reported *Smash Hits* – which spent six weeks in the Top 5 of the UK singles chart between April and June, including two consecutive weeks at number two, held off the top spot by 1979's bestselling single, Art Garfunkel's 'Bright Eyes'. In their review of 'Pop Muzik', *Smash Hits* further described the single as a 'contrived but extremely clever electro-energised, robotic-rock-cum-disco chant', while *Melody Maker* enthusiastically declared, "'Pop Muzik' throws in everything but the kitchen sink, Euro-references, disco beat, 'la-la-la' chorus, even mildly subversive touches.' 'The most exciting record for me this year has been M's 'Pop Muzik' which I recognise as a really innovating record,' producer Martin Rushent would tell *Record Mirror* at the end of 1979, adding, 'Tubeway Army and Joy Division are also a sign of things to come.'

Cut from the same cloth, and wearing its disco influence only slightly less conspicuously, was another of 1979's most successful UK singles, 'Video Killed The Radio Star', which was released at the beginning of September and topped the UK singles chart just six weeks later. Inspired by a short story written by science fiction author J. G. Ballard, and heavily influenced by Kraftwerk's album *The Man-Machine*, 'Video Killed The Radio Star' was the debut release from Buggles – initially a three-piece consisting of Trevor Horn, Geoff Downes and Bruce Woolley, although Woolley left the band before the single's release and in fact recorded his own version of 'Video Killed The Radio Star' with his new project, Bruce Woolley & The Camera Club, a band which incidentally featured Thomas Dolby in its line-up – and was born from similar conceptual beginnings as Daniel Miller's Silicon Teens, as Trevor Horn later explained to *People* magazine: 'In our heads, the Buggles were a fantasy group that had been dreamt up by a record label that had this huge computer in the basement.'

Prior to becoming artists in their own right, Trevor Horn and Geoff Downes came from backgrounds which had seen the duo variously dabble in production, songwriting, session playing and jingle-writing: 'We used to be track repair men, song repair men,' Horn told the *NME*'s Paul Morley at the beginning of 1980. 'If you've got a duff demo or song and £300 you'd come to us and we'd make it into a presentable record.' 'Before I started Buggles I was a sort of loser record producer,' Horn told *The Face* in 1982. 'I spent four years producing records for various people without ever making any money out of it or having any success at all. Eventually I got so fed up doing things that weren't successful I decided that if I couldn't find a good artist and a good song then I'd write it myself and become the artist.'

Although Geoff Downes' synthesiser work underpins the sound of 'Video Killed The Radio Star', it wasn't Buggles' intention to make an overtly electronic record. 'We use synths to fake up things and to provide effects,' Horn explained to *Smash Hits*' Fred Dellar in February 1980. 'We won't use them in the manner that somebody like John Foxx does. He's dominated by synths but we're not.'

'Video Killed The Radio Star', with its bright, glossy, modern sound and sci-fi lyrics, was in fact the culmination of all of Horn and Downes' studio and musical experience at the time. 'We felt that it was about time that somebody started making good, well-produced pop records again,' Horn told Dellar. 'We believe in perfection – we sometimes get criticised for being too professional – but then, people also criticise if you make things rough. There's no way of winning really. So we try for perfection as far as we can get it in recording.' And that need for perfection was all-consuming: 'I once worked out it would take twenty-six people to recreate the single live,' an incredulous Horn marvelled in an interview for *The Guardian* in 2018. Talking to *Record Mirror*'s John Shearlaw the week following the *Smash Hits* feature, Horn was in a more reflective mood: 'You can be really confident about your own music, especially working the way we work. But that doesn't mean you're confident that it will be "a hit". As a matter of fact I'm still surprised, not just about the hit, but about the whole process behind it.'

It would be an understatement to say that 'Video Killed The Radio Star' was a hit. The single went on to sell in excess of five million copies and claimed the number one spot in sixteen countries, including the UK, over the course of the following year. Despite further success with their second and third singles – 'The Plastic Age' reached number sixteen in the UK singles chart in January 1980, and 'Clean Clean' peaked at thirty-eight in April – and an album, *The Age Of Plastic*, which reached twenty-seven in the album charts, 'Video Killed The Radio Star' would always overshadow those achievements, forever relegating Buggles to the category of one-hit wonders. 'We decided we would work on it as one great big cheap gimmick from beginning to end,' Trevor Horn told *Record Mirror* at the end of November. 'That doesn't mean we're a silly band like, say The Flying Lizards – no disrespect intended – we're just out to make music fun again.'

31 March 1979   US $1.10c/Canada 80c   20p

JAM tour exclusive / LIZZY in Paris

NEW MUSICAL EXPRESS
NME

JONATHAN RICHMAN
The Ice Cream Man Cometh
P.23

Springtime For
SIOUXSIE P.28

HUMAN LEAGUE

Synthesizers in the snow...

P.7

1979.2 The Human League / The Men / Tubeway Army / Joy Division / Devo / Orchestral Manoeuvres In The Dark / Gary Numan

HAVING ALSO BEEN VOCAL in their assertion that their own brand of quirky electronic pop owed more than a small debt to the influence of disco, in 1979 The Human League were ready to serve up their most unabashed tribute to the disco genre in the shape of a quirky one-off single released under the name The Men. But before that, their next release as The Human League would be one of the least disco-influenced and most uncommercial releases of their career.

Since the release of 'Being Boiled' a little over a year earlier, The Human League had scaled up their ambition in all directions. They had expanded their line-up to a become a four-piece; had toured extensively, including a prestigious support tour with Siouxsie & The Banshees; and in January 1979 signed publishing and recording contracts with Virgin which they followed in April with the release of their second single, an EP entitled *The Dignity Of Labour*.

Having spent much of the time since the release of 'Being Boiled' on the road honing their live show, The Human League had recruited a new member with specific responsibility for the band's onstage presentation. Adrian Wright, a former ice cream man and an avid collector of sci-fi and pop culture ephemera, had been drafted in for the role, bringing with him an eclectic collection of slides which were projected behind the band while they played. As Ian Birch wrote in *Melody Maker*, 'The overall effect is one of science-fiction romance: *New Scientist* diagrams cheerfully collide with shots from *Fireball XL5*, Hammer Horror movies and Sunsilk-shampoo-styled erotica.'

Picking up reviews as they went, The Human League's early live shows amazed and confounded in equal measures. *Sounds'* Mick Middles attended a show at Manchester's Factory at the start of February and came away with favourable impressions of some parts of the show – 'Layer upon layer of synthesizer sound was thrown at us with calculated precision' – but remained baffled by others – 'the first five numbers rarely rose above the nondescript electronic drone that is as limiting as three guitars and a drumkit' – before ending with the confession, 'I'm not exactly certain whether or not I enjoyed myself.'

A fortnight later the *NME*'s Adrian Thrills attended the first of two nights of Human League shows at The Nashville in London. Describing the band as 'fun' and recognising pop roots which 'owe more to Giorgio Moroder and Pete Bellotte than they do to Brian Eno or Can', Thrills was less convinced by the 'ragbag of contradictions' he felt informed The Human League's live shows. Worrying that – despite Wright's considered slide show – Ware, Marsh and Oakey's low-key and deadpan performance style was at odds with the accessible, human and pop elements to be found in the band's music, and that their reliance on pre-recorded backing tapes left them with very little scope for improvisation or spontaneity, Thrills summed up the show as 'a case of admirable intentions that don't quite bridge the manifold limitations of the chosen instruments'.

The *NME* wasn't alone in identifying that when it came to crossover potential, The Human League had plenty: also at The Nashville that night was one David Bowie, who had swooped into the venue with his entourage as part of his ongoing efforts to keep up with music's most interesting twists and turns. Talking to Adrian Thrills after the show Bowie was most enthusiastic about the band: 'They were great. I was watching from behind the lighting desk so that I could see the audience as well as the group. It was like watching 1980!'

Asked about their moment in the presence of rock greatness a couple of years later, Phil Oakey recalled Bowie coming backstage before and after the show, leaving the Sheffield quartet impressed by his friendly modesty, despite one notably awkward moment which Martyn Ware recalled in an interview with Paul Morley for the *NME*: 'Before we went on, he asked us how long we were working for. "Huh? Oh, about four years, I suppose," and he said, "No, how long are you on for?"... "Oh, 43 minutes and 23 seconds."'

Also in The Nashville's audience that night was Gary Numan, just weeks away from the release of 'Down In The Park' and on a similar mission to educate himself about the emerging electronic acts who were about to become his peers. A huge fan of Bowie at the time, Numan would later recall that starstruck night in his autobiography, *Praying to the Aliens*: 'I was standing on a chair at the back and couldn't resist touching the top of his head as he walked past.'

With Virgin's blessing, *The Dignity Of Labour* was released as a four-track twelve-inch EP on the Fast Product label containing four thematically linked instrumental tracks, 'The Dignity Of Labour Parts I–IV'. Initial quantities of the release included a free flexi-disc which contained a recording of a meeting between the band and their manager, Fast Product's Bob Last, in which the topic of discussion was whether to include a flexi-disc with the single, and if so what to include on it. Such mischief wasn't unusual for Fast Product, who were already known for their high-concept ideas, which were widely admired by their peers, including Factory Records' Tony Wilson, who made no secret of the esteem in which he held Fast Product, describing them as 'the first really arty, clever label'.

Lacking the pop elements that had started to endear The Human League to the media, *The Dignity Of Labour* wasn't a hit, channelling as it did the more obscure of the band's krautrock influences at the expense of the polished pop sensibilities of Giorgio Moroder and Donna Summer. In his 1982 biography of The Human League, *Perfect Pop*, Pete Nash even went so far as to describe the release as 'a miserably drab item, despite its electric noodling around… literally swathed in arty pretence and foppery.' Chris Westwood was more encouraging in his review of the single for *Record Mirror*: 'Four parts, four slabs of credible, hummable synthesiser structures, three of which are adaptable, distorted, special dance music fodder.'

Radio play was not forthcoming, with even John Peel committing to just a single play each of two of the four tracks on the single. Fortunately the band's expectations for the EP had been fairly low. Talking to *Melody Maker* about the release a couple of weeks prior to the release of *The Dignity Of Labour*, Martyn Ware went on record to state that The Human League 'are fairly confident that the rock press is going to hate it'. As it happened the single did catch the attention of the media, whose positive reactions included *Smash Hits*, who weren't able to review the single because its EP format fell outside the parameters of their review page, but nonetheless awarded it unofficial Single of the Week status, writing 'Pride of place really belongs to The Human League with their splendid 'Dignity of Labour' twelve incher on Fast Product.'

Sounds were equally enthusiastic and proclaimed *The Dignity Of Labour* their Single of the Week, writer Chris Westwood describing the release as 'a minor masterpiece; moody, evocative, provocative. It fulfils with a (subtle?) vengeance so much of what's been scrawled about the League so far whilst exposing a new facet of both their capabilities and interest.' 'Fun, interesting and entirely disposable,' declared *Melody Maker*, describing *The Dignity Of Labour* as 'four instrumentals which hover between the spontaneous and the self-conscious, the corny and the beguiling'. 'This record is not The Human League as such, but The Human League exploring and letting no one down,' was the *NME*'s take on the release. 'Don't expect anything radically provocative, but there's a lot of compulsive synthesizer noises that are best played dead loud in the dark.'

The *NME* review also quoted The Human League themselves on their decision to release an EP of instrumental compositions – 'We never get the chance to play instrumentals on stage, mainly because we don't want to bore our audience to death. So we thought we'd bore them on record' – but with the benefit of some perspective, the band's Phil Oakey did later admit that the release may have been ill-conceived: 'It was a bad mistake doing it at that time, because everyone had decided we were a pop band, and we put that out and it sounded like Amon Düül or something.'

For their next release The Human League took full advantage of the 'full artistic control' clause they had built into their agreement with their new label, and released a single, 'I Don't Depend On You', under the name The Men. An eccentric move, even by The Human League's standards, 'I Don't Depend On You' showcased a very different side of the band's sensibilities to those on display on *The Dignity Of Labour* a few months previously, and the new release represented a very deliberate flirtation with a mainstream commercial sound.

Popular wisdom holds that the overtly commercial approach was the result of pressure from Virgin Records, but the reality was that the idea came from the band themselves who, without label backing, had never previously been in the position to afford the necessary session musicians to allow them to experiment outside their self-imposed electronic constraints. 'We thought for it to really be disco it should have proper drums and bass and therefore it couldn't be The [purely electronic] Human League,' Phil Oakey told The Arts Desk in 2011. Recalling the release of 'I Don't Depend On You' today, Martyn Ware compares the single's foray into disco as The Human League's equivalent of David Bowie's pre-Ziggy Stardust project, Arnold Corns: a safe environment out of the public gaze in which they could experiment with new directions. 'We were super keen on trying out a secret mission to see if we could do proper disco outside our own self-imposed The Human League "electronic instruments only" rule, and Virgin thought it was a cool idea and were happy to fund the experiment.'

Smash Hits journalist Red Starr was an immediate convert to the new cause and reviewed 'I Don't Depend On You' at the end of July, correctly identifying The Human League – their line-up supplemented for the single with session musicians and backing singers – as the true artists behind the release. Starr was also enthusiastic about the single's theme of female empowerment, describing 'I Don't Depend On You''s 'tongue in cheek disco' as 'difficult fun' before signing off with the slightly desperate promise, 'It's also really good, so persevere if it doesn't hit you immediately.' Meanwhile the *NME*'s Danny Baker professed himself baffled by the release, which he described, inauspiciously, as 'Sort of moody Chicory Tip with Peter Skellern overtones.'

Now, with the benefit of much hindsight, it's possible to see the prescience of 'I Don't Depend On You', which not only predicted the shiny commercial sound and female backing vocals which would be such an important part of *Dare*, but was also a nod towards the looser, more collaborative style which saw Heaven 17 later abandon The Human League's rigid electronic manifesto in favour of session musicians and traditional instruments. But at the time, and despite *Smash Hits*' unswerving support, 'I Don't Depend On You' failed to pick up much else in the way of press or radio support, and the single quietly fell by the wayside, leaving The Men to metamorphose back into The Human League.

Although it didn't represent such an obvious change of style, Gary Numan's next choice of Tubeway Army single was an equally curious one. Clocking in at almost five and a half minutes, 'Are 'Friends' Electric?' was too long to reasonably expect much in the way of radio play, and the song was schizophrenic to the extent that it was essentially two songs stuck together: 'I had a verse from one, the chorus from the other, and was struggling to mix them together,' Numan later admitted to *The Guardian*. 'I got so fed up, one day I played them one after another and suddenly they sounded right.'

Continuing to mine the sci-fi subject matter he had explored in 'Down In The Park' – 'all my early songs were about being alone or misunderstood' – Numan would later admit that the lyrical themes running through his work at the time were inspired by his own science-fiction writing. 'The lyrics came from short stories I'd written about what London would be like in thirty years,' he explained. 'These machines – "friends" – come to the door. They supply services of various kinds, but your neighbours never know what they really are since they look human. The one in the song is a prostitute, hence the inverted commas.'

'Are 'Friends' Electric?' was released on May 4th in an initial run of limited-edition picture discs, a relatively unusual format at the time, which were quickly snapped up by his expanding fanbase, enough to propel it into the lower reaches of the chart, where it began to catch the attention of radio and media. John Peel – for whom Tubeway Army would record a second session at the end of May – was once again on hand to bring the single's strange sounds to his band of listeners, at one point musing that Tubeway Army might, in fact, be a Pink Floyd for the eighties. *Smash Hits*' Cliff White was also a fan of the song and, in what was perhaps Tubeway Army's first positive national press review, wrote, 'A dark, threatening wall of synthesized sound throbs ominously behind a gloomy song of paranoia and loneliness. Gripping stuff, but cheerful it isn't.'

As the single slowly gathered momentum, fortune smiled upon Tubeway Army, and the band – now boosted for performances by the addition of Chris Payne alongside Ultravox's Billy Currie – was booked to perform two songs on BBC2's influential music TV show *The Old Grey Whistle Test*. Numan was determined to capitalise on the appearance: 'It was a major opportunity and I intended to make the most of it. I worked out every move the night before in front of a mirror. Every glance, every hand gesture, everything was pre-planned.' Numan's meticulous planning paid off and, in fact, laid the foundations for a second, even more important television performance.

Each week *Top of the Pops* would present one promising up-and-coming band, chosen from the lower reaches of the UK singles chart, with the opportunity to showcase their potential with a performance on the show. Under consideration for that 'Bubbling Under' performance that week were Simple Minds, whose 'Life In A Day' single was at number sixty-two, and Tubeway Army, whose 'Are 'Friends' Electric?' was at seventy-one. Tubeway Army were selected, and the call came through while they were still in the *Old Grey Whistle Test* studio following their recording. In his memoir, *Praying to the Aliens*, Numan would write, 'Someone has since said that it was the name that swung it for us – they thought it was a more interesting name. I don't know if that's true. We were bubbling under that week and so we were on.'

While *The Old Grey Whistle Test* catered to dedicated fans of music, at the end of the seventies *Top of the Pops* was a far more commercial proposition. Broadcasting on primetime BBC1 every Thursday evening the show was a national institution which, on one of only three television channels available, would reach an audience of millions. As an opportunity it was beyond the wildest dreams of Tubeway Army, particularly for the release of such a lengthy and strange song. Numan was over the moon. 'I couldn't believe it. *Top of the Pops* had been a part of my life for as long as I could remember. Just being on it was to have made it, as far as I was concerned.'

Alongside performances from Elvis Costello, The Shadows, Dollar, The Damned, and Liner, plus videos of Blondie, David Bowie and ELO, Tubeway Army's *Top of the Pops* debut was beamed into millions of homes on May 24th, 1979. Numan, determined to make the very most of the unexpected opportunity, had instructed his band – supplemented again by Payne and Currie, and this time with an old friend of Numan's, Garry Robson, miming guitar – to dress in black, to not smile, and to not play to the camera, as he would recall: 'I may have been very calculating about the look of the performance, about the image, about everything really, but I was more terrified than you can possibly imagine when the time came to do the song. The pressure of the scale of opportunity was heavy on my shoulders, the realisation that so much could hinge on the next few minutes.'

After the show the band headed into central London to celebrate their achievement with a trip to Rusty Egan and Steve Strange's Blitz club. Sadly, despite 'Are 'Friends' Electric?' having joined 'Down In The Park' on the Blitz playlist, the party were left outside the club, in the rain, with only Numan and Currie passing Strange's muster on the door, an experience which certainly dampened Tubeway Army's night and earned the club Numan's ongoing antipathy as a result. 'He spoiled what should have been a major celebration and I was very angry about it,' remembered Numan, who was later able to put his disappointment into perspective with the revelation that 'Are 'Friends' Electric?' was by then selling around 40,000 copies a day.

The combined effect of the *Old Grey Whistle Test* and *Top of the Pops* appearances was enough to propel the single twenty-three places up the singles chart, from seventy-one to forty-eight, with sufficient momentum that 'Are 'Friends' Electric?' then entered the Top 40 a week later at number twenty-five. Moving up the chart steadily, by June 30th the single was number one. 'It was Martin Mills from Beggars Banquet who rang me at home and said,

"You've done it, you're number one." When I put the phone down I leapt around the room for a bit. I went back into the front room and carried on watching the telly,' Numan would remember. 'I was smiling, though.' In the space of less than a month, Tubeway Army, and Gary Numan in particular, had been propelled from relative obscurity to full-blown pop stardom.

One of the first of the emerging artists to successfully recognise the importance of what would today be described as 'brand', Gary Numan's efforts to ensure that all the facets of his career, from music to image, were presented in parallel had paid off. 'I was very aware of how all these things should work together, like a well-geared machine, but all the parts – what you say, how you look, what you wear, the covers, the lyrics, the music obviously – it all has to work together to make a cohesive package. And I think I got it right.'

Numan's calculated approach was perfectly in step with the times. Advances in print technology meant that colour printing was suddenly faster and cheaper, which in turn had made it more accessible to the music press, and the black-and-white imagery that had accompanied punk gave way to a demand for striking colour images which perfectly showcased Numan's visual presentation: 'I had the whole image thing going, the make-up and so on. I think I looked right for that sort of music,' he declared later.

'Are 'Friends' Electric?' remained at number one for four weeks, selling a reported million copies in the process. On July 21st, while 'Are 'Friends' Electric?' was still at the top of the UK singles chart, the second Tubeway Army album, *Replicas*, which had been quietly released in May, climbed to number one on the UK album chart, a rare feat, particularly from a previously unknown act. *Smash Hits* made *Replicas* their Pick of the Week in the middle of June, awarding the record eight out of ten for its 'Strong futuristic imagery, simple but catchy melodies and riffs, haunting synthesiser work – all delivered in distinctive fashion. Intriguing and definitely different.'

Recorded at the start of 1979 over a five-day period at Gooseberry Studios in London's Gerrard Street, and mixed over a further three days, the album showcased the first batch of Numan's songs to be entirely written and composed with synthesisers in mind, and featured the singles 'Down In The Park' and 'Are 'Friends' Electric?', as well as an additional eight tracks which included more polished versions of the songs 'Me I Disconnect From You' and 'I Nearly Married A Human' that Tubeway Army had previewed on John Peel's radio show in January. 'The first album had been a guitar-based album that had electronics welded onto it. *Replicas* was an electronic album from the very beginning,' Numan would later note. Amazingly, budget restraints imposed upon the project by Beggars Banquet meant that the band – Numan, with Paul Gardiner and Jess Lidyard – were only able to hire in synthesisers for three of the five days they were in the studio.

Freely admitting his debt to the bands who influenced the sound of *Replicas*, Numan was particularly effusive in his praise of Ultravox, telling *Melody Maker*'s Chris Bohn that much of *Replicas* was inspired by their music. 'What sets him [Numan] apart from most other plagiarists is that he admits and acknowledges his sources, pre-empting criticism,' marvelled Bohn. 'Because of Ultravox's perennial unpopularity, Numan claims that nobody even noticed his debt to them until he pointed it out.' The Human League, David Bowie and Kraftwerk were other influences Numan declared at the time. 'I don't listen to stuff as a fan, I listen to stuff to get ideas from,' the singer explained to Bohn, 'I listen to what other people are doing with tones with synthesisers, with rhythms, the way they use structural ideas and the way they link things up.'

'Tubeway Army's approach puts them, inevitably, in a clique. But they are sufficiently adept and individual to secure their own corner within it,' decided Chris Westwood in his review of *Replicas* for *Record Mirror*. 'It is visual, evocative, occasionally wringing with excellence but also damaged by intermittent lapses into pretentiousness,' Westwood added, awarding the album four stars out of five and concluding, 'When the machines rock... they will sound like this.'

James Truman, reviewing the album for *Melody Maker*, reported that '"Replicas' is not particularly rewarding. Too clever and stylised for its own (limited) ambitions, it makes all the right gestures but fits them in the wrong place and, most importantly, is unlikely to transform Gary Numan into the star he evidently desires to be,' but by the end of July *Replicas* had gone gold with UK sales of over 100,000 copies. The album spent over half a year in the UK album charts, including nine weeks in the Top 10.

With *Replicas* and 'Are 'Friends' Electric?' riding high in the charts, Beggars Banquet took full advantage of the appetite for product from electronic pop's first mainstream star by reissuing the first two Tubeway Army singles – 'That's Too Bad' and 'Bombers' – in a gatefold double-pack in June 1979. A reissue of the *Tubeway Army* album followed in August, this time peaking at number fourteen in the UK album chart in the middle of September and spending a total of ten weeks in the Top 75 courtesy of the legion of new fans who were playing catch-up with Numan's career.

The reissued *Tubeway Army* album, repackaged in a brand new sleeve featuring the now iconic Gary Numan face graphic designed by Numan's friend Garry Robson, also picked up a new round of reviews. Summing up *Tubeway Army* as 'raw', *Smash Hits* awarded the release seven out of ten, noting similar lyrical themes to *Replicas*, but placing its importance firmly in the past and describing the 'cruder and punkier' sound of the reissue as 'interesting to look back on rather than a must for the present'.

In the same issue of *Smash Hits* as his review of *Tubeway Army*, Red Starr also turned in a positive review of Joy Division's debut album, awarding *Unknown Pleasures*' 'bleak nightmare soundtrack' an enthusiastic eight out of ten for its 'mysterious gloomy lyrics amidst intense music of urgent guitar, eerie effects and driving rhythms', which he further described as 'the sound of feelings talking'.

In the *NME*, Max Bell identified threads running through *Unknown Pleasures* which sonically connected the album to the work of the early krautrock artists, and to Can in particular, describing Martin Hannett's input as 'distorting the orthodox conceptions of sound level, balance and attack' and *Unknown Pleasures* as 'something memorably psychotic', before proclaiming the album an 'English rock masterwork'. *Sounds* took a more novel approach in their piece, writer Dave McCullough wrapping his review inside a pretentious, if chilling, piece of short fiction which revolved around a tragic, lonely character called Andrew – 'Andrew looked out through the misty, musky curtains and saw that morning was on its way like a messenger of doom…' – who listens to *Unknown Pleasures* before attempting to take his own life. While the piece lacks much in the way of literary merit, the review does provide a neat dissection of the album's elemental parts: 'Clicking electronic drums hissed and spat, a bass rumbled in, fat and heavy, a guitar pinged trebly into a weaving, jittery pattern of ragged chords.'

One might think that in the face of such an enthusiastic critical reception Joy Division would have been similarly delighted by their album debut. Posing the rhetorical question, 'Were we happy with *Unknown Pleasures* when it was finished?' in his memoir *Record Play Pause* Stephen Morris would answer, 'No, generally speaking, were we fuck.' Feeling that Martin Hannett's production had failed to capture the raw power of Joy Division's live shows, leaving behind a mere ghost of the band they were on stage, frontman Bernard Sumner was equally unequivocal in his own autobiography *Chapter And Verse*: 'The production inflicted this dark, doomy mood over the album: we'd drawn this picture in black and white, and Martin had coloured it in for us.'

It's interesting that the majority of the reviews of *Unknown Pleasures* – alternative titles for the album considered by the band included *Systems Of Collapse*, *Bureau Of Change*, *The Aura* and *Convulsive (Compulsive) Therapy* – were quick to draw attention to the electronic and synthesiser sounds that infused the record when in fact the album was almost entirely recorded using traditional instruments – vocals, guitar, bass and drums – and many of those perceived sounds came courtesy of producer Martin Hannett's preoccupation with sonic experimentation and manipulation, coupled with his obsession with pushing audio technology to new limits.

Although certain factions within Joy Division were resistant to Hannett's use of electronics – 'If we want fucking keyboards we'll get a fucking keyboard player' was Peter Hook's reaction upon learning that Hannett had overdubbed a synthesiser on the album track 'Day Of The Lords' – *Unknown Pleasures* wasn't entirely without electronic input from the band. Both Bernard Sumner and Stephen Morris had contributed to the band's gradual embrace of electronics, adding a Powertran Transcendent 2000 synthesiser and a Synare 3 electronic drum pad, respectively, to Joy Division's sonic arsenal.

The Transcendent 2000 had been hand-built by Sumner from an electronics kit as a hobby project to pass the nighttime hours during a bout of insomnia and, prior to the recording of *Unknown Pleasures*, its use had been mainly confined to providing the electronic sounds on a song loosely known as 'the synthesiser one' – before briefly becoming known as 'The Visitors' before finally becoming the album's closing track, 'I Remember Nothing' – with which Joy Division would frequently end their live sets.

The flying-saucer shaped Synare 3 not only fulfilled Stephen Morris's dual fascinations with the German 'krautrock' bands and with electronic gadgetry, but was also used more widely across *Unknown Pleasures* and in concerts, as Morris would later write. 'We used it for the sci-fi whup-whup siren intro in the live version of 'Disorder', noise washes in 'Shadowplay', chi-chi sounds in 'She's Lost Control' and, more alarmingly, for the disco drum and ray-gun blaster break on 'Insight'. On a good night, it would sound like ray-guns. On a bad night, if I got the switches wrong, it sounded like a flock of enraged pigeons.'

Looking back on *Unknown Pleasures* for a *Mojo* magazine feature in 2006, journalist Jon Savage, a key supporter and confidant of the band, would neatly clarify the standoff between band and producer: 'Hannett's magic trick was to give Joy Division the recorded sound that they did not know they wanted… They were a gift to a producer, because they didn't have a clue. They didn't argue.' Talking to *ZigZag* in May 1980, Hannett would attempt to explain his aural process, telling the magazine, 'With Joy Division the thing is, there's an ideal acoustic environment where you would see them – it's probably not a [real] place – and you try and arrange it to create the illusion you're in that place. It's probably a sinister place.'

Today, with the benefit of a great deal of perspective, the surviving members of Joy Division are much more comfortable with *Unknown Pleasures'* sonic qualities. 'We wanted it to be like how we were live, the guts and the power,' Peter Hook told *Mojo*. 'But what he [Martin Hannett] did was make it timeless. So you could listen to it in 1979 and 2009. If me and Barney had got to produce it, we wouldn't be here now.' Hook has even gone so far as to make peace with Hannett's keyboard work on 'Day Of The Lords': 'He was right though, Martin. The keyboards sweeten it and make it better.'

Joy Division's sudden elevation to darlings of the music press came at the same time that the tides were starting to turn on a previous media favourite. Released at the same time as *Unknown Pleasures*, Devo's second album, *Duty Now For The Future*, was received with a marked shift in media enthusiasm following the band's audacity in delivering a record that was markedly different to *Are We Not Men?* the previous year. 'The most striking feature is the slickness of its sound. Eno's experimental approach has been replaced by the clean-cut professional thrust of Ken Scott, a producer normally associated with the likes of Supertramp,' marvelled *Melody Maker*'s Ian Birch before summing up *Duty Now For The Future* as 'art pop that has lost its claws and started to feed off its own eccentricities'.

Smash Hits also reported that on *Duty Now For The Future*, Devo's sound had become 'standard, mainstream rock', and were disappointed to discern a noticeable lack of 'the zany magic of old', awarding the album just six out of ten and rueing that 'strong tunes are in short supply'. 'They're not clever so much as cunning,' mused the *NME*'s Paul Rambali in a thoughtful review. 'They won't give their game away because they'll have no game left to play.'

Duty Now For The Future had been preceded by a June single, 'The Day My Baby Gave Me A Surprize' [sic]. 'Poor dear Devo: too wacky for the mainstream, too drab for the new adventures of the New Frontier,' lamented Charles Shaar Murray in the *NME*. *Smash Hits'* Cliff White was equally unimpressed, finding nothing surprising about the track, and writing 'Ho hum. I realise that Devo have been darlings of New Wave chic but this is nothing to rave about.'

Actually, this time around, Devo were in broad agreement with their detractors, and laid the blame for the failure of *Duty Now For The Future* firmly at the feet of the album's producer, Ken Scott (who had famously produced David Bowie's album *The Rise And Fall Of Ziggy Stardust & The Spiders From Mars*). 'Musically less sudden and dynamic than its predecessor,' noted Paul Rambali in his *NME* review, 'recorded more in keeping with mainstream production values by producer Ken Scott who tries to curb what Eno tried to exaggerate.' 'He was totally the wrong producer,' Devo's Jerry Casale later admitted to *Electronic Sound*. 'He took those raw, nasty, intense songs and took all the balls out, took all the passion out, and did his little, twee, English-style dissection.'

Following the album's lukewarm critical reception – *Duty Now For The Future* peaked at a lowly forty-nine in the UK album charts at the end of June – Devo's star dipped a little further in September 1979 when *Smash Hits* reported that the band had been forced to postpone the four UK dates they had planned to play in October, intimating that the album's relative lack of success was to blame but citing 'difficulties presenting their extravagant new stage act at small European venues' as the reason for the band's decision to defer the shows until the following spring.

By July Joy Division had reunited with Martin Hannett and, after a demo session at Manchester's Central Sounds studio – 'Right next to the best kebab shop in town' according to the band's Peter Hook in his book *Unknown Pleasures* – returned to Strawberry Studios to record a single which would allow them to capitalise on the positive reaction to *Unknown Pleasures*. For reasons that are now vaguely attributed to either a principled desire to offer their audience new material, or to a dogged mistrust of traditional music industry practice, Joy Division deliberately chose to record brand new tracks for the single instead of using a track from the album the single was supposedly promoting. 'Considered from a purely commercial perspective this might seem naive, stupid or puzzling,' Stephen Morris would later muse in his book *Record Play Pause*. 'All I can say is that it made sense to us back then.'

'Transmission' was a track that the band had been playing live for a while, and which they had earmarked as a possible single on the very straightforward basis that the lyrics for the song contained the word 'radio': 'I thought it was Joy Division's first pop record,' Stephen Morris claimed later. 'It mentioned the radio, and that's got to get played on the radio. They like that.' For the single's B-side the band also recorded a new version of an even earlier track, 'Novelty'. According to Morris the band's choice of B-side was more pragmatic than artistic: 'I don't think we had a particular soft spot for 'Novelty' – it was an old song harking back to the days of Warsaw – but in the spirit of want not, waste not… 'Novelty' it would be.' In his own book, *Unknown Pleasures*, Peter Hook added a further important note to the recording of 'Novelty' which demonstrated the direction in which Joy Division found themselves heading: 'It was an interesting song for us, though, being the first time the band had used a synthesiser.'

Having received Martin Hannett's final mix of 'Transmission', Joy Division found themselves at an impasse similar to the one they experienced after hearing his mix of the *Unknown Pleasures* album. Except, according to Stephen Morris, it wasn't just Bernard Sumner and Peter Hook who were opposed to this mix, but the entire band: "Transmission' was the first time we were unanimously unhappy with Martin's mix. Ian was especially displeased and for once Martin seemed to take our views on board. I don't think he was satisfied with it either.' Hannett duly returned to the studio to remix his initial efforts into a version the band were more comfortable with, and with which Factory Records were particularly delighted.

Joy Division kicked off the 'Transmission' single project with an incendiary performance of the song as part of a two-song live performance for the BBC2 TV show *Something Else*, filmed in Manchester in September. The other band on the show were The Jam, whose frontman, Paul Weller, antagonised Joy Division by describing them as The Jam's support band. Interestingly, choosing his favourite singles for *Smash Hits* in December, a couple of months after recording the show, and a month after 'Transmission''s release as a single, Weller picked the track as one of his 'All Time Top Ten' song selections.

'Transmission' was released as a seven-inch single in November and such was Tony Wilson's enthusiasm for the track, and his complete belief in the single's commercial potential, that he ordered a 10,000-copy initial pressing in anticipation of massive demand for the release. Not for the last time, Wilson's enthusiasm proved unfounded, and a year after the release of 'Transmission' around 7,000 copies remained in the Factory Records warehouse unsold. Wilson hadn't been alone in hailing the single a masterpiece, however; hot on the heels of their effusive reactions to *Unknown Pleasures* the music press were equally impressed by the release and showered it with praise.

'Joy Division's pop is the pride and the passion of the moment, a potent fusion of moral fervour and strident rock'n'roll, and it's the most exciting thing I've heard in a long while,' pronounced *Melody Maker*'s Chris Bohn.

'This is an awesome disc, easily the most powerful dance-floor record of the week,' extolled Adrian Thrills in the *NME*. 'The simmering production is crisp enough to push 'Transmission' into the chart – with the right breaks, this could easily be a hit.'

Earlier, in support of the release of *Unknown Pleasures*, Joy Division embarked on a series of live dates around the country, including a number of Factory Records shows designed to showcase the fledgling label's roster which frequently saw Joy Division playing shows alongside labelmates Orchestral Manoeuvres In The Dark, who were also being well received by audiences and critics alike, although that feedback wasn't always as welcome. To the duo's deep discomfort, *Melody Maker*'s Chris Bohn, in his review of a Factory Records show at London's Acklam Hall in May, described Orchestral Manoeuvres In The Dark as 'a cute pop duo… like Kraftwerk during their lighter moments.'

Factory's Tony Wilson also subscribed to the theory that the music that Orchestral Manoeuvres In The Dark – their name now frequently abbreviated in the media to OMITD – were crafting was predominantly a new type of pop, an opinion which Humphreys and McCluskey, who viewed their work rather differently, found troubling: 'He'd gone from not liking it to saying, "You guys are the future of pop music." To which we replied, "Fuck off, we're experimental. Don't call us pop."' True to Factory's stated philosophy of acting as a launchpad for new bands that would allow them to move from the Manchester independent to a bigger label, Wilson duly sent copies of 'Electricity' to his industry contacts in the hope of securing the duo a major-label deal.

Wilson's efforts paid off. By July Orchestral Manoeuvres In The Dark were firmly in the sights of a new label, DinDisc – an offshoot of Virgin Records which was managed by Carol Wilson, who had signed The Human League in her previous role at Virgin Publishing, and had been instrumental in the Sheffield act's subsequent signing to Virgin Records – who had received a copy of 'Electricity' from Factory's Tony Wilson (no relation) and, after some exploratory conversations with the duo, were sufficiently interested to set up a meeting with the band. 'Carol Wilson from Din Disk [sic] came round to Paul's house 'cos we didn't have any gigs booked,' Andy McCluskey remembered in Jacki Florek and Paul Whelan's history of Eric's, *All The Best Clubs Are Downstairs*. 'She and the A&R man sat on the sofa in the back room and we played them the set, all seven songs, maybe twenty-five minutes long.'

Despite the unconventional nature of the audition, DinDisc were impressed by the band's efforts and by the potential on display in OMD's latest demo, which consisted of rough versions of the tracks 'Bunker Soldiers', 'Red Frame/White Light' and 'Messages' alongside an updated version of 'Julia's Song'. At the end of July, Carol Wilson travelled from London to Blackpool, where Orchestral Manoeuvres In The Dark were appearing alongside Joy Division and Section 25 at a special Year of the Child benefit concert at the town's Imperial Hotel. Although weekend traffic delayed her from catching anything of OMD's performance, before Wilson left the venue she presented the band with a contract offer, an event which Andy McCluskey still remembers with incredulity: 'It was amazing, driving home from Blackpool with a contract offer in our hands. How we didn't crash I don't know, because I'm sure we were all just screaming.'

Just a fortnight later, on August 13th, 1979, Orchestral Manoeuvres In The Dark were to have another career-changing stroke of luck. In London to play a Factory Records show at The Nashville alongside Joy Division and A Certain Ratio, Humphreys and McCluskey found themselves playing to an audience which included Gary Numan, a fan of the 'Electricity' single, who was on the lookout for a support act for the first tour under his own name, and his first live dates since the twin successes of 'Are 'Friends' Electric?' and *Replicas*, scheduled to start at the end of September.

The choice of opening act was something that Numan, as with all aspects of his career, would take extremely seriously: 'Finding the right support band, one that would enhance each concert evening, was extremely important.' Numan knew that he was looking for an electronic act with a unique sound and good songs, and after seeing their set that night he was confident that OMD would fulfil all his criteria perfectly. In addition OMD were also a good choice for altogether more prosaic reasons, which Andy McCluskey would later acknowledge: 'We suited his purpose, it was electronic music and he felt comfortable with it, and we weren't going to get in the way of his humongous stage set.'

In addition to the forthcoming tour, Beggars Banquet's flurry of Tubeway Army reissues only served to heighten anticipation for new material from Numan and, at the end of August, a brand new single, 'Cars', was finally released. 'Cars' was not entirely unfamiliar to Numan's fanbase as an early version of the song had been broadcast, alongside proto versions of three other new songs – 'Films', 'Airlane' and 'Conversation' – on BBC Radio 1 in

June, as part of Tubeway Army's second live session for DJ John Peel, which had successfully assisted a pre-release buzz around the new album and single.

The first record to drop the Tubeway Army name, 'Cars' was released under the name Gary Numan, a transition the singer had been working towards since the release of the *Tubeway Army* album the previous year, having started to recognise a disconnect between his band's punk origins and its new electronic trajectory. 'Tubeway Army was only ever a vehicle for me to get somewhere else,' Numan would explain. 'As soon as I found synthesisers and started making electronic music, I told Beggars I didn't want to be called Tubeway Army any more.' Having invested in the Tubeway Army name, the label were initially resistant to the idea of a name change, but the success of *Replicas* had shifted the balance of power in Numan's favour, and the change was finally approved by the label, as the singer would later tell *Billboard*: 'By being so successful, I could then say, "Right, now that this punk thing is gone and it's purely electronic, I'm going out as Gary Numan," and further qualifying the shift by explaining that 'It was a clear-cut decision to try to make a mark as electronic.'

The 'Cars' single was also the first release to showcase an expanded musical line-up which now featured Chris Payne on keyboards and saw Numan's uncle, Jess Lidyard, replaced on drums by Cedric Sharpley, to allow Lidyard, who had always considered his role in the band to be temporary, to return to a more regular life. The line-up was also boosted for the album sessions with the addition of Ultravox's Billy Currie, whom Numan had met through a mutual contact at Beggars Banquet. Numan later wrote in his first autobiography how awed he had been to have Currie in his band: 'I saw him as the synthesiser expert and myself as the young pretender, so to have him in the band was amazing.' The timing was also perfect for Currie, who was looking for something to distract him after the implosion of Ultravox earlier in the year. 'It was quite nice for me not to be in Ultravox and just have some fun,' he would admit later.

Structurally as strange a song as 'Are 'Friends' Electric?' before it, 'Cars' emerged from the twin challenges Numan had set himself during the writing sessions for the new record: firstly that the album would entirely sidestep the use of guitars in favour of synthesisers; and secondly that he would write a song on a bass guitar, a process he would later explain in an interview for Lori Majewski and Jonathan Bernstein's book *Mad World*: 'I'd never written a song on the bass. So I went to Shaftesbury Avenue in London and bought myself a cheap bass called a Shergold Modulator. I've still got it – it hangs on a wall in my studio. I took it home, got it out of its case and the very first thing I played was [sings the first four notes of 'Cars']. That was it. The first four notes I played on that guitar, and I thought, that's all right. The whole thing took about half an hour, from opening the case to having the finished bass line, arrangement, lyric and vocal line sorted out. It was the most productive thirty minutes of my life.'

The single, which came in a picture sleeve featuring what has now become an iconic image of a besuited Numan posed like a mannequin and holding an invisible steering wheel, was an instant success and immediately entered the UK Top 20 singles chart after just one week of sales. 'It's about the way I think of the modern motor car more as a personal tank,' Numan would reveal of the song. 'I can always drive away at the first sign of trouble.'

Smash Hits found the single a disappointing follow up to 'Are 'Friends' Electric?' but posted a positive review rejecting the media belief that Numan was little more than 'a plastic synthesised noise machine' while praising 'Cars'' 'distant haunting message of doom.' He picked up on the single's shorter lyrics and sharper vocals in comparison to the material on *Replicas*, and expressing their belief that the single would become a big hit. 'Numan's no fool,' wrote the *NME*'s Max Bell, also predicting a hit, 'he hasn't changed a winning formula. The callous, digital memory bank is as smooth and soulessly seamless as ever.'

The reviews were correct. Four weeks after its release, 'Cars' followed in the footsteps of 'Are 'Friends' Electric?' and went to the top of the UK singles chart. 'I think 'Cars' is probably the best pop song I've ever written. In many ways it's quite possibly the only pure pop song I've ever written,' Numan stated later. *Melody Maker* agreed, and their Ian Birch made 'Cars' their Single of the Week: 'After loathing 'Are 'Friends' Electric?' first time around, I gradually succumbed to its ludicrously synthetic charm. This continues in exactly the same vein with that formula synthesizer loop and Gary's absurdly intoned, cut-up words.'

Numan followed 'Cars' with the release of a brand-new album, *The Pleasure Principle*, which took its name from a 1937 painting, *Le Principe du Plaisir*, by the surrealist artist René Magritte, which had recently caught Numan's eye. The painting, itself named after a psychoanalytical theory suggested by Sigmund Freud, depicts a man in a suit sitting at a table contemplating a piece of rock, but where the man's head should be is an explosion of bright light which entirely obscures his features. On the front of the album sleeve, Numan's features are left intact and, instead of a rock, the singer, dressed for the shoot in a demure business suit to echo the figure in the painting, is pictured gazing intently at a small pyramid which appears to be glowing red. On the back of the album Numan is standing, holding the pyramid over his face.

The pyramid motif was echoed through the rest of the project, extending as far as the creation of two pyramid-shaped robots – affectionately known in the Numan camp as Huey and Duey – to feature as part of the elaborate staging for the tour to support the album. While Numan would talk about the power and stability of pyramids over the course of the publicity for the album, the real reason for the inclusion of the pyramid was actually far more prosaic: 'The reason why I'm looking at a glowing pyramid is that it just happened to be lying around the studio and I thought, that looks cool.'

The first copies of *The Pleasure Principle* hit the shops in the middle of September, three weeks after the release of 'Cars' and just a few days before the opening night of the first Gary Numan tour. Perhaps predictably, *The Pleasure Principle* met a similar critical reaction to *Replicas*, the media generally turning on Numan for having the audacity to be successful without their patronage, a reaction that US music magazine *Creem* later noted with interest from their detached transatlantic perspective: 'The immediate success of 'Are 'Friends' Electric?' and, subsequently, 'Cars' satisfied fans but riled critics who, as always, perceived anyone who could rise to fame so fast as a charlatan, a huckster out for dollars while starving artists were out for art.'

Smash Hits' Red Starr attempted to be objective, praising Numan's lyrics and awarding *The Pleasure Principle* seven out of ten but ultimately admitting, 'I'm not greatly sold on this. It's not bad, mind you – a smoother, almost discoish version of 'Replicas' – but much too similar to it and not as adventurous.' *Record Mirror* noted *The Pleasure Principle*'s 'overpowering sense of claustrophobia, of being trapped' but nevertheless defaulted to the media's well-worn suspicion of the new technology and working methods which underpinned the album when the paper's Simon Ludgate summarily dismissed the record with the words 'I'm wary of anything that is as calculated and cold as this. Every tiny detail has been carefully planned and inspected with a clinical detachment, leaving nothing to chance.' Interestingly, in Ray Coleman's 1982 book *Gary Numan – The Authorised Biography*, Numan was given the opportunity to revisit those comments, and responded to *Record Mirror*'s words by pointing out the publication's hypocrisy in 'criticising me for paying attention to every tiny detail, yet another band that take care over their work would be praised for it. I'm criticised for taking care!'

Unexpected press support for *The Pleasure Principle* came from the *NME*, where the frequently caustic Danny Baker applauded Numan's success, if not his actual creation, opining, 'Simply, Numan is making intelligent music for people who aren't intelligent.' To his credit Baker had opened his review for the paper by addressing his peers' criticisms head on: 'Let's forget the threadbare rock'n'roll bitch that it's all been done before by "proper" artists – Bowie this, Kraftwerk that – because, although the groundwork was laid down by lots of clever folk long ago nobody has done what Gary Numan is doing right now.' Baker also praised Numan's production as 'excellent', the music on the album as 'easy and listenable', and predicted another number one record.

For Gary Numan's burgeoning fanbase, however, the media's lukewarm reaction to the album was of no importance whatsoever, and their unwavering support propelled *The Pleasure Principle* to the top of the UK charts in September 1979, the album entering the chart at number one in the very same week that 'Cars' topped the singles chart, marking the second time in just nine weeks that Numan had simultaneously topped both charts. The chart double also marked the start of Gary Numan's tour in support of *The Pleasure Principle*, a sixteen-date UK outing in front of over 40,000 people under the banner *The Touring Principle*.

The Touring Principle opened at Glasgow's Apollo Theatre on September 20th, 1979, where Gary Numan's rapid elevation to the status of electronic pop's first superstar ensured that it launched in fine style, the singer later recalling, 'Glasgow was coming apart at the seams. You could actually see the balcony moving up and down on what I assumed were hydraulic dampers as the fans danced along to the music. It was genuine pop hysteria and it was everything I'd ever imagined. People were fainting, girls were screaming and crying, people were dressed up like me, same haircut, same clothes, they copied my movements, such as they were, they mimicked my stare, my posturing, everything. It was a truly amazing experience.'

In June, prior to the start of the tour, Numan had outlined his live plans to the *NME*, telling Paul Morley, 'I've always thought of it as a very glamorous business, the whole thing about putting on a show. All the anti-hero punk thing, it went against everything I've ever wanted to do.' Picking up the same theme in *Smash Hits* shortly after the tour Numan would further explain the lavish staging: 'I thought there was no point in going out unless you were going to give people something to remember and to make it worthwhile. There's no point in being top of the pile unless your show's going to be top of the pile as well.'

Addressing the extravagance of that first solo tour in his 1997 autobiography *Praying to the Aliens*, Numan, with characteristic honesty, was able to be more forthright about his true intentions, writing, 'I thought the money spent on the tour would make me an even bigger star. The shows would be so spectacular that even the press, clearly hostile towards me, would see the light.' If that had truly been his expectation then Numan must have been sorely disappointed by the press reaction to *The Touring Principle*.

Reviewing the opening show of *The Touring Principle* in Glasgow, Jon Savage turned a sympathetic and sensitive review in to *Melody Maker*, a thoughtful piece which opened by Savage calling out his media peers for their inability to celebrate, embrace or even properly acknowledge Numan's success: 'The press don't hate Numan: worse, they underestimate or patronise. He's committed the cardinal sin of not being "authentic", or even "artistic", and what's more, becoming very successful without the writer's imprimatur. It's an object lesson in the unimportance of the press, which Numan displays while laughing, with his record company, all the way to the bank.' The review continued on a similarly positive note, Savage taking the time to praise the production for its 'use of careful pacing, stunning stage sets and a constant supply of changes and toys to keep the audience constantly amused'.

Elsewhere in the press Jon Savage's concerns about Gary Numan's standing in the media were realised. *Sounds* reviewed the Gary Numan tour twice, sending Ian Ravendale and Phil Sutcliffe to report from different shows. Ian Ravendale, present at the second night of the tour at Newcastle's City Hall, was cautiously positive, but chose to pull the show's weaknesses into focus rather than to celebrate its strengths, and in the process dedicated a significant proportion of his review to presenting Numan's music and performance as style over substance, comparing and contrasting Numan's work with David Bowie's flirtations in the same electronic arena, before grudgingly concluding that if Numan were 'able to synthesise Bowie's chameleon qualities as well as he's absorbed his theatrics, Gary Numan will live long and prosper'.

There was little doubt in either *Sounds* review that the production was spectacular, or that it successfully won the admiration of the respective crowds. Phil Sutcliffe, attending one of two sold-out nights at London's

Hammersmith Odeon, outlined the elaborate lighting rig and stage set with enthusiasm, describing how the Gary Numan live band – the core line-up of Paul Gardiner, Cedric Sharpley and Chris Payne supplemented for the tour by the addition of Billy Currie on synthesisers, and Rrussell [sic] Bell, newly recruited to provide extra guitar and assorted keyboards – were 'set diagonally in the legs and cross-piece of a gorgeous H of golden bars of light which had no sooner been admired than they began an astonishing sequence of rhythmic variations and strobe flashes'.

Something all the publications agreed upon was the sensational reaction of the Gary Numan audiences. Despite their personal reservations about the experience, Ian Ravendale did acknowledge Numan's hold over the Newcastle audience, and equally Phil Sutcliffe noted how the show had captivated the London concertgoers. In *Melody Maker*, Jon Savage wrote of the 'rising hysteria' that Numan teased from the Glasgow crowd, partly as a result of the show's spectacle and partly through the singer's 'clever, realistic showmanship'. Savage also found much to compliment in the show's sense of spectacle and entertainment, and applauded Numan as 'the perfect icon'.

Having praised the quality of the presentation of the shows, and the audience's satisfaction with the production – which from the point of view of the band and the audience was surely the whole point of the exercise – it was when the reviewers moved from the objective to the subjective that things became more difficult, as neither *Sounds* reviewer could resist systematically picking the experience apart, each dismissing Numan's performance as derivative, uneven and gauche, and his material as one-dimensional and flimsy. Attempting to look beyond the show's 'visual razzle-dazzle', Sutcliffe's review became an analysis of each song performed, delivered alongside a rather condescending list of seven additional songs from the Tubeway Army and Gary Numan catalogues that Numan had omitted from his setlist but which Sutcliffe felt should have been included.

Opening act Orchestral Manoeuvres In The Dark came in for similar criticism when Phil Sutcliffe turned in a separate review of their set at London's Hammersmith Odeon for *Sounds*. After describing OMD's onstage performance – Paul Humphreys 'at a stack of keyboards', Andy McCluskey 'tying his hands and arms in nervous knots while singing' – Sutcliffe professed to find himself horrified by the onstage presence of the band's third member, Winston, the tape machine which provided the parts his human bandmates were unable to generate themselves, causing the writer to exclaim, 'It's one thing to use machines and quite another to replace people with them.'

Sounds' horror at Winston's presence, and the fact that the tape machine was positioned in a way that gave it equal billing to that of its human bandmates, was essentially triggered by what Sutcliffe perceived as a lack of essential humanity within Orchestral Manoeuvres In The Dark's music: 'There was no room for emotional traffic, no contact or natural response,' Sutcliffe wrote, before dismissing the set-up entirely, writing, 'This was "live" music translated into the production line.'

Interestingly the review wasn't hostile to the band themselves, or to their use of synthesisers − Sutcliffe acknowledged the 'heart and fire' at the core of OMD's music and complimented Andy McCluskey for his 'forceful, passionate voice' − the problem lay with Winston, whose role in the band imposed an unnecessary lack of spontaneity on Humphreys and McCluskey's performance, eliminating the opportunity for the 'brains and souls' of the duo's human elements to engage in 'creative action and interaction'. 'I longed for their tape to snap and leave them stranded in human reality,' Sutcliffe wrote. 'It's not that they are cold personally, but for the moment they have been suckered by a cold theory.'

Numan treated his support act generously, allowing Orchestral Manoeuvres In The Dark to travel on his own bus, arranging for their gear to be transported with his own equipment, and permitting them free use of his sound and lighting technicians. Andy McCluskey later recalled his experience of opening for Numan with great fondness. 'I enjoyed the Gary Numan tour. No pressure − we just trotted out onto the stage with Winston,' further adding, 'We thought we'd gone down really well. I suppose it's all relative, and maybe we didn't! But polite applause from 2,000 people can sound louder than enthusiastic cheering from just 200.' Numan was also impressed, and a little awed, by his support act: 'Most nights I would sneak out to the side of the stage while they were on and, from my little hiding spot, would listen to some of the best pop songs ever written.'

It was during the Gary Numan tour that Orchestral Manoeuvres In The Dark signed both publishing and recording contracts with DinDisc, committing themselves to a seven-album deal in exchange for a combined advance variously reported to have been between £40,000 and £50,000. Budgeting for failure, the duo promptly invested the advance in setting up their own studio, The Gramophone Suite, in Liverpool, a move Andy McCluskey would explain as 'When they drop us, at least we'll have a recording studio, then we can carry on making some records and go indie or whatever.' *Sounds* would later applaud the decision to use the advance money to build the studio as 'more far-sighted than shoving it in or up any of the usual orifices'.

Once contracts were signed in September, DinDisc lost no time in putting out their first OMD release, and by the end of the month a new edition of the 'Electricity' single was in record shops, just in time to coincide with the band's final dates with Gary Numan. The DinDisc release of 'Electricity' differed from the Factory Records version in that the label swapped out the band's own recording of 'Electricity' in favour of Martin Hannett's Martin Zero mix, the band having reconsidered their position on the 'romantic, swirling, melancholy' of Hannett's work: 'We hated it to begin with but then we got to thinking "That's pretty cool, actually!"'

DinDisc wisely decided to spare their printer the combustion-risk associated with 'Electricity''s original thermographic black-on-black artwork, and instead adapted the original sleeve design to use more traditional print techniques which converted those elements that were previously printed using thermographic ink to appear as more conventional white print on a black sleeve, a process made easier by the fact that DinDisc had recently appointed Factory's Peter Saville as their art director. Having completed his studies in Manchester, Saville had relocated to London to find paid work, saying later, 'Factory was not a business and wasn't in a position to employ me. It was vocational; we were doing it for the love of doing it, not for the money.'

A friend and ally of the band since the Factory release of 'Electricity', Saville's influence on Orchestral Manoeuvres In The Dark extended beyond simply providing the artwork for their releases, and it was he who first suggested the duo reinvent their image, something Paul Humphreys would acknowledge in an interview for the *NME* in 1980: 'When we first met him [Saville] we looked awful, we dressed really badly, looked scruffy and dirty. He said to us, "Well, listen, you're getting on now, you can't keep up that really scruffy image. If you don't want to do anything really outrageous, at least look smart and tidy." Which is what we did. He didn't really tell us what clothes to wear, we just wore what we felt comfortable in.'

Smash Hits, recognising Orchestral Manoeuvres In The Dark from their supporting role on the Gary Numan tour, gave the DinDisc release of 'Electricity' their seal of approval in October: 'Unlike most synthesiser specialists… these two aren't afraid of a tune and a bit of fun and this bubbling electrobop could see them in the charts.' DinDisc's Carol Wilson was convinced the single was going to be number one, but although the music press were encouraging, mainstream radio – and in particular the powerful playlist committee at Radio 1 – was less convinced, a frustration Andy McCluskey would later recall: 'Unfortunately all the people at Radio 1 thought we were jumping on the Numan bandwagon.' Although the single sold well it nevertheless failed to become the hit the band and their new label were hoping for, and instead became a cult classic which features, to rapturous reception, on the band's live setlist to this day.

Steve Strange (Visage), 1980.

1979.3 Cabaret Voltaire / The Human League / Gary Numan / Musicians' Union / Ultravox / Visage / Simple Minds

THE INJECTION OF CASH that Factory Records received for the Orchestral Manoeuvres In The Dark deal – reportedly around £3,000 – was a welcome boost to the label, whose independent status meant that finance was often in short supply. It was a situation which had previously impacted on Cabaret Voltaire, who had been interested in continuing their relationship with Factory after the success of *A Factory Sample*, but had found the label unable to commit to the costs of making their album.

Assisted by journalist Jon Savage, who had already championed them in the press, Cabaret Voltaire instead entered into exploratory talks with Throbbing Gristle's Industrial label – who were keen to support the Sheffield three-piece but who also lacked the necessary funds to commit to an album – before coming to an agreement with Rough Trade, who had released the band's debut EP and who were sufficiently solvent to able to upgrade the band's technology for the project. As Cabaret Voltaire's Stephen Mallinder would later explain: 'What Rough Trade allowed us to do was buy a Tascam four-track, which meant we could do the *Mix-Up* album. It was "If you can buy us a four-track, we can do an album", so signing to them was a no-brainer.'

Armed with their new four-track system, the first music to emerge from Cabaret Voltaire's Western Works studio following the *A Factory Sample* release was a new single, 'Nag Nag Nag', in June, a track which the band initially recorded in Sheffield before recording a second version at Berry Street Studio near London's Barbican.

'Nag Nag Nag' was born of an unusual collision of musical influences. As Stephen Mallinder would explain to *Electronic Sound* later, Cabaret Voltaire had recently added an interest in psychedelic 1960s garage rock to their ongoing list of influences as they worked on their debut album: 'We were obviously listening to a lot of electronic and avant-garde music, like Can and the early Kraftwerk, but we were also listening to a lot of American sixties garage records, people like The 13th Floor Elevators and Red Krayola.'

This new musical influence had already led to Cabaret Voltaire recording a version of The Seeds' 1966 underground classic 'No Escape' as a key track on their debut album but, having made the decision to follow the example of early Roxy Music and not release a single from the album, they wanted to record a standalone track as a single. 'We were big fans of the first two Roxy Music albums and one of the things that Bryan Ferry said was that they never took singles off albums. We liked that philosophy, so we adopted it too,' Stephen Mallinder would explain to *Electronic Sound* magazine in a retrospective feature about 'Nag Nag Nag' in 2019. 'We didn't want to bring out the Seeds track as a single, so we were like, 'We'll do our own version of 'No Escape',' Mallinder explained to the Red Bull Music Academy in 2006, and so 'Nag Nag Nag' was born.

By coincidence Red Krayola guitarist and frontman Mayo Thompson was in London when Cabaret Voltaire arrived to record their single, already working with Rough Trade on records for Scritti Politti and The Raincoats, and was duly drafted in to provide nominal production duties for the Cabaret Voltaire session, a synchronicity which delighted not only the band, but also Thompson himself who later, and rather gleefully, reported, 'When we mixed 'Nag Nag Nag' we basically blew the desk. What we were trying to achieve could not be achieved short of driving the machines mad.'

Successful in their mission to twist 1960s psychedelic rock into vicious and distorted electronic shapes of their own making, 'Nag Nag Nag' has since become one of Cabaret Voltaire's best-known songs, and is rightly hailed as a classic, perfectly encapsulating the band's intent, later outlined by Stephen Mallinder: 'There was a part of us that didn't want to compromise, we had a particular sound and we just wanted to shape that into a regular pop song, but in a warped way.'

Standing somewhere between the intractable experimentation of much of Cabaret Voltaire's earlier recordings and the proto-electro of their later work,

'Nag Nag Nag' was maligned by most of the press. 'Their record is as flat as a witch's tit,' wrote the *NME*'s Danny Baker. 'It's dull, unusable and quaint but it does have a good title. Probably about a horse race.' The band were unperturbed: 'All we really knew about how the record was received was that it sold pretty well,' Mallinder told *Electronic Sound*. 'You weren't sure who your audience were until you turned up and did a gig, so the only barometer you had of anything you released was via the three weekly music papers.'

Cabaret Voltaire's debut album, *Mix-Up*, followed at the end of October and the *NME*, in their review, took the omission of 'Nag Nag Nag' as evidence of the rapidity of Cabaret Voltaire's musical maturation since the single's April release. Hailing 'Nag Nag Nag''s 'cretin simplicity' as the quintessential electronic garage-band single of the year, journalist Andy Gill praised *Mix-Up* for its ambition and complexity, and the band for their refusal to fall back on a proven commercial formula. 'Instead of concentrating on the easy hook and the instant rhythm, the Cabs here concentrate on emotional soundscaping, offering several alternatives to the pure noise/pure pop furrows endlessly ploughed by latterday synthesizer bands,' Gill wrote, before ending his review on a similarly high note: 'In other words, they've refined their product to an acceptable 'professional' standard, whilst retaining the integrity and spirit of amateurs.'

Melody Maker's Chris Bohn delivered a joint review of *Mix-Up* alongside *Reproduction*, the debut album from The Human League, which was released around the same time, but was distinctly uncomfortable with the pairing. 'Previously such groupings were helpful to both the artists and followers, giving them the feeling of belonging to a movement,' Bohn explained in the introduction to his piece, 'but it doesn't help much in the post-Numan world, in which fields have polarised around the two respective flags of experiment and pop.' Placing *Mix-Up* firmly in the experimental category, Bohn continued, 'Cabaret Voltaire have always worked in isolation. They have gone on doing what they do, seemingly regardless of outsiders' opinions… 'Mix-Up' gives the impression that it lives for itself first – take it or leave it. Sometimes it degenerates into listenable noise, but mostly it's quite captivating.'

Reproduction, meanwhile, Bohn filed under pop – 'The music is always attractive, never threatening, usually optimistic. Bright, breezy and open airings over synthesized handclaps and syn-drums' – but was concerned that The Human League were in a particularly tricky position in the wake of Gary

Numan's recent stellar success: "Reproduction' is initially disappointing, because it's no longer new and the songs aren't really individual or strong enough to stand out in the pop market,' he began, adding: '[The Human League] want to be a successful pop band and try possibly too hard at it to succeed. They know too well what it takes and have artfully fitted together all the components, but somehow it doesn't convince. Contrived art-pop, pretty colours, pleasant swathes of sound and it's about as substantial as candy floss. Tastes nice though.'

The idea that the success of Tubeway Army and Gary Numan had relegated The Human League to the role of electronic also-rans also underpinned the *NME*'s review of *Reproduction*: 'Every TV appearance Gary Numan makes must be like a dagger to the heart of The Human League, every radio-play a bit more salt in the wound,' wrote Andy Gill. 'And they've only themselves to blame for not striking whilst the iron was hot.' In his review Gill also made it abundantly clear that he was neither a fan of The Human League, or of their music, before embarking on a savaging of *Reproduction* Gill first dismissed the band's recent *The Dignity Of Labour* release as unnecessary and pretentious, and their project under the name The Men as an 'embarrassingly half-assed' debacle. Phil Oakey's voice came in for a moment of faint praise, before the singer's actual vocal performances on the album were subsequently rejected as 'overly restrained, impersonal, and distanced from the subject-matter… There's an unavoidable flatness, blandness, and lack of emotion and dynamics,' Gill continued, 'because their progressions and climaxes are so obvious, so predictable, and so colourless. Pop music should be just that – fizzy, sweet, and bad for your health; *Reproduction* is as flat, neutral and unappetising as a glass of Coke that's been standing for too long.'

Sounds' Garry Bushell turned in a slightly surreal review of *Reproduction* in which he tried to view the album through the eyes of an alien called Zarki whose extraterrestrial musings were very positive. 'Excellent synthesiser pop, perfect for listening to on headphones in the dark,' was the verdict, with Zarki allegedly in favour of the 'electronic pop fun' and 'bizarre comedy' the album contained, particularly in comparison to the output of some of The Human League's peers, who were considered by the alien to be 'grimmer, austere and morose young people painting their bleak, ice cold New Musick portraits with an intensity that couldn't be good for their health'. Phil Oakey's vocals received further faint praise, Zarki finding the frontman's performance 'unattractive but strangely magnetic', before the second half of the review inexplicably dissolved into a tale of exploding genitals and an exploration of murderous, psychopathic alien tendencies.

Smash Hits' Red Starr came down broadly in favour of the band's musical manoeuvres – 'Sheffield's excellent Human League will certainly be among the leaders of the '80s' – and while he considered *Reproduction* 'a grower' and 'a definite goodie', Starr was forced to admit that the album 'suffers badly from lifeless presentation'. None of which stopped the increasingly irreverent magazine from turning a mischievous eye towards the album's artwork, described in Alaska Ross's book *The Story of a Band Called The Human League* as an image of 'new born babies being trampled underfoot by a bunch of stiletto-heeled adults'. A couple of weeks after their review, *Smash Hits* reported, entirely erroneously, that 'one or two of those babies had well known parents. Simon King of Hawkwind was one proud father, while Slade leader Noddy Holder's offspring is also believed to have been around someplace.'

Concluding his review of the album for the *NME*, Andy Gill declared, 'The Human League story, so far, is one of missed chances combined with unclear thinking and lack of forethought. Rather than redressing the balance, *Reproduction* only serves to throw their shortcomings into sharper focus.' Unfortunately it wasn't long before The Human League would agree. 'Doing it was great,' explained the band's Ian Craig Marsh, remembering how the album had sounded in the high-tech environment of the studio. 'We thought "Wow, this sounds fantastic, great". But it was only a few months later when we listened to it on our normal systems that we decided it was lacking in quite a major way in several areas.'

'Empire State Human', the sole single to be taken from *Reproduction*, was released shortly after the album and, while the single fared a little better than the album in the press – 'If we have to have all this Teutonic synthesiser stuff,' David Hepworth wrote in *Smash Hits*, 'let it be said that The Human League have a sense of humour and fairly catchy choruses' – it failed to gain much traction in terms of radio play or sales. Focusing on the kind of electronic glam rock stomp that was a particular strength of The Human League at the time, *Record Mirror*'s Robin Smith reviewed 'Empire State Human' in October: 'Lurking behind the wall of pretentious poop which has built around the League, there lurks this good single. Kraftwerk meets Slade, if such a peculiar amalgam can be imagined.'

Unlike Gary Numan, whose success with *The Pleasure Principle* had allowed him a certain satisfaction in the face of the critics, The Human League were denied the gratification of seeing the public defy the wisdom of the music press by rushing out to purchase either *Reproduction* or 'Empire State Human', and initial sales for both were sufficiently poor that a proposed headline tour of the UK in November was cut down from eleven shows to just one date at The Lyceum in London. 'It seems the League have been thinking long and seriously about their music and future directions, and have decided on radical changes,' stated the *NME*'s news page when announcing the cancellations, adding, 'A new Human League product will be touring in the near future.'

Garry Bushell, attending the Lyceum show for *Sounds*, identified 'Empire State Human' as a highlight in the live set, describing the song as 'true mutant pop', but was not impressed overall. 'I'm afraid the novelty value's worn well thin,' Bushell wrote, ending his review on a sombre note for someone who had previously been supportive of the band – 'tonight's sad performance left me wondering if they'd blown it' – although Bushell did undermine his own credibility somewhat by adding an update on the unusual proclivities of Zarki, the extraterrestrial colleague who had previously featured in his review of *Reproduction*. Adrian Thrills also attended the show for the *NME* and reported, 'Enigmatic as ever, the League gave no hints as to what direction their planned "re-programming" would take.'

Undeterred by their treatment at the hands of the press, The Human League duly revealed their new live direction when announced as support to Talking Heads across the latter's short UK tour at the end of November and the beginning of December. Sensing a conceptual opportunity, the band had set upon an unusual way of fulfilling their touring commitment with the American act, and gleefully issued a press release to outline their plans: 'The Human League, intrigued to experience their own performance themselves, have designed a remotely controlled touring entertainment. Therefore, 30 Human League minutes will be available on the upcoming Talking Heads tour. The League themselves may well join the audience on some evenings to savour the occasion. The arrangement will allow them on other evenings to continue working on their second album in their Sheffield workshop.'

At the point where adverts started to appear in the music press – 'The Human League present a unique automated cabaret! The entertainment will feature specially taped songs and rhythms with synchronized moving pictures and snapshots instead of The League themselves. Catch this 30 minute cinema you can dance to on the Talking Heads tour' – the headliners changed their minds about having The Human League on the bill and the support found themselves suddenly off the bill. The news reportedly came in the form of a telex: 'Regret must cancel Human League appearance on Talking Heads tour in deference to ticket buyers due to format of League's show.' 'It was too much for them,' a still gleeful Martyn Ware recalled later. 'Maybe they thought they were going to be upstaged.'

Crucial among the music press's criticism of the new wave of electronically influenced acts – The Human League amongst them – was the question of a lack of rock'n'roll authenticity within this broad electronic genre, a preconception that ownership of a synthesiser would be enough to overcome a lack of talent, a misconception so common that OMD frontman Andy McCluskey would still be debating it in an interview for the BBC's *Synth Britannia* documentary many years later: 'The number of people who thought that the equipment wrote the song for you, "Well anybody could do it if they had the same equipment you've got." Fuck. Off. Believe me if there was a button on a synth or a drum machine that said "Hit Single" then I would have pressed it as often as anyone else had. But there isn't. It's all written by real human beings and it's all played by hand.'

In his unofficial, and certainly unwanted, role as an ambassador for 'something new', by the end of 1979 Gary Numan's escalating problems with a music press which insisted upon viewing his work in comparison with the heft of rock'n'roll history, much of which was irrelevant in relation to the new electronic vanguard, were at a peak. Not only did Numan's music fail to invoke the authenticity of the artists who had gone before him, but the singer was also disarmingly frank about his lack of musical prowess. 'I was no good on guitar and the synthesiser was dead easy to play,' Numan told *Melody Maker*'s Ray Coleman the following year. 'So my only talent musically is as an arranger of noises.'

And it wasn't only the media that was struggling with the new ways of working that were starting to emerge in connection with electronic music. Further resistance to Gary Numan's electronic odyssey came courtesy of the Musicians' Union, many of whose members were struggling to fully assess the perceived threat of affordable synthesisers. In August 1978 a story entitled 'Synthesisers – Friend or Foe?' had appeared on the cover of *Musician*, the journal for Union members, and, unfortunately for Numan, debate on the subject was still raging as the singer's singularly electronic approach was propelling him up the charts.

The *Musician* feature had been written by Bruce Graham – a multi-instrumentalist who had made the transition to synthesisers from his first instruments, the piano-accordion and the bagpipes – who was vocal in his support of his new instrument after having encountered difficulties during a West End theatre engagement where he had been suspected of creating synthesised string sounds at the expense of actual string players: 'It is my opinion now that anyone who specialises on electronic instruments – especially the synthesiser – is getting a raw deal from the Union, due to pressure from ill-informed members.'

At its heart the Musicians' Union's rules, as quoted by Graham, dictated that while it was permitted for 'instruments and devices incorporating pre-recorded sounds or producing sounds by electronic means' to be used 'to produce sounds that cannot be produced by conventional instruments', the use of synthesisers in situations where the instrument might 'replace or reduce the employment of conventional instrumentalists' was forbidden. Graham argued that 'the synthesiser does not come into this category, as it is a manually played instrument, and where an operator is controlling the instrument by manpower there should be no objections'. After all, Graham asked, 'How many times have we heard flutes imitating piccolos, tom-toms imitating timpani, piano imitating harp or trombones imitating horns?' The central message of Graham's article was a call for the Musicians' Union's rules on synthesisers to be amended on the grounds that the organisation's current regulations were vague and out of date.

The 'Friend or Foe' piece immediately struck a chord and the letters page of the next edition of *Musician*, in November 1978, was almost entirely turned over to further debate on the issue. Reader A. E. Rodda correctly surmised that the article was likely to 'open up a debate which will be argued for a long time to come'. Nevertheless, most viewpoints were reasonable and balanced, Union member Alan Townsend, for example, speaking for many by writing in defence of the practical reasons behind his use of a string synthesiser 'without apology or guilt', safe in the knowledge 'that the working mens' club where I am resident would never dream of increasing the band from a two-piece'.

Notably less ambivalent, another member, Richard Tomalin, took the opportunity to express his own resistance to the use of synthesisers by quoting

George Orwell and writing: 'It isn't only the synthesiser that threatens us. It's the whole concept of industrialism, of progress towards a materialist Utopia and of our blind obedience to "Reason",' before ending his letter on the sepulchral note, 'Let's hope the human race will be able to pull itself out of the vortex before it's too late.'

The timing of the ongoing debate couldn't have been worse for Gary Numan, whose rapid rise to stardom was happening in parallel with the ongoing controversy within the Musicians' Union, a quarrel which, as poster boy for the emerging electronic pop movement, Numan was inevitably brought into. Still indignant about his treatment at the hands of the MU at that time, Numan remains weary today when he reports, 'The Musicians' Union tried to ban me for about the first year because they said I was putting proper musicians out of work,' his tone sombre when reflecting how close the dispute came to derailing his career before it had even begun: 'Caused me no end of grief.'

As if the resistance to his music from the music press, and from the Musicians' Union, wasn't enough, Numan's dramatic and sudden success had also taken his peers by surprise, and artists who had been operating in the electronic arena for some time were, at best, disconcerted by the realisation that Numan had apparently arrived in their sphere from nowhere and had unexpectedly stolen the march on everyone. 'All this time we were convinced that it was just a matter of time before we had a number one record – part arrogance and part stupidity – and then somebody comes out the blue and does it,' rued Martyn Ware in the BBC documentary *Synth Britannia* in 2009.

At the time most of the emerging acts experimenting with synthesisers had evolved from a partial vacuum that was essentially peerless, but by the release of 'Are 'Friends' Electric?' those bands had started to learn of the existence of similarly minded artists. As John Foxx would explain in the same documentary: 'In the late seventies in London, Sheffield and Manchester there was a very early beginning of electronic music in Britain. Just a few people excited by similar thoughts and possibilities. These cells knew very little of each other at the time, but later evolved into a genuine movement.' Orchestral Manoeuvres In The Dark's Andy McCluskey concurred: 'People like ourselves, and Cabaret Voltaire and The Human League had all just got used to the fact that we existed, and there was somebody else sharing our space.' Echoing the thoughts of many of his 1979 peers McCluskey would also add his own reaction to Gary Numan's success: 'We wanted to hate him. We'd been grafting away writing songs since we were sixteen and we were like, "Where did he come from?"'

Numan – who had previously considered himself to be at the vanguard of something entirely new – was similarly surprised to discover the existence of so many likeminded up-and-coming acts and artists. 'Far from being the first person to discover electronic music, I seemed to be one of the last,' he wrote in his second autobiography, *(R)evolution*, in 2020. 'The more I looked into it the more electronic artists I found, people who had been doing it long before me.' With characteristic honesty Numan would go on to defend his success, writing, 'All I can say in my defence is I just wrote some songs, wrapped them in an image, gave them a persona and went for it. I didn't do anything that they couldn't have done before.'

Numan's saving grace in the eyes of his peers was the quality of his music. 'I really liked Gary's music, he made the best records of that time,' John Foxx reflected later. 'I think that he, if anyone, really condensed it into a form that was perfect at that point.' The Human League were equally impressed: 'I was gutted when 'Cars' came out,' Martyn Ware deadpanned on *Synth Britannia*, 'I thought it was really good.' As it would turn out, rather than stealing the opportunity to carve their own paths, his success actually had an opposite effect, as Numan would recollect with some satisfaction: 'My success opened the floodgates for electronic music, and soon every label was signing up their token electronic band.'

A final Gary Numan single, 'Complex', was taken from *The Pleasure Principle* in the middle of November. Although mostly overlooked on the review pages in favour of the usual desperate flurry of festive single releases, 'Complex' was nevertheless championed by *Melody Maker*'s Chris Bohn – 'The yearning weariness of the tune beautifully eases out on an expanding synthesiser line, leading into the regrettably short song' – who hailed the track as his favourite from *The Pleasure Principle*. *Record Mirror* ruled that 'Complex' was 'very neo-modern classical' but surprisingly short, and chose instead to celebrate the single's B-side, a live version of Tubeway Army's 'Bombers' recorded at London's Hammersmith Odeon earlier in the year, and specifically Billy Currie's 'stunningly atmospheric violin'.

The *NME*'s Nick Kent pulled no punches and rejected 'Complex' as 'more of the same formula', to which he added, 'It's so vacuous it's really nothing more than muzak, a fact that makes me feel increasingly uneasy about this wretched clone's considerable following.' With number one hits behind him for the *Replicas* and *The Pleasure Principle* albums, and for the 'Are 'Friends' Electric?' and 'Cars' singles over the course of the previous few months, Numan's devoted fanbase ensured that the single soared into the UK singles charts, where it peaked at number six at the start of December after just two weeks on sale.

Before 'Complex' had even left the Top 10, and less than three months after the release of *The Pleasure Principle*, the music press was already reporting that, as a result of his prodigious work ethic, Gary Numan was already staking his claim on the imminent new decade with an announcement that the singer was putting the finishing touches to yet another new album, *Telekon*, which which was to be released in September 1980.

The release of 'Complex' marked the end of Billy Currie's sojourn as a member of Gary Numan's band, a period Currie looks back on with affection, recalling it as a time when he could temporarily trade the pressures and challenges facing Ultravox for 'Special Guest' billing and the responsibility-free luxury that came with his role as a session musician in a successful act.

Prior to Currie meeting Numan – during a night out to see Magazine play London's Theatre Royal on their *Secondhand Daylight* tour in May 1979, a show which also featured support act Simple Minds playing their first ever show in the capital – Ultravox had followed their split from Island Records with a trip to America at the start of 1979, where they spent six weeks touring the country and quietly imploding. By the time of their return to the UK at the end of March, John Foxx had left the band, Robin Simon had decided to settle in America, and Ultravox had been reduced to just Warren Cann, Chris Cross and Billy Currie.

It was while Ultravox considered their next move that Billy Currie had taken advantage of the hiatus in Ultravox activities to spend some time catching up on life outside the band, doing some socialising, and exploring whatever opportunities might present themselves. 'We just wanted to forget Ultravox,' Currie recalled in an interview with *Record Mirror*'s Daniela Soave the following year. 'We'd been kicked off our record label, we were down to three members, we just didn't want to know.'

Meanwhile, having previously brought him to Billy's and then to the Blitz, Currie's socialising had also led to his befriending Rusty Egan. Gratified that Egan – who was at the time also the drummer in Rich Kids, Glen Matlock's post-Sex Pistols power pop project – was raving about Ultravox's music, which was regularly featured on his Blitz club playlists, Currie was sufficiently intrigued by the emerging scene to make the Blitz a regular haunt, in the process falling in with Egan's bandmate, Rich Kids guitarist Midge Ure, who was also a regular at the club.

'Rusty came up with a million ideas a day, and one was, "Wouldn't it be great to have a band with all our favourite musicians in it?"' Midge Ure would recall in his autobiography, *If I Was*, in 2004. 'And I went, "OK, stop. Let's do that." And that was Visage.' Outlining the idea further, Ure went on to explain, 'All the musicians we wanted to work with in Visage were working in other bands. Dave Formula, Barry Adamson and John McGeoch were in Magazine, and Billy Currie was in Ultravox. So Rusty approached them, and they were all up for the idea of doing this simply as a studio project, as a collective.'

In *If I Was*, Midge Ure also explained that he came up with the name Visage on the grounds that it 'sounded very romantic, very European', but in the often blurry world which is Visage's history, some other members of the collective remember it rather differently. Steve Strange made the same claim in his own autobiography, *Blitzed!*, In 2002: 'I came up with the name of Visage,' he declared. '"Vis" stood for the visual elements of the band, "Visa" represented the fact that we were going to be a global band, and "age" symbolised our part in a new age of music.'

Visage began by taking advantage of some unused studio time at EMI Studios which was owed to the Rich Kids, and the collective, joined by Rusty Egan's Blitz club partner Steve Strange on vocals, recorded cover versions of Zager & Evans' 'In The Year 2525' and Barry McGuire's 'Eve Of Destruction'. The collaboration was a creative success and those recordings not only formed the basis of Visage's first demos, but also provided Egan with new material for his Blitz playlist, where the nascent Visage were heartened to see their tracks enthusiastically received.

Upstairs from Blitz, Martin Rushent was naturally intrigued by the unusual, alternative crowd which flocked to the club each Tuesday. Although his personal style was somewhat at odds with the flamboyance of the club's crowd – 'I'd gone right through the punk era with a beard,' the producer told Simon Reynolds later, describing himself as the most unfashionable person anyone could meet and adding, 'I wear what I want to wear, and if you don't like it you can fuck off' – Rushent nevertheless became a regular at

Blitz and was intrigued by the cutting-edge sounds gracing Egan's turntables. Keen to explore the commercial potential of this emerging scene, Rushent was immediately interested in the Visage demos and offered the band the opportunity to work up some more ideas in Genetic's recording studio with a view to signing with his label.

In reality, Genetic Studios, located at Rushent's home in Streatley, Berkshire, were far from finished and at the time consisted of little more than a MCI mixing desk in a portable building in his garden, but Billy Currie thoroughly approved of the desk – identical to the one Ultravox used at Conny Plank's studio in Germany when recording *Systems Of Romance* – and Visage jumped at the chance of studio time there. Initial sessions included the tracks 'Tar' (described by Steve Strange as being about 'the pleasure and pain of nicotine') and 'Frequency 7', which were released on Genetic Records in November 1979 as the debut Visage single, 'Tar'.

Although 'Tar' picked up some encouraging reviews, Nick Kent's for the *NME* wasn't one of them. 'It's a load of over-synthesized drivel overburdened by layer upon layer of clumsy electronic icing that attempts to come to terms with the topic of cigarette smoking and succeeds only in sounding like a bunch of inept and uninspired young posers.' *Smash Hits* were kinder, describing Visage as 'a new electro-supergroup', and while they considered 'the sax, the synthesisers, the bass, the vocal, the clothes' to be Bowie cast-offs, they nevertheless voted the single 'strong enough to be a hit'.

In fact, 'Tar' failed to pick up much in the way of radio play and wasn't a hit, which in retrospect may have saved the band from all manner of legal problems. On the single, 'Tar' – and its B-side 'Frequency 7' – is credited entirely to Visage, a collective credit which covered the entire band. However, Steve Strange's previous group, a power pop act called The Photons later claimed that although Strange had written the lyrics to 'Tar', that song, and a second track that Visage would go on to record, 'Mind Of A Toy', were actually theirs, although were unable to prove it. Interestingly, in an interview for Ultravox fanzine *Extreme Voice* some years later, Billie Currie recalled that both 'Tar' and 'Mind Of A Toy' started as tracks which had originated from Ultravox sessions only to be abandoned after disagreements with John Foxx.

Fortunately, Midge Ure at least had a new challenge to concentrate on, one which he'd had in his sights for some time. 'All the time we were writing and planning for Visage I kept asking asking Billy what was happening with Ultravox. I was continually dropping really heavy hints, asking if they had found a new singer almost every day,' Ure confessed to *Record Mirror* later. The penny finally dropped with Ultravox and an audition was duly arranged. 'I remember immediately feeling energised by just being these four people,' remembered Currie of that first meeting. 'I know three of us were in the previous line-up but it was suddenly like an injection of life and we started writing right away and went out and performed those tracks straight away. We were just keen to get on with it.'

On November 1st, 1979, Midge Ure officially joined Ultravox as the band's new frontman, although the process hadn't been without its frustrations: though the decision to join the band had been made several months earlier, it had taken almost six months to jump through the necessary legal hoops that would allow him to leave the Rich Kids. 'The first time I plugged in and made a noise with Ultravox was in April 1979 at a rehearsal room in the Elephant and Castle,' Ure remembered. 'Right from the first minute I knew I had come home. This noise was what I had been searching for, not only could these people make that noise, but they also could teach me how to make it. It felt so right I drank it all in.'

In a similar spirit of reinvention, Simple Minds put out their second album of the year at the same time. *Real To Real Cacophony* was a release which couldn't come fast enough for the Scottish five-piece, who were desperate to move on from their April debut. 'Two months after *Life In A Day* came out, we were really embarrassed by it,' Jim Kerr remembered later. 'It was very, very poppy, and we realised we were drowned in influence. We had to try to get our own sound… we had to stop messing about.' Simple Minds' guitarist Charlie Burchill concurred, and in an echo of The Human League's experience following the release of *Reproduction*, explained, 'It's very frustrating when you go into a studio for the first time and it all sounds great, then it comes out on vinyl and you think, "What the fuck is this?" We thought that album would give us a face and get us off to a good start, but the end result showed us being naive in the studio and naive in general. It's taken us this time to develop and feel what we're doing now is the right direction for us.'

Having considered making an approach to Gary Numan to produce the new record, Simple Minds eventually recorded *Real To Real Cacophony* at Rockfield Studios in Wales with *Life In A Day* producer John Leckie in the producer's seat, but the new direction that Simple Minds were keen to explore ensured that their time in the studio was spent very differently to the way they had approached their first album. Keen to explore a more spontaneous and organic approach to the writing and recording of their new material, the band had deliberately entered the studio without many preconceptions of what they might deliver: 'All we had were cassettes with little bits on. We just went in and did it,' Jim Kerr would explain shortly after *Real To Real Cacophony*'s release, adding, 'That's going to be our attitude from now on. On edge, where you have to make decisions. It wasn't safe, and that felt good.'

The band's fresh approach worked and it was an invigorated Simple Minds who headed out on a short European tour in October, followed by UK dates around the release of *Real To Real Cacophony* in November. In a review of the band's show at Edinburgh's Tiffany's for *Sounds*, Johnny Waller spotted the shift in mood: 'No longer do the Minds sulk in the shadows amid accusations of Roxy/Magazine cloning, and their own new-found direction and maturity asserts itself through the music and its presentation.' Observing that no less than eight tracks from *Real To Real Cacophony* had made it onto Simple Minds' setlist for the show, Waller welcomed the band's new direction, and noted with approval how the latest material 'explored a greater range of emotions, utilising different rhythms and experimenting with various styles and tempos', before ending on the optimistic and upbeat note, 'I'm looking to the future and I want it now!'

In the same edition of *Sounds*, John Gill turned in a similarly positive review of the *Real To Real Cacophony* album which he praised for its considerable and brave progression: 'Where *Life In A Day* was tentative and predictable, *Real To Real Cacophony* is self-assured and explorative,' he declared, and encouraged his readers to 'File under impressive.' Ronnie Gurr in *Record Mirror* was similarly effusive, hailing the release as 'a quality album' and writing, 'This is a mighty progression. One of the signs of a fine second album, and there are few of those around, is the fact that it leaves that debut redundant. 'Real To Real Cacophony' lays waste to 'Life In A Day' which was itself a promising little slice of occasional magic.'

Only Paul Du Noyer, reviewing *Real To Real Cacophony* for the *NME*, was less than convinced by the new direction. 'It's the smug, callow, facile facade of inscrutability which irritates, and it's the long, ponderous, pointless musical meandering which bores,' he wrote. 'There's neither the energy nor the emotive capacity to sustain either album side, and any intellectual consistency remains too obscured for this reviewer to detect. Serious, cold and contrivedly [sic] clever, the results stretch your patience rather than your mind.'

Real To Real Cacophony also resonated across other parts of the media. John Peel, whose support of *Life In A Day* had amounted to just a single play of the 'Chelsea Girl' single, became an enthusiastic champion of the new album and played almost all the tracks from *Real To Real Cacophony* over the course of December 1979 and January 1980. Peel also invited the band to record a prestigious live session in December, and their performances of the tracks 'Changeling', 'Premonition', 'Citizen (Dance Of Youth)' and 'Room' were broadcast at the beginning of January. *The Old Grey Whistle Test* booked the band for a second performance and this time filmed three tracks – 'Factory', 'Changeling' and 'Premonition' – at Simple Minds' first-ever US show, at Hurrah in New York at the end of October. Their footage was broadcast in November, alongside a short interview with the band conducted by Bob Harris and filmed on the streets of New York, in which the band enthused about their new direction and expressed their gratitude to Gary Numan, whom they described as a friend, for opening doors for Simple Minds and other emerging bands who were experimenting with electronics.

Echoing Peter Saville's concept for the Factory Records release of Orchestral Manoeuvres In The Dark's 'Electricity', initial copies of *Real To Real Cacophony* came packaged in a blue sleeve, entirely plain except for discrete lettering to announce the name of the band and the title of the album, and enhanced with a series of thermographically printed raised designs. While no stories have circulated about Simple Minds' thermographic printing process causing a fire at the printers, the elaborate sleeve nevertheless proved too expensive for Arista, who switched to a simplified design, without the raised elements, for all subsequent pressings.

Despite the positive critical reaction to the album, as well as the support of John Peel and *The Old Grey Whistle Test*, *Real To Real Cacophony* failed to make an impact on the UK album charts, and the sole single from the album, 'Changeling', released at the start of January 1980 to coincide with the second leg of Simple Minds' UK and European *Real To Real Cacophony* tour dates, also failed to chart. Backed with a live version of 'Premonition' from *The Old Grey Whistle Test*, the 'Changeling' single slipped out during the immediate post-Christmas period, and while the release didn't chart, it did attract some positive attention from the music press: 'Best track from 'Real To Real Cacophony',' proclaimed *Record Mirror*, and identified the single as a contender for the imminent new decade.

TRANSITION

1980 & 1981

'There are some days when you turn on the radio and every record begins with a bleep or a bubble. Not just the plastic Top 30, three minutes at a time and expensive matching video, but groups which want us to take them seriously, groups it is necessary to admire in order to stay up to date.'

NME, August 2nd, 1980

Midge Ure (Ultravox), 1980.

1980

1980.1 John Foxx / Ultravox / Gareth Jones / Japan / Orchestral Manoeuvres In The Dark / The Human League / Johnny Logan / Telex

HAD IT BEEN LEFT to his new label, Virgin Records, John Foxx would have debuted his first solo project at the end of 1979 with the release of a single, 'A New Kind Of Man'. However, after work was completed on one of the final tracks for the album, Virgin, with Foxx's support, decided instead to release the new track, 'Underpass', and the project subsequently moved to early 1980, to the delight of Foxx. 'I'm glad it wasn't the last record of the seventies and was the first record of the eighties,' Foxx told *Electronic Sound* later.

At the start of January 1980 *Smash Hits* ran a news piece announcing the project: 'John Foxx, former lead singer with Ultravox! and a personal hero of one Gary Numan, has formed his own label called Metal Beat with the intention of signing and helping young bands with similar interests to his own. Metal Beat, which is distributed by Virgin, gets off the ground in January with a Foxx album called *Metamatic* and a single entitled 'Underpass'.' (The distractions and responsibilities involved in running a label would very quickly prove too much for Foxx, who admitted the fact in an interview for his fan club magazine *The Service* later. 'I've realised that if I did this seriously, I'd be forced to become another record executive rather than a musician,' he wrote in response to a question about the label from a fan. 'It would cut down my freedom and I don't want that.') Foxx's original plan had been to call his album *Fusion Fission* but settled upon *Metamatic* after discovering a series of intriguing kinetic sculptures created under that name: 'There was an artist called Jean Tinguely who made self-destructing machines, they were amusing things that pull themselves apart eventually, and I thought that was a pretty good description of what I was like, they had a sense of humour, they were called Metamatics, and that was their mission; self destruction. And I thought, "Alright, let's have some of that then."'

Given Gary Numan's visibility and profile at the start of the new decade, it was inevitable that his name would crop up again and again in reviews and interviews across the *Metamatic* project. Red Starr award *Metamatic* a robust seven-and-a-half stars out of ten and addressed the question of any implied plagiarism on Foxx's part in his review of the album for *Smash*

Telex at the Eurovision Song Contest, 1980.

Hits: 'Copying Gary Numan? Hardly – John Foxx started it all! And after the chronically pretentious Ultravox, this restrained and melodic album of synthesised music and (surprise, surprise) futuristic visions comes as an impressive step forward.'

"Underpass' is so close to Gary Numan that it could almost be a parody, which is pretty ironic since Foxx's Ultravox! were his biggest influence,' noted Chris Bohn in his review of the single for *Melody Maker*. Professing himself equally unnerved by the similarities to Gary Numan's recent output, Mike Nicholls, reviewing *Metamatic* for *Record Mirror*, nevertheless awarded the album the maximum five stars 'for effort, integrity and ongoing determination', adding that neither Numan nor Foxx 'can really be accused of plagiarising from the other as both are quite obviously tuned in to the same cold wave length. Exit people and enter machines. Screw emotions, just give us that good old sheet metal logic.'

Recognising Gary Numan's high-profile support of Ultravox in the media as an opportunity to connect with a broad potential audience, Foxx remained sanguine about the spectre of Numan that hovered over *Metamatic*. In one of his very first interviews as a solo artist, Foxx was asked by *Record Mirror*'s Mike Nicholls how the singer felt about being such an important influence on Numan's musical journey and subsequent success: 'Well, I don't mind much because he's acknowledged his source and for that, I like him,' Foxx replied. 'He wanted to meet me and I was glad to meet him, too. Yes, there was some talk about us collaborating.' (While the duo first met in Numan's studio during the making of *The Pleasure Principle* album, Foxx and Numan wouldn't actually manage to work together for another thirty-five years when, in 2016, they finally collaborated on a track entitled 'Talk (Are You Listening To Me?)' for Foxx's career-spanning compilation album *21st Century: A Man, A Woman And A City*. 'He's extremely smart, a very interesting man to spend time with,' Numan would say of Foxx in an interview about the collaboration for The Quietus.) In response to the same question from *Melody Maker* a few weeks later, Foxx was more wry, calmly telling Chris Bohn, 'I'm very glad that the ideas I put down then haven't been ignored or wasted. It means, I suppose, they've got some validity.'

Equally inevitably, over the course of the *Metamatic* project the media was curious to know why Foxx had left Ultravox. In Mike Nicholls' interview for *Record Mirror* Foxx was initially vague about his reasons for going solo: 'I decided the band format was too difficult to work in. Like there were some songs where I wanted, say, no guitar or drums, so I thought it would be easier to work alone.' Nevertheless Foxx was unable to resist taking a quick swipe at his former bandmates, adding, 'Plus the fact that there were certain people in the band that simply lost interest, and it was a lot of pressure having them there not doing anything.'

When the *NME*'s Paul Morley asked Ultravox for their side of the story later that same year, the band's Billy Currie concurred with Foxx's explanation of the split. 'I'm a very headstrong character,' Currie admitted. 'It was just a clash between me and [Foxx]. He wanted to go into this minimalist thing… and I wanted to develop more, open up more. I didn't like what was going on, that he considered it was his band.' 'I still like them as individuals,' Foxx clarified in an interview with *Melody Maker*'s Chris Bohn, and by the time of a second interview for *Record Mirror* in April, in the way of those who are repeatedly asked the same question, Foxx had distilled his response into a smooth soundbite: 'One of the reasons I left Ultravox is because I realised that I could do all the parts more efficiently myself and I wanted to be totally electronic.'

In part inspired to explore the possibilities of that stripped-down sound – synthesisers, drum machine, vocals – by recent releases from The Normal, Robert Rental and Thomas Leer (whose 'Private Plane' Foxx selected as one of his 'All Time Top Ten' tracks for a *Smash Hits* feature in March 1980), coupled with a desire to explore the potential of working alone, Foxx had already developed the concept which went on to shape the sound of *Metamatic* before leaving Ultravox: 'I decided that the only thing you could do to make a good record at that time was to clear the decks and start again, limit myself to eight tracks, three instruments and a drum machine. So it was a very firm design construct, if you like. I'd learned from art school that if you limit your palette you get better results. Get to know one thing well and you get the best results.'

Working within this minimal manifesto, *Metamatic* was written and recorded over the course of 1979, Foxx working on the songs at his home in North London before taking them to nearby Pathway Studios – 'a swift cycle ride' away – to record them on his own. 'With this magic kit, I realised I could make an album all by myself. This was an entirely new development,' Foxx told Dylan Jones later. 'Bands were a pain, and the future looked mobile and agile. One or two guys with a synth, a drum machine, a tape machine and some imagination, and you were away.'

While Foxx was familiar with Pathway from previous sessions at the studio with Ultravox, for *Metamatic* he was introduced to the studio's assistant engineer Gareth Jones – described by Foxx as 'a bit of a hippie, highly intelligent, and completely dedicated to sonic adventures of every kind' – whose enthusiasm for Foxx's proposed experimentation became essential in realising Foxx's sonic vision. '[Jones] was the other arm and that was really important,' Foxx would later tell *Electronic Sound*. 'He was great as he wasn't really interested in pop music but more esoteric stuff. Also, because he was so new to it, he was really excited by it and I fed off that.' 'John seemed vastly experienced, focused and elegant in his pursuit of a minimal aesthetic,' Gareth Jones warmly recalls of their first meeting today, 'He was a great mentor for me, and I was delighted to get my first opportunity to record and mix an album with him.'

Metamatic was released on January 18th, two weeks after 'Underpass', sporting a sleeve inspired by a short story Foxx had recently written about a man with the ability to step into and out of a film screen. As he had done for Ultravox's *Systems Of Romance* album the previous year, Foxx, a former student at London's Royal College of Art, also took on creative duties for the *Metamatic* project, which included art-directing the photo session that resulted in the album cover image with photographer Chris Gabrin, who had also been responsible for the cover of The Human League's *Reproduction* album the previous year. Hitting the Top 30 of the UK album chart just a fortnight after release, *Metamatic* subsequently went on to become a Top 20 hit for Foxx when it later peaked at number eighteen over the course of its seven-week chart run.

Whether as a result of good fortune or good planning, at the same time John Foxx was releasing and promoting *Metamatic*, Ultravox chose to make their return to the public eye, playing a one-off show at London's Electric Ballroom in February. At odds with the enthusiastic media reaction afforded to Foxx's new direction the Ultravox show was savaged by Chris Westwood in his review for *Record Mirror* the following week. 'New Ultravox are a dull, characterless fiction – a cold, hard, sluggish calculation,' Westwood wrote of the new line-up, deriding the band for putting style before substance, and adding that the addition of Ure to the line-up 'has succeeded in mutating this Ultravox into a sort of grotesque, mangled synthetic Rich Kids'. The review entirely failed to mention any of the music played, which included airings of a number of new compositions – among them 'Sleepwalk', 'All Stood Still', 'Astradyne' and 'New Europeans' – alongside reworked versions of fan favourites from the old Ultravox catalogue.

The Electric Ballroom show was the band's first date in London since Foxx's departure and followed the new Ultravox line-up's first tour of the USA, which had taken place at the end of 1979. The American dates, which the band had arranged and self-financed courtesy of a loan from the National Westminster Bank, had been set up with two goals in mind: firstly to give the new line-up a chance to test their live show, and their new line-up, out of sight of their home audience: 'We chose America because it was available,' Billy Currie told *Record Mirror* later. 'We had no financial backing behind us and you can actually tour America on a budget because all the clubs have their own PA systems so you don't have to lug that around.' The second reason for choosing America came from the band's belief that their live show might help persuade an American label to take them on and offer Ultravox a contract which would secure their future.

While the American tour was successful in that the band played well and attracted decent-sized crowds – 'We actually made money!' Midge Ure proudly told *Record Mirror*'s Daniela Soave a few months later – Ultravox's plan to dazzle the American music industry with a five-night residency at Los Angeles' legendary Whiskey a Go Go venue at the end of December fell rather flat, as Chris Cross would later recall: 'What we didn't realise was that LA is a desert at Christmas and New Year. Everyone goes away. The shows all sold out, but none of the people there were record company people.'

Returning to England at the start of January, and still in desperate need of a label to finance any future activity, Ultravox decided to put on the show at the Electric Ballroom as a showcase for any UK labels who might be interested in the band. To further their cause, prior to the concert the band and their management circulated a rumour that Ultravox were about to sign an American deal. 'It was a classic management scam,' Midge Ure would later explain in his autobiography *If I Was*. 'There never was an American deal.'

On the evidence of the London show, coupled with the threat of losing them to a fictitious American deal, Chrysalis Records were intrigued enough to open discussions about signing the band, and offered Ultravox a couple of days in the studio to demo some of the unreleased material which formed the backbone of their new live set. 'We went into the studio with Conny Plank as engineer,' Warren Cann told Jonas Wårstad later, 'and decided not to do the usual thing of recording three songs to "demo" status, we would use the allotted studio time to concentrate on doing one song well and hand them a "master".' The track Ultravox chose to record was 'Sleepwalk' and fortunately the one-song recording was enough to convince Chrysalis to offer the band a deal.

Inevitably there was tension between Ultravox and John Foxx as they each went about their respective careers, but perhaps not as much as has been supposed. Foxx attended Ultravox's London debut at the Electric Ballroom – 'standing in the shadows at the back' according to *Smash Hits* – where Midge Ure dedicated 'Quiet Men' to the band's former singer. Around the same time, 'Touch And Go' and 'He's A Liquid' – tracks which Foxx had written for Ultravox and which had been developed by the rest of that band to the extent that they each appeared on the setlist of their final tour with Foxx – appeared, in new stripped-back versions, on *Metamatic*, while Ultravox in turn repurposed part of 'Touch And Go' in a new song called 'Mr. X', without either use referring to the other party, or becoming a public issue. Talking about his own use of those tracks almost forty years later in an interview to promote a remastered and expanded edition of *Metamatic*, Foxx explained further: 'I didn't really feel they'd reached their potential until they were synth and drum machine only.'

The comfortable truce between Ultravox and John Foxx fractured somewhat in May 1980, when *Record Mirror* reported that Ultravox's original label, Island Records, was to condense tracks from the band's three John Foxx-fronted albums for the label into a single album compilation, *Three Into One*. 'Foxx, now a successful solo artist, objected to certain credits on the album which were worded: "All lyrics John Foxx, all compositions Ultravox,"' reported the paper, adding that Foxx had 'Issued writs against all the present four members of the band and Island in an attempt to injunct the album.'

Foxx's efforts ultimately came to nothing and *Three Into One* was released in June, earning the band some surprisingly positive reviews in the process. In a five-star review of the album, *Record Mirror* reassessed the charges of pretension and of taking themselves too seriously which had dogged Ultravox's early career: 'Weren't these same charges applicable to the vastly more hip Human

League and Tubeway Army?' wrote Mike Nicholls, while praising the *Ultravox!* and *Ha! Ha! Ha!* albums for being ahead of their time, and adding, 'There must be a lot of people around scratching their heads wondering why they didn't get into Ultravox.'

Coinciding with the end of *Metamatic*'s chart run, Foxx released a second single from the album on March 21st. Featuring 'No-One Driving' from *Metamatic* as its lead track, the single came out as a double pack which included a further three non-album tracks, 'Glimmer', 'This City' and 'Mr. No', across the two discs, all for a recommended retail price of £1.19. Despite the value-for-money package, the *NME* were positive but unenthusiastic – 'A hit of course, but a complete dead-end,' wrote Andy Gill. *Melody Maker*'s Chris Bohn redressed the balance somewhat by declaring, 'Where others missed the passion and the point of the electronic age's innovative, distanced vocals by merely mimicking humanoid voices, Foxx sings with commitment and love, which brings a new dimension to the form.'

Sitting side by side with the reviews of 'No-One Driving' across the music press were reviews of a new single from Japan. 'I Second That Emotion' picked up some of Japan's best reviews to date. The *NME*'s Andy Gill made the single his 'Cover of the Week' and wrote, 'Beneath all the prattish glam-rock revivalist visuals, there appears to be a decent band struggling to get out of Japan. Their version of the old Smokey Robinson number treats it with the respect and sympathy it deserves; the result is just as sad and gentle as the original, but refreshingly different.'

Released to promote Japan's third album, *Quiet Life*, 'I Second That Emotion' was an odd choice of single because the track wasn't actually featured on the album, although the track 'Quiet Life' was included as the single's B-side. The choice of single had been made by Japan's label, Hansa, and illustrated a widening gap between the band and the label. Japan themselves weren't keen on the track, bassist Mick Karn going so far as to say, "I Second That Emotion' was a bad indication of what to expect from the new album and, for my tastes, the worst recording we have ever made.'

The original plan had been to release a three-track single featuring 'Quiet Life', 'A Foreign Place' and 'European Son', but fearing that the new material wasn't commercial enough for a single Hansa lost their nerve and instead insisted that the band select a well-known song to cover. The whole chapter was summed up best by writer Anthony Reynolds in his impressive 2015 biography of Japan, *A Foreign Place*: 'A promo video was made at Shepperton and was shown nowhere. The single garnered no airplay. Both Japan and their record company must have wondered at the point of it all.'

Quiet Life had been released in the UK on January 18th, the same day as John Foxx's *Metamatic*, and was the first Japan album to chart in their home territory, albeit peaking at a lowly seventy-two and spending just two weeks in the UK album chart. However, *Quiet Life* had already been released in the two markets which had most enthusiastically embraced Japan's previous album: Japan and Canada. To coincide with the Canadian album release the band had headed to Toronto in late November 1979 to play two shows. *Record Mirror*'s Rosalind Russell tagged along to do a combined interview and review piece in which she reported that *Quiet Life* was selling 'like candles in a power strike'. Russell was also struck by the scale of the show in contrast to the venues the band played at home, noting the capacity audience crammed into the 1,400-seater Ryerson Theatre and the crowd's enthusiastic reaction to Japan's show.

As was the case with 'I Second That Emotion', 'Life In Tokyo', Japan's previous single, had also been omitted from the *Quiet Life* tracklisting, which placed the album in the curious position of being bracketed by singles which weren't actually on the new record. Nevertheless *Quiet Life* attracted some of the most positive reviews the band had seen to date. Mike Nicholls, reviewing the album for *Record Mirror*, awarded it four stars. 'Hard work, a little imagination and more than a little opportunism have broadened their scope and they are maturing fast,' he noted. 'Thoughtful and adventurous, the band neatly summarise a lot of what has gone before them, whilst still pointing in a forward direction.' The *NME*'s Ian Penman, however, had heard it all before: 'Although they may seem full speed ahead, seamlessly "European" to you, it all sounds slyly studied Roxy 'Stranded' to us ancients, Ferry's smokey closures accentuated and crowded into one watery fiction.'

In fact the band had been keen to bring in Roxy Music producer Chris Thomas to take charge of production duties on *Quiet Life*, only to learn that he was already booked for a different project. However, Thomas had recommended that the band meet Roxy Music engineer John Punter as a possible alternative. 'There was obviously a conscious decision to go down the Roxy Music route,' Richard Barbieri admitted to *Classic Pop* magazine later. 'We were all Roxy fans, John Punter had produced their *Country Life* album and engineered on their earlier albums.'

A fortnight after *Quiet Life* hit its 1980 chart peak, OMD's debut album, *Orchestral Manoeuvres In The Dark*, started a chart journey of its own, entering the UK albums chart at fifty-three, the first step on an impressive six-month chart journey over the course of which it would peak at twenty-seven on three separate occasions.

Since coming off the road with Gary Numan in October, OMD had spent the last part of 1979 using their DinDisc advance money to build their own sixteen-track recording studio a stone's throw away from the site of Eric's club in Liverpool. Once work on the studio, which the band christened The Gramophone Suite, was complete OMD had just three weeks in which to record their debut album in time to meet the production deadlines DinDisc had imposed upon them for a February 1980 release. Pulling what they considered the best ten tracks from their repertoire to date, the album was performed by Andy McCluskey and Paul Humphreys, alongside Mal Holmes, Martin Cooper and Dave Fairbairn, who were recruited to add extra elements of percussion, saxophone and guitar, respectively.

With their first European tour dates set for early in the new year, McCluskey and Humphreys also had plans to expand OMD's live line-up, and with that in mind the duo ended 1979 with a special show at Liverpool's Eric's on December 28th. Billed as 'A Tribute to Winston', the show saw OMD play a final live show backed by Winston, their trusty reel-to-reel tape recorder. The end of an era for OMD, it would be another thirty-five years before Winston next appeared with the band, reprising his onstage role in 2014 at a one-off concert at the Museum of Liverpool, where Winston is now part of the permanent collection in the museum's Wondrous Place gallery.

A week after OMD's farewell to Winston, the music press announced that the duo would put out a new single, 'Red Frame/White Light', in advance of the release of *Orchestral Manoeuvres In The Dark*. Possibly the first pop song on the subject, 'Red Frame/White Light' was written about a telephone box located between McCluskey and Humphreys' childhood homes on the Wirral. 'The phone box was our office,' Paul Humphreys would recollect for OMD's 2019 book *Pretending to See the Future*. 'Neither Andy or I had a house phone, neither of our families could afford one. We used to have people call us at a certain time at the phone box, and we would keep other people out of the box because we were waiting for a call.' Located outside The Railway

Inn in Meols the telephone box subsequently provided an unlikely moment of inspiration for McCluskey: 'I was going through a stage where I was writing about inanimate objects – I was actually phoning up a venue to get a gig, and I was getting this engaged tone all the time. It sounded great. I ran back to Paul's, and for a month later we were just doing this song that went [*imitates an engaged tone*] all the way through.'

Adrian Thrills was unenthusiastic about 'Red Frame/White Light' in the *NME*, finding the single a disappointing follow-up to 'Electricity' which neither innovated or irritated, but Thrills nevertheless dismissed the release as little more than bandwagon jumping: 'The majors continue to muscle in on the electronic pop purveyors worldwide in the vain hope of unearthing the next Gary Numan, but to little avail.' *Melody Maker* were significantly more positive, however, and described 'Red Frame/White Light' as 'Synth-pop of the new sensibility, which incorporates humour, emotion and a healthy awareness of disposability.'

Following his enthusiastic support of the Factory Records release of 'Electricity' the previous year, John Peel had already given 'Red Frame/White Light' its first Radio 1 play when the DJ broadcast OMD's debut radio session, recorded for his show in October 1979. Peel was equally supportive of the track when it appeared as the band's new single in February 1980, although lacking the support of Peel's daytime colleagues 'Red Frame/White Light' ultimately failed to cross over to daytime play on the station, and although the single entered the UK charts at sixty-eight and then climbed to sixty-seven, it subsequently dropped out of the charts entirely.

As 'Red Frame/White Light' burned through its short chart life OMD, now expanded to a four-piece for live shows with the addition of Dave Hughes on synthesisers and Mal Holmes on electronic drums, embarked on an extensive UK tour, which kicked off at Eric's in Liverpool. *Melody Maker*'s Penny Kiley was on hand to file a report: 'It's the opening night of an important tour, on home ground (almost), and the message is there. It's there in the queues outside the door, in the club full of strangers, and in the slick new equipment waiting on the stage.' Noting the band's transition to a four-piece from their former live presentation of 'two men/one machine and a set of fluorescent tubes', Kiley found it difficult to embrace this upscaled OMD, fearing a move away from the band's early DIY approach might rob them of what made them unique: 'A year ago what the band was aiming at seemed radical, but sounds are fast assimilated into the TV consciousness of the populist; and now their music suggests all the tedious comparisons with others sharing the genre.'

Presumably Kiley included Gary Numan among those 'tedious comparisons'. In the same way that John Foxx's recent releases had been overshadowed by comparisons to Numan, it was also inevitable that OMD, particularly after opening Numan's tour the previous autumn, would receive the same treatment. Reviewing *Orchestral Manoeuvres In The Dark* for *Record Mirror* the following week, Simon Ludgate argued that OMD were a notable exception to that rule: 'Paul Humphreys and Andy McCluskey survived a thorough tarring of the same brush as Gary Numan, even playing on his tour. Not only have they survived this almost certain kiss of death, but they are thriving.' In his four-star review of the album Ludgate further declared that 'OMD are one of only a few bands of their genre which have any emotional content' and praised the album for being 'Replete with rich, though tastefully restrained, synthesiser, structured by conventional percussion and some real guitar.'

Smash Hits were similarly enthusiastic, and the frequently irascible Red Starr awarded *Orchestral Manoeuvres In The Dark* a solid seven and a half out of ten: 'An odd album from an odd duo, sometimes briskly clean synthesiser pop, sometimes strange and intriguing electronic excursions.' Even the *NME* was full of praise for the duo's debut album. 'The LP works well as a cumulative effect, gradually revealing how much Orch Man can do with their vivacious electronic sensibility, how fine and different their melodies can be, how detailed and distinctive their song structures,' Paul Morley enthused. 'Orchestral Manoeuvres are very wonderful. Take them as seriously as you want.'

Packaged in an ingenious cover courtesy of Peter Saville, *Orchestral Manoeuvres In The Dark* sported a bold industrial aesthetic inspired by a perforated steel door Ben Kelly (who went on to design the Haçienda for Factory Records) had designed for a London boutique. On the initial print runs the orange of the album's inner sleeve showed through a design of 144 holes cut in a blue outer sleeve. 'Peter Saville came up with this sleeve that was basically a grill. The exterior cover was bright blue with a series of lozenges, grill holes, punched into it so you could see this bright orange interior. It was a very unusual sleeve for its time,' explained Andy McCluskey later. 'The album will appear in specially designed "high tech" sleeves,' *Smash Hits* announced before release. 'And each batch of twenty thousand will appear in different colour combinations.'

Keen to maintain momentum around the album, DinDisc decided to release the latest version of OMD's September 1979 single 'Electricity' in the hope it would become the hit they believed it to be. Swapping the Martin Hannett version of 'Almost' on the B-side for the more recently recorded album version, 'Electricity' was released as a single for the third time on March 31st. Despite featuring the mischievous message 'Will Radio 1 Like It' scratched into the single's run-out groove, mainstream radio, and the opportunity for commercial success that comes with it, remained elusive and the release soon fell by the wayside.

Having caught the ear of reviewers of *Orchestral Manoeuvres In The Dark* as a standout track from the album, 'Messages' was chosen as the next OMD single. Concerned that the album version of 'Messages' wasn't polished enough to fulfil its potential as a single, DinDisc suggested that McCluskey and Humphreys try recording a new version of the song with a producer. 'We always tended to think that producers would distort the vision we had of our music,' McCluskey stated in 1987 biography *Messages*, before confessing, 'We knew that we weren't very good at getting a really professional sound in the studios. Yet somehow we couldn't trust an outsider.'

OMD were duly booked into London's Advision Studios with Mike Howlett in the producer's chair and a plan to record the single and its associated B-sides. Fortunately their new producer was already a fan of the band, and of 'Messages'. 'The hook-line for the song was superb, and so was the vocal melody,' Howlett enthused in *Messages*, recalling that the session went well from his perspective. However, Andy McCluskey had a very different view. 'I absolutely hated it,' the singer admitted later. 'We'd worked on it for two days. It was the worst case of demo-itis. I was terrible in recording studios. I'd write a song and have a vision of it, but my ears never heard in the final version what I'd originally imagined.'

Having persuaded McCluskey that the new version of 'Messages' passed muster, OMD signed off on the recording and DinDisc launched a promotional campaign around the single. *Smash Hits* were immediately enthusiastic and their reviewer – allegedly one Mrs Esmé Sprigg of Hounslow – commended the release as 'haunting stuff' and praised its 'gentle touch and masterly restraint', 'plaintive vocal' and 'interlocking melodic ideas', ending the review, 'While all the competition are slapping poster paint everywhere, OMITD work with watercolours. More power to them.'

'Messages' was released on May 2nd, 1980, two weeks after the band performed the track live, alongside 'Dancing' from *Orchestral Manoeuvres In The Dark*, on *The Old Grey Whistle Test*. Appearing on the same show was the American rock act ZZ Top who subsequently became fans of Humphreys and McCluskey, and of electronic pop in general, to the extent that they went on to play the *Orchestral Manoeuvres In The Dark* album over the PA before taking the stage at their own concerts, on their way to adopting some of those electronic influences into their own music, and later admitting to having even copied Andy McCluskey's distinctive dancing style.

The *Old Grey Whistle Test* performance, combined with the support of the OMD fanbase, some early reviews, and tentative support from daytime radio was enough to place 'Messages' at number fifty-three in the UK singles chart after just one week of sales, enough to convince *Top of the Pops* to offer the band a last-minute opportunity to take the same 'Bubbling Under' slot that had so effectively launched Gary Numan the previous year. 'That was an amazing feeling doing *Top of the Pops*, a show we'd watched as kids,' Paul Humphreys said in *Pretending to See the Future*. 'To actually stand on that stage, we were absolutely terrified. But we did it and that was such a milestone.' *Top of the Pops* worked its magic and 'Messages' started an ascent of the charts which would see the single peak at number thirteen while enjoying an eleven-week chart run, assisted by a second *Top of the Pops* appearance two weeks later.

Also making their *Top of the Pops* debut on May 8th were The Human League who, similarly to OMD, had been hovering tantalisingly outside the UK Top 40 with their *Holiday '80* EP, a seven-inch double pack featuring four tracks across the two singles and advertised as being limited to a run of just 10,000 copies. Released on April 16th, and intended to pave the way for the release of The Human League's second album, *Travelogue*, *Holiday '80* was greeted with unusual enthusiasm in some quarters of the press. *Smash Hits* declared The Human League 'the band who, along with OMITD, seem to be able to use synthesisers without getting used by them', although the declaration may have lost some credibility in being credited to 'A Small Creature (In Shorts)'. Meanwhile *Sounds* were in raptures about the EP, trumpeting, 'The finest electronic band of all time finally release the goods. A double single that clearly defines all four angles of synthesised madness,' and making the recommendation 'To be taken in large doses. To be played to life.'

Despite preceding the release of The Human League's second album by just a few weeks, *Holiday '80* is a curious release in that of all the tracks it contains only one appears on the *Travelogue* album, and that track, 'Being Boiled', is itself a rerecorded version of The Human League's 1978 debut single. Of the other tracks the 'Rock'N'Roll' and 'Nightclubbing' medley consisted of cover versions of those songs – originally recorded by Gary Glitter and Iggy Pop, respectively – lifted from The Human League's live set, and 'Dancevision' was originally recorded by Martyn Ware and Ian Marsh's The Future in 1977, before The Human League had even formed.

It was a bold move, and one which ultimately failed to pay off. The Human League now found themselves playing catch-up to artists like Gary Numan, John Foxx and OMD, a fact which didn't go unnoticed in *Sounds' Holiday '80* review: 'Eighteen months ago The Human League stood on the brink of altering the course of British pop music. Their humour and conviction combined to create an aura of (until then) unknown commercial excitement… Had the Sheffield funsters swallowed their hip pride and attacked the singles charts, they would have created a devastating impact on the British pop music(k) scene.'

Having made the promising leap to fifty-six from *Holiday '80*'s debut UK singles chart position of seventy-two, The Human League were duly invited to appear on *Top of the Pops*, but the choice of track they would perform was not so straightforward. Despite the band's intention that 'Marianne' was the lead track on the *Holiday '80* EP, Virgin Records had other ideas, and The Human League were persuaded to perform 'Rock'N'Roll' instead. 'The label just didn't "get" 'Marianne',' Martyn Ware sighs, looking back at the release today. To add insult to injury Virgin then scaled the double-pack *Holiday '80* EP down to a regular single-disc seven-inch single which dropped 'Marianne' and 'Nightclubbing' from the tracklisting entirely, and resequenced the songs so that 'Rock'N'Roll' became the new A-side.

On the day of the *Top of the Pops* recording The Human League delivered an eccentric performance which alternately focused on a made-up Phil Oakley, demure and static, and a bearded Martyn Ware, excitable and animated, while Adrian Wright abandoned his usual slides and films in favour of a synthesiser. In the usual way of things a band with a *Top of the Pops* performance under their belt would expect their single to shoot up the charts the following week, but The Human League once again flew in the face of fashion and their appearance lost them eight places, *Holiday '80* dropping to number sixty-four, rallying briefly the following week before vanishing from the charts.

Alongside The Human League and OMD on that same episode of *Top of the Pops* was Irish singer Johnny Logan, whose ballad 'Just Another Year' was sitting at number two in the Top 40 on its way to topping the UK singles chart the following week. Although Logan contributed little to the story of electronic pop, 'Just Another Year' had recently won the Eurovision Song Contest, which had recently taken place in The Hague. If things had gone very differently at the competition then it's entirely possible that Belgian act Telex might have graced the *Top of the Pops* stage alongside their Sheffield and Liverpool peers instead.

Sneaking their eccentric version of electronica into the mainstream consciousness, Telex had been picked to represent Belgium in the 1980 Eurovision Song Contest, an event which broadcast to an estimated live television audience of around half a billion people across Europe. It would be fair to say that Telex were an interesting choice to participate in the show, but their record label believed that the band's quirky electronic pop might have a genuine chance of success. 'At first we thought it was a stupid idea. Not our type of music, nor our audience, and we didn't really want to show ourselves on TV, thinking that it was the music that was more important,' the band's Michel Moers told *Electronic Sound* in 2019. However after some consideration the trio began to see the artistic merits in taking part and revised their position on the contest: 'We thought it would be interesting to go,' Moers admitted. 'After all we were making "pop music" and Eurovision was the epitome of that, plus subverting clichés was something we enjoyed.' The band's participation came with one caveat, however: 'We thought the only meaningful result was to come first… or last.'

With victory, or defeat, in their sights, Telex set about crafting their entry for the show, a song they cunningly entitled 'Euro-Vision'. 'The song was a kind of "international situationist" I suppose. Putting a little worm in an apple. It was about this glittering contest taking place in old Europe, opening borders virtually, if only for a few hours,' Moers explained to *Electronic Sound*, adding with satisfaction that Telex had deliberately included 'a few Eurovision clichés' in their composition, among them a few notes of the Eurovision Song Contest's own theme music, which appeared at the end of the track. 'A mixture of Kraftwerk robotics, Human League vigorousness, maybe a soupcon [sic] of Yellow Magic, topped with smooth vocals/vocodings reminiscent of Serge Gainsbourg,' was Betty Page's analysis of the single in *Sounds*.

Spectacularly failing in their attempt to subvert the Eurovision Song Contest from the inside by winning the competition, Telex also conspicuously failed to come last. On the night 'Euro-Vision' scored a total of fourteen points – including a resounding ten points awarded by Portugal – which saw Telex finish seventeenth of the nineteen participating acts. 'My favourite memory was speaking to the eventual winner Johnny Logan backstage before the show,' Michel Moers told *Electronic Sound*. 'I told him he was going to win. He said, "Well, if I win it's good for me, but if you win, it's good for music!"'

By June 1980, with OMD having completed touring and promotional duties for *Orchestral Manoeuvres In The Dark*, DinDisc, keen to maintain the momentum the band had built over the course of the year, sent the duo to start work on their second album. Arriving back at The Gramophone Suite less than a year after recording their eponymous debut, Andy McCluskey and Paul Humphreys found themselves with just one new song, 'Enola Gay', a track which had been written too late to be included on *Orchestral Manoeuvres In The Dark*, but early enough to have already been performed on OMD's recent tour. Tackling the situation head on, over the course of June and July 1980 Humphreys and McCluskey wrote an entire album's worth of material which DinDisc decided to release before the end of the year.

Chosen as the first single from the new album, 'Enola Gay' was the cause of some considerable disquiet within the band, and had been for some time. 'Paul and myself are starting to form different ideas as to what we want,' Andy McCluskey had told *Record Mirror*'s Chris Westwood in April. 'I know we've had a lot of altercations lately about this song 'Enola Gay'.' Written by McCluskey, working on his own, 'Enola Gay' was summarily dismissed as 'pop-crap' by OMD manager Paul Collister. 'That was the first time I think there'd been a real split in the camp,' McCluskey confessed in *Pretending to See the Future*. 'For Paul, it was an adopted song. It wasn't really his baby. And Paul Collister thought it was absolute cheesy shite. The two Pauls were saying, "We don't want that. That's not cool. That's pop rubbish. Forget it being a single. We don't even want it on the album."' Nevertheless DinDisc were delighted with 'Enola Gay', the label viewing the song as evidence of the essential contradiction at the heart of OMD: 'They could never decide between credibility and commerciality,' label head Carol Wilson would say a few years later. 'We always said they didn't know whether they wanted to be Joy Division or ABBA!'

In an interview for *Sounds* after the release of the single, writer Dave McCullough described 'Enola Gay''s pop sensibilities as 'a form of gentle subversion' and was interested in exploring the overlap of pop and credibility in OMD's work. 'Tony Wilson of Factory said to us after we'd done 'Electricity', "Give up your day jobs and go out there and make hit singles,"' McCluskey told the writer, before admitting, 'We didn't believe him at the time… We know also that we have a depth to our music,' the singer continued, 'but it's a different depth than Joy Division.'

'Enola Gay' presented a further challenge in its choice of subject matter. The song was named after the plane which dropped the atomic bomb on Hiroshima during the Second World War in 1945, McCluskey having become interested in the subject after coming across a reference to the plane while researching Messerschmitt fighters for the song 'The Messerschmitt Twins', which had appeared on the first OMD album. In the same *Sounds* interview Dave McCullough also dug a little deeper into McCluskey's defence of 'Enola Gay': 'I think it works in the end because it's perverse. It's a disgusting theme in a jolly little pop tune, one for the housewives to do the washing up to,' the singer explained. 'And that is a parallel to what actually happened with the bomb. This guy who dropped it named it after his mum. If anyone tells me that single is perverse, then that's my answer: compare our little record with that disgusting event.'

Released in September 1980 as the first single from OMD's second album, *Organisation*, 'Enola Gay' was met with mixed reviews. Unaware of the internal struggles OMD were facing, *Melody Maker*'s Allan Jones was extremely positive, noting that 'Orchestral Manoeuvres stride forward with confidence and a sure sense of their own identity.' The *NME* praised the single's 'glorious melody' but, apparently forgetting that the latter had reached number thirteen on the UK singles chart, gloomily predicted that the release 'seems destined to follow 'Red Frame White Light' and 'Messages' into chart oblivion', and awarded the single just four out of ten.

'Enola Gay' entered the UK singles chart at fifty-nine a week after release, and the following week it broke into the Top 40 where its number thirty-five position was enough to secure OMD another *Top of the Pops* appearance, which also showcased a change in the the way the band presented themselves. Gone was McCluskey's unfashionable explosion of hair, and the band's vaguely eccentric and mismatched clothes had been replaced by matching shirts and ties and the kind of casual knitwear, in a palate of understated but coordinated greys and whites, that was ubiquitous at the time.

Despite being banned from the influential BBC Saturday morning TV show for children *Multi-Coloured Swap Shop* over suspicions that the word 'Gay' in the single's title might be a reference to homosexuality, *Top of the Pops* alone was sufficient to propel the single to eighteen the following week, and then to twelve, at which point a repeat of the *Top of the Pops* performance, plus the release of the *Organisation* album, put it into the Top 10, where it sat for a month, peaking at number eight as part of a fifteen-week chart run that would see the single still clinging to the Top 75 at the start of January 1981.

Although McCluskey and Humphreys had already recorded initial versions of most of the material that would appear on their second album at The Gramophone Suite – this time with minimal input from Paul Collister, whose relationship with the band was starting to fracture under the weight of their success – most of the tracks that would make it onto the album were subsequently remade from scratch over a four-week session at Ridge Farm Studios in Dorking where, encouraged by his work on the 'Enola Gay' single, the band had reunited with producer Mike Howlett. 'We wanted to try working with another producer and engineer,' Paul Humphreys told *Record Mirror* after the release of the album. 'You lose perspective producing yourself, and this has given us a more professional sound.'

As they headed into the *Organisation* project, the band's intention was to try and escape from the upbeat electronic pop of the *Orchestral Manoeuvres In The Dark* album and instead explore some of the more experimental areas that were currently holding their interest. 'We're getting really primitive. Buzzes and wails drifting on, going back to our earlier days,' Andy McCluskey told *Record Mirror* after the release of *Organisation*, explaining that he and Humphreys had grown tired of the lightness and melody of their debut which they now considered was 'not really the thing for the eighties'.

Nevertheless the band's work on *Organisation* paid off and the album was well received by OMD's growing band of media supporters following its release in October. Dave McCullough, on hand to review the album for *Sounds*, wrote, 'OMITD are warmer than your so-called "warm" bands, your Springsteens and your Parkers could ever be. They reflect the young horror of where and how we live but, in their songs at least, they face the problems with an irrepressible intuitive sense that makes the best pop of any time.' *Melody Maker*'s Lynden Barber was similarly impressed: 'With their second album, OMD have produced not so much a collection of songs as a pervading mood, a feeling of restfulness spiked by an unsettling edge that never allows the music to descend into complacency.'

Awarding *Organisation* just five stars out of a possible ten, *Smash Hits* came out firmly in favour of OMD's pop sensibilities. 'If only this twosome would cease clinging to the idea of being a serious "experimental" band and go all out for the shameless synth-pop single, then at least we'd be spared these endless retreads of a rather limiting format,' Mark Ellen grumbled. 'They haven't the substance to sound convincing when attempting to be anything but clever and superficial.'

To illustrate how far OMD's fortunes had risen over the course of 1980, their tour in support of *Organisation* started in November at a sold-out Friars club in Aylesbury, a little over a year since the band had supported Gary Numan at a similarly sold-out gig at the same venue in 1979. Joining McCluskey and Humphreys on the road for the Scottish leg of the tour for an *NME* feature, journalist Paul Morley was impressed by the band's transition to bigger venues for the *Organisation* tour. 'Their show is unexpectedly spectacular, even disturbingly grand. It commands,' he declared. Further illustrating how far OMD had developed in a very short time Morley also noted with surprise that 'Their audience is, surprisingly, teen orientated and predominantly female,' and reported marathon autograph signing sessions at the stage door after each show, which made him marvel, 'For a group with minimum obvious visual sparkle, who not long ago looked so drab, their impact now is fantastic.'

In exploring OMD's unexpected transition further, Morley also touched on the same struggle between art and commerce that had dogged the band over the course of the *Organisation* project. 'Without even trying OMD have surged through into the mainstream,' Morley observed, contrasting the shift in tone and mood between *Orchestral Manoeuvres In The Dark* ('definite and dandy electro-pop') and *Organisation* ('more mood than melody'), and noting a similar shift in the band themselves: 'Within a year, OMD had glided from one extreme to another – and were uncomfortable with both.'

Following a similarly prodigious work ethic to that of OMD, Japan released their own second album of 1980, *Gentlemen Take Polaroids*, at the same time OMD released *Organisation*. Preceded by a single of the same name which had come out out in a double seven-inch package in October, the November album release found Japan newly invigorated having finally extricated themselves from their deal with Hansa and signed a new deal with Virgin Records. Neither the 'Gentlemen Take Polaroids' single or album was a hit, each spending just two weeks apiece in their respective charts, where the single peaked at sixty and the album at fifty-one.

Record Mirror were first to savage the single. Disregarding the lead track's title as awful, and treading familiar territory by rejecting 'Gentlemen Take Polaroids' as a 'mellifluously nondescript Roxy rip-off', the paper described the overall release as 'truly turgid and tasteful... ideal stuff for shampoo adverts'. *Smash Hits'* Steve Taylor took a similar, but significantly more positive, line when he described the 'attractively smooth and syrupy' single as an 'elegant retread of mid-period Roxy Music.'

Two weeks later Japan were on *Smash Hits'* cover with the same image that featured on the front of the album, a striking image of a beautifully lit and immaculately made-up David Sylvian sheltering under an umbrella, which was accompanied by a three-page feature, also penned by Taylor, in which the band discussed the genesis of the *Gentlemen Take Polaroids* album and the 'long legal tussle' which followed *Quiet Life* and which eventually allowed their transition from Ariola's Hansa label to 'the more commercially-orientated' Virgin Records. Taylor was also keen to discuss Japan's image and made much of their use of make-up, despite the topic being summarily dismissed as inconsequential by the band themselves, keen to use the opportunity to discuss the new project instead. 'It's part of everyday life, an individual way of looking. You'd put it on every morning whether you were going out or not,' Mick Karn dismissed airily.

The band's working process on *Gentlemen Take Polaroids* drew a lot from their experience of making *Quiet Life*, as Richard Barbieri would tell *Electronic Sound* later: 'The *Gentlemen Take Polaroids* album is an extension of *Quiet Life* really. With *Quiet Life* we'd found a way of doing things and a producer we liked working with, so *Polaroids* was about perfecting a new style we'd developed.' As with *Quiet Life* most of the songs on *Gentlemen Take Polaroids* were born out of rudimentary ideas which David Sylvian took to the band's rehearsal room and which the band developed together until there was enough material arranged to justify taking the finished songs into the studio to be recorded. 'I'm like the catalyst which sparks off inspiration in the rest of the band, but I'm a terrible musician so we really need each other,' explained Sylvian.

Although the making of *Gentlemen Take Polaroids* was generally an enjoyable experience for Japan, David Sylvian's increasing need to be in control was starting to put a strain on some of the relationships within the group. 'I tend to be too much of a perfectionist,' Sylvian would later admit. 'It caused a lot of problems in the studio.' Returning to the question of tensions during the *Gentlemen Take Polaroids* sessions in January 1981 in an interview for the Japanese magazine *Music Life*, Sylvian was sombre: 'We're coming to a turning point and as far as I'm concerned, a dramatic change has already happened to me. I think a similar thing might have happened to the other members too, or it'll happen to them in the future.'

While Sylvian's relationship with Mick Karn was a particular area of friction, Rob Dean found himself in the unenviable position of having his role increasingly marginalised within the band. In an echo of the way Ultravox's increasing electronic leanings had seen them dispense with Stevie Shears' punk-influenced guitar in 1978, Japan now appeared to be treading a similar path. 'The band was moving more towards electronic music, with YMO, Eno and Kraftwerk being the strongest influences,' Dean would tell *Classic Pop* magazine later. 'And a distorted guitar started to feel more intrusive than complementary.'

'If Brian Eno rather than Bryan Ferry had rerouted the original direction of Roxy Music, this might well have been the result,' was Steve Taylor's take on the *Gentlemen Take Polaroids* album in *Smash Hits* in October. *Record Mirror* awarded the album two-and-a-half stars out of five and fell back on the all too familiar theme of Japan's apparent debt to previous acts: 'This record should appeal to 'Generation Game' lovers. Only instead of trying to recall what rubbish went past on the conveyor belt, it's a case of memorising how many other artists you thought they were listening to.' In addition, reviewer Mike Nicholls found the record lacking in comparison with its predecessor: ''Quiet Life' might have been similarly derivative, but it was at least substantial and an adventurous departure. This is just a patch-work quilt of half-digested influences that will do nothing to solve the group's dilettante image problem.'

Mike Nicholls would also be sent to review Japan's November 27th concert at London's Lyceum, the band's final show of 1980, and revised his opinion of the new material based on their live performance, writing, 'On stage none of the influences are nearly so apparent, the superb rhythms fusing with Richard Barbieri's improving synthesiser to produce some of the most insidious dance music imaginable.' Nicholls also reassessed the popular view of Japan by ending his review on an unusually encouraging note: 'It was an unimpeachable show, Japan confirming that they aren't just a bunch of pretty faces and shameless plagiarists but a group of talented, maturing musicians who wed dance to romance in the most stylish way.'

ISSN 0144-5804

RECORD MIRROR

BRAVE NEW FACE

STEVE STRANGE
SPANDAU BALLET
SHOCK
NAKED LUNCH
SOFT CELL

WIN COPIES OF ROCKSTARS UNDERPANTS

1980.2 Blitz / Mick Jagger / David Bowie / Musicians' Union / The Face / i-D / Blitz (Magazine) / The Gentry / Spandau Ballet / Visage / Ultravox

AS THE BLITZ BECAME increasingly well known, it also became increasingly busy, attracting the attention of several generations of London's glitterati desperate to check out the latest sensation. In addition to the new generation of clubbers, Molly Parkin, Peter York, Zandra Rhodes and Andrew Logan were all regulars and through them key members of Steve Strange's entourage were welcomed into more exclusive echelons of London nightlife, where they lived off canapes and champagne as they were paraded from soiree to soiree.

A high public profile, however, wasn't enough on its own to secure entrance to this increasingly exclusive world, and undoubtedly one of the key events cementing the Blitz's reputation was a night in 1980 when Mick Jagger, reportedly rather the worse for wear after a night out drinking, arrived at the club and demanded admission. Whether he ever actually uttered the words 'Don't you know who I am?' or not remains apocryphal, but the fact remained that he wasn't allowed in and the subsequent altercation was witnessed by a journalist from *The Mirror*, who gleefully reported the story in his paper two days later. The real story – that Blitz was under threat of closure by the authorities for being too full that night, and that Strange simply couldn't allow anyone else inside, whoever they were – is more prosaic and less glamorous, but either way the headline merely added fuel to an already burning fire.

While Mick Jagger's presence, or otherwise, went unnoticed by the majority of the Blitz regulars, it would be another matter entirely when the club was visited by another of rock's elder statesmen, David Bowie, the star whose picture had adorned the bedroom wall of almost everyone in the room and certainly the one person who could claim the most influence on this emerging new generation. Despite his having been smuggled into Blitz, news of Bowie's presence quickly spread. The exact details of his visit vary depending on who's telling the story, but one thing that everyone agrees upon was the impact Bowie's presence had on the club.

'He was probably the reason most people at the club had got into pop music in the first place,' Steve Strange wrote of David Bowie in his memoir *Blitzed!*, noting Bowie's direct impact on the styling of the Blitz regulars themselves: 'He had changed his look and his sound so many times, there were more than enough images to go round.' 'It was different when Bowie arrived. Bowie melted the cool at the Blitz just by coming in the door,' Midge Ure recalled in *If I Was*. 'I was standing at the bar and all of a sudden there was this huge buzz; all the cool people were just flapping about, bitching and bickering as to who could sit next to him. The Emperor, the king of cool, walked in and everybody realised they were not wearing any clothes.'

'It was very odd going down to the Blitz club and seeing all these kids who had grown up with me, who were dressing like me, trying to make records like me!' Bowie told Dylan Jones later. 'Which is why I wanted some of them in the video for 'Ashes To Ashes'.' Before leaving the club and heading back into the night, Bowie recruited Steve Strange, plus a further three members of that evening's clubbing elite – Judi Frankland (who had designed and made her own ecclesiastically-inspired outfit, as well as the black wedding dress sported by Strange), Darla Jane Gilroy (in a similarly ecclesiastical black velvet outfit and hat) and Elise Brazier (dressed as a ballet dancer) – to appear in the video for his new single. The Blitz contingent were instructed to be dressed in their clubbing outfits, and to be waiting outside the Hilton hotel in London at 6.30 a.m. the following Thursday morning, when they were transported by coach to Pett Level, a beach near Hastings in East Sussex, where the video shoot for 'Ashes To Ashes' was to take place.

In their 1983 book *Who's Who in Rock Video*, MTV were right to applaud the 'trailblazing' video for 'Ashes To Ashes' – which, as he was at pains to point out to the *NME*'s Angus MacKinnon in September, Bowie had conceived and directed himself: 'this one I storyboarded myself, actually drew it frame for frame' – and praised the video for its 'innovative editing techniques and surreal images'. By September, however, Bowie was less sure of his creation: 'There're an awful lot of clichéd things in the video but I think I put them together in such a way that the whole thing isn't clichéd... some feeling of nostalgia for a future,' he mused in his interview with MacKinnon. 'I've always been hung up on that; it creeps into everything I do, however far away I try to get from it. It does recur and it's something I have to admit to and I can't... and that's obviously part of what I'm all about as an artist.' In *Strange Fascination*, writer David Buckley sums this up perfectly: 'One reviewer would later comment that on *Scary Monsters* David Bowie "ate his young". By jumping on a bandwagon full of Bowie clones (if only for one video) he was copying a copy (new romanticism) of a fabrication (glam rock, Ziggy) of the real David Jones.'

Upon 'Ashes To Ashes''s release in August *Record Mirror* delivered a damning verdict which concentrated more on the variety of available formats than it did on Bowie's latest musical turn. 'Should you be moderately interested, our Dave is doing slightly different things with a silver slipper on three slightly different sleeves. Inside you get four sheets of stamps with textured Bowie art work splattered all over their pointless fronts. All very dull really,' yawned Ronnie Gurr while summarily rejecting the single as 'Tosh.' Deanne Pearson reviewed the single for *Smash Hits* the following week, writing that despite being rather a strange choice for a single – 'It sounds like it's been lifted from the middle of an album, where it should have been left as it needs things around it' – there was much to admire in 'Ashes To Ashes'. 'An interesting collection of sounds rolled into a clean, fluid melody punctuated by a hollow echoey snare drumming and Bowie's beautiful voice just gliding and flowing and mixing with perfect skill and clarity... Not a hit,' she added confidently, 'but bodes well for his next album in September.'

In a stroke of luck for Bowie, 'Ashes To Ashes' was released on August 1st, 1980, the very same day on which a standoff between the Musicians' Union and the BBC came to an end. The dispute, which had been triggered by the BBC's decision to reduce the number of live musicians who played across their various orchestras, had led to the Musicians' Union's subsequent withdrawal of their members from all BBC recordings, which in turn meant that in common with all shows with a live music element, *Top of the Pops* had been off the air since the end of May. For an unprecedented nine weeks the *Top of the Pops* audience was forced to console itself with reruns of the BBC television comedy *Are You Being Served?* before *Top of the Pops* finally returned on August 7th. The music industry reacted to the strike with concern: 'Record sales, already in decline, have taken a further dive following the absence of

'Top of the Pops' from the nation's television screens,' reported *Sounds* at the end of June. 'No official figures have yet been compiled but Don McLean's Number One hit 'Crying' is estimated to be selling a quarter of the number of copies normally reckoned to be needed to top the charts.'

As *Top of the Pops* returned to British television screens, Bowie was in America, acting in the stage version of *The Elephant Man*, a commitment which ruled out any live UK television performances in support of the 'Ashes To Ashes' release. In the UK that meant *Top of the Pops*' airing of the video on August 14th was even more crucial to the success of the single. Although 'Ashes To Ashes' had entered the UK singles chart at number four after just one week on sale, the *Top of the Pops* exposure ensured that the single shot to the top of the UK singles charts the following week, earning Bowie his second-ever UK number one single, his first since a reissue of 'Space Oddity' had topped the chart in 1975, a satisfying symmetry given that 'Ashes To Ashes' was a continuation of the story of Major Tom, the astronaut Bowie had launched into space on the original release of 'Space Oddity' in 1969.

While the video was undoubtedly an important part of the artistic and promotional package around the release of 'Ashes To Ashes', it's arguable that it was even more important as a vehicle for presenting the new generation of musicians this story is about. Having appropriated the stylings of the Blitz and woven them into his own creative vision for 'Ashes To Ashes', Bowie managed to simultaneously present himself at the cutting edge of fashion while also standing to one side of the movement so as not to become tainted by the association. In *Strange Fascination*, David Buckley makes the succinct point, 'The video was also the first time that a mainstream pop audience had been confronted with new romanticism.'

It seems extraordinary now that, with the exception of Visage's 1979 single 'Tar' and Ultravox's 'Sleepwalk' in June 1980, Bowie had managed to completely steal the thunder of the entire emerging movement by sweeping in and appropriating the Blitz sound and aesthetic from under their very noses, and with four of their number willingly complicit in his cultural appropriation. But how did the new generation feel about Bowie's actions? 'He was the inspiration and it was his right to do that, he is and has always been the god,' Rusty Egan emphatically declared later. 'It was his right!'

Aired on *Top of the Pops* three times over the course of the single's initial chart run, the video provided excellent exposure not only for Bowie's new album, *Scary Monsters (And Super Creeps)*, but also for the stylings which showcased and legitimised the Blitz aesthetic during its furious journey from the underground into the public eye. 'That 'Ashes To Ashes' thing was all inspired by Blitz,' Steve Strange confided to *Sounds'* Betty Page during a Visage interview at the end of the year. 'It sounds immodest, but I know it's true, 'cause he's very clever, got a lot of suss.'

With a number one single for 'Ashes To Ashes' firmly tucked into the frilly pocket of his Pierrot suit, Bowie released *Scary Monsters (And Super Creeps)* on September 12th in a blaze of advertising courtesy of his label RCA, who accompanied their press for the album with the slightly defensive headline 'Often Copied, Never Equalled', a slogan widely thought to be aimed at Gary Numan, whose considerable success was thought by many to be a direct plagiarism of Bowie's various influences. The day after the album release the *NME* ran Bowie's interview with Angus MacKinnon, one of the very few the star had given in support of *Scary Monsters* – most of which were also opportunities to promote *The Elephant Man*, an important project for Bowie, who declared the production 'the first piece of legitimate acting I've ever done' – accompanied by an Anton Corbijn shot of a pensive Bowie on the cover.

In his interview Angus MacKinnon also took advantage of Bowie's candour to ask if the *Scary Monsters* track 'Teenage Wildlife' – popularly thought to be about Gary Numan – was written about anyone in particular? 'No, if I had my kind of mythical younger brother, I think it might have been addressed to him,' Bowie mused. 'It's for somebody who's not mentally armed. The shellshock of actually trying to assert yourself in society and your newly found values. I guess the younger brother is my adolescent self.' Bowie's response may have been a disappointment for Numan who, despite being wounded by the accusations that he had worn his influences too obviously, had never made a secret of his admiration for Bowie, and professed to being flattered to think that he was the subject of a Bowie song. 'I was quite proud about it at the time, to be honest,' Numan told David Buckley later. 'Even though I'd fallen out with him it still made me feel, Wahey! I'm in a Bowie song. That's cool.'

Interestingly, just two months after 'Ashes To Ashes', Bowie was already distancing himself from the Blitz, feigning disinterest in the scene in his interview with the *NME*: 'I was taken to one extraordinary place by... Steve Strange? God, what was it called? Everybody was in Victorian clothes. I suppose they were part of the new new wave or the permanent wave or whatever.' However, in the same interview, when asked how he felt about 'Gary Numan and John Foxx and all the other little Diamond Dog clones?' Bowie was more charitable: 'Foxx – I think he gives himself a wider berth; I think there's more diversity in what he does and could do. Numan? I really don't know. I think what he did – that element of 'Saviour Machine' – type things – I think he encapsulated that whole feeling excellently. He really did a good job on that kind of stereotype, but I think therein lies his own particular confinement. I don't know where he intends going or what he intends doing, but I think he has confined himself terrifically.'

In fact the suggestion that he was somehow responsible for a vapid wave of apparent imitators clung to Bowie, to the extent that he was still being questioned on the subject in 1983. In an interview for the official book to commemorate that year's *Serious Moonlight Tour*, Bowie responded to the question frankly, but wearily: 'I never, ever wanted to be regarded as the leader or the forefront of any movement. Ever. Never wanted it. I did want to be regarded as an individualist. But that's about it. And I never wanted to be trapped into a particular kind of music, or perceived as presenting a kind of music. That's why my music goes back and forwards, from rhythm and blues to tech-rock or whatever. Because I never wanted to be pinned down. I'm wary about this, because I am not the leader of any school of rock. I've always been an entertainer, but that's not a school, that's just a new way of doing songs.'

While *Scary Monsters (And Super Creeps)* was received with broad enthusiasm by most of the music press, Charles Shaar Murray, in a positive review for the *NME* – 'The album is harsh, strained, inelegant, cluttered, verbose, elliptical, yet Bowie communicates with an honesty and directness that suggests that an informed pessimism can be more inspiring – in real terms – than any obtuse optimistic fantasy' – took a moment to remind his readers that although Bowie did exert an enormous influence over the generation of artists coming of age at the start of the eighties, it shouldn't be forgotten that he also had form for absorbing his own influences in a similarly public way. 'His snapshots are taken from angles sufficiently unlike those selected by others to enable him to use the devices they pioneered without plagiarising their work,' mused Shaar Murray, 'and he leaves enough debris in his wake for younger artists to make their names by tidying up after him.'

While the reviews of *Scary Monsters (And Super Creeps)* may have been shorter and less considered elsewhere, they were no less enthusiastic.

Record Mirror's Simon Ludgate went so far as to award *Scary Monsters* an unprecedented, and mathematically challenging, seven stars out of five for its 'brilliant, innovative, visionary, articulate, eloquent, inconsistent, unpredictable, majestic, frigging genius'. *Smash Hits* kept within the bounds of traditional scoring, but David Hepworth nevertheless gave the album nine out of ten: 'Not just his most rounded effort since 'Station To Station', but possibly his most consistently effective long player of all since it doesn't get hung up on one musical style and encompasses most aspects of his talent. His melodic gifts are as much in evidence as his lyrical talents and the result is a fierce, imaginative piece of work that seems to speak more directly than any Bowie album in years. Complex, disturbing and streets ahead of the imitators.'

Scary Monsters (And Super Creeps) entered the UK albums chart at number one, retaining the top spot for a second week on its way to spending five weeks in the Top 10 and an impressive thirty-two weeks on the charts. The album's chart life was further boosted by a second single, 'Fashion', which was released in the last week of October, during which Bowie and his band recorded a video to accompany the single at New York City's new wave club, Hurrah. Revolving around a performance of the song from the club's tiny stage, the 'Fashion' video, which Bowie directed, was considerably less surreal than the one the same team delivered for 'Ashes To Ashes'. Nevertheless 'Fashion' did reprise some elements from 'Ashes To Ashes', including Bowie using the exaggerated bowing movement that Steve Strange had demonstrated on the beach at Pett Level, and the inclusion of a small cast of elaborately styled young people, presumably representatives from Manhattan's version of the Blitz scene.

Supported by no less than four successive showings on *Top of the Pops*, plus an initial week where Legs & Co. – the show's resident dance troupe at the time – performed a choreographed routine to the track, 'Fashion' was another huge success for Bowie and underlined his immediate ownership of the new decade. The single immediately entered the UK singles chart at number twenty in the first week of November and climbed slowly but steadily to a two-week peak position of number five at the start of December, remaining a chart fixture until well into the new year.

In his *NME* interview Angus MacKinnon had picked up on the reference to the Goon Squad in the lyrics for 'Fashion', and asked Bowie if the single was in fact about fascism, only to be told that it really was about fashion. 'I was trying to move on a little from that Ray Davies concept of determination and an unsureness about why one's doing it,' Bowie explained. 'But one has to do it, rather like one goes to the dentist and has the tooth drilled. I mean, you have to have it done, putting up with the fear and the aggravation. It's that kind of feeling about fashion, which seems to have in it now an element that's all too depressing.' Returning to the subject in an interview for *Rolling Stone* magazine in November, Bowie elaborated further, telling journalist Kurt Loder that 'Fashion' was 'about the sort of grim determination that's swept into modern "now" culture – the high-tech thing, which I think is a farce. Forget your high-tech. We're not gonna be prancin' around in silver suits or anything like that.'

Although his commercial reach was the most impressive, Bowie wasn't the only one to identify the spirit of something interesting emerging from the Blitz, and from similar clubs and underground scenes around the country. Before the end of 1980 no less than three different magazines would emerge, each a natural fit for this new audience, and each approaching the new movement from a slightly different perspective.

The Face was the brainchild of Nick Logan, who had been editor of the *NME* when the paper was selling around 250,000 copies a week at its early seventies peak, and who had gone on to create *Smash Hits*, which he also edited for the first year of the magazine's existence. Inspired by *Smash Hits*' use of glossy paper and colour printing, Logan set out to create a magazine which combined music with fashion, style, art and culture. 'The premise which made – and still makes – *The Face* unique was that youth and pop culture should be treated with the sort of reverence and critical intelligence that prior to May 1980 was almost exclusively associated with the highbrow,' wrote *The Face*'s Richard Benson in 1997.

The Face launched in spring 1980, perfectly in step with the Blitz crowd's transition to the mainstream, and perfectly placed to capture the colourful style-led movement which until then had been underrepresented in the traditional music press. 'This is *The Face*, issue numero uno, licensed to thrill. The first new rock magazine of the 1980s, and an independent at that. A totally new slant on the Modern Dance. Available monthly from all good newsagents, while stocks last,' frothed the introduction to the first issue. The magazine quickly fell into step with everything that was spinning out from the Blitz and the first few issues included pieces on The Human League, Ultravox, David Bowie, Bryan Ferry, Spandau Ballet and Steve Strange, as it eighteen months after it began, and while they would continue to run clubs, none could, or would, match the seismic impact of Blitz.

In the course of those eighteen months the duo, their club, and their peers had been instrumental in changing the face of popular culture in the United Kingdom and were in the process of spreading their influence around the globe. In the areas of fashion, media and graphics, but particularly in music – and Blitz still had one more musical trump card to play. In addition to Visage, who had released their debut single at the end of 1979, the club was also responsible for the launch of another band, then in the process of transitioning from their power-pop roots as The Gentry on the way to reinventing themselves as Spandau Ballet.

In direct response to the influence of the Blitz scene, in which they had immersed themselves, London band The Gentry purchased a Yamaha CS-10 synthesiser with the express intention of moving the band's sound away from what singer Tony Hadley described as 'high-energy, thrashing, catchy pop' towards a more sophisticated sound, which incorporated the electronic stylings and influence of Rusty Egan's Blitz playlist into their own music. 'These new songs would be to a disco beat; there would be a cull of all the old power pop stuff; our future sound had to be like the one we heard every Tuesday night,' wrote The Gentry's guitarist and songwriter Gary Kemp in his 2009 memoir, *I Know This Much*.

Rusty Egan's Blitz playlist had alerted The Gentry to the fact that there were other acts already operating in the same musical and creative space they had designs on, and the entire band were all too conscious of the fact that they needed to move fast in order to assure themselves a place on the frontline of the next cultural zeitgeist. 'If we were to attempt to be the band that represented this new cult, then we had to be absolutely ready,' wrote Gary Kemp of his band's preparations for this new journey.

Despite being key participants in the razzmatazz that was the Blitz, The Gentry were under no illusion that the insular scene – which they saw as an essential launching pad for their new band – would be easy to infiltrate if their ambition to present themselves as the movement's first new band was to succeed. Fortunately, manager Steve Dagger had a plan. 'Dagger knew that we couldn't play any of the regular venues – this crowd would never come – and in any case, in such intolerant times, the way we all looked was extremely dangerous,' acknowledged Gary Kemp. 'If this was to work, then we needed the approval of the cognoscenti, so a private show was how Dagger saw our reveal.'

New Order, 1989. © BOB BERG / GETTY IMAGES

Nine Inch Nails, 2013. © TIM MOSENFELDER / GETTY IMAGES

Spandau Ballet, 1980. © FG/BAUER-GRIFFIN / GETTY IMAGES

Orbital, 2017. © MIRRORPIX

Soft Cell, 1981. © FIN COSTELLO / GETTY IMAGES

Japan, 1981. © KOH HASEBE / SHINKO MUSIC / GETTY IMAGES

Ultravox, 1977. © ESTATE OF KEITH MORRIS / GETTY IMAGES

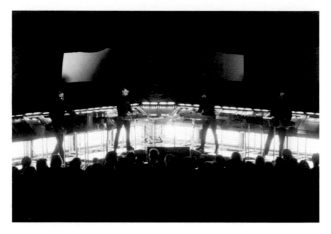

Kraftwerk, 1981.

Erasure, 1990.

The Human League, 1981. © PETE STILL / GETTY IMAGES

Depeche Mode, 1986. © ULLSTEIN BILD / GETTY IMAGES

Orchestral Manoeuvres in the Dark, 1983. © ULLSTEIN BILD / GETTY IMAGES

Devo, 1979. © MICHAEL OCHS ARCHIVE / GETTY IMAGES

Eurythmics, 1983. © JOEL SELVIN / GETTY IMAGES

Duran Duran, 1983. © FIN COSTELLO / GETTY IMAGES

The Prodigy, 2008. © STEVE THORNE / GETTY IMAGES

Gary Numan, 1980. © PETER NOBLE / GETTY IMAGES

Pet Shop Boys, 1986. © ULLSTEIN BILD / GETTY IMAGES

In November 1979 The Gentry invited a select number of movers and shakers from the Blitz scene to their rehearsal room at Halligan's Band Centre on London's Holloway Road where the band played a forty-minute showcase – covers of Iggy Pop's 'Funtime' and John Barry's 'On Her Majesty's Secret Service' breaking up a set of new original material – including a synthesiser-led standout track, one of The Gentry's latest songs, 'To Cut A Long Story Short'. 'The set went down well,' frontman Tony Hadley would remember in his own memoir *To Cut A Long Story Short* in 2005. 'But you have to remember we were playing to people who prided themselves on being cool. While they were appreciative, they didn't exactly jump up and down.'

A better measure of the showcase's success came when band and audience decamped to the pub after the performance and The Gentry immediately received two offers to play their first live shows since their reinvention, the first of which was to be a live set at the Blitz Christmas party just a few weeks later. 'The people we invited were very hypercritical people. Critical of themselves and critical of the way they, and other people, dress,' Gary Kemp assured *Melody Maker*'s Steve Sutherland later. 'There's no way they were gonna say we were any good if we weren't.'

Rusty Egan was gratified to learn that the band had heeded his previous advice. 'I explained to Gary Kemp in the DJ booth that young people were into dancing but not disco,' Egan recalled later. 'I was playing The Human League every week so he knew that a guitar, bass and drum band sounded as relevant as The Beatles.' But there was more to the transition than just the music, and Egan was also impressed that the band had those bases covered too. 'All the fashion designers loved them and all the girls loved them too,' he added with approval.

While The Gentry's musical output and sartorial statement managed to pass muster with the assembled group of Blitz scene tastemakers, there was concern over the suitability of the name The Gentry for the next chapter in the band's history. It was a decision which sat easily with the band. 'I'm not sure where the name [The Gentry] came from in the first place,' Tony Hadley wrote in his memoir. 'We all seemed to hate it.' At the suggestion of their friend, aspiring journalist Robert Elms, recently returned from a trip to Germany, The Gentry changed their name to Spandau Ballet that same afternoon. 'He had seen it scrawled on the wall of a toilet in Berlin, and thought it had a ring to it,' recalled Hadley of their new name. 'It was preposterous but edgy; arty but aggressive; obscure but assured,' enthused

Gary Kemp later. 'It encapsulated all of the arch preciousness we aspired to and we immediately loved it.'

In much the same way as Joy Division and New Order, Spandau Ballet conspicuously failed to consider any unintentional political statements that their new name might make to the uninitiated. 'When Bob had suggested our name it never occurred to us that some might query its Germanic origin,' Gary Kemp clarified. 'It was only later that we learned Spandau was the town where the Nazi war criminal, Rudolph Hess, was imprisoned. Naively, to us it had just sounded exotic.' 'Spandau Ballet was just a name,' Tony Hadley shrugged. 'There were no sinister hidden meanings. We just happened to like the sound of it.' There was also a less serious consequence of the new name. In his 2000 memoir *True*, the band's bassist, Martin Kemp, remembered audience members arriving at Spandau Ballet shows expecting to see a German dance troupe. 'These people stood out a mile from the rest of the audience,' Kemp wrote. 'And watching their faces from the stage when we launched into the opening songs was hilarious.'

Potential political minefields aside, from the moment they accepted their new name Spandau Ballet were unshackled from their power-pop past and were now able to present themselves as a band with no history, a group entirely made in the moment and as modern as it was possible to be, all of which played into manager Steve Dagger's ambitions for his charges: 'I would have bet my house on this scene becoming culturally important, and in the context of that I wanted a band to go with it. I was absolutely convinced that in a year's time, the whole of London and the UK would be moving in that direction musically.'

'I remember the manager of Spandau Ballet being frightfully serious about all of this stuff. There was someone who didn't crack a smile,' writer and cultural commentator Peter York told Dylan Jones later, and when it came to Spandau Ballet, Steve Dagger was deadly serious. With the change of name and the change of sound, Dagger's plan was to position Spandau Ballet as trailblazers within the deliberately insular and exclusive scene that had sprung up around the Blitz, and while all five band members were already regular faces, the first real rung on the ladder of the band's ambitions had to be climbed on December 5th, 1979 when Spandau Ballet played their first ever public show at the Blitz Christmas party.

Although the band were already starting to attract record company interest they made it a policy not to court the music industry like other acts. 'If they wanted to see us, they had to tune in to what was happening on the club scene,' Tony Hadley explained with satisfaction. 'Even if they heard about a gig, there was no guarantee they'd get in. Most of the clubs operated a strict – and peculiar – dress code.', 'No demo tapes were sent out, and although our name was spreading quickly around town and beyond, very few people knew what we sounded like,' Gary Kemp added in *I Know This Much*. 'It made them want to hear us even more.'

Steered by Steve Dagger, Spandau Ballet continued to foster a live following within the exclusive circle of the Blitz scene, deliberately shying away from the traditional route of extensive touring in the hope of building a following and attracting the interest of a record label. Spandau Ballet were playing a different game, preferring to play a small number of highly focused one-off events in non-traditional venues. As was Dagger's intention, each show the band played added to the air of mystique and excitement that was starting to surround Spandau Ballet. 'Instead of begging A&R men and journalists to come down, we did the opposite, and were perversely thrilled by them not being allowed in,' Gary Kemp recalled with obvious satisfaction.

In March, Spandau Ballet hosted their own night at the Scala Cinema in London's Fitzrovia. 'The venue, better known for obscure art-house films than pop bands, suited us down to the ground. It was about as unconventional as we were… There was no support band, just some cult film with sub-titles,' is how Tony Hadley remembers that night. (Gary Kemp recollects two films – Luis Buñuel and Salvador Dalí's *L'Age d'Or* and *Un Chien Andalou* – being shown at the Scala in lieu of a traditional support act.) 'Instead of the Scala's usual crowd of earnest film buffs, were people from the Blitz. In their midst, doing their best to blend in, but not quite managing it, were those record company executives who'd managed to get hold of tickets.'

To further fuel the fire, the *NME* subsequently published a review of the show at the Scala, a less than objective review penned at Steve Dagger's behest by Robert Elms. 'Dagger had decided Bob should put his pen where his mouth was and fashion a review of the event,' Gary Kemp explained later. 'Dagger stood over Bob's shoulder, prodding, adding, deleting, until both were happy with it.' Steve Dagger and Robert Elms delivered the piece to the *NME* by hand: 'We said "You should print this. Your paper is shit; you don't know this is going on. There's this whole scene." And they did.'

The impact of the *NME* review, along with similarly enthusiastic pieces in *The Daily Star* and *Record Mirror*, brought Spandau Ballet to the attention of

London Weekend Television's *Twentieth Century Box*. Dedicated to reporting youth interest stories, *Twentieth Century Box* – whose theme music, John Foxx's '20th Century', was subsequently released on the B-side of Foxx's 'Burning Car' single in July – was the brainchild of producer Janet Street-Porter and featured a young Danny Baker as presenter. Steve Dagger remembers taking that initial call: 'He said, "We are London Weekend Television and we would like to make a documentary film about the band and the scene surrounding it and film your next performance."'

'Millions of people were told that we were the hottest, most exciting new musical property around,' marvelled the band's Martin Kemp in retrospect. Transmitted in black and white – 'Paradoxically, it made it all look a bit more expensive, masking our tawdry reality,' Gary Kemp remembers wryly – the portrait of five aspirational working-class boys from Islington with the ambition to rise to the peak of their game had an immediate effect. 'The Sunday it was screened on London Weekend Television, it antagonised many,' Kemp mused later. 'To mix popular art and the immodest desire for money and success was quite a subversive cocktail in a post-punk era.'

While Spandau Ballet's naked ambition might have been anathema for some, the band's appearance on *Twentieth Century Box* pushed the music industry into a frenzy and the telephone in Steve Dagger's parents' home in Holborn, which also served as Spandau Ballet's base of operations, went into meltdown as the band received overtures from a swathe of labels including EMI, Phonogram, Magnet and Arista. 'It was as if the heavens had opened up and it was raining record deals,' Martin Kemp marvelled in *True*, 'and we were soaking wet.'

On October 10th, 1980, Martin Kemp's nineteenth birthday, Spandau Ballet signed with Chrysalis Records, the label the band felt understood them, and the new cultural landscape they represented, best, and who were willing to meet the band's rigorous demands financially and creatively. 'The band secured an unprecedented package,' journalist David Johnson told Dylan Jones in *Sweet Dreams*, '14 per cent against the norm of 8 per cent; their own record label, Reformation, to manage publishing rights and merchandising; a promotional video and a twelve-inch club mix with each single, which were firsts for a British band.'

With the ink on the Chrysalis contract still drying the band wasted no time in recording their debut single. 'There was no huge fanfare,' Tony Hadley reported of the signing. 'We had a glass of champagne, posed for a few photographs, and left. As with most things, the reality rarely matches the expectation. That afternoon, I went into the studio and laid down the vocal for our first single, 'To Cut A Long Story Short'.'

When 'To Cut A Long Story Short' was released at the end of October, Peter Powell was an immediate convert and threw his support behind the single at Radio 1, and on the station's record review show, *Roundtable*, Roxy Music's Bryan Ferry gave the release his blessing, describing the song as smart and witty. At the same time the twelve-inch mix of the track hit the clubs, Spandau Ballet's insistence on releasing the format paying off in spades as the track made huge waves on dance floors around the country.

Record Mirror reviewed the single twice in their November 15th issue, once on the regular singles review page where Mark Cooper wrote, 'Their debut single features a cute synthesiser riff that pretends to be profound and is pure pop with a vocal that verges on the operatic,' before summing up 'To Cut A Long Story Short' as 'an ordinary short story trying to become a novel'. The issue's second review appeared on the page dedicated to reporting on the latest disco and dance releases, which must have been gratifying for the band, who had always maintained that they were making white European dance music, and simply reported the track's beats per minute (143) for DJs and described the single as 'Straightforward uncluttered "Covent Garden" electronic dance music.'

'We'll be keeping an eye on the progress of 'Cut A Long Story Short' to see if the record companies are correct in their belief that Spandau Ballet will be the trailblazers of a new kind of music and a whole visual style,' *Smash Hits* declared at the end of October. The magazine's staff were presumably impressed by the single's rapid trajectory up the UK singles chart because in December they published their first Spandau Ballet cover story, which reported that 'To Cut A Long Story Short' was 'sprinting up the thirty with hair-raising speed' while 'shifting up to 23,000 copies in a single day'.

In addition to the reviews of the single, the music press were falling over themselves to talk to Spandau Ballet and, between the release of 'To Cut A Long Story Short' and the end of the year, interview features appeared in all the major publications, an irony that wasn't lost on the *NME*'s Paul Rambali: 'Spandau Ballet didn't go begging at the door of the rock press; they didn't play the Marquee week in, week out; and because of that, the jealous, conservative rock establishment is deeply suspicious. It hasn't won our endorsement, they say, so it must be a hype. But if Malcolm McLaren was pulling the strings, they'd all be applauding!'

Rambali's refreshingly honest Spandau Ballet interview and feature appeared on November 11th and, in the absence of much music upon which to judge the band, revolved mostly around the band's style, the scene from which they came, and their aspirational working-class roots. 'None of them particularly likes rock music,' Rambali reported, 'which is why they didn't do any of the things a rock band is supposed to do. They're into dance music, parties and clothes, not especially in that order, and rock'n'roll in all its grey, earnest, high-handed importance hates them for it.' The interview ended on an optimistic note for the band, but less so for the music publications playing catch-up: 'Like Roxy Music before them, Spandau Ballet have come out of nowhere, fast. Right now, they're going somewhere even faster. What's more, they could seize the imagination of a lot of young kids who aren't all that interested in what the *NME* puts on its cover each week, because they're brash, loud, young and fun.'

'There are a lot of very confused opinions around about us at the moment, about what we sound like, because so few have actually seen us,' Gary Kemp told *Sounds'* Betty Page. 'It's not weird electronic music at all, it's dance music. In fact, there's only one synthesiser in it and it's not even dominant.' Interviewed for the feature alongside Kemp, Steve Dagger, the band's manager and unofficial sixth member, was equally quick to separate Spandau Ballet from the emerging wave of earnest new synthesiser acts: 'The synthesiser's used as an instrument, not a modus operandi; it's an easy instrument on all the disco stuff. It's just a question of using it imaginatively.'

Propelled by the onslaught of press and radio support, after just two weeks on sale 'To Cut A Long Story Short' entered the UK singles charts at number forty-three, high enough to qualify Spandau Ballet for the same 'Bubbling Under' position on *Top of the Pops* which had already won Gary Numan, Orchestral Manoeuvres In The Dark and The Human League their debut performances on the same show. 'That first appearance still ranks as one of my best memories,' Tony Hadley would write in his memoir in 2004. 'Appearing on the *Pops* was a dream come true. It was validation.'

As a result of the band's *Top of the Pops* appearance 'To Cut A Long Story Short' accelerated twenty-four places up the charts to number nineteen the following week before rising to number eleven, assisted by a repeat showing of their performance, before eventually peaking at an impressive number five.

Tony Hadley estimates that the single sold in the region of 400,000 copies. 'We had proved we could shift records in the kind of numbers no one had anticipated. For Chrysalis, it was a sign of things to come.'

Boosted by the success of Spandau Ballet and the increasing public interest in the Blitz scene, Polydor Records announced a reactivated Visage at the end of November 1980 with *Smash Hits* reporting: 'Visage, the brainchild of Steve Strange and featuring Midge Ure, Billy Currie, John McGeoch, Rusty Egan and Dave Formula release a single 'Fade To Grey' this week. There will be a limited edition released in a picture bag.' That 'Fade To Grey' was in fact the follow up to Visage's first single, 'Tar', a full year previously, wasn't lost on *Record Mirror* who, when reviewing the single the following week, mischievously reported, 'Not to be outdone by Spandau Ballet, here is the annual single from Visage.'

The long delay between the September 1979 release of 'Tar' on Genetic and the November 1980 release of 'Fade To Grey' on Polydor had been the source of much frustration for the collective of musicians who made up Visage. Problems with Genetic Records' parent label, Radar, had led to Genetic's collapse shortly after the release of 'Tar', by which time the band had at least come out of the experience with close to an album's worth of material recorded at Martin Rushent's studio. Arguably Rushent also came out of the situation well. Having built a state-of-the-art studio at his Berkshire home, the experience of working with Visage had opened his eyes to the new electronic scene, an area which would soon catch his full attention and imagination. 'It didn't look like anything more than a shed in a rather large garden,' Steve Strange wrote later. 'Yet some fabulous music came out of there, and not just ours.'

After the implosion of Genetic, Visage struggled to find a new label, an understandable but frustrating situation which Midge Ure would recall in *If I Was*, writing, 'I was really peeved when we couldn't get a record deal for Visage. For a year we had this finished record from the hottest club in the UK, and nobody was interested in releasing it.' Ure was nonetheless able to be objective enough to see that Visage was not an easy proposition to sell to labels: 'Not surprisingly people fought shy of the whole concept of Visage: they couldn't grasp the idea of an invisible group, a band that wasn't a band. Visage was seven people, five of whom were signed to other labels, fronted by a very strange gay guy.'

Billy Currie, in a space between Gary Numan and Ultravox projects, had taken advantage of his access to Genetic Studios to spend some time there with his Numan band colleagues Chris Payne and Cedric Sharpley to record a track the trio had been collaborating on during soundcheck across *The Touring Principle* shows. 'Toot City' was born from a chord progression which Chris Payne had conceived and which he'd been playing during soundchecks on the Gary Numan tour, and when drummer Cedric Sharpley added a simple drum riff one day it caught Currie's attention. The trio continued to work on the track over the course of the Gary Numan dates and Currie and Payne headed to Genetic the day after the end of the tour to record it.

Although they had approached the recording session with the vague idea of releasing 'Toot City' as a Billy Currie & Chris Payne collaboration, that release failed to materialise, perhaps because, as Currie would later remember, 'It had no lyrics, just me shouting 'Toot City' like a lunatic over the backing track.' Before putting the 'Toot City' recordings to one side, however, Currie played the track to Midge Ure. 'I'd always thought it was a fantastic bit of music,' Ure said later, recalling how, after Visage's Polydor deal was done, he had taken their self-titled album into Mayfair Studios to mix it and realised that *Visage* needed one more track: 'I asked Billy for his tape, I went home, sat up all night, came up with the top line and wrote the lyrics.' The track was retitled 'Fade To Grey', and Visage had the single they needed to relaunch themselves after the false start they'd had with 'Tar'.

Just a couple of months after his appearance in David Bowie's 'Ashes To Ashes' video, Steve Strange found himself in another studio filming the promo for 'Fade To Grey'. The resulting video, made by Godley & Creme, was sufficiently striking and innovative that it is still admired today. 'With the directors Kevin Godley and Lol Creme I came up with a storyline for the video in which make-up came to life and changed my body,' claimed Strange in *Blitzed!* 'My eyebrow turned into a snake, and my arms were painted like snakeskin. My arms went round a girl, played by my friend from Blitz, Princess Julia [Julia Fodor], making her arms become snakes. Then my arms became a snake, the snake bit me and I died and faded to grey.' 'It was incredibly cheap and groundbreaking at the same time,' Midge Ure recalled in his memoir in 2004. 'Godley & Creme did it for £1,500, most of which went on the makeup artists for Steve.' 'They're all our ideas,' Lol Creme told *Smash Hits* the following year. 'Which is why I was a bit hurt to hear Steve saying he was responsible for some of his videos, which just isn't true.'

The *Visage* album was launched, appropriately given Strange and Egan's standing in clubland, with a special party at London club The Venue. On

December 6th *Record Mirror* listed the 'beautiful people' among the attendees as including Steve Jones, Molly Parkin, Billy Idol, Tony James, Shock, Richard Strange, Hall & Oates and Cherry Vanilla, boosted by the extensive line-up of musicians and creatives behind the Visage project, all of whom were treated to the first public play of the *Visage* album. Spandau Ballet, whose 'To Cut A Long Story Short' single was at its UK singles chart peak of five the same week, were also in attendance. 'They nodded in encouragement, but you could sense the rivalry,' Steve Strange recalled later, adding, 'We had stolen the march on the rest of the New Romantic scene, getting our debut album out long before Spandau Ballet released theirs. There was always an element of friendly rivalry between us. We didn't mind the others doing well, as long as we did better.'

With the 'Fade To Grey' video complete and the album and the single released, Steve Strange was unleashed on the music press, and all the major publications printed interviews with the frontman before the end of the year, each of which drew heavily on the fashion aspects of the band rather than on their music. Betty Page's interview for *Sounds* was the first to appear, the issue, with Strange on the cover, hitting newsstands a few days before the album and single releases. The interview consisted of a potted history of the band and their aspirations for the future, and also allowed Strange his first opportunity to trot out some rather hackneyed soundbites which would continue to crop up in his interviews for the duration of the first album project, the first being the origin of the name Visage. 'The meaning of Visage, apart from being French for face, is that the Vis is for the visual side of the band, the Visa… well, although we can't tour at the moment, as it's impossible to get everyone together, we will do, and the Age is the new age in dance music,' Strange enthused. 'That's how I see it.'

That Visage shared the same Blitz club roots, audience and aesthetic as Spandau Ballet was also a frequent topic of conversation in those initial interviews. 'I don't mind being bracketed with the Ballet. They're my friends anyway,' Strange told Betty Page, and any similarities to the influence of Ultravox didn't go unnoticed: 'I know we sound a bit like Ultravox but we've got our own sound as well. The album was recorded around the same time as theirs, but there's obviously a Magazine influence too. Me, I'm a newcomer, I learnt a lot from recording this. Next album I'm going to get a lot more across, I'm going to change, move on from this; I've got ideas, different but still dance music.'

Despite their readiness to feature Visage in their publications the critical reaction to *Visage* from the mainstream music press was decidedly muted. 'Despite the illustrious cast of backing musicians,' wrote *Smash Hits'* Beverly Hillier, 'Steve Strange's debut album is a bit of a non-event. Their branch of "white disco", although technically competent, tends to be dull and uninspiring. They mimic the likes of Bowie, New Musik, M etc quite professionally but seem to lack any real identity of their own.' *Record Mirror*'s Mike Nicholls was more positive, noting the album's musical parallels – 'modern wallpaper muzak' – with Ultravox's *Vienna* and enthusing, 'This is a highly listenable album of quality background music and the fruit of a useful collaboration amongst talented like-minded musicians.'

Packaged in equally striking and stylish covers, 'Fade To Grey' and *Visage* were both released on November 10th. 'Fade To Grey' would be Visage's most successful single, not only scoring the band a Top 10 hit in the UK when it peaked at number eight in February 1981, part of a fifteen-week chart run, but also earning them number one singles in Germany and Switzerland as well as Top 5 singles in France, Belgium and Austria. The *Visage* album performed similarly well in Europe but failed to enter the Top 10 of the UK album chart, peaking number thirteen at the beginning of April 1981 during a sterling twenty-nine weeks in the album charts.

Although less obviously influenced by Rusty Egan's playlist, or by Steve Strange's sartorial inspiration, Ultravox's Midge Ure and Billy Currie, both of whom also had a foot in the Visage camp, were regulars at Blitz, and inevitably both elements filtered through to Ultravox's music and presentation.

Using a slightly different mix of the same recording of 'Sleepwalk' that the band had submitted to Chrysalis as their demo, and which had secured Ultravox their contract with the label, 'Sleepwalk' was released as a standard black vinyl seven-inch single and as a limited-edition transparent seven-inch single on June 16th, with a non-album track, 'Waiting', on the B-side. (Ultravox would go on to release further singles on transparent vinyl, a decision based not on aesthetics so much as for reasons of optimum sound quality, for the band had discovered that releasing a transparent record was a good way to ensure getting the best quality vinyl possible, because transparent vinyl wasn't going to be pulled from vinyl stocks that might include previously pressed records which had been returned and then melted down for reuse. 'I like to believe it really made some degree of difference to the listening quality of the records,' Warren Cann would tell Jonas Wårstad in 1997.) While the two tracks on

'Sleepwalk' signposted Ultravox's new musical direction, a reinvention of a different kind was evident in Peter Saville's sleek sleeve design, which saw the confrontational, glam-punk stylings of previous Ultravox releases replaced by a more sophisticated and streamlined aesthetic revolving around a moody black-and-white photograph of the new line-up.

The band's musical and stylistic reinvention worked. 'Ultravox return to vinyl after a long vacation, poppy side up, punching along an attractive mekkanik [sic] dance tune in infectious fashion,' enthused *Smash Hits* in their review of 'Sleepwalk'. 'It seems that when John Foxx departed he took the majority of the melodrama with him and left behind a leaner machine streamlined enough to get on the radio.' *Smash Hits*' prediction proved correct and 'Sleepwalk' provided Ultravox with their first-ever hit single, spending seven weeks in the UK Top 40 and peaking at number twenty-nine on two separate occasions, boosted by encouraging radio play and an August appearance on *Top of the Pops* alongside the premiere of David Bowie's 'Ashes To Ashes' video.

Recorded over the course of just ten days at RAK Studios in London, and mixed over a further two weeks at Conny Plank's studio outside Cologne in Germany, Ultravox's first album release following the departure of John Foxx came out while 'Sleepwalk' was peaking in the singles charts. According to Midge Ure, writing in his autobiography *If I Was*, the album was recorded as *Torque Point* – 'That was Billy's idea, because he didn't want to focus on any one track on the album' – but was subsequently retitled in response to enthusiasm for the album track of the same name, and was released as *Vienna* on July 16th, 1980.

The nine tracks that featured on *Vienna* generally emerged from extended jam sessions in Ultravox's rehearsal studio in King's Cross, sessions that the band recorded in order that they could listen back to the tapes later and pick out any elements they felt might be worth developing further. 'Our method of writing was a simple one,' Warren Cann told Jonas Wårstad. 'We would jam about with our collective ideas and throw things back and forth until something sparked. We'd take the idea, work on it, and polish into a song structure.'

Despite the arsenal of synthesisers evident during Ultravox's *Top of the Pops* performance of 'Sleepwalk', *Vienna* wasn't the electronic album that the single had led parts of the media to expect. Talking to *Sounds* for a cover feature in July, Billy Currie offered his own take on where the miscommunication had swiftly became the reading matter of choice for an emerging generation with a passion for fashion and style to match their appetite for the new electronic music emerging from Blitz and from similarly trailblazing scenes around the country.

By the autumn of 1980 a second publication had arrived to serve a similar audience. Embracing a different aesthetic to *The Face*'s sleek glossiness, *i-D* launched in September as little more than a fanzine; a handful of black-and-white A4 pages, printed landscape and roughly stapled beneath a stark red-and-black cover which featured nothing but the magazine's winking-face logo. *i-D* was the creation of Terry Jones, who had previously worked at *Vanity Fair* and then *Vogue*, but had left the latter after failing to persuade his colleagues to share his enthusiasm for punk, and the post-punk explosion of street styles. The magazine set out to celebrate ordinary people who were making individual fashion statements and the first few issues were dominated by photographs of punks, mods, post-punks, rockabillies, Blitz kids, retro style fetishists and anyone making an interesting fashion statement, among them Boy George, Rusty Egan, Steve Strange and Soft Cell, all of whom appeared in 'straight-up' photographs, designed to capture their entire look, across the first few issues alongside interviews with an equally diverse selection of up-and-coming musicians including Fad Gadget, Adam Ant, Spandau Ballet and Duran Duran.

A third publication, *Blitz*, debuted at the same time as *i-D*. Launched in Cambridge by Carey Labovitch, *Blitz* had no connection to Steve Strange and Rusty Egan's club of the same name: 'I had no idea about the Blitz club in London because I wasn't part of that,' Labovitch told Dylan Jones later. *Blitz* was ultimately interested in reflecting the post-punk culture the magazine had emerged into, and was most interested in seeing how punk's DIY inspiration had spilled into other walks of life and had precipitated similarly exciting revolutions in fashion, style and design as well as in music.

The cumulative effect of such mainstream exposure to their underground world put the Blitz club regulars in the surreal situation of watching Bowie, and this new section of the media, take their movement public, a transition they viewed with a mixture of pride and trepidation. Pride that their backstreet revolution had caught the imagination of their hero and subsequently the world; but trepidation that the tiny club was already starting to fracture under the weight of such mainstream attention. Steve Strange and Rusty Egan's residency at the Blitz came to an end in October 1980, just slightly over taken place: 'When Gary Numan said he'd been influenced so much by us, we got this reputation of being a synthesiser band, but we never were, totally. If you listen to our albums it's like a rock band, basically, with one or two totally synthesised tracks.' In her interview with the band for *Melody Maker* a few weeks later, writer Penny Kiley made a similar distinction when she described Ultravox as 'a rock band who happen to use synthesizers' and, not being a particular fan of electronic music herself, asked the band, 'Why do I hate synthesisers and not hate Ultravox?' 'We're a rock band,' Billy Currie explained. 'We use the technology but we don't let it push us around. We use whichever instrument we think is necessary to get the effect and sound that we want,' Midge Ure added. 'Whether it's a guitar, bagpipes, whatever, it doesn't matter as long as we get the desired effect.'

Equally, and contrary to various opinions in the media, Ultravox hadn't become the latest Midge Ure vanity project either. 'I didn't make it better, I didn't make it worse,' Ure clarified in *Classic Pop* later. 'It was simply different because I was now in the band.' The new Ultravox was a democracy in which all writing credits were divided between the four band members equally. 'There were no lines of demarcation,' Warren Cann explained later, looking back at those sessions after Ultravox reunited their *Vienna* line-up in 2009. 'Midge would suggest a drum part; I'd suggest a keyboard part and so on. That fluidity between the four of us was the first thing I remember about what a magnificent noise we were making.'

The change in personnel had shifted the band's post-Foxx dynamic for the better, something Midge Ure touched on in an interview with *The Face* in August: 'They just needed somebody to come in and give them a hand, give them a boost again, a kick up the backside. And that's what I think I've done.' 'I remember how focused we were,' Warren Cann recalled later. 'We were quite manic about it.'

Despite Ultravox's newly discovered democratic process Midge Ure was very much the focus of interest for the media. In a positive review of *Vienna* for *Smash Hits* in July, Steve Taylor wrote, 'The addition of talented Midge Ure, ex-Slik and ex-Rich Kid, has done these leading lights of electro-pop nothing but good.' But while Taylor awarded the album eight out of ten stars, and described *Vienna* as 'synthesiser music with backbone and muscle', some of his journalistic peers were less convinced by Ultravox's new direction, and the responsibility for that was also laid at Ure's feet. 'This album is polished and full of competent songs but it is still a big disappointment,' shrugged Philip

Hall in *Record Mirror*. 'With Midge Ure replacing John Foxx I expected to hear more variety from Ultravox. But 'Vienna' never equals the sparkling electronic heights reached by Numan and Foxx.'

In an overwhelmingly upbeat assessment of *Vienna* – 'Ultravox deserves success. This should do the trick' – Penny Kiley nevertheless cautioned her *Melody Maker* readers that for all that was positive about it, *Vienna* was a record that lacked frivolity. 'Electronic clichés are no worse than guitar clichés, but they're more likely to sound pompous,' she wrote. 'We're left in no doubt that this is the serious side of electronics.' In common with other reviewers Kiley also selected the title track 'Vienna' for special attention. 'A welcome change comes with the epic title track, which is varied in pace as well as instrumentation... real strings and lots of atmosphere,' she enthused, adding, 'Top marks for effort.' And even Philip Hall managed to find something to admire in the title track which he described as 'a little bit special'.

Ultravox knew 'Vienna' was special. In *If I Was* Midge Ure recalled the band's early affection for the song, to the extent that immediately after they recorded it they kept returning to it in the studio: 'We played it at the end of every day's recording because we all got this huge buzz hearing it. It was so unique with the big overblown powerful ending. It was everyone's favourite track.' In their hearts the band felt that 'Vienna' was a potential hit, but they also knew that it was an unconventional choice for a single and Chrysalis were, as yet, uncertain of its commercial possibilities. 'It was too slow, too long and there was a violin solo, the antithesis of a commercial single,' Ure acknowledged wryly.

Despite the lacklustre reactions to the album from the music press *Vienna* entered the UK album chart at number fourteen after just one week on sale and went on to spend eleven successive weeks in the charts, six of which were in the Top 20, making *Vienna* Ultravox's most successful album by some considerable margin. Encouraged by the chart success of the album, and of the 'Sleepwalk' single, Chrysalis selected 'Passing Strangers' as the second single from the album.

Following twenty-two dates across the UK in August in support of *Vienna*, Ultravox then took the tour to the USA, and 'Passing Strangers' was released in the UK in October to keep the album project active while the band was out of the country. Following the success of 'Sleepwalk', encouraged by sales of the album, and in the absence of the band's availability for promotion, Chrysalis decided to invest in a video to support 'Passing Strangers', and

Ultravox enlisted the help of up-and-coming director Russell Mulcahy to oversee filming.

Shot mostly in black and white, 'Passing Strangers' echoes the classic film noir aesthetic of the 'dead men's clothes' styling the band had recently adopted, and which featured across the single and album artwork created across the *Vienna* project. Mulcahy delivered a suitably melancholic video, set in and around a decaying warehouse, the shoot revolving around a couple dancing robotically before dramatically fleeing from a moodily-lit Ultravox, swathed in dry ice, who turned in deadpan vocal performances while casting dramatic shadows against the walls. In *If I Was*, Midge Ure remembered the video less for its retro-cinematic stylings than for everyone's disregard of health and safety protocols: 'On 'Passing Strangers' we managed to set fire to an extra's hair. We had painted a tree with petroleum jelly so that it would ignite properly and used a bit too much.'

Chrysalis released 'Passing Strangers' on October 15th, reprising the limited-edition transparent-vinyl seven-inch format that had worked so well with 'Sleepwalk'. *Record Mirror*, reviewing the single on September 27th, found that they were unable to even play the advance copy they had been sent. 'It's amazing that for a band with such hi-tech aspirations, the hole in the centre of their single is too small to straddle my humble hi-fi,' grumbled Mike Nicholls, who continued, 'Anyway, since it's from the flatulent 'Vienna', I can tell you it's typically soporific, superficial post-Foxx Vox, but with a hook melodic enough to combine with their image of accessible futurist chic to grant them minor hit status.'

Despite Chrysalis's investment in the video, and the addition of an extra twelve-inch single format, 'Passing Strangers' failed to live up to even Nicholls' gloomy prediction. Unable to engage the attention of radio, or catch the public ear in the way 'Sleepwalk' had previously, 'Passing Strangers' entered the UK singles chart at number sixty-six, after which it took a further fortnight to ascend to a chart peak of fifty-seven before dropping out of the charts after just a month.

Honed by a vigorous US tour in September, October and November, Ultravox were in fine shape when they returned to the UK live circuit in December to play nine further shows in support of *Vienna*, this time making the transition from the club-level venues they'd played in August to the significantly larger theatres, and finishing their 1980 with a triumphant show at London's Hammersmith Odeon. In fact such was the quality of the

Manchester show that even *Record Mirror*'s Mike Nicholls was moved enough to report, 'They're in control of what they're doing and are experimental without being unnecessarily esoteric. Ultravox will be heroes for more than one day. Their time has come.'

Gillian Gilbert (New Order), 1981.

1980.3 The Human League / Joy Division / The Independent Charts / Cabaret Voltaire / Deutsch Amerikanische Freundschaft / Silicon Teens / Fad Gadget / Gary Numan / Robert Palmer / Simple Minds

AT THE BEGINNING OF May 1980 *Smash Hits* announced that The Human League would be releasing their second album, *Travelogue*, on May 14th and, as an incentive to fans, the first 10,000 copies of the album would be available at a special price of £3.99 instead of the regular price of £5.25. *Travelogue* subsequently entered the UK album chart at its peak position of sixteen after just one week on sale. The album would spend a fortnight in the Top 40 as part of an initial nine-week residency in the Top 75.

Smash Hits' Red Starr was first to review *Travelogue* and scored the album eight out of ten, despite its 'Sluggish production and fussy over-arrangements', praising the 'accomplished all synthesiser line-up' for their strong tunes and excellent lyrics, and predicted a great future for The Human League. In a more detailed review for *Record Mirror*, Chris Westwood was less certain of the band's prospects and argued that The Human League had fallen into the trap of making 'an album The Human League would expect people to expect from The Human League', and had thus already missed the 'synth-as-pop' boat. 'When The Human League choose sterile, well-meaning blandness instead of instinctive spontaneous sounds, they sound very, very dull,' Westwood sighed. 'I don't want to turn The Human League off, I just wish they'd turn themselves on.'

Sounds' Dave McCullough was also gloomy in the face of *Travelogue*, awarding the album just three out of five stars, and opening his review with 'This is an irritating album. Mostly it's prostitutional, dreadful or averagely condescending.' McCullough struggled particularly with those tracks – The Human League's cover of Mick Ronson's 'Only After Dark', and 'Life Kills' in particular – which he felt were nothing but retreads of conventional rock, rather than the bold and revolutionary electronic statements he was expecting. 'They can't rock and roll and it's embarrassing hearing them trying to get down and boogie, like seeing a juggernaut walk a tightrope,' McCullough lamented.

The Human League headed out on a seventeen-date UK tour around the release of the new album, and the outing provided them with an opportunity to engage with the media. Given *Record Mirror*'s recent savaging of *Travelogue* at the hands of Chris Westwood, it must have come as a relief to the band when the paper instead dispatched writer Ronnie Gurr to attend the first two shows, in Portsmouth and Birmingham. 'The League are essential dance-mongers, an audio-visual delight, and pure zestful entertainment. Messrs Marsh, Oakey, Ware and Wright are intelligent pop perfectionists,' Gurr enthused. 'One day all pop bands will be made this way.'

The *NME*'s Charles Shaar Murray joined The Human League for their shows in Sheffield and Derby for a similar piece which would appear in July: 'In Sheffield Top Rank, a capacity audience welcomes them with that combination of warm encouragement and ferociously critical scrutiny which hallmarks the hometown audience.' Shaar Murray also attended the band's London show at the Hammersmith Palais, and was struck by the difference between each show's audience, describing the crowd in the capital as 'a legion of exquisitely detailed glamrockers of a demented dandyism', adding: 'Dotted hither and yon are youth units with the beginnings of Philip Oakey's haircut: cropped on one side, elegantly flowing on the other.'

Smash Hits' David Hepworth was impressed by The Human League's presentation on stage, and lauded Adrian Wright for his efforts. 'As the slides flit about on Adrian's four screens, you feel as if a hand had reached out of your TV to drag you through time. The world shoots by you in the shape of old movie stills: the entire plot of Hitchcock's *Psycho* in just four minutes, ancient telly adverts, characters from *Star Trek* and *Thunderbirds*, heroes and villains of world politics and various other less specific ideas.' But the band were also quick to acknowledge that Wright's visual spectacle played a further important role by taking the attention away from the rest of the group. 'It's different for other groups because at least they're leaping about. We're just not very moveable,' Ian Marsh explained to the *NME*, while Martyn Ware acknowledged the same in *Smash Hits*: 'Watching people play synthesisers on stage is not the most exciting thing in the world.' But the stage show didn't just mask the static nature of The Human League's performance, the need for visual distraction went deeper, for Oakey at least. 'If it weren't for the slides I wouldn't be on stage, I'd be embarrassed to death,' the singer admitted to *The Face* in August.

Throughout their on-the-road pieces the various journalists found The Human League bickering amiably and in good spirits, as noted by Shaar Murray in the *NME*: 'Their combination of the grandiose and the silly, the trivial and the significant, the trashy and the classic is as perverse and unusual as anything else in its immediate cultural vicinity. Their blending of childish glee and adult scepticism is alarmingly appealing.' In *Smash Hits* David Hepworth was equally charmed: 'They're also open, friendly and intelligent people with a good ear for an argument. No sooner will one of them have delivered you up a comprehensive, well thought out summary of their plans and aims than along comes another to stick his oar in and neatly contradict the lot.'

While *Record Mirror* ran their tour feature around the release of *Travelogue* in May, *Smash Hits* and the *NME* held theirs until July to coincide with The Human League's next release. In another decidedly eccentric choice of single, Virgin sidestepped the new album entirely in favour of reissuing 1979's 'Empire State Human' from the band's first album, *Reproduction*. As a concession to the new album, Virgin also announced that the first 15,000 singles were to be accompanied by a second seven-inch featuring two tracks from *Travelogue*, The Human League's cover of Mick Ronson's 'Only After Dark' on one side, and instrumental track 'Toyota City' on the other.

In June, prior to the release of the new 'Empire State Human' single, *Record Mirror* additionally reported that Virgin planned to follow that release with a further single from *Travelogue*, the band's favourite track from the album, 'Marianne'. In the event, a single release of 'Marianne' conspicuously failed to emerge; it seems likely that Virgin's announcement was merely an attempt to placate the four members of The Human League, who were reportedly less than happy with their label's release plan. In an interview for *Sounds* the following year Phil Oakey confirmed, 'We did a nice version of 'Marianne', much better than the *Holiday '80* one – I think it was great, one of the best things we've done, but they wouldn't put it out because they didn't like it.'

Reading between the lines it would appear that Virgin had decided to release 'Only After Dark' as the next single without consulting the band, who felt that following their cover of Gary Glitter's 'Rock'N'Roll' on *Holiday '80* with a Mick Ronson cover was a bad career move. 'If you make it on other people's songs you're not giving people good reason to want to listen to what you do,' Phil Oakey reasoned when Sheffield fanzine *NMX* asked about the band's cover versions. 'We never wanted 'Rock'N'Roll' to come out as a single off the double EP, although we agreed to it,' he added. 'After that we didn't want to release another cover version for a couple of records.'

The band's subsequent discovery that Virgin's plans were more advanced than they had originally thought – 'They'd already shrink-wrapped 'Only After Dark' with 'Empire State Human' without telling us,' Oakey told *NMX* – was the cause of 'a very big argument' between band and label which eventually resulted in a compromise of sorts. 'We knew it was going to be released,' Oakey continued, 'so we said, "We're not against re-releasing 'Empire State Human' so can't you make that the single to be pushed?" and they gave in to it.'

The shrink-wrapped double single, 'Empire State Human' and 'Only After Dark', was released in the middle of June to mixed reviews. Fresh from his on-the-road adventure with the band in May, *Smash Hits'* David Hepworth delivered a positive review which acknowledged the quirky choice of single but ultimately welcomed it, writing, 'The important thing is that 'Empire State Human' is probably the catchiest item in their rich repertoire, tailored almost along the lines of a crazed rugby song.' *Record Mirror*'s Chris Westwood, however, was less inclined to be as generous and, pulling no punches, described the release as 'dull', 'lazy' and 'utterly disposable'.

It probably came as no surprise that, despite coming after a successful album and tour, the idiosyncratic nature of the 'Empire State Human' single, and the associated confusion as to how the release related to the *Travelogue* project, ensured that although the single entered the UK singles chart at number sixty-two at the end of June, it fell one place the following week and subsequently dropped out of the chart, leaving the relationships within the band, and between band and label, tense at best.

Despite a news piece in *Record Mirror* in October stating that The Human League were 'holed up in their native Sheffield creating yet another musical

evocative and interesting taster for the band's forthcoming album, *Closer*, which was to follow in July.

Produced by Martin Hannett, *Closer* had been recorded at Pink Floyd's state-of-the-art Britannia Row Studios in London, Joy Division decamping to the capital for two weeks in March 1980. Despite their ongoing concerns over Ian Curtis's epilepsy, and the complications of the singer's domestic and romantic lives (having met London-based Belgian journalist Annik Honoré in 1979, by the time of the *Closer* recording sessions Ian Curtis was partially estranged from his wife Deborah, and he and Honoré used the downtime in the band's studio schedule to live together in the London flat the band had rented, and to deepen their relationship; it is sometimes alleged that Honoré was the inspiration for the lyrics of 'Love Will Tear Us Apart'), the time spent at Britannia Row was a happy period for the band, who enjoyed the trappings that came with working at the studios – 'I remember them bringing sandwiches in and tea and stuff like that,' Bernard Sumner told Jon Savage – and with being away from home. 'We felt like we were free down there,' Sumner added. 'We didn't have day jobs then, we had a couple of weeks to record it in, and we had fun down in London. We were going out to clubs and restaurants. Living together as a band was quite a lot of fun.'

Closer was released in July 1980 to overwhelmingly positive reviews from the UK media. 'Naturally, the events surrounding Curtis's strange and violent action of three months ago cling unavoidably around *Closer*,' wrote Paolo Hewitt in a considered review for the *NME*, highlighting that the album contained 'some of the most irresistible dance music we'll hear this year' and applauding Joy Division's increased reliance on synthesisers to create the album's moods of shadow and light. *The Face* were similarly moved by the band's increased use of electronics. 'Gone are the hard bass lines, the punchy disco drum beat,' wrote Mick Middlehurst for a retrospective feature on the band in November, 'replaced by an icy, sensitive, synthesizer and a general breaking down of the band's previously self-imposed boundaries.'

'When *Closer* came out we didn't promote it at all, didn't even read the reviews,' Peter Hook recalled in *Substance* later. 'Why bother? It was over and done with. We were much too focussed on trying to cope without him.' As far as the three surviving members of Joy Division were concerned the idea of continuing to make music was never in question, but they were equally unanimous that without Ian Curtis in the line-up any further music would need to be released under a new name. 'People were interested in us because obviously we were Joy Division, but it was a burden in that we couldn't be Joy Division. We had to reinvent ourselves, but we weren't very good at that,' Bernard Summer told *Uncut* in 2016, with the benefit of hindsight. 'We didn't have a clue really.'

The process of reinvention was made more difficult by Joy Division's success. *Closer* peaked at number six on the UK albums chart in August, where it spent a total of six weeks in the Top 40 and topped the independent album charts for eight weeks on the back of the success of 'Love Will Tear Us Apart', which in itself claimed the number one position in the independent singles charts for ten weeks, scoring a record for the longest-ever run in the independent singles, where it racked up an astonishing 195 weeks over the course of the next few years.

The independent charts had been founded in January 1980 as a way of recognising the success of the thriving post-punk independent music scene. 'To have indie status, a record – or the label on which it was released – has to be one which was independently distributed: produced, manufactured, marketed and put into the shops without recourse to the corporate framework of the major record companies,' explained Barry Lazell, the original compiler of the independent charts, in his 1997 book *Indie Hits 1980–1989*. As a result some independent labels – Beggars Banquet, home to Tubeway Army and Gary Numan, among them – whose releases employed the support of major labels were excluded from the independent charts, but nevertheless both charts played a hugely important role in recognising labels and artists who might otherwise have been overlooked.

At the end of the eighties Rough Trade would emerge as the decade's most successful independent albums chart label, having chalked up eighty-four weeks at number one across eighteen different albums. In fact when the independent albums chart launched in the week ending January 19th, 1980, Rough Trade had released three of its Top 10 albums, and had a stake in distributing six more. At number twelve in that first ever independent albums chart sat Cabaret Voltaire, whose album *Mix-Up* had been released in October 1979 but was still attracting steady sales. By February, *Mix-Up* was joined in the chart by the first of Cabaret Voltaire's two 1980 albums. *Live At The YMCA* was an 'official bootleg' of a show the band had played at the YMCA on London's Tottenham Court Road in October the previous year. The album featured nine tracks, seven original Cabaret Voltaire compositions alongside covers of The Velvet Underground's 'Here She Comes Now' and The Seeds' 'No Escape'.

'This is a much better showcase than their recent stuffy studio LP,' wrote *Smash Hits*' Red Starr of *Live At The YMCA*, awarding the live release seven out of ten, and going on to add, 'Far more accessible with the addition of rhythm, their eerie experiments with electronics and effects are further out than most but their sense of urgency does hold your attention throughout. Well worth checking.' *Record Mirror*'s Chris Westwood was equally enthusiastic, giving the album – which he described as 'a rough, brash alternative' to the band's 1979 album *Mix-Up* – four stars out of a possible five and offering the supportive thought, 'Critics will keep dubbing Cabaret Voltaire bleak, grey, industrial and esoteric – and Cabaret Voltaire will keep laughing at the critics, and they'll keep producing music in their own little vacuum, oblivious to rock and roll and all the rest of these silly, creaking traditions.'

Cabaret Voltaire's second studio album, *The Voice Of America*, was released in the summer of 1980 and shared one track with *Live At The YMCA*, 'Untitled', which appeared on the new record in an updated and more streamlined form as 'Damage Is Done'. Fortunately for the band, Chris Westwood was assigned the task of reviewing *The Voice Of America* for *Record Mirror*, bestowing the album with four-and-a-half stars out of five and describing it as 'more scattered, more indistinct than what has gone before... There's an odd spontaneity running through it,' Westwood continued, 'where ideas are lightly sketched, then discarded quickly in favour of more substantial patterns of noise. The music is full of ironies, paradoxes, sharp turns, short bursts, loopholes.'

In the same week, *Smash Hits* also reviewed *The Voice Of America*, the sole album review on their Independent Bitz page, and were equally enthusiastic. 'They are now close to having something really significant to show for their constructive approach,' ran the uncredited review, likely the work of the paper's Red Starr. 'The result is really surprisingly listenable and melodic. The rhythm tracks are subtle but strong enough to make the music accessible, while all the distorted vocals, taped effects and electronically treated noises hang together in a quietly effective way, expressing a "feel" more than a precisely stated object.'

In addition to being admired, Cabaret Voltaire were also becoming an influence. 'We seem to inspire people to go out and do things for themselves,'

Richard H. Kirk told Paul Morley in an interview for the *NME*. 'We get a lot of tapes from people, some are appalling, some are good. Geoff Travis at Rough Trade says that each week they get tapes of ten or twelve Falls, and ten or twelve Cabaret Voltaires.' One artist inspired by Cabaret Voltaire and their peers was Meat Beat Manifesto's Jack Dangers who looked back at the impact of *The Voice Of America* for *Electronic Sound* magazine in 2017: 'As an album, I think this is the best of the period, the best of all the music that came out of Sheffield. It was subversive, there was a real punk element to it, although they actually had nothing to do with punk.'

Experimenting with formatting and convention, as well as with their musical output, Cabaret Voltaire also put out a rather confusing release in the space between *Live At The YMCA* and *The Voice Of America*. Introduced as 'the world's longest single' by *Record Mirror* at the end of April, 'Three Mantras' played at 33 1/3 rpm, was pressed on twelve-inch vinyl and, although it contained just two tracks – 'Western Mantra' and 'Eastern Mantra', each lasting a little over twenty minutes – was frequently mistaken for an album. Reviewed as a single by the music press, the release prompted *Melody Maker* to note yet another change in Cabaret Voltaire's musical direction: 'Unusually direct, CV have this time pared down their hypnotic drone music to emphasise the mantric qualities of an insistently repetitive beat.' *Record Mirror* were unsure of the new sound – "'Eastern Mantra' is persistent, rhythmic Berlin waiting room music while 'Western Mantra' features sounds from a Jerusalem market place' – re-stating the boast that 'Three Mantras' was the world's longest single, noting its bargain price of £1.78 and ending on the note, 'Now is this obscure or am I missing the whole point?'

While Rough Trade would emerge as the eighties' most successful independent album chart label, the most successful independent singles label crown would go to Mute Records, who would score 106 weeks at number one across twenty-nine different singles. At the very start of the decade that success was still some way off, and at the beginning of 1980 Daniel Miller was working towards Mute's first album project.

Deutsch Amerikanische Freundschaft, their name frequently shortened to D.A.F., released 'Kebabträume', their first single for Mute, in March. *Smash Hits* were less than impressed. 'Kebabträume is a piece of German electronic nonsense that doesn't actually do anything or go anywhere but is pleasant enough,' they wrote in their Independent Bitz column. 'The 'B' side 'Gewalt (Violence)' is all World War 2 noises amid swooshing synthesisers and yelled vocals. Doubtless somebody's impression of something, it ends up somewhere between boring and irritating.'

D.A.F.'s *Die Kleinen Und Die Bösen* ('The Small And The Evil') album – the band's second long-player, but their first for Mute – duly followed in June, and D.A.F. played some live shows to promote the release. Gill Smith headed to the Notre Dame Hall in central London to review the show for *Record Mirror*. 'DAF can only be described as sheer force,' wrote Smith, who likened the experience to watching a war, and went on to describe the physical assault of D.A.F.'s live show: 'Gabi shrieked and leapt up to the ceiling, while the rest of them all but attacked the crowd. Throbbing synthesised rhythms, primal screams and a drummer like an overwound clockwork toy, shook the walls in a most unholy manner… I came out shell-shocked but thoroughly entertained,' Smith concluded.

Reviewed alongside *Die Kleinen Und Die Bösen* was an advance look at Mute Records' second album release, Silicon Teens' *Music For Parties*. The review started promisingly enough: 'They've made some extremely neat singles recently with synthesised reworkings of rock'n'roll oldies,' *Smash Hits*' Independent Bitz enthused, but when it came to the album as a whole the review took a chillier tone: 'The whole collection, especially with interpretations so faithful to the original as these, simply invites the comment – very pretty, but so what?' Nevertheless the inclusion of some original compositions alongside the selection of covers which made up *Music For Parties* was noted with approval: 'The three original tracks, though not much more daring than the covers, are certainly more interesting and more even old/new balance would have done the band much better justice.' (In addition to 1979's debut single release, the Silicon Teens' cover of 'Memphis Tennessee', the band had released two further singles, 'Judy In Disguise' in January 1980 – '"For that really up-to-date sound," they say. I'll buy that: more great fun from the Teens,' enthused *Record Mirror* – and 'Just Like Eddie', which *Record Mirror* reviewed in June, saying, 'As pure sickly pop it's vastly more successful than the Human League because it doesn't [pretend] to take as much on. It works insidiously well on any level you want, on a background muzak level, as soundtrack for underwater documentaries, as anything light and throwaway.')

Fad Gadget's debut album, *Fireside Favourites*, came out as Mute Records' third album release in October. *Smash Hits* had already given the April single 'Ricky's Hand' a positive review, noting how "'Ricky's Hand' shows off more of his [Fad Gadget's] black humour lyrics and hustling synthesised pop to good effect.' The eccentric, industrial and electronic nature of the single was further underlined on the credits on the back of the sleeve, where Fad Gadget was credited with 'Synthesizer, Vocals, Tapes, Black & Decker V8 Double Speed Electric Drill', Daniel Miller with 'Synthesisers', and BJ Frost (Fad Gadget's wife, Barbara Frost) was listed for 'Choir Girl Effect'.

Smash Hits' affection for Fad Gadget extended to *Fireside Favourites* when it appeared in October, the magazine's Independent Bitz column stepping up to review the release: 'There's been such a buzz about him that I didn't expect the rather tame Numanisms of the first side. Turn over though and you'll find him recovering much of the lost ground with four more original tracks that include a dreamlike trip through major surgery called 'Arch Of The Aorta' and the comedy of 'Insecticide' in which Fad becomes a housefly who spins round a lightbulb prior to landing on your sandwich.'

Fireside Favourites' title track was also released as a single to promote the album, and gave *Smash Hits* another opportunity to wax lyrical: 'Fad Gadget looks like he could give The Human League a run for their money in the smart electronic pop stakes,' enthused the single review, praising the release for its 'clever, black humour lyrics and nifty tunes,' and adding, "Fireside Favourites' pointedly combines the home fire, the atom bomb and an insanely jolly cakewalk, while 'Insecticide' views life from an insect's point of view with some clever effects. Highly recommended.'

Sounds' Adele-Marie Cherreson was positive about the single. 'Another Iggy soundalike,' she wrote, 'but with a definite character and lots of ideas.' In turn *Melody Maker*'s Paul Strange reviewed *Fireside Favourites* and decided that, such was the influx of new electronic sounds at the time, while the album was contemporary, it was also derivative. 'Despite the title it's rather a cold and dreary album, drawing influences from early Numan, current electronic bands and (vocally) Syd Barrett.'

That Gary Numan had a new album in the pipeline had been public knowledge for some time. The singer's setlist on the UK leg of his tour in support of *The Pleasure Principle* had already provided a taste of the new project in the form of new track, 'Remember I Was Vapour'. As early as December 1979 *Smash Hits* had reported that Numan was close to finishing his third album, which the magazine not only named as *Telekon*, but also confidently printed a six-song tracklisting and reported that the album wasn't set for release until September 1980, adding, 'We also hear that Gary is planning a series of ten four-minute videos and film version of the 'Replicas' album.'

A film project was in the works, and by April of 1980 *Record Mirror* reported that Numan had become 'the first top rock act to have a video cassette on general sale to the public'. Priced at £19.99 for the standard VHS and Betamax versions, and an eye-watering £29.99 for Sony and Philips formats, the release featured eleven tracks filmed at Numan's Hammersmith Odeon show the previous September alongside the promotional video for the 'Cars' single. 'We did release the first ever [commercial] music video, consisting of the 'Cars' promo clip and treated footage from 'The Touring Principle' UK tour,' recalled Numan in *Praying to the Aliens*. 'It's a small thing really, but I'm quite proud of the fact we beat Blondie's 'Eat To The Beat' video by a few weeks.'

Smash Hits caught up with Numan around the time of the video release and found the singer restless following the end of his international dates in support of *The Pleasure Principle*, which had seen three more new songs – 'We Are Glass', 'I Die: You Die' and 'Remind Me To Smile' – added to the setlist. 'I don't even feel confident that I can go on writing songs sometimes,' Numan told Frank Drake and Peter Gilbert. 'I'm back to looking for something again, like I was before. Now I sit here for hours and hours, day after day, looking for something more.' Fortunately for Numan, distraction was on its way with the release of a new single, 'We Are Glass', the first to be released in the countdown to the release of *Telekon*. 'I'd written the song about how I felt in the wake of my success. Fragmented, transparent, hard, brittle, cold, sharp and just about ready to break into a thousand pieces,' Numan wrote in *Praying to the Aliens*.

Rosalind Russell was among the first writers to review 'We Are Glass', admitting to not being a fan of Numan's previous work in her review for *Record Mirror* but nonetheless acknowledging that 'It's an excellent song, arranged with precision and care, and its shuffling half swing beat is quite compelling.' Deanne Pearson, reviewing the single for *Smash Hits*, was less enthusiastic, writing, 'The Numan humanoid becomes the human Numanoid, that is to say he's getting a bit predictable now. But he keeps churning them out in his (fairly) inimitable fashion, and on this alone sales are guaranteed. A hit? Maybe that's getting predictable too.'

Predictable or otherwise 'We Are Glass' scored Gary Numan another significant hit. Assisted by a *Top of the Pops* play of the 'We Are Glass' video the previous week, the single entered the UK singles chart at number ten at the end of May, starting a seven-week chart run which saw it peak at number five. The 'We Are Glass' video also caused some mild controversy, and some TV shows with a young audience chose not to play it because it contained 'violent' scenes of Numan smashing through glass walls and destroying television sets with a sledgehammer.

That their first look at the *Telekon* project, via the 'We Are Glass' video, featured Numan prominently holding, and playing, an electric guitar, was also of concern to some factions of Numan's audience following the pure electronic sounds running through *The Pleasure Principle*. 'I re-introduced a heavy, choppy guitar riff because I was interested in blending different sounds and instruments together,' Numan explained later. 'Synthesisers had become very accepted very quickly and within a year of 'Are 'Friends' Electric?' it seemed as though everyone had one. After all the song and dance about them it was no longer valid to stand next to a keyboard and say, look at me, I'm different because I use a synthesiser.'

Of more concern to his audience was the announcement, around the same time as the release of 'We Are Glass', that Numan had also been collaborating with the decidedly non-android Robert Palmer. 'Gary Numan is helping out Robert Palmer with his new album being recorded at Compass Point studios in Nassau, Bahamas,' reported *Smash Hits* in May. Palmer, it seemed, was a fan of Numan's work to the extent that he had incorporated versions of 'Cars' and 'Me, I Disconnect From You' into his live set, which in turn had led to a meeting between the two artists, something Palmer described to the *NME*'s Ian Penman in November 1980: 'I was doing three of his tunes in my live show about eighteen months ago and he came and saw the show with his dad. We got on really well so I suggested that... well, actually he suggested that we work together, so we did.'

The fruits of the collaboration between Numan and Palmer subsequently appeared on Palmer's album *Clues*, which was released in September in tandem with Numan's *Telekon*, and both albums featured versions of a new Gary Numan track, 'I Dream Of Wires'. *Telekon* naturally contained the original version of the track, which Numan had finished writing during his time in Nassau with Palmer, while *Clues* featured Palmer's take on the song alongside Numan providing the keyboard parts. *Clues* also included one track co-written by Palmer and Numan, 'Found You Now', while a second co-write, 'Style Kills', appeared as a B-side of the twelve-inch single release of Palmer's 'Looking For Clues' single.

Clues was generally well reviewed, although its release did provide Numan's many detractors in the media with yet another opportunity for a snide comment. "I Dream of Wires' is given a new lease of life in comparison with the turgid version on 'Telekon',' wrote Mike Gardner in *Record Mirror*, while the *NME*'s Nick Kent sniffed, '*Clues*... has the strength to suggest that, the spectre of "Gazza" notwithstanding, Robert Palmer may finally be in the right place at the right time.'

A second Gary Numan single, 'I Die: You Die', was released in August, entering the Top 10 once again and this time peaking at number six. 'I Die: You Die' was aimed squarely at the music press: 'The press had come at me so hard, so aggressively and without a single pause for breath that I felt very hostile towards them,' Numan wrote in *Praying to the Aliens*. 'I thought that such severe hostility towards performers in general made the business bloody depressing. Everything you read, about virtually everybody, was bitching and sarcastic. I got it the worst but it was pretty much the same story across the board.'

Numan also took the new project as an opportunity to reinvent his image, and was presented on the 'I Die: You Die' single cover gripping a metal baton while clad in a black leather jumpsuit decorated with two parallel red belts, and two parallel red lines from shoulder to waist, a motif that would run through the imagery for the entire *Telekon* project. 'I'm holding a silver object which vaguely looks like a weapon of some kind,' Numan would later reveal. 'It's actually a tube from my mum's Hoover, the ends were airbrushed so you couldn't tell it was hollow.'

Whether the single's swipe at their profession impacted the release's reception at the hands of the media or not is difficult to assess, but 'I Die: You Die' was universally savaged by the music press. *Record Mirror* dismissed the single outright, writing, 'Same old sandpapered voice, same old *Doctor Who* noises. Once again the Numan phenomenon eludes me.' Even *Smash Hits*, usually a supporter of Numan's work, professed to find themselves disappointed with the release: 'Even an outsider like me, who really doesn't understand what all the fuss is about, can detect that this effort lacks the commercial clout of previous singles,' wrote David Hepworth, before adding, 'Backing track reminds me of ELO. Song reminds me of being asleep.'

'I don't read papers any more because each week they're tearing me down and that gets on my nerves after a while,' Gary Numan had told *Smash Hits* earlier in the year, a strategy which presumably sheltered him from some of the media's vitriol at that time, although worse was to come in the form of the reviews for Numan's latest album *Telekon* in September.

In the *NME*, despite a moment of fleeting admiration for the track 'Sleep By Windows' – 'possibly the most effective Numan piece since 'Cars'' – Charles Shaar Murray was brutal, writing, 'All non-musical considerations temporarily to one side, I'd say that it was a woefully dull and monotonous album, pompous in the extreme.' *Record Mirror*'s Chris Westwood awarded *Telekon* – 'a collection of the "right" sounds, gestures and postures' – one star out of a possible five, and wrote '"Telekon' is Gary Numan playing at Gary Numan. It's redundant, and the fact that this legend is built on nothing in particular makes it all the more fearsome.'

Sounds' John Gill attempted to restore the balance and wrote, '*Telekon* sees Numan fleshing out his sound, perhaps a little belatedly. Back in the mix unusual things are beginning to happen, new levels of interest, new layers of sound, both formal and free.' In a succinct review for *Smash Hits*, reviewer Red Starr also took something positive from *Telekon*'s ten tracks: 'In short, this is better than 'The Pleasure Principle' but not so good as 'Replicas'. Numanoids everywhere will adore it since the essential ingredients – lonely lyrical themes, plaintive synthesisers and distinctive vocals – remain... No one will be disappointed but there won't be many new fans either.'

Whether *Telekon* attracted new fans or not was a moot point because the album effortlessly topped the charts in the middle of September after just one week on sale, securing Numan his third number one album in the space of just fourteen months. In an attempt to offer as much value for money as possible to Numan's loyal fanbase, the vinyl version of *Telekon* omitted both 'We Are Glass' and 'I Die: You Die' to make room for more new tracks, although both singles were included as bonus tracks on the cassette edition of the album. 'I had a surplus of new songs and I wanted to give the fans the best possible value for their money. It probably wasn't the smartest thing to do as it made the album less attractive to people who weren't part of my hardcore fanbase,' Numan mused later, admitting, 'I didn't give it that much thought at the time.'

Telekon sold 150,000 copies in just two months to achieve gold record status, and remains one of Gary Numan's own favourites from that imperial delight for our aural receptors' and had David Bowie in mind as producer for their next project, the reality was that things were not so rosy at the band's Monumental Pictures headquarters. In *The Story of a Band Called The Human League*, biographer Alaska Ross summed up the mood in The Human League camp at that time: 'By now, on the verge of a make or break year, the strains on the band were beginning to tell. Never the most complementary of characters, the in-fighting on everything from group policy to the kind of animal skin jacket Bryan Ferry wore on Roxy Music's first 'Old Grey Whistle Test' appearance had become unbearable.'

On the other side of the Peak District, Joy Division were having more serious problems. The band had been working on writing and recording their second album between bursts of touring and – with the exception of a spring single, grandly titled 'Licht Und Blindheit' but featuring the tracks 'Atmosphere' and 'Dead Souls', which had been released only in France – had released no new material since 'Transmission' the previous November. John Peel had continued to support Joy Division, however, and had taken it upon himself to throw his support behind the import release of 'Atmosphere' and 'Dead Souls', each of which he played multiple times on his shows throughout March and April, in order that fans who were unable to locate or afford expensive import copies could still enjoy the release.

As a result, Joy Division's profile was relatively high when they put out their next UK release in June 1980. 'Love Will Tear Us Apart' also provided the band with their first mainstream hit when it peaked at number thirteen in the UK singles chart and spent six consecutive weeks in the Top 40. While the band knew that 'Love Will Tear Us Apart' was their most commercial offering to date, the success mostly passed them by because, on the night of May 18th, at the age of just twenty-three, Joy Division frontman Ian Curtis had taken his own life. 'The long-awaited 'Love Will Tear Us Apart' single came out, but we hardly noticed,' recalled Peter Hook later.

In true eccentric Joy Division style, while the single was released in advance of a new album, *Closer*, 'Love Will Tear Us Apart' didn't actually appear on the album but stood alone as a way of introducing the world to the band's sophomore effort. 'This single has been invested with sad significance after singer Ian Curtis' tragic suicide. Joy Division were, and still may remain, an innovative and courageous band,' wrote Martyn Sutton in a sombre review for *Melody Maker*, in which he applauded 'Love Will Tear Us Apart' as an period of his career: 'Musically I thought *Telekon* was a big step forward from *The Pleasure Principle*, with the guitars back to add a rawness that had been missing on that album, and a new level of production and writing.' At the time, however, the singer was worried: 'I was very aware that, although it seemed to be continuing the phenomenal success of the previous year, *Telekon* had actually sold a lot fewer. About half of what *The Pleasure Principle* had sold in fact.'

At the end of November, as he brought a twenty-date North American leg of the *Teletour* to a close, Numan announced that a final single from *Telekon* would be released on December 12th. The last song to be written for the album, 'This Wreckage' was released into the busy festive market but nevertheless entered the UK singles chart at number thirty-five the week before Christmas, which secured Numan another *Top of the Pops* performance as the single slowly climbed to a peak position of twenty over the course of the next four weeks.

Smash Hits printed the lyrics to the song along with a small news piece to report that the Japanese words in the lyrics translated to 'I'm leaving now', which Numan had included as a thinly veiled reference to his intention to stop touring at the end of the *Telekon* project. 'I was already sure that I was finished with touring so it was a disguised way of saying goodbye to the fans, long before I announced it for real,' Numan wrote in his 1997 memoir, although he had actually announced his plans to retire from touring earlier in 1980 in an interview for Capital Radio, telling a caller 'It takes up too much time. One tour takes six months out of the year and I just can't afford that sort of time. There are other things I want to do.'

The music press wasted no time in voicing their opinion that 'This Wreckage' lacked obvious single qualities. *Record Mirror* reviewed the seven-inch as part of a trio of releases, examining Numan's latest alongside Bauhaus's cover of T. Rex's 'Telegram Sam' and In Camera's 'IV Songs'. 'These are the culprits that drag us down, making rock/pop what it is today,' wrote Chris Westwood. 'In Numan's case, it can't be helped – he's finally succumbed to his own problems, now making static stereotype music on the production line.' In the event Numan got off relatively lightly, leaving Bauhaus on the receiving end of the brunt of Westwood's vitriol: 'People like Bauhaus are the cause of all this disgusting post-modernist mythery, hiding behind layers of inconsequential noise, even desecrating 'Telegram Sam' (the only T Rex single I ever loved) and doing Bolan's memory no favours.'

Among the credits on Gary Numan's *Telekon* sleeve was one for Simple Minds in recognition of their assistance on the album when they provided 'handclaps' after finding themselves working in the same studios as Numan. Simple Minds were happy to be of service to Numan, with whom they were already friendly after supporting the star on a short run of German dates earlier in the year. Shortly after those dates Simple Minds played two shows at Edinburgh's Nite Club, during which they reportedly played a number of new songs for the first time. Billy Sloan was on hand to witness one of the shows for a review which appeared in *Record Mirror* a couple of weeks later. Mentioning new songs 'Pulse', 'New Warm Skin', 'Here Comes The Fool' and 'Gods', alongside live staples from the *Life In A Day* and *Real To Real Cacophony* albums, Sloan's review was rapt, and his admiration of the band was evident as he signed off his piece with the tantalising, 'So Simple Minds more than indicate that the foundation has been well and truly laid for that crucial third album, and through his riveting performance Jim Kerr takes another step towards becoming a star.'

Behind the scenes, however, things were not quite so rosy for Simple Minds, whose relationship with their label was decidedly strained after Arista's lacklustre support of *Real To Real Cacophony*. 'We were in debt to the record company to the tune of £150,000 but they were reluctant to drop us,' explained Bruce Findlay, Simple Minds' manager at that time, in an interview for Simple Minds' 2020 book *Heart of the Crowd*. 'So they said, "Make a third album."' Simple Minds subsequently headed back to Rockfield Studios where, with John Leckie once more in the producer's seat, they started work on the album which would eventually become *Empires And Dance*. Asked about that time in an interview for *Record Collector* magazine in 2019, Simple Minds' Jim Kerr concurred with his former manager. 'We'd amassed some debts. The whole picture wasn't looking good. Though it wouldn't be fair to say we were hoping to get dumped, we thought a clean slate mightn't be a bad idea,' Kerr recalled, before attributing some of Arista's newfound interest in Simple Minds to an unexpected ally. 'But then Rusty Egan started championing us and suddenly we began to register in the futurist charts. Arista thought that they may be on to something.'

That wasn't to say that Simple Minds were entirely comfortable being bracketed with the new futurist crowd. During an interview with the *NME*'s Chris Bohn in support of *Empires And Dance* in October, Jim Kerr and Charlie Burchill touched upon the subject again, Kerr saying, 'Look, with the electronic thing you can switch the synthesizer on and get really appealing tunes, to which you could sing typical science fiction lyrics and things like that... The record company would have loved it if we chose something so direct.' Warming to his bandmate's theme, Burchill then added, 'We could have all worn the same futuristic clothes, splashed wires and capacitors across the album cover and all that.'

Simple Minds were right. Although their music came drenched in electronics, they were an uneasy fit with the bands who were suddenly considered to be their peers, and *Empires And Dance* made a very different musical statement to the ones being put out by those acts who were riding on the peacock coat-tails of the Blitz. Rather than containing inconsequential pop songs, *Empires And Dance* was a more substantial and weighty release, informed by the band's recent travels and experiences, and looking to communicate those thoughts to a wider audience. 'We were seeing the picture postcard stuff, statues, parks and galleries – but bombs were going off, the Red Brigade had struck, or Baader Meinhof, or one time when we were in Paris, a synagogue had been set fire to – there was danger in the air,' Kerr told The Quietus in 2012. 'Against that backdrop, you've got classical Europe, you're reading Graham Greene and Albert Camus and back in London there were so many independent cinemas showing these great Italian and French classics – it all fed in, that and our own experiences.'

'I Travel' was chosen as the first single from *Empires And Dance*, and was greeted with enthusiasm by the media. Simple Minds' then Manager Bruce Findlay remembers BBC Radio 1's Peter Powell, Kid Jensen and John Peel all being very supportive, and the music press were similarly impressed. 'The impudent accessibility of 'I Travel' is no insulting gesture,' wrote Paul Morley in the *NME*. 'Simple Minds have always been potentially an important group, and they move into play with something close to the plausible freak out to show that they now have the sense and essence of their music under control.' Talking to Morley's *NME* colleague Chris Bohn in October, Jim Kerr expressed a similar line of thought: "I Travel' is an important development for us,' he began, warming to the idea of smuggling his message into the minds of his audience. 'I think if we can do a song that's appealing, but with an edge so that it doesn't get too comfortable, people might listen to what's being said.'

Reviewing *Empires And Dance* for *Smash Hits* at the beginning of October, David Hepworth awarded the release nine out of ten alongside an extremely positive review. 'In which one of Britain's most gifted and imaginative young bands exchange drama for dance and promote synthesiser over guitar without losing any of their melodic instinct or emotional impact,' reported Hepworth. 'The result has the dance rhythms of disco, the energy of new wave, haunting melodies with fleeting lyrical glimpses of a troubled modern Europe (but minus the usual 'modernist' posing) – and a touch of genius at its very human heart. Brilliant – buy it.'

Ultravox! On the set of the 'Reap The Wild Wind' video shoot, 1982.

1981

ULTRAVOX FINISHED THEIR 1980 by taking a new single, the title track from *Vienna*, to UK radio. Whether as a result of good planning or good fortune, the timing proved excellent, as frontman Midge Ure later explained in *If I Was*: 'In 1980 nobody bothered to release a new record just before Christmas. The Radio One playlist was shut down; the charts froze and they kept on playing the same old crap for weeks. 'Vienna' was taken to radio ten days before Christmas. They lapped it up, played it all the way through January.'

While radio was supportive of 'Vienna', the reaction from the music press was less effusive. Ian Penman was given the task of reviewing the single for the *NME* in January and wasted no time in attacking the 'precipitously clichéd' artwork and the 'extremely silly' delivery of the sounds the release contained. '"Vienna' is an unbearable po-faced trek,' he wrote. 'A load of extremely portentous airy fairy nonsense.' Robin Smith's thoughts on the single for *Record Maker* were decidedly more oblique: 'Full blown futurism on a real sod's opera that soars for 2,000 feet before you can look around and lands with a cataclysmic bump. The acceptable face of post modernism,' pronounced Smith, before issuing an ominous warning: 'If Genesis were young again this is how they would have started.'

Sharing the music press's concern that 'Vienna' might not be ideal chart material was Ultravox's record label, Chrysalis. 'We were determined that it would be our third single and fought with Chrysalis over it,' the band's Warren Cann told Jonas Wårstad. 'They thought it was far too long at six minutes, too weird for a Top 30 chart hit, and too depressing and too slow. Other than that, they liked it.' Having let themselves be persuaded that 'Vienna' should be a single, Chrysalis then refused to fund a video to accompany the release, leaving the band, who were certain that video was the way to go, to finance the filming themselves.

'The video is designed to show a society that's cracking, literally. Which is why you see the upper classes dancing and enjoying themselves, but when they turn to the camera, they're all a bit wrong,' Billy Currie told *Smash Hits*' Steve Taylor at the time, also revealing that he hadn't always been as confident about the merits of 'Vienna'. 'When Midge first sang it in the rehearsal room, I thought, "What is he going on about, singing about bloody Vienna?"' Currie confessed, attributing his subsequent change of heart to the extra input provided by Ultravox's producer, Conny Plank, who talked the band through the history of the city of Vienna, 'how it had once been a really grand city producing epic music and then both had gone into a decline... Suddenly he [Plank] put the song all in perspective,' Currie continued. 'Things like those cymbal crashes at the end of the song – almost over the top, but very grand – that gives it the feeling of something impressive that's on the edge of decay.'

And Currie wasn't the only one to question what the song was all about. 'People always wonder what 'Vienna' was about,' Midge Ure would say later. 'We lied about it at the time. In interviews with the *NME* I talked for hours about the Secessionists and Gustav Klimt, all the stuff that was going on in turn-of-the-century Vienna. That was all rubbish designed to make us sound interesting.' The truth was altogether more prosaic. 'It was a love story,' Ure admitted, 'the story of a holiday romance, about going to a beautiful place and meeting somebody special. You have this huge holiday romance, that you vow is going to continue forever, but, once you get back home and start living your nine-to-five job again, it just fades away.'

On Valentine's Day 1981 'Vienna' hit number two in the UK singles charts, where it would spend four successive weeks, initially kept off the top of the charts by John Lennon's 'Woman' – reissued as a tribute following the assassination of the former Beatle in New York the previous month – and then, more famously, for a further three weeks by Australian singer Joe Dolce's novelty hit 'Shaddap You Face'. Although it failed to top the charts, 'Vienna' was nonetheless a bona fide hit and enjoyed fourteen weeks in the UK singles chart, including an impressive ten weeks in the Top 20. The band's belief in the track had paid off and Chrysalis had even stepped up to pay for the video. 'It's just the right time for 'Vienna',' Billy Currie told *Smash Hits* with satisfaction, 'that kind of feeling, this time of year. It feels just right for us, this moody European sound.'

While 'Vienna' continued its chart journey it was an upbeat Ultravox who decamped to Conny Plank's studio in Germany to start work on a new album, a plan Billy Currie had explained to *Smash Hits*' Steve Taylor in February: 'We've booked five weeks in the studio, so that there's enough time to actually write songs there. 'Vienna' was the start of a new group; we're more of a unit now. We've done all that touring together. When we get an idea we seem to click together straight away.'

Alongside their reviews of 'Vienna', the music press also delivered their various verdicts on Spandau Ballet's second single, 'The Freeze', which was released the following week. Having scored a substantial Top 5 single success with 'To Cut A Long Story Short', which was still sitting comfortably within the Top 20 of the UK singles chart, any pressure the band might have felt to prove that they were more than a one-hit wonder was swept away when 'The Freeze' entered the charts at number forty-five on its way to a peak position of seventeen.

In an unusual display of enthusiasm the *NME*'s Adrian Thrills awarded 'The Freeze' the accolade of 'Long Fringe Single of the Week'. (The 'Short Fringe Single of the Week' went to The Shakin' Pyramids' 'Reeferbilly Boogie', and 'Institution of the Week' to David Bowie's single release of the track 'Scary Monsters (And Super Creeps)'.) 'When they signed Spandau Ballet in the autumn, Chrysalis made one or two ridiculous claims about their new employees being the most vital force for the '80s, the future of modern dance as we know it. You know the sort of thing,' wrote Thrills. 'There is still some way to go before they are able to justify that sort of billing, but the band themselves have quickly and quietly dispelled most of our remaining preconceptions, prejudices and blind spots in the best way possible.'

Spandau Ballet set about promoting 'The Freeze' with a video to accompany the single. Unashamedly pretentious – 'I was unshaven with my hair slicked back, wearing a vest, glasses, and a second-hand leather jacket I'd picked up in Belgium,' Tony Hadley later recalled of the filming. 'A scarf knotted at the throat competed the look. John Keeble teamed his gymslip with a new shirt. A girl lay on a sofa in a cobweb shroud' – the video for 'The Freeze' was a worthy successor to the one Spandau Ballet had delivered for 'To Cut A Long Story Short', and provided them with the means by which they could disseminate the aesthetic aspects of their message to a wider audience than they could reach with the photographs of their ever-changing styles which they were regularly supplying to the music press.

In the middle of February, Spandau Ballet appeared on the cover of *Sounds* for an interview feature to promote their debut album, *Journeys To Glory*. In the accompanying piece, *Sounds*' Betty Page, one of the band's most ferocious champions, was present while various members of Spandau Ballet examined DJ reaction forms reporting on how the twelve-inch format of 'The Freeze' was performing in the clubs. 'Only one DJ in 20 claimed that 'The Freeze' received anything less than "excellent" on the audience dance-o-meter,' she reported, noting Spandau Ballet manager Steve Dagger's obvious satisfaction with the reactions: 'They're a great indication of how things are going – better than any airplay charts,' Dagger explained. 'That's where the real record buyers are – on the dance floor. You go to clubs to pick up on new sounds, much more so than listening to the radio.'

Treated to an advance play of *Journeys To Glory* as part of her time with the band, Page also reported that Spandau Ballet's debut album was a 'quite simply stunning' channelling of their white funk and disco influences: 'Spandau have picked it all up and shaken it by the scruff of its neck, fed in a European beat and 80s technology to produce a different breed of syncopation, injecting disco with the oomph and excitement it's been lacking for too long.' Unsurprisingly, when it came to submitting *Sounds*' official review of the album a couple of weeks later, Page awarded the release a maximum five stars. "Journeys of Glory' will appeal to the many nationwide who recognise the value of creativity, style, self-respect, imagination, passion and escapism, who realise music can't change the world but can influence personal attitudes,' she enthused. 'Spandau Ballet are here for those who take their enjoyment seriously. Be one of the happy people.'

While no other reviews quite matched Page's for enthusiasm, and despite being something of an easy target for the music press, *Journeys To Glory* generally avoided a savaging at the hands of the critics, although both the *NME* and *Record Mirror* professed themselves underwhelmed. 'To cut a long story short, Spandau Ballet have made an awfully ordinary record. Given the enormous pretensions which surround this music, the extravagant claims made on its behalf, it's admittedly easy to seize the instant-backlash opportunity which the long-play debut provides. But in all honesty, 'Journeys To Glory' is an unremarkable affair by any standards. Not bad, but modest,' wrote Paul Du Noyer in the *NME*. 'More colour, more life, and some genuine passion are required to flesh out the undoubted musical promise of Kemp's work,' wrote Sunie in her three-and-a-half stars out of five review for *Record Mirror*. 'At present, what comes over is a more than fair debut album with some good songs, and a couple of duff ones, a talented set of musicians and a singer who needs a tragic love affair or something to put a little humanity into his performance.'

One aspect of the album's release that most publications seized upon was the album's striking sleeve. Betty Page enthusiastically described *Journeys To Glory*'s cover as oozing style, but *Record Mirror* was less sure. 'Let's look first at the packaging, which in the Spandau scheme of things must be counted important,' wrote Sunie, who described the sleeve as 'a classy white-on-white affair, with a cod classical design embossed upon it. Said design is of a naked male form, looking suitably noble and muscular.' A second aspect of the release to be put under the microscope were the unashamedly pretentious sleeve notes provided by the band's chief scribe, Robert Elms. 'Elegantly dressed as a Peter Saville-like design of frigid classicism,' wrote Paul Du Noyer in the *NME*, 'the LP suffers rather than boasts cringe-inducing blurb by the ubiquitous Robert Elms.'

The combination of the classical aesthetic of the *Journeys To Glory* album sleeve with Elms' quasi-intellectual rhetoric caused both *Melody Maker* and *Record Mirror* to take a longer look at Spandau Ballet's manifesto. 'Fascist overtones?' questioned Lynden Barber in the former. 'Remember those British Movement stickers urging the release of Rudolph Hess from Spandau jail? Just what's needed for adding that hint of danger, that sense of momentous import.' *Record Mirror*'s Sunie was also concerned by what she perceived as potentially fascist undertones suggested by the artwork and in Robert Elms' notes. 'The most striking thing,' she wrote, 'is Spandau's increasing promotion of the ideal of the "beautiful and clean", heroic young man; and so forth that Elms lays out on the sleeve. The last thing on earth that Spandau need is to link themselves with some sort of Aryan Youth ideal, smacking hideously of Hitlerian master-race notions.'

The week following the appearance of Sunie's review, Spandau Ballet and Robert Elms each hit back at the accusations they felt had been hurled their way by *Record Mirror* in the form of a pair of smouldering letters sent to the paper. 'Dear Sunie, thanks very much indeed for nothing, for just stopping short of calling us Nazis in your review of our album last week, that was really wonderful of you,' opened the letter from the band, who carefully addressed each point of concern, before stating, 'Yours is the ignorance in not realising that heroic and classical imagery has been used in many other contexts, too numerous and varied to mention.' Elms's letter, which appeared directly below the band's own comments on the *Record Mirror* letters page, ploughed a similar furrow: 'The suggestion that either myself, or the band, are fascists – or that we are toying with pseudo-fascist imagery – is so unfounded that it is almost fraudulently laughable.'

In his autobiography, *I Know This Much*, Spandau Ballet songwriter Gary Kemp later addressed the choice of album name. '*Journeys To Glory* was the title of a book I had read on religious obsessives – people who'd crucify or flagellate themselves in the name of their beliefs. It seemed the perfect title for our first album: as well as being wonderfully pompous and presumptuous, it was made to irritate the enemy and clearly stated our intentions.' Looking back at the same period in his own memoir, *To Cut A Long Story Short*, the band's frontman Tony Hadley remembered, 'The music press had a field day. The cover, coupled with a few words about sharp youth – plus the name of the band – proved our fascist leanings beyond all reasonable doubt. Allegedly.'

Buoyed by the success of 'Fade To Grey', and keen to capture some of the Blitz impetus that was fuelling Spandau Ballet's march on the charts, Polydor wasted no time in releasing a new Visage single, 'Mind Of A Toy', at the end of March. 'In keeping with its title, the song has a distinctly boyish feel, a disjointed, puppety construction with all sorts of nooks and crannies, danceable (of course), thoughtfully garnished and completed by an attractive tune that takes root more with every play,' enthused *Melody Maker*'s Carol Clerk, who also described 'Mind Of A Toy' as 'an exceptionally imaginative single'. 'Harder and more gritty than 'Fade To Grey' this is the tougher side to their collective personality,' wrote *Record Mirror*'s Simon Ludgate, who also praised the twelve-inch release as value for money and for being 'beautifully produced and very loud'.

'Mind Of A Toy' was accompanied by the now obligatory video designed to celebrate the all-important visual aspects of Visage's presentation, and by the middle of March had entered the UK singles chart at thirty-two, where four weeks later it would peak at a very respectable thirteen as part of of an eight-week chart run – the same week that the *Visage* album, boosted by the release of the single, hit its own chart peak of thirteen in the UK album chart.

The release of 'Mind Of A Toy' also provided Steve Strange with the opportunity for another round of interviews, most of which entirely sidestepped any discussion of Visage's music and instead focused on Strange's image, lifestyle, and ambitions for the band and himself. Talking to *Record Mirror*'s Daniela Soave for a front cover feature in April, Strange revealed that work was about to begin on the second Visage album both musically and visually: 'I think I'm going to change my image in a drastic way. I want to go upmarket, in a way which will shock people.'

Meanwhile *Journeys To Glory* entered the UK album charts at number seven and peaked at number five the following week, remaining in the Top 20 for the next eight weeks, and becoming a fixture in the album charts until the end of September, but Spandau Ballet were already in the process of moving on. In her interview piece for *Sounds* Betty Page had already cautioned that the album was 'conceived in part up to two years ago, and recorded last year, thus meaning that this is not state-of-the-art Spandau'. Tony Hadley concurred, confirming that *Journeys To Glory* 'more or less comprised the set we had been playing in the months leading up to the deal with Chrysalis'. According to the *NME*'s gossip page, Gary Kemp had also started distancing himself from the popular view of his band before *Journeys To Glory* had even been released. 'I'm sick of us being labelled a synthesiser band!' Kemp was reported as saying. 'I reckon that it will really surprise some people that our album is not all dance music. There are a lot of slower tracks on it, and not even that many synthesiser tracks. It pisses me off that everyone's going on about funk being the new thing right now, when six months ago no one wanted to touch it.'

The first evidence of this shift in their musical thinking came with the release of Spandau Ballet's next single, a double A-side release which featured 'Muscle Bound' from *Journeys To Glory* on one side, and a brand new track, 'Glow', on the other. 'We'd started to strip back some of the synthesisers on tracks and develop the guitar parts,' Gary Kemp explained later. 'I sat with my guitar in my bedroom and with the sound of the Fatback Band and Dr Buzzard in my head, I ground out a groove and made an attempt to write a song that combined funk with the stark European music that we had created already. The result was 'Glow'.'

The 'Muscle Bound'/'Glow' single was released at the end of March on seven-inch and twelve-inch formats, each containing different mixes the band had made with *Journeys To Glory* producer Richard Burgess. "Glow' shrivels the LP under its heat, makes those other singles sound like tinny teenypop jingles,' wrote the *NME* approvingly, describing the twelve-inch release as 'such a vivid, vaulting chunk of growth, such a bursting tumble through the undergrowth, such a dose of undaunted exertion'. 'They swing into a chain gang rhythm, painting a vivid picture of Eastern Bloc labour, more by the music than by the words,' enthused Rosalind Russell in *Record Mirror*. 'The Russian sounding break in the middle adds to the Red Army Choir impression just enough to stir the imagination. Another Steppe in the right direction.'

The positive reviews no doubt served to give the band a confidence boost because behind the scenes, despite their assured public swagger, Spandau Ballet were concerned as to whether they could maintain the forward momentum that had propelled *Journeys To Glory* into the Top 5 of the albums chart. "The Freeze', our second single, had worryingly sunk before it made it into the Radio 1 top ten,' Martin Kemp confided in his memoir *True*. 'It's well known that the most dangerous time for any band is between those early singles. The enthusiasm for a new group can die just as fast as it was born.' Fortunately 'Muscle Bound'/'Glow' entered the UK singles chart at number fifty-three after just one week on sale, steadily climbing over the next few weeks until it broke into the all important Top 10, where it peaked at number ten over the course of a respectable ten-week chart run.

And as 'Muscle Bound'/'Glow' dropped out of the singles chart, Ultravox's 'All Stood Still' entered at number forty-six at the start of June before climbing to a chart peak of number eight, scoring Ultravox another significant hit despite the usual wave of indifference from the music press. 'This is a jabbering rush of brittle electronic squeals; an animated bluster that almost makes me yearn for the tedious grandeur of 'Vienna',' reported *Melody Maker*'s Allan Jones, and the *NME*'s Max Bell turned in a similar sentiment: 'Ultravox and Conny Plank vamp up some surreal trickery but the joke wears thin second time around. That's when you realise it is only another heavy metal record after all.'

Basking in the halo effect of his production work for Spandau Ballet, producer Richard Burgess lost no time in launching a musical vision of his own or, more precisely, in reshaping a long-running project to fit the current climate. In January 1981 Landscape, the band Burgess had been a part of since 1975, announced the release of their latest single, 'Einstein A Go-Go', much to the initial discomfort of the music press. 'Yeah, *that* Landscape,' reported *Sounds*. 'Those boring Old Jazzrock Farts who were around for donkeys doing nothing till someone gave them robot suits and synthesisers to rapidly trendy themselves up.'

Smash Hits were similarly fascinated by Landscape's transition. 'Three years ago Landscape were being called a jazz-rock outfit. They were playing pubs and clubs on a well-worn circuit in London,' observed writer Steve Taylor. 'There were no vocal numbers, just a huge number of high-octane instrumentals that sounded like the product of a miniaturised – and electrified – jazz orchestra with a funk rhythm section.' Having failed to get anywhere on the jazz-rock circuit, Landscape finally took a break to reassess what they wanted to achieve next and, influenced by the Blitz scene which Burgess had made his home, decided to explore a more overtly electronic pop direction, which in turn would mean that their new material was going to require vocals.

'We deliberately held up the release of this album for what will be about six months because we're now identified with the Blitz scene,' Burgess told *Melody Maker*'s Steve Sutherland at the time, expressing his hope that the success of Ultravox, Spandau Ballet and Visage might 'prepare people's ears' for Landscape. 'Not that we're exactly like those bands,' Burgess was quick to add. 'I think perhaps we're a little more quirky – but they're unusual too and I think people's ears will start getting used to the kinds of sounds that we're making,'

Sounds unexpectedly declared themselves delighted by the new Landscape. 'Now they're unrecognisable, completely electronic,' enthused Betty Page in her review of 'Einstein A Go-Go' in January. 'This is worthy of your time mostly due to its wondrous danceability and synth doodlings.' Mark Total, reviewing the single for *Record Mirror*, was significantly less generous about Landscape's transition from jazz to the dance floor: 'The futurist movement doesn't need another anthem,' he shrugged. 'This is Landscape cashing in, pure and simple.'

'Einstein A Go-Go' – 'possibly the only novelty pop song about global religious nuclear terrorism,' Landscape's John Walters pointed out to *Electronic Sound* magazine in 2017 – entered the Top 40 of the UK singles chart in the middle of March and four weeks later spent a fortnight at a peak chart position of number five, assisted by a memorable video – 'A drum kit which appeared to be made from human heads… a mad scientist and a pied piper, a surreal housewife in a Cubist living room, a hamster in a wheel and a box with a head that sang 'Einstein A Go-Go',' marvelled *Smash Hits*.

Towards the end of February, while 'Einstein A Go-Go' was still climbing the charts, Landscape released a new album which peaked at number sixteen on the UK album charts for a fortnight, part of a twelve-week chart run under the unwieldy title *From The Tea-Rooms Of Mars… To The Hellholes Of Uranus*. At the end of February *NME*'s Chris Bohn was among the first to offer his verdict: 'Their sudden, whole-hearted embracing of binary systems is a definite improvement on their previous directionless fusions,' Bohn announced cautiously, 'but though it's a step forward for them personally, it's not necessarily a giant leap for mankind.' *Sounds*' Tony Mitchell managed to be more positive about Landscape's new trajectory. 'Suddenly, Landscape are no longer a bunch of old fogeys doing impersonations of Weather Report,' he wrote with approval. 'It is now very prudent to see them as very much to the fore of the hi tech revolution, using synths, computer hardware and assorted electronic percussion in a way practically unrivalled elsewhere.'

Having failed to secure themselves a *Top of the Pops* performance with 'Einstein A Go-Go', Landscape finally managed to debut on the show in support of the next single to be taken from *From The Tea-Rooms Of Mars*, 'Norman Bates', inspired by the character of the same name played by Anthony Perkins in Alfred Hitchcock's infamous horror movie *Psycho* in 1960. 'Norman Bates' was released in the middle of May and immediately entered the lower reaches of the UK singles chart, despite being greeted by a selection of lukewarm reviews from the music press. 'Landscape make my flesh crawl, put snakes in my stomach and make my bowels twitch,' wrote *Sounds*' Mick Middles in an unambiguous review in which he went on to reject the band as 'a minor talent destined for the scrap heap not long from now'. The review was prescient, however: despite Landscape's appearance on *Top of the Pops*, 'Norman Bates' was destined to stall at number forty in the UK singles chart.

But it wasn't just London's Blitz scene that was responsible for the deluge of sparkling electronic pop that was lighting up the charts in 1981. Emerging from a similar scene that had coalesced around Birmingham's Rum Runner club the previous year, Duran Duran found themselves hailed as another bright new hope for the new year. In January *Record Mirror* and *Sounds* both ran reviews of a recent show at the Birmingham Cedar Club, the former's Kevin Wilson praising Duran Duran's 'raunchy techno pop' and predicting that the band would 'never again be so close to their audiences' such was the potential on display in their performance. Carolyn Spence, reviewing the show for *Sounds*, was also enthusiastic. 'They're good,' she declared, 'tight and rhythmic, clever vocals, and the disco bass runs work. But the best thing is, you can dance to it.' Spence also singled out 'Planet Earth' for particular praise, identifying the track as Duran Duran's first single and enthusing that of all the songs in the band's live set it was the one that best epitomised Duran Duran's 'peculiar blend of disco/funk/jazz/punk'.

Reviewing Duran Duran's debut single a fortnight later, Spence's *Sounds* colleague Valac Van Der Veene was more circumspect in his enthusiasm: 'Perfect night music for those of the elite who want vacuous romance, style – and nothing else,' he wrote before describing the single as a 'tempting taster' for Duran Duran's forthcoming album. 'This isn't just dull. It's an old kind of dull,' was *Smash Hits*' caustic view of 'Planet Earth', while *Melody Maker*'s Patrick Humphries directed just eleven words towards the single: 'As empty as a Marcel Marceau soundtrack. Lacking soul and originality.' In *Record Mirror* Sunie was similarly brief: 'It's not hard to see why this lot have been compared with Spandau Ballet, but the song isn't anywhere near as memorable as the latter's hits. The lyrics are painfully mundane sci-fi.'

The *NME* was the first of the mainstream music press titles to feature Duran Duran, Chris Salewicz joining the group in a Putney rehearsal studio. Spandau Ballet's name came up again. 'They're okay but they've had such hype that anything they do's bound to be a let-down,' Nick Rhodes responded when asked about any parallels between the two bands, adding 'they're much better than anything else new that I've heard. At the same time though, I must say they're pretty flimsy.' Mark Total also wanted to sound out Duran Duran about Spandau Ballet being a possible influence in a piece for *Record Mirror*, to Nick Rhodes' patient response: 'How can they possibly be an influence on anyone when they've only had two singles?' 'We like Spandau Ballet – honestly,' John Taylor told *Melody Maker* in April. 'They're better than 99 per cent of the new bands around at the moment but they're nothing to do with us really.'

But Spandau Ballet provided an easy comparison point for Duran Duran that the music press couldn't resist returning to over and over again. 'What we're doing is European white disco,' Duran Duran bassist John Taylor told *Smash Hits*' Kasper De Graaf in the band's first feature for the magazine in March. 'What we wanted to do was just pick out all the elements of various musics,' explained Nick Rhodes. 'Disco's pretty good on its own, but a lot of the vocals wreck it. We're just trying to make a much more interesting dance music, as well as keeping one foot well lodged in the obscure end of things.' 'What Duran Duran have in common with Visage and Spandau Ballet is perhaps that they responded to the need for their own kind of music in the clubs,' reasoned De Graaf, and instead asked frontman Simon Le Bon about Duran Duran's 'Planet Earth' single. 'It's been labelled as a sci-fi thing but it's not really got much to do with that,' explained the singer. 'The fact is that at one point I just had this idea of what would it be like if you were coming in and seeing this place for the first time. In my head was also the idea of being born, but at an age and with the kind of mentality where you can actually see what's going on. It's all about waking up really.'

In support of 'Planet Earth' Duran Duran headed out on a short UK tour, and it was in their live presentation that their true influences revealed themselves. *Melody Maker*'s Steve Sutherland saw the band at The Sundown in London: 'A short, sweet set of memorable, unpretentious pop songs that pack real punch live and will sound so great on the radio that they'll put the rest of their chosen contemporaries to shame,' he reported warmly. *Sounds*' Betty Page attended the same show. 'Duran claim to merge disco with rock and achieve a new hybrid but observers whispered that icky phrase that is anathema to most: "They're just a rock band!"' she wrote. 'They incorporate elements of new stylish/glam/pomp and even HM, so they've well and truly covered their options,' Page continued more promisingly. 'They do possess true crossover potential and shouldn't have any trouble in shifting the units.'

Duran Duran remained nonplussed by such accusations. 'If rock means power and drive and excitement and showbiz, then yeah, we are a rock band and we're only too happy to be called that,' John Taylor told *Melody Maker* in April. 'I think what we've tried to do with Duran Duran both visually and musically, is put on a show that would have excited us five years ago if we'd gone to see ourselves play.'

In the *NME*, Lynn Hanna attended Duran Duran's show at Nottingham's Rock City on the same evening that the band's debut *Top of the Pops* appearance had aired and reported that Duran Duran were brimming with confidence as a result. Combined with early support from Radio 1, the *Top of the Pops* appearance had been enough to propel 'Planet Earth' from the lower reaches of the UK singles chart into the Top 40, where it would continue to climb until it reached an impressive chart peak of twelve a fortnight later. The subsequent release of a twelve-inch extended 'Night Version' of the single then ensured that 'Planet Earth' remained in the charts for an admirable twelve weeks, before dropping out of the chart after the release of Duran Duran's second single, 'Careless Memories'.

'Sounds like another winner from this cuddly Birmingham-based band,' wrote *ZigZag* of 'Careless Memories'. 'Slightly more uptempo than 'Planet Earth', this should have them bopping in the discos. I like it.' 'We seem to have a meaty, beaty, big and bouncy chart smash on our hands,' exclaimed *Sounds* in their review of the single. 'Buried beneath layers of silk finish is a contraction so staggeringly basic you wonder if their punk roots don't extend back to the Dry-Ice Age,' mocked *Smash Hits*. 'Programmed by computers, played by androids, listened to by robots,' exclaimed *Melody Maker*. 'That's a bit unfair, actually, because this is pretty good of its type. It's by no means exciting or novel but it's performed well enough.'

The lukewarm reviews of 'Careless Memories' were accompanied by a dip in enthusiasm for Duran Duran from radio and, despite a second appearance on *Top of the Pops* and encouraging initial sales from Duran Duran's emerging fanbase, the single stalled at the bottom of the Top 40, spending two weeks at number thirty-seven and dropping out of the charts after just four weeks. Unperturbed, Duran Duran stuck to their guns and at the end of May announced that their debut album, *Duran Duran*, would be released in June, accompanied by a run of European festival appearances and a second UK tour which would include the band's first headline show at London's Hammersmith Odeon.

Despite the cautious reaction to 'Careless Memories', by the time Duran Duran released their eponymous album in the middle of June their efforts were rewarded when it soared into the Top 10 of the UK albums chart at the end of the month, the start of a forty-five-week chart run which included ten weeks in the Top 10, and a peak position of number three in September, in step with the band's third single, 'Girls On Film'.

'Initially, the murky production, lame-brained lyrics, tinny, trippy aural effects and overall blandness of the whole affair had me almost fooled enough to trash the bloody thing,' muttered *Melody Maker*'s Steve Sutherland in his review of *Duran Duran*, describing the record as 'a poor man's Ultravox', until he looked beyond his own preconceptions of the band and came to the realisation that Duran Duran were in fact 'painlessly pointless, bouncy, bright and brilliant' and could be enjoyed purely on those merits. Betty Page, in her review of *Duran Duran* for *Sounds*, was in agreement: 'Wiped clean of all the hype, the music speaks for itself and shines brightly.' Page also drew a parallel with Ultravox, but a more positive one: 'Duran are a great pop/rock band in the fine tradition of Ultravox, blending pop tunes with clear, clean-cut hooks, chunky, hard guitar and disco/funk based rhythms,' she proclaimed, ending, 'Duran World Domination starts here.'

Duran Duran subsequently embarked upon their second UK tour of the year and found themselves playing to an audience dominated by young girls. 'As the smoke clears to reveal [Duran Duran] in grey suits, suede boots, and striped T-shirts, they remind me instantly of an older, flabbier Bay City Rollers,' scoffed the *NME*'s Kirsty McNeill, who came away from Duran Duran's Glasgow show unimpressed. 'They scrape the surface of a variety of styles without a hint of imagination,' she continued. 'The set is laden with pompous, tedious synthesizer parts, Gillanesque guitar; their material is completely inadequate: the performance laborious.' 'This is good time, naive, even teeny-bop in places,' wrote *Sounds*' Ian Ravendale, whose largely positive review of the band's Newcastle show echoed previous opinions that Duran Duran were essentially a rock band in a sleek, new contemporary package. 'Don't be misled by the style or the mechanics, like the atmospheric twiddles of synthesiser operator Nick Rhodes,' Ravendale warned. 'This is still rock 'n' roll to me.'

'Give us that hour on stage we can convince people that we don't need to be labelled to help us,' Nick Rhodes told the *NME*'s Paul Morley, who attended Duran Duran's hometown Birmingham show. 'I think honesty wins through in the end.' Equally the band weren't unhappy about their new pop audience. 'On this tour the audience has been incredibly young, they're all really enjoying themselves, and as long as we can play to people enjoying themselves and if we're enjoying ourselves, I don't see any harm in what we we do,' Rhodes added in the same interview.

John Taylor was also sanguine about Duran Duran's new audience, and in an interview for *Melody Maker* at the end of the year declared himself comfortable with the band's fanbase, and with the company they kept. 'The kids who come to see us – I know who they like,' Taylor told Steve Sutherland, 'I can see their badges; it's us, The Human League, Orchestral Manoeuvres.' Spandau Ballet, he added, were conspicuously absent from the list and for good reason: 'When we started, we were just five men in a boat rowing out to sea, but Spandau got a motor boat and roared past us out into the middle. Now they've run out of petrol and we've got our oars, we're rowing past them all and they're just sinking.'

In fact, on the day of Duran Duran's show at Birmingham's Odeon on July 11th, Spandau Ballet were riding high in the UK singles charts with their new single 'Chant No. 1 (I Don't Need This Pressure On)' at number four, having slipped a place from its peak the previous week. 'Chant No. 1 (I Don't Need This Pressure On)' was the first Spandau Ballet single to take a step away from the predominately electronic sound which had pigeonholed them inside the New Romantic scene, in favour of a funkier more organic sound. 'It was a different sound for us, with a horn section by the jazz-funk trio, Beggar & Co,' wrote Tony Hadley later, adding that the single also marked the first time that Spandau Ballet guitarist Steve Norman had appeared on record playing the saxophone, the instrument for which he would become best known.

'Chant No. 1 (I Don't Need This Pressure On)' was a turning point for Spandau Ballet, who were now keen to move towards a more funk-orientated sound, and who also wanted to put some distance between themselves and the rapidly cooling New Romantic scene. 'We wanted to get back to soul again because that was genuinely the music that most of us were into,' Gary Kemp told the *NME*'s Adrian Thrills in a front-cover feature at the beginning of August. 'It was back to the feeling that you were doing something different to most kids. The reason that electronic music was played was basically just to prove that we were a different scene.'

Spandau Ballet unleashed their new sound at the start of July to the immediate delight of the media. 'Spandau has taken the spirit of '75 – Kool, Fatback and (especially) Brass Construction – and slammed it, complete with soulful dress, straight into the heart of 1981,' reported Adrian Thrills in the *NME*, going on to praise 'Chant No. 1 (I Don't Need This Pressure On)' as 'a dazzling dance floor stormer as demonic as anything else we're likely to contort ourselves to this summer'. *Record Mirror* also came down in favour of the release, which they described as 'White European disco coloured by what sounds like the Earth, Wind and Fire brass section trumpeting away,' before declaring the single 'a rare classic of its genre'.

In fact asking Earth, Wind & Fire to guest on 'Chant No. 1' had been Spandau Ballet's intention prior to recording the single, until the latter changed their plans after meeting Beggar & Co – the three-piece brass section who had recently split from Light Of The World – at *Top of the Pops* and immediately discovering a great deal of common ground. 'They're mates of ours, young Londoners, and they have the same influences as us,' Gary Kemp told *New Sounds New Styles* later. 'They know what's going on.' 'The original rhythm track was never that strong as a disco track until the horns made it what it was,' Beggar & Co's Neville 'Breeze' McKreith told *Record Mirror* modestly when asked about their contribution to Spandau Ballet's new sound.

A final Visage single, the title track from *Visage*, came out alongside 'Chant No. 1' at the beginning of July. In addition to the twelve-inch remix format that was becoming so fashionable at the time, 'Visage' was also released as a standard seven-inch single, which Polydor issued in three different sleeves – each limited to a single print run of 25,000 copies – as an incentive to fans to purchase multiple copies. Supported by a video shot in and around Blitz, and featuring a cast of characters from the club, the ploy worked and gave the band their third single hit of the year when it spent two consecutive weeks at a chart peak of twenty-one in August.

This time the press was less supportive of Visage and reviews for the single were dogged by comparisons to their increasingly successful peers. *Smash Hits'* Red Starr, reviewing the twelve-inch release, declared Visage a second-division Ultravox, but was encouraged somewhat by the single's upbeat and danceable nature, reporting, 'another near-instrumental with loads of swooping synthesisers and somebody muttering something about "my visage".' 'It pales beside Spandau's 'Chant', the most obvious yardstick,' rued Adrian Thrills in the *NME*, while *Melody Maker's* Steve Sutherland considered the release a cynical cash-in to fund Steve Strange's wardrobe and lavish lifestyle, and to fill in time while the rest of Visage worked on other projects. 'I know, let's wack out a 12 inch remix with oodles of effects. That should keep the damn punters happy and bring in the odd bob or two,' Sutherland wrote. 'Sorry Steve, not this time. It stinks.'

Steve Strange had meanwhile been dispatched to New York in an attempt by their record label for Visage to take America by storm. Not wanting to be outdone by Spandau Ballet, who had embarked on a similar campaign earlier in the year, Strange conceived a spectacular launch, the jewel in the crown of which was to be his arrival at the venue riding on an elephant, a plan which had to be scaled down to his arriving on a camel as there were no readily available elephants in Manhattan at the time.

While the rest of the band had gone into the project knowing that Steve Strange would be the public face of Visage – 'We made Steve Strange a star and that was the deal,' Billy Currie told the *NME* in February – Midge Ure in particular was struggling with what he saw as the frontman's inflated sense of his own importance, which came to a head during that New York trip. Writing in his autobiography *If I Was* Ure recalled being in London at the time of the New York launch and hearing about the camel. 'I flipped,' he admitted. 'It had just got so ridiculously over the top. Visage had ceased to be fun any more, and fashion and pomp had taken over.'

For Ure it was the beginning of the end. After completing work on the second Visage album, *The Anvil*, which would be released the following year, Ure left the band, preferring to concentrate his creative energies on Ultravox instead. 'I was happy to leave when I did, as the bubble had burst,' Ure confessed. 'Ultravox was the real thing. Visage the bit of fun that led up to it.'

On the back of their *Faster Than Light* tour Duran Duran dropped their third single, 'Girls On Film', which overtook 'Visage' in the UK singles chart on the way to becoming a number five hit at the end of August. After 'Careless Memories" lacklustre reception, Duran Duran were no doubt relieved when 'Girls On Film' immediately caught the ear of radio, press and their audience alike. 'Champion team effort, full marks for loose, flowing danceability. Who's cornering more markets than anyone else, then?' asked Betty Page in *Sounds*, once again professing particular admiration for the twelve-inch extended 'Night Version' of the track. 'By far their best yet, this sees Duran in a much more funky mood,' reported a similarly enthusiastic Alan Coulthard in *Record Mirror*, although not everyone shared his enthusiasm. 'The first five minutes are the worst,' wrote *Smash Hits*' Johnny Black. 'After that it goes into a bit of decline.'

The release of 'Girls On Film' coincided with the launch of a new American cable TV channel which had been set up in recognition of a new visual era for music. Launched at midnight on August 1st, 1981 and choosing Buggles' 'Video Killed The Radio Star' as its first video, MTV initially broadcast to a limited number of homes across New Jersey but was attracting around two million viewers within a year, and ten million viewers after two. As a showcase for new music MTV was revolutionary but it was a revolution that depended entirely on artists making videos available to the channel. In 1981 it was British artists who were the pioneers in the field of video, and as MTV was hungry for new content, it was the new wave of colourful, visual and frequently electronic acts coming out of the UK who dominated the channel.

Duran Duran's relationship with MTV began with 'Girls On Film', for which the band produced a racy, semi-pornographic video which featured them performing the song alongside a boxing ring which variously hosted sumo-wrestling, mud-wrestling, pillow fights, massage oils, models dressed in lingerie and swimwear and sometimes less, and – most controversially of all – a scene where an ice-cube is applied to a female nipple. 'Video to us is like stereo was to Pink Floyd,' Duran Duran's Nick Rhodes told *Rolling Stone* in 1984. 'It was new, it was just happening. And we saw we could do a lot with it.' Made with club video screens in mind, the controversial video was banned by television, but an edited version still managed to shock. 'The original idea, I guess, was an ironic take on exploitation, because that's what the song was about,' director Kevin Godley explained later. 'We were trying to stay true, in our own way, to what the song was about and be ironic about it. But particularly in America, irony isn't a hugely popular thing, so maybe it just went over people's heads and all they saw was naked women.'

By October Duran Duran had reportedly sold over 100,000 copies of their debut album in the UK, and announced a celebratory third UK tour for the end of 1981 with news of a further twelve shows across the country – including two nights at London's Hammersmith Odeon. The success of *Duran Duran* and its three singles had even started to thaw a few journalistic hearts. A new single, 'My Own Way', the first from the band's second album, was released in November to capitalise on Duran Duran's success and to provide the band with their fourth single hit of the year when it reached number fourteen in the Christmas UK singles chart, spending almost three months in the Top 75 as 1981 gave way to 1982.

Despite dismissing 'My Own Way' as 'second division competent white funk-pop', *Record Mirror*'s Sunie found herself sufficiently enamoured to proclaim, 'If they'd stop all that cloddish pouting and allow themselves a grin or two, they'd be rather loveable.' 'Carefully designed for mass appeal, it's pleasant-ish and melodic, not so inoffensive as to be offensive, but light enough to be superfluous and/or instantly disposable,' was Lynden Barber's take in *Melody Maker*. 'The only instantly recognisable feature of Duran Duran is the singer's voice, otherwise they have no personality, no individuality, no quirks of style. I think this is what is known in some quarters as "good pop".'

Spandau Ballet also had a new single out in November. 'Paint Me Down' was the second single to be taken from their second album but failed to capitalise on the stellar success of their previous releases when it peaked at a lowly number thirty. The relative failure of 'Paint Me Down' took everyone by surprise, including *Top of the Pops*, who had pre-recorded a performance in anticipation of the single performing to a similar level as 'Chant No. 1', a performance which was subsequently never used.

"Paint Me Down' is lumpy and clumsy where 'Chant' was nimble and bright, and it's built around a very rudimentary and stubborn baseline which means the song sticks in the head but stays rigid and unexpressive,' declared the *NME*'s Gavin Martin. 'A skilfully stitched tapestry of influences – maybe – but it has a drab constitution with no new resource or imagination added. Too much fashion, not enough style.' 'They should have been content to be one hit wonders,' mocked *Smash Hits*' Johnny Black. 'This cringeworthy blooper can barely crawl out of the grooves of its own lethargy. Drunk on funk? Dipso on calypso more like.'

ISSN 0144 5804

AUGUST 29, 1981. 30p

MODERN ROMANCE • UB40

RECORD MIRROR

ORCHESTRAL MANOEUVRES

Sparks in the dark

GENESIS DATES • CASTLE DONINGTON REPORT

CLASSIX NOUVEAUX • HAZEL O'CONNOR • SIMPLE MINDS

ORCHESTRAL MANOEUVRES PIC BY ERIC WATSON

1981.2 Some Bizzare / Stevo / Depeche Mode / Soft Cell / Orchestral Manoeuvres In The Dark / Laurie Anderson / Blancmange

AT THE END OF January, *Sounds* reported that 'A dozen Futurist bands have been garnered together for a compilation called 'Some Bizzare Album' which has been put together by futurist DJ and entrepreneur Stevo,' to which they added, 'To coincide with the album's release 20 "Bizzare Evenings" have been lined up at clubs around the country and two of the bands appearing on the album will be playing at each event.' The piece also listed the dates and venues for nineteen shows, of which the first ten also appeared in a series of display adverts in the concert pages of the music press. 'Different bands on different nights' enthused the adverts, which then went on to list the twelve acts involved under a large picture of a fish: Fast Set, The Loved One, Blah Blah Blah, Illustration, Depeche Mode, The The, B-Movie, Jell, Blancmange, Soft Cell, Neu Electrikk and Naked Lunch. 'Which bands will be appearing where hasn't been revealed,' the report continued. 'Stevo says that it doesn't matter "because people should be into the whole scene and not just individual groups".'

The following week, reviews of the *Some Bizzare Album* started to appear in the music press. The release scored just two of a possible five stars from *Record Mirror*'s Chris Westwood, who suspected that the album was simply designed to profiteer from the 'futurist' fashion that was being spearheaded by Spandau Ballet, and rejected the release in his brief review as a collection of 'stale and trivial and – above all – loveless songs wrapped around cold, hollow images, no flair, no fight'. *Sounds*, more promisingly, gave over most of a page to their review of the album, which Betty Page mischievously ran under the title 'Q: Are We Not Men? A: We Are Stevo', a nod to the founder of the Some Bizzare label, and the sometime compiler of *Sounds*' new Futurist Chart, Stevo Pearce. Opening her review with an introduction to the eccentric maverick behind the release, Page wrote, 'In the dim and distant early months of 1980, a lone figure entered the *Sounds* scenario. Self-styled electro-entrepreneur Steve, complete with his half a lank fringe, offered up a chart the like of which had never before been witnessed,' she deadpanned. 'Full of bands who didn't fit the alternative label, weren't smart enough to be on Rough Trade.'

Page identified three tracks from the *Some Bizzare Album* for particular praise: Depeche Mode's 'Photographic' – 'the only featured band to make their synths go with beauty, bouncy energy and harmony'; B-Movie's 'Moles' – 'much more rock'n'roll than the rest'; and the 'quite charming' 'The Girl With The Patent Leather Face' from Soft Cell, whose 'crooning vocals from Marc Almond soar away close to the edge singing a stunningly visual fetishistic lyric'. *Sounds*' review was overwhelmingly supportive of the Some Bizzare project, Page ending her piece by celebrating the album's 'balance between fun, dance and thoughtfulness'. 'They do it with a certain panache,' Chris Bohn wrote of Soft Cell's 'The Girl With The Patent Leather Face' in the *NME*, which he went on to describe as 'mock grotesque, mildly amusing/insulting clockwork pop'. Depeche Mode and Blancmange he considered more mainstream highlights, praising the former's contribution, 'Photographic', for its 'very assured, neatly structured and entwined synth melodies' and the 'persistent quiver of a rhythm line' which ran through the track; and Blancmange's 'Sad Day' as a 'beautiful, wistful instrumental'.

Unfortunately the promising response to the album failed to extend to the Some Bizzare Evenings and, a week after their review of the album, *Sounds* reported that the tour had collapsed after playing just two shows, at Leeds' Electro Disco and Sheffield's Limit Club, each featuring The Loved One and Depeche Mode. In the report Stevo was quoted as saying, 'The tour hadn't been well organised, but we decided that the bands shouldn't appear in such normal pub and club venues because they are part of the rock'n'roll lifestyle and just rip off bands.'

Sounds further fuelled the myth of Stevo by publishing an interview with the Some Bizzare label head, and also by reporting on its gossip page that, during negotiations with Phonogram to secure distribution for the *Some Bizzare Album*, Pearce 'refused to put pen to paper until a most important rider had been included in his contract: 40p a week sweetie money. And so the world held its breath until the moguls finally gave way to this drastic demand.' Having so thoroughly championed the *Some Bizzare Album* in her review it was Betty Page who was dispatched to interview Stevo to find out more about Some Bizzare. 'The Bizzare philosophy is that nothing is going to sound the same,' explained Stevo of his nascent label, while taking exception at attempts to dismiss the compilation as cashing in on a new fad. 'You can't call it all futurist just because it's electronic,' stated Pearce. 'Electronic music isn't fashion – it's a style of music... I think it [Some Bizzare] will be the biggest independent label album of this year or last year,' Stevo promised by way of a conclusion.

In fact, as Some Bizzare was manufactured and distributed by Phonogram, the label's releases didn't qualify for the independent charts, and although the *Some Bizzare Album* did spend a single week at number fifty-eight in the UK album charts in March, the release wasn't the commercial success Stevo predicted. However, the album represented the first mainstream exposure for both Depeche Mode and Soft Cell, whose combined sales by the end of 1981 were sufficient to count the album as a hugely important stepping stone in the development of electronic pop.

Despite a persistent rumour that Depeche Mode finalised their initial line-up after hearing singer Dave Gahan performing David Bowie's 'Heroes' in the adjacent rehearsal room at Basildon's Woodlands School, founding member, Vince Clarke is emphatic in his rejection of the story. 'That's not true,' Clarke shrugs today, 'We didn't hear Dave singing in the room next door, we didn't rehearse at Woodlands School either.' 'I don't really remember how we met Dave,' Clarke continued, 'He was one of those people that was one of the cool kids, and we weren't, we definitely weren't cool, not me, or Martin or Fletch.' What is less contentious is that Depeche Mode emerged from the ashes of two Basildon bands, Composition Of Sound and French Look, and consisted of Vince Clarke, Andy Fletcher and Martin Gore, each on synthesiser, and Dave Gahan on vocals, the band calling themselves Depeche Mode in time for a show at The Bridgehouse venue in Canning Town at the end of September 1980. 'We just liked the sound of "Depeche Mode",' the band would tell *Smash Hits'* Ian Cranna in their first interview for the paper some six months later, explaining that the name came from a French magazine, adding, 'It has no meaning at all.' Impressed by their performance at The Bridgehouse, Terry Murphy, who owned the venue, continued to book shows for Depeche

Mode, an arrangement which led to the band playing in Canning Town roughly once a fortnight until the end of the year.

In the middle of November 1980 Murphy booked Depeche Mode as support for Mute Records' Fad Gadget, who was promoting his debut album *Fireside Favourites*. Mute Records' Daniel Miller was at the show to look after the sound for Fad Gadget and watched Depeche Mode's set with increasing interest and enthusiasm. 'I saw them at the soundcheck and I thought they were a right bunch of spotty pseudo-New Romantics. But as soon as they started playing I thought "What the fuck is this? It's incredible!"' Miller recalled in the Mute Records book *A Visual Document*. 'It was exactly the the kind of thing I'd been hoping would happen. These were teenagers – seventeen or eighteen years of age – they'd chosen synthesisers as their instruments and they were making great pop music.' Miller introduced himself to the band after the show and arranged to see them play again, after which he proposed they make a single together.

The first Depeche Mode single, 'Dreaming Of Me', followed in February 1981 and Betty Page wasted no time in awarding it *Sounds'* Single of the Week, praising the release as 'Refreshing for its total lack of anything deep, meaningful, heavy or arty. Very much an instant now sound.' In the same review Page also lauded Depeche Mode as 'among the best of the new breed of techno poppers and this wistful, melodic, soft ditty, verging on electro-folk, is destined for Silicon Teens-style success'. Red Starr, in *Smash Hits'* Independent Bitz column, proclaimed himself delighted by Depeche Mode in general – 'On the fringes of the Blitz Kids scene by virtue of their electronic music and evident taste for make up and flash clothes, Depeche Mode in fact far outshine many a better known name by virtue of their ability to write great tunes and treat them right' – and by 'Dreaming Of Me' in particular, describing the single as 'Simply wonderful… tasteful and tuneful, danceable and intelligent… it deserves to be utterly huge.'

Record Mirror's Philip Hall was less certain of the merits of the single's 'drum machine, humanoid vocals and synthesised hand claps' – which he ultimately dismissed as 'Floppy fringe music' – but nevertheless paid 'Dreaming Of Me' a backhanded compliment by noting that Depeche Mode's debut was 'as predictable and well crafted as any Ultravox song'. The *NME*'s Chris Bohn, while significantly more charmed by the single, also chose to compare Depeche Mode with another of their influences. 'As sweetly unassuming a slice of electronic whimsy as anything by early Orchestral Manoeuvres.'

While both Ultravox and OMD were tangible influences on Depeche Mode, the fledgeling band remained spiky about their inspirations. 'We wouldn't like to be categorised with them or associated with them at all,' Dave Gahan told Betty Page, who had made the mistake of comparing Depeche Mode with OMD in an interview with the former for *Sounds*. The reality was that OMD, and in particular their 'Electricity' single, had exercised a profound influence on Depeche Mode songwriter Vince Clarke. 'When I first heard 'Electricity' in 1979 I could immediately relate to it,' Clarke explained later. 'Here was music I could work out and play... and the B-side, 'Almost', made me realise electronic music need not be robotic and cold but emotional and indeed, soulful.'

The February release of 'Dreaming Of Me' was supported by a run of Depeche Mode features across the music press. 'They are bass synth player Andrew Fletcher, an insurance man; David Gahan, lead vocalist, electronic percussionist and trainee window dresser; the silent Martin Gore, synthesist and banker; and Vincent Clarke, writer, synthesist and otherwise unemployed,' introduced Chris Bohn in his interview piece for the *NME* a couple of weeks after the release of the single. 'Due to their extremely shy natures,' Bohn continued, 'the four have chosen to be chaperoned by producer [Daniel] Miller, whom they refer to as Uncle Daniel.' It was Miller who outlined the challenge that Mute Records had ahead of them. 'We're making every sort of legal effort to make it a hit,' Miller explained. 'We have had some experience with the Silicon Teens in terms of marketing and how best to approach it. I think we're at a stage now where we can make a really concerted effort – hopefully doing the right things at the right time. In a way it's a sort of test case.' And as a test case the release of 'Dreaming Of Me' was a positive one. The single quickly topped the new independent singles chart and even spent a month in the UK singles chart, where it peaked at an encouraging number fifty-seven.

Having made advances to Depeche Mode to join his Some Bizzare roster until he lost them to Mute, by April Stevo was nevertheless ready to release the first Some Bizzare single, although that wasn't the straightforward proposition it might have been. Soft Cell – Dave Ball and Marc Almond ('We couldn't have been more contrasting,' Almond noted in his memoir *Tainted Life* later, 'Dave in a denim jacket, jeans and desert wellies, tall and stocky with black curly hair; me in gold-lamé trousers, a leopard-skin T-shirt on a small skinny frame with a blond crop.') – who Stevo was also managing, were to release two singles, the first a seven inch of 'A Man Can Get Lost' with 'Memorabilia' on the B-side; and the second a twelve-inch single of 'Memorabilia' with 'Persuasion' on the B-side a couple of weeks later.

Betty Page, one of Soft Cell's earliest champions, reviewed both singles for *Sounds* at the beginning of April. 'A Man Can Get Lost' she made one of her '7″ Grooves of the Week', praising its 'warm, tongue-in-cheek type of electro-funk dabbling' and declaring the release 'Cool as a mountain stream and just as refreshing.' On the same page the 'Memorabilia' twelve-inch single was included in Page's '12″ Tips for the Top'. 'Have a ball in your own backroom with the spine tingling, euphoric, toe-tapping, spirit-lifting Soft Cell,' Page enthused.

'Memorabilia' quickly became the track that the media chose to focus upon. ''Memorabilia' is an excellent record, with Marc's voice playing clever tricks over the assorted hardware,' *Record Mirror* applauded. 'Soft Cell clearly listen to funk and dub as well as the required masters of practical electronics, and the result of their homework is a very tasteful hybrid.' But not all the reviews were quite so generous. 'Dull and soulless "electro-disco",' was the *NME*'s uncompromising take. 'The fact that many of London's funksters are dancing to things like this and Heaven 17 proves they have no funk in them at all,' sniffed the review. 'If it's just beat they need, why don't they amplify a giant metronome?'

Produced by Daniel Miller, 'Memorabilia' quickly caught the ear of clubland and wasted no time before it was topping the various 'futurist' charts of the time. '[Daniel Miller] seems sympathetic to our ideas, and hasn't taken over in the studio,' Dave Ball told Betty Page in Soft Cell's first interview for *Sounds*, before describing the duo's output as a 'danceable sort of pop music… That's always been our idea, doing sad sort of songs, nothing bleak, no grinding grating noises,' explained Ball, a theme Marc Almond then developed in the band's first interview for the *NME* in May: 'Both of us have always enjoyed listening to dance music, and we wanted to interpret disco in our own way. We wanted to make good quality soulful electronic dance music, more biting than the usual bland disco stuff.'

Soft Cell played a few shows to promote the release of 'A Man Can Get Lost' and 'Memorabilia', including a performance at Rusty Egan's new club night in Dartford. 'I don't think I've ever experienced such strength, richness and rhythm emanating from two blokes, one syn-drum, one synthesiser and a tape recorder before,' declared *Sounds*' Tony Mitchell, despite Marc Almond cheerily telling his colleague Betty Page that 'Most of the live set is taped, about 95 per cent. We look on live gigs as making a personal appearance with our music, still if we had to do everything live we'd have loads of people in the group – the Soft Cell Synthesiser Orchestra.' Instead Mitchell concluded, 'They're fun to watch, fun to listen to and provide ultimately, an irresistible motive force for limbs both ancient and modern.'

Given the duo's shared art-school background it was perhaps unsurprising that Soft Cell's live presentation included films and slide projections, which in turn led to critics drawing parallels with some of Soft Cell's peers. 'We've been compared to Orchestral Manoeuvres, Gary Numan, Human League etc. Just because we use synthesisers and slides,' Marc Almond told the *NME*. 'I don't think we're like any of those bands.' In fact by the time of 'Memorabilia''s release in March, Soft Cell were already limiting their use of film footage. 'We used to have two films going continuously all the way through the set, but now we really like people to get involved in moving about and actually dancing,' Almond told Betty Page. 'People were just standing there watching the films,' added Dave Ball. 'We're more like a cabaret than a rock band really,' confessed Almond.

'Memorabilia''s lack of mainstream chart success was of concern to Soft Cell's paymasters, Phonogram, and plans for further releases from Soft Cell, and in particular the go-ahead for the duo to record their debut album, were put on hold while a new round of negotiations took place between band and label. It would take another three frustrating months before Marc Almond and Dave Ball were able to release a second Soft Cell single for Phonogram, and even then the label had resisted committing to an album until they had seen some success in the singles chart. 'We've got everything ready and prepared, but we're being held back,' Almond told Betty Page at the end of July. 'It's a very frustrating and worrying time.'

Set up by the February release of 'Dreaming Of Me' and a run of live shows, Depeche Mode released their second single in June. 'New Life' trod a similar pop path to its predecessor and was quickly picked up by Radio 1's Peter Powell and Richard Skinner in addition to a largely positive set of reviews from the music press. 'Another winner,' enthused *Melody Maker*'s Paul Colbert. 'A drawn out synth figure suddenly gallops into full techno rhythm fury, looking fatter and more interesting at every passing moment.' 'A very attractive tune, shamelessly commercial,' agreed *Record Mirror*'s Simon Ludgate, leaving it to the *NME*'s Julie Burchill to take an opposite view: 'The Depeche Mode is a maggoty old pumpkin masquerading as a glass coach.'

'New Life' immediately entered the lower reaches of the UK singles chart, where it spent fifteen weeks in the Top 75, six of which were spent in the Top 20, on its way to an August peak position of eleven, earning the band no less than three performances on *Top of the Pops* and reported sales of around a quarter of a million copies. Not that Depeche Mode had much time to contemplate their success. In June *Sounds'* Betty Page visited the band at South London's Blackwing Studios to interview them for their first cover feature to find them already at work on a third single, a promising piece of work entitled 'Just Can't Get Enough'.

Marvelling at the difference in the band since her first encounter with them in January, Page reported that Depeche Mode were now '100% more confident, talkative, witty and brighter'. With 'New Life' firmly in the charts, Page found the band invigorated by their success and learning fast. 'We learned a lot from 'Dreaming', came in here and just did a better job on the next one,' explained Dave Gahan, who also featured on the issue's front cover, posing with a microphone stand and striking a defiant rock'n'roll frontman pose. The interview also tackled the tricky question of how to pronounce Depeche Mode. ''Depeche-ay', if you please. It's probably grammatically wrong,' said Vince, 'but we like it that way.'

Although things weren't quite as rosy in their camp, Soft Cell remained publicly optimistic despite the perceived failure of 'Memorabilia'. 'I think we're pleased in a way that it wasn't a hit – it would've put a stamp on us,' Almond told *Sounds*. 'It's nicer for it to be a cult thing, a sort of classic in a way. It left us free to take a slightly different direction.' And Soft Cell's different direction was to prove a shrewd move. 'Tainted Love' – a cover of Gloria Jones's northern soul classic – was released in July in seven-inch and twelve-inch editions, both of which featured a cover of The Supremes' 'Where Did Our Love Go?' on the B-side. In the case of the extended twelve-inch mix the two tracks were mixed together allowing 'Tainted Love' to flow seamlessly into 'Where Did Our Love Go?', a technique which particularly impressed the *NME* who, in their review of the single at the beginning of August, wrote, 'The wind-down segue into The Supremes' 'Where Did Our Love Go?' is so wonderful I'm still reeling.'

The *NME*'s review – which proclaimed Soft Cell 'once daft, suddenly splendid' – also went on to praise 'Tainted Love' for its 'sharpness, clarity and streamlined class', while Betty Page turned in an equally positive review for *Sounds*, in which she applauded Soft Cell's 'surprisingly minimal but eccentric and loveable' cover for its 'deliciously forceful and soulful vocals... Purists will hate it!' Page exclaimed. 'I love it!' *Melody Maker* meanwhile reviewed the single twice, which allowed them to cover both bases: initially Lynden Barber dismissed the single as 'Some of the most appallingly limp music it's ever been my misfortune to hear,' but a fortnight later the paper's Neil Rowland redressed the balance by issuing *Melody Maker* readers with a stern warning to dismiss Soft Cell as 'just another electronic group' at their peril. 'Don't take them for granted, don't under estimate them because of the sound – it has nothing to do with nonsensicals like Duran Duran or Depeche Mode – it has real anguish,' Rowland proclaimed. 'This is dance – I love it as an exorcism of the soul.'

Talking to Rowland's *Melody Maker* colleague Steve Sutherland a few weeks later, Soft Cell concurred with Rowland's suggestion that Soft Cell operated on genuine emotions. 'The main thing about us is our variety; we're heading for a minimal, sort of spacious sound,' asserted Dave Ball. 'The thing that singles us out is that it's got a lot more feeling than a lot of the other futurist music.' Marc Almond agreed, adding, 'We've got a lot of intense emotion, and we believe in un-narrowness, in taking inspiration from lots of different sorts of music and things that have gone before and things that are happening now.'

Marc Almond expanded on this theme, while also attempting to disassociate Soft Cell from their perceived 'futurist' peers, later that year in an interview with *Sounds*' Dave McCullough. 'When people say, "Oh Soft Cell are a futurist band" I find it astonishing! Because we always write about things that are very current, from say two seconds ago in a newspaper. And we blend that into music that has its roots in the sixties,' Almond explained. 'It's in fact anything but futuristic... That way we have it good both ways. We're very "now" and very nostalgic at the same time. That's why I think 'Tainted Love' was so successful. It mixed the two ingredients.'

And 'Tainted Love' was successful. Combining the overwhelmingly positive press reviews with enthusiastic support for the song from radio – which kicked off with a prestigious Radio 1 live session for Richard Skinner at the end of July – the single wasted no time in hitting the lower reaches of the UK singles chart on its way to a sixteen-week chart run which included no less than seven weeks in the Top 10 and two weeks at the top of the charts in September. In fact 'Tainted Love' racked up sales of over one million copies for Soft Cell in 1981, making the track the UK's bestselling single of the year. Over the course of the next six months the single also went on to be a hit in most parts of the

Western world, and achieved number one positions in Germany, Australia, South Africa and Canada in addition to breaking in the USA, where it peaked at number eight in *Billboard*'s main Hot 100 singles chart.

Success at such an intense and global level presented its own set of problems for Soft Cell, the main one being financial, as Dave Ball would write in his autobiography *Electronic Boy* in 2020. 'Over the years, that decision to record two cover versions and not one of our own songs on the B-side was to cost Marc and me about a million quid each in lost writing-credit royalty earnings,' Ball revealed. 'It was like the anti-Midas touch struck from day one, inversely snatching failure from the jaws of success.' And for all their success, Soft Cell never saw themselves as a commercial proposition: 'We like writing songs about sex and trash. We did that consciously to get a dirtier image really,' Marc Almond confessed to the *NME*'s Chris Bohn. 'Our writing is getting more personal, a bit deeper and a lot sadder. It's about reaching into the stuff and writing about things that you have to feel.'

Soft Cell's exploration of dark themes, combined with Almond's unthreatening candour, enamoured the band to a portion of the significant new pop audience, attracted to the duo's acceptable alienation. But Soft Cell's appeal wasn't just about the music. In Marc Almond, Soft Cell's audience had been delivered an easily imitated style which was rapidly picked up by disaffected youth everywhere, and revealed in Almond's penchant for black clothes, black eyeliner, costume jewellery and an armful of bangles. From their first *Top of the Pops* performance of 'Tainted Love' in the middle of August, the band began to notice that their audience was largely made up of clones of themselves. 'Within days, all over the UK, tens of thousands of teenagers, male and female, were copying his look,' marvelled Dave Ball of his bandmate. 'Sales of black jeans, black T-shirts and mascara must have gone through the roof.'

Alongside 'Tainted Love' in the Top 5 of the UK singles chart in the second half of September was 'Souvenir', the first single to be taken from OMD's new album. 'Souvenir' had started it's ten-week chart journey at the end of August and had peaked at number three in September, one place behind 'Tainted Love', which itself had been displaced from the top of the charts by Adam & The Ants' 'Prince Charming'. In fact the success of 'Souvenir' was such that OMD quickly announced a seventeen-date UK tour in November, and were also invited to perform the single on the Christmas Day edition of *Top of the Pops* at the end of the year.

Soft Cell, 1983.

With the exception of a *Smash Hits* front cover in March when the band supplied the magazine with a live version of 'Pretending To See The Future' for a free flexi-disc, OMD spent the first half of 1981 out of the UK eye. Partly they used that time to work on material for their third album, but mostly OMD took their live show to the USA and Europe, where they also undertook promotional duties for 'Enola Gay', which was proving particularly successful in Italy, Spain, France and Switzerland. In fact it wasn't until the beginning of August that Humphreys and McCluskey were able to announce a new single, 'Souvenir', for the middle of the month, and an album for October. 'Because they haven't seen you on TV in nine months and they haven't heard any records from you, they think you must have been slouching around in The Bahamas or something, living off your ill-gotten gains,' Andy McCluskey told *Smash Hits*. 'And all we've ever done is work!'

Having been off the music radar for the best part of eight months, and given the band's success with *Organisation* and its associated singles, anticipation for OMD's new material was high when 'Souvenir' was released in August to widespread bafflement on the part of the UK music press. 'The Manoeuvres get trickier by the minute,' declared Colin Irwin, reviewing 'Souvenir' for *Melody Maker*. 'It opens so like an Ennio Morricone soundtrack you expect

Clint Eastwood to come shambling on to the screen, and then slips into 'Exodus' piano, before settling into a haunting song that's both intense and understated.' *Record Mirror*'s Sunie also picked up on the cinematic nature of the single: 'Very reminiscent of French movie music,' she offered, 'you know the stuff, rain against windowpane, wistful blonde, empty beach, crowded railway platform.' 'I preferred them when they were still OMITD,' wrote Pete Silverton in *Smash Hits*, gleefully setting himself up for the punchline, 'Since then, they seem to have lost IT.'

"Souvenir' took eight or nine months to develop. I started writing it immediately after 'Organisation',' Paul Humphreys told *Record Mirror*'s Daniela Soave later in the year. 'To begin with it was so abstract and really, really choral and slow. If you'd have said it was a single then I'd have laughed. David Hughes came round with some tapes of choirs which I made into chords, then I wrote the tune when I was sitting around in the studio. It stayed like that for several months, until one day I got a voice for it.'

In September, capitalising on their return to the public eye, OMD announced that their new album, the grandly titled *Architecture And Morality*, was to come out at the beginning of November. At the same time Andy McCluskey and Paul Humphreys embarked upon another round of interviews in support of their new project. In an interview for *Record Mirror*, which saw OMD back on their front cover, Mark Cooper found Humphreys and McCluskey preoccupied with the need keep evolving the OMD sound. 'The danger lies in repeating yourself because then you get bored with what you do. We wouldn't be able to repeat something like 'Enola Gay' even if we wanted to,' McCluskey explained, to which Humphreys added, 'Nothing would be worse than if the record company could put out a compilation of five albums by us and you couldn't tell the difference between the songs in terms of when they'd been recorded.'

Asked how the duo managed to avoid the trap of repeating previous formulas, OMD revealed that the sound of the new album had been underpinned by paranoia and technology. 'Paul and I wonder constantly if we're doing the right thing. If your integrity's intact. If we still enjoy what we're doing,' McCluskey confessed. 'This new record is nothing like the last one. There's a couple of tracks on it that are good solid pop songs in the OMD mould but the rest are all different.' 'One of the best things about having made a bit of money is that we've been able to afford new instruments to play around with. There's all kinds lying around the studio now,' added Humphreys. 'Whenever we go into the studio or pick up an instrument, we try to think, what haven't we done before, what could we try that's new.'

The band also revealed that an important aspect of the spirit of experimentation that led to the creation of *Architecture And Morality* was the band's own naivety. Paul Humphreys: 'One of the things about us two is that even after six years our level of musical competency is dreadful. We're not trained and we're not musicians. As a result, we're always discovering things a musician would be unable to think of because his training and its conventions make some steps inconceivable. If it works, it works, we don't know the rules so we can't follow them.'

Hot on the heels of 'Souvenir' came the third single from Depeche Mode, a track which would become one of their most classic and recognisable hits. Recorded at London's Blackwing Studios in June, 'Just Can't Get Enough' hit the ground running upon release and was immediately propelled into the lower reaches of the UK singles chart, the band's new fanbase ensuring that it entered the chart a few places shy of the Top 40 just one week after release. Given the previous success of 'Dreaming Of Me' and 'New Life', Radio 1 scented a further hit and was quick to get on board, and the music press remained broadly positive in the face of Depeche Mode's latest musical statement.

'Bubblegum is back!' enthused Sunie in *Record Mirror*, awarding 'Just Can't Get Enough' Single of the Week and describing the track as 'Hugely enjoyable, bouncy and boppy.' *Sounds'* John Gill praised the single as a 'shiny pop anthem… It's firmly set in the '78 School of Electronics; foursquare pulse, funny-funky time signatures,' Gill observed while comparing the song favourably to The Human League's early output. *Melody Maker's* Patrick Humphries was unconvinced, however: 'I can. You will,' he declared in response to the title.

Fuelled by a quirky *Top of the Pops* appearance featuring the band playing along to the single's brass section on plastic trumpets, and a bare-chested Martin Gore, his nipples obscured by carefully positioned braces, 'Just Can't Get Enough' earned Depeche Mode their first Top 10 single when it climbed to number eight in the UK singles chart in October as part of a ten-week chart run, in the process picking up in excess of 200,000 sales by the end of the year.

Before the release of *Architecture And Morality* in November, and as 'Just Can't Get Enough' began its slow decent of the UK singles chart, DinDisc decided to release a second OMD single, 'Joan Of Arc', one of two songs on the album inspired by the 13th-century saint. 'It starts all angelic voices from the balcony of a draughty cathedral: fortunately a glockenspiel and a drum machine drift in to save the simile and the Orchs take off on a moody fantasy of myth and martyrdom,' revealed Paul Colbert in a cautious review of the single for *Melody Maker*. 'The backing is as soft as the vocals are wispy, but it's not strong Manoeuvres material and fades like the spoke of its inspiration.' The *NME* was less ambivalent: 'I expect more from Orchestral Manoeuvres, but they appear to be spitefully set on becoming the witless stainless wimps enemies erroneously used to suggest they were... I think they've gone mad.'

'Joan Of Arc' followed 'Souvenir' into the UK singles chart where it spent a month in the Top 10 – which included two weeks at a peak position of number five – remaining in the charts until well into the new year and selling in excess of 250,000 copies in the process. Once again OMD were invited onto *Top of the Pops*, who showed their performance twice, once at the end of October, when 'Joan Of Arc' was still ascending the chart, and again when the single was at its chart peak in November, in the very same week that *Architecture And Morality* was released.

'Hallelujah! OMD are literally back on song, reigning in their more ambitious ideas into concise but varied and imaginative arrangements that actually boost instead of swamp their wonderful melodies and intelligent lyrics,' was Ian Cranna's exuberant opinion of *Architecture And Morality* in a nine-out-of-ten review for *Smash Hits*. *Record Mirror*'s Daniela Soave was also upbeat, although more cautiously so. 'It is not so blatantly poppy as the first album, nor is it as overtly bleak as 'Organisation',' she mused. 'And because it falls between creating one overall mood and a collection of classic pop – 'Architecture And Morality' requires more effort on the listener's part before the layers and textures can be enjoyably recognised.'

'Are Orchestral Manoeuvres scientifically testing just how serene, solemn, poignant and grave serious popular music can get and still stay popular?' Paul Morley demanded in his review for the *NME*. 'The ten songs lack laughs, lumps, lines: these are guiltless hymns to dying glory, rock steady studies of immensity and the sense of sacredness in time and space... OMITD have lost themselves to a dream,' Morley proclaimed.

Morley's accusations of OMD's pretentiousness weren't entirely without foundation. Interviewed by Morley's *NME* colleague Paul Du Noyer the following week, Andy McCluskey was asked about the *Architecture And Morality* album title. 'It sounds very pretentious,' the singer admitted. 'I'm sure if we hadn't used it for our title I would have thought it was pretentious for anyone else. But it seemed to make sense for us.' In fact, the title emerged from a conversation between McCluskey and Martha Ladly, formerly of fellow DinDisc act Martha & The Muffins and girlfriend of OMD designer Peter Saville, in which Ladly revealed that she had considered using the name – inspired by the title of David Watkins' 1977 book *Morality and Architecture: The Development of a Theme in Architectural History and Theory from the Gothic Revival to the Modern Movement* – for a project of her own before abandoning it to OMD. 'I haven't read the whole book, largely because I got bored to tears with it, it's such a dull book,' McCluskey told *Sounds'* Johnny Waller at the beginning of December. 'But the phrase 'Architecture And Morality' seemed to sum up the way we used to work, in a musical sense, it was like the architecture of the machine-orientated rhythm track, plus the morality of the words and melodies.'

Less pretentious was OMD's live presentation of *Architecture And Morality*, the band playing a sold-out UK tour in November to the delight of band, audience, and media alike. 'This is the first time we've ever had to choose what we play,' Andy McCluskey told *Melody Maker*'s Steve Sutherland shortly before the start of the tour. 'Before, we've always had to play everything. It's the dawning of a new era!' 'Sixty minutes of intelligent, accessible, danceable pop – well planned, well played and completely irresistible,' was *Smash Hits'* Steve Bush's verdict on one of the band's London shows.

Architecture And Morality entered the UK album chart at number five after just one week on sale and peaked at number three the following week – OMD's highest album placing to date – remaining in the charts for a further eight months, during which the album spent twelve weeks in the Top 10. Indeed *Architecture And Morality* would return to its peak position of number three again in February 1982 in response to the success of the third and final single to be taken from the album in January 1982.

Despite appearing on *Architecture And Morality* as 'Joan Of Arc (Maid Of Orleans)' for the single the song was retitled 'Maid Of Orleans (The Waltz Of Joan Of Arc)' to avoid being confused with 'Joan Of Arc'. 'I like Joan of Arc as a historical character because no one really knows anything about her and that's part of my fascination with things that aren't black-and-white, things you can't quite put your finger on,' Andy McCluskey told *Sounds* in December. 'My view of her seems to fall into two differing categories. There's

273

the little Catholic girl, the virginal saint led on by her voices; and there's also this Amazonian crusading figure – possibly even a man… there's so many great, interesting things about her and I was simply drawn to her.'

In one of his final media pieces of 1981 Andy McCluskey selected one of 1981's most unexpected electronic hits as one of his six 'Star Choice' tracks for *Record Mirror*. Alongside tracks from Kraftwerk, La Düsseldorf and Leonard Cohen, McCluskey recalled being 'stunned speechless' after first hearing Laurie Anderson's October single release, 'O Superman'.

'O Superman' had already caused a minor furore earlier in the year when import copies from the USA had caught the ear of those in the know. *Sounds* ran a short piece on the record in September in which Chris Burkham noted 'ripples of interest from labels as diverse as Daniel Miller's Mute and Alan Horne's Postcard', before reporting that Rough Trade had stepped up as the official UK distributor of the single on behalf of the release's US label, One Ten Records. 'Laurie Anderson is a performance artist (hold back those derisive chuckles) from New York, who manages to keep her performances free of the usual arty-tarty conceptualising that those of her ilk are associated with,' revealed Burkham.

Burkham's piece helped fuel an already increasing interest in the record, and WEA subsequently picked it up for a full domestic release at the end of September, the single scheduled to tie in with Anderson's first-ever UK appearances at London's Riverside Studios. Reviews of the single from the UK music press were varied: 'Anderson weaves around a machine that's grabbed a central slot on modern media consciousness: the answering machine. With it, disembodied voices of parents, friends, lovers, strangers, assault you with their conflicting messages every time you touch home base. Anderson is oblique, evocative, not afraid of silence. She is daring and very funny indeed,' enthused Vivien Goldman in the *NME*.

Melody Maker's Paolo Hewitt was personally unconvinced, writing, 'This sickly little record is apparently in great demand. I can't imagine why. Unbearably coy, Miss Anderson discovers studio effects and breathes out an eight minute little ditty to Superman through her phone answering machine,' but nevertheless Hewitt thawed sufficiently to admit to the record having 'a certain charm', and predicted that with radio support it could end up a hit: 'All it will take is one of those wimpy little jockeys to pick up on this record and shove it down our necks every hour.' By the middle of October, Hewitt's worst fears had been realised. 'Early reactions have already been hysterical,' reported *Smash Hits'* Ian Birch. 'Peter Powell can scarcely get through his [Radio 1] afternoon show without going bananas over it.'

'O Superman' entered the UK singles chart at number eighteen in the middle of October and immediately leaped to its peak position of number two before dropping out of the chart by the end of November. 'So what's it gonna be like being a pop star?' *Melody Maker*'s Steve Sutherland asked Anderson. 'I haven't the slightest idea,' she replied. 'Y'know, I always wanted to be a librarian.'

Reviewed alongside OMD's *Architecture And Morality* in the *NME*, Paul Morley turned in an upbeat review of Depeche Mode's debut album, *Speak & Spell*, released at the same time, and which Morley described as 'a simple sample of generous, silly, susceptible electro-tickled pop.' 'A charming, cheeky collection of compulsive dance tunes, bubbly and brief like the best pop should be,' acclaimed Sunie in her *Record Mirror* review, praising Depeche Mode for lighting up 'a dull chart landscape' and celebrating the band's 'bubblegum simplicity': 'Their chief skill lies in making their art sound artless: simple synthesiser melodies, Gahan's tuneful but undramatic singing and a matter-of-fact, gimmick-free production all help achieve this unforced effect. But a good listen to their first LP reveals smartness beneath the simplicity.'

'So obviously bright, so clearly sparkling with new life, it's a wonder they don't burn permanent dancing shadows onto the walls,' enthused *Melody Maker*'s Paul Colbert in his review of the album. *Sounds*' Betty Page also professed to being charmed by *Speak & Spell*, which she described as 'A perfectly uncontrived pop soufflé… These boys have a sense of humour, a sense of simplicity and a sense of what's good and natural,' Page wrote, adding: 'Synthetic textures and natural harmony make one highly vibrant whole. It's perfect, un-prepossessing, unpretentious pop, but not so insubstantial that it just floats away.'

While Depeche Mode had played a number of dates around the country over the course of 1981, the band didn't embark on their first proper tour until after the release of *Speak & Spell*, when they played a run of shows in October and November in support of the album. *Record Mirror*'s Mike Nicholls sat down with Martin Gore, Dave Gahan and Andy Fletcher in the cafe of Littlewoods department store in Basildon and asked why the tour was so short. 'We get tired after two nights,' replied Gahan, revealing that the band's agent had hoped to put in double the number of shows. 'But we reckon thirteen will be enough,' the singer explained affably, his confidence faltering slightly as he added: 'Or fourteen if we do a second night at the [London] Lyceum.

Depends if we can sell it out or not.' As it would turn out, Gahan had nothing to fear: a second show at the Lyceum was quickly added to the run of dates and Depeche Mode played to capacity crowds at every show.

Support act at all the shows of that first tour was Blancmange, a duo who had been hovering on the edges of the electronic scene for a while and who, along with Depeche Mode, had been one of the standout acts on Stevo's *Some Bizzare Album* when it came out at the start of the year. Blancmange's contribution to the Some Bizzare release had been the wispy, instrumental track 'Sad Day'. 'Our track on the album was recorded two years ago and is totally unrepresentative,' exclaimed Blancmange's Stephen Luscombe in an interview about the compilation for *Sounds* in February. Blancmange had come to Stevo's attention via a limited-edition six-track EP, *Irene & Mavis*, which the duo had financed themselves and released on their own Blaah Music label in 1980. Stevo had got the EP from Rough Trade and liked what he heard enough to contact the band with the offer of playing at some gigs he was organising, which in turn led to his offering Blancmange the chance to contribute to the compilation.

In his review of Depeche Mode's hometown show at Basildon club Raquels on November 10th, the *NME*'s Dave Hill introduced Blancmange's Stephen Luscombe and Neil Arthur, respectively, as 'one man and his machines and tapes, and another man with his voice, his suit, a Bogart way with a cigarette, and an exaggeratedly gaunt frame and features', before going on to applaud the duo's short set. 'Together, they mould a weighty storm of atmospheres and pulses, add a little guitar, and the voice, harrowing, crawling from the tight extremes of a broad mouth, is a siren buried in the deluge,' Hill enthused, concluding, 'Blancmange, a little hard to take, could equally become hard to resist.'

Moving on to the main attraction, Hill was equally enthusiastic: 'Depeche Mode have truly humanised the man-as-machine connotations of synthi-pop, whilst taking advantage of its unique properties,' he wrote. 'They did not act like heroes,' declared *Melody Maker*'s Steve Sutherland after a show at London's Lyceum in December. 'They are to be embraced with affection, enjoyed for their enjoyment and the way they suggest enjoyment. Innocence is not as disposable as it may seem, and Depeche Mode are a warm breeze which whispers in your ear. Their debut album's a collection of will-be greatest hits and their live show's the same but with slightly shakier vocals... Depeche Mode are pop at its purest.'

Testament to their success over the course of the year, Depeche Mode ended 1981 with a coveted spot on the prestigious Christmas Day edition of *Top of the Pops*, where they joined OMD, Soft Cell, Ultravox and Spandau Ballet to deliver a line-up which would leave no one in any doubt that electronic pop had become a force to be reckoned with. The appearance, which was recorded earlier in December, and which featured Martin Gore with his shirt on, would prove bittersweet for the band as it would mark Depeche Mode's last public appearance with Vince Clarke, who had announced that he was leaving the group just a couple of weeks earlier.

Having become increasingly disenchanted over the course of the *Speak & Spell* project, Clarke's departure was announced in a press release issued by Mute in December and picked up by all the main music publications. 'The reason for leaving is that he wants to concentrate on being simply a song writer, rather than go on the road or take part in Depeche Mode's other activities,' explained *Record Mirror*. 'However the band will still use his songs and he will not be replaced.' While the various news pieces were unable to provide any specific information about what Clarke might do next, the paper trod the party line and sought to assure its readers that business for Depeche Mode would continue as usual. 'A new single also comes out in January, but the group have yet to decide on a title,' they added. 'A spokesman would only reveal, "the single will be a little different to what they've played before. I think it will be a nice surprise."'

Given its astonishing success earlier in the year it came as no surprise that *Top of the Pops* requested that Soft Cell perform 'Tainted Love' on the show's festive edition. However, by the time the show aired on Christmas Day 1981, Soft Cell were celebrating another major hit with their second Parlophone single, 'Bedsitter', which had peaked at number four in the UK singles chart at the beginning of December. 'With the phenomenal international success of 'Tainted Love', we had inadvertently made a Faustian pact with the Devil and it was gonna be a very hard act to follow,' admitted Dave Ball later. 'Where do you go after number one? Unless you were very lucky or happened to be The Beatles, the only way was down.'

Packaged in a picture sleeve featuring a Peter Ashworth image of Soft Cell posed against a wall upon which a selection of kitchen implements had been fixed – an image which is today part of the National Portrait Gallery's photographic collection – 'Bedsitter' was released at the end of October while 'Tainted Love' was still in the Top 40. The new single was an original Soft

Cell composition which explored another aspect of the band's sound, and was inspired by their own experiences. "'Bedsitter' was a forties image grafted on to something personal to me. Which was living in really grotty bedsitters in Leeds,' Marc Almond told Dave McCullough for *Sounds*. 'Going out at night to clubs looking glamorous and I suppose pretending to enjoy yourself. Sort of mixing reality with the fantasy, the glitter with the squalor.'

On the back of Soft Cell's success with 'Tainted Love', 'Bedsitter' was immediately and enthusiastically playlisted at radio, even if the music press was less supportive. 'This sounds a bit foot-tied after 'Tainted Love',' suggested *Smash Hits*' Dave Rimmer. 'Catchy chorus,' acknowledged *Record Mirror*'s Sunie, 'otherwise, a teeny bit nondescript musically.' Unusually it was the *NME* who were most enthusiastic: 'Soft Cell are the essential teases of the modern bop, at once winsomely witty and coyly touching,' declared Chris Bohn, who went on to describe the band as 'the great soul duo of the moment: sexy, suggestive and soppy'.

As 'Bedsitter' climbed to a UK singles chart peak of number four at the start of December, Soft Cell's debut album, *Non-Stop Erotic Cabaret*, was released to a flurry of excitement and, with a reported 200,000 advance orders for the album received from UK record shops, expectations for the release were running high. Joining the band in Paris, where they were holding court with the French media, *Record Mirror*'s Simon Tebbutt asked Soft Cell what kind of album they'd made. 'There's many sorts of different moods and directions, it's gutsy and loose edgy, there's atmosphere, a dirty atmosphere... it's sleazy, dirty,' Marc Almond began hesitantly. 'It's the whole nightclubby scene. Sort of smokey and sort of souly. The jazz and the wet streets.'

Mark Cooper awarded *Non-Stop Erotic Cabaret* a maximum five stars in his review for *Record Mirror*, declaring, 'Rock is dead and the most intelligent and human music is coming from these amateur experimentalists who are all making a warm and glossy pop whose ultimate mood is the sadness of the human confronted by machines.' Touching on the album's appeal for Soft Cell's emerging fanbase of disenfranchised souls, Cooper summed the record up as 'a non-stop tour of the world of the frustrated and the isolated', and predicted great things for the band: 'Soft Cell are a surprise and a success. 'Tainted Love' was only the beginning.'

Sounds' Betty Page hailed *Non-Stop Erotic Cabaret* as a milestone for the rapidly emerging electronic scene, and also gave the album a five-star review. 'I think it's no coincidence that the Human League and Soft Cell are two of this year's success stories, they both have powerful character, singers that croon from the heart, one writing of a more wholesome love, the other of grubby, messy affairs and sordid, secret sex,' Page mused. 'Both are Soft, both are Human, expressing feelings that connect with a satisfying simplicity of electronic melody.'

After just one week of sales, *Non-Stop Erotic Cabaret* entered the UK album charts at number fifteen before taking up residence in the charts for almost a year, during which time it would peak twice at number five, in February and then March 1982, on the back of the release of Soft Cell's third single for Phonogram, the album's closing track 'Say Hello, Wave Goodbye', at the start of the new year. By the end of 1982 Soft Cell were presented with platinum discs in recognition of over 300,000 sales of *Non-Stop Erotic Cabaret* in the UK alone.

1981.3 The Human League / British Electric Foundation / Heaven 17 / Martin Rushent / Hot Gossip

IN NOVEMBER 1980, *SOUNDS* had announced some important news about The Human League, reporting, 'Synthesiser players Ian Marsh and Martyn Ware have left [the band] to form their own production company, British Electric Foundation, leaving vocalist Phil Oakey and visual director Adrian Wright as the nucleus of the new Human League.' 'Oakey and Wright will be recruiting new members for live shows, and they're likely to be a backing vocalist and another keyboards player,' added *Record Mirror* the same week, while also revealing that British Electric Foundation's intention was to 'work with other vocalists as a production and composing team', starting with a record featuring singer Glenn Gregory.

Very little in the way of additional information about the split was revealed at the time other than a rather bland explanation courtesy of The Human League's manager, Bob Last: 'The League didn't split up for the usual corny musical-and-personal differences reasons: they simply no longer had an adequate working relationship. Neither party was happy and no one fulfilled, but this way both sides will produce far more satisfactory and commercial work.' It would take more water under the bridge, and the necessity for both parties to properly launch their new projects, before more details could be extracted from either side.

'It'd got very stale, everyone was a bit sick, of everyone,' Phil Oakey told *Sounds*' Betty Page in March 1981. 'I've known Martyn a long time and periodically we do have very big arguments. Twice in the past I didn't talk to him for a whole year, which is a bit silly. But they're nice lads. Ian still comes in the studio when we're in and I see Martyn quite a lot.' *Sounds* caught up with Martyn Ware and Ian Marsh a few weeks later: 'I think that it became very apparent over the last three to four months that the second [Human League] album was the one to make us very successful, or the one to "put the boot in", as it were,' Martyn Ware mused. 'And it became increasingly apparent that there was no internal cooperation at all. I remember the feeling when I was getting out of it – I was elated! I still am actually. I'm really glad it happened.'

Although the band's financial debt to Virgin was divided equally between the two sides, Oakey and Wright, having retained The Human League name, had also inherited The Human League's existing live commitments, which amounted to a handful of concerts booked for December 1980. Therefore the first task for the new version of The Human League was to recruit new members, and by the end of November *Smash Hits* published the first picture of the band's new line-up, reporting that Phil Oakey and Adrian Wright would be joined for live performances by Ian Burden on synthesisers, and two teenage singers, Joanne and Susanne, on 'backing vocals and dancing'.

It is the stuff of legend that Joanne Catherall and Susanne Sulley were recruited on the dance floor of Sheffield nightclub The Crazy Daisy after Phil Oakey spotted them dancing to the likes of Gary Numan and OMD at the venue's regular futurist night. 'I went in looking for someone to join the group,' Oakey clarified later, having been inspired to introduce a female singer to the line-up after listening to Michael Jackson's *Off The Wall* album. 'We needed a high voice just to cut through and add things on record or sing leads occasionally.' 'At every stage, The Human League have always done the exact opposite of what was expected of them,' Oakey told *Record Mirror* later. 'When Martyn and Ian left, the obvious thing was to recruit some musicians because everybody who could play had quit, right? So we did the opposite, we went out and recruited two schoolgirls who'd never sung a note before.' 'He wanted a tall black singer,' laughed Sulley. 'And he got two short white girls who couldn't sing.'

The recruitment of Ian Burden was an easier proposition: not only was Burden already a familiar face on the Sheffield scene as the bassist for local 'anti-pop' group Graph, but his girlfriend also lived in the same shared house as Oakey and was able to make the necessary introductions. 'Ian was roped in because we had four days before a German tour and we had nobody to play synthesiser on stage,' Adrian Wright elaborated later in Alaska Ross's biography. 'If we hadn't got him we'd have had to have gone out with tapes of me and Philip – which we wanted to do at one point but we chickened out because we thought they might kill us!' Burden was recruited on an informal two-month trial period to cover the band's existing commitments in exchange for a modest weekly retainer.

Having debuted the new line-up with a short run of relatively low-key shows in the UK and Europe, The Human League's next challenge was a high-profile London show at the Hammersmith Odeon on December 4th. *Record Mirror* were in attendance to report on the show, which writer Simon Ludgate reviewed under the headline 'Oakey Cokey'. Ludgate was considerate enough to temper his review in the light of the rather fraught circumstances The Human League had recently found themselves in – 'Trying to put a new format together only two weeks before the start of a tour must have been a pain in the arse' – and found much to admire in the show, which included particular praise for the band's opening number, an unlikely cover of Judas Priest's 'Take On The World', which he described as a 'stroke of genius, executed with real panache'.

Two new songs were included on the band's Hammersmith setlist, a 'messy' rendition of 'I Am The Law', and 'Boys And Girls', which had already been identified in the press as a possible new single. Simon Ludgate's generous review didn't extend as far as The Human League's new backing singers, however: 'The girls' singing ability hovers somewhere around the zero mark and they destroyed most of the songs with admirable finality,' he rued. Faced with a similar opinion from *Sounds* the following March, Phil Oakey's response was admirably diplomatic: 'When people are expecting a certain thing it's very hard to introduce new people, especially who've never been on a stage before.'

In February *Smash Hits* announced that 'Boys And Girls' would be The Human League's new single, their first since the split with Marsh and Ware the previous year, with an as-yet untitled new album set to follow in August. In the same breath the magazine also announced that Heaven 17, the latter's new project with Glenn Gregory, would issue their first single, '(We Don't Need This) Fascist Groove Thang' in March, alongside the first product from their British Electric Foundation project, a cassette entitled *Music For Stowaways*, rather bafflingly described as 'a preliminary manifesto of the musical intent of BEF for at least the next several minutes'.

Sounds declared 'Boys And Girls' 'A gothic, echoing epic with more than a ring of teen opera to it.' *Smash Hits* and *Melody Maker* were also positive, although both expressed similar concerns about the structure and pacing of the song. 'The song is neat enough and sung with the sort of skill and taste that you expect from Phil Oakey but it doesn't, er, get anywhere,' wrote David Hepworth in *Smash Hits*. 'I fear that until some kind of dull, boring and conventional rhythm section is employed Human League product will always sound like one long, drawn out intro, wound up and threatening to burst but never quite getting there.' *Melody Maker* trod a similar path: 'Declamatory vocals over stirring electronic backdrop. Sparse but lively, with the jerking momentum of a fit of hysterics. The arrangement pleases itself, takes the scenic route to its final destination, but still manages to arrest your attention.'

Embarking on a round of publicity to promote 'Boys And Girls', The Human League sat down with Betty Page in March for a *Sounds* interview that also saw them claim the magazine's front cover. Page found the band in high spirits, apparently invigorated by the split, and energised by the release of the single. 'We came back from the last tour in a complete daze and thought what on earth are we going to do,' Phil Oakey confessed, 'but we did 'Boys' and the next two are going to be so strong compared to that.' Asked about the inspiration for 'Boys And Girls', Oakey was happy to offer an insight into the song: 'It's about people growing old and pretending they're not. It's pretty serious actually.' And while The Human League were justifiably proud of 'Boys And Girls', they already had an eye on what was coming next. 'The new stuff's going to be stronger,' Oakey declared. ''Boys And Girls' was a sort of start.'

The following week *Record Mirror* published their own interview with the band. 'The trouble with so many ideas in such a small space is that there has to be an explosion, and there was,' wrote Simon Fowler of the split. Once again The Human League made light of the situation and explained that the two bands still saw each other on a fairly regular basis: 'We share our studio with Ian and Martyn,' Phil Oakey explained to Fowler, revealing that the original line-up's Monumental Pictures studio, built using advance money given to The Human League to make their early albums, had remained a shared asset, and had been pressed into service by both bands while they each worked on new material. Of the studio sharing arrangements Oakey would later tell the *NME* that his former bandmates were 'not as tidy as they might be'.

When Heaven 17 released '(We Don't Need This) Fascist Groove Thang' at the end of February it was entirely natural that the single would be held up against 'Boys And Girls', and the media didn't disappoint. 'Where the Human League got lost in a fantasy world of '50s science fiction movies and '60s trash aesthetics, Heaven 17 have absorbed the grittier language and spunk of funk,' wrote the *NME* approvingly, while in an interview with the band a fortnight later the paper's Paul Morley went as far as to ask, 'What's the difference between Oakey and Wright's Human League and your British Electric Foundation?' Martyn Ware's response was swift, cool and provocative: 'We've got talent. They haven't.'

Morley also asked about the title of the single. If he was expecting a hefty intellectual treatise to match the weighty title he was to be disappointed. 'We were going through the disco charts in *Record Mirror* picking out all the words from those absurd disco titles. We were laughing at those phrases, thinking they're pretty good, and then we chucked in 'How Much Longer Must We Tolerate This Groove Thang', a spoof on The Pop Group, and then Martyn changed that to 'How Much Longer Must We Tolerate This Fascist Groove Thang',' Ian Craig Marsh revealed. 'We were pissing ourselves for days. Glenn had to sing it line by line in the studio. We've got loads of out-takes of him cracking up while singing.'

Despite the band's apparent levity, the single, written in response to Ronald Reagan's election as President of the United States of America, was indeed a political item – a 'superbly funky piece of electronic lefty propaganda' according to *Record Mirror*'s Sunie. 'There was the joke aspect to it,' Ware admitted in the *NME*, 'being too dogmatic about politics, and then extra fun to imply that to get across to a mass audience it's no use preaching to the converted. It was like a hangover from the time the Presidential elections were on TV.'

Unsurprisingly '(We Don't Need This) Fascist Groove Thang' raised more than an eyebrow or two, and the lyrical content of the single impacted heavily upon radio play for the single, particularly from the most influential UK station, BBC Radio 1. At the beginning of April the *NME* ran a short story on the situation, speculating that 'radio stations around the UK are showing a marked reluctance to play it, presumably because of its title and lyrics – and although the BBC won't officially give reasons, it's obvious that Radio 1 is not devoting air-time to the single proportionate to its success.'

More solid evidence that radio stations were sidestepping the release in response to its provocative content came when Virgin tried to book advertising on commercial stations across the UK and ran into problems with the Independent Broadcasting Authority. 'The IBA claims the lyrics breach its advertising guidelines, which state that no ad "may show partiality regarding political, religious or industrial controversy",' explained the *NME*, adding, 'Heaven 17 have now recorded a slightly different set of lyrics, to remove the offending reference… They say they've consented to alter the words because they believe that radio play and *TOTP* will enable them to reach a far wider audience – who, when they buy the record, will still be getting the original version with its message intact.'

Sadly Heaven 17's efforts to smuggle their subversion into the mainstream came to nothing and, hampered by the lack of radio play, '(We Don't Need This) Fascist Groove Thang' failed to take the band as far as the *Top of the Pops* studios. Instead the single stalled before entering the UK singles chart Top 40, when it peaked at forty-five as part of a brief five-week chart run – a small improvement on 'Boys And Girls', which peaked at forty-eight for The Human League as part of just four weeks in the charts.

Despite the setbacks around the release of '(We Don't Need This) Fascist Groove Thang', the single nevertheless picked up a selection of impressive reviews from the music press. In *Melody Maker*, Lynden Barber was sufficiently enthused by the single's 'red-hot slice of funkatronics' that he made it one of his Singles of the Week: 'Human League refugees Ware and Marsh have finally gotten their shit together, transcended the WED ['White Elektrik Diskow'] genre and got down.' Robbi Millar made the single *Sounds*' 'Finger Popping Single Of The Week', declaring, 'I love this single!' But not everyone was quite as swayed by Heaven 17's new electronic funk posturing. 'A slightly forced attempt to mate bubbling, repetitive funk with poker faced electronics,' ran *Smash Hits*' take on the release. 'Some interesting things arise from the marriage of looping funk bass and shuddering keyboards but overall I'd put this down as a promising failure.'

Released alongside '(We Don't Need This) Fascist Groove Thang' came British Electric Foundation's first album, *Music For Stowaways*, a release designed by the band as music to listen to on the personal cassette players that were then becoming popular. Named after the Sony Stowaway, a precursor to the soon-to-be ubiquitous Sony Walkman, the album was intended as a soundtrack for life on the move. Released as a limited-edition run of 10,000 cassettes, *Music For Stowaways* was released to a flurry of approval from the music press.

New Sounds New Styles' Dave Rimmer described *Music For Stowaways* as 'a collection of moody instrumentals designed specifically for mobile listening' and concluded, 'The effect was like wandering around in your very own Fassbinder movie.' Divided into two distinct sides to match different moods, *Music For Stowaways* was also well received by Red Starr in *Smash Hits*. 'The 'Uptown' side is really great – melodic, funky, inventive, energetic, danceable, optimistic and further good adjectives well into the night,' enthused Starr, awarding the release nine out of a possible ten stars, and adding, 'The 'Downtown' side, by contrast, is a rather less essential stab at impressionism and atmospherics, albeit with tongue in cheek, but it occupies the time very nicely while winding back to hear side one again.' 'Take a bow, guys. This is the strongest, most diverse and human electronic album to come out of Europe in ages,' effused *Sounds'* John Gill in a five-star review of the release. 'Put it to any litmus test you usually apply to music and it'll emerge with an arrogant grin on its face. This is it folks – accept no substitutes.'

The *NME* sat down with Marsh and Ware in March to find out more about *Music For Stowaways*, and found themselves seduced by the duo's ambitious plans under the British Electric Foundation banner: 'BEF is freedom to move, freedom to stay still, freedom to think, a control that is pure-punk complete. It's the flexibility Ware and Marsh once expected with the League, the chance to maintain assiduity, trust their own judgement, frame their own inventions.' 'It's set up as a production company,' explained Marsh. 'We've signed a contract that is between the production company and Virgin Records, not us as individuals, to deliver a number of LPs per year. A maximum of four and a minimum two, and related singles.'

April saw the announcement of a brand new single from The Human League, 'The Sound Of The Crowd', which was to be released in four different versions across its seven-inch and twelve-inch editions. 'It's credited to Human League Red,' reported *Sounds*, 'which is some vague reference to the fact that future singles from the band will be colour-coded.' The *NME* published a similar announcement, also noting that 'The Sound Of The Crowd' was the first collaboration between The Human League and their new producer Martin Rushent, while *Sounds* provided the additional information that Ian Burden – who had written the original track before finishing it as a co-write with Phil Oakey – had become a full-time member of the band.

Sounds published a second story the following week designed to shed more light on The Human League's decision to colour-code their releases, explaining, 'Punters puzzled by the latest Human League offerings being described as "Human League Red" should note that this colour-coding is present to indicate the type of music on vinyl – ie dance/pop/ballad etc. Red, naturally, means irresistibly danceable.' The *NME*'s Lynn Hanna later pushed the band for an explanation of the system. According to Susanne Sulley, red was for posers – 'For Spandy [Spandau Ballet] types', Joanne Catherall added helpfully – while Phil Oakey added, without further explanation, that blue was 'for ABBA fans'.

Sounds complemented their explanation with a stellar review of 'The Sound Of The Crowd' penned by Tony Mitchell. 'This is where all would-be futuramists should sit down and listen; this is How It Should Be Done,' proclaimed Mitchell. 'It's intended, and functions perfectly, as a dance record, with stunningly simple synthesised riffs, an unforgettable vocal hook and the kind of driving, swaying rhythm that gets its edge from that wonderful slap sound of the percussion.' *Smash Hits* concurred with Mitchell and declared the single a future classic: 'I see it now… the year is 2000! Revivalist groups are trying to reconstruct the genuine sound of the synthesiser. This they achieve by banging a hammer on a corrugated roof in time to an assortment of fog-horns, humming kettles and finely-tuned cake tins. Much like this in fact. And very good it is too.'

Certainly The Human League's shiny new sound had as much to do with their producer, Martin Rushent, as it did with the band's new line-up. By March 1981, having resolved his problems with Radar Records, work was finally complete on the producer's Genetic Sound studio, and Rushent and his business partner, fellow producer Alan Winstanley, had revived the Genetic label with backing from Island Records. The *NME* interviewed the duo for a feature which appeared in September, and noted the importance Rushent attached to the social dynamic between artist and producer with particular reference to The Human League: 'He believes that this camaraderie is essential: without it people can't make the free-and-easy, almost silly, suggestions which often turn out to be strokes of genius.'

The Human League also approved of Rushent's work ethic, which chimed with their own. 'It's his attitude,' explained Oakey. 'A lot of people I've worked with won't take any little dodges to get round something and make it easier. If something could be played by hand, they'd say, "Keep doing it, you'll do it eventually", and you'd end up wasting six hours, whereas Martin just feeds it through the computer. At every stage, he always goes for the easiest way of getting the best idea down.'

While the bearded, garrulous Rushent was the first to admit that he wasn't a natural sartorial fit for the increasingly fashionable electronic scene, he remained evangelical about the possibilities the movement signposted. 'Electronic music, without giving it a futurist tag or whatever, is very important to me,' Rushent told the *NME*. 'So far we've only nibbled around the edges. Most electronically based records are quite simple.' 'Martin really knew what pop was. He could take your mad sounds and they'd still be mad sounds but he could put them in places that made them pop,' Oakey told Simon Reynolds later. 'Really horrible things come out of synthesisers and that's what I like about them. But somehow Martin could make them work within a pop context, and I don't know how he did it.'

'The Sound Of The Crowd' was The Human League's first significant hit, and peaked at number twelve in the UK singles charts at the end of May, by which time Heaven 17 had released their second single, 'I'm Your Money'. 'Just like Kraftwerk once sounded – conscious humour and all. Not as obviously funny as Fascist Groove Thang but stronger and harder,' wrote Pete Silverton in *Smash Hits*, expressing a positivity not always shared by his peers. 'A danceable solution to teenage revolution?' asked Patrick Humphries in *Melody Maker*. 'Well, no, actually. The 'Fascist Groove Thang' hitmakers turn their synthesisers towards fiscal problems and almost manage to convince with their relentless riffing. Almost, but not quite.' 'This is getting boring,' yawned the *NME*, already keen to start a Heaven 17 backlash following the rapturous reception afforded to their debut: 'A vapid and disposable synthesiser workout from the British Electric Foundation offshoot, lacking even the redeeming lyrical virtues of the over-rated 'Fascist Groove Thang'.'

That 'I'm Your Money' failed to chart while The Human League appeared on *Top of the Pops* twice with 'The Sound Of The Crowd' as part of their single's ten-week run in the charts must have rankled with Heaven 17, who had to stand by and watch as their former colleagues were hailed as new pop heroes. And the gap between the two bands only grew wider when The Human League's next single, 'Love Action (I Believe In Love)', peaked at number three in the UK singles chart in August and spent an impressive six weeks in the Top 10.

'Love Action (I Believe In Love)', released as a double A-side single with 'Hard Times' on the flip, continued the electro-disco swagger that had made 'The Sound Of The Crowd' a hit, and came out in seven-inch and twelve-inch editions, although it was the latter, which featured extended versions of both tracks on one side, and a dub mix of the two tracks together on the reverse, which really caught the attention of the media. 'This is more like it,' applauded *Smash Hits*' David Hepworth. 'First couple of times through I suspected that they'd already lost the confidence that made 'Sound Of The Crowd' such a cracker, but that was before a splendidly loping chorus and staccato synth fill had got their hooks in, and before Phil Oakey's distinctive baritone had soared through the song. Sterling stuff.'

Record Mirror's Sunie agreed, dubbing the single a 'megahit' and declaring it her 'Undisputed Single of the Week'. 'The "A" and "B" sides of the 7in are welded together to form a killer 12in,' she explained. 'This is tasteful, tuneful, witty and danceable, and you can't ask for much more than that from a single.' In fact, so convinced were they by 'Love Action', *Record Mirror* put The Human League on their cover at the beginning of August and dispatched Mark Cooper to interview the band for the accompanying feature. Cooper was immediately interested to find out more about the circumstances behind The Human League's bright new pop direction. 'We're more competent now,' was Phil Oakey's frank reply. 'We didn't do it before because we didn't know how to do it. We always wanted to be hugely popular but we couldn't play well enough to get what we wanted. Now we have choruses and stuff and a proper producer to make sure we get what we want.'

Talking to *Sounds*' Dave McCullough, Oakey also revealed that 'Love Action' was actually an amalgamation of two songs. 'The 'Love Action' bits you can throw out. It's really a song called 'I Believe In Love' – the chorus 'Love Action' is from another song which is about going to a cinema and watching Sylvia Kristel,' Oakey explained, confessing, 'It completely wrecks the whole meaning of the song. Lyrically it's wrong… but if we hadn't put the chorus in nobody, or at least much fewer people than did, would have brought the record.'

The third single from Heaven 17, 'Play To Win', was released at the end of August, and entered the UK singles chart at fifty-nine the same week that 'Love Action (I Believe In Love)' peaked at number three for The Human League. 'Play To Win' came out as a seven-inch 'pop' single and a twelve-inch 'disco' single, with each format featuring a remixed version of the lead track entitled 'Play' as its B-side. In fact it was this alternative mix that caught the ear of *Melody Maker*'s Paolo Hewitt, whose review of the single – which described the A-side as 'a promising slice of moderne dance music' – was much more enthusiastic about 'Play', 'a far funkier clubland delight which eschews the electronics for a great disco mix'.

'Play To Win' demonstrated yet another facet to Heaven 17's sound, as Sunie noted in her review for *Record Mirror*: 'Forsaking the groove thang for a disco beat, the BEF turn out a hoarse rap, superbly produced.' Pete Silverton, who had previously rejected 'I'm Your Money' in *Smash Hits*, remained unforgiving in his review of 'Play To Win': 'A tedious example of what happens when intellectual boys discover disco rhythms. They find the beat, they hook up the synthesisers just so... but they forget the song.'

Coming on the back of the unfulfilled potential of '(We Don't Need This) Fascist Groove Thang' and 'I'm Your Money', the commercial and critical reaction to 'Play To Win' was enough to finally put Heaven 17 in front of the *Top of the Pops* cameras when they joined Depeche Mode (performing 'Just Can't Get Enough') and Japan ('Quiet Life') on the show at the end of September. The appearance wasn't enough to give the single the boost it needed, however, and despite being featured on the show again a fortnight later, the single peaked at a lowly forty-six.

With four *Top of the Pops* appearances already under The Human League's belt since the departure of Ware and Marsh it was inevitable that parallels would be drawn between the two bands, and Charles Shaar Murray, in his review of 'Play To Win' for the *NME*, didn't disappoint: 'In which Ian Craig Marsh and Martin Ware [sic] ignore the fact that the other half of the Great Sheffield Schism (the unhip ones with the slides and the haircut) have taken the chart biscuit despite the fact that they were supposed to have curled up and died shortly after the admittedly superb 'Fascist Groove Thang' came out.'

In a loose continuation of the concept that had underpinned their *Music For Stowaways* release earlier in the year, Heaven 17's debut album, *Penthouse And Pavement*, featured themed sides, but that was where the similarities between the two albums ended, as Lynden Barber noted in his review of the former for *Melody Maker*. 'Rather than continuing the overt experimentation started on 'Stowaways', Martyn Ware and Ian Marsh have cleverly decided to apply the expertise they've gained through their left-field explorations to the melodic pop sensibility they originally developed as one half of the Human League, resulting in a record that sparkles with irresistible tunes.' The remainder of Barber's review continued in a similarly fervent tone as he pinned his colours firmly to Heaven 17's mast: 'So far ahead of the competition that it degrades them to be even mentioned in the same category. Heaven 17 occupy that rare space in contemporary pop reserved for true originals. Heaven 17 are, quite simply, in the Superhuman League.'

Vince Moren awarded *Penthouse And Pavement* a five-star review in *Sounds*: 'Not only have they produced a collection of danceable funk tunes worthy of the group that produced 'Fascist Groove Thang', but also side two of this LP is the timely follow-up to the Human League's classic 'Travelogue' LP.' Drawing parallels between the twin trajectories of The Human League and Heaven 17 since the split, Moren declared the latter victorious: 'Heaven 17 have produced the last word in trump cards and they are bound, I am sure, to take the very large prize that is the prerogative of the victor... So here you have it, commercial success on a plate for Heaven 17, and they haven't even had their nipples pierced.'

A fortnight after their album review appeared, *Sounds* published an interview with Heaven 17 in which Betty Page attempted to decipher the band's intentions, and discovered that Moren's analysis of *Penthouse And Pavement* wasn't far off the mark. 'We thought half of it should be a follow on to *Travelogue*, and half of it a new direction,' explained Martyn Ware, who went on to add, '*Travelogue*'s still a fairly new direction even now, as judged by the number of people who're going out and buying it. We were a bit worried it wouldn't work, actually. Well, I was. Ideally it would be the perfect thing for the press to slag off, but fortunately it turned out well and I don't think they will.'

Penthouse And Pavement came packaged in a sleeve which depicted Heaven 17's Glenn Gregory, Ian Craig Marsh and Martyn Ware pictured in a spoof advert boasting 'Heaven 17 – Sheffield, Edinburgh, London' and featuring the subtitle 'BEF: The New Partnership – That's Opening Doors All Over The World'. 'It came out of a copy of *Newsweek*, it was an ad for a multinational American firm,' Marsh told Betty Page when asked about the album cover. 'It was one of those classic drawings, a guy with a pipe, cigars, case, contracts, lots of people in the background and telecommunications satellites all merged, and a slogan about keeping ahead since 1881 and being ready to meet the challenge of yet another century. So I thought that sounded like a good idea to use for a cover.'

In the middle of October 1981, *Melody Maker* ran a news piece which reported an unlikely and unexpected collaboration between British Electric Foundation and *Top of the Pops* dance troupe Hot Gossip. The result of the collaboration, a Hot Gossip album entitled *Geisha Boys And Temple Girls*, was scheduled for release at the beginning of November and was to be preceded by a single, Hot Gossip's take on 'Soul Warfare', from Heaven 17's newly released *Penthouse And Pavement* album. The album – 'which features the BEF on musical instruments and three boys and three girls from Hot Gossip on vocals' – was an attempt by the dance troupe to replicate the pop success Hot Gossip had recently enjoyed with Sarah Brightman on their collaborative hit 'I Lost My Heart To A Starship Trooper'. 'It is very hard for Hot Gossip to be taken seriously but then once you're known for something then it's very hard to change people's minds on it,' explained Hot Gossip creator and choreographer Arlene Phillips. 'They drove us very hard in the studio,' she added of the recording sessions with BEF. 'It took a week to record it.'

Interviewing Heaven 17 for the *NME* at around the same time, Ian Penman asked the band about their work with Hot Gossip and discovered that initial sessions for the project had been produced by Landscape's Richard James Burgess but were shelved following DinDisc's fears that the material was somehow at odds with Hot Gossip's image. 'They were desperately scrabbling around for some way of salvaging the situation,' explained Marsh and Ware. 'Carol Wilson at DinDisc just happened to have heard *Penthouse And Pavement* – they played it to Arlene, who really liked it, plus in the past they'd all been Human League fans anyway, early Human League material. So their album was put together comprising three old Human League tracks, a couple of tracks off our album – 'Soul Warfare' and 'Geisha Boys And Temple Girls' and a few other covers, a Sting song and Talking Heads' 'Houses In Motion'.'

The release of Hot Gossip's version of 'Soul Warfare' coincided with the release of a new Heaven 17 single, their album's title track, 'Penthouse And Pavement', which frequently led to the two records being reviewed side by side. 'No apologies for this odd coupling,' announced the *NME*, who added, 'Neither of them is up to much as far as I'm concerned.' *Smash Hits'* Dave Rimmer also reviewed the two tracks together: "'Soul Warfare' sounds just like the original with Gossip's vocals instead of Glenn Gregory's,' was Rimmer's disappointed verdict, 'while their own re-mix seems actually to decrease the dance rating by emphasising the wrong bits. Shame.'

'Penthouse And Pavement' fared better on the single review pages when it wasn't coupled with Hot Gossip's musical excursion. 'An adventure on plastic. A dance virus. A running, jumping, never standing shift of excitement in an otherwise dim and dreary week,' was *Melody Maker*'s Paul Colbert's verdict on the single, while in *Record Mirror* Sunie reluctantly decided against making 'Penthouse And Pavement' her Single of the Week as it had already appeared on the album, but nevertheless declared the release 'Excellent stuff.'

Hot Gossip's *Geisha Boys And Temple Girls* was released in November, and Charles Shaar Murray was savage in his review of the album for the *NME*:

'This album is not simply cheap, exploitative dreck, but it's cheap exploitative dreck that even lacks the guts and flash that has been the redeeming feature of great trash throughout the 20th century. Trash without energy is unforgivable, and this doesn't even have enough drive to crawl into its own grave.' *Geisha Boys And Temple Girls* was not a hit, and neither were the 'Soul Warfare' or 'Penthouse And Pavement' singles, although the latter fared best when it spent three weeks in the UK singles chart, peaking at an underwhelming fifty-seven.

If anything the release and the success of *Penthouse And Pavement* – the album entered the UK albums chart at number twenty after one week on release and peaked at fourteen the following week, remaining a fixture in the lower reaches of the chart for most of the next year – served to heighten anticipation for the October release of The Human League's new album, *Dare*.

A fortnight before the release of *Dare*, The Human League released another single. Slightly overshadowed by the arrival of the album, 'Open Your Heart' was nevertheless well received by a music media who were starting to mellow to the new pop incarnation of the band. 'This is a number one,' declared *Smash Hits'* Ian Birch. 'It's got everything – strong chorus, instant appeal and dreamboat topping.' Sunie made the release her Single of the Week in *Record Mirror*, praising Phil Oakey's performance and gamely attempting to understand the band's new colour-coding initiative which had dubbed the release 'blue': 'His voice stretches with an aching sincerity that forever damns the idea of the Human League (blue?) as a bunch of coldhearted engineers.'

Although it failed to become the number one hit that *Smash Hits* had predicted, 'Open Your Heart' spent two weeks at a very respectable chart peak of six at the end of October in advance of the release of *Dare*, alongside the announcement of an ambitious seventeen-date UK tour in November and December, including two shows at The Rainbow in London, which would be the first public outing for The Human League in their latest line-up: Phil Oakey, Adrian Wright, Susanne Sulley, Joanne Catherall, Ian Burden, and the band's latest recruit, Jo Callis – who had previously played with The Rezillos – who had written 'Open Your Heart' with Oakey. 'He can do anything,' Oakey told the *NME*'s Lynn Hanna when asked about Callis's contribution to The Human League. 'He's the best keyboards player in the group, which is quite good when you consider he's not a keyboards player. No one who can play with two hands has ever been in our studio before.'

The recruitment of Callis was the final piece in the puzzle of The Human League's reinvention: 'Listening to the old Human League was like listening to electronic music,' Callis explained in an interview with the *NME*, 'but now when I hear a Human League record, it sounds like a pop record that just happens to have all been done on synthesisers and electronically.' The distinction was crucial. In the space of less than a year Phil Oakey and Adrian Wright had successfully transformed the band into a bright new pop proposition. Not that the transformation had always been easy: 'I thought then we might easily blow it completely. I agreed with everyone else. I thought we were the ones without the talent as well,' Oakey told Lynn Hanna in the *NME* shortly before the release of *Dare*, although Wright, talking to *Sounds'* Dave McCullough the same week, was more sanguine: 'We seem to have gone through all these different stages. First we were the Industrial Band, then we were the Electronic Band, then Fathers Of The Futurists. I think we'll survive whatever the flavour is.'

Despite briefly considering calling the record *Jihad*, The Human League released *Dare* on October 16th, 1981 to a round of encouraging reviews. Simon Ludgate conferred a maximum five stars on the album in his review for *Record Mirror*: 'With advance orders for this album rumoured to be nudging the 200,000 mark, the extent of the League's ever-increasing fan club's faith is obvious. But will they be disappointed? No, they won't. The rough edges of old have been smoothed away, and a lot of the famous diffidence has evaporated, but the strong, commercial sound which was always there really is now much more in evidence.' "Dare' is one deliciously, definitively daft album,' wrote Steve Sutherland in *Melody Maker*. 'I think it's a masterpiece. Sure to upset some, sell to millions more and so it should the way it tramps all over rock traditions. A trite sound, a retarded glam image and a mock respect. All the appeal in the world.'

Reviewing the album for the *NME*, Paul Morley agreed. 'It's the first Human League greatest hits collection,' he exclaimed, presumably to the satisfaction of the band, whose intentions had been outlined in a *Smash Hits* interview a fortnight previously: 'We wanted an album full of singles, like a Michael Jackson or ABBA LP,' explained Phil Oakey. 'We've moved away from textures to tunes. It's tunes every time.' With the scent of revolution in his nostrils Morley continued to lionise the band: 'The Human League could be the first pop group broken in by punk and who are in touch with the deeper elements of art rituals, pop skills, political illusion and love codes who have burst through into the mainstream dominated by the likes of Genesis and ELO,' he wrote, 'in many ways it challenges the very conventions of pop music and the essence of innovation.'

In an echo of the the sleek professionalism that characterised the sound of *Dare*, the album came packaged in an elegant sleeve which owed more to the glossy sophistication of the fashion world than it did to rock tradition. 'Most covers date,' Susanne Sulley told *Record Mirror*'s Mark Cooper later in October. 'The idea was that when you're going through the racks two years later, this cover should still stand out. That's why nobody went over the top with the make-up, it was meant to be classy.' Phil Oakey concurred, adding, with a sideswipe at some of The Human League's 1981 peers, 'It's real class, not fake class, none of this ridiculous stuff that designers have been doing on covers like classical statues or ridiculously naive stuff like that.'

The shiny surfaces and smooth edges that characterised the look and sound of *Dare* also extended to the band themselves. Interviewing The Human League in September in support of the album, *Sounds*' Dave McCullough was unsettled by a change in the band's own attitude. 'The Human League proved almost certainly the most serious and self-conscious group I'd ever talked to,' he reported. 'They had planned the interview, I realised half way into it, as much as they could.' Phil Oakey led the media assault, smoothly unrolling a list of slightly unlikely artists The Human League considered their influences and their peers: ABBA ('They've always been our heroes'); Dollar ('They're very modern, the first LP especially − the way they use the synthesiser... it's what The Human League always wanted to do!'); and Kim Wilde ('I think we've a lot of similarities with Kim Wilde − the synths, the very modern sound, the great production'). Oakey also managed to distance the sound of the old Human League from the new by confessing that he now found the production on the band's *Travelogue* album to be outrageous. 'I think it's disgusting that anyone should pay six quid for it − for something as bad as that.' Asked whose fault that was, Oakey's response was immediate: 'Mine and everyone who was in the HL at the time. We were uneducated. There's less arrogant people in the HL now as well. Except me that is, I'm the only arrogant one left.'

Despite their newfound coolness, and Oakey's self-confessed arrogance, The Human League nevertheless bristled at accusations of selling out, itself an outdated concept which couldn't be properly applied to the band's new vision. 'We're writing pop songs because we want to and at the moment we can shelve everything else,' Oakey told the *NME* in an attempt to defend the band's position. 'I don't think we're selling out because that's part of what we want to do, although it's not all we want to do. At the moment it makes a lot of sense to write the best pop songs we can.'

Dare entered the UK album charts at number two at the end of October and the following week hit the very top of the charts for the first time on its way to racking up an initial sixty-nine weeks in the charts. A fixture in the Top 10 of the album chart until the end of February, *Dare* would in fact return to the number one position for another three weeks in January 1982, but it would take the success of The Human League's next single, the last to be taken from the album, to put them back there.

'Don't You Want Me' was released at the end of November and immediately entered the UK singles chart at number nine, propelled by the excitement surrounding the release of *Dare*, the avalanche of publicity the band had done around both releases, and the success of The Human League's UK tour. 'To say they've improved in recent months is something of an understatement. They're a million times better in every respect,' lauded Mark Ellen in *Smash Hits* after seeing the band's London show. 'Get used to them if you aren't already. They'll be around for a while.'

Despite being familiar with 'Don't You Want Me' since the release of *Dare*, the media were enthusiastic. 'A first-class pop song that combines wit and sincerity, together with the all important Catchy Bit. A monster hit, put your shirt on it,' declared Sunie at *Record Mirror*. 'Classic heart-string duo pop, like a synthesised, new romanticized Sonny & Cher, it underlines the Human League's arrival as purveyors of perfect pop singles,' celebrated *Melody Maker*'s Colin Irwin. 'Number one at Christmas?'

Both predictions were correct. 'Don't You Want Me' was a monster hit which reached number one in the UK singles chart after just two weeks on sale, and remained there for five consecutive weeks, earning The Human League the coveted Christmas number one as well as a platinum disc for in excess of 600,000 copies by the end of the year. 'It's the best song I've ever written. It's a proper song like the kind that Earth, Wind & Fire or ABBA would write,' Phil Oakey told *Smash Hits'* Ian Birch with obvious pride when *Dare* came out. 'It's the story of *A Star Is Born*.'

1981.4 Pete Shelley / New Order / Simple Minds / John Foxx / Ultravox

AFTER COMPLETING WORK ON *Dare*, producer Martin Rushent turned his attention back to a project he had been working on prior to his sessions with The Human League, and which he hoped to release on his recently reactivated Genetic Records label. Pete Shelley had headed to Rushent's Genetic Sound studio in Berkshire in February after an aborted recording session with Rushent in Manchester with Shelley's band Buzzcocks, and had fallen back in love with electronics in the process. (Recorded in 1974 before the formation of Buzzcocks, Pete Shelley's first solo album, *Sky Yen*, was an experimental and entirely electronic DIY affair, which Shelley released on his own label, Groovy Records, in 1980.) Combined with the difficulties which had derailed the Buzzcocks' Manchester sessions – which mostly revolved around a financial dispute between the band and their label – Shelley found the process of working on his own sufficiently invigorating that in March he announced that he had left the Buzzcocks, and was concentrating on solo material instead.

The *NME*'s Lynn Hanna happened to be interviewing Shelley at Genetic Studios the same day that news of the Buzzcocks split broke, and found the former frontman in good spirits, exuding 'the positive aura of a man with a new enthusiasm for his music'. 'I've been getting back to doing things rather than just thinking about them,' Shelley explained about his newfound energy and enthusiasm. 'It was using the tools at our disposal. The computer's like a very obedient musician, and it saves having to learn all the parts... I've never been proficient at being proficient,' he added, 'I found I was far happier on my own.'

In August Pete Shelley's first solo single emerged as the debut release on Genetic Records. Obliquely dealing with Shelley's own sexuality, 'Homosapien' was a coming out record in more ways than one. *Melody Maker* were similarly enthusiastic, Paolo Hewitt hailing the single 'a promising new beginning' and describing 'Homosapien' as 'an electronic pop song that meshes together Shelley's pop instincts with an attractive urgency'. Betty Page praised the single's 'cheeky, risqué vocal', and in her review for *Sounds* summed up the release as 'Fruity, memorable electropop,' regretfully declaring, 'Severe absence of airplay is predicted.'

Page was right. Pete Shelley's arch but playful lyrics were enough that mainstream radio programmers gave 'Homosapien' a wide berth, although the release was well supported by shows with less regard for a commercial audience. John Peel played the record, and tracks from the subsequent album, on his BBC Radio 1 show, as did his Radio 1 colleague Annie Nightingale, who later confirmed that 'Homosapien''s 'risqué' lyrics were noted at the time. 'Didn't stop me playing it on my radio show,' she added. Without the requisite radio airplay in place, however, 'Homosapien' failed to chart, although it performed well in the independent chart, and retains a well-deserved cult status to this day.

Meanwhile, in Shelley's native Manchester, in an attempt to free themselves from the weight of history, tragedy and expectation, and determined not to repeat the mistake of adopting a new name as controversial as Joy Division, New Order was picked from a list of possible names presented to Peter Hook, Stephen Morris and Bernard Sumner by manager Rob Gretton. 'One thing's for sure,' Gretton told the band at the time. 'We don't want another name with any fascist connotations after all the hassle we had with Joy Division. New Order. It's completely neutral.' Picked from a list of potential names which allegedly also included The Witchdoctors Of Zimbabwe, Khmer Rouge, The Shining Path, The Sunshine Valley Dance Band, Fifth Column, Stevie & The JDs, Black September, Mau Mau, The Immortals and Man Ray, New Order was an abridged version of the original suggestion, The New Order Of The Kampuchean Rebels. 'Never at any point did any of us consider a certain Mr Hitler and his bloody *Mein Kampf*,' Peter Hook wrote in his memoir *Substance* in 2016. 'Shows you how daft we were. We just thought it summed up our new start perfectly.'

Armed with their new name, New Order were starting to shape their future plans. Unable to countenance the idea of recruiting a new singer to replace Ian Curtis, the surviving members of Joy Division looked closer to home, and in the early stages of their transition to New Order instead chose to provide any vocals themselves, an arrangement which stayed in place across their first live shows, in the USA and in the UK, since losing Curtis. *Smash Hits* updated their readers on Joy Division's reinvention, reporting that the band – 'currently working under the name New Order but a further name change is likely, it seems' – were recording in the USA with a view to releasing their first single in December. In fact, between live dates in Hoboken and Manhattan, the band had taken advantage of the favourable exchange rate to put down their first recordings as New Order, commuting from Manhattan to the Eastern Artists Recording Studios in New Jersey to reunite with Joy Division producer Martin Hannett, who was working there with A Certain Ratio on their *To Each...* album.

It was at EARS, as the Eastern Artists Recording Studios were popularly known, that the band recorded the tracks 'Ceremony' and 'In A Lonely Place', the last two songs they had written with Ian Curtis, and the final songs they had demoed with Curtis in early May, just days before his death. Initially titled 'Little Boy', 'In A Lonely Place' – 'probably one of the most doom-laden tracks we'd ever written – and we'd written a few,' Bernard Sumner would say of the song later – was renamed after a film, the poster for which – 'pillaged from the Kant Kino gig in Berlin' according to Stephen Morris – Joy Division had on display on the wall of their rehearsal room.

Despite having played 'Ceremony' live as the opening number at Joy Division's last-ever concert in Birmingham at the beginning of May – a performance which can be heard on the 1981 Joy Division compilation *Still* – preparing to record the New Order versions of the two songs would prove tortuous. 'We had none of Ian's lyric books,' Stephen Morris wrote in *Record Play Pause*. 'So in order to work out what exactly the words to 'Ceremony' and 'In A Lonely Place' were, we booked a day in a studio to try and decipher them from what tapes we had. It was grim. The closest thing I could imagine to a sonic autopsy. Listening to Ian's words so closely was like reading a suicide note over and over again.'

Using the Joy Division demos as a close template for the New Order recordings, when it came to putting vocals on the single Peter Hook, Stephen Morris and Bernard Sumner each recorded a vocal before leaving it to New Order manager Rob Gretton to make the final decision. 'Everyone was worried about singing in Ian's place,' reported Sumner after the band's US dates. 'I got shitfaced most nights to try and take my mind off it but we all had a go, while Rob watched from the sidelines, stroking his chin.' Morris has similar memories from those initial US shows: 'I think Hooky was secretly the least indisposed to the idea and went at it with gusto. Bernard's approach of having a few drinks and keeping his eyes closed worked well in a don't-give-a-fuck kind of way. I went about it by not trying too hard to sing, more drunkenly shouting or failing that mumbling what lyrics I could remember.'

By the time of the band's next run of shows at the end of the year, Rob Gretton had made the decision that Sumner would be the band's singer, despite the impact of that decision on the band's onstage dynamic, as Sumner found himself unable to sing and play the guitar at the same time. 'I think, on the American tour, Rob had spotted that all of us doing something new was making the band different, but not as good. It was changing the sound too much and taking us out of our comfort zones,' Peter Hook mused in *Substance*. 'It was obvious something had to change.' Stephen Morris wrote of the decision, 'At the few gigs we'd done there'd been an awful lot of instrument juggling going on.'

With this in mind Gillian Gilbert was recruited to New Order on guitar and synthesisers for several important reasons: she had already cut her musical teeth as guitarist in The Inadequates; she was already known to the band because both groups used the same rehearsal space; but most of all she was Stephen Morris's girlfriend. 'I think they wanted someone without any knowledge of guitar whatsoever to remind them of when they started and couldn't play,' Gilbert told the *NME* later, Morris adding, 'If we got someone in who could, he might not fit in with the way we write songs and stuff, so we decided the best thing to do was get someone in fresh.'

Shortly before Christmas, *Record Mirror* teased their forthcoming review of a Rotterdam show, scheduled to appear the following week, with the first mention of an expanded line-up: 'New Order, the remaining three-quarters of Joy Division, had Dutch hearts a-pounding over the weekend when they played a sold-out gig in Rotterdam. Swelling their ranks was a girl answering to the name of Gillian who played keyboards and some guitar. Expect to be astounded by their 'Ceremony' single in the new year.' The following week the promised review appeared. 'First things first, New Order are not a Joy Division re-incarnation, second-coming or anything else to do with that great band,' writer Gordon Charlton opened, before going on to report that, despite problems with the band's live sound, he was excited by New Order's short, nine-song performance, further eulogising that 'Ceremony' was 'destined to be a classic of the same kind as 'Transmission" and finishing, 'Through all the chaos it was still hard to mistake that touch of something brilliant which very few bands have. Welcome to the New Order.'

Having spent the earlier part of 1981 playing live shows around the UK, New Order's debut single, 'Ceremony', was finally released at the beginning of March. Following the death of Ian Curtis, and the subsequent deification of Joy Division, expectations of what New Order might deliver were running high. In his review for *NME* of New Order's debut London concert, which took place at the capital's Heaven nightclub on February 9th, Paul Morley observed a band in a state of flux: 'They are starting again but transmuting certain energies: a new group who have a tradition all of their own to re-direct,' he mused. 'They have slowly and without bother achieved a majestic balance between extending suggested possibilities from that disturbed past and embodying novel principles and fresh threatening passions.'

Joy Division was naturally a touchstone in the various reviews that appeared of 'Ceremony' in the music press. 'This week's most important release is also the most impressive,' *Smash Hits'* Red Starr declared. "Ceremony' by New Order finds the three instrumentalists of Joy Division not only surviving but sounding better than ever, and showing just how much they contributed to that highly influential band. The sound is pretty much the same – grand, dark designs – but simpler, clearer and more confident than before.' But not everyone was so sure. 'I clasp my hands and hope for forgiveness when I say that this single strikes me as less than revelatory,' confessed Carol Clerk in *Melody Maker*. 'It hasn't changed the course of my life.'

Radio 1 DJ John Peel came out as an early supporter of New Order and started playing both 'Ceremony' and B-side 'In A Lonely Place' several weeks before release, continuing to give airtime to both tracks over the course of the next few months. In fact Peel's support was enough to place 'Ceremony' in fourth place in his annual Festive Fifty at the end of the year, alongside no less than eight Joy Division tracks, including 'Atmosphere' at number one and 'Love Will Tear Us Apart' at three. It seems likely that Peel's support was also instrumental in getting 'Ceremony' to the top of the independent singles chart after just one week on sale. Despite a distinct lack of support from daytime radio, 'Ceremony' also crossed into the UK singles chart, where it entered the Top 40 at thirty-nine after just a week on sale, and peaked at thirty-four the following week.

On the back of the success of 'Ceremony' New Order embarked on another run of UK dates where they continued to gain fans and media support. 'New

Order show a sharpness and flexibility that Joy Division didn't have for me,' wrote *Sounds*' Rab in his review of the band's Bristol show. 'New Order are marvellous! Bloody amazing!' exclaimed Dave McCullough in *Sounds* after experiencing the band's second London concert at The Forum in Kentish Town in May, a show which also impressed *Melody Maker*'s Ian Pye, who wrote, 'Certainly they seem to have improved considerably since I last saw them… achieving a degree of intensity in their subtly climatic songs that was genuinely breathtaking.'

The show at The Forum was also notable as the venue for New Order's first ever press interview, which the band granted to *Melody Maker*'s Neil Rowland after having studiously avoided interviews since the death of Ian Curtis the previous May. 'Our attitude to interviews is that we've nothing to say,' Bernard Sumner had explained to *Record Mirror*'s Simon Tebbutt. Inevitably much of Rowland's questioning revolved around the death of Ian Curtis. 'Continuing was the most natural thing to do, there were no doubts,' admitted a reluctant Peter Hook. 'Yes, Ian's death was a surprise, it was totally unexpected. And the first meeting after it happened was short and very difficult. But we had to continue.' 'I will never be able to cope,' confessed Bernard Sumner. 'Ian's death will affect me for now, and forever. I will never be able to forget it.'

In September New Order took another step forward with the release of a new twelve-inch recording of 'Ceremony', this new version featuring Gillian Gilbert, alongside a seven-inch of their second single, 'Procession', with 'Everything's Gone Green' on the flip side, although obtaining that information from the packaging proved a challenge, as *Smash Hits*' Ian Birch discovered when he reviewed the single: 'The artful sleeve and the absolute minimum of information (which is the A-side?) can only mean one band – New Order,' he noted wryly, nevertheless delighting in the music the package contained: 'Whatever you feel about the religious adoration that surrounds them, here are two bewitching songs – urgent, interesting and confident.' Sunie was also impressed, calling the single 'sterling stuff' and making an important point about the band's trajectory in her review for *Record Mirror*: 'The important thing is that New Order are proving themselves on their own merits, and that even if you'd never heard of the noble shade who haunts their reputation, you'd judge this a very good record indeed.'

Sunie's review of 'Procession' also drew parallels with the progressive electronic sounds of Tangerine Dream, a genre comparison which Garry Bushell also noted in his review for *Sounds*, where he wrote, 'Despite all the

sharper – you can hear the words too, hooray!' McCullough enthused, going so far as to banish further accusations of New Order's apparent debt to progressive rock: 'This is great stuff and effectively wards off those leaden, Genesis-of-our-age fears.'

Treading a similarly uncompromising path of their own were Simple Minds, who started their 1981 by attempting to extricate themselves from their record deal with Arista. 'Simple Minds have parted company with Arista Records. Or they haven't, depending on which side of the increasingly complex band/label argument you believe,' reported *Sounds* at the end of January, alongside news of a new Simple Minds single, 'Celebrate', coming out on Arista towards the end of February.

'Not so much dance music as a record to gently massage your hips and shoulders by warming, seductive and haunting, swaddled in abundant wraps of humanity,' Lynden Barber wrote of 'Celebrate' in *Melody Maker* in the middle of February. 'It makes me wonder what sort of a world we live in where Gary Numan can make millions and Simple Minds, who work in the same seam with double the invention, can barely make a crust,' added *Smash Hits*' David Hepworth. 'The archetypal Should But Won't Be A Hit,' lamented Dave McCullough in *Sounds*.

While 'Celebrate' proved McCullough correct, the single was to be Arista's last new material from Simple Minds. 'Simple Minds have found a new home at Virgin. April should see the release of their first single under the new contract,' reported an upbeat *Smash Hits* later. In the same week, *Sounds*' Betty Page turned in a review of the band's recent show at The Venue in London, where she witnessed a reinvigorated Simple Minds: 'A faultless mixture of energy, passion and technical ability. That's surely the mark of a band reaching its peak. Simple Minds have ploughed their own fields, sowed their own seeds, knowing they have perhaps been ahead of their time.'

Simple Minds' first release for Virgin came in May when 'The American' was released as a seven-inch and twelve-inch single, the band's first release to have been produced by their new producer, Steve Hillage, a pairing which immediately raised eyebrows. 'Steve Hillage producing Simple Minds is like Rolf Harris producing Splodge,' quipped Dave McCullough in a tepid review of the single for *Sounds*. 'It opens promisingly enough,' reported the *NME*'s Adrian Thrills. 'But the song soon develops into a typically harsh, teutonic treatise built around some jerky synthesisers. Plenty of punch but no real tune.'

By July Simple Minds' plans were starting to take firmer shape and the band announced that their first album for Virgin would in fact be two albums, *Sons And Fascination* and *Sister Feelings Call*. 'Simple Minds' next release – this is very complicated – is a double LP that, after the requisite limited edition has run out, will be available as two separate single LPs,' *Smash Hits* explained. 'They will probably come out together in a limited edition of 20,000 first and will then be sold as two separate records.' 'The main album is *Sons And Fascination*,' Jim Kerr told *ZigZag*'s Louisa Hennessy when asked about the unconventional release later, 'but during the recording we had a lot of tracks, backing tracks and surplus stuff which although we didn't think were substandard, it was just that we were changing direction, and to try and combine both albums and put them on one record, the whole thing would have been out of focus.'

Peaking at a lowly fifty-nine in the UK singles chart, 'The American', which was taken from the *Sister Feelings Call* portion of the album release, was followed by Simple Minds' new single, 'Love Song', taken from *Sons And Fascination*. 'How long before these people get a hit, I wonder, I mean, what do they have to do?' exclaimed Sunie in her review of 'Love Song' for *Record Mirror* in August. 'This is their fourth superb single in a row.' 'These poor darlings are still bogged down in sombre electro-disco when just everyone knows funk is where it's at,' sneered Garry Bushell in *Sounds*. 'They're so uncool they've even got the horrendous Steve Hillage producing.' 'Quite a lot of people have slagged us since we used [Hillage],' Jim Kerr told *Sounds*' John Gill in September. 'Not because of the sound or anything, but because they thought we should use some ultra-trendy producer. We thought, "Fuck that!"'

'Love Song' subsequently peaked at forty-seven in the UK singles chart, the best position the band had achieved for a single to date, and two weeks later the *Sons And Fascination/Sister Feelings Call* double-pack entered the UK album chart at fourteen on its way to a chart peak of eleven the following week. 'I think it's time that we began to get the kind of recognition that we deserve and that we've earned. I'm just getting fed up with a lot of pretenders getting all the limelight while we have to struggle,' Jim Kerr told *Record Mirror*'s Mark Cooper after the release of the albums.

In fact Cooper had awarded *Sons And Fascination/Sister Feelings Call* four out of five stars in his review of the album for *Record Mirror* at the end of August: 'Plucked bass and shimmering synth-string riffs wind their way in and out of Brian McGee's solid and yet imaginative drumming. Jim Kerr sings like an arty trouper mixed far enough back to intrigue with his solemn waxing.'

And Cooper wasn't alone in his praise of Simple Minds' latest direction. 'To describe the metronomic beat, the twittering synths and the pulsing bass, or even to single out specific songs for special attention, is to miss the point of this music,' declared *Smash Hits'* Johnny Black, who also awarded the release eight of ten, concluding, 'a double album with so much content, so much restrained passion and so much going on that it captivates at first listen.'

A final single, 'Sweat In Bullet', taken from *Sons And Fascination* but backed by '20th Century Promised Land' from *Sister Feelings Call*, followed in November. In common with the previous singles from the albums, 'Sweat In Bullet' picked up good reviews but failed to score Simple Minds the hit they were chasing when the single peaked at fifty-two in the middle of the month. 'This is still instantly recognisable Simple Minds, but more catchy and commercial than they've ever been,' wrote *Record Mirror*'s ever-supportive Sunie. 'They need no more eulogising, they need to Top 20, so I'll shut up. Yes, really. Our fingers are crossed for you boys.' Chris Bohn made 'Sweat In Bullet' Single of the Week in the *NME*: 'No other group is capable of keeping such clear heads while being so passionate and only a few can match disco calculation and youthful naivety with such unabashed honesty. 'Sweat In Bullet' is Simple Minds soaking up the nightmare American experience.'

'I think there is a connection between *Empires And Dance* and this album,' Jim Kerr told *Sounds'* John Gill in a cover feature on the band in early September. 'Whatever we do next, album-wise, I'm sure we don't have any idea now of what it will be like. I'm sure it'll be something radically different.' Kerr returned to the same theme of transition and change in an interview for *Melody Maker* which appeared the same week. 'Subconsciously, I feel the new album's the end of a phase for us although we didn't realise it or speak about it at the time,' Kerr confessed to Steve Sutherland. 'I think we were subconsciously clearing everything out so that next time we go in to record, I'm sure – though I've no idea what it will be just now – it'll be on a totally different level altogether.'

Exploring a similar path of reinvention, John Foxx, disenchanted by the current musical fashions, had already set out on his new musical course. 'I'd grown tired of being a frozen electrician and gone off on a walking tour of England. Then to Italy where I was thawed in a big way,' Foxx recalled in the notes to accompany his 1992 compilation album *Assembly*, adding, 'After 1981 everyone and his dog went electro, so I became Max Ernst dressed as Lord Lost, exploring the overgrown and abandoned city of London. To a psychedelic ecclesiastical disco soundtrack.'

A psychedelic ecclesiastical disco soundtrack was an extraordinary mission statement to unleash on 1981's electronic landscape, now populated by an explosion of new acts with obvious debts to Foxx's earlier work. Foxx's own new single, 'Europe After The Rain', and the album from which it was taken, *The Garden*, was announced in August and was reported upon by most of the main music publications. 'John Foxx has just completed work on his second album, 'The Garden', which should surface on the Metal Beat label in September,' announced the *NME*, noting that for the new project Foxx had apparently abandoned the solo electronic format in favour of working with a band playing traditional instruments – 'a line-up formed from Joe Dworniak (bass), Duncan Bridgeman (keyboards), Phil Roberts (drums) and Robin Simon (guitar)'.

Melody Maker also ran the story, and were able to add some information about the unconventional nature of some of the sessions which led to *The Garden*: 'It was recorded in a country house in Surrey,' reported Carol Clerk. 'And some of the material was put down in the open air because Foxx apparently believed the presence of trees and leaves improved the recording.' Looking back at the making of *The Garden* in the notes to accompany *Assembly* a little over a decade later, Foxx recalled the experience as a real pleasure, and confirmed *Melody Maker*'s assertions. 'Delightful, mysterious things were happening,' he remembered. 'We recorded outside in the gardens, catching the dawn chorus on the title track. Everything fell quite naturally into place. A very good time.'

'Europe After The Rain' was released on August 21st to mixed reviews. 'The presence of trees and leaves during John Foxx's recording sessions have obviously influenced his music, as he claimed,' wrote *Melody Maker*'s Carol Clerk, unable to resist the pun, 'It's sap.' Clerk continued: 'Ordinary in the extreme, the song skitters along with a notable lack of individuality, and despite the fact that he's using more musicians than machines these days, it still sounds mechanically lifeless.' 'I'm not sure it actually clicks in the pastoral way he intended,' mused *Sounds*' Betty Page, picking up the same theme and going on to describe the single as 'a cold wash of Foxx synthetics blended with piano, acoustic guitar and a overly wistful melody', and ending her review with more than a touch of mischief: 'Don't anyone mention Vienna.'

The single scraped into the UK singles chart but peaked at number forty after just two weeks, enough to earn Foxx a place on *Top of the Pops*. A *Top of the Pops* performance, particularly a good one, was generally a guarantee that a single would comfortably ascend the charts the following week, but despite an assured performance from Foxx – dressed in the kind of pale, frilly costume that suggested the romantic hero in a period drama, playing an acoustic guitar while backed by two synthesiser players and a pianist, on a stage decorated with statuary and greenery – 'Europe After The Rain' subsequently dropped one place to forty-one and fell out of the charts completely just two weeks later.

Not only was John Foxx styled differently around the release of *The Garden*, the new Foxx, like the music he was now making, appeared softer and more human. In one of the first interviews Foxx gave in support of the album, *Record Mirror*'s Mike Nicholls discovered 'a suitably mellower, more relaxed individual, softly spoken and smiling'. In the same interview Foxx enthused about books, art and photography and talked about gathering each of those strands together in the creation of *The Garden*, explaining that the music contained on the record would be supplemented in initial quantities of the record by a sixteen-page glossy booklet entitled 'Church', which would contain Foxx's own photographs and prose. 'I got the idea from the French photographer Atget, he was a solitary man who just took photographs of churches and gardens,' explained Foxx, while Nicholls described the imagery of the booklet as 'stained glass windows, crumbling statues, ivy-infested archways and other related semi-ecclesiastical images'.

In the same week that *The Garden* was released, the *NME* published an interview with Foxx in which the singer confessed to being nervous about how the album might be received, while also discussing his rediscovery of the psychedelic flavours of early Pink Floyd, which had underpinned some of his earliest musical experiences and provided a tangible influence on his latest work. 'It was very mysterious, optimistic and very English – nothing American about them – a strange mixture of traditional churchy things, but with young people involved,' Foxx told Chris Bohn. 'That kind of feeling, the summery, open air feeling hasn't been in music for a long time, and I'd like to see it incorporated in whatever happens next, which doesn't mean a pastiche of what has gone before. That openness is how I feel at the moment and *The Garden* was an attempt to rediscover those feelings that had been neglected in me for a long time'

Released at the end of September *The Garden* attracted another round of largely indifferent reviews. *ZigZag* were unambiguous in their opinion. 'This is precious, pretentious, derivative, self-important crap of a kind rarely encountered. The embodiment of all that's wrong with "Modern Music".

A free glossy book about a bleedin' church! Acres of synths, drums, all as empty as my wallet.' 'Despite a promising start with the lighter, more human, band sound of 'Europe After The Rain', [Foxx] is still peddling the same old improbably pseudo-mystic melodrama about "fading" and "shadows" to predictable synthesisers and monotonous vocals,' wrote *Smash Hits'* Ian Cranna, assigning the album five stars out of a possible ten. 'Not that this album doesn't have its moments,' added Cranna, 'but there's nothing he hasn't done better previously. Beautiful accompanying booklet, though.'

On October 30th, the same week *The Garden* slipped out of the Top 40 of the UK albums chart after just five weeks – during which time it peaked at twenty-four – John Foxx released a second single from the album, 'Dancing Like A Gun'. Despite evidencing a harder and more overtly electronic edge and being supported by a video replete with faux symbolism, a cast of mysterious and enigmatic characters and a wind machine, 'Dancing Like A Gun' became the first John Foxx single to fail to chart, and reviews were also unpromising. 'Despite his recent success, Foxx hasn't lived up to his early promise,' wrote Johnny Black for *Smash Hits*. 'This has all the ingredients – the pips and the peel – but without the juice.' Reviewing 'Dancing Like A Gun' for *Record Mirror*, Sunie wrote, 'John Foxx aggravates me. I want to see him laugh, eat chips, boil eggs, dance – like a gun or anything else he cares to impersonate – but all he does is stand next to that bloody statue and sneer.'

Despite the underwhelming critical and commercial response to *The Garden*, Foxx remained upbeat and supportive of the emerging electronic scene. When asked about the wave of electronic artists who had followed him into the charts since the success of *Metamatic* he took an avuncular tone: 'The more the merrier, although it was inevitable, really,' Foxx told *Record Mirror*'s Mike Nicholls, adding, 'I'm really glad to see The Human League doing well at last.' But the question that everyone wanted to ask, was how Foxx felt about Ultravox's recent success. 'I'm very pleased they've done well,' the singer confessed to Nicholls, 'excited even.'

Ultravox announced the release of a new album, *Rage In Eden*, in August, a couple of weeks after *Record Mirror* had featured the band in a two-page round-up of the movers and shakers of the current wave of electronic acts, waggishly entitled 'Sine of the Times'. The feature included short pieces on Ultravox alongside similar reports on Duran Duran, Depeche Mode, Rusty Egan and Soft Cell. 'In retrospect they can be seen to have been the founding fathers of futurism, or whatever expression you wish to use for the synthesised brand of soulful electro-pop they purvey,' enthused the article, before providing an early glimpse of Ultravox's new material courtesy of a quote from frontman Midge Ure: 'It's a lot meatier than 'Vienna',' Ure disclosed. 'There's a year-and-a-half's difference and it shows.'

Rage In Eden was written and recorded at Conny Plank's studio in Germany in the spring of 1981, and while Ultravox were delighted with Plank's production work, and were grateful to him for his input into the project, the location presented some challenges. 'Conny Plank's studio is like a farmyard forty kilometres outside Cologne in the middle of the country. And there's nothing to do,' Ure told *New Sounds New Styles* in October. 'There's no TV. You can't listen to the radio, the radio's crap. We had maybe half a dozen videos. No women. Loads of drink.' 'Three months in a farmyard in the middle of Germany is nobody's idea of fun,' Ure added in an interview with *Smash Hits*' Ian Birch later. 'We got a gymnasium horse and tried to tunnel out a couple of times but it didn't seem to work.'

On the back of the success of *Vienna*, Ultravox had departed for Germany with the intention of working in a different way. Instead of writing the songs in advance and then taking them into the studio to record them, the plan for *Rage In Eden* was to write and record the songs in the studio. 'We didn't think it would take so long, you think something's gonna be simple then it gets more intricate as whole new aspects of the song start opening up,' Midge Ure admitted to *Record Mirror*'s Mike Nicholls later. 'So instead of taking a couple of days to write a song, it might take two weeks. We actually went over to Conny Plank's studio in Germany for six weeks but ended up staying three months!' But the band were justifiably proud of the results, as Ure would tell *Smash Hits*' Ian Birch: '*Rage In Eden* has some depth to it. In ten years' time somebody will pick it up and go, "This still stands up and makes sense".'

Ultravox preceded *Rage In Eden* with the release of a new single, 'The Thin Wall', in August. 'Why do Ultravox records always make me think of film scores to foreign language movies about gay maths tutors who drown themselves in cyanide?' asked Colin Irwin, reviewing the single for *Melody Maker*. 'A hugely clever exercise in production, but otherwise a whining narcissistic romp into emptiness – it's like eating a plate of garnished, pretty-patterned cardboard.' "The Thin Wall' continues the harping Ultravox melodrama,' sighed Gavin Martin in the *NME*. 'Such a confused, trumped up mess this is! Electro bleeps and blops, fuzz guitar and pseudo-crooning all get put into the synths-blender.'

'The Thin Wall' went straight into the UK Top 40 on its way to a two-week peak position of fourteen over the first two weeks of September, part of a seven-week chart run which also earned Ultravox a *Top of the Pops* appearance, the band presenting the track through billowing dry ice, Midge Ure sporting Oxford bags and an oversized tweed cap, Warren Cann impassive with a single drum and a bank of electronics, and an unusually animated Billy Currie and Chris Cross on hand to provide theatrical synthesiser gestures.

Reviews of *Rage In Eden* were also mixed upon its release in September. 'The promise of 'Vienna' is delivered,' applauded *Sounds* in their review, adding, less auspiciously, 'I worry sometimes that they seem to take themselves too seriously.' 'This album is safe Ultravox shine and glory, with hints of busting out,' was *ZigZag*'s cautious take. 'The rock'n'roll treadmill never changed, they just dressed differently and swapped guitars for synths.' 'It sounds like mature, devilishly clever Duran Duran – lush arrangements, obtuse, absurd lyrics,' wrote Steve Sutherland in *Melody Maker*.

Despite such an underwhelming critical reception, *Rage In Eden* nevertheless entered the UK album chart at its two-week peak of number four after a single week on sale, and the album remained in the charts for an impressive twenty-three weeks, boosted by the October release of a second single from the album, 'The Voice'. *Record Mirror* were nonplussed by the new single, reviewer Sunie writing, 'By releasing this single, which is an Ultravox single for better or worse and sounds exactly like an Ultravox single, no more or less, they have left me unable to think of anything to say.' 'I'm still totally stumped by the Ultravox appeal,' shrugged Gavin Martin in the *NME*. 'Can anyone tell me what it is Midge Ure is getting worked up about? Out of the blandest stream of neutralised electro gloop he always starts raging or moaning about something which is never qualified or reasonable reconciled with the rest of the record.'

Undeterred by the indifference of the music press 'The Voice' was another hit for Ultravox when it peaked at sixteen in the UK singles chart at the beginning of December 1981. The final single to be taken from *Rage In Eden*, 'The Voice' ended what would be the most successful year of Ultravox's career. Over the course of 1981 the band spent a total of forty-four weeks in the UK singles chart with sales of over half a million records; and *Vienna* and *Rage In Eden* spent a combined sixty-three weeks in the UK albums chart with over 400,000 album sales. 'It was a brilliant time to be in a band, and Ultravox were a brilliant band to be in,' declared a satisfied Midge Ure later.

GARY NUMAN KICKED OFF 1981 with a January edition of his official fan club magazine, and the singer's introductory letter started by setting the story straight about recent reports that he was about to quit music. 'I'm not quitting the music business, I'm just not going to tour anymore. I will still make records and do the occasional TV and radio show,' Numan wrote, before revealing that there was already a new record in the pipeline: 'The next album should be ready by September '81 and will feature mainly new people. Mick Karn from 'Japan' is playing bass and sax, and there will be several other guests appearing on it.' Having confirmed elsewhere in the same newsletter that Japan were currently his favourite group, Numan also revealed further plans involving them: 'I'm off to Japan soon for a promotional tour with the band 'Japan',' he enthused, 'I'll be guesting on stage a few times and hopefully doing some writing with Mick and David Sylvian.'

A couple of weeks later the music press announced that Numan was to retire from live performance with two final shows planned at London's prestigious Wembley Arena at the end of April. 'These are intended to be his last ever public performances as he plans in future to concentrate exclusively on films, videos and recording,' reported the *NME*. A second story, a fortnight later, followed with the news that, as a result of extraordinary demand for tickets, a third show had been added to the Wembley residency.

Numan also announced that he was planning to release two limited-edition live albums designed to mark his retirement from live performance. The two albums, *Living Ornaments '79*, featuring live tracks recorded on Numan's *The Touring Principle* tour, and *Living Ornaments '80*, featuring live tracks recorded on the *Teletour*, would be available either as individual albums or together in a box set alongside a bonus single featuring two extra tracks. 'They will be deleted a month after release, thus causing maximum pandemonium and purchasing activity among his fans,' reported *Sounds*.

Around the same time, *Sounds* also published an interview with Japan bassist Mick Karn which reported that the Numan and Karn collaboration had already started, and had resulted in the recording of five tracks which were being considered for inclusion on Numan's next album. The piece also revealed that the duo had been introduced at the launch of an exhibition of Karn's sculptures in London, and that Numan had subsequently attended a Japan concert at the Lyceum in London at the end of 1980 before extending an invitation to Karn to work on material for his new album. 'I think he'd found it hard to break away from his standard sound and wanted someone new from outside to come and give it new perspective,' Karn told *Sounds'* Valac Van Der Veene of the offer, adding, 'We get on, and the combination's working really well.'

A few days after the *Sounds* interview appeared, Japan headed to the country that was their namesake for a short tour, where they were greeted by levels of teenage hysteria more usually associated with mainstream pop sensations. Despite the thrill of such a rapturous reception from their Japanese audience, the band were starting to distance themselves from their Japanese success. 'The audience has changed a great deal in Japan,' Mick Karn told *ZigZag* upon his return to the UK. 'Something we've been trying to do since we broke over there is to get rid of young girls and trying to reach the male audience and grown-ups and it seems to have slowly picked up and worked.'

True to his January intentions, Gary Numan was in Tokyo at the same time, presumably to honour his commitment to appear on stage with Japan, at which point the story becomes somewhat opaque. 'It was a fairly loose arrangement, but I flew out to Tokyo and waited. They were supposed to call me when they arrived for us all to meet up. I didn't hear anything, and I was sent on a wild goose chase to catch up with them,' Numan wrote in his memoir *(R)evolution*. 'Maybe I had it wrong and hadn't really been invited, or maybe they'd gone off the idea of me guesting with them and no one had the courage to tell me.' 'There were never any plans to have Gary join us on stage,' Mick Karn stated later. 'I wonder how he thought that at all possible as nothing had been rehearsed musically or vocally.'

Any residual awkwardness that may have arisen from the Japanese encounter seems to have been quickly forgotten by Karn. Asked by *ZigZag*'s unexposed flirting-with-nazi-imagery around them, New Order are actually the true new Psychedelia. Pink Floyd ten years on.' Nevertheless 'Procession' followed 'Ceremony' into the lower reaches of the UK singles chart, earning New Order a second consecutive hit when the single spent two weeks in the Top 40, peaking at number thirty-eight in the middle of October.

Unsurprisingly the shadow of Joy Division also fell across the reviews of New Order's album debut, *Movement*. 'In a real sense 'Movement' fails so severely both because of the links it's broken with JD and those it's kept,' wrote Dave McCullough in *Sounds*. 'It is all unconscious I am sure, but in effect New Order are a band decapitated.' Adam Sweeting's review for *Melody Maker* trod a similar path: "Movement' feels stricken and defeated, neither exploiting the advances JD were once held to have pioneered nor veering radically from them in an effort to establish new criteria or identities.'

Record Mirror awarded the album four out of a possible five stars and declared 'New Order have created a spell-binding record', not only proclaiming *Movement* a triumph but also full of praise for the album's production: 'Hannett has captured New Order's metallic majority extremely well, especially with the trickling keyboards and rich synthesised percussion.' "Movement' really is the direct descendent of mid-'70s Pink Floyd LPs like 'Dark Side Of The Moon',' observed the *NME*'s Danny Baker, while *Sounds*' Dave McCullough rued the fact that some tracks on the album were 'almost comically ruined' by studio effects that were 'pure Pink Floyd'.

The studio effects came courtesy of *Movement* producer Martin Hannett, rather than from the band themselves. 'Maybe they should have kept Hannett off the case. His production has condensed all the contents into a forbiddingly arid, stark potion, steering away from primary colours and opting instead for hallucinatory shades of grey,' mused Adam Sweeting, while Dave McCullough noted Hannett's 'rigidly safe, arid, stifling production' and added, 'It would be so easy to blame the huge disappointment of this debut New Order album on the production of Martin Hannett, but it wouldn't be anywhere near the entire story. A good, obvious part of it, yes. 'Movement' is astonishingly flat sounding.'

While 'Procession' was released on seven-inch only, the single's B-side, 'Everything's Gone Green', was released via Factory Benelux as a twelve-inch single in December. Dave McCullough, who had previously been so disparaging about Martin Hannett's production on *Movement*, found himself pleasantly surprised by the producer's work across the tracks on the 'Everything's Gone Green' twelve-inch. 'The production is sprightlier,

Louisa Hennessy shortly after Japan's Japanese tour how he felt about Gary Numan as a person, Mick Karn's answer was open, and even affectionate: 'I can't really see how you can dislike him really,' stated Karn, 'unless you don't know him.' Hennessy was also curious about the results of the collaboration between the two musicians. 'He just wanted to go in the studio with me and play around and have some basic tracks,' explained Karn, who went on to expand on the process: 'When we did the basic tracks I was a little worried that it sounded too much like Japan because I wanted to get away from sounding like that if I could help it. By the time it was all finished and [Numan] added all the electronic effects and his vocal, it's got much more of him in it now, but it is a clash, it doesn't really go together.'

It seems doubtful that, after his return from Japan, Numan was quite as comfortable with the situation. Interviewed by Ray Coleman for a *Melody Maker* front cover feature in May, at around the same time as *ZigZag*'s interview with Mick Karn, Numan reframed the reasons behind his Japanese trip, which Coleman reported in the piece as a holiday alongside some promotional duties for his own releases. While Coleman also noted that Numan had apparently taken up sword fighting whilst in Japan, and had spent time with the band Queen, who had been there at the same time (a meeting which led to Queen drummer Roger Taylor subsequently guesting on two tracks for Numan's album), no mention was made of Numan spending time with Japan, or of his collaboration with Mick Karn.

Conducted at the rehearsals for his final shows at Wembley, in the interview Coleman found Numan excited about the prospect of bowing out of live performance on a high, despite being predicted to lose an estimated £150,000 on the three shows, which Numan had conceived as his most spectacular to date. And for once the music press was in agreement. 'Seventy-two sheets of Perspex, 1692 light bulbs, 300 theatre lights, and three tons of other suspended lighting going up and down over Gary Numan's head,' enthused Karl Dallas in *Melody Maker*. 'It was the largest, most spectacular stage set I've ever seen,' exclaimed the *NME*'s Barney Hoskyns, who was also full of praise for the sound: 'Every number is rendered note perfect, and every sound comes over with crystal clarity: the icy lacquer of the keyboards, the pulverising throb of bass.' 'Credit where credit's due. The shortcomings of Numan's music and of his appearance are compensated by the lavish trappings which surround him,' admitted Sunie in *Record Mirror*. 'He gives his audience their money's worth and more.'

Living Ornaments '79 and *Living Ornaments '80*, released just two days before Numan's three-night stand at Wembley, were nevertheless received with a characteristic lack of enthusiasm by the music press. 'I don't want to rehash all the old criticisms you've awkwardly cringed away from whilst scurrying all the way to the bank,' opened Nick Kent in the *NME*, before doing precisely that: 'Listening to all four sides of your parting bouquet, all the old adjectives are summoned forth once more: the eerie synthesisers, the dank, drab metronome of a pulse-beat, your whining vocals, the empty gestures, the numbing bombast.' 'I imagine if you like him you'll enjoy this,' wrote an obviously baffled Adam Sweeting in his review for *Melody Maker*, 'but it's hard to tell what difference the live setting makes because the music seems identical to its studio-recorded counterpart.'

'Musically I don't think I fit in anywhere at the moment,' Numan told Ray Coleman. 'I don't listen to anything any more. I don't try to find out what trends are coming and beat them to it.' But the day after the final date at Wembley, Coleman reported that Numan would be back in the studio, putting the finishing touches to the final track for his next album, which he revealed would be called *Dance*. 'See, I can go on now and do whatever I like as long as I don't join in or try to start a new direction,' explained Numan. 'I've done all that. I want no tags to weigh me down. It puts me out on my own a little bit but I think it's for the best.'

Despite the strange turn his relationship with Mick Karn had taken, the first – and, as it would turn out, only – single from the new Gary Numan album was one of the songs that Numan had worked on with Karn. 'She's Got Claws' was released at the end of August to the obvious glee of the music press, who wasted no time in delivering their verdicts. 'The world's least charismatic pop star discovers funk,' sniffed *Smash Hits*' Pete Silverton. 'A dreary affair, this, plodding slowly along and not helped a great deal by that ludicrous, unvarying whinge of a voice,' wrote Sunie in *Record Mirror*, while *Sounds*' Robbi Millar added, 'Gal is still a-whining electro-stylee, still forgetting to blow his nose and still threatening to Give It All Up. Hurry up, mate.'

Karn's contribution to 'She's Got Claws' gave the single a certain added credibility for *Melody Maker*'s Colin Irwin: 'An impressive sax line recurs to make this a bit less cosmic than [Numan's] previous efforts, despite the characteristic passing spaceships and waves of vacant staring.' Unusually it was left to the *NME* to offer a hint of positivity for Numan's latest, even if that acclaim was delivered in a decidedly backhand manner. 'The presence of

Japan's Mick Karn on bass and sax adds elasticity to Numan's impenetrable electro-plating,' declared Lynn Hanna, before adding a rare moment of faint praise: "She's Got Claws' is poised between his usual hollow pop and something infinitely more interesting.'

By the time the further results of his collaboration with Gary Numan surfaced on Numan's new album, *Dance*, in September, Mick Karn was distinctly frostier about their work together than he had been previously. In *ZigZag*'s review of the album Karn was quoted as saying, 'I'm really disappointed with the album. I played it to a friend last night and his only comment was what he's thought all along, which is that Gary Numan is not a musician, that's basically it.'

'This isn't his 'Young Americans', this is his "shoring up failing reputation with excellent musicians from fave band and ripping them off in the process" album,' wrote Betty Page in her review of *Dance* for *Sounds*, awarding the album just three-and-a-half stars out of a possible ten. *Record Mirror*'s Daniela Soave had been a notable supporter of the new electronic pop, but when it came to *Dance* she shared Page's misgivings and assigned the album just one star out of five, writing, 'I would like to be able to say that Numan is the ABBA of synthesiser music, presenting the lighter, poppier side to it. But ABBA make brilliant music and Gary Numan doesn't.'

Only the *NME* were prepared to give *Dance* a more balanced review, Paul Morley stepping up to offer a considered and sympathetic piece which sought to examine the album in relation to Numan's position as an elder statesman of electronic pop while a raft of new acts were jostling to occupy the same electronic niche. "Dance' is Numan's attempt at getting his music's energy accepted as a serious force, not just a disintegrating teen-type thing, easily excusable and easily avoidable,' Morley mused. "Dance' is a thoughtful response to the new competition. Numan self-controlled and sophisticated.' In identifying Numan's desire to be taken seriously as an artist, Morley also identified what he considered to be *Dance*'s greatest flaw: 'By responding to the new competition, by searching for a more satisfying respect, by trying to lift himself out of the teen pool, Numan has ended up in the middle of nowhere. In ways this matters. He's too restless to be satisfied with his new automatic pop parade placings; too inhibited and imprecise to achieve the kind of inspirational resonance he desires.'

Dance was an album which showed a more human side of Numan. Gone were the fantasy sci-fi worlds created for his previous releases, and in their place Numan explored an altogether more relatable subject, the fragility of the human heart. 'There was a 'little incident' in February that involved one particular person who thought she could make an awful lot of money out of saying what it was like to be with me for six months,' Numan told *Smash Hits* after being asked about the album's theme. 'You don't expect that. I was all set for, y'know, the ring – the lot! I thought "That's it. My life's complete" and then it turns round and hits you like an atom bomb. And that's what the album's about.' 'Where *Telekon* had been dark and oppressively inward looking, angry and lashing out, *Dance* was haunting and full of sadness,' Numan contemplated in *Praying to the Aliens* later. 'I thought I was taking a brave, more personal direction after the oppressiveness of *Telekon*. The subject matter of the new songs was full of reflections on the previous two years.'

With the change in subject matter came an accompanying change in image. For *Dance*, Numan dropped his alienated android image in favour of a 1930s suit and trilby hat combination inspired, he told *Smash Hits*, by a TV documentary about eccentric American aviator and tycoon Howard Hughes. 'I loved the ambience of the old Sinatra and Bogart films and I thought the 1930s were, visually, a really cool era,' Numan wrote in *Praying to the Aliens* later. 'It was the last age when everyday men looked stylish just going to work... The new look was actually on the cover of the *Replicas* album back in 1979,' Numan added. 'There is a grey man outside the window, dressed in a trilby and long grey overcoat.'

Despite its savaging at the hands of the music press *Dance* entered the UK album chart at number four after a week and peaked at number three the following week on its way to spending seven weeks in the charts. But sales were down on those for *Telekon*, and dramatically down on those for *Replicas* and *The Pleasure Principle*, and Gary Numan was feeling the pressure. 'I can't accept that the lack of sales for that album was because of the music,' the singer told Ray Coleman. 'It was one of the best, most adventurous things I've done, I'm sure of that. I worked hard on it.'

The same week that *Dance* peaked in the UK albums chart, a new compilation started its slow climb to becoming Japan's most successful chart album to date. Although Japan were now signed to Virgin, their previous label, Hansa, were keen to exploit the band's catalogue and, having decided that the time might finally be right for Japan's unorthodox sound, hit upon the idea of a retrospective release, *Assemblage*, which would compile the best tracks from the band's time on the Hansa label. While *Assemblage* wasn't released until September, Hansa's campaign for the album had started earlier in 1981 with a May reissue of Japan's 1979 single 'Life In Tokyo'.

Curiously, Virgin also chose May 1st, the release date of the 'Life In Tokyo' reissue, to release a brand new Japan single, 'The Art Of Parties'. *Melody Maker* reviewed both singles together and duly rejected 'Life In Tokyo' as little more than a cynical cash-in, adding, 'If life in Tokyo is as drab as this single suggests I certainly wouldn't want to live there.' Describing 'The Art Of Parties' as 'a distinct improvement' on 'Life In Tokyo', *Melody Maker* nevertheless dismissed the new single as dull, adding for good measure, 'If Dr Robert Moog had ever imagined his brainchild, the synthesizer, would fall into the hands of Japan he would probably have jacked the whole project in and joined his local dole queue.' By comparison *Sounds* also reviewed both releases together and Betty Page made them her joint Singles of the Week, reporting the release of 'Life In Tokyo' – 'it has a lazy sensuality and self-assurance that belies the age of the young men who produced it' – as 'by popular demand' following recent support in the clubs, before turning her admiration to 'The Art Of Parties': 'Its effortless fluidity and silky-smoothness is hip-wrigglingly danceable and that bubbly Karn bassline gets you every time.'

'The Art Of Parties' subsequently scored Japan their biggest hit to date when it peaked at forty-eight in the UK singles chart a fortnight later, while 'Life In Tokyo' conspicuously failed to chart. Nevertheless the release of the singles contributed to the success of Japan's nine-date *The Art Of Parties* tour in May, providing further evidence that for once Japan appeared to have fallen into step with the times from a style perspective, if not a musical one. 'By gum, the local theatrical shop never had it so good,' wrote Mike Nicholls of Japan's audience in his review of the band's show at Manchester's Apollo Theatre, and continued by praising Japan for their skill as musicians, but coming away disappointed by their show's lack of excitement.

Interestingly, Japan didn't disagree. In an interview with David Sylvian and Mick Karn for the *NME*, conducted in Norwich after the band's show there, Sylvian admitted to hating touring in England. 'This style of rock touring is extremely boring,' he confessed to Max Bell. 'Our music is much more effective on record, it's not designed for playing live. On stage we try to reproduce our sound exactly, we use tapes and treatments... Most people don't like that idea,' he continued. 'I'd like to use film focused on a mesh in front of the band, that way you won't concentrate on the band. You'll see the musicians' shadows but you'll ignore them.'

In the same interview Bell sounded out Karn and Sylvian on the idea of the times finally catching up with Japan, only to find the band resistant to the idea. Asked if he liked the futurist movement, Sylvian was dismissive. 'No. I feel neutral about it mostly. I don't see them and what I hear on the radio I don't care for.' 'We could have had spiky hair and done punk stuff. We avoided that,' added Mick Karn. 'Now the category is for futurism and people are saying this is your time, your time has finally come! We deliberately avoid it. If we become really successful now people will only say {Oh! You're part of *that*" and when that dies we'll die with it.'

A month later, and with the tour behind them, Japan were on the front cover of *Sounds*, and Betty Page's accompanying interview with David Sylvian found the singer in a more sanguine mood about prevailing fashion. 'The audience has changed quite a bit, because of the futurist interest, people began associating us with it, saying we started it off, so a lot of kids have been coming along, doing the whole posing bit, which is unfortunate,' Sylvian declared. 'But they went away having really enjoyed it.' Page also asked the frontman whether Japan's new direction, as evidenced by 'The Art Of Parties', was a deliberate attempt to capture the interest of this new audience. 'No, not at all. Changes are instinctive, if you begin to think about changing, it doesn't work,' Sylvian responded. 'We've been wanting to do that for a long time – something really funky – because the last two albums had the whole muzak thing. The idea was to totally break away from that and do something really dynamic.'

Following the release of 'The Art Of Parties', Japan returned to the studio to work on the follow-up to 1980's *Gentlemen Take Polaroids*, the timing of which provided Hansa with another space to revisit the band's back catalogue. In August the music press reported that Japan's 'Quiet Life' single would be reissued in advance of September's *Assemblage* compilation. 'This is Japan firing on all (sophisticated) cylinders,' enthused Betty Page of the reissued single in *Sounds*, 'an exotic, heady mixture as fresh as the day it was born, a spot on balance between danceability, pop sensibility and technical grace.' The timing was right for the release and 'Quiet Life' slowly started to ascend the UK singles chart, giving Japan their first bona fide hit as the single entered not only the Top 40 but also the Top 20, where it spent two weeks at a peak position of number nineteen.

Assemblage duly followed 'Quiet Life' into the charts and peaked at thirty in the UK albums chart at the start of October, making it Japan's most successful album to date. A compilation of ten tracks recorded during Japan's time on the Hansa label between 1978 and 1980, *Assemblage* drew mainly on tracks gathered from the band's *Adolescent Sex*, *Obscure Alternatives* and *Quiet Life* albums alongside a couple of B-sides and Japan's non-album singles 'Life In Tokyo' and 'I Second That Emotion'. 'If you're looking for an introduction to the band, you couldn't find a better way of getting acquainted,' volunteered *Smash Hits*, while Paul Tickell, re-examining the band's early material in a review of the album in the *NME*, ventured that the earliest Hansa material might even be superior to Japan's more recent releases.

The unexpected successes of 'Quiet Life' and *Assemblage* combined to put Japan in a strong position when they announced the release of a new studio album at the end of October. *Tin Drum* was scheduled for a November 13th release, and was to be preceded by a new single, 'Visions Of China'. 'Sylvian's vocals are much improved and this neat cakewalk suggests they're developing into something worthwhile, offbeat and distinctive,' enthused *Smash Hits* in their review of the single. 'It remains solidly a la mode but the maturity of their new work comes as a pleasant surprise.' *Sounds* struck a similar stance in their review. 'Japan are quite uncompromising in their musical stance, and probe still further into unusual tonal and rhythmic concepts,' they noted with approval before delivering their final verdict: 'Calm, measured, and not a hit, but a tribute to perseverance.'

In fact 'Visions Of China' was a hit, and followed 'Quiet Life' into the UK singles chart, where it peaked at number thirty-two on two separate occasions as part of a healthy twelve-week chart run. The single also provided Japan with the perfect springboard from which to launch their new album, *Tin Drum,* which in turn entered the album chart at number twelve after just one week on sale and remained a fixture in the chart for almost a year.

Reviews of *Tin Drum* were unusually positive, a fact that was as much of a surprise to the music press as to the band themselves. 'Following a parallel course to that run by Ultravox, Japan have of late gone from sneered-upon glam cult status to chart success and popular acclaim,' wrote a startled Sunie in *Record Mirror*, awarding the album four out of five stars and praising *Tin Drum* as 'a very accomplished musical exercise'. 'The funk flirtation has passed, with a heavy absorption of recent Oriental electronica and not so recent traditional elements having take its place,' enthused Betty Page in *Sounds*, further reporting, 'It's a cleansing experience that reflects Japan's quiet discipline. Haunting but sensually pleasing. Calming and carefully structured, but ultimately maintaining the balance between cold calculation and human feeling.'

Having spent the previous three years watching a new generation of electronic acts take the charts by storm, in April 1981, after three years away from the spotlight and anxious to reclaim the crown that was being stolen by the young pretenders, Kraftwerk announced that they would release a new album, which they would promote with a run of UK concerts in May. The album was to be called *Computer World* and would be preceded by a new single, 'Pocket Calculator'. Although the *Computer World* tour was subsequently delayed after Kraftwerk ran into problems with the video screens they had commissioned for their tour, 'Pocket Calculator' was released in early May to a waiting music press.

'The great Grandaddies of teutonic techno pop return from retirement, their reputation unexpectedly enhanced in their absence, and deliver one humdinger of a dance-track not to be bettered in eons,' exclaimed *Melody Maker*. 'Blip and beep perfect for the the nouveau robot manoeuvres currently in vogue at the discos, it takes mechanical minimalism one step nearer non-existence with deadpan vocals, meaningless lyrics, and a sparse, basic beat.' *Smash Hits*' Peter Silverton declared 'Pocket Calculator' 'silly' and wondered if Kraftwerk were still the pioneers they had once been. 'Clearly, they have been surpassed by technology,' he declared.

'Pocket Calculator' limped into the UK singles chart at number seventy-three the week after its release and peaked at thirty-nine just two weeks later when it fell away after the release of Kraftwerk's *Computer World* album in the second half of May. *Computer World* in turn achieved a respectable Top 20 chart position when it peaked at fifteen in its first week in the UK albums chart, and remained in the charts for a further thirteen weeks. The *NME*'s Andy Gill started his review of *Computer World* by wondering if Kraftwerk had been away for too long since releasing *The Man-Machine* in 1978. 'The intervening three years have seen their lead whittled away somewhat by lesser – but more prolific – exponents of synthesised pop,' deliberated Gill, concluding that Kraftwerk 'though undoubtedly field leaders, are in the curious position of having to do a bit of catching-up'. *Computer World*, Gill decided, didn't represent a significant step up for the German band, but could be considered a success nonetheless: 'Even slightly substandard Kraftwerk's preferable to the half-assed posturing of latter-day "Futurist" synthesists, the majority of whom won't even come close to understanding what makes Kraftwerk special.'

Kraftwerk's position as pioneers of 1981's emerging electronic scene was a theme that was also picked up elsewhere, although not always in such a positive way. 'Considering how many bands have filched their sound and ideas since the last Kraftwerk album three years ago, you'd have thought the time was ripe for another Great Leap Forward, the kind of album that would leave their imitators in the shade,' wrote David Hepworth in *Smash Hits*, where he awarded *Computer World* just four out of a possible ten stars, adding, 'Sadly, this isn't it.' In his assessment of *Computer World* for *Sounds*, Dave McCullough agreed, and while his star rating of three out of five was slightly more favourable than *Smash Hits*', his review pulled no punches: "Computer World', betrayed by its own colossally small title, is an album by a band trying to squeeze back into a context that's long been lost. Its central conceits, once new and funny and dangerous, now seem self-conscious and second-hand.'

In July Kraftwerk finally arrived in the UK for their first UK tour since 1975 and, while the press reactions to the *Computer World* album had sometimes been lukewarm, the *Computer World* tour was universally hailed a success. Featuring an innovative stage presentation which included a light show, video screens, audience participation during 'Pocket Calculator', and a 'performance' from Kraftwerk's famous dummies, the show was as cutting edge as it could be given the technological limitations of the day. 'Kraftwerk put together a stunning show that encapsulated their idea of a robotic future; and was more of a statement of fact than a futurist manifesto,' exclaimed *Record Mirror*'s Mark Total of the band's Sheffield show. 'It's a perfect imperfect mix of pop fun and crafted work,' concluded the *NME*'s Ian Penman in Newcastle.

Kraftwerk capitalised on the success of the *Computer World* tour by releasing another single from the new album. 'Computer Love' was released at the beginning of July, entering the UK singles chart at sixty in the middle of the month and climbing slowly to a peak position of thirty-six a fortnight later before falling back out of the charts by the end of August. 'Relying heavily on a sugary, sentimental, sensitive melody it glistens with the human factor of the synthesiser in an "epilogue" style and I can easily imagine the New Romantics taking it to heart as their very own Last Waltz,' was Robbi Millar's take on the single in her review for *Sounds*. Steve Sutherland was also enthusiastic in his review for *Melody Maker* the same week. "Pocket Calculator' was '81's should-have-been biggie that inexplicably never was,' Sutherland lamented. "Computer Love' is hardly less compelling; tongue well and truly in socket, tape tucked neatly in cheek while a gorgeous tune loops the loop to a percussive soft shoe shuffle.'

Sutherland's review also noted the presence of 'The Model', a track from Kraftwerk's 1978 album *The Man-Machine*, as 'Computer Love''s B-side, and exhorted his readers to also check out the vintage track. *Record Mirror,* perfunctory in their assessment of 'Computer Love' – 'Doesn't possess the riveting monotony of which they are capable' – also called attention to the flip side, adding, 'Backed with 'The Model', though, which may well make it an essential buy.' In the *NME* Adrian Thrills was more forthright, declaring, 'The 'Werk's sleepy, bleepy 'Computer Love' is shown up terribly by the 1978 meisterwerk 'The Model', which sparkles on the flip.'

Radio stations agreed and started playing 'The Model' in preference to 'Computer Love', and in response EMI reassessed their campaign. On December 12th *Melody Maker* ran a short news piece announcing that EMI were releasing 'a special dance floor version' of 'The Model' in a new double A-sided single with 'Computer Love' the same week, and a fortnight later, on Boxing Day 1981, the single re-entered the UK singles chart at fifty. By the following week, in the first chart of 1982, the single had shot to twenty-one, and three weeks later it topped the charts, marking the first time an entirely German act had been at number one in the UK. 'We found that our music, electronic language, is universal. We only just discovered that,' Kraftwerk's Ralf Hütter told *Smash Hits* with satisfaction. 'Electronic music is now breaking through and that's good.'

MAINSTREAM

1982 & 1983

'Suddenly every major label wanted to sign an electronic band or two, in the same way they did with punk bands and rock'n'roll bands and heavy metal bands and funk bands when they were the new thing. This is how record companies apparently work and always have done.'

Dave Ball, *NME*, December 25th, 1982

Afrika Bambaataa, 1982.

1982

HAVING QUIETLY BUT CONSISTENTLY placed in the various music press readers polls for best band, best live act, best synthesiser player and best album of 1981, Orchestral Manoeuvres In The Dark kicked off their 1982 with the release of a third single from *Architecture And Morality*. 'Maid Of Orleans (The Waltz Of Joan Of Arc)' – retitled from the album version of the track, 'Joan Of Arc (Maid Of Orleans)', to avoid the release being confused with OMD's previous single, 'Joan Of Arc' – was released in January. *Smash Hits'* Ian Birch was encouraging: 'Once again the dreamboat duo come up with a scintillating intro before settling into a stately canter which becomes more hypnotic with each listen. It could easily be their 'Mull Of Kintyre'.' 'Second instalment of OMD's love affair with Joan of Arc, this one being in waltz time and, to these ears at least, a better listen than the last,' was Sunie's positive take on 'Maid Of Orleans'. 'Top three with no bother,' she added confidently.

But not everyone was so supportive. *Sounds'* Sandy Robertson was significantly less enthusiastic about the single, the singer, and OMD in general, and identified the echo of a far less promising song in the grooves of 'Maid Of Orleans (The Waltz Of Joan Of Arc)'. 'The main theme has that epileptic dingbat "singing" over what sounds like a mutated electronic version of the 'Skye Boat Song',' Robertson declared. In the *NME*, Julie Burchill reviewed the single alongside new singles from The Stranglers, Japan, Tom Robinson and Spandau Ballet, the combination of which had caused her to embark on a rant against the easy-listening muzak qualities that had crept into music generally, and which spilled into her verdict on 'Maid Of Orleans' specifically: 'The point these anaemic young men missed is that it's only interesting if the tune being muzaked is a unimpeachable, incorruptible classic.'

Although 'Maid Of Orleans (The Waltz Of Joan Of Arc)' missed fulfilling *Record Mirror*'s prediction of a Top 3 chart position, the single nevertheless peaked at number four, one place higher than OMD's previous single, 'Joan Of Arc', and spent a healthy nine weeks in the UK Top 40, five of which saw the single nestled comfortably in the Top 10 amid rumours that OMD were on the verge of splitting up. In a cover interview for *Record Mirror* published on February 20th under the headline 'Ominous Miserable Despairing', Mike Nicholls had travelled to watch OMD play in Düsseldorf and reported that Kraftwerk's Ralf Hütter and Karl Bartos had met Paul Humphreys and Andy McCluskey after the show, a meeting which left the latter, questioning the value of his work and struggling with his relationship with DinDisc, despondent. 'Speaking to Kraftwerk last night made me realise how disorganised we are… something's gonna have to change,' McCluskey told Nicholls. 'This OMD incarnation is definitely at an end. We're going to turn into butterflies or lizards. You know what I mean? Metamorphosise.'

While the potential demise of OMD had cropped up in previous interviews – Andy McCluskey had told *Smash Hits* that towards the end of 1981 the duo had come close to calling it a day: 'We asked ourselves whether we really enjoyed what we were doing, and there was a long period – from September to October – when we weren't,' he said, adding, 'The night before the last British tour began, me and Paul were in the studios 'til 3.30 in the morning recording what we both thought then would be the last song we'd ever write' – the news piece was enough to trigger a panic amongst OMD's audience, and the music press scrambled to print the band's denial that they weren't splitting, but were instead planning to step back from work for a while. 'Orchestral Manoeuvres In The Dark are not breaking up,' reported *Sounds*. 'They're just taking a break to "rethink their live approach to their music and live presentation". Andy McCluskey said this week that quotes of his were taken out of context in another paper and there's no question of he and Paul Humphreys not working together again.'

Reviewed alongside 'Maid Of Orleans (The Waltz Of Joan Of Arc)' in the pages of the music press was 'She Loved Like Diamond', the third single from Spandau Ballet's forthcoming second album. 'This soft-shoed lilting shuffle is somewhat marred by an embarrassing operatic warble from the man they're all calling "Foghorn" Hadley,' smirked *Smash Hits*' Mark Ellen in his review. 'The b-side's the same song without him. An improvement.' 'Glamour?' questioned Sandy Robertson in *Sounds*. 'They look (and sing) like labourers in mom's curtains.' 'A pleasant song, though it's not helped much by some naively pompous lyrics,' opined Sunie in *Record Mirror*, describing the vocals as 'execrable' but nevertheless declaring the single 'a welcome break away from the funk rut that 'Paint Me Down' got stuck in'.

The general public concurred with the lukewarm press and 'She Loved Like Diamond' failed to become a hit following its release at the end of January, spending just four weeks in the UK singles chart and peaking at an underwhelming forty-nine. Spandau Ballet remained nonplussed by the single's reception and announced that their second album, *Diamond*, would be released in March as a standard vinyl and cassette album, and also as a limited-edition set of four twelve-inch singles featuring the eight album tracks, five of which would be presented in special remixed versions. The band also announced concerts in Scarborough, Brighton and Bournemouth but shied away from embarking on a traditional tour. 'There isn't a full tour as such,' explained Spandau Ballet manager Steve Dagger. 'But we will be playing secret appearances, which people will find out about by word of mouth.'

'Everyone assumed 'Chant No. 1' was representative of what was to come on *Diamond*. They were wrong,' Tony Hadley wrote in *To Cut A Long Story Short* later. In *Smash Hits*, Red Starr agreed and awarded *Diamond* just three out of ten: '[The album] is a repeat of the last two singles (included here); painfully pretentious lyrics whose irritation is doubled by those awful stilted vocals, some overblown, heavy-handed muzak arrangements plus a couple of mock Oriental pieces to boot... Not only is it contrived rubbish, it's boring contrived rubbish.' 'Most of the album grooves along quite harmlessly, though it'll take more than the ragged vestiges of a bunch of die-hard soul boys to make this a spectacular success,' offered Mike Nicholls in *Record Mirror*. 'The band have become victims of their obsessive stylisation and unless they break free from their neurotic need to be super-hip, they will soon stagnate beyond the point of no return.' "Diamond' is a cold hotch potch of a terribly studio-sounding album that is "light" in the sense it doesn't want to be, both sounding unconvinced and being, simply, unconvincing,' declared Dave McCullough in *Sounds*. 'At last we can all stop pretending to hate Spandau and start really hating them.'

The concept of releasing *Diamond* across four twelve-inch dance singles came as a saving grace in some quarters at least. In the *NME*, Richard Cook, who had found himself disappointed by *Diamond* – 'It seems like Spandau ballet are having trouble, and they're not sure how to face up to it' – was pleasantly surprised by the set, and the remixes helped to turn his review around. 'What comes close to being startling is the way the tracks have been developed for twelve inch consumption,' Cook reported. 'Instead of taking the obvious course of padded dance mix extensions – doubled choruses and spendthrift percussion-only interludes – producers Kemp and Richard Burgess choose to dismantle the basic tracks and reassemble them with a different subversion in mind.' 'These sides represent the group at its best,' agreed Cook's colleague Paul Du Noyer in a separate review of the 'Paint Me Down'/'Chant No.1' and 'Coffee Club'/'Instinction' discs for the *NME*'s singles column. 'Whether that's good enough is something you've doubtless decided already.'

But the remixed versions weren't to everyone's taste. In his review of the set for *Melody Maker*, Adam Sweeting found himself perplexed by Spandau Ballet's move, and possibly by the modern world in general: 'All this "remix", "dance mix" and "special 12 inch version" scam is the perfect ploy for this blighted age,' he grumbled. 'It doesn't matter what you sell as long as you package it properly... Spandau Ballet have nothing to say musically,' Sweeting continued. 'Everything they do has been done much better. They make sure they nod in the direction of any trend that has or might proved fashionable/lucrative... For all the talk of style and being young, most of this music groans like a terminal patient.'

Despite the wave of negativity sent their way by the music press, *Diamond* proved more resilient than any of their detractors predicted and spent an encouraging seven weeks in the Top 20 of the UK album charts, where it peaked at number fifteen, picking up a silver award for 60,000 copies of the album sold by the end of April, and a gold award for 100,000 copies by the end of the year. 'I thought the LP reviews were good!' Gary Kemp told *Sounds*' Chris Burkham in an interview to support the album release. 'I know you'll just think I'm saying that, but when we released the LP I knew that there was no way we would ever get a good review. The editors would give the LP to people who they knew would just rip it to shreds... I think that getting half a page of insults is a lot stronger than getting a quarter page of wishy-washy nothing.' 'I still think we break down conventions and we still enjoy doing that – it's a bit perverse really and I think we do go against ourselves commercially at times,' Kemp told *Record Mirror*'s Billy Sloan in a cover feature on the band that appeared at the same time. 'But hopefully we're not a band who has to rely on our last single.'

In Spandau Ballet's case it would be their next single which would see them regain some of the chart swagger that had been lacking after the disappointing sales of 'Paint Me Down' and 'She Loved Like Diamond'. 'Instinction' represented another important step for the five-piece. Realising that they needed a change of approach if they were going to maintain their previous upward trajectory, Spandau Ballet decided to approach producer Trevor Horn for a remix of 'Instinction' which they could release as their next single. 'You didn't have to look very far to realise that Trevor Horn was doing some of the best things in the charts,' Gary Kemp told Billy Sloan at the time, 'and what he did was come in and polish the song up.'

'All credit then to Trevor Horn for another dazzling production job,' wrote an approving Paul Simper in his review of 'Instinction' for *Melody Maker* at the end of March. 'This track now leaps out at you with almost indecent gusto and shows what a fine voice Tony Hadley has.' 'Let it be said instantly that the difference [Horn] makes is beyond measure; with the bright, classy sound they've always needed, Spandau are an altogether more attractive proposition,' enthused Sunie in *Record Mirror*, adding 'all round this is the best Ballet 45 for ages – in fact, to date.' 'The band's last few singles were justifiable flops. They junked toe-tapping tunes in favour of self-conscious whimpers,' declared *Smash Hits*' Ian Birch. 'But Horn has put them back on course. He's turned this track inside out and added all those magical ingredients like synthesised drum cracks and chattering percussion. The real follow-up to 'Chant No.1'.'

Trevor Horn's remix of 'Instinction' put Spandau Ballet back in the Top 10 of the UK singles chart for a week in May when the single peaked at number ten, and demonstrated significantly more longevity than the band's recent singles when it spent ten weeks in the charts, four of them in the Top 20. 'Instinction' also marked the end of Spandau Ballet's association with Richard Burgess. 'We have enjoyed working with Richard but both parties felt we had taken the relationship as far as we could,' Steve Dagger told *Sounds*. 'Richard now wants to concentrate on Landscape and we are looking forward to working on further products with Trevor [Horn].'

Undergoing a similarly seismic musical transition of their own in 1982 was Simple Minds, whose first new material of the year was announced in March as a single, 'Promised You A Miracle', to come at the start of April. Featuring 'Theme For Great Cities' from Simple Minds' 1981 album *Sister Feelings Call* on the B-side, the genesis of the new single saw Simple Minds working in a new way. 'This is the first time we've recorded a single isolated from an album,' Jim Kerr told *Sounds*' Mick Sinclair in April. 'We took ten days to practice and made all these cassettes full of riffs. We played what became the single for about one hour, thought it sounded good and then we went on to do something else. But later that night it was going round and round in our heads so we thought we'd just take a couple of days and do it, not get precious about it, just see what happens.'

By not overthinking the process, in 'Promised You A Miracle' Simple Minds had created their first proper pop song, and were ready to take on the world. 'We used to believe that we were gonna be a small band, we'd get a little bit of hipness or something, but I can see us becoming much more of a force,' Jim Kerr told *Melody Maker*'s Adam Sweeting in a cover feature for the magazine at the end of March. 'Before, it was always like someone else was driving us, you know, the record company or the press, or we had to prove this or we had to be hip to this kind of audience. But now I think we really are driving ourselves and can do anything we want without feeling in debt to anyone or scared of letting anyone down.'

Produced by Pete Walsh, who had impressed the band with his remix of 'Sweat In Bullet' the previous year, 'Promised You A Miracle' was made Single of the Week in both the *NME* and *Melody Maker* at the beginning of April. 'This is not only Simple Minds' most danceable record since 'I Travel' but also their finest pop shot ever,' declared the latter's Lynden Barber. 'The one that might just break the Minds,' asserted *Smash Hits*' Ian Birch. 'It's a brassy performance with Jim Kerr in formidable form, a hip-swivelling dance beat and a jumbo helping of "atmosphere".' But not everyone was convinced by Simple Minds' leap into pop. 'It's still unmistakably Simple Minds, but in a less ponderous way than usual,' acknowledged *Record Mirror*'s Sunie, while *Sounds*' Johnny Waller described the release as 'a desperate, but honourable, disappointment'.

On a par with their previous singles, 'Promised You A Miracle' entered the UK singles chart at fifty-nine after its first week of release, but this time, to the delight of the band, the single started to pick up radio support. 'We could get a chance to do *Top of the Pops* soon,' Kerr enthused to *Sounds*' Mick Sinclair at the time. 'I think it's time for a dark horse again. There's Human League, Soft Cell, Haircut 100, we can be as bouncy and boyish as any of them but we've also got an undercurrent that we're proud of.' Simple Minds subsequently made their first *Top of the Pops* appearance in the middle of April and 'Promised You A Miracle' continued its climb up the charts, where it eventually peaked at thirteen four weeks later. 'Right now, for us, for Simple Minds, it's time to take everything by the neck. I used to think great bands ought to be cults, they're not for the masses,' Jim Kerr told *New Sounds New Styles* in June. 'Now I'm interested in clearing the board, sweeping the world.'

Despite existing commitments to complete the final legs of their *Sons And Fascination* tour in Europe and the UK, Simple Minds continued the momentum and intent which had fuelled the creation of 'Promised You A Miracle' and, with Pete Walsh in place as producer – 'I still find it hard to believe that Pete was only 21 years old when he produced that record,' Kerr reflected later, adding, 'The guy youngest in the room, the rest of us were 22' – set about writing and recording their new album in any gaps between shows. 'We've been through our period of searching for experimental sounds and doing virtual double albums,' Kerr told *Sounds*' Mick Sinclair in April. 'We're due eight or nine songs where every one is a really focussed piece, really up front. The sound will be a lot more obvious but it's the feeling that's changed.'

At the beginning of August, Simple Minds announced that their sixth album, *New Gold Dream (81-82-83-84)*, would be released in September in the wake of a second single from the album, 'Glittering Prize'. "Glittering Prize' is a definite step forward,' enthused *Record Mirror*'s John Shearlaw, 'convoluted (as always) but clean, more of a treat than an all-out attack on the senses.' 'The confused state they explored before with such curiosity and intelligence has cleared up with the success of the dizzy 'Promised You A…', but just how do you follow up a miracle?' Chris Bohn asked the readers of the *NME*. 'Easy. Dangle a glittering prize some ways in the distance and Simple Minds will always chase after it.' "Glittering Prize' is bitterly disappointing, all glossy, impressive-looking packaging and very little solid substance,' reported *Sounds*' Geoff Barton, while The Jam's Paul Weller, reviewing that week's singles in *Melody Maker*, went even further and declared that Simple Minds were making 'Modern hippy music; if they wore cheese cloth and clogs you lot wouldn't look twice at 'em.'

In the wake of the success of 'Promised You A Miracle' both Radio 1 and *Top of the Pops* were supportive, and as a result of the support of the former, and two appearances on the latter, one of which was subsequently repeated, 'Glittering Prize' spent almost three months in the UK singles chart, where it achieved a peak position of sixteen in October. As 'Glittering Prize' peaked, Simple Minds' new album *New Gold Dream (81-82-83-84)* was already riding high in the UK albums chart, where it would remain until the end of February 1983, peaking at number three after a fortnight on sale and earning the band a gold album for 100,000 UK sales by the end of 1982. 'In the past, Simple Minds have always been associated with the darker side of things. I think we encouraged the association because it made us seem profound. But there's always been other sides to our personalities and we haven't allowed them to come out,' Jim Kerr told *Record Mirror* in September, shortly before the release of *New Gold Dream (81-82-83-84)*, when the band's new confident and accessible direction earned Simple Minds their best set of album reviews to date.

'Let's face it, it's a glorious achievement to produce something that works generously in the usual sweet way tucked inside the trivialised pop context, yet that stretches far beyond those coloured walls to stand strong as an exhilarated canny comment on the "state of the world's flow", on the position of hope and anxiety,' was Paul Morley's enthusiastic but characteristically opaque view of *New Gold Dream (81-82-83-84)*. 'Simple Minds have found a smoothness that translates their big beat into a big treat, a summertime dream romance with love itself,' enthused *Sounds*' Johnny Waller, who also awarded the release four and a half of a possible five stars. 'They've got a considered approach which has so far managed to avoid the ever ready traps of pretension and heavy going. Meanwhile the lyrics are prettily abstracted visions of love, requited and unrequited, for and against,' wrote Christine Buckley in a four-out-of-five review of the album for *Record Mirror*. 'All in all an aural feast which teeters on the edge of getting lost in its own coolness, but still preserves and essential integrity.'

A final single from the album, 'Someone Somewhere (In Summertime)', reached thirty-six in the UK singles chart at the end of November as the band capitalised on their new-found success with a tour which took them across the UK, Europe, Australia, New Zealand and North America before the end of the year. 'I reckon that in two years time if we keep to the same rate, people looking back on our albums will be talking about two different bands – pre 'New Gold Dream', and after,' Jim Kerr told *Record Mirror*'s Billy Sloan at the end of the year, 'We're not trying to be smug, but we know that we have to top it next year – we seem to have a weird competitiveness with ourselves. 'New Gold Dream' has set a standard.'

Similarly interested in setting standards were Soft Cell. In January, Marc Almond and Dave Ball had revealed that they were about to travel to New York to start work on *Non Stop Ecstatic Dancing*, described in the music press as 'a special disco mini-album' which was expected to feature 'six non-stop segued, remixed and re-edited tracks'. The same press stories also reported that Soft Cell were kicking off 1982 with the release of a new single from *Non-Stop Erotic Cabaret*, the album's epic closing track, 'Say Hello, Wave Goodbye'.

'Magic,' enthused Sunie in her review of 'Say Hello, Wave Goodbye' for *Record Mirror*. 'This record will sell in vast quantities and quite possibly take Soft Cell back to square (ie number) one and make even more little girls sigh over Marc and make Stevo a rich and happy man and perhaps even get David Ball noticed, and the nation will hum it wistfully on its way to work and it's slow and sad and quite wonderful.' 'Best track on the elpee,' enthused Betty Page in *Sounds*, declaring the release her Single of Next Week and describing it as 'poignant, heartfelt, stunning, magnificent, swelling… you know the sort of thing'. 'That seedy stuff becomes a stereotype too easily, but this inhabits another space altogether, a real runny eyes and handkerchief job – old romantic, not new, if you ask me,' concluded *Melody Maker*'s Lynden Barber.

The final single to be taken from *Non-Stop Erotic Cabaret*, 'Say Hello, Wave Goodbye' ensured that the album bowed out on a high when it reached number three in the UK charts in the second half of February, earning Soft Cell a silver disc for sales of over 200,000 copies and remaining in the Top 40 for eight weeks. Supported by a suitably tawdry neon-drenched video which was played on *Top of the Pops* two weeks in a row, the soft and sensuous 'Say

Hello, Wave Goodbye' attracted new fans for Soft Cell while also providing a signpost towards another life for those who were watching closely. 'Seeing Marc Almond on *Top Of The Pops*, taking off his dark sunglasses on 'Say Hello, Wave Goodbye' and revealing thick black eyeliner just blew me away,' confessed Erasure's Andy Bell, then starting to question his own sexuality. 'I thought he was very beautiful and I just couldn't figure out why I was so intrigued.'

Remaining coy about his own sexuality – 'For me, sexual ambiguity was always more interesting than being obviously straight or gay,' he wrote in in *Tainted Life*, adding, 'Hadn't all the stars that I'd ever loved been sexually ambiguous, mysterious or enigmatic? I wanted to be like them' – Marc Almond was nevertheless experiencing a transition of his own. 'I feel we're a lot maturer now, it's time to stop saying "tits and ass" and start saying "heart and soul" instead,' he ventured in an interview for a *Record Mirror* cover feature. 'I still write about the same things but I'm approaching them in a much more sensitive way now... I'm looking more into the heart of it as opposed to the surface. Getting much more into the heart of the lowlife land, that underground other world with its different set of rules and codes and languages and everything.' In the same interview Almond also talked enthusiastically about how *Non Stop Ecstatic Dancing* was progressing: 'It's nice to be able to do that now, after a few months of the album being out so we can listen to the tracks and think of alternative ways of putting them over, to take songs and ideas to various extremes.'

In May, Soft Cell followed the success of 'Say Hello, Wave Goodbye' with the release of a brand new single, 'Torch'. '"Torch' sees Soft Cell at their sentimental best,' acknowledged *Sounds*' Dave McCullough. 'A trumpet passage that sounds like it belongs in some great, forgotten '60s ballad leads into this typically tearfully tale of a romantic encounter in a bar,' was *Smash Hits*' take on the single, Dave Rimmer further praising the release as Soft Cell's 'most lavish production yet'. 'A sound production and the usual irreproachable performance from Marc Almond are its strengths,' wrote a more cautious Sunie in *Record Mirror*, 'not nearly as memorable as 'Say Hello' and will inevitably suffer by comparison.'

In fact 'Torch' beat 'Say Hello, Wave Goodbye''s chart peak of number three by one place when it hit number two in the middle of June, held off the top spot by Adam Ant's 'Goody Two Shoes', by which point it had already earned Soft Cell another silver disc for sales in excess of 200,000 copies. 'We

were outselling Adam & The Ants three to one yet we got to number two…
which is like a million miles from number one,' Dave Ball grimaced in his
memoir *Electronic Boy* in 2020, reporting 'an apparent fuck-up with the chart
return shops' and adding wryly, 'We was robbed by a dandy highwayman.'

Released towards the end of the month, *Non Stop Ecstatic Dancing* entered
the UK album charts at number seven in the last chart of June and peaked at
number six the following week on its way to selling in excess of 100,000 copies
by the end of 1982. 'A scintillating, motivating, stimulating, disco-mating
blend of grinding, squirming rhythms and yearning, oozing vocals specifically
designed for bodily celebration,' applauded Johnny Waller in a maximum
five-star review for *Sounds*. 'A new set of clothes on last year's tunes for this
week's party,' wrote Pete Silverton in *Smash Hits*, awarding the album six out
of ten and continuing, 'There are odd electronic noises, babbles of female
voices, squawks of saxophones and enough echo to fill The Albert Hall. Is it a
mini LP or an EP with ideas above its station?'

Nevertheless *Non Stop Ecstatic Dancing* gave Parlophone the opportunity to
release another single, 'What', and this time Marc Almond was determined
that the single would be the end of Soft Cell's latest chapter. "'What' ties up a
whole year for us. We started a year ago with a Northern Soul thing that had
people dancing. We've gone through a full circle and before the second era
starts with a new sound and a new album, we have a bit of a breather and a
dance with 'What', another soul number,' Almond explained to *Smash Hits'*
Neil Tennant in advance of the single release.

Record Mirror were immediately enthusiastic, Simon Tebbutt making
'What' his Single of the Week in August: 'This, like 'Tainted Love', is an old
Northern Soul number given the inimitable treatment with shifts of mood
and changes of pace, and combining all those dancing to and listening to
qualities that have become the Soft Cell hallmark.' *Sounds* provided the single
with another Single of the Week, Johnny Waller declaring, 'These words may
not win you true love, but I promise you that for the duration of this record,
this pulsating, exciting record, you simply won't care.' 'The real follow-up
to 'Tainted Love',' exclaimed Neil Tennant at *Smash Hits*, 'this is Marc and
David at their most friendly and least bizarre with a touching version of a
Northern Soul favourite.'

Soft Cell's sixth Top 5 hit in row, 'What' entered the charts at thirteen
in late August and peaked at number three in the final chart of the month,
remaining in the Top 20 for five weeks and earning Marc Almond and Dave

Ball their third silver single of the year and another *Top of the Pops* appearance as they laid the *Non-Stop Erotic Cabaret* project to rest. 'It's the one single we've released – and we've released a lot – which was not totally true to ourselves,' Almond told *Melody Maker*'s Steve Sutherland when asked about 'What' the following year. 'It should have stayed an extra on the dance mix album, as it was intended to be. It shouldn't have been a single for the simple reason that it was very commercial and poppy, and we don't like to do the obvious. Allowing it to be released, I felt, was like a moment of weakness, a lesson learnt on our part, which is not to give in to moments of weakness at all.'

Asked by the *NME*'s Chris Bohn whether he considered any of the bands loosely considered to be Soft Cell's peers were displaying similar artistic integrity at the time, Almond alighted on The Human League. 'If anybody could break down barriers, turn people's heads, it's them. They're much more stable than we are. God, they could really surprise everybody. I don't mean in terms of outrage; I just mean in terms of doing something a little different,' Almond exclaimed. 'People will listen to them because they're The Human League. I mean, use the name! Use it! You don't have to do things that will change the world. Just do a little bit.'

At the beginning of June the *NME* caught up with The Human League in New York, San Francisco and Los Angeles, where the band were on tour in support of an attempt to break America in the same way that they'd broken the UK the previous year. Tony Stewart, while discovering that Phil Oakey had now cut his trademark asymmetric hair short, found the band in no hurry to release new music on the back of the success of *Dare*. 'The old Human League was a careless bunch, we would do good enough things and then we'd put them out. But from the split me and Adrian said we would never ever do that again. We're never ever gonna do good enough, we're going to do the best or else it's going to stay where it is,' explained Oakey, who added: 'We've got the money to do it this time round. *Dare* was a budget album, we had to rush it. This time we'll finish the tracks off and if I think that the synthesiser strings could have been better, we'll go back and we'll hire a string section.'

Not that a lack of new material had kept the band out of the public eye. At the end of January, a reissued edition of The Human League's 'Being Boiled' single had peaked at number six, and a reissued edition of their Holiday '80 EP – a single seven-inch release which featured 'Being Boiled', 'Marianne' and 'Dancevision' – had grazed the charts in February when it beat the chart placing of its original 1980 release by ten places, reaching number forty-six, much to the band's chagrin. 'We just don't want it out,' Oakey told *Smash Hits* at the time. 'We hate all that old stuff. Virgin said they were doing it to stop 'Being Boiled' being successful. If so, they've done it too late.'

As part of their attempt to refocus the record-buying public on the correct line-up of The Human League, at the beginning of June the band announced that in lieu of new material they were to take a leaf out of Spandau Ballet and Soft Cell's books and would release remixed versions of tracks from their 1981 album *Dare* instead: 'The album will be called 'Love And Dancing' and is set for release on June 25 under the name of The League Unlimited Orchestra,' reported *Record Mirror*.

The League Unlimited Orchestra was effectively *Dare* producer Martin Rushent assisted by his studio engineer Dave Allen, and the inspiration for the release came from The Human League's practice of doing dub mixes to use as B-sides and additional tracks across the various *Dare* singles. 'The dub mixes started because we didn't have time to do B-sides,' Rushent told *Sound On Sound* later. 'When it was all finished I had four or five remixes. Phil wasn't sure about releasing them on an album and left me to make *Love And Dancing* on my own. It was mixed on a board, so I had the multitrack of *Dare* feeding in, a Harmonizer on send one, delay lines and phasers everywhere and I'd flick it about. I'd do a section and if I liked it I'd make a tape cut and splice it in. There were thousands of edits on the master and it took forever to do.'

Melody Maker's Paul Simper found himself an immediate convert and his review of *Love And Dancing* heaped praise on Rushent's wizardry at the end of June: 'Martin Rushent's great bonus of course is that he has some lovely tunes to work with. All the singles revolve so easily round their riffs that the job of distortion is simple and instantly dramatic. Stick the parts together in a different order and suddenly it's a whole new song.' 'It's 'Dare' through the looking glass,' declared Paul Morley in the *NME*. 'Mr Rushent has cautiously dynamited 'Dare' – leaving gasping rhythms, gaping intervals, groping shrieks, concrete bleeps, disembodied voices and cricket balls that have been used for 85 overs.' '"Love And Dancing' is itself a very successful exercise,' wrote Sunie in *Record Mirror*. 'Unlike the nastily robotic capering that were so vogueish last year, this is real Electronic Dance Music.'

Released at a special low price – 'The whole point of *Love And Dancing* is that we did it only as a bonus to fans who would like it,' Phil Oakey told *Melody Maker* at the time, adding: 'It's there if they want it but it's supposed to be sold cheaply, as a little extra, and that's why we haven't had it advertised or anything' – *Love And Dancing* entered the UK album charts at number four in the middle of July, the first step in a fifty-two-week journey through the charts, which included nine consecutive weeks in the Top 10, eventually earning a platinum album for 300,000 UK sales, much to the satisfaction of Martin Rushent. 'Making *Love and Dancing* was the most creative experience I've ever had in my life,' the producer told Simon Reynolds in an interview for *Totally Wired* later. 'Something that has been difficult to top. I haven't gone anywhere near it since. That's probably why I gave up record production for so long. It's like why astronauts go a bit loopy after they've got back from the moon. You've walked on the fucking moon, what are you gonna do now?'

Rushent was also able to give The Human League due credit for the material from which *Love And Dancing* was created. 'I can't make good records with lousy artists, I help them achieve the ideas they start out with,' the producer told *Record Mirror*'s Mark Cooper in June. 'People like The Human League are marvellous to work with because we [Genetic Studio] have the sound and they have the songs. They have such strength of writing power.' 'In a dance-mix you can put in all the ideas you leave off the singles because they'll put the radio planners off,' Rushent added. 'I have to admit I've learned an awful lot about dance mixes from New York clubs. I started doing them after hearing Grandmaster Flash over there. Now everybody wants dance-mixes because they give bands a foothold in America.'

Grandmaster Flash & The Furious Five were responsible for one of 1982's most influential hits when their single 'The Message' reached number eight on the UK singles chart in the second half of September, despite Radio 1 imposing what *Record Mirror* described as a 'semi-ban' on the record for including the word 'pissing' in its lyrics. In *Melody Maker*, Lynden Barber correctly recognised something of cultural importance in the record: 'The Grandmaster's seething anthem of inner city blues and militant black consciousness tells a different story, an attempt to heave rap out of the ghettoes of harmless fun and into the tradition laid down by such milestones as James Brown's 'Say It Loud, I'm Black And I'm Proud'.' "The Message' is a devastating return, going far beyond "rap" or "protest". So far in fact that it's one of the most mesmeric records you're ever likely to hear. Ever,' stated Gavin Martin in the *NME* with obvious approval.

Although by 1982 there was a growing market for compilations of American rap tracks 'The Message' was only the second rap single to properly cross over into the UK mainstream after The Sugarhill Gang's number three hit

'Rapper's Delight' at the very end of 1979. A third rap single – Grandmaster Flash's epic twelve-inch 'The Adventures Of Grandmaster Flash On The Wheels Of Steel', an influential DJ mix which featured excerpts from songs recorded by other artists – was equally innovative upon its release in 1981, introducing new audiences to the radical new DJ techniques of scratching and mixing, and although it wasn't a commercial hit in the UK it nevertheless took second place in the *NME*'s 'Tracks of the Year' ranking at the end of 1981.

Although 'Rapper's Delight', 'The Message' and 'The Adventures Of Grandmaster Flash On The Wheels Of Steel' all fall outside the category of electronic pop, the trio of releases became the foundation stones for what would soon become known as hip-hop, which in turn took electronic music in a brand new direction. As 'The Message' broke into the Top 10 of the UK singles charts in September 1982, New York's Afrika Bambaataa & The Soulsonic Force entered the lower reaches of the same chart with an equally groundbreaking release of their own, 'Planet Rock'. 'Europe was a lot into synthesiser music, but it wasn't strict funk. I said "What if I could take a break off that, blend boundaries of funk and like a new wave beat or something?"' Bambaataa told *Melody Maker* the following year. 'I was just looking to just please people that was into hip-hop and people into new wave, but then it just took off.'

Prior to 'Planet Rock', Afrika Bambaataa had been a DJ, playing parties in the Bronx alongside luminaries like Grandmaster Flash and DJ Kool Herc, but what made Bambaataa special was the breadth of his musical knowledge and his eclectic record collection. Not content with simply serving up the same funk and disco tracks favoured by his peers, Bambaataa would mix extracts from records by The Beatles, The Rolling Stones, Led Zeppelin and The Monkees, alongside European electronic records. 'In the early eighties I liked electronic bands such as Depeche Mode and Ultravox! But Kraftwerk and Gary Numan were special to me because they made funk music,' Bambaataa is quoted as saying in a Gary Numan fan club magazine later. 'It's all related – Sly Stone, James Brown, George Clinton, Bootsy Collins, Kraftwerk and Gary Numan.'

While 'Planet Rock' only made it to fifty-three in the UK singles chart, its impact was immeasurable, despite the entire single being constructed around replayed, unlicensed riffs from Kraftwerk's 'Trans-Europe Express' and 'Numbers'. 'I don't think [Kraftwerk] even knew how big they were among the black masses back in '77 when they came out with 'Trans Europe Express',' Bambaataa told *The Face* in 1984. 'When that came out I thought that was one of the best and weirdest damn records I ever heard in my life.'

'At first I thought it was peculiar, these black kids getting off to this music, very technical, very German; but it's more general, in society everyone is getting very technical, with all the video games, hardware, boxes, tape recorders,' 'Planet Rock' producer Arthur Baker told the *NME* at the time, also revealing that the single had already sold in excess of 700,000 copies in the USA. 'So the kids liked 'Numbers', I liked Kraftwerk – we knew it would get over to the New York kids, but we didn't see it catching on like it did. I mean, I had a feeling I'd done something better than I'd ever done before, but it wasn't the type of thing where we took a lot of time, we didn't concentrate that much, we just had real fun doin' it.'

'I wanted it to be the first black electronic group... and it just took off,' Bambaataa told Frank Broughton in 1998. 'With the elements of the Kraftwerk sound and then the hard funk bass, and a beat underneath it... I decided the name of this sound is the electrofunk sound,' Bambaataa declared in the same interview. That name – frequently shortened to simply 'electro' – stuck, and a new electronic genre was invented. 'Electro was born when New York's rappers discovered computer technology, mixed it with a love of early video games and comic culture, then added a certain electronic influence from groups like Kraftwerk and Yellow Magic Orchestra to create the first computerised strain of black music,' explained *i-D* magazine later. 'Combined with breakdancing, body-popping and graffiti art, electro was exported throughout the world and formed the first wave of global hip hop culture.'

'This is a rap effort grafted on the top of the tune from Kraftwerk's 'Trans-Europe Express' without the courtesy of a credit. It's not a crime is it?' asked *Smash Hits'* David Hepworth in his review of 'Planet Rock' at the start of September. 'Well yeah, it is a crime...' 'A lot of people think we sampled Kraftwerk but it's just not true,' declared Bambaataa later. 'John Robie [co-writer] was a bad-ass synthesiser player, so he was just so good in playing stuff, that it sounded like they sampled the record.' 'What we're doing now is the true jazz music, I think, because jazz artists of the past, they wouldn't always particularly write new songs; they would take standards and do something new to them,' 'Planet Rock' producer Arthur Baker explained to the *NME*'s

Ian Penman. 'Rap to me is jazz; it takes something familiar – a beat or a melody – and has fun with it.' Kraftwerk took a less romantic view of the plagiarism of their work and subsequently took legal action against Tommy Boy Records, who had released 'Planet Rock', winning a reported $1 royalty for every copy sold.

Hot on the heels of 'Planet Rock' came a rush of similarly pioneering electro tracks from New York, most of which remained underground, although some would occasionally cross over into the UK singles chart. In fact the two new entries in the last UK chart of the year, announced on Christmas Day 1982, were a pair of key crossover records: Tyrone Brunson's 'The Smurf' and Whodini's 'Magic's Wand'. 'The biggest and best of all the electrophonic phunkers,' declared *Record Mirror* of 'The Smurf', which the *NME* simultaneously dismissed as 'ineffectual funk'. 'Magic's Wand' was more interesting for being one of the very first electro records to come, in part, from the UK. 'This involves the talents of that jack-of-all-trades, Thomas Dolby,' announced *Record Mirror*, who reported that the single was also 'bursting out all over the clubs'.

'I built up the groove and chord sequence in late night sessions, and the backing tracks were sent to the USA, where a pair of black college graduates called Whodini added a rap,' Dolby explained in his memoir *The Speed of Sound* in 2017. He also revealed that 'Magic's Wand' was the first twelve-inch single to sell a million copies in the USA. Dolby had been matched with Whodini through his publishing company, Zomba, who also represented Whodini, and 'Magic's Wand' was the first release on their new label, Jive Records. Whodini were keen to bring something distinctive to their sound, something that would make them stand out against their New York peers, and were not only keen to see what Dolby could bring to the table, but also approached Conny Plank to produce some of the tracks for their subsequent album.

Thomas Dolby wasn't the first UK artist to have identified something interesting and inspiring in the hip-hop and electro scenes coming out of New York; Dolby had also been recruited to play on the first homegrown hit to emerge from the influences of hip-hop and electro: Malcolm McLaren's *Duck Rock*, which was preceded by a first single, 'Buffalo Gals'. McLaren had been taken to see Afrika Bambaataa play a show in New York and had immediately recognised something innovative and important not only in the music but also in the broader rapping, scratching, graffiti and electro scenes in which he suddenly found himself.

Duck Rock was born from an ambitious project conceived by Malcolm McLaren and produced by Trevor Horn, the latter on a golden streak after working on highly successful records for ABC, Dollar and Spandau Ballet. McLaren and Horn weren't an obvious match, and in fact Horn was recruited on the urging of the record label. 'At the beginning I didn't have any say in it, he was the company's guardian angel. But I did choose him ultimately,' McLaren told *Sounds*' Dave McCullough at the time. 'In the company's eyes, he lessened the risk that I presented.' However, the unlikely combination somehow worked: 'I find that he [McLaren] has a way of looking at things that is similar to mine as regards its perversity,' Horn told the *NME*. 'This project is such a good idea. I don't know if it will work, we're both taking a bit of a fling on it.' 'What intrigued me initially was what he said about how black kids in New York were listening to Depeche Mode. I'd got this probably erroneous idea that black people in America were listening to soul music,' Horn confessed to Simon Reynolds later. 'He said, "Oh no," and told me about scratching. He had a cassette of the The World Famous Supreme Team, and I'd never heard anything like it. He also had a record by Afrika Bambaataa, 'Planet Rock'… so we were on the same page right away.'

Initially entitled *Folk Dances Of The World*, *Duck Rock* was McLaren's attempt to extract the revolutionary magic from traditional indigenous music from around the world, identify and amplify the seismic proto-rock'n'roll moments, and then celebrate them in a new modern context. 'It's using the "debris" of old music,' McLaren told *The Face* at the time. 'Finding little beats inside other people's records and mixing them together to form another composite, another piece of music, and then adding to it by using other technology such as a rhythm box. It doesn't follow the old-fashioned format of verse-chorus either. It's an adventure story, it goes off at tangents. That's what makes it one of the most inventive, the newest and most interesting types of music being made today. Scratching is probably the newest urban folk music.' 'He wants to get kids dancing to folk music, very basic music, music from the Americas,' Trevor Horn told the *NME*'s Paul Morley. 'He wants to see them square dancing. Dances where you actually have to learn something, where people are actually dancing together…'

'Malc's debut combines scratch DJ techniques from NYC with square dancing styles from the country. The two collide then collapse in a heap on the floor,' wrote *Melody Maker*'s Mark Cooper of 'Buffalo Gals' when the single was released as the first introduction to *Duck Rock* in November 1982. 'This is little short of utter madness, particularly the A-side which is a ridiculously fragmented dub-wise Trevor Horn production extravaganza,' proclaimed *Sounds*' Geoff Barton. 'I'd like to say that MMc has gone completely round the twist and that such behaviour hasn't a cat in hell's chance of becoming a dancehall trend... but I can't help feeling that, yes, he is on to something.' 'A "Wheels Of Steel/Soulsonic Force" workout, with the Supreme Team scratching themselves silly while Malcolm warbles the directions of the dance in the background,' enthused Gary Crowley in *Melody Maker*. 'It's itchy and irresistible.'

'A Buffalo Gal was a pioneer, an adventurer, someone cowboys in the Wild West sang about at barn dances when they were trying to get a girl: that's what the square dance is on the B-side of the record. Square dancing in the last century was their rock'n'roll, long before rock'n'roll existed. I wanted to show that, exposed properly, it has as much vehemence,' McLaren told *Smash Hits*' Neil Tennant in January 1983 when 'Buffalo Gals', having entered the UK singles chart at thirty-eight at the start of December 1982 and steadily climbed the charts through Christmas and the New Year, hit its chart peak of number nine.

Meanwhile, in addition to his unexpected role as a pioneer of hip-hop and electro, Thomas Dolby was working to establish himself as an electronic music artist in his own right, a process he had started the previous year with an independently released single, 'Urges', before signing himself, and his Venice In Peril label, to EMI in the spring of 1981. Dolby's first single for EMI, 'Europa And The Pirate Twins', was well reviewed in the music press – 'This is so good you couldn't get a scalpel between the ideas, they're packed that tight,' enthused *Melody Maker*'s Paul Colbert – and peaked at number forty-eight in the UK singles chart in October 1981, when Dolby embarked on the usual round of promotion, which included a front cover feature for *Sounds*. Revealing that Dolby – 'Distinguishing features: Professional demeanour, poor eyesight, absent mind, bow tie' – had already worked with artists as diverse as Foreigner, Lene Lovich, M and Joan Armatrading, in addition to playing alongside 'Video Killed The Radio Star' co-writer Bruce Woolley in The Camera Club, the feature reported that he was now ready to embrace his future as a solo artist in his own right.

Two further Thomas Dolby singles, 'Airwaves' and 'Radio Silence', followed in January and April 1982, respectively, and while both were accompanied by innovative videos, which emphasised Dolby's endearing, eccentric boffin image and attracted another round of enthusiastic reviews from the music press – 'Mark this man down as a star of the future,' predicted *Smash Hits'* Red Starr in his review of 'Airwaves', while 'Radio Silence' was declared 'marvellous stuff' by *Sounds'* Johnny Waller – neither made any inroads on the singles chart. 'I'm quite content to remain what's euphemistically called a "cult figure",' Dolby told *Record Mirror* later, 'but obviously I'm not about to make a duff record to be quite sure of keeping out of the Top 10. If it happens, it happens.'

Thomas Dolby's debut album, *The Golden Age Of Wireless*, followed in May and spent three weeks in the lower reaches of the UK album chart. Tony Mitchell awarded *The Golden Age Of Wireless* five out of a possible five stars in his review for *Sounds* and enthused, 'Being one of the relatively few who know the impact Dolby is very soon going to have on modern British music is like being part of an exciting conspiracy to pervert the course of pop into something entirely new and unashamedly glorious.' 'This is another Dolby system that will enhance listening pleasure,' added Mike Gardner in a four-out-of-five-star review for *Record Mirror*.

Released in the slipstream of *The Golden Age Of Wireless* came a fourth single, 'Windpower', which finally put Thomas Dolby back in the UK singles chart and, when the single reached number fifty-six at the end of August, Dolby was invited to perform the single on *Top of the Pops*. 'The *TOTP* production crew had pulled out all the stops for my performance. There were massive wind machines surrounding my small stage, bold monochromatic lighting, stroboscopes, and enough fog to cause a collision at sea,' Dolby recalled of his *Top of the Pops* debut in *The Speed of Sound*. 'I sprang around between multiple keyboards and Simmons drum pads, spectacles askance, hair blowing in the wind, in a dapper fawn suit.' As a result of *Top of the Pops'* boost, 'Windpower' continued a slow climb to a peak position of thirty-one in the middle of September, the success of the single also pushing *The Golden Age Of Wireless* album to its chart peak of sixty-five the same week.

Determined to capitalise on the success of 'Windpower', but having already taken four singles from *The Golden Age Of Wireless*, Thomas Dolby set to work on the song which would become one of the commercial cornerstones of his career, a track which began life as a video concept rather than a piece of music. 'I began dreaming up a scenario for a music video set in a Home for Deranged Scientists, including a mad psychiatrist and his hot Japanese lab assistant,' Dolby revealed in *The Speed of Sound*. 'My character would arrive at the clinic astride a classic vintage motorbike with sidecar. After an initial session on the analyst's couch, I would be drugged and wheeled into the operating theatre for some sort of corrective procedure. There followed a surreal dream involving sinister schoolboy twins and a waltz with a female lab assistant in a Magritte-style cello gown. I was to be put out to pasture with the other deranged scientists, but I escaped in a straitjacket, and the psychiatrist got his comeuppance.'

'She Blinded Me With Science' was subsequently written over a single weekend as the soundtrack to accompany the video concept and, with TV personality Dr Magnus Pyke on board to perform the part of the mad psychiatrist on the record and in the video, the single was released at the end of October. 'The best from Mr Dolby yet,' *Melody Maker*'s Caroline Harper reported, 'thoroughly danceable, but laced with the usual class one expects from this electronic wizard.' Robin Smith's take on the single for *Record Mirror* was distinctly more unfriendly: 'I don't like Thomas Dolby at all. He's like a smart arse kid at school who used to get all the answers right during science tests. As if Dolby's not bad enough on his own, he's signed up Magnus Pyke, the old duffer who waves his arms around on BBC shows.'

Interestingly, although 'She Blinded Me With Science' became one of Thomas Dolby's best-known songs, it failed to become a substantial hit in the UK and spent two weeks at a chart peak of just forty-nine in November 1982. A re-release of the single the following year fared no better when it failed to rise above fifty-six, despite a *Top of the Pops* showing of the 'She Blinded Me With Science' video. In North America, however, the eccentric track and its equally eccentric video ploughed a very different furrow: 'She Blinded Me With Science' became a number one hit for Thomas Dolby in Canada and peaked at number five in *Billboard*'s Hot 100 chart.

Yazoo, 1982.

1982.2 Depeche Mode / Yazoo / Blancmange

KEEN TO FIND OUT more about the circumstances which had led to Vince Clarke's departure from Depeche Mode the previous November, *Smash Hits* put a picture of the latter's three-piece line-up on the cover of their second issue of 1982 and dispatched writer Mark Ellen to meet both parties to find out what had happened. 'All the things that come with success had suddenly become more important than the music,' Clarke explained, in a separate interview to his former bandmates, stating that his expectations for Depeche Mode had never factored in the kind of success they had enjoyed the previous year. 'We used to get letters from fans saying: "I really like your songs"; then we got letters saying: "Where do you buy your trousers from?" Where do you go from there?'

Ellen found Andy Fletcher, Dave Gahan and Martin Gore in a more upbeat mood than their former colleague, until the interview touched on Clarke's departure. 'There's a bit of a block between us… it's a Him and Us situation,' the band admitted, but Depeche Mode found themselves closer as a band as a result. 'Before we used to rely on Vince; now we've got to try a lot harder. And it'll be different,' Fletcher acknowledged, particularly now that songwriting duties would fall mainly to Gore. 'Martin writes music around his words, whereas Vince used to write the tunes first and then fit the lyrics to them… words were never Vince's strong point.' 'He's a genius but he doesn't know it,' Clarke declared of Gore, and also generously praised the new Depeche Mode single 'See You', the first to be penned by Gore, as 'the band's best ever'.

A few pages further on in the same issue of *Smash Hits*, Mark Ellen made 'See You' his Star Single. 'Light years ahead of the rest. Listening to this you can hardly believe that – even a year back – the mention of 'synthesised pop' conjured up images of doomy one-dimensional treks to the space-lab,' Ellen wrote. "'See You' sounds warm, colourful and surprisingly durable… if it doesn't make Number One I'll write and complain.' 'Imagine the dewy-eyed, soft focus pictures of Dave Gahan you've seen transmuted into sound, and you'll have a fair idea of what 'See You' sounds like,' added Sunie in *Record Mirror* the following week, describing the song as 'a softly attractive song without their usual hard, poppy edge'. To which *Sounds'* Robbi Millar added, "'See You' shows the Mode taking a leaf out of Soft Cell's dog-eared booklet and creating warm, compulsive pop instead of antiseptic hit fodder.'

Released in early February – which allowed Depeche Mode to take advantage of an ongoing British Rail strike to film a winsome video to accompany the single at Hounslow's deserted railway station – 'See You' became the band's biggest hit to date when it spent seven weeks in the Top 40. The single peaked at number six in the middle of March, by which time the band had completed a UK tour – their first with Alan Wilder, who had been recruited to take Vince Clarke's place for live appearances – as well as a show at the BBC's Paris Theatre which was recorded for Radio One's *In Concert* series.

'Every day there seems to be something,' Dave Gahan told the *NME*'s Lynn Hanna at the end of March, in an echo of Vince Clarke's own objections to the high-pace lifestyle of the modern pop star. 'Up to a certain point you get used to it,' Gahan continued. 'But you do begin to wonder what good it actually does.' 'The only point of bitterness really is the fact that we're working really hard and promoting his [Vince Clarke's] material and he's doing what we want to do but can't,' added Andy Fletcher. Ironically Clarke was about to become similarly busy as he launched a new project of his own, one he had touched upon in his interview with *Smash Hits* earlier in the year. Contrary to earlier reports from Mute Records, Ellen had reported that Clarke no longer had plans to contribute songs to Depeche Mode, but was instead working with a new singer, Geneviève Alison Moyet, under the name Yazoo.

'I met her as she floated ashore on a boat from Afghanistan, heard her singing and formed the band…' Clarke told Ellen of his new bandmate. 'Oh alright then, she comes from Basildon.' 'If it's any help,' Ellen added, 'the rest of the band call her 'Alf'.' 'Yazoo are Vince Clarke and Alf. Vince is male and short. Alf is female and tall. Vince floated to the top of the pops pile in the Depeche Mode bubble, while Alf barely survived the gruelling bars'n'grime circuit of Southend and Canvey Island blues clubs and bars,' explained Chris Bohn in the *NME*'s first interview with Yazoo. 'We're not setting out to do anything in particular like blending blues and pop,' explained Clarke hurriedly. 'The stuff we're doing in the studio, well neither of us would've done anything like it a year ago.'

'Only You', Yazoo's debut single, was a track which Clarke had originally written with Depeche Mode in mind, but when his former bandmates turned the song down he decided to record it himself. 'When I left the band I didn't intend to do anything, but I got bored so I decided to do a one-off single of a particular song I'd written some time before,' Clarke told *New Sounds New Styles'* Robert Elms later. 'It was going to be a one-off thing, then we decided we wanted to carry on and see what else we could come up with,' Alison Moyet explained to *Record Mirror*, at the same time shining a light onto the genesis of Yazoo's name: 'I just hate the way so many groups have these fashionable names. I like Yazoo because it means nothing, so with luck it won't date. I got it from an atlas – it's a small town in America.'

And how was Vince Clarke going to cope with the possibility of a second flush of success, after so roundly rejecting the first? 'The way things generated around Depeche Mode, I felt we'd lost control over it, but now I feel I've got a lot more freedom,' Clarke told *Record Mirror*'s Sunie in May. 'I'm not afraid of success really, it's just that I need to be more careful to keep things in perspective,' he elaborated in an interview with *Smash Hits'* Neil Tennant. 'It's not so much what you do as how you view it, placing the right amount of importance on the right things. Then you get satisfaction out of what you're doing.'

Released in March, 'Only You' was an immediate hit for Yazoo, peaking at number two in the UK singles chart in May – kept off the top spot by the 1982 Eurovision Song Contest winner Nicole's 'A Little Peace' – and topping the independent singles chart. 'The Captain and Tennille of electronic pop?' wondered *Record Mirror*'s Sunie. 'Lovely stuff.' Richard Cook was equally enthusiastic in the *NME*: 'The emotional dial is on yearning and it trips through a melodic multiplication table that charms a passage to the heart by the end. Sweet.'

While 'Only You' blazed it's fourteen-week chart journey, Mute also released 'The Meaning Of Love', the second single from Depeche Mode's first album following Vince Clarke's departure. Under normal circumstances 'The Meaning Of Love' could be considered to have performed well, peaking at number twelve in the UK singles chart and at number two in the independent singles chart, but in comparison to Yazoo's debut it came off as decidedly second-best despite some sterling reviews, including one from ABC frontman Martin Fry reviewing the singles for *Smash Hits* at the end of April:

'It's watertight and nearly perfect, as damn near perfect as a record can be… what else is there to say except truly scrumptious.'

Despite Fry's optimistic declaration, in some quarters the tide was starting to turn on Depeche Mode's colourful pop. 'The youth of Basildon present their least shiny record so far,' noted Charles Shaar Murray in the *NME*. 'Another band with its hit formula wearing a little thin… it's too sugar sugar for me,' wrote *Melody Maker*'s Mike Andrews, while *Sounds*' Valac Van Der Veene was apologetic in his dismissal of the single: 'I'd be a terrible spoilsport to observe that the lead melody line is musically identical to their last hit. And to suggest their harmonies are trite and the rhythms lumpen would condemn me to the post-juvenile scrap-heap – yes?'

In turn 'Don't Go' provided Yazoo with a second Top 5 hit when their sophomore single spent three consecutive weeks at a chart peak of number three in July and August, racking up another eleven weeks in the UK singles chart and a second number one in the independent singles chart. Awarded Single of the Week status in *Smash Hits*, the *NME* and *Melody Maker* at the start of July, the release established Yazoo as much more than another one hit wonder. 'A sharp successor to the delicious 'Only You'. Vince coaxes a sterling song out of his synthesiser while Alf balances its metallic clip with a deep, emotion-packed vocal that gets better with every hearing,' extolled *Smash Hits*' Ian Birch. 'A slice of soul melodrama that knocks the rest of this week's releases into a cocked hat in terms of impact and intensity,' declared Adrian Thrills in the *NME*. *Flexipop* meanwhile turned their page of singles reviews over to The Girls of Oxford High School and their teacher, Mr Crisp. 'It's a sort of powerfunk, but with soul,' decided Mr Crisp. 'It'll do well in the charts,' continued one of his pupils, Jane, to which another pupil, Isobel, added, 'All the trendies will go out and buy it.'

At the end of July, Yazoo were on the cover of the *NME* for the first time and, in the accompanying interview, Adrian Thrills took the opportunity to ask Vince Clarke about his recent split from Depeche Mode, discovering that distance had indeed made the heart grow fonder. 'It wasn't really a personal thing. It would be out of order for me to say that their attitude was wrong. It was just very different to mine,' Clarke began. 'At first there were a few bad feelings, but that seems to have died down now that everybody concerned feels more secure about what they're doing now.'

In an interview with *Record Mirror* a few weeks later, it seemed that Depeche Mode were of the same mind. 'We still see Vince quite a lot. He pops in when we're recording,' Dave Gahan told journalist Simon Tebbutt, and Depeche Mode professed themselves quite taken by Yazoo's recent success. 'We're really pleased, especially for Alison. She's got a great voice,' Andy Fletcher revealed. 'Martin was at school with her and we've known her for ages. She's been working hard for years. A long time before we started.' 'I don't think of Yazoo as a continuation of Depeche or even as an improvement on Depeche. It's a completely new project and fortunately it has always been taken as that,' Clarke added in the *NME*.

In fact Depeche Mode were about to take their first significant step away from the bubblegum pop that characterised their work with Clarke in favour of a darker, more considered direction of their own on a new single, 'Leave In Silence'. 'It's getting away from dance music,' Martin Gore told Simon Tebbutt in *Record Mirror*. 'It's not that you can't dance to it – it's just that the charts are getting too dance orientated.' 'It's a lot weightier, not so lightweight and poppy,' Andy Fletcher mused of Depeche Mode's new direction. 'A lot of people who liked us before might not like it because it isn't bouncy – a lot of the songs are very moody.'

'Leave In Silence' was greeted with cautious enthusiasm upon its release in August, providing Depeche Mode with another independent singles chart number one and peaking at eighteen in the UK singles chart despite its change in musical direction, and garnering some encouraging reviews. *Record Mirror* made the release their Single of the Week: "Leave In Silence' is a tower of glory. Whoever said that synthesisers are only good for pretty little ditties will have to eat their words,' enthused Daniela Soave. 'This pounds with atmosphere, creating a dramatic soundtrack for a film which is created in your mind's eye.' "Leave In Silence' is a wonderful, deserted love song, which has Dave Gahan manfully tackling pending departure without collapsing in tears,' proclaimed the *NME*'s Chris Bohn. 'A softly stated rhythm and muted synth horns lead Depeche Mode out of the idiot chattering seasick electro-trough they were threatening to fall into.'

Aware of the dangers of being too closely associated with a transient scene, Bohn's words were exactly the reaction to 'Leave In Silence' Depeche Mode were hoping for. 'The sort of people who buy Duran Duran or Spandau Ballet records might buy ours as well,' allowed Dave Gahan in an interview for *Smash Hits*, 'but I think we're in a slightly different market. A slightly older market. There's not so many New Romantics in our audience as there used to be. Not so many frilly shirts.' Gahan returned the same theme in a later interview for *Record Mirror* when, apparently still troubled by the popular perception of his band's immediate peers, he added, 'It's much better that people associate us with The Human League and Soft Cell rather than Duran Duran and Spandau Ballet. I hope gradually people will stop associating us with others and we will get our own name and identity.'

Unencumbered by such preconceptions, Yazoo released their debut album in August to the overwhelming approval of the press and of the public. In the independent singles chart, *Upstairs At Eric's* – 'Eric is our engineer and co-producer, but "Upstairs" we just liked the sound of it,' Alison Moyet told *Sounds* later, adding: 'The studio is a one-story church, so there isn't any upstairs!' – spent twelve consecutive weeks at number one in the independent albums chart, and entered the UK albums chart at number two in the first week of September, a position it maintained for a further two weeks – kept off the top spot on all three occasions by The Kids From Fame's eponymous album – remaining in the Top 10 for eight weeks as part of an enviable sixty-week chart run.

'Clarke's light and essentially cheerful electro-pop shuffles are given another dimension by a voice that takes something disposable and very nearly lifts it out of the sphere of an effervescent everyday entertainment into a truer, purer category,' was Lynn Hanna's take on *Upstairs At Eric's* in the *NME*. 'Vince Clarke and Alison 'Alf' Moyet have turned in a debut that's rich, satisfying and shows more promise in songwriting, lyrics and playing than any album this year,' applauded Simon Hills in a five-out-of-five-star review for *Melody Maker*. 'Whoever said synthesiser music has no feeling can start eating their heart out now.' 'It's one hell of an album,' added *Sounds'* Johnny Waller, who also awarded *Upstairs At Eric's* a maximum five stars. 'Three cheers for something unpredictable,' added *Smash Hits'* Ian Cranna. 'I can't stop playing it.'

Yazoo embarked on their debut tour of the UK, which kicked off with two warm-up shows at Basildon's Raquel's club in August – 'The instant Vince and Alison stepped on to the purpose-built stage, it was sheer perfection from the computer-controlled music, lights and film to the informality and warmth of Alf's banter with the audience,' wrote *Sounds'* Helen Fitzgerald of the first show – and ended with three dates at London's prestigious Dominion Theatre at the end of November. Interrupted briefly by a quick trip to the USA to play three shows in New York at the end of October in support of the enthusiastic American reaction to *Upstairs At Eric's* and its associated singles, Yazoo played twenty-two sold-out shows across the UK before the end of the year.

'At the beginning when 'Only You' came out and Vince was on every front cover, "Vince and Alf", "Alf and Vince", "Alf's voice" and everything – even going into the Mute office, everything was Yazoo this, Yazoo that – it was hard,' Martin Gore admitted to *Melody Maker*'s Steve Sutherland when Depeche Mode released their second album, *A Broken Frame*, in October. 'We've basically faced the fact that they're massive now.' And while Clarke was back on cordial terms with his former bandmates as they released their first album without him, Depeche Mode remained unable to strike out on their own without Clarke's shadow falling over everything they did.

'After Vince left and went to form Yazoo, we were getting ready to record a new album. Alan started playing with us but we wanted to make certain that any change in direction in our music wasn't attributable to Alan joining,' Martin Gore explained to *ZigZag* in November. 'We needed to show we were capable of musical alteration by ourselves. So we recorded *A Broken Frame* with that in mind.' In fact, despite the band's best efforts, *A Broken Frame* struggled to move the band away from the bubblegum pop of their debut. 'In attempting the balance that Yazoo get away with, the new Depeche Mode overstep the mark. Vince is adept at conjuring musical moods and Alf's voice is earthy and human enough to con us there's emotion behind their candy floss, but the Mode remain essentially vacuous,' wrote *Melody Maker*'s Steve Sutherland regretfully, adding: 'The boys' pluck should be applauded and we should be grateful that they refuse to tread water. But the plain fact is, they're drowning.'

'The songs of Depeche Mode are not bad and they are, pathetically at times, nice. But, is that all there is?' asked Chris Burkham in his review of *A Broken Frame* for *Sounds*. 'It is possible to accept this calculated kind of blandness when it is just a three minute stab at the charts, because then you know that it isn't going to last that long. But the very attempt to put together a whole LP's worth of these songs shows their shortcomings.'

'For me the Mode talk about the passing pleasures with an ace precision, and are a consistently excellent illumination of pop's mystical ability to ravish the senses through a combination of sweet regrets and agile delight,' declared Paul Morley of *A Broken Frame*. 'And with Depeche Mode it is their potential that excites as much as anything.' And Depeche Mode agreed. 'I don't think *A Broken Frame* is the tester, really,' Andy Fletcher told *Melody Maker*'s Steve Sutherland at the beginning of October. 'I mean, I hope a lot of people will go out and buy it because it's us and it's got three hit singles on it. I think the next album will be the real teller...'

Undeterred by the music press's perfunctory reaction to *A Broken Frame*, Depeche Mode set off on a twenty-date tour of the UK and Ireland in support of the album in October, which saw them play to near-hysterical audiences everywhere they went. 'The audience was young and very lively, going bloody bonkers every night,' remembers Neil Arthur of Blancmange, who played support to Depeche Mode on their dates earlier that year. 'I remember there was always masses of teddy bears that had been given to the band at the back of the coach.' 'It's good in a way, 'cos they're not embarrassed,' Dave Gahan told Lynn Hanna in the *NME* when asked about Depeche Mode's young audience earlier in the year. 'I remember going to gigs and being embarrassed to move 'cos it's not cool to dance. I remember seeing Gary Numan at Hammersmith and just sitting through the whole gig.'

On a short break from his own UK dates with Yazoo, and a couple of days before heading to the USA for their New York shows, Vince Clarke watched one of Depeche Mode's two shows at London's Hammersmith Odeon at the end of October and, although he reported the experience of seeing his former band's performance in *Smash Hits* as 'Weird,' he was also impressed: 'I thought: "So that's what we sounded like,"' Clarke told Dave Rimmer. 'But I enjoyed it.' *Smash Hits* enjoyed it too. 'Depeche Mode have grown up,' they reported in their review of the band's show in St Austell. 'They perform their bright, slight pop with a newly-found sophistication which belies their wimpish style.' 'The nervousness David [Gahan] used to reflect has gone,' added *Sounds* approvingly in their review of the band's Brighton show. 'Now, he jerks and boogies almost puppet-like, each movement provoking swoons and screams.'

In addition to providing swoons, screams and gifts of soft toys at the live shows, Depeche Mode's loyal audience were also on hand to support *A Broken Frame* which, in parallel with the start of the tour, charted at number ten in the UK album charts at the start of October. *A Broken Frame* spent a subsequent ten weeks in the charts, peaking at number eight, and selling over 60,000 copies in its first fortnight on the way to earning the band a gold disc for 100,000 copies by the end of the following year.

Despite the success of the album, Depeche Mode subsequently distanced themselves from *A Broken Frame*, starting the following year when Dave Gahan told *Record Mirror*: 'The whole album was written by Martin and it was the first opportunity to write a large amount of songs in a short period of time. There was so much pressure involved in that album.'

On the back of the success of *Upstairs At Eric's*, Yazoo released one more single from their album at the end of the year, and enjoyed their third single hit of 1982 when 'The Other Side Of Love' peaked at thirteen in the run-up to Christmas. This time it was the turn of Clarke and Moyet to be compared to Depeche Mode. 'This is bouncy, catchy, but deeply unsatisfying; pleasure and irritation result, in equal proportions. And it's regressive too,' noted *Sounds'* Tony Mitchell, 'just when you thought he was on the point of exploring new directions, Vince comes up with a rehash of an early Depeche Mode b-side, with all its lightweight, bubblegum implications.' *Smash Hits* agreed. 'A lighter pop song than their last offering, more closely related to Depeche Mode's 'Just Can't Get Enough' than 'Don't Go',' declared Neil Tennant. 'The third Yazoo single departs from the pomp and circumstantial drama of 'Only You' and 'Don't Go' in order to essay a fast, sexy dance tune that gives this year's major new pop voice a chance to show off her soul chops,' wrote Charles Shaar Murray in the *NME*.

Blancmange kicked off their 1982 by reconnecting with Depeche Mode on the latter's UK dates in support of 'See You' in February. Having also supported Depeche Mode on their last tour with Vince Clarke at the end of 1981, Blancmange were well placed to witness any changes in the band as a result of Clarke's departure and their subsequent engagement of Alan Wilder as an extra synthesiser player. 'Going on tour with them again was quite easy, because we already had a relationship with them,' Blancmange frontman Neil Arthur remembers today, without recalling any particular tension after Clarke left the band. 'We got on well with all of them. We had a real laugh on both tours, with Vince, and when Alan joined and Vince left.'

Between their support duties for the two Depeche Mode tours, Blancmange were also recruited to open for Japan on the band's *Visions Of China Tour* in December 1981. 'My memory of the Depeche Mode tour is that their audience really warmed to us, I mean we were the support act so we weren't expecting much. To be honest it was an opportunity to have one or two weeks off work, but the audience seemed to like us,' remembers Arthur today. 'Japan's audience was receptive to us, but they were less hysterical than Depeche Mode's audience. There was a sophistication to Japan, they were a big band but they weren't necessarily a singles band with a pop audience like Depeche.' On a personal level the Japan dates weren't the enjoyable social occasions that Blancmange had enjoyed with Depeche Mode. 'It wasn't the friendly happy family like it was with Depeche Mode,' Arthur continues, remembering that Blancmange had very little contact with most of Japan over the course of the tour, although they did bond with Japan's recently recruited new guitarist, David Rhodes, who relocated any beer delivered to Japan to Blancmange's dressing room, as the rest of Japan were not beer drinkers.

Blancmange's efforts to build an audience through their live work, and in particular from appearing alongside high-profile acts like Depeche Mode and Japan, paid off, and at the start of 1982 they signed a deal with Decca's London Records label. By March, Blancmange were ready to announce their first single and embark on their first headline tour. Their debut single for their new label was a double A-side featuring 'I've Seen The Word' on one side and 'God's Kitchen' on the other – although it was the latter track which became the one which press and radio focused their attention on – which was released in the middle of March to coincide with the tour dates. In fact 'God's Kitchen' came from a very personal place. 'My mum's dad died when he was still reasonably young and I remember her saying to me, "If God's so good and wise why did he take dad away just when I needed him most?" That made a lasting impression on me,' Neil Arthur told *Record Mirror*'s Simon Ludgate in response to a question about the inspiration for the single. 'It put me off in the same way that people dress up in their best clothes and go to church every Sunday. Why should God only exist in church? The kitchen is a far more down to earth place.'

Record Mirror's Sunie was part of the panel of guests reviewing 'God's Kitchen' for BBC Radio 1's review show *Roundtable*, where she suggested 'Echoes of David Byrne, and a bit of Ian Curtis?' before handing over to fellow panellist, Haircut 100's Nick Heyward, who also heard something of Talking Heads in the record, and declared of Blancmange 'they are a band that are really trying to get on and they probably will'. 'Blancmange are part of the Some Bizzares that got left behind when Soft Cell and Depeche Mode stormed the charts. However, 'God's Kitchen' with its lazy, funky dance beat and whimsical lyrics makes for an appealing pop consciousness,' was Robbi Millar's upbeat take on the single in her review for *Sounds*.

Propelled by the media's generally positive reactions, alongside equally positive notices for their tour in support of the single, Blancmange were delighted to see their debut major label single spend two weeks in the lower reaches of the UK singles chart, both weeks at an encouraging number sixty-five. 'The whole thing's incredible. Neither of us are proper musicians, we've had no training at all,' Stephen Luscombe confessed to *Smash Hits*' Rosalyn Chissick, and *Melody Maker*'s Steve Sutherland came away from the duo's London show full of optimism for the group: 'The time is right for Blancmange,' he noted with approval. 'Vince Clark [sic] drops their name, they've just finished a tour with the Mode and their amusing angst expands Cell's 'Bedsitter' into a set's worth of adolescent self-questioning, intuitively tuned to contemporary taste.'

Vince Clarke even mooted the idea of Yazoo and Blancmange collaborating on a cover of Marvin Gaye and Tammi Terrell's soul classic 'It Takes Two'. The proposed collaboration, which got as far as being mentioned in interviews and in news reports in the music press at the time, was subsequently abandoned, but not before it had been discussed as an ongoing concern, to the extent that, at the end of May, the *NME* went as far as announcing, 'A new single duet available shortly featuring the combined talents of Yazoo and Blancmange getting their choppers round an old Motown classic made famous by Marvin Gaye and Tammi Terrell.' 'Yes. We went into Blackwing to do it but it just didn't come together,' recalls Vince Clarke. 'We started in earnest, recording 'It Takes Two', but it descended into hysterics and never went any further,' corroborated Neil Arthur, who also dashed any hopes that the recording might ever see the light of day: 'If I had a cassette of it, I would never let you hear it. We never got close to finishing it. It sounded like a Morecambe & Wise sketch after a while.'

By the summer of 1982 London Records were ready to release Blancmange's second single for the label and chose to put out 'Feel Me' in the first half of July to another round of largely positive reviews. 'Blancmange stand out a mile as a life-saving raft of pure pop pizzazz on a dark sea of sludge,' enthused *Sounds*' Dave Lewis approvingly. 'This is what good dance records are supposed to sound like.' At *Melody Maker* the single was reviewed by Richard Butler of The Psychedelic Furs, who happened to be the guest reviewer that week and who came down firmly on the side of Blancmange: 'I'm a sucker for this sort of thing,' Butler declared. 'Talking Heads meet Joy Division, somewhere between Depeche Mode and Soft Cell. I think they deserve a break.' 'Feel Me' entered the UK singles chart at fifty-five at the very end of July, an encouraging ten places higher than 'God's Kitchen', and climbed to a peak position of forty-six the following week before gracefully sliding out of the charts three weeks later.

In September, Blancmange announced that their debut album, *Happy Families*, would be released at the end of the month. 'Who would have thought that the bosom buddies who self-consciously disguised themselves as 'Mavis' and 'Irene' on their long-ago first venture on to vinyl could one day release an album as roundly delightful and as soundly devastating as 'Happy Families'?' exhorted *Sounds'* Mick Sinclair, whose enthusiastic five-star review of Blancmange's debut continued: 'Cupid's amorous arrow was well-aimed when it brought these two together. One of the pop world's more inspired pairings. A classic oddball partnership.' "Happy Families' is a calmly assured collection of work: maybe not stamped with greatness, quite, but there's not a number in the whole ten that's without appeal, intelligence and warmth,' was Paul Du Noyer's verdict on *Happy Families* for the *NME* at the beginning of October.

The most curious review of Blancmange's debut album came courtesy of *Flexipop*, who set up a review swap which saw Blancmange's Stephen Luscombe review rock act Diamond Head's new album *Living On Borrowed Time* while Diamond Head singer Sean Harris in turn provided a review of *Happy Families*. Neither side came off particularly well, Harris declaring that Blancmange reminded him of A Flock Of Seagulls – 'Thankfully not so bland, but at the same time, probably less commercial' – before delivering a damning verdict on *Happy Families*: 'For me the album never gets beyond intolerable boredom simply because the melodies are horrendous and utterly forgettable.' Luscombe in turn described *Living On Borrowed Time* as 'dull, reactionary and pompous' and noted the album's 'lack of dynamics, imagination and adventurousness'.

Happy Families peaked at number thirty in the UK albums chart, where it remained a fixture in the lower reaches of the chart for the best part of a year, earning Blancmange a gold disc for 100,000 copies sold in the process. In the inevitable round of interviews Blancmange gave to support the release of *Happy Families*, *Melody Maker*'s Lynden Barber asked the duo what made Blancmange different from their electronic peers? 'Probably our approach,' decided Stephen Luscombe. 'Ours is a lot more textured – probably because of the way we are as people. We've always made a conscious attempt to make it a bit more earthy rather than clean and electronic sounding. I personally feel that synthesisers have got an awful lot to offer and they haven't been properly exploited for their emotional uses. We have tried to do that.'

In an interview with Carole Linfield for *Sounds*, Luscombe also admitted that he was broadly happy with the way *Happy Families* had turned out, although his bandmate was less sure. 'There are things about the album I'm not happy with,' mused Neil Arthur, who also revealed that the duo were always motivated by looking ahead to the next challenge, and added 'if I was totally satisfied with it I'd stop here'. 'We're writing new material too, for the next album which will be more minimalist,' added Luscombe. 'We want it to be a bit simpler – not any less powerful, but less complicated.' Was commercial success important to Blancmange, asked Linfield? 'It's probably more important to Decca than it is to us, but it would be nice,' admitted Luscombe. 'If 'Living On The Ceiling' is a success it could give us more power, that extra gateway,' he explained before predicting a flaw in his plan: 'Unless it works the other way and people say "just do another one".'

In October, hot on the heels of *Happy Families*, London Records released a third single from the album, 'Living On The Ceiling', and expectations that the release might provide Blancmange and their label with their first single hit proved correct. 'Living On The Ceiling' entered the UK Top 40 after just two weeks, leapt into the Top 20 the following week after Blancmange's debut appearance on *Top of the Pops*, and spent three consecutive weeks at a peak position of seven as part of an impressive twelve-week residency in the Top 40. Interestingly, after their largely positive support of the previous two Blancmange singles, and of the *Happy Families* album, the music press response to 'Living On The Ceiling' was curiously lacklustre.

'Blancmange once more come up with an interesting rhythmic idea and throw it away as an indifferent song,' wrote David Hepworth in *Smash Hits*. 'The K-Tel answer to Simple Minds,' wrote Ian Pye in his review for *Melody Maker*, 'the revolting Blancmange have found themselves a mould and of course a shape follows. Pink, soft and powdery to taste, this will remind you of school dinners and other things too unpleasant to mention here.' And were Blancmange concerned by this critical about-turn? 'I'd already learned not to read reviews. I would have known but maybe I just wasn't bothered about it,' Neil Arthur remembers today. 'We were really busy, 'Living On The Ceiling' was going up the charts, the album was in the Top 30 for however long, and I was just savouring it all really. It's probably a good job I didn't see them.'

A curious and unexpected footnote to the *Happy Families* story is that the record was, in part, allegedly responsible for the break-up of Liverpool band The Teardrop Explodes. 'What finally made my mind up [to break up the band] was on hearing the new Blancmange album,' Teardrop Explodes' Julian Cope told *Melody Maker* at the end of November 1982. 'I hated it, skated round the floor on the record itself, then burnt the sleeve on the electric ring on the cooker. It's pinned to my wall as a reminder of how much I'm bored with the current music.' 'I do remember that!' Arthur laughs today. 'My first question was, did he buy the record? If he bought the record then he could do what he liked with it.'

5 June 1982　　US $1·95 (by air)　　30p　　OF RECORDED SOUND, 29 EXHIBITION ROAD.　　ISSN 0028 6362

NME

MUSICAL EXPRESS

30p

NEW ORDER

HUMAN LEAGUE

HUMANS INVADE AMERICA SHOCK!
Exclusive Report by Tony Stewart

World's largest selling music weekly

ANTIPASTI

BLUES MASTERS

PhD

LINDSAY ANDERSON

AT THE BEGINNING OF February 1982, news started to circulate of a new British Electric Foundation project which was to kick off with a collaboration with sixties singer and icon Sandie Shaw. The track would be the first single from BEF's debut album, a collection of collaborations with a diverse range of artists entitled *Music Of Quality And Distinction*. 'The rumours breaking out make it sound like an edition of 'Ready, Steady, Go',' teased *Melody Maker*'s gossip page at the time. 'Dagenham songbird Sandie Shaw turns in a version of the old Dionne Warwick hit 'Anyone Who Had A Heart', the BEF's Glenn Gregory lends his larynx to Glen Campbell's 'Witchita Lineman' and Shadows supremo Hank B. Marvin is contributing guitar. Billy Mackenzie of the Associates is allegedly in there somewhere too, with versions of Bowie's 'Secret Life Of Arabia' and Lou Reed's 'Perfect Day', from 'Transformer'. The king of circus'n'roll, Gary Glitter, is also rumoured to be in attendance.'

To clear the decks for *Music Of Quality And Distinction*, BEF announced at the same time that they would bring Heaven 17's *Penthouse And Pavement* project to a close with the release of a fifth and final single from the album, a remixed and re-cut version of 'At The Height Of Fighting (He-La-Hu!)', in the middle of February. 'It's a mystery why this infinitely superior, complex half of the old Human League isn't doing better,' pondered *Sounds*' Sandy Robertson in his review of 'At The Height Of Fighting (He-La-Hu!)'. 'Perhaps too clever for its own good, 'Height' still dazzles.' 'It doesn't quite match the magnificent

'Penthouse And Pavement' single but it's pretty fab nonetheless,' added *Record Mirror*'s Sunie the same week. *Melody Maker*, struggling to identify the substance beneath 'At The Height Of Fighting (He-La-Hu!)''s surface sheen, declared, 'Listening to 'Height Of The Fighting' is a little like trying to tattoo an ice-cube; you can't grip it, and it's always sliding away.' Radio programmers and the great British public seemed to agree and, without the support of radio or the Heaven 17 fanbase, 'At The Height Of Fighting (He-La-Hu!)' failed to chart.

Now able to concentrate fully on the March release of British Electronic Foundation's *Music Of Quality And Distinction*, Martyn Ware and Ian Craig Marsh turned their attention to the release of the first single from the project, a new version of 'Anyone Who Had A Heart', originally a 1964 number one for Cilla Black, featuring Sandie Shaw on vocals, Martyn Ware on synthesisers, Beggar & Co's David 'Baps' Baptiste on saxophone and Hank Marvin on guitar. Released in the last week of February, 'Anyone Who Had A Heart' not only failed to chart, but it also elicited a cautious response from the music press. 'Even hard-core Shaw supporters are going to wonder why it shows no improving updates on the Cilla Black opus,' ventured *Sounds*' Robbi Millar. 'For all the cleverness of the arrangement, Shaw's more than fair vocal and some smashing cocktail piano, this version simply isn't exciting,' mused Sunie in *Record Mirror*, 'and for that reason, I'd gladly trade it for the brash splendour of Cilla's rendition. Cheap passion beats sophisticated artifice every time when it comes to delivering a trashy epic such as this.'

It wasn't the start to *Music Of Quality And Distinction* that Marsh and Ware had been hoping for, but British Electric Foundation did the rounds of the music press to talk up the project in advance of the release of the album nevertheless. 'Choosing the songs for the LP worked in two ways,' Martyn Ware told the *NME* for a front cover feature on the release. 'Sometimes we thought, that's a great song, and tried to think who could do a good vocal for it; and sometimes we wanted to work with people and it was a question of finding a song.' Perhaps on the back foot after the lack of success for 'Anyone Who Had A Heart', Ware also pre-empted any criticism of the album in advance by adding, 'I'm convinced that there are going to be quite a few people who don't like the album. I think it's more likely to be in the music business, because they'll regard it as a smart-aleck project.'

The inspiration for *Music Of Quality And Distinction* actually dated back several years. 'When we were with The Human League, right from the inception we did cover versions and they tended to be the more popular things we did, although cover versions weren't fashionable at all at that time,' Ware explained to the *NME*. Inevitably the legacy of The Human League also fell across the project. 'They're alright,' admitted Marsh when asked about his former bandmates in an interview to accompany a *Melody Maker* cover feature. 'They're fine,' added Ware. 'If I was disconnected from them, if we'd had no connection with them in the past, I'd look upon them as an entertaining diversion. They are entertaining, there's no doubt about it and that album [*Dare*] is a good album.' Marsh and Ware's cautious goodwill towards their former bandmates might also be explained by the windfall they each received in the wake of the success of *Dare*, something the *NME*'s gossip page touched upon in February: 'When they left Human League about 18 months ago Messers Marsh and Ware sold the rights to the group title to Phil and co. for one per cent of returns.' 'The royalties are compensation for allowing Phil Oakey and Adrian Wright to retain the name after the 1980 parting of the ways which saw Marsh and Ware forming Heaven 17 and the British Electric Foundation to pursue their own brand of funk,' explained a *Record Mirror* chart analysis published at the same time, which also estimated that March and Ware had each earned over £20,000 from *Dare* so far, adding, 'Heaven 17's own records have not received the same level of popular acclaim as the more recent Human League output and it's wholly likely that Marsh and Ware have been paid more royalties for work they haven't done than for that which they have!'

Upon its release at the start of April, *Music Of Quality And Distinction* was greeted coolly by the music press. 'Too much strategy; not enough substance,' wrote *Smash Hits*' Ian Birch, awarding the album six-and-a-half out of ten, and finding himself underwhelmed by the release: 'Rather than the excitement lying in the music itself, it's generated by outside issues like who sings what, how they've tinkered with the originals and how they organised all the contracts.' 'As a covert cultural manoeuvre, Ware and Marsh's concept is misguided and has led them to uninspired treatments which for the most part only succeed in smudging the imprint of their originals,' lamented Barney Hoskyns in the *NME*, while *Sounds*' Chris Burkham was similarly unimpressed. 'The initial reaction is that it is not that dissimilar from a low budget Music For Pleasure compilation of chart hits. The versions of the songs on the lp on the whole follow the lines and form of the originals, with perhaps a dash too much respect,' Burkham noted sadly. 'BEF have not added anything to the original, they have just dusted the cobwebs off their memories and carried out an exercise in polishing.'

Music Of Quality And Distinction spent just six weeks in the UK album chart, entering the chart at twenty-six after its first week of sales, and peaking at twenty-five the following week before dropping out of the Top 40 entirely. Marsh and Ware appeared to take note of the criticisms *Music Of Quality And Distinction* received at the hands of the press. 'Perhaps we approached the album in too high-profile a manner. People should have heard the album for themselves instead of hearing about our ideas about the record,' Martyn Ware told *Record Mirror* in November. 'We went for broke with that record and it didn't pay off.' In the *NME* Ware also addressed the criticism that BEF's versions of the songs on the album might be too close to the originals: 'There would be no point in us employing all these people and spending a lot of money if we were going to submerge it under an array of electronic effects, it's getting away from the bigotry of electronic music,' Ware explained. 'Ironically, even though we're called the British Electric Foundation, we're moving towards acoustically based instruments.'

In the middle of October, Heaven 17 announced the release of 'Let Me Go', the first single to be taken from their sophomore album which was to follow in early 1983. The following week all the main music publications ran their reviews, and once again the general feeling was cautious at best and dismissive at worst. *Sounds*' Carole Linfield provided the most positive take on the single when she described 'Let Me Go' as 'A harmonious, addictive record,' while at the other end of the scale the *NME*'s Gavin Martin reported, 'This is a depressing song full of mock sorrow and refined angst. Glenn Gregory comes on like a caller on LBC Radio's Problem Hour and the group are similarly inspired dragging everything far down into the depths of despair with a steam hammer beat, monotonous drones and a melody it would be kind to call ponderous.'

'Let Me Go' earned Heaven 17 their highest chart position to date when it peaked at number forty-one in the UK singles chart in the second half of September, but that success was surely dulled for the band by the news that a brand new single from The Human League, 'Mirror Man', their own first new music since the spectacular success of *Dare*, had entered the same chart at number eleven the same week. Outwardly, at least, the band remained upbeat: 'Fortunately we're not in a position where we need to worry too much about how many records we sell because we've got quite a lot of money coming in off the royalty on *Dare*. We don't have to be quite so paranoically obsessed with making money,' Martyn Ware told *One Two Testing* magazine in November.

'Relax everyone. The New League single's alright,' reported a relieved Neil Tennant in his review of 'Mirror Man' for *Smash Hits*. 'It's been a year since their last release but the drive to world domination hasn't stopped them being able to polish off a shiny new dance song with traces of both Tamla Motown and ABBA.' 'The strong, powerful tune and memorable riffs can't disguise the fact that progress-wise, it's a big step forward into yesterday,' wrote Tony Mitchell in *Sounds*, making 'Mirror Man' his Single of the Week and conceding, 'It's a bloody good record, and if there is such a thing as the proverbial pure pop, instant smash-hit sound, then this is probably it.' 'We've been waiting all this time for this?' demanded *Record Mirror*'s John Shearlaw. 'The new offering from the Sheffield gold mine is nothing more than a limp early seventies sounding rock song callously bumped out over a crass sub Motown backdrop, and boy does it go on. A tiresome, repetitive listen, and one that shows that the bubble might indeed have burst.'

'Mirror Man' subsequently spent the next three weeks at its chart peak of number two (kept from the top of the charts by Eddy Grant's 'I Don't Wanna Dance' for the first week, and then by The Jam's 'Beat Surrender' for the next two weeks), and remained in the Top 20 for another month as part of an eleven-week chart run through Christmas and the New Year. The single also saw The Human League embark upon a limited number of press interviews, which included Jo Callis talking to *Melody Maker*'s Tony Bacon for the paper's 'Musician's World' page, where the conversation, unsurprisingly, turned to the fact that the band had used a guitar on 'Mirror Man'. 'They definitely had a fear of guitars then, a fear of instruments, because no one else could play them, I suppose. Ian could play bass and that, but no one in the old group could play instruments,' Callis mused. 'Now I think the emphasis has changed more to songwriting and obviously an identifiable sound. The Human League aren't to me now a synthesizery-sounding group. I'd say it's still an electronic group.'

Record Mirror put Phil Oakey on their cover at the end of November and caught up with The Human League for the first time in almost a year. 'If you're doing something of quality then you'll always sell, regardless of the time you take doing it,' Oakey pondered, in response to a question about the band taking their time to release new material in the wake of their success with *Dare*. 'Music is important. It's something that colours every person's attitude and life. Our mission is to stop it from ever becoming mediocre.' And what did the band think of the state of the music scene in 1982? 'I think I would rather die a thousand deaths than sound like Depeche Mode or Yazoo,' declared Oakey.

A fortnight later, Soft Cell's Marc Almond was asked exactly the same question in an interview for *Melody Maker* and, without naming any names, managed to be similarly dismissive: 'I feel that these people aren't making stands, aren't trying to be risky or adventurous or maybe truly what they are,' Almond explained to Steve Sutherland. 'They feel they've got a nice situation in the pop charts and they're happy to keep on churning 'em out. But it's not very interesting.' Almond's answer also hinted at Soft Cell's own need to deliver something more substantial and authentic on their second album, which was due for release in January 1983 under the title *The Art Of Falling Apart*. 'There was time when Soft Cell fell apart, it really fell apart,' Almond confessed. 'I mean, I must have quit so many times and finished it so many times, and I know Dave and I got confused and very lost because I didn't really like being a pop star.'

'Where The Heart Is' was announced as the first single from *The Art Of Falling Apart* and was released a fortnight after The Human League's 'Mirror Man'. 'This will be massive,' wrote *Record Mirror*'s Mark Cooper of 'Where The Heart Is' at the end of November, describing the single as 'more substantial and more sentimental' than their previous work, a view shared by both the *NME* and *Sounds*, each of whom declared the new single an improvement over 'What'. 'This one should safely give the boys a respectable chart position over Yuletide,' predicted Paul Du Noyer in the *NME*, adding, 'Sad symphonic waves of melody lap lightly over a nostalgic essay of childhood.'

In fact, despite a *Top of the Pops* performance the previous week, 'Where The Heart Is' peaked at a disappointing number twenty-one in the same week that 'Mirror Man' sat at number three for its third week, although the reaction to their new single might have been less of surprising for Soft Cell, who were determined to explore a more authentic approach to their music. 'A lot of records in the charts settle for the icing without the cake. I'd like to see writers try to paint more challenging pictures. I hate the tweeness of pop,' Marc Almond told *Record Mirror* in a cover feature for the magazine's last issue of 1982. 'The records I've loved are the ones you can feel deeply about as well as dance to and hum.'

Given Soft Cell's extraordinary international success with *Non-Stop Erotic Cabaret* over the previous year, it is perhaps unsurprising that *The Art Of Falling Apart* found Almond and Ball keen to move away from their pop success. 'There's always the people who want to hear the endless 'Tainted Love' or whatever, which is depressing, I wish people would realise there's more there and more to offer,' Almond admitted to *Sounds'* Tony Mitchell at the beginning of December. 'If anyone asked what I honestly think of 'Tainted Love' – I appreciate it for what it's done but to be honest I f---ing well hate it!' 'The pressure we've had that's built up over the past year since the last album, comes out in the music,' Dave Ball explained to *Record Mirror*'s Simon Tebbutt. 'We've channelled it, making the album much deeper, stronger and harder. We both feel we've got something to say about life but we've come closer to realism this time.'

The Art Of Falling Apart was released in January 1983 and managed to walk a difficult line between critical and commercial success, peaking at number five on the UK albums chart after one week and earning Marc Almond and Dave Ball a gold award for sales of over 100,000 copies in its first month on sale. ''The Art' is a stunning display of the duo's range and diversity,' applauded Barney Hoskyns in the *NME*. 'The glimpse and giggle peepshow of 'Non-Stop Erotic Cabaret' has finally been left behind. This album aptly titled 'The Art of Falling Apart' shows the deeper and darker and more developed side of Soft Cell,' commended *Record Mirror*'s ever-supportive Simon Tebbutt, who awarded the album a maximum five stars and continued, 'Soft Cell take risks. Look at things most people try to ignore. Speak of the unspoken. That's why they're still one of the most interesting groups making music today.'

Some forty years before his own collaboration with Soft Cell as part of the Pet Shop Boys on 2022's 'Purple Zone', Neil Tennant penned an enthusiastic review of *The Art Of Falling Apart* for *Smash Hits*. 'The new Soft Cell sound is epic and detailed, weaving trumpets and pianos into a backdrop of synthesisers. Pretty tunes flutter out of a hard mix while Marc Almond's vocals sound both charming and malevolent,' Tennant exclaimed, awarding the album eight out of ten stars and continuing, 'To be able to put over with such conviction the teenage angst, excitement and traumas of everyday life is no mean achievement.'

'I think we owe it to people to mean what we're doing and not just say "Oh, here's another nice pop song for you." We're not just another pop band; it's just that we started off being marketed like that and we've survived being marketed really. *The Art Of Falling Apart* is not repeating what we've done, it's improving and extending it,' Dave Ball told *Melody Maker*'s Steve Sutherland in January 1983 as Soft Cell unveiled their uncompromising new vision. 'The first album was a terrifying situation, because we had this collection of songs and had this massive record company putting pressure on us – they know you're naive, they know your weaknesses – and so we thought, "Well, we've gotta have pop tunes because they want singles." I'm not saying I disown any of that material because I don't – some of it's good – but I can allow myself a bit more leeway now, and I've tended to experiment a bit more.'

Had Soft Cell's dark turn been a shock to Soft Cell's audience, Steve Sutherland asked the duo? 'I hope so!' exclaimed Ball. 'You gotta bring out things that people don't expect you to,' Almond added. 'I hate to think that people are gonna predict your every next little move – it's so boring! We're having a row with Phonogram at the moment over our next choice of single which they're not particularly enamoured of – 'Numbers'... The title was actually nicked from a John Rechy book called *Numbers* where he goes to Los Angeles and just sees how many people he can have in a weekend, one after another,' Almond explained. 'It's a soundtrack of loveless sex, the succession of one night stands and the feeling at the end of it.'

Released at the beginning of March, 'Numbers' was a calculated risk on the part of Soft Cell, and not one that their label was comfortable with. 'I'd feel good if that one's a success rather than one of the more obvious singles on the album. It's a little dicey perhaps, but I hope people will think about it, what's there,' Marc Almond told the *NME*'s Chris Bohn, relishing Soft Cell's position at the time: 'Because we're Soft Cell, Radio 1 will at least give us a hearing, so we can take a chance by not putting out the obvious single. I just don't understand this need for the obvious all the time. So what if you fail? That's just incentive to build again!'

'Numbers' spent four weeks on the UK singles chart in March where it peaked at twenty-five, making it Soft Cell's least successful Phonogram single to date, despite the best endeavours of the label who, without the knowledge of the band, had attempted to make the release more attractive to record buyers by offering a free twelve-inch of 'Tainted Love' with every twelve-inch of the new single. When they discovered their label's attempts to soften 'Numbers'' uncommercial edge the band and their management were furious. 'I was enraged,' Soft Cell manager Stevo told *Melody Maker* the week after 'Numbers'' release. 'I'm supposed to have full control over marketing and I knew nothing about this. I mean I would never have stooped to such a trick – I mean 'Tainted Love' was good at the time but that was then and it does both singles a disservice to put them together. It reflects badly on us and it lets down the fans.' Stevo also claimed that, with Marc Almond in tow, he had confronted Phonogram about their dubious marketing activities and in the process the duo trashed two offices, set a fire extinguisher on an employee and smashed the silver, gold and platinum sales awards that lined the label's walls, although Parlophone played down the incident telling the *NME* that 'the damage was minimal and, furthermore, no fire extinguishers were set off or windows damaged'.

In December Dave Ball was asked by the *NME* to contribute his thoughts on electronic music in 1982 for the paper's final issue of the year. 'I think 1982 has definitely been the year that people realised the possibilities and potential of the synthesiser as a 'real' musical instrument, especially with the rapid advance of technology available,' Ball wrote before addressing one of the strangest things to happen to electronic music over the course of that year: 'The Musicians' Union attempt to boycott synthesisers earlier in the year clearly illustrated that electronic music is being taken seriously. It seemed that the MU considered the synthesiser a threat to traditional instruments – although I can't see any reason why all instruments cannot co-exist.' As membership of the Musicians' Union was a requirement for all musicians appearing on *Top of the Pops*, Ball had already had a personal run-in with the organisation the previous year in advance of Soft Cell's debut appearance on the show. 'I found out when I got to the MU offices in Clapham that I couldn't join as a synthesiser player because they didn't officially recognise it as a real musical instrument,' Ball recalled in *Electronic Boy*, evidently still incredulous forty years later. 'I often wondered what early synth pop pioneers like Kraftwerk, Giorgio Moroder and Brian Eno put down as their instruments back in the seventies,' before admitting, 'I towed the line and registered as a keyboard player/bass guitarist instead of synthesist.'

Sounds had been the first to report on the extraordinary news that in May 1982 the London Branch of the Musicians' Union had put forward a motion 'to ban electronic instruments from live recordings, studio work and live performance' in order to protect their members' jobs. 'Could this be the scrap heap for Soft Cell, Depeche Mode and the Human League?' demanded *Melody Maker* the following week, updating the story with the news that 'By a vote of two to one at the branch's regular meeting, MU members decided that synths and drum machines were doing musicians out of work. They decided to recommend to the executive committee of the MU – motto "Working For Today's Musicians" – that a ban be placed on anyone using synths or drum machines from recording studios, from live shows and from radio or television programmes like 'Top Of The Pops'.' Noting that the success of the vote at the London Branch meeting wasn't sufficient to change Musicians' Union policy, *Melody Maker* sought clarification on the situation from the union's 'Rock Organiser', Mike Evans. 'From what I gather the resolution passed by the branch was intended to stop people from using things like string machines on sessions for advertising jingles – things like that. I don't see it as a threat to bands like Depeche Mode or Soft Cell because these people are using synthesisers as musical instruments in their own right,' explained Evans. 'Our attitude is that we only disagree with the use of synths or drum machines if it's obvious that they're depriving working musicians of work.'

But the London Branch's actions had already sounded alarm bells among the electronic community. In the same *Melody Maker* piece, Landscape's Peter Thoms spoke for his peers: 'What we're concerned about, as a band who use synths, is that the resolution might almost sneak through simply because not enough people know it's on the cards. I'm interested in getting maximum publicity for this so that at the next meeting – the district meeting – this vote won't get any further.' Thomas Dolby, who had been present at the London Branch's vote, wrote a slightly tongue-in-cheek piece about the experience for *Sounds* the following week: 'The meeting on May 20 of the Central London branch of the Musicians Union was a tragic-comedy affair which I sat through huddled among a small group of worried synthesiser sympathisers exchanging insults with various bedraggled-looking characters I took to be bricklayers, but who turned out to be other members and, as it happened, a working majority at that.'

The original proposal, Dolby reported, had been made by Musicians' Union member Neil Lancaster 'who expressed his concern that the mindless megalomania of greedy synth-players was gradually taking away the livelihoods of serious musicians and threatening to stamp out real music within ten years… The gravity of the situation was outlined with examples like the Barry Manilow Orchestra and the forthcoming West End production of *The Pirates Of Penzance*, either of which could so easily have accommodated another thirty-seven or so Celtic harp players were it not for the spotty Casio owner who did it all with one finger… Joking aside, though,' Dolby continued, 'what I witnessed was a democratic body setting out to protect and promote its own interests and livelihood and falling flat on its eggy face. By the time the MU realises the immense futility and impracticability of any attempt to halt the advance of electronic music by force, it will already have further alienated the same energetic and open-minded musicians whose involvement it so desperately needs if similar situations are to be avoided in the future.'

In the middle of June, *Melody Maker* announced the formation of 'The Union of Sound Synthesists' by an organisation called Electronic Syntheziser Sound Projects, whose spokesperson declared, 'We feel this particular motion by certain MU members is probably based on paranoia of their own musical capabilities and certainly suggests a lack of understanding towards the role of synthesisers in the development of music. We think it is reasonable to prepare to make a stand against the activities of members of a union that promotes its activities under the banner "Advancing Today's Music".' Meanwhile *Sounds* were quick to point out that The Union of Sound Synthesists was 'not a union in the conventional sense', to which the *NME* added, more prosaically, 'The USS is, so far, a list of names and addresses of persons prepared to get publicly upset if the motion progresses any further.'

'The MU seems to be acting very selfishly on its own behalf. How they can think banning synthesisers can do any good is quite beyond me,' ran a reader's letter in *Melody Maker* the same week. 'Depeche Mode, The Human League, Yazoo, Kraftwerk and Tangerine Dream would have to leave all their pioneering work behind them and perhaps go on the dole.' But not all *Melody Maker* readers were quite as sympathetic. 'All this fuss about the Musicians' Union trying to ban synthesisers seems a little hysterical to me, and strangely enough most of the silly noises seem to be originating from the opposition,' exclaimed Deke Roberts from Oxford in a letter of his own the following week. 'As I understand it, the MU is not trying to ban synthesisers per se, they're trying to ban machines that synthesise the sounds of other musicians, ie string synths, rhythm boxes etc. As such they're only doing the same as any other union would do.'

At a later meeting of the Musicians' Union Central London Branch a second motion was proposed by member Keith Armstrong and subsequently passed: 'Recognising the need for unity within our own union in this time of crisis and recognising that all synthesiser players are musicians who are entitled to equal rights with all other union members, this Central London branch requests the executive committee that synthesiser players should be allowed to work without impediment, providing that they are not being employed in preference to two or more musicians; and that a drum machine would be permissible providing that a member of the union is controlling the machine and playing no other instrument while the machine is in use,' reported *Sounds* at the end of July, before noting, 'No-one within the MU has yet presented proof that there are actually less musicians in work now than when the "synthesiser revolution" began. The likelihood is in fact that there are many more, because the micro-chip and modern manufacturing methods have made it easier and cheaper to become involved in the creation of music.'

In response to the second motion, The Union of Sound Synthesists quickly made an announcement of their own, which *Melody Maker* reported the same week: '[The Union of Sound Synthesists] set up an active pressure group to monitor the activities of anyone who aims to restrict the use of computers and synthesisers in recording or in live performance.' Meanwhile the public response was less earnest. 'I say congratulations to synthesisers!' celebrated *Melody Maker* reader Al Doggett at the start of August. 'They've enabled lots of talented songwriters to escape unemployment and become "musicians".' 'The Union of Sound Synthesists, formed in the wake of the Musicians Union's bid to outlaw synthesisers, has compiled a defence case against the MU which could be used in court to fight a Restraint Of Trade law suit if any action is taken by the MU to restrict the sale, use or development of electronic instruments,' reported *Sounds* in October following months of silence on the matter on the part of the Musicians' Union. 'The Union has compiled a petition, correspondence and taped conversations as evidence for a possible court case and has also launched a variety of campaign material such as stickers, sweatshirts and badges.' The USS's efforts were ultimately unrewarded in the face of any further comment on the situation from the Musicians' Union.

The MU's General Secretary John Morton was nevertheless forced to break his silence in regard to the activities of The Union of Sound Synthesists the following spring when the *NME* ran a tongue-in-cheek story at the start of April 1983 reporting having received a press release from the USS – 'suspiciously dated April 1st' – which claimed that the Musicians' Union, in collaboration with the Arts Council, were planning to lobby the Department of the Environment to have a 'special tax' added to sales of synthesisers in Britain. 'The implication is that said parties are in cahoots to thwart the electro-revolution, in favour of traditional music and musicians,' added the *NME*. 'It's all absolutely a load of cock; absolute rubbish. I'm not sure anybody at the Arts Council has ever even heard of synthesisers,' declared Morton in the same report, evidently failing to appreciate the April Fool. 'But most of those musicians who use them are our members and it's their work we're protecting too.'

But the music industry had more immediate concerns than the USS's tomfoolery. 'Welcome to 1982 and the first bad news of the year is that there's likely to be an across-the-board increase in the price of records,' announced *Melody Maker* in February. While seven-inch single prices escaped unscathed, the feature reported that WEA had been first to announce price increases – twelve-inch singles would cost around £1.99, albums around £4.26 and double albums £6.50 – with EMI, Polydor and Phonogram following suit, and smaller labels forced to fall into line behind them. The BPI (British Phonographic Industry) followed the news of the new pricing structure with their annual report in May which reported further struggles within the music industry. '[The report] speaks of an "unprecedented" sales decline in the past three years leading to a one-third reduction in staffing, and the closure of several factories,' reported the *NME*. 'The main reason for the cutbacks, says the BPI, has been the sharp fall in LP sales, from a peak of 91.6m in 1975 to just 64m last year.' 'Home taping is blamed for the massive drop,' added *Record Mirror* in their own reaction to the BPI report the same week. 'Blank tape sales have increased from 50 million a year in 1978 to 70 million last year.'

In 1982 the threat of home taping was coming to a head as more and more domestic audio systems offered the capability to record records, and the music industry was running scared. 'Technology has overtaken the law in the audio-visual field and chaos has resulted,' declared the BPI in July, estimating that record sales were down £305 million a year as a result of home taping. 'The BPI says new copyright laws are needed because the present Act Of Parliament was introduced in 1956 and, they pointedly remark, that the cassette recorder hadn't been invented then,' reported *Melody Maker* in the wake of the British government rejecting a proposal to add a levy to blank tape sales to offset the losses for the music industry and its artists.

The BPI, in collaboration with the Musicians' Union, the MCPS (Mechanical Copyright Protection Society) and the MRS (Mechanical Rights Society) launched a campaign to educate the general public on the illegality of home taping while putting pressure on the government to address the issue in the same way as the authorities in Germany, Austria, Hungary and Scandinavia were doing. The initiative was launched at the end of 1981 under the banner 'Home Taping Is Killing Music', which was spearheaded by a series of press advertisements across the music and general press signed by a selection of artists from different parts of the music industry, including Debbie Harry, Elton John, Vladimir Ashkenazy, Cliff Richard, Dame Margot Fonteyn and Gary Numan.

In the wake of his participation in the 'Home Taping Is Killing Music' campaign, Gary Numan started his 1982 more positively with the January announcement of a new album, *I, Assassin*, preceded by a February single, 'Music For Chameleons'. At the start of February, in advance of the release of the new single, Numan also took steps to undo his previous decision to retire from live performance. Attending the music industry conference MIDEM, Numan was asked if his retirement had actually been a hype; *Melody Maker* reported Numan's response as 'If it was, then it was a bloody stupid one. I've got to work very hard now to undo all the damage I've done.' At the same time, Numan revealed that his new album was to take an unexpected direction: 'I'm going to make my music happier so people can dance to it, I used to be a miserable sod.'

Further unexpected news came with the revelation that 'Music For Chameleons'' B-side, a non-album track entitled 'Noise Noise', featured additional vocals from Thereza Bazar of Dollar, whose David Van Day also received a less substantial credit on the single for 'Helpful Hints'. An unlikely connection had developed between the two acts, who had encountered each other through sharing the same distribution company. 'He's so shy. And just the last few weeks we've really gotten quite close,' Bazar told *Record Mirror* of Dollar's friendship with Numan in August 1981, explaining how the relationship was also beneficial to both parties: 'Because he wants to be more a part of the areas we're involved in a lot, that very showbizzy kind of image, in the papers a lot. And we want to be a bit more credible and respected for our music instead of being slated all the time. So it's quite interesting. We've got quite a lot in common.'

'Music For Chameleons' was released in the second half of February, and while the single didn't feature Mick Karn, who had helped to shape the sound of the previous Gary Numan album, *Dance*, it did feature a similar fretless bass sound, provided for the new project by up-and-coming talent Pino Palladino. 'After listening to him play on some of the *I, Assassin* songs, I decided to make the bass a lead melody instrument instead of just underpinning the grooves, which is the way it is usually employed. It gave the album a very different sound and feel to anything I'd done before, and I was massively proud of it,' Numan wrote in his memoir *(R)evolution* later. Nevertheless, the similarities to Karn's playing were enough to attract frequent comparisons to Japan from the music press. 'Thanks to Mick Kahn [sic], our Gazza now sounds like he's fully recovered and turned not a little Japanese in the process,' wrote *Melody Maker*. "Music For Chameleons' would sit really rather nicely on Japan's last album.' 'Sub-Japan drivelling, revealing the conceited turnip for the giftless charlatan he always was,' declared Sunie in *Record Mirror*.

At odds with Numan's usual treatment at the hands of the press, 'Music For Chameleons' also attracted a couple of reviews that were broadly enthusiastic. 'It may be music for chameleons but Gary hasn't changed colours. He still provides dark, dark music for chameleons to change their clothes and dance to,' proclaimed *Smash Hits*' Neil Tennant. 'Lots of people are eager to write him off but listen to the loose bass playing, the Human-esque sound effects and chorus and watch the dance floor fill up. Sometimes you can be happy feeling sad.' 'Typically grey but nicely enhanced by double beat drum punches, the best for a while,' mused Mick Middles in *Sounds*. 'I'd even consider liking it if those bloody swirling keyboards didn't push the song back into that old, old Numanic tradition.'

Inspired in part by Stephen Sondheim's classic 'Send In The Clowns' – '['Send In The Clowns'] had always touched a nerve in me – you've had your career, your best days are gone and there comes the time when you walk out on stage and no one has come,' Numan wrote in *Praying to the Aliens* – 'Music For Chameleons' reached number nineteen in the UK singles chart and saw Numan perform the track twice on *Top of the Pops*, continuing the trilby-hatted gangster image which he had used on *Dance*, and which also defined the single's striking video. 'Right now I'm confident about my career again. And I feel good about the music I'm writing at the moment,' Numan told *Flexipop* in May. 'It's great to know I've still got a lot of fans out there.'

A second single from *I, Assassin*, 'We Take Mystery (To Bed)', was released at the beginning of June and was once again dogged by comparisons to Japan in the music press. 'Is it the Japan single?' asked The Sound's Michael Dudley, reviewing the single for *Melody Maker*. 'It's the kind of record that if a deejay put it on you'd try and persuade him to take it off,' added Dudley's bandmate Graham Bailey. Betty Page dismissed the 'Karn-klone' bass sounds evident on the single in her review for *Sounds*, adding, 'His poor little voice keeps disappearing into the bowels of the song in its attempts to be all enigmatic and Sylvian and ends up sounding like he wants to go to the toilet.' 'A joke,' announced *Record Mirror*'s John Shearlaw. 'The game's up, it's got to be!' But the joke was on the press. 'We Take Mystery (To Bed)' scored Gary Numan his sixth Top 10 hit when it peaked at number nine in the UK singles chart in the middle of July.

'White Boys And Heroes' was released as the third *I, Assassin* single in August to a tepid reception from the music press – 'No words can describe the tediousness of Gal's latest dirge,' cautioned *Record Mirror*'s John Shearlaw, while Chris Bohn in the *NME* demanded, 'White boy? He's presently positively anaemic! Not even a heft dab of Japan blusher can cover Numan's cheek' – and earned Gary Numan another place on *Top of the Pops* and another hit single when it reached number twenty in the UK singles chart in the same week that *I, Assassin* entered the UK album chart at number eight.

Inevitably the press reaction to *I, Assassin* was less than kind. 'Gary Numan has some excellent musical ideas,' *Flexipop* began promisingly. 'Unfortunately he put all three of them onto an album called 'Replicas' and has been making a fortune out of repeating them ever since. There's really nothing on this insipid collection to relieve the boredom of repetition.' ''I, Assassin' highlights Numan's basic inability to stretch much further away from his initial synth doodling,' opined Chris Burkham in a two-star review for *Sounds*. 'The continuity and regularity of Numan's music gives it a background feeling; it doesn't do anything, it just is. Implacable and slightly cold, it is a shiny surface, a real gloss job.' 'Just what is it, I wonder, that makes Gary Numan so repulsive?' demanded Charles Shaar Murray in the *NME*. 'The whole album is one long paean to numbness, only Numan doesn't extract anything from said numbness, he simply wallows in it.'

'I thought *I, Assassin* was the best thing I'd ever done. It was a lot more accessible than *Dance* and I was sure it would turn things around,' Numan admitted in *Praying to the Aliens* later, a decision which in part led to his planning a return to live performance with a nineteen-date American tour in October and November. 'I've had my year off, now it's back to my old habits again: music and touring. Last year I didn't feel like doing any more live shows, this year I do,' the singer told *Record Mirror*. 'And now I feel that I can handle things better – I've grown up in the pop world – there's no pressure any more.'

Similarly reliant on playing live as a way of building and maintaining an audience were New Order, who continued their policy of playing one-off shows and short tours throughout the year, a strategy which was starting to pay off and allow the band to finally emerge from the shadow of Joy Division. 'First the resounding echo of the cumbersome mythology surrounding this group, then the subsequent, inevitable dismissals and sneers,' wrote *Melody Maker*'s Lynden Barber in a January 1982 review of a recent New Order gig at the North London Polytechnic. 'Now, perhaps for the first time, it's possible to listen to New Order freely, untainted by excessive hopes or prejudices… New Order may only have just begun.'

New Order's first single of 1982 came in May with the release of 'Temptation', which scored the band their biggest single hit to date when it peaked at twenty-nine in middle of June, propelled in part by a subtle change in musical direction. Sunie reviewed the 'Temptation' twelve-inch for *Record Mirror* in May and immediately spotted the band's new course: 'The sound is familiar, but the mood certainly isn't. There's a pop song in here somewhere, and if there's a seven-inch available, it's probably a fairly commercial proposition.' *Melody Maker* were also enthusiastic: 'Spartan, but moving fast enough to leave a trail of dust visible from miles away, airy but cunningly melodic, this is a subtle and continuously maturing brew,' declared their review warmly. 'Everything is allowed its place, including vrooming bass and wiry guitar which turns into a nasty weapon when required, plus mechanised synth, a huge drum sound and the best New Order vocalising to date.'

'"Temptation' is shaded to the paler edge of the emotional spectrum; politely unreproachful, quietly respectful and almost world-weary,' mused Lynn Hanna in the *NME*. 'This sounds like the musical equivalent of a soft sigh: personal poignancy safely evaporated without ostensible effect.' And *Sounds*' Chris Burkham was also unconvinced: '"Temptation' shows New Order slipping back into the Joy Division shadow, a pointless direction to follow,' he declared, adding, for good measure: 'New Order are for students, for people who think they are being "different" and "rebellious" before they settle down into their jobs as stockbrokers, or lawyers, or members of Echo And The Bunnymen.'

As 'Temptation' left the UK singles chart at the beginning of July, it made way for one of 1982's most eccentric electronic hits, Trio's 'Da Da Da' – or to use its full title, 'Da Da Da (I Don't Love You You Don't Love Me Aha Aha Aha)' – which had already been a hugely successful record in Germany and Switzerland and had been released in the UK at the end of June. 'A deliberately dumb synthesiser pattern and equally loony words make it infuriatingly catchy,' wrote *Smash Hits'* Ian Birch, predicting a hit but ending his review on the plaintive note, 'I hate it.' 'A blip-blop record from three ugly Germanic souls aspiring to a sense of humour,' was Mark Cooper's savage dismissal of 'Da Da Da' in *Record Mirror*, although unlikely support for the record came from the frequently caustic Garry Bushell in *Sounds*: 'Futurism can be fun! And this weird but wonderful German three-piece prove it by being dry all the way to the bank,' Bushell enthused. 'Even money says it's Top Three.'

Bushell was proved correct when 'Da Da Da' peaked at number two in the UK singles chart, held off the top spot by Irene Cara's 'Fame' and spending ten weeks on the charts, earning Trio a silver record for sales of over 100,000 singles by the end of the year, assisted by a quirky *Top of the Pops* appearance that saw the studio audience holding up black-and-white cartoon versions of their faces in an echo of the primitive cartoons of the three band-members – Peter Behrens (drums), Gert 'Kralle' Krawinkel (guitar), and Stephan Remmler (vocals) – on the artwork of the single and subsequent album.

Although 'Da Da Da' was powered by a simple, insistent electronic beat, Trio weren't in fact an electronic band, as *Melody Maker*'s Lynden Barber discovered when Trio released their debut album in August: 'Synthesisers are largely junked for an energetic, skeletal (no bass) rock thrash that would fit neatly into the scheme of things '77, but which now seems a little pointless.' 'Minimalist Teutonic, industrial, grey, dull, boring, humourless, ironic, repetitive, innovative... O.K. I haven't got a clue how to try to sum up the music that Trio make,' reported *Flexipop* in their September issue. 'In summary, this sounds a bit like "Kraftwerk Meets The Tweets."'

Discovered and produced by former Beatles collaborator Klaus Voormann, 'Da Da Da' was a deliberate, if tongue-in-cheek, attempt at a minimal sound, as Trio's Stephan Remmler explained to the *NME*'s Chris Bohn in July. 'Novelty is the right word for it. But we didn't plan it as a hit song. You can't do that. It was just part of our development. Anyway, I think it's a great song. It has broken everything down to essentials. Kralle is playing a classic rock and roll riff. Peter is playing a standard beat and I just speak. I think it is very good that we can bring ourselves to this minimal point where we are doing nothing superfluous.' But generally Trio gave little away in the interviews they gave in support of 'Da Da Da' and of their eponymous album, which failed to be successful in the UK. 'We don't talk about anything that happened before Christmas 1980,' Stephan Remmler told Garry Bushell in an interview for *Sounds* in July. 'We are all thirty-three,' Remmler added. 'We have all been thirty-three for three years and will continue to be so as long as Trio exists.'

THE *NME* KICKED OFF 1982 with David Sylvian on the front cover of their first issue of the new year, and the headline 'Solo For Sylvian?'. Ian Penman interviewed Sylvian for the accompanying piece, conducted during Japan's *Visions Of China Tour* the previous December. 'We've got no plans for Japan after the tour. It's just got to the point where we need to break away from each other,' Sylvian explained. 'We've been with each other – with or without the band – for ten years. Which is a long time to spend working together, no matter how good the relationship is.' Penman also found the singer to be at a crossroads as he contemplated his next move. 'You don't realise you have the choice, that's the problem. You start doing things in a set way that you're not really aware you're doing, until a couple of years later, you realise you've been doing something for the past couple of years that you really don't like,' Sylvian added. 'I'm just taking myself up to the end of this year doing the things that are expected and then I'm going to stop and just work out exactly what I want to do and what I enjoy doing and work from there on.'

The week following the publication of David Sylvian's *NME* interview, speculation as to Japan's future was discussed across the music press, as Virgin Records sought to minimise the impact of the story. 'In the couple of years they've been with Virgin they've been on the verge of splitting up three times,' a Virgin spokesman told *Sounds*. 'The fact is that right now they've finished all their current projects with this tour and they've no plans for anything else at the moment.' And Sylvian went on the record again in the *NME* a week later, commenting on the furore by saying, 'It's all due to over-exaggeration. Contrary to belief that all is doom and desperation with the band, we are actually quite happy.'

As reports of an imminent split swirled around Japan, their former label, Hansa, once again took advantage of the band's rising profile and recent commercial success to continue to release material from the Japan back catalogue, starting with a January single. 'Japan upgrade the b-side of the 'Life In Tokyo' single, 'European Son' to an a-side which they'll be releasing on Hansa Records on January 8,' reported *Sounds* at the start of the year, adding that the track had been remixed by David Sylvian and Steve Nye. Despite the implicit suggestion that the remix represented his endorsement of the single, Sylvian was unhappy with the release and expressed his disapproval to *Sounds'* Betty Page later in the year, admitting that Japan's relationship with Hansa had 'fallen to pieces' as a result.

To the relief of Japan, 'European Son' failed to translate into a significant hit, and although the single reached a chart peak of thirty-one in February, it failed to pick up much support from radio or enthusiasm from the music press: 'All the usual Japan hallmarks in tow – jazz bass and tones of arty sound textures that fail to combine into an overall sound,' reported *Smash Hits'* Mark Ellen. *Record Mirror* and *Sounds* both held 'European Son' up against Japan's more recent output and found it lacking. 'Give your cash, if you must, to Branson's '82 model,' an unimpressed Sandy Robertson advised the readers of *Sounds*. 'Considerably less interesting in just about every way, than their current output,' declared Sunie in *Record Mirror*, before admitting, 'It's actually pretty good, but I'd rather listen to 'Ghosts'.'

From their recent *Tin Drum* album, 'Ghosts' was Virgin's first Japan release of 1982 when it was released as a single in March. 'You know what it sounds like,' grumbled the *NME*. 'David Sylvian has a bellyache and so we all have to hear about it.' But elsewhere 'Ghosts' was received more positively: 'Arguably the best thing they've done – slow, spare and mesmerising,' enthused *Smash Hits'* Tim de Lisle. 'This single is a clever manipulation of sounds and senses, a pull and a push, but never letting go,' observed *Sounds'* Chris Burkham, while *Melody Maker*'s guest reviewer for the week, Jennie Bellestar, praised 'Ghosts' for 'good lyrics, nice vocals, well produced'.

'Ghosts' provided Japan with what would become the biggest hit of their career when it peaked at number five in the UK singles chart in April, to the obvious delight of the band. '[The success of] 'Ghosts' is just really satisfying because of what it is,' David Sylvian told *Sounds'* Betty Page at the time. 'I couldn't pick another song from the whole catalogue that I would rather have in the charts.' Capitalising on the success of the single, and perhaps to scotch rumours of an imminent split, at the end of April Japan announced a twenty-two-date tour of the UK for October and November 1982, as well as shows in Europe, Japan and the Far East. But Japan's efforts at solidarity floundered when *ZigZag* magazine subsequently published an interview with Mick Karn which included the revelation that, shortly before embarking on December 1981's *Visions Of China Tour*, Karn's girlfriend had left him for David Sylvian and solo projects were firmly on the cards. 'After the tour we realised that the band was beginning to become successful and if we did want to do any solo projects we'd have to carry on with Japan otherwise Virgin wouldn't let us do anything on our own,' Karn told Louisa Hennessy, 'so the band isn't splitting up but there's definitely a feeling that as soon as anything better comes up we're taking the first chance we get.'

'The things we disagree on aren't big things. We still socialise together, probably more than most bands do, and especially after ten years. We all have flats in the same square in Kensington, so we're in and out all the time,' David Sylvian told Sunie in a cover feature for *Record Mirror* which came out at the same time as Mick Karn's *ZigZag* interview. 'Being unsettled unnerves me a bit – I don't know what I'm doing after this, though I'm not short on ideas,' Sylvian continued. 'The Japan situation is really weird. I'm not bothered by it existing or not existing, but I would like to know either way, and we can't tell until the end of the year. It's sort of exciting, but it doesn't mean I'm happy.'

Japan's pleasure at the success of 'Ghosts' was subsequently tempered by their despair over Hansa's next catalogue release, a reissue of Japan's 1980 cover of Smokey Robinson & The Miracles' 'I Second That Emotion'. 'I've always hated that song. Me and Steve have always hated it – not the song, but our rendition of it. It's got such a gloomy cotton-wool-wrapped-round-it atmosphere, and our playing is really safe, uninteresting,' Mick Karn told *Record Mirror*'s Sunie later, adding with a note of despair, 'It's got nothing to do with us now at all.' Nevertheless 'I Second That Emotion' was a Top 10 hit for Japan when it peaked at number nine in the UK singles chart for two weeks at the end of July, and would forever remain the band's most successful chart single after 'Ghosts'.

In a reflection of Japan's internal struggles, both Mick Karn and David Sylvian released solo singles over the summer. Mick Karn's 'Sensitive' was the first to come out in June, when it received next to no radio play and a selection of insipid reviews: 'Karn's mixture is pure cup-cake, a hobbit jamming with fairies and goblins at the bottom of Jaco Pastorius's garden,' was Lynden Barber's dismissal in *Smash Hits*, while *Sounds*' Hugh Fielder described 'Sensitive' as an 'insipid song that would be laughed out of sight if it was by Ken Dodd or Val Doonican'. 'Sensitive' failed to chart, although a subsequent reissue, remixed by Karn with producer Colin Fairley at AIR Studios in London, spent one week on the UK singles chart when it peaked at number ninety-eight at the end of January 1983. 'Released before anyone's noticed it ever went away, and remixed to highlight the dulcet tones of the now more vocally confident Mick,' noted *Record Mirror*'s Betty Page at the start of the new year.

David Sylvian's first single outside Japan, a collaboration with Yellow Magic Orchestra's Ryuichi Sakamoto entitled 'Bamboo Houses', fared a little better after its own release at the end of June when it spent three weeks in the UK singles chart, including one week at a peak chart position of thirty. 'Something a darn sight more palatable than Karn's dismal solo effort,' *Record Mirror*'s Robin Smith wrote of the single. 'Sylvian's vocals are kept to a bare minimum – thank the stars – on a quirky, infectious tune.' 'Do you think Mick Karn's single deserved to do as well as yours?' *The Face* asked David Sylvian in October. 'I think I feel the same way that Mick feels about it,' Sylvian replied diplomatically. 'I don't think Mick particularly liked the single very much but it was something he had to do, it's the first thing he's written and it was done at a time when he was very confused.'

Also emerging from London's AIR Studios at the start of 1982 were Duran Duran. At the beginning of April, *Smash Hits* put the band's Simon Le Bon on their cover and dispatched writer Ian Birch to sit down with the singer to find out about the band's new album, *Rio*. 'The word looks great, sounds great and makes people think of parties, rivers – it's Spanish for river! – foreign places and sunshine,' enthused the frontman, before adding a more oblique revelation: 'We've discovered that our real strength lies in what we are and not what we want to be. It's like a jigsaw with five pieces. But the puzzle doesn't have curly edges. Instead there are rectangles and pentagons and triangles and they all have to fit together. The outside must be a perfect circle because that is the strongest shape and there everything is equal. We've had to fill in all the gaps inside and round off all the corners on the outside and still reconcile the true shapes of what we are within.'

Rio was scheduled for release in May and was preceded by a brand new single from the album, 'Hungry Like The Wolf'. 'It's neither the best nor the worst of Duran Duran's singles so far, but a solid, well-crafted continuation of their hit formula,' was Sunie's take on the single in her review for *Record Mirror*, although the *NME*'s Gavin Martin was less keen. 'Duran Duran, the dustbin men of the new fad, are certainly very ordinary; very, very ordinary, numbingly ordinary, excruciatingly ordinary – ordinary to the point of being relentless bores. This is another copy cat, dogeared, patchwork of endless electro fidgets, piled on thick and fast (and thicker and faster than all the rest of their efforts) with a minimum of style and class.' Ultravox's Midge Ure, guest reviewer for *Flexipop*, was also unimpressed: 'This song is incredibly normal. Duran Duran are a funny sort of group. If they hadn't latched onto that New Romantic look, they'd just be one more band from Birmingham, indistinguishable from thousands of other bands.'

Fortunately for Duran Duran, both *Top of the Pops* and Radio 1 were immediately enthusiastic, and both were swift to put their support behind the single, which, in combination with the band's increasingly passionate and supportive fanbase, was enough to ensure that 'Hungry Like The Wolf' entered the UK singles charts at thirty-five on its way to twelve weeks in the charts, including five weeks in the Top 10 and a peak position of number five at the end of June. *Rio* – released a week after 'Hungry Like The Wolf' – subsequently entered the UK album chart at number four, and peaked at number two the following week before spending most of the next two years in the album charts and earning Duran Duran a platinum award for sales of 300,000 albums by the end of the year.

The commercial success of *Rio* must have been a huge relief to Duran Duran, who later admitted to having initially struggled with the follow-up to *Duran Duran*. 'In January we were going through a very paranoid sort of period, and thinking we should write an album for the people who bought the first album, or maybe one for America – it was absolute madness,' John Taylor confessed in an interview for *Sounds* at the end of May. 'We ended up going back into a four-track studio, back to basics, as if we'd never done the first album.' 'I think we've done more subtle pop. It's difficult to explain, but I think each song in its own way is commercial, as opposed to the first one, which perhaps wasn't quite…' added Nick Rhodes in the same interview. 'The way I viewed it was that we should just write an album to please ourselves first, which is the way we usually work and what we ended up doing, 'cos if you think about things to please other people you end up doing something highly disastrous.'

The critical reaction to *Rio* from the music press was varied. 'If there's a catch, it's that – honest to God – 'Rio' is so good, and defines such an exuberant majesty, where the hell do they go from here?' applauded *Melody Maker*'s Steve Sutherland, awarding the album a maximum five stars. But not everyone was as awed by the record. 'It's an indisputable fact that Duran Duran's limited talents look mighty thin when stretched over an LP,' mused Sunie in *Record Mirror*. 'The band go through the toons, lacking nothing in workmanlike proficiency and everything in imagination.' 'Another well-dressed but not totally satisfying album,' wrote *Smash Hits*' Fred Dellar, not unkindly. 'Third time lucky? Could be. Could be.'

But what 'Hungry Like The Wolf' did do was to set a new bar for what bands could achieve through the medium of video. Its accompaniment to the single was arguably a bigger part of Duran Duran's success story than the song itself. Having embraced the concept of the pop video, and having already befriended MTV in America, Duran Duran were perfectly placed to become superstars. Having considered and conceived the visual aspects of *Rio* on a par with the music, the band scheduled a stop in Sri Lanka on their way to Australia to start a year-long world tour in support of the album. In Sri Lanka, Duran Duran would shoot three videos – for 'Hungry Like The Wolf', 'Save A Prayer' and 'Lonely In Your Nightmare' – over the course of a few days. 'There is no doubt that the work we did in Sri Lanka created a huge shift in the way we were perceived by the global music-buying public,' John Taylor wrote of the 'Hungry Like The Wolf' video in his own memoir, *In the Pleasure Groove*, in 2012. 'We were no longer just an urban club band, famous for our sharp clothes and snazzy haircuts. We were, thanks to that video, transformed.'

Meanwhile Midge Ure's insipid review of 'Hungry Like The Wolf' had been delivered while the Ultravox frontman was promoting a new project of his own, a solo single which he released on June 8th. The release, featuring Ure playing all the instruments on the track as well as producing the single and directing the video, was a cover of Tom Rush's 'No Regrets', best known as The Walker Brothers' biggest hit, which Ure had worked on in between producing other artists during breaks in Ultravox activities. 'I got tired of doing it for other people and decided I'd do something for myself,' Ure told *Sounds*. 'Originally I rang up Phil Oakey to see if he'd be interested in doing a duet with me on that number and he was really into it, you know, a bit of a Walker Brothers update, but The Human League were touring at the time so I went ahead anyway and did it on my own,' he explained in an interview with *Flexipop* later.

'No Regrets', which broadly followed the musical template that had already been successful for Ultravox, was a Top 10 hit for Ure in July 1982 when it peaked at number nine in the wake of a *Top of the Pops* showing of the video the previous week. 'A brilliant mixture of the big emotional American ballad with the kind of clean cut and almost cold precision we've come to associate with Mr Ure,' enthused *Record Mirror*'s Simon Tebbutt. 'With a lovely piano and misplaced guitar solo, Midge stalks the baroque alleyways by lamplight.' 'An undeniably superb song is predictably given the 'Vienna' treatment – swathed in synths that swamp most of the sublime sensitivity of the original,' reported the *NME*'s Adrian Thrills. 'This is the type of stuff Tony Blackburn plays,' despaired The Exploited's Wattie Buchan, reviewing the singles for *Melody Maker*, before imploring, 'Midge, stick to Ultravox – they're better than this.'

While new music from Ultravox was already in the pipeline, the next Midge Ure project to hit the public consciousness was the second Visage album, *The Anvil*, and its associated singles. By coincidence the same edition of *Top of the Pops* that had aired Ure's 'No Regrets' video in July also featured Visage opening the show with a performance of the second single from the album, 'Night Train', a performance which featured just Steve Strange on stage alongside two backing vocalists miming to a new version of the original album track remixed by American DJ and producer John Luongo, to Ure's considerable displeasure. 'It sounds like bad American disco to me. When you start feeling half-hearted about something, then you know it's time to go,' Ure told *Smash Hits* in June, and revealed that he had requested that his name be removed from the single's credits. *Smash Hits* also asked about Ure's continued involvement in Visage: 'I have nothing to do with Visage any more,' Ure responded sadly. 'There are too many cooks and no chefs… During the last album I kept hearing phrases like "commercial" and "appealing to the American market",' he added with a shudder.

'In amongst all the week's funky stuff, this is the sassiest, the flashiest, the most eminently danceable,' proclaimed *Sounds*' Robbi Millar of 'Night Train', which, despite Midge Ure's reservations, scored Visage a significant hit when it reached number twelve in the UK singles chart at the end of July, the peak of a ten-week chart journey which saw the single remain in the Top 40 for a highly respectable seven weeks. Not all the critics were quite as enthusiastic, however. *Record Mirror*'s Mike Nicholls rejected 'Night Train' as 'Totally predictable electronic flotsam,' while the *NME*'s X Moore – the journalistic nom de plume of The Redskins' Chris Dean – was even less circumspect: "Night Train' is cack.'

'It was not intentional to jump on the bandwagon and produce funky music because it's fashionable. From the initial feel of the song it just ended up like that,' Steve Strange told *Record Mirror*'s Sonia Ducie in a cover feature in March. 'The album's a progression in that it has a different theme, nightclubs, and this being the second time we have all worked together it has come out even better. It's dance music for European nightclubs – or for when you're having a smoke late at night.' 'The musical concept around the album all centres around nightclubs – it's about going out and having a good time,' Strange continued. 'I spent a lot of time on the American nightclub scene last year, especially visiting the gay discos and that inspired me. The album title, *The Anvil*, comes from a nightclub in America. It is actually notorious for its wild nightlife.'

Rumours that Midge Ure had quit Visage had been circulating in the music press since the start of 1982. 'There's also a rumour that Midge is bidding adieu to Visage,' *Smash Hits* had reported in February, although Steve Strange allegedly set the record straight: 'Midge hasn't really left, although it's a bit up in the air at the moment. He's just letting me do what I want, taking more control over the group.' By April, however, the dynamics within the band appeared to be floundering. 'I wouldn't say I like the set-up with Midge at the moment,' Strange told *Melody Maker*. 'Maybe it's just going through a bad patch.' Strange's assertion that Ure had left Visage in order to allow the singer to take more control was one he would continue to return to in interviews. 'I'm a lot more confident on my own now, that's why Midge left Visage,' Strange told *Record Mirror* in July. 'At the beginning I didn't know too much so I tended to take a back seat, but now I've acquired more knowledge I want to use it. The trouble with that was that both Midge and I are very, very stubborn and neither of us would back down to the other's ideas. One of us had to go.'

In fact before leaving, Ure discharged all his duties relating to *The Anvil* and not only produced the album with the band – 'I had got it into my head that you got more respect if you produced the music as well, created it from scratch,' Ure confessed in *If I Was*, adding: 'The first two albums say: 'Produced by Visage & Midge Ure'. That little credit led to a huge ruck with Rusty, so huge we fell out for years' – but, with Chris Cross, directed the video for its first single, 'The Damned Don't Cry', which had been released in March. 'We were trying to recreate the mood of the Orient Express,' Steve Strange remembered in his memoir *Blitzed!* 'The whole video was supposed to be this surreal dream, as I go through different carriages and see ghosts appearing. At one point, I see a party going on, but only two people there are real, the rest turn out to be mannequins. In the buffet car, the barman offers me a drink, then turns out not to have a reflection.'

Boosted by a *Top of the Pops* showing of Midge Ure and Chris Cross's creation, 'The Damned Don't Cry' peaked at eleven in the UK singles chart at the beginning of April. Inspired by the Dirk Bogarde film 'The Damned', the single was released to some acclaim from the music press. 'A whispy wedge of pop electronique not a million miles away from the fine 'Fade To Grey' in terms of mood and melody,' wrote Adrian Thrills in the *NME*. 'If ABBA had made this record, it would probably be hailed as a pop masterpiece.' 'It does the various musicians involved credit that although it's a part-time interest for most of them, Visage have a sound of their own and are quite distinct from Ultravox or Magazine,' opined *Smash Hits'* Tim de Lisle. 'If you liked 'Fade To Grey' you'll enjoy this.' Bananarama, however, reviewing the single for *Flexipop*, were vocal and unanimous in their love of 'Fade To Grey', but disappointed by 'The Damned Don't Cry'. 'This one is pretty uninspired,' announced the band's Siobhan Fahey. 'I mean it's very pleasant but it's not what you'd call exciting is it?'

Released the week following 'The Damned Don't Cry', Visage's second album, *The Anvil*, resplendent in a Peter Saville sleeve featuring striking black-and-white photography courtesy of the iconic fashion photographer Helmut Newton, entered the UK albums chart at its peak of number six, spent sixteen weeks in the charts, and earned Visage a silver record for sales of 60,000 albums by the end of April. The press response was largely positive. "'The Anvil' is actually fluent, melodic, entertaining dance music,' wrote *Record Mirror*'s Sonia Ducie, who awarded the album four and a half out of a possible five stars. 'The new album – and it galls me to say it, more than it does you to hear it – is better than the first,' admitted the *NME*'s Paul Tickell. 'It's more professional, more danceable, much more of an exhortation to take to the floor.' 'In spite of its occasional lyrical pretensions and the obvious vocal limitations of Strange's voice, when all is said and done 'The Anvil', with its impressive collection of musicians and excellent siren harmonies by backing vocalists Perry and Lorraine, is an excellent LP which is potentially as vital and influential in its field as the Human League's 'Dare' or Heaven 17's 'Penthouse And Pavement',' declared Paul Simper in *Melody Maker*, singling out Midge Ure's 'much matured' production and Rusty Egan's 'understanding of the logistics of hard danceable music' for particular praise.

'Night Train' was not only the final single to be taken from *The Anvil*, it also marked the end of Midge Ure's involvement with Visage. Ultravox subsequently announced that their new single, 'Reap The Wild Wind', would be released on September 17th and their new album, *Quartet*, produced by George Martin, best known for his pioneering work with The Beatles, would follow in mid-October.

'I thought *Rage In Eden* was still drifting a bit,' Billy Currie had told *Sounds'* Hugh Fielder earlier in the year when asked about the direction of the new material. 'I think what's building up is a desire for more power on the next album. For me that means less subtlety… I'm not in that mood right now. I want to blast out a bit more.'

'It's not an instant record but, the more I hear it, the more I like it,' enthused Duran Duran's John Taylor, reviewing 'Reap The Wild Wind' for *Melody Maker*, before mischievously adding, 'It's a good record; one I would have bought anyway – even if Midge didn't like 'Hungry Like The Wolf'.' 'Pompous,' declared *Record Mirror*'s Simon Hills. 'Cue dry ice and huge banks of lights for this mass of swirling synthesisers wrapping pure commercial pop.' 'Ultravox have tried and failed to become the first credible futurist heavy metal band with 'All Stood Still' and are now reverting to what they do best,' volunteered the *NME*'s Adrian Thrills, who further described the single as 'a mild Kraftwerk pastiche' while acknowledging 'Reap The Wild Wind''s 'shockingly decent melody line and tune'.

'It starts, it goes on a bit, it fades out. Nothing happens,' was Johnny Black's dismissal of the single in *Smash Hits*. 'Maybe it will have a great video.' And the single did have a great video, which was shown on *Top of the Pops* twice in lieu of performances by the band, assisting 'Reap The Wild Wind' to a peak chart position of twelve in the second half of October. Directed by the band's Midge Ure and Chris Cross, the video – intercut with vintage footage of World War II fighter pilots and planes and featuring Ultravox themselves dressed as pilots from the same era engaged in the construction of a dramatic monument on a cliff as Spitfires flew overhead – was intended to be a bit of fun, but instead fed into the accusations of pomposity that seemed to dog Ultravox's every move. 'It's great fun except when people take it seriously and start asking "What's all this with Spitfires?" and so on,' Midge Ure told *Sounds'* Hugh Fielder later in the year. 'We're just a bunch of big kids, that's why. It's like being given three wishes and you go "gee thanks" and have a Spitfire whizzing over your head while you're standing out in a field and building a thirty-foot structure on the edge of a cliff. It's kids stuff and we really enjoy it.'

While Ultravox were disappointed by 'Reap The Wild Wind''s journey through the singles charts – 'It wasn't poppy enough for the British charts,' Billy Currie told Hugh Fielder. The single set up *Quartet* beautifully, and in the week that the single hit its peak, the new album soared into the UK albums chart at number six. This was the highest position in the six-month period the album remained in the chart. It earned Ultravox a gold record for selling over 100,000 albums in the UK before the end of 1982, despite an underwhelming, if not unexpected, response from the music press.

'I find the music paper criticisms a bit sad,' Midge Ure admitted to *Sounds* in November, following a press response which largely accused Ultravox of treading water and failing to develop their sound, while dismissing *Quartet* as a triumph of style over substance. 'Through years of practice, Ultravox have perfected the art of taking the vacuous phrase and making it sound like profound philosophy,' sniffed the *NME*'s Leyla Sanai. 'At the moment they're too composed and self-conscious to seriously threaten emotional complacency, and too grandiose to be an elevating pop hope.' 'The infuriating aspect of it is that they're well-equipped to be making music that could enthral, inspire and seduce,' added *Sounds*' Johnny Waller. 'Instead, they're stuck in a post-seduction phase of merely stroking a lover's forehead when a little more stimulation is required.' 'You have to hand it to Ure, Cann, Cross and Currie: their synthesis is just right and this gleaming music could dazzle even Trevor Horn. Producer George Martin has clearly brought his technique in line with the demands of the moment', reported Ian Pye in *Melody Maker*, 'Ultravox aim straight for the target. They score all right, but it's a triumph of expediency and an easy victory is easily forgotten.'

The second single to be selected from *Quartet* was 'Hymn', which Ultravox released in the second half of November. 'This sort of thing should have been left frozen in an ice floe to be unearthed by bemused archaeologists along with the last mellotron,' sniped Charles Shaar Murray in the *NME*. 'Ultravox are the Barclay James Harvest of the '80s.' 'The pomp and insincerity of Ultravox's music reaches new heights,' continued *Sounds*' Tony Mitchell. 'It's executed perfectly well and it's a pretty memorable song, but I just don't experience any of the human feeling that attracts me to music in the first place,' lamented Gary Crowley, reviewing the single for *Melody Maker* the same week.

Despite the underwhelming media response, 'Hymn' remained in the UK singles chart for almost three months, and spent eight weeks in the Top 20 over Christmas and the New Year, eventually beating 'Reap The Wild Wind' by one place when it peaked at number eleven in the middle of January. 'Hymn' was supported by another tongue-in-cheek Midge Ure and Chris Cross video, in which the individual members of Ultravox each sign a contract with a mysterious and shadowy figure with glowing green eyes who briefly makes their dreams come true before destroying their ambitions. The video earned

'Hymn' the single's *Top of the Pops* debut and the band subsequently delivered a performance on the show which was shown twice as the single made its way up the charts.

Similarly fascinated by video, Duran Duran followed 'Hungry Like The Wolf' with a second single from *Rio* in August. 'Save A Prayer' presented a more introspective, soulful side of Duran Duran to mixed reviews. 'Get yourself into the most soppy, lugubrious mood possible and pretend that you can hear something medium and ploddy with too many acoustic guitars, a tear-jerking synth line and a song equally remarkable for its portentousness, its blandness and its utter vacuity,' ran Charles Shaar Murray's dismissive review for the *NME*. 'If you have followed these instructions faithfully, you have just imagined the new Duran Duran single.' But both *Smash Hits* and *Sounds* were cautiously encouraging: 'Dropping their usual top twenty bounce, Simon and the boys hold back the tears with a bravely romantic ballad. Listen with a stiff upper lip,' instructed *Smash Hits*' Neil Tennant, while *Sounds*' Johnny Waller declared "Prayer' mellows out through a drifting quasi-Japan melody and some stirring, soaring synth. Another hit, and I approve.'

Accompanied by Duran Duran's second Sri Lankan video – set on the island's beaches alongside footage of the band strolling through an ancient fortress and a ruined Buddhist temple, in contrast to the Indiana Jones-style jungle themes of 'Hungry Like The Wolf' – 'Save A Prayer' became Duran Duran's biggest UK single hit to date when it peaked at number two in the middle of September, held off the top spot by Survivor's 'Eye Of The Tiger'. "Save a Prayer' and 'Hungry Like the Wolf' are like mini-movies in their own right, yet they each cost less than £20,000, which illustrates how video allowed us to do things that we otherwise could not have done. It helped us to connect with our audience,' Andy Taylor wrote in his autobiography *Wild Boy* in 2008. 'The flipside is that a lot of people still thought we spent all our time messing about on yachts.' *Top of the Pops* showed the video twice in lieu of a studio performance from the band, and it was a more mature and sophisticated Duran Duran that embarked on another round of interviews to support the single and the *Rio* album. 'I can't relate to the old Duran Duran. I look at the 'Planet Earth' video or the frilly shirts or the make-up, which isn't that long ago, and think, for crying out loud,' John Taylor told *Smash Hits*' Ian Birch at the end of August. 'At first I didn't want anyone to be put off by the fact that I had deep cherry lip liner on. Now, if they don't buy our records because we haven't got frilly shirts on, I'm not interested.'

Capitalising on the success of 'Save A Prayer', Duran Duran chose the album's title track, 'Rio', released at the start of November, as their next single. 'Duran Duran have become masters at giving the people exactly what they want in carefully measured doses and one's immediate reaction is yes, they do write good toons, don't they? But listen again. Is there really anything that special about this one?' asked *Sounds*' Tony Mitchell the following week, while *Record Mirror*'s Jim Reid was more direct in his rejection of the charms of 'Rio', which he described as having 'All the joie de vivre of an ingrowing toe nail.'

The single was reviewed by the Anti-Nowhere League in *Melody Maker*, where Duran Duran found unlikely allies. 'I like it. I like Duran Duran and I like the bass sound on this. I reckon the bass player's brilliant,' proclaimed Anti-Nowhere League bassist Winston, while frontman Animal correctly predicted, 'It's going to be Top 10. There's no doubt about it.' 'Rio' peaked at number nine in the middle of December, assisted by a *Top of the Pops* studio performance on release, followed by a showing of the 'Rio' video a fortnight later. Revolving around footage of Duran Duran, dressed in pastel-coloured Anthony Price suits, sailing on a yacht off the coast of Antigua, the 'Rio' video was a defining moment in the band's career. 'It was a surprisingly controversial, polarising video. It became our most iconic video, making MTV's all-time Top Ten, but it also perceived by many in Britain as an arrogant portrayal of the worst traits of Thatcherite self-interest,' John Taylor wrote in *In the Pleasure Groove*. 'There would be no going back to the underground after that one.'

Things weren't looking quite so rosy for Visage however, who announced a new single, 'Pleasure Boys', in October, the first release from a new album which was to follow in January. *Sounds* were initially enthusiastic about the new Visage. 'This has got real guts to it – a two-finger gesture to the overblown pomp of Ultravox and worthy sequel to 'Night Train',' applauded Tony Mitchell in his review of 'Pleasure Boys', but his peers were less effusive. 'This record is just as soulless as its predecessor. Steve is a great populariser, and good luck to him, but I do wish he'd stop making records,' wrote *Record Mirror*'s Jim Reid. Radio 1 were equally unenthusiastic, and without the benefit of their support, 'Pleasure Boys' floundered, spending just three weeks in the UK singles chart at the end of November and peaking at a lowly forty-four.

'The single, our first track that Midge had not co-written, was released on 5 November 1982, but there weren't many fireworks,' Steve Strange confessed in *Blitzed!* later. After the success of *The Anvil* and its associated singles 'The Damned Don't Cry' and 'Night Train' earlier in the year, the release of

'Pleasure Boys' was a disappointment to everyone involved although the band tried to put on a brave face. 'Now that Midge has left, we've turned over a new leaf,' Strange told *Record Mirror*'s Mark Cooper in December. 'We're gradually going to get a heavier, raunchier, more aggressive sound. I want to get in a good guitar player and be more of a rock and roll band.'

As Visage faltered, Japan appeared to be going from strength to strength as their *Sons Of Pioneers* tour made its way across the country, playing to packed venues and attracting positive reviews on the way to finishing the UK leg with six sold-out shows at London's Hammersmith Odeon. Both Hansa and Virgin scrambled to take advantage of Japan's momentum by each releasing a single in quick succession. First came Hansa's release of a remixed version of 1979's 'Life In Tokyo', which came out at the end of September and peaked at number twenty-eight in the UK singles chart as part of a six-week chart run. A few weeks later Virgin released 'Nightporter' from Japan's *Gentlemen Take Polaroids* album, which peaked at number twenty-nine at the start of December, and attracted a mixed bag of reviews. 'An arresting and unexpected single in the wake of their 'Tin Drum' LP,' wrote *Melody Maker*'s Paul Simper. 'Shaped round some elegant piano and with Dave Sylvian's vocals returning to the impressive emotional depths of 'Ghosts'.'

Just three days after Japan's final *Sons Of Pioneers* UK concert at London's Hammersmith Odeon, as Japan headed to the Far East to play the final leg of the tour, *Smash Hits* announced the news that everyone had been expecting but dreading. Ian Birch had met David Sylvian in Manchester for the feature, which was teased by a picture of a laughing Japan on the magazine's cover accompanied by the headline 'Japan – A Happy Ending?' 'Are Japan calling it a day?' asked Birch in his introduction to the piece. 'The answer is an unhesitating yes. After a brief tour in Japan itself, the band will go their separate ways at the end of January.' 'We're growing apart,' Sylvian explained. 'As musicians Japan was four people working together on an equal basis but on the creative side – the concepts, writing, that way an album goes in the studio – it was mainly my project. That was the whole concept of Japan and it got better over the years. That can't work any more because of ego problems. People no longer want to work under me, so to speak, and I never want to force anyone to play things they don't want to play.'

Howard Jones, 1984.

1983.1 Sampling / Top Hats / OMD / Howard Jones / Smash Hits / Duran Duran / Spandau Ballet / Simple Minds

AT THE START OF 1983 the *NME*, in their rundown of the best and worst of the previous year, compiled a list of 'Last Year's Things', which included Spies, Snooker, Ten-Inch Singles, Lumberjacks, No Socks and Deely-Boppers, alongside a list of 'Next Year's Things', which included Bio-Technology, Socks, Dickensian Chic, Folk Dancing, Top Hats, Paranoia, Real Drums and Emulators. While the paper's accuracy in their prediction that Top Hats would be an important feature of 1983 remains a moot point, they were correct in that 1983 would be the year in which more and more electronic musicians would turn to the Emulator. 'An Emulator looks, at first sight, like any other portable synthesiser. But it isn't a synthesiser at all. It's a small computer connected to a piano keyboard,' explained the *NME*'s Paul Rambali in a short technical feature the previous October. 'Unlike a synthesiser, it doesn't generate any sound itself. You simply record two seconds of sound through a microphone input, and there it is. It can be any sound at all: any musical instrument, any note, or a spoken word, or the sound of a Ferrari in second gear, or a dog barking, or a train, or the wind howling, anything,' he continued. 'Using digital circuitry similar to the Eventide Harmoniser, which changes the pitch of a note, the Emulator takes this 'sample' and recreates it for each of the 12 tones and across four octaves. You could, if you wished, play a Mozart sonata on Waterford crystal, or a Human League tune on a tuba, or a heavy metal riff on a cathedral organ.'

The advertising for the E-mu Emulator was equally upbeat: 'Finally there's nothing standing between you and the sound you want. Any sound you want.

Instruments. Voices. Sound effects. Animals. Machines. Anything. Sounds that sound real because they are real. Not synthesized simulations but the actual digitally recorded sounds,' enthused an advert which appeared in *Keyboard Magazine* in 1982, and continued, 'You can start with a selection of pre-recorded sounds from the extensive Emulator sound library. Or exercise your creativity. Plug a microphone or line level source into your Emulator and sample a sound of your choice. Instantly it is digitized, stored in memory, and available to be played polyphonically on the keyboard. You can record the sound of any existing instrument exactly as you want it. Or create entirely new instruments from everyday sounds around you. But recording your sound is only the beginning. Use the Emulator's controls to edit, filter, and tune it. Store it on diskette as part of your personal sound library. Experiment with it. Add vibrato or pitchbend. Use the Emulator's doubling mode to combine it with other sounds. Or activate backwards mode and play it in reverse. Overdub parts on the built in polyphonic sequencer. Create complex multitrack compositions and effects tracks without the need for a multitrack tape recorder.'

Designed as an affordable alternative to the Fairlight CMI system favoured by successful musicians with deep pockets, the availability of E-mu Systems' Emulator was a crucial turning point in the development of electronic music. 'Sampling was very important,' Daniel Miller confirms today. 'The E-mu Emulator was the first semi-affordable sampler. Before that there was the Fairlight and the Synclavier but they were both very expensive. The Emulator was still pretty expensive for most and it wasn't really until later, with the release of the Akai S900 and similar models that the sampling revolution really kicked off.' 'Sampling changed everything, it was revolutionary,' muses Vince Clarke today. 'Samplers changed the sound of lots and lots of records.'

Having spent an inordinate amount of the first six months of 1982 touring in support of *Architecture And Morality*, by the second half of the year OMD found themselves back in the studio ready to start work on their next album. Lacking a clear new direction, Paul Humphreys and Andy McCluskey looked to technology to show them a way forward. 'As usual, the impetus came from random experimentation and idle curiosity,' wrote Johnny Waller and Mike Humphreys in their 1987 OMD biography *Messages*. 'Just as the choir tape-loops had propelled them towards 'Souvenir', so their continuing fascination with emulators led them towards another new style, away from the ballads and moody anthems.' 'We changed instruments again, using an emulator digital sampling keyboard,' Paul Humphreys acknowledged. 'We were looking for alternatives obviously, asking ourselves questions about what to do next.'

In January 1983, OMD announced the first fruits of their labours, a new single entitled 'Genetic Engineering' which was to be released at the start of February, with a new album, *Dazzle Ships*, to follow at the start of March. The band also announced that the producer for the new project would be Rhett Davies, best known for his work with Roxy Music, alongside Paul Humphreys and Andy McCluskey. Despite the quiet confidence with which they delivered the announcement, OMD were feeling far from happy. Their record label, DinDisc, had closed down and their contract had been transferred to DinDisc's parent company, Virgin Records, OMD found themselves very much operating in the dark. 'Virgin inherited us from DinDisc and didn't give us any guidance,' Paul Humphreys recalled later in *Pretending to See the Future*. '*Architecture And Morality* sold five million copies and some stupid person at the record label said, "Okay, all you have to do is *Architecture And Morality* No. 2 and you're the next Genesis." Andy and I looked at each other and went, "Well, let's not do *Architecture And Morality* No. 2 then. We don't want to be the next Genesis! Let's do something radically different."' Both parties were still feeling their way forward with the new arrangement. 'They said, "How does this work?" and we said, "You let us go to our studio and we write an album. When we're ready, we say, 'We want to work in that studio with that person' and you give us the money, we give you the record and it sells millions." And they said, "Okay,"' recalled Andy McCluskey. 'Then we delivered *Dazzle Ships* and they thought, "Well, they must know what they're doing."'

In a February interview with *Record Mirror*'s John Shearlaw to promote the 'Genetic Engineering' single, OMD were swift to communicate their misgivings and manage any expectations of the new project. 'I've got no idea what to expect, no idea how people will react apart from raising their eyebrows,' Paul Humphreys confessed when asked how he thought OMD's new material would be received by the general public. 'Do you think that's brave?' Humphreys asked a little tremulously. 'Or just silly?' 'We were given enough rope to hang ourselves and we may well have done it with this album,' Andy McCluskey added. 'Really we're just having fun. If we're going to go down we're going to laugh all the way to bankruptcy.'

Released on their own label, Telegraph, through Virgin Records, 'Genetic Engineering' was met by mixed reviews. 'Well worth the wait. OMD's knack of coming up with exhilarating singles has not been affected by their year off,' applauded *Smash Hits*. 'When you marry such sentiments to a great tune, even your goosebumps get goosebumps.' 'OMD have been biding their time as the platoons of lesser electronic talents have encroached on their patch, only to re-emerge one year on sounding as mundane as all their bastard sons,' wrote an underwhelmed Adrian Thrills in the *NME*. 'Their, almost embarrassing, desire to write yet more songs about technology has got beyond a joke,' declared *Sounds'* Dave Henderson. 'They've either run out of ideas completely or they've become totally infatuated with computers.'

"Genetic Engineering' had to be the first choice as a single, rather than an obvious "OMD are back" single. It's a piece of positive propaganda – at least I hope it is. And to justify its existence it's got to be a hit,' Andy McCluskey told John Shearlaw. And 'Genetic Engineering' was a hit, spending a respectable eight weeks in the UK singles charts, but failing to rise above a chart peak of twenty in the middle of March, making it the least successful OMD single since 'Red Frame/White Light' three years previously. 'Every song has a massive background. We're quite proud of the fact that we create hit pop songs from potentially unpromising ideas,' McCluskey told Shearlaw. 'Like the single; the idea is for people to associate the phrase genetic engineering with a happy pop song.'

In the wake of 'Genetic Engineering', Humphreys and McCluskey's confidence dipped even further. 'It's been quite a sticky year for a lot of bands who came from our era,' McCluskey told Mark Ellen for a *Smash Hits* cover feature on the band – now officially expended to a four piece with the promotion of Martin Cooper and Malcolm Holmes to the core OMD line-up – in February. 'Most of us came up in '78, post-punk, and always felt there was a sort of positiveness born out of – I don't know – naivety that made us think we weren't going to sell out or whatever even if we had hits. And now we've become the Establishment.' 'We were lacking mental energy,' McCluskey told *Sounds'* Johnny Waller the following week. 'When you worry too much, you can't focus on what you want to do. If we'd had some great songs early last year, then a lot of the worries would have disappeared, but because the songs weren't right, the more the worries increased – and the more the worries increased the less likely it was that the songs would ever be finished.' 'It's an album moving in a new direction, moving towards another album. Maybe the next album will be the important one in the same was that *Organisation* was a step towards *Architecture And Morality* from the first one,' McCluskey added hopefully.

Released at the start of March, *Dazzle Ships* was propelled by OMD's loyal audience to number five in the UK albums chart after a single week of sales, and the album remained in the Top 20 for the next five weeks, earning a gold record for in excess of 100,000 sales in the process, despite a markedly unenthusiastic reaction from most of the music press. 'Having stepped away from the more grandiose sweeps of sound on 'Architecture And Morality' to the sweeter and simpler songs of 'Dazzle', OMD are still not that sure of themselves as purely pop artistes. The clever-clever trickery is like a salve to their conscience – to give the impression that here is something of lasting quality,' wrote Chris Burkham in a thoughtful review for *Sounds*. 'Though there are rewards in repeated listening and benefits from concentration, the sad truth is that OMD have few good songs to wrap around their musical test tubes. For all their efforts to change ground 'Dazzle Ships' too readily slips into the timekeeping synths and levelled vocals of previous workouts,' cautioned Paul Colbert in *Melody Maker*. *Smash Hits*' Johnny Black also recommended repeated listening in his review, in which he awarded *Dazzle Ships* eight out of ten stars: 'On first listen this is an unlikely, spiky successor to 'Architecture And Morality'. Persistence pays, though. The songs are waiting to be found and are as melodic, passionate and vital as ever. These people are originals and should not be underestimated – even if they oblige us to work for our pleasure.'

That the tracklisting for *Dazzle Ships* – named after the wartime practice of painting battleships with bizarre designs in order to confuse enemy submarines – included two songs previously released as single B-sides ('The Romance Of The Telescope' was the B-side to 'Joan Of Arc' and 'Of All The Things We've Made' appeared on the reverse of 'Maid Of Orleans' in 1981 and 1982 respectively) seemed further evidence that OMD had struggled for content to include on the album. 'They're on there because we don't wish them to be forever neglected,' McCluskey explained to *Sounds*. 'I agree that they are two of the best songs, but they're not the only good songs on the album.' 'It would seem that OMD have squandered the chances they had with 'Dazzle',' Chris Burkham continued in his review of the album. 'Perhaps because they themselves cannot be that sure about exactly what direction they should now take. The project that is 'Dazzle' is too sketchy, too unsure and wobbly to be worth much.'

More successful was the striking artwork which Peter Saville had devised for the project, although that had presented problems of its own. 'I found the cover very difficult. I'm not the best person for doing camouflage. I'm too reductive,' Saville confessed in *Pretending to See the Future*. 'Every time I tried there was nothing left by the end of the day. I ended up giving it to Malcolm Garrett, saying "Could you do this again, because there's no camouflage left – I've taken it all away."' Working with Saville at the time was Australian architect Ken Kennedy, who then translated the artwork into a stage set for the band's international *Dazzle Ships* tour, which kicked off in the UK in April, supported by a second single from the album, 'Telegraph', released at the start of the same month.

Despite being a more straightforward proposition than 'Genetic Engineering', 'Telegraph' was ultimately unsuccessful as a means of getting OMD back into the charts when it stalled at a peak of number forty-two two weeks into an underwhelming four-week chart run. 'A well-recorded piece of nonsense that doesn't show any ideas apart from starting and ending,' ran *Record Mirror*'s entire review. 'Don't know what to say about this actually, because it made no impression on me whatsoever,' confessed Dave Rimmer in *Smash Hits*. 'Jolly, jangly, deliberately obscure and dull as proverbial dishwater. A bit like 'Genetic Engineering' in fact.'

'*Dazzle Ships* wasn't wrapped in the candy coating of the melodies and the beauty, and people went, "Ow! That's not what I want to hear!" Nowadays, we're accustomed to samples and hard edits and mash-ups but, thirty years ago, *Dazzle Ships* was out on a limb and a lot of people didn't get it at all,' Andy McCluskey told *Classic Pop* magazine in 2013, adding that the band had fallen back in love with the album in recent years, as had the public and the media. 'We're accustomed to channel surfing, to multi-tasking with our computers, phones, radios, iPods and TVs. We consume things in a much more multiplied and fractured way, and we're accustomed to songs made of samples and broken bits of music reconstituted. So I think people find it easier to digest the album now,' McCluskey added in an interview for *Electronic Sound* the following year.

In the wake of their disappointment at the reception of *Dazzle Ships* from the press and from the public, OMD instead focused their attention on their live show and spent three months touring in the UK and across Europe throughout April, May and June before retiring to the studio in the summer to start work on a new album. The first fruits of the band's efforts were soon ready to play live, and OMD announced a short UK club tour in September in order to try out some of their new ideas in front of a live audience. *Melody Maker*'s Frank Worrall attended the band's show at Manchester's Haçienda on September 9th and decided that OMD's efforts had paid off: 'OMD offered a tasty menu of lively new songs that may well turn out to be their best ever material when put on record. Many are still untitled and are being given their first airing tonight.'

Sounds were also in attendance at the Manchester show and, while Mick Middles was less effusive in his praise of OMD, he nevertheless found something of interest in the band's new material. 'I'm certainly not about to cast them away into a sea of former glory,' Middles reported. 'Watch them.' Support act Howard Jones came over less well: 'Howard Jones supplies us with a tedious drone from a synth while a mime artist impersonates a Zulu war dance onstage,' wrote Middles. 'The effect is numbing in the worst possible sense of the word.'

Although still a relatively unknown artists at the time he joined OMD for their short jaunt around the UK, Howard Jones had recently released his first single, 'New Song', which entered the lower reaches of the UK singles chart at ninety-two the week the OMD dates commenced, and rose to seventy-six the day after they finished. 'I couldn't believe it when I was asked to play five support gigs with OMD in September 1983,' Jones recalled in OMD's *Pretending to See the Future* in 2019. 'I was a huge fan, so much that the only cover I played in my early Eighties set was 'Enola Gay', but I didn't perform it [with OMD] in Nottingham, Cardiff, Bradford, Manchester's Hacienda and Liverpool.'

Mick Middles' resistance to Howard Jones's presentation as a modern, electronic one-man band would prove to be a stumbling point for the traditional music press in general, as the more established writers struggled to adjust their preconceptions of how music should work. 'I used to play in bands when I was younger, but I couldn't stand the arguments and fighting that bands usually have so I thought I'd have a go on my own. I just started with one synth, then got another and just built it up like that,' Jones told *Record Mirror* in September. 'I was presented with an impossible task in a way. When I started off playing on my own, people said, "You can't do it, you've gotta have a band"... I was determined to have a go,' Jones added. 'I believe that anything is possible – it just takes a bit of time and effort. If I've got anything to say it's that. Whatever anyone wants to do they should just go out and have a crack at it.'

Howard Jones had been operating on the fringes of the live circuit for some time, and in fact the Christmas Day 1982 edition of the *NME* had featured an oddly phrased, strangely punctuated, tongue-in-cheek advert in support of Jones's upcoming show at the Marquee in London on January 3rd: 'Howard Jones cordially does not invite you to come and listen to his fabulous display of musical genius and to listen to his songs generally beloved by saints, kings, prime ministers etc also you are not granted the opportunity to hear the most original lyrics ever (probably in the whole world) and to witness a breathtaking display of mime by Jed Hoile arguably one of the most untrained and therefore most original mime artists in the cosmos so if you don't want to be part of the wonderful experience you'd better drop in at The Marquee.' Although most of the shows weren't advertised in such a curious way, Jones continued to play dates here and there, including a three-night run of shows at the ZigZag club in April – a spin-off from the music paper of the same name – and a support slot on China Crisis's UK tour in May and June.

Newly signed to WEA Records, Howard Jones released 'New Song', at the end of August, and much was made of Jones's choice of Colin Thurston as producer in the subsequent single reviews. 'Another in the long line of pretty-boy popsters, Howard is apparently rather big in High Wycombe,' reported *Record Mirror*'s Eleanor Levy. 'This first offering is produced by the same man as Duran Duran and Kajagoogoo and will probably be massive. It's squeaky-clean disco-pop with lots of whoops and whoos in the background. You can't fault it.' '[Howard Jones] sings all about being individual and anti-herd, but just to be on the safe side he ropes in the producer of Duran Duran and Kajagoogoo,' smirked the *NME*'s Paul Du Noyer. 'The result is just as individual and anti-herd as you'd expect.'

But Howard Jones's upbeat modern pop didn't need the approval or patronage of the music press and, with the enthusiastic support of Radio 1, 'New Song' went from strength to strength, remaining in the UK singles chart for an impressive fourteen weeks, including a month in the Top 10 and a peak position of number three in the middle of October. *Sounds*' Carole Linfield went to see Howard Jones play at the Marquee at the end of August and was forced to review her position as a result: 'This is the future of pop that so many people dread, that bland impersonality that stretched from the Durans through to even the brilliant Dolby. But Howard proves just how this power pop can, against the odds, captivate and control. Quite frightening, but so listenable.'

Howard Jones's second single, 'What Is Love?', followed in November and spent a further fifteen weeks in the UK charts over Christmas and the New Year, peaking at number two in the middle of January 1984 and earning Jones *Smash Hits'* the Most Promising Act For 1984 award in their annual poll, an accolade which saw the singer grace the cover of the magazine's Christmas edition in December 1983. 'What Is Love?' received a predictably lukewarm

reception from the music press – 'Throughout the centuries, artists by the dozen have tried, through their work, to answer the above question [What is love?],' noted the *NME*'s Paolo Hewitt, adding, 'None, though, could have done it as facetiously as Howard Jones has done on this imminently disposable record' – although Jones found unlikely support in the shape of Status Quo's Francis Rossi, reviewing the singles for *Melody Maker*, who declared, 'This is quite likeable – there's a pleasant melody at least, but it's not as strong as 'New Song', which is an excellent record.' Further celebrity support came from former Squeeze keyboardist, and presenter of Channel 4's new music show *The Tube*, Jools Holland, who reviewed the single in *Smash Hits* and reported, 'This is a well-produced song that sounds great loud.'

Although it was Howard Jones who claimed the cover of the prestigious 1983 *Smash Hits* Christmas edition in recognition of his achievements over the course of the year, inside the magazine, a different band cleaned up across the award categories. Duran Duran topped the polls for Best Group, Event Of The Year (for a charity concert at Birmingham's Aston Villa Stadium), Best Male Singer, Most Fanciable Male (John Taylor won the category but Simon Le Bon, Nick Rhodes and Roger Taylor all placed in the top ten) and Best Video for 'Union Of The Snake'. The band's two single releases in 1983, 'Union Of The Snake' and 'Is There Something I Should Know?', placed at two and three, respectively, in Best Single (bettered only by Culture Club's 'Karma Chameleon'). Duran Duran were voted Twits Of The Year and only failed to chart in the Most Fanciable Female (won by Tracie Young), Best Female Singer (won by Tracey Ullman, although Boy George claimed tenth place) and Album Of The Year categories as their 1983 *Seven And The Ragged Tiger* release came out too late to qualify for the poll.

Duran Duran's first release of 1983 was an interim single, 'Is There Something I Should Know?', designed as a bridge between the band's second and third albums, and which was released in March. 'The thing about Duran Duran is that they always put out really infectious pop records and, whether you love 'em or hate 'em, you end up going round singing them all the time,' was Marc Almond's take, reviewing the single for *Melody Maker*, and adding less promisingly, 'This is them at their most unmemorable.' That the single would be a success was not in any doubt; 'This'll crash in at Number One,' predicted Betty Page in *Record Mirror*, 'it's well-crafted, crushingly memorable and possesses their unique youthful vibrancy.' 'Is There Something I Should Know?' was also the first Duran Duran single to not be produced by Colin

Thurston, and was instead produced by the band themselves with help from Ian Little, who had previously worked on Roxy Music's album *Avalon*.

As predicted, 'Is There Something I Should Know?' entered the UK singles chart at number one at the end of March, a position it maintained for two successive weeks before spending a further seven weeks in the charts and earning the band a gold record for sales of over 400,000 by the start of April. Although 'Is There Something I Should Know?' was Duran Duran's first number one, it nevertheless followed the chart-topping success of Kajagoogoo's 'Too Shy', which had been produced by Nick Rhodes alongside Duran Duran producer Colin Thurston. Was it frustrating to Rhodes that Kajagoogoo had had a number one single before Duran Duran, asked *Smash Hits*? 'I was waiting for this one!' Rhodes responded. 'I'm very glad I produced Kajagoogoo, I'm proud of them being number one and I hope their success continues. The only thing I'd say is that I'm glad Duran Duran didn't go straight to number one because you then have so much to live up to.'

Duran Duran announced in July that their third album, recorded in France, Montserrat and Australia, would be titled *Seven And The Ragged Tiger*, the title inspired by Simon Le Bon's imagining of the band, plus their managers Paul and Michael Berrow, as a gang in search of adventure in the manner of a children's book. 'Simon reimagined us as a twisted Enid Blyton creation,' John Taylor later wrote in *In the Pleasure Groove*, 'the five band members plus Mike and Paul were the seven, and the ragged tiger was that intangible phenomenon that was beginning to swallow us up – fame.' 'This is probably the album we wanted to make first time around but it takes a few to get it right,' Andy Taylor admitted to the *NME* in 1983. 'I dunno what we do after that. We'll have to wait and see what everybody else is up to! This is the first time we've made an album with a sort of blind naivety – if it sounds good, that'll do.' 'I can't listen to the first two albums now. The first one was very original for its time. But *Rio* was only a very small step forward. It didn't achieve anything,' Nick Rhodes confessed to *Smash Hits* later in the year. 'I'm pleased with the new one though. It's not too obvious, we've done a lot of new things. It's great.'

With work finally complete on *Seven And The Ragged Tiger* – which was produced by Alex Sadkin, whose previous work had included projects for Grace Jones and Talking Heads – Duran Duran announced that the album would be released in November and would be preceded by a single, 'Union

Of The Snake', at the end of October. Despite the chart-topping success of 'Is There Something I Should Know?', reviews of the first single from the new project were not promising. 'Fastidiously humourless, 'Union Of The Snake' threatens to never end: chattering guitars find nothing much to say; the drumming sounds like something that just drifted in from the soundtrack of a documentary on carpet laying; the bass line pouts heavily and Simon Le Bon's warthog vocal hangs over the musical rubble like a dark pall of smoke over a crematorium,' ran Allan Jones's dismissal of the single in *Melody Maker*. 'It's a case of too many cooks (in too many places) complicating the recipe,' wrote *Smash Hits*' Ian Birch. 'The idea is to make a glossy, international, funk-drenched dance number but the result is a clutter of effects that drown out the song.' In *Sounds*, Johnny Waller was less circumspect and described the release as 'over-produced, over-ambitious, meaningless nonsense'.

Despite the number one success of 'Is There Something I Should Know?', 'Union Of The Snake' confounded expectations that it would do the same when it entered the UK singles chart at number four, before rising to a peak position of number three in its second week of sales. While it sold considerably less copies than 'Is There Something I Should Know?' 'Union Of The Snake' nevertheless managed to sell around a quarter of a million singles in the UK by the end of the year, and earned the band *Smash Hits*' Best Video award in December. In recognition of the increasing importance of video in music, *Sounds* reviewed a selection of the current crop of videos in April and found themselves cautiously impressed by 'Is There Something I Should Know?': 'A promising start with heavy hints of surrealism, but rather too much emphasis on Simon miming in his smart blue outfit in between the good bits which include Magritte-style "half men" in bowler hats.'

Video had remained crucial to Duran Duran's vision of how they should present themselves visually, and the band's love affair with the medium had already led to the release of an eleven-track video album, *Duran Duran*, in March. 'With preposterous pretensions to sophistication yet the instincts of naughty schoolboys, they make pop equivalents of James Bond movies – every punter's fantasy pools win,' wrote *Melody Maker*'s Steve Sutherland of the video release, 'you can't help feeling, as you watch them grapple with beauties on some tropical isle, that if you were them, you'd do much the same.'

The video for 'Union Of The Snake' saw Duran Duran take a step back from the surreal, quasi-intellectual stylings of 'Is There Something I Should Know?' and return to the epic themes of adventure that they had explored to great effect in the now-classic videos to accompany 'Hungry Like The Wolf' and 'Save A Prayer'. In 'Union Of The Snake' the band are seen trekking across a post-apocalyptic desert landscape where they are observed by a half-man, half-lizard creature as they pursue mystery women, descend to the depths of the earth by way of a special lift full of birds where they find a settlement, are given a map, engage in a great deal of stylised and heavily-choreographed fighting, and escape back to the desert, the underground lair apparently exploding behind them as the band make their escape. 'It takes a few looks to really work out what's going on,' Simon Le Bon admitted to *Melody Maker*'s Steve Sutherland in October, 'it's a sort of journey of discovery I suppose.'

Seven And The Ragged Tiger was released hot on the heels of 'Union Of The Snake' and generally received a savaging at the hands of the music press. 'Their aim, as I understand it, was to bring Chic and punk together, but it is, of course, nothing of the sort,' wrote the *NME*'s Paolo Hewitt. 'It is the grandeur of deceit, all chunky, boring rhythms and precious little melody, bolstered by the big sound and production of Bowie's 'Let's Dance'.' *Record Mirror* and *Sounds* both awarded *Seven And The Ragged Tiger* one star of a possible five: "Seven And The Ragged Tiger' is bad. Not bad as in naughty and nasty, but bad as in pathetic, useless, no good,' declared Jim Reid in *Record Mirror*. 'It's pretentious, pompous and possibly the first chapter in their decline.' 'I should hit it for six with a few sweet witticisms,' added Dave McCullough in *Sounds*, 'and what do I feel? I feel pity for Duran Duran. It's as if 'Seven And The Rancid Ravings' is so assuredly awful it breaks new ground in badness.' But not everyone was so quick to dismiss the release. In a reasoned and thoughtful review for *Melody Maker*, Michael Oldfield found much to admire in Duran Duran's latest direction. 'Having been given (seemingly) endless amounts of time and money to make 'Seven And The Ragged Tiger', it's a pleasure to report that they have refused the offer to cross over into safe pop, all sulky pouts and moody looks, and come up with an album of unrelenting Eighties dance music,' to which he added, "Seven And The Ragged Tiger' restores danger and menace to a band that was veering dangerously close to the insipid.' *Smash Hits*' Peter Martin was also positive. 'The arrangements are watertight, the melodies razor sharp and every number is drenched with the mystique of a James Bond theme,' he noted. 'A classy concoction. It should ensure that they'll be around for quite a while yet.'

Seven And The Ragged Tiger entered the UK albums chart at number one, and within two weeks it had achieved platinum status for sales of over 300,000 records, staying in the Top 10 for the remainder of 1983 and in the album charts for the best part of a year. 'The critics tried to kill this band and, in not succeeding, it just shows how powerless they are even though they hold themselves in such high esteem,' Andy Taylor told the *NME* with satisfaction the same year. But Taylor's robust attitude would prove short-lived. By the time of the release of Duran Duran's next studio album, 1986's *Notorious*, he had left the band in a blaze of animosity. At the end of 1983, however, that was all in the future, and not only did *Seven And The Ragged Tiger* become a huge international hit for Duran Duran, the band also enjoyed two further UK hit singles from the album in 1984. 'New Moon On Monday' was a Top 10 single when it spent two successive weeks at number nine in the UK singles chart in February, and 'The Reflex' provided Duran Duran with their second, and final, UK number one single when it spent four consecutive weeks at the top of the chart in May 1984.

Although still pitched as arch rivals by the media, 1983 saw Duran Duran and Spandau Ballet's respective musical journeys move further apart, to the extent that such parallels were essentially meaningless. Since embarking on the funk trajectory they had so successfully explored on their 1982 hit 'Instinction', Spandau Ballet had continued to move in a blue-eyed soul direction that they harnessed again, and to even greater effect, with the release of 'Lifeline', which spent a fortnight at a UK singles chart peak of seven in October 1982. In February 1983, Spandau Ballet released another new single, 'Communication', which Nick Rhodes was called upon to review in *Melody Maker*. 'Their first release with the help of Imagination producers Tony Swain and Steve Jolley – a definite positive move,' Rhodes noted approvingly, 'melodies come over well, good for clubs, good for radio.' 'Communication' reached number twelve, but it was Spandau Ballet's next single which was to become a milestone in their history. Four weeks after Duran Duran topped the charts with 'Is There Something I Should Know?', Spandau Ballet knocked David Bowie's 'Let's Dance' from the top spot with the title track from their new album, 'True', which then spent four consecutive weeks at the top of the charts in April and May.

Released in March, it took nine weeks – seven of which were spent in the Top 10 – for Spandau Ballet's *True* album to reach number one in the UK albums chart in May, hitting the top in the same week that their single of the same name topped the UK singles chart. *True* certified platinum for 300,000 albums sold before the end of May and became a fixture in the UK album charts, where it remained for the best part of the next two years. 'Music has changed, become more visual, more glossy. There's no division now between pop and what used to be called progressive, more credible stuff,' Martin Kemp told *Melody Maker* in June in an echo of Duran Duran's similarly image-orientated manifesto. 'Duran Duran have done very well for themselves. They've stood the test of time and proved their worth. They write good songs – good luck to them,' Spandau Ballet's John Keeble told *Smash Hits* in August. 'There's obviously rivalry between us but there's plenty of room for both of us.'

Spandau Ballet's latest turn came with significantly less focus on the electronic elements which had underpinned some of their previous work, and they moved away from the club-orientated focus of their previous albums in favour of the smoother soul sound that had always been an influence. That transition echoed a similar change in the work of another UK act in the process of reinventing themselves to similarly spectacular commercial success. Although their 1983 was spent mostly on the road, capitalising on the success of their album *New Gold Dream (81-82-83-84)*, Simple Minds' next four album releases would each top the UK charts, in the process establishing the band as one of the most successful international artists of the eighties.

Where Spandau Ballet turned to soul for their new direction, Simple Minds turned to rock, and the first release to display the latter's new intent was their sole 1983 single, 'Waterfront'. 'Scottish songsters suffering from acute Heavy-Metal-Syndrome,' reported *Record Mirror* in their review of 'Waterfront' in November. 'Built around a shuddering backbeat shot through with guitar chords that will take your head off, and overlaid with those haunting keyboard lines, 'Waterfront' is remarkable even by Simple Minds' own high standards,' declared Mark Steels in *Smash Hits*. 'Pretentious, pompous and progressive,' proclaimed the *NME*'s Paolo Hewitt, less encouragingly. 'Simple Minds are (simply) mind over matter. And that's the matter.' 'Waterfront' spent ten weeks in the UK singles chart between November 1983 and January 1984 and peaked at number thirteen at the start of December in the wake of Simple Minds' first *Top of the Pops* appearance for over a year. 'We've changed a lot the past year, but certainly not in a contrived way,' Jim Kerr told to *Smash Hits* in November. 'We just constantly played live, moving towards this heavier sound and suddenly it's like we've woken up and found we're there.'

Depeche Mode, 1984.

1983.2 Eurythmics / Yazoo / Reset Records / The Assembly / The Flying Pickets / Depeche Mode

THE RELEASE OF EURYTHMICS' *Sweet Dreams (Are Made Of This)* album in the first week of January 1983 set an immediate high bar for the new year. 'A sparkling, gem-studded collection of the finest material that the Eurythmics can currently muster, 'Sweet Dreams' is all that I hoped for and more. Go out and buy one of the most important albums of '83,' applauded *Melody Maker*'s Paul Strange on January 22nd. The band's Dave Stewart agreed. 'I would say that our album *Sweet Dreams (Are Made Of This)* is one of the most important records of 1983,' he declared in an interview for *Record Mirror* in February. 'To us, the lyrics are so cutting and poignant, and it's been very carefully structured. We're not interested in creating anything unless it's really powerful.' But for all of Dave Stewart's optimism and swagger, the success of *Sweet Dreams (Are Made of This)* had never been a certainty.

Eurythmics' Annie Lennox and Dave Stewart had previously been part of The Tourists, with whom they had enjoyed Top 10 single successes with 'I Only Want To Be With You' and 'So Good To Be Back Home Again' in 1979 and 1980, respectively, before the group subsequently spilt in February 1981. 'We were greatly relieved by the decision to call it a day. Our musical attitudes were becoming gradually polarised as well as having to cope with our steadily deteriorating personal relationships,' explained Lennox in a press release issued at the time, which announced not only the demise of The Tourists but also the genesis of Eurythmics, originally conceived as a collective project. 'Though Stewart and Lennox are "the nucleus", Conny Plank is on one-third of the royalties and will do some performing as well as all the production,' reported the *NME*, who also revealed that Lennox, Plank and Stewart had been recording at Plank's studio in Germany with a number of 'satellite members' of Eurythmics, including Blondie drummer Clem Burke, D.A.F.'s Robert Görl, and Can's Holger Czukay and Jaki Liebezeit.

The result of those initial sessions, Eurythmics' debut album *In The Garden*, failed to chart upon its release in October 1981, and of the two singles released from the record – 'Never Gonna Cry Again' and 'Belinda' – only the former enjoyed any sort of chart activity when it spent two weeks at a peak position of sixty-three in the UK singles chart in July of that year. 'The arrangements are delicately hypnotic; the duo's writing goes for a sophistication that doesn't try too hard, soothingly evocative of moods and atmospheres,' wrote an encouraging Paul Du Noyer in his review of the album for the *NME*. 'And while the melodies are strong, Annie Lennox's vocals are mellow and understated – making for an often intriguing combination.' 'I saw the garden as a place of growth and death – a cycle – and I see life as an on-going thing of birth and re-birth, total circles,' Lennox told *Melody Maker*'s Paul Strange in December 1981. 'And I felt that *In The Garden* was a growth place for me and Dave as well, a nice place to be.'

'This Is The House' and 'The Walk', the first singles to be taken from *Sweet Dreams (Are Made Of This)* – which saw Eurythmics slimmed down to just Lennox and Stewart – also failed to become hits after their releases in April and June 1982, respectively, and a third single, 'Love Is A Stranger', only reached number fifty-four at the end of the year, despite some encouraging notices from the music press. 'Quite tasty this,' *Melody Maker*'s Adam Sweeting wrote of 'Love Is A Stranger', while *Sounds*' Johnny Waller described the single as 'quite possibly the best slice of cultured pure pop in the pile and deserves to be a hit'. 'Not the subversive slab we'd been promised the Eurythmics were concocting although bubbling underneath the unremitting "quality" production this has a savage hook that could launch this into the hearts of millions,' added *ZigZag*.

Anxious to fit Eurythmics into a convenient category, the press were quick to identify superficial parallels with Yazoo. 'When the Eurythmics' Dave Stewart heard Yazoo's 'Only You' he nearly flipped. For he and partner Annie Lennox had been locked away for some 18 months working on their electronic bluesy sound and it looked like they'd been beaten to it,' wrote Simon Tebbutt in *Record Mirror*'s first feature on the Eurythmics in December 1982. 'Ours is a much more organic sound. Not the deliberate contrast between the minimal electronics and the soulful voice,' Stewart responded patiently. 'If you were to play a Yazoo track and then a Eurythmics one, you'll find there's a very different feeling,' a similarly patient Lennox asserted in an interview for *Melody Maker* the following month. '[Alison Moyet] sings in a certain way and my voice is completely different.' 'I really like the Eurythmics,' Alison Moyet told *Record Mirror* in July 1983. 'I think Annie Lennox has got a brilliant voice. It's got a direction to it, it works a song, it doesn't just sing along to it with a bit of an edge. She's a far better singer than I am.'

Sweet Dreams (Are Made Of This) was released to a round of encouraging reviews at the same time as a new single, the album's title track, 'Sweet Dreams (Are Made of This)'. 'Annie Lennox once told me Eurythmics were driven on by sex and love, which – next to money – are the most motivating things in people's lives,' recalled *Sounds*' Johnny Waller in his review of the long-player. 'This album virtually fulfils that motivation and interprets that emotion, combining the thrilling anticipation of pre-sex excitement and the unrivalled contentment of post-sex relaxation,' Waller continued. 'For mere music, that's not bad going.' The 'Sweet Dreams (Are Made of This)' single, however, received short shrift at the hands of Waller's *Sounds* colleague Edwin Pouncey the same week. 'A lifeless plod of a song that drones on like a flood warning siren,' Pouncey wrote, while in *Melody Maker*, Duran Duran's Nick Rhodes, reviewing the singles the following week, came to a similar conclusion: 'It passes without noticing. I've already forgotten how it goes and don't expect to be remembering it in the near future.'

Fortunately for Eurythmics, Radio 1's reaction to the 'Sweet Dreams (Are Made Of This)' single was significantly more positive than their counterparts in the press, and the station's enthusiastic support was enough to earn the release a place in the lower reaches of the Top 40, and the duo their first appearance on *Top of the Pops*. Eurythmics' appearance on the show in the last week of February – mainstream Britain's first glimpse of Annie Lennox's sleekly contemporary androgynous image and Dave Stewart's maverick eccentricity – was enough to win the hearts of a nation, although the band failed to understand why they had caused such a furore. 'There's nothing new or shocking about androgyny,' Lennox told *The Face* later in the year, 'there are obvious people like Bowie and Boy George. That's wishful thinking. I don't fit that bill.'

Nevertheless, image and presentation were crucial to the success of Eurythmics, not just because of how Lennox, in particular, presented herself, but because of why she chose to do so. 'When I started wearing mannish clothes on stage it was to detract from what people had come to expect from women singers, the height of which was Debbie Harry, who I loved. But I felt I couldn't be a sex symbol. That's not me. So I tried to find a way to transcend that emphasis on sexuality,' Lennox told *Rolling Stone*. 'Ironically, a different kind of sexuality emerged from that. I wasn't particularly concerned with bending genders. I simply wanted to get away from wearing cutesy-pie miniskirts and tacky cutaway push-ups.'

The week following Eurythmics' *Top of the Pops* debut, 'Sweet Dreams (Are Made Of This)' leaped to number twenty-one on its slow climb to a peak of number two in March, part of a fourteen-week chart run which also saw *Top of the Pops* air the single's striking video on two separate occasions. Video was a medium which fascinated both Annie Lennox and Dave Stewart and had quickly become a crucial way for Eurythmics to present themselves. While 'Sweet Dreams (Are Made Of This)' wasn't the duo's first excursion into video, it was nevertheless an important glimpse into the visual side of Eurythmics' presentation, and also into the mischievous side of Lennox and Stewart's personalities. The video features the duo in a record company boardroom, dressed in suits and making forceful business points, holding yoga poses, and footage on a boat and in a field, where Eurythmics are surrounded by cows who also appear in further scenes in the record company boardroom. 'It's a bit off the wall,' Dave Stewart conceded in an an interview with *Smash Hits* later. 'Everybody is scrabbling around the world looking for things; businessmen looking for more money, gurus looking for more spiritual awareness and so on, so the video is just symbolising that, but it's up to people to look at it and interpret it how they want. Of course, to some people it might look like a pair of nutcases messing around in a boat and freaking out in a field with a bunch of cows.'

The perfect synergy of the various elements that made up the release of the 'Sweet Dreams (Are Made Of This)' single – the song, the artwork, the video, the band's performances – fed directly into the the public appetite for style and presentation which was starting to define the eighties. On the coattails of the success of the 'Sweet Dreams (Are Made Of This)' single, the *Sweet Dreams (Are Made Of This)* album followed a similarly startling trajectory and reached a UK albums chart peak of three, earning silver, and then gold, sales awards in recognition of sales of 60,000 and 100,000 albums by the end of March. Whether they liked it or not – and mostly they didn't – Eurythmics had become bona fide pop stars. 'When you're famous, it's a bit like having an extra leg,' Annie Lennox told *Smash Hits*' Neil Tennant later. 'You can't forget about it because other people don't let you forget about it – there's always an extra thing around you.'

Eurythmics' record label, RCA, followed the success of 'Sweet Dreams (Are Made Of This)' with a reissue of 'Love Is A Stranger', which reached number six in the UK singles chart at the end of April. Talking to *The Face*, Annie Lennox described 'Love Is A Stranger' as an 'emotionally sadomasochistic' song: 'It's not the love act, nothing so literal, but it is taken from my experience. It's about falling for people who never want you and feeling ambivalent towards the people who do want you. I've hurt people and felt totally cold about them but when it's happened to me... I can't take it.'

With four singles already taken from the *Sweet Dreams (Are Made Of This)* album, Eurythmics were soon ready to release the first music from their next album project, and in June announced that they would release a new single, 'Who's That Girl?', at the start of July. 'This single shows that they'll be able to build on their 'Sweet Dreams' album and give their image more substance. I think I see a career in the making here,' reported Hugh Fielder in an optimistic review for *Sounds*. 'Already my favourite Eurythmics single,' enthused *Smash Hits*' Dave Rimmer, who also admitted to concerns over the single cover: 'Who's that bloke is what most folk'll wonder when they clock Annie's latest look.'

'Who's That Girl?' played directly into Eurythmics' themes of blurred androgyny that had served the duo so well across the *Sweet Dreams (Are Made Of This)* project, and the new single's sleeve featured a characteristically tousled Dave Stewart, dressed in white, posing with a bequiffed and dark-haired Annie Lennox in black shirt and tie, channelling the spirit of Elvis Presley with a roguish, and highly masculine, Teddy Boy look. 'Yes, well, the make-up's all very clever, but what the blazes does it have to do with the music?' demanded *Record Mirror*'s Paul Sexton in his review of 'Who's That Girl?' 'Possible answer: it's supposed to make us forget this tedium which has none of the winning melody of their previous hits.' 'Lennox's voice, an exceptionally rich and fiery instrument, is capable of leaving lasting burns. All it needs is the right song,' declared the *NME*'s Chris Bohn in his own review. 'This cautious electronic simulation of sap soul isn't it.'

For all of the caution about the single's merits in certain quarters of the press, radio was not in agreement and, with Radio 1's full support, 'Who's

That Girl?' soared into the Top 30 after just one week on sale and spent the next five weeks in the Top 10, where it peaked at number three at the very end of July. *Top of the Pops* showed the video twice, setting up Eurythmics' forthcoming album admirably, although the band themselves remained tight-lipped, giving little away. 'I could say three words to you to describe it,' Dave Stewart teased *Melody Maker*'s Helen Fitzgerald when she asked about the band's new material during an interview in July, 'but that would be giving the game away.' Nevertheless Stewart did provide some tantalising clues as to their new material: 'The backing – the rhythm is going to be quite different, darker, but the songs will still have the soul element of Annie's strong vocal textures. There'll be lots of melody as well – it'll be like a combination of various polemic musical devices that should be quite startling.'

Eurythmics' next single, 'Right By Your Side', came at the end of October. 'The Eurythmics are definitely sticking their necks out with this one,' admitted *Smash Hits*' Peter Martin. 'Annie's sweet soul voice commandeers the unique electro calypso backing that also boasts a shiny African juju guitar and the whole shebang sounds really fab.' 'Eurythmics have bravely forsaken the smooth seductive tones of 'Sweet Dreams' and 'Who's That Girl' for a South Sea Island dance number complete with steel drums effect,' marvelled *Sounds*' Johnny Waller, who added, 'A vast leap forward for the Eurythmics in terms of versatility – and fun for all the family!' 'This is gorgeous,' declared Blancmange's Stephen Luscombe, reviewing the singles for *Melody Maker*, and bandmate Neil Arthur concurred: 'As usual, lovely melodies, arrangements and production, Annie's voice wandering like a beautiful multi-coloured snake through the music, whooping and curling.'

At the end of October, Eurythmics also announced that they would be releasing a third album, *Touch*, in the middle of November, while Dave Stewart continued to marvel at the duo's musical development since recording *Sweet Dreams (Are Made Of This)* on an eight-track TEAC recorder in a rented room above a picture framing workshop in North London's Chalk Farm. 'People think that album [*Sweet Dreams (Are Made Of This)*] is so high tech,' Stewart told the *NME*. 'But we couldn't even afford a claptrap – the classic disco thing, you know, that goes ckkk-ckkk-ckkk. It's just me and Annie banging on the wall with a handful of picture frames. If we'd had the money, of course we would have used a claptrap. But not having it made us a lot more inventive.'

In addition to access to bigger studios and better technology, *Touch* also saw Eurythmics working in a different, more spontaneous and organic way: 'I think what Annie and I wanted really was to go straight in and get on tape the very first thing, as if it's the demo, but carry on working on it. Often when we'd made tapes before we'd found the demos were like eleven times better than the actual master – the master sounded blanded out and nicely in proportion but had lost that initial spontaneity,' Dave Stewart explained to *Melody Maker* in an interview which ran the same week the album was released. 'That's why it took such a short time,' he added. 'We just went straight from nothing to the master. In that way, I think we've captured on this album a particular feeling of freshness and enthusiasm straight on the tape, in the sound of it, in the actual way it's mixed, and also in Annie's vocals and all the playing.' 'It's like a piece of clay I suppose, that you just play with until a shape starts to appear,' Annie Lennox speculated in the same interview, 'and from that you get the idea of what kind of thing you've got and what's gonna develop from that.'

If Lennox and Stewart had experienced any vestiges of doubt about their new material they needn't have worried. 'What's required now is an album that proves they're something more than flavour of the month,' cautioned the *NME*'s Paul Du Noyer in his review of *Touch*. 'And bless their carrot tops and platform boots, they've done it.' 'One of the most classy albums to be released for ages,' agreed Lisa Anthony in a nine-out-of-ten review for *Smash Hits*. '"Touch' is a perfect, carefully balanced tonic for the newly conscripted troops,' applauded *Melody Maker*'s Paul Strange. 'Dave and Annie have done it again.' Only *Record Mirror* was uncertain about Eurythmics' latest chapter. 'Perhaps I was expecting just too much… 'Touch' promised the world,' pondered Graham K. Smith. 'Promised, but failed to deliver.'

'At the beginning of Eurythmics I did say to RCA that we wanted to be successful in a way that people wouldn't know what the next record was going to be,' Dave Stewart had told *Sounds* earlier in the year. 'It's a bit like Bowie, nobody ever has a clue what he's going to do next.' In the eyes of the public, *Touch* was an immediate success, and the album entered the UK chart at number eight a week after release, where it bobbed around the Top 20 for the rest of the year before climbing back into the Top 10 in January on its way to spending two weeks at number one in February, and the best part of a year in the album chart, courtesy of the Top 10 success of a January 1984 single, 'Here Comes The Rain Again'.

For all their success the previous year, Yazoo were also struggling with their newfound fame and success. While a February news story in the *NME* wasn't explicit about the situation that Vince Clarke and Alison Moyet now found themselves in, it did sound a note of caution that things might not be as they should be. 'Yazoo's Alf is set to form a new band later in the year, once her current recording commitments with Vince have been completed,' reported the piece, which allegedly stemmed from an informal conversation Moyet had had with an *NME* writer who quoted the singer as saying, 'As we're not planning to play live at all this year, Yazoo will probably only take up about two months of the twelve, so I've got to find something to do with the rest of my time.' By the following week, Mute Records had put out an announcement to address the situation: 'The blues band project is still on the cards,' read the statement, 'but Alf has decided that outside projects should take a back seat until the Yazoo album is done. That should be in about two or two and a half months, although it might be quicker since they've made fast progress already and they've only been in the studio for 12 days.'

The first new music from those springtime recording sessions was announced as a new single, 'Nobody's Diary', in the middle of May, alongside the news that Yazoo's 1982 debut album *Upstairs At Eric's* had recently been certified platinum for sales of 300,000 copies in the UK. 'Nobody's Diary' was an immediate hit and entered the UK singles chart at twenty, climbing the chart for the next three weeks until it reached a peak position of three in June, part of almost three months in the charts, seven weeks of which the single spent in the Top 40. 'We've waited a long time for this – I quite like it, but I would like now to hear a different kind of backing track,' admitted Radio 1 DJ David 'Kid' Jensen, reviewing 'Nobody's Diary' for *Melody Maker*, but nevertheless adding, 'I'm sure it'll be a big, big hit.' 'A sad love-gone-sour song written by Alf,' noted *Smash Hits'* Neil Tennant. 'Strong on emotion and weak on melody but the combination of ringing synths and bluesy singing is still a winner.' 'A cleverly infectious happy song which Alf manages to inject passion and heartbreak into, by virtue of the "love's labours's lost" lyrics,' noted *Sounds'* Carole Linfield with enthusiasm.

The week following the release of 'Nobody's Diary' the *NME* announced that Yazoo were to split. 'After 15 months together as Yazoo, the duo have decided to go their separate ways, at least for the time being,' ran the story, alongside a quote from Moyet to clarify the situation: 'Towards the end of the first album the atmosphere was getting heavy and we weren't enjoying it too much. We decided the initial excitement had gone, and we've both got other things we want to do.' The following week the story appeared across the rest of the music press. 'No official statement has been issued yet but the two are understood to be parting on good terms,' noted *Smash Hits*, while *Record Mirror* reported 'Vince Clarke will probably form his own label and work more as a producer and songwriter. Partner Alison Moyet will be doing more blues numbers like those she was singing before joining Yazoo.'

Alison Moyet appeared on the cover of the *NME* in the last week of May, a chance for her to present her side of the story to the paper's Don Watson: 'The main reason for the split, I suppose, is simply that the magic that we had at first just seems to have gone. I mean, when we started off, it was just so spontaneous,' Moyet explained. '"Only You' was the first track we ever did; it was just straight into the studio and on with it. 'Don't Go' was the second. It was all new and fresh and exciting. As you get successful, though, you're expected to bring out singles and you're expected to bring out albums and it all begins to lose its sparkle… I really loved playing live, but I didn't feel that Yazoo worked terribly well as a live band,' Moyet continued. 'Then Vince decided that he didn't want to tour any more, and he didn't want to do any promotion work. So what people wanted us to do was leave Vince to work in the studio and have me going out, working and doing the interviews and the photo-sessions. Which was totally not on.'

In turn, Vince Clarke appeared on the cover of *Melody Maker*. 'The truth is that Yazoo happened by chance, happened very well and now doesn't happen any more,' Clarke told Paul Colbert for the piece. 'We did have a serious talk about it. We did talk about it quite a lot after the last album. She's become far more self-confident, she used to be terrible, no confidence in herself or her abilities… I think this album was more planned, and to be honest that's the way I like to work,' Clarke continued. 'It's not a "band" where you can jam and save the best take. If it's two people it needs to be worked out. For Alison that probably lost its spontaneity. I think it's because of her background in the blues, she likes spontaneity.'

Yazoo's swansong was their second and final album, *You And Me Both*, which was released in early July. 'Undiminished by a few minor quibbles and despite its posthumous release 'You And Me Both' is a record of loss, yearning, warmth, anger and defiance, and it stands as one of 1983's major achievements,' wrote Gavin Martin in a warm review for the *NME*, in which he described the release as 'a brave, ambitious work'. *Sounds*' Carole Linfield was equally supportive, writing, '"You And Me Both' is assured a status in the memory as a classic example of resonant pop, fun and yet not throwaway, deep but not depressing.' 'The uneasy musical balance between Vince Clarke and Alf Moyet was the whole point of Yazoo and it's sharply in focus here,' observed *Smash Hits*' Neil Tennant while awarding the release a positive seven-and-a-half out of ten. "You And Me Both' is a pointless album, perhaps even one that neither party wishes they had made,' decided *Record Mirror*'s John Shearlaw. 'Reeking strongly of effort and obligation the tracks are split down the middle – Moyet then Clarke on side one, Clarke then Moyet on side two. Very neat, very self-conscious.'

If there was any residual tension still remaining between Vince Clarke and Alison Moyet, neither party were admitting to it. 'There's no hard feelings between us, it's something we both wanted to do,' Moyet told *Record Mirror* in a cover feature in support of *You And Me Both* in July. 'If anything we get on better now than at the beginning.' 'I really want to do something with more of a band line up and gig a lot and do some recording,' Moyet told the *NME* in response to being asked what her immediate plans were. 'But basically, I just like the idea of liking every track that I do, just the joy of being able to put your heart into every song, which hasn't always been the case with Yazoo.' 'I'm starting a record label with my partner – Mr Radcliffe – and a studio,' reported Clarke when asked the same question by *Melody Maker*.

Sounds' Johnny Waller caught up with Vince Clarke at the end of July to find out more about Reset Records, Clarke's label partnership with Eric Radcliffe, to find the pair cautious about their initial plans: 'At the moment – for the first year – we want to keep Reset to just two artists, and we're aiming to do a track every six weeks, that's like two albums and six singles a year,' Clarke explained. 'We think this arrangement is truly splendid. At the moment we don't want to stretch ourselves too far too soon and will be concentrating on working with Robert Marlow and Peter Hewson. It's a case of small is beautiful for the time being.'

Robert Marlow came to the attention of Reset Records through Vince Clarke – Marlow had not only grown up with Clarke in Basildon, where the pair were friends and had been in bands together, but he had also played alongside Alison Moyet in her pre-Yazoo band The Vandals – and Peter Hewson through Eric Radcliffe. Reset signed the distribution and administration aspects of the label over to RCA and set about releasing three singles over the course of 1983 – Robert Marlow's 'The Face Of Dorian Gray' and 'I Just Want To Dance', and Peter Hewson's 'Take My Hand' – and one in 1984 – Marlow's 'Claudette' – but none were commercially successful, and

Clarke eventually handed the label over to Radcliffe in 1985 after forming Erasure with Andy Bell.

In 1983, however, while launching the Reset Records project, Vince Clarke and Eric Radcliffe were working on another project together: The Assembly. 'Vince is teaming up with EC Radcliffe, the co-producer of Yazoo's old albums, and they've called themselves The Assembly,' explained *Record Mirror* in October. 'The idea is to work with guest vocalists and they've so far recorded a single with ex-Undertones vocalist Feargal Sharkey. The as yet untitled single will be out in late October. An album is likely to follow, but nothing has yet been confirmed.' 'Feargal Sharkey became involved after a spurious gossip item in a paper speculated that he was working with Vince. They weren't, but both parties decided after reading it that it might be a good idea,' added a similar piece in *Sounds* the same week.

By the second half of October, The Assembly were ready to announce that their collaboration with Feargal Sharkey, a single entitled 'Never Never', was to be released on Mute Records at the end of the month. The three principles – Clarke, Radcliffe and Sharkey – appeared on the cover of the *NME* on October 29th and Gavin Martin interviewed the trio about the release for the accompanying feature. 'That was the main thing that rubbed off working with Alf, what a good singer means to a song, what a difference it makes,' Clarke began. 'You don't really appreciate a good singer until you've been in the same room listening to them. Like with Feargal it was great, I've never seen anyone taking singing so seriously. You can write lyrics and try to write some emotion into them, but until you get someone who can sing it with some emotion the benefit of the whole thing doesn't come across.' 'It was strange because with The Undertones we had this way of working that everyone criticised everyone else,' added Sharkey. 'Vince and Eric just left it up to me to decide. If they were all as easy as that I'd be well happy. I think it will surprise a lot of people both on my part and Vince's.'

'It's nice to see them all bounce straight back after the sad demise of their recent bands,' *Smash Hits'* Mark Steels announced in his review of 'Never Never' in November, adding, 'It sounds just like another Yazoo record except that Feargal lacks Alf's vocal range and passion.' *Record Mirror's* Graham K. Smith disagreed: 'The meeting of Vince and Feargal was obviously one of those perfect liaisons forged in heaven above, the ex-Undertoner stepping into Alf's vocal booth in a majestic fashion. The electronics are as understated and insinuative as ever and Mr Sharkey milks the tune without erring into overkill.' 'Never Never' is a song perfectly suited to the tremulous power of Sharkey's matured style,' declared the *NME*'s Charles Shaar Murray, 'everybody whose emotional life is either arid or messy will buy this record and play the shit out of it for months.'

By the end of November 'Never Never' was in the Top 5 of the UK singles chart, where it peaked at number four and sold around a quarter of a million singles for The Assembly, earning the trio a *Top of the Pops* performance. But Vince Clarke's year wasn't quite over. In the same week that 'Never Never' hit number four in the charts, an unlikely cover version of Yazoo's 'Only You' claimed a new entry at sixty for a cappella act The Flying Pickets. 'Scrupulously fashioned and very clever acapella arrangement of the Yazoo classic. The textures are smooth as ice, the harmonies crystal clear,' the *NME*'s Gavin Martin wrote of the single. A fortnight later, and with 'Never Never' still in the Top 10, The Flying Pickets' version of 'Only You' was at number one, a position it retained for five successive weeks, earning itself the coveted Christmas number one and sales of around half a million records.

While the spectre of Vince Clarke still cast a shadow over Depeche Mode – 'Our success last year was overshadowed by Yazoo's success,' Andy Fletcher admitted to the *NME*'s Mat Snow in March 1983 – the band's continued musical development was finally starting to widen the gap between the two parties. At the start of the year *Record Mirror* had interviewed an upbeat Depeche Mode, whose line-up was now expanded to include Alan Wilder, promoted from playing at the band's live shows to full band member. 'I'm optimistic about our material and the way we're going to progress and get stronger, but whether the material will sell as well is hard to say,' confessed Martin Gore as Depeche Mode announced their new single, 'Get The Balance Right', in January. 'I think it's a lot harder, more powerful and more direct,' added Gore of the new single. 'It's quite moody too.' 'It's about telling people to go their own way,' Dave Gahan told *Smash Hits*. 'It also takes a dig at people who like to be different just for the sake of it. You've got to reach the right balance between normality and insanity.'

'This is exactly the sort of single they do better than anyone else – a sweeping ditty of a melody, with clever arrangements and subtle little noises underneath,' reported an enthusiastic Johnny Waller in his review of 'Get The Balance Right' for *Sounds*, further declaring the track 'A brilliant pop song.' 'Maybe not the most instant record that the Mode have ever despatched but one that's rewarding enough in the synth-riff department to ensure chart status, and fascinating enough structurally to keep it around longer than most,' noted *Smash Hits'* similarly positive Fred Dellar around the release of 'Get The Balance Right' at the start of February.

'Get The Balance Right' entered the UK singles chart at thirty-two after its first week of sales and peaked at thirteen three weeks later on the way to spending eight weeks in the charts. 'Luckily we're in the position where we know we're going to get a certain amount of radio play just on the strength of reputation, which means that you can take slightly more of a risk than maybe a band putting out their first single,' Alan Wilder told the *NME* in March, and in the case of 'Get The Balance Right' that position and reputation extended to *Top of the Pops,* who booked Depeche Mode to perform on the show at the very start of the single's chart journey in February. Despite Martin Gore's half-hearted attempt to make it appear that he was using a hammer to strike percussion sounds, with the exception of Dave Gahan's leather trousers, Depeche Mode's *Top of the Pops* performance of 'Get The Balance Right' presented a band looking for all the world like they had chosen their clothes from their mothers' mail order catalogues.

Sartorial considerations aside, it was a more thoughtful, considered, and mature Depeche Mode who hit the promotional trail around the release of 'Get The Balance Right'. 'We want to get more into the album-orientated market but it's still important for us to have [singles] hits. Bands like Echo & The Bunnymen and Simple Minds do well in both charts,' Martin Gore explained to *Smash Hits* in March. 'We just want to produce a really fine album that will hopefully establish us as a major act. Another year like the last two should seal our success and enable us to stick around for quite a while,' he added hopefully.

A second 1983 single, 'Everything Counts', followed in the middle of July and attracted another eclectic round of reviews. 'Dependable as the postman, Depeche Mode deliver another little packet of impeccable pop which I was happily prepared to hate, but couldn't,' admitted *Melody Maker.* 'The contents are as expected: a whacking great thud of a beat with twiddly bits jumping all round it; a nagging chorus; rich vocal contrasts; a thoughtful production and an arrangement that guarantees the final sparkle.' 'Depeche Mode have perfected the art of making disposable singles. Like candy floss it melts in your mouth when you think you've sunk your teeth into something substantial. While it seems musically sophisticated their melodic sense seems to have deserted them,' mused Mike Gardner in *Record Mirror.*

Nevertheless 'Everything Counts' scored Depeche Mode a number six hit in the second half of August, matching their previously most successful chart single 'See You', which had peaked at the same position in February the previous year. *Top of the Pops* were again supportive, showing the 'Everything Counts' video early in the single's chart run, and then booking a performance a fortnight later when the single entered the Top 10. The band's presentation on *Top of the Pops* was more uniform than some of their previous appearances and saw Gahan in a jacket, shirt and tie, and Fletcher and Wilder in striped shirts. A particularly cherubic-looking Martin Gore was topless behind the only synthesiser on stage, Andy Fletcher and Alan Wilder miming with a shawm (a type of oboe) and a xylophone respectively. While the sounds of both those instruments did feature on 'Everything Counts', in both cases they appeared on the record as samples, rather than having been played organically. 'We could be a conventional band if we wanted to,' Andy Fletcher had told *Smash Hits* earlier in the year, 'but really, we're not interested in the instruments, just the sounds they make. We still think synthesisers produce far more interesting sounds than traditional instruments, so we'll carry on using them.'

Depeche Mode released their third album, *Construction Time Again*, in August, and the release attracted some of the best reviews of the band's career to date. 'Basildon boys who sing pretty electro pop songs about love, right? Wrong,' declared *Smash Hits*' Peter Martin. 'The songs are still electronically based, but the brilliantly melodic and bouncy edge is contrasted by a brooding 'Tin Drum'-type sparseness. A brave departure.' 'This LP is so good, it cannot be described in relation to the previous Depeche albums, which now seem to be mere sketches compared to this masterpiece,' announced Johnny Waller in his maximum five-star review for *Sounds*. 'Make no mistake, this is truly subversive music… 'Construction Time Again' is the most surprising album this year. Quite simply, it's also one of the best.' Betty Page also awarded *Construction Time Again* five out of a possible five stars in her review for *Record Mirror*: 'This album will surprise a lot of people,' she wrote. 'The tunes are still pure and simple, but their machinery's gone into top gear to give the sound an underlying sinister feel… There's a real maturity in all departments, especially in the richer textures they've discovered.' 'Easily their best yet,' applauded the *NME*'s Mat Snow. 'The sounds and textures Mode's Gore, Fletcher and Wilder coax from their synthesisers and associated hardware are so rich and various that Messrs Heaven, League and Clarke appear by comparison someone primitive.'

And for once Depeche Mode were in agreement. 'We've got a really unique sound now, no one else sounds like us – especially our latest stuff – and we're really improving,' Andy Fletcher told *Sounds'* Johnny Waller in advance of the release of *Construction Time Again*. 'This album should be the one really, it'll be one of the albums of the year, I think.' 'We feel a lot more confident now – and I think it shows in the new album, it comes across more,' added Dave Gahan. 'I feel a lot more confident about doing my vocals now, we've moved on so far from our first album.' Interestingly, in the interviews the band gave around the release of *Construction Time Again*, neither they or the interviewers made much of the reasons for Depeche Mode's new, tougher and more textured sound.

Recorded at John Foxx's recently opened studio The Garden in London's Shoreditch, and produced by Daniel Miller with the band, the album saw Depeche Mode introduced to engineer Gareth Jones, whose input was crucial. 'We used a new engineer, Gareth, who showed so much enthusiasm, which was missing with the last album. If no one is sharing any enthusiasm with us in the studio it's impossible to record a good album,' Alan Wilder told *Record Mirror* in September. Jones, along with Depeche Mode producer Daniel Miller, was instrumental in introducing the band to the possibilities of the latest sampling technology. 'We used the E-mu Emulator and the Synclavier extensively from *Construction Time Again* onwards,' Miller remembers today, 'we didn't sample other records though, instead we used found sounds and sampled unusual instruments. Of the two we preferred to use the Synclavier as it had a much longer sampling time and much better sound quality.' Consequently Depeche Mode were sent out onto the streets of London to collect sounds for sampling, Andy Fletcher recalling 'smashing corrugated iron and old cars' in an interview for *Melody Maker* the following year.

Depeche Mode released a third and final single from *Construction Time Again* in September. The 'Love In Itself' single featured a remixed version of the original album track and was released to another round of positive reviews. 'A fabulous pop song that purrs with the humanity and sex and prowess and power that has always lain dormant inside their machines just waiting to be discovered,' was Lynden Barber's enthusiastic take on the single in *Melody Maker*, in which he also recognised that Depeche Mode were travelling on an important trajectory: 'There's an obvious maturing process going on here, a growing toughness that doesn't sacrifice their vulnerability as much as make it seem more touching, more acceptable.' The *NME* also picked up on the band's evolution in their review the same week: 'In 1983 power will come not from the barrel of a gun but the knowledge stored in a microchip. 'Love In Itself' catches Depeche Mode in transition from lovesick schoolboys to men made aware they hold the future in their hands.'

ON JANUARY 26TH, 1983 New Order played a one-off hometown concert at the Haçienda in Manchester. 'They've thrown off the shackles of Joy Division. They're creating music that is of a new order: new in its direction and ordered in its rich discipline. In fact, New Order are finally living up to their name,' reported an enthusiastic Frank Worrall in a review of the show for *Melody Maker* in the first week of February, to which he tantalisingly added, 'New Order have suddenly become the greatest band in the world.' In the same week, *Smash Hits* were the first to announce that New Order had completed work on their second album, *Power, Corruption & Lies*, which would be released later that month.

In fact the first new music to come from the reinvigorated New Order arrived in March with the release of one of electronic music's greatest singles, 'Blue Monday', although the music press entirely failed to recognise the magic of the track upon its initial release. The *NME*'s Julie Burchill was the first to review the single, and set a trend for her peers when she declared, 'It calls itself a double A side but it's a double B side.' *Smash Hits*' David Hepworth's review was the next to be published. 'New Order have dumped moody, repetitive guitars in favour of moody, repetitive synths and a drum kit with a pronounced stutter,' Hepworth reported. 'After the first twenty minutes or so, it starts to cause a tense, nervous headache.' 'The old-New Order's skittering squall of rumpled guitars is mostly off-menu. Like a well-produced backing track, this. Too much trouble spent on the packaging and not enough on the product,' was Dave Anderson's take on the single in *Sounds*. Soft Cell's Marc Almond, reviewing the singles for *Melody Maker,* also failed to identify the pioneering spirit of 'Blue Monday'. 'This is a boring old standard electro-disco riff with a few standard electronic effects thrown in, put over a wet, weary, soulless vocal totally devoid of any passion whatsoever and wrapped in a suitably annoying Factory package,' Almond declared. 'They're doing something new for them but it's very, very dated. It would be preferable to have your head run over by a steamroller – both give you a headache but at least the steamroller ends it quickly.'

New Order marked the release of 'Blue Monday' with a one-off London show at the Brixton Ace, where *Melody Maker*'s Lynden Barber was significantly more encouraging about the band's emerging electronic sensibility than Marc Almond had been in the same paper. 'No longer dogged by past associations and inclinations, New Order have not only followed the routes signposted by the sublime 'Everything's Gone Green' and 'Temptation', but are fruitfully exploiting the vistas that lay beyond, tapping the surges of electricity that were unleashed by Kraftwerk, Moroder, DAF and Suicide and spitting them out with an intense self-assurance that borders on a strange sense of possession,' Barber announced confidently.

Undeterred by the underwhelming reviews, or by the fact that at almost seven-and-a-half minutes long 'Blue Monday' was inherently unsuitable for daytime radio play, New Order's escalating fanbase ensured that the single entered the UK singles chart at thirty-nine, from where it steadily climbed over the next five weeks to an initial peak of number twelve at the end of April. The success of the single also earned New Order their first appearance on *Top of the Pops*. 'We did get asked to play on *Top of the Pops*,' recalled Peter Hook in his memoir *Substance*. 'Well, I say play, more mime in fact, and we did not mime so we said no. We will only play live. They said no. They asked again the next week, same reply both ways. Then they asked a third time and said yes, you can play live.' Having scored their principled victory, New Order subsequently turned in a live performance that Stephen Morris, in his book *Fast Forward*, described, accurately, as 'the dampest of damp squibs'. New Order mythology dictates that as a result of their *Top of the Pops* appearance 'Blue Monday' plummeted down the charts the following week, whereas the reality is that the single actually rose three places from seventeen to fourteen, a position it maintained for a second week before rising to its peak. 'Blue Monday' also topped the independent singles chart for a record thirteen weeks, remaining on the charts for 186 weeks, second only to the 195-week record the band also set as Joy Division with 'Love Will Tear Us Apart'.

Another New Order legend states that the complicated cut-out sleeve for 'Blue Monday', inspired by the design of the floppy discs used by the band's E-mu Emulator, was so expensive that New Order and Factory Records lost money on every sale of the single. 'Nobody is that daft,' stated Stephen Morris in *Fast Forward*, declaring, 'Apparently by the end of 31 May 1983 Blue Monday had sold 230,340 copies and had made £113,477.78.' Fortunately, despite conspicuously failing to display the name of the band or the album, the sleeve for *Power, Corruption & Lies* was a much more straightforward proposition – at least it was once you were in the know. 'It seems that witty Peter Saville, whilst designing the sleeves, decided on a series of coloured squares to represent the letters thus giving him the opportunity to write all manner of rude things on the sleeves and only those in the know could decipher them,' revealed *Sounds* in July. 'Finally it can be revealed that the single sleeve says New Order: 'Blue Monday' and the LP says, yes, you've guessed it 'Power, Corruption And Lies'… The key to the code is the colour wheel on the back of the LP sleeve,' the piece continued. 'The outer two rings correspond to the letters of the alphabet and taking the double green ring as A you too can be a Factory trendy, and write your own colour coded message to other Factory trendies.' 'The cover artwork was reputedly Peter Saville's favourite,' Peter Hook reported in *Substance*, alongside the fact that the album sold '75,000 copies in the UK in its first two months of release. Unlike *Movement*, reviews are very good.'

Power, Corruption & Lies was released at the start of May. 'If you're expecting this new one to be in the same White Disco vein as 'Blue Monday', you'll be disappointed. I was,' cautioned *Smash Hits*' Neil Tennant. 'This is really the New Order of old, sweeter on some tracks and more cheerful on others but mainly murky and dull.' In true New Order style 'Blue Monday' wasn't among the album's eight tracks, although the track '5-8-6' does share some stylistic elements with the single. 'New Order have patiently fashioned a sound where keyboard programmes become the main element of their vocabulary. It's a sound that is logically, painfully, right,' reported *Melody Maker*'s Mark Brennan, who further added, 'If anything, it is more patchy even than 'Movement'. But it has its moments, and they are moments when time stands still.' 'The new sound is vigorous and exhilarating, brisk and stripped of undue preciousness. The synthesised lines that provide its major characteristic keep a disciplined electric rhythm but they still pulsate with life and colour,' wrote Paul Du Noyer in the *NME*. 'It will sell well and long, of course, and it deserves to, because I suspect it'll prove one of the best records made in England this year.'

Power, Corruption & Lies entered the UK album charts at its peak position of number four in the middle of May and spent a month in the Top 20, remaining a fixture in the lower reaches of the chart for most of the year, sustained in part by another single, 'Confusion', which, like 'Blue Monday', wasn't taken from the album but which kept the band's name in the public consciousness. 'I think this is stunning. One of those brilliantly conceived records that challenges and confuses and achieves new highs in terms of production, technique and arrangement,' enthused Colin Irwin, reviewing 'Confusion' for *Melody Maker* at the beginning of September. 'In spite of the trendiness of just about every aspect here, one has to admit it has a certain muscle-popping charm,' reported Sandy Robertson in *Sounds*. 'An aggressively sharp sounding mix for New Order with more of a tune than their previous outing and, as the record plays on, a familiar drum pattern echoes 'Perfect Beat', 'Hip Hop' and 'IOU',' observed *Record Mirror*.

That 'Confusion' shared similar sonic territory to Afrika Bambaataa & The Soulsonic Force's 'Looking For The Perfect Beat' and Freeez's 'I.O.U.' comes as no surprise when you consider that Arthur Baker, who produced both those records, had been selected to work on the single with New Order. The band travelled to New York in January 1983 without any song ideas, assuming that Baker would lead the sessions, and were immediately dispatched to a holding studio by Baker with instructions to come up with some ideas while the producer finished work on 'I.O.U.' with Freeez. 'It's the only time we ever sat down to write, and God, was it hard!' Peter Hook told the *NME*'s Chris Bohn in July. 'Arthur Baker just stood there staring at us, sort of going, go on go on, write something, and we were walking around in circles thinking, fucking hell, isn't it time to go home yet? We don't normally work well under pressure.' 'He'd start a drum machine off and send one of us in saying have a go on that synthesiser, see what you can come up with. So you're standing there thinking what the fucking hell am I doing?' added Bernard Sumner in the same interview. 'You'd do something and he'd go, that's alright, turn off the drum machine, start the tape rolling and say, right play it again.'

In fact New Order and Arthur Baker had more in common than either first thought, something that Peter Hook admitted later: 'We thought Arthur

Baker was going to be this technological genius creating these dance records, and really he was just a punk let loose in a recording studio, who didn't know what the fucking hell he was doing – he was just pushing sliders up and down. We were terrified of going over there to meet him, but when we got there we realised he was just like us. We thought he was the bee's knees, and he thought we were!' 'I thought they were going to be some sort of really flash, polished English band and they thought I was a flash, polished American producer,' Baker told the Red Bull Music Academy later. 'So, we were both wrong!' Against the odds, New Order's short time in the studio with Arthur Baker resulted in not just 'Confusion' but also in a second track, 'Thieves Like Us', which would become the next New Order single in April 1984.

'Confusion' followed 'Blue Monday' into the UK singles chart, where it peaked at twelve in early September, spending seven weeks in the national chart and sixteen weeks on the independent singles chart, which included four weeks at number one. As with 'Blue Monday', 'Confusion' received little in the way of radio support, and *Top of the Pops* confined themselves to playing the track over footage of the audience dancing instead of inviting the band to appear on the show, or showing the video the band had made to support the single. Said video showed Arthur Baker in his studio, apparently finishing 'Confusion' and taking the master tape to New York club the Fun House, where it was played to a rapturous breakdancing crowd who were also treated to a live set from New Order, filmed travelling to the venue, relaxing in their dressing room and performing at the club.

As 'Confusion' peaked in the charts, *Record Mirror* reported that New Order's 'Blue Monday' – which had remained a constant in the lower reaches of the chart since its release in March – had re-entered the Top 40. 'New Order's 'Blue Monday' single this week extends its continuous chart residency to 30 weeks,' *Record Mirror* wrote. 'In the whole of chart history only 13 singles have enjoyed longer uninterrupted period of tenure.' 'Blue Monday' continued to climb the chart, reaching a new peak position of number nine by the middle of October following a repeat of New Order's *Top of the Pops* appearance from earlier in the year. In their piece *Record Mirror* further added that 'Blue Monday' had now sold 'over 350,000 copies in Britain, and is nudging the 800,000 sales mark globally'.

In an echo of New Order's experience's with Arthur Baker earlier in the year when the producer was briefly working with both band's simultaneously,

'Confusion' was released hot on the heels of Baker's previous project, Freeez's 'I.O.U.', which had been released in June and which was still sitting comfortably in the Top 30 when 'Confusion' entered the national charts in September. 'Times have changed and we've come up with something different,' Freeez's John Rocca explained to *Smash Hits* in July, in response to a question about the duo's new musical direction since enjoying success with 'Southern Freeez' and 'Flying High' in 1981. 'It's still along the same lines – but today's version. I think that when 'Southern Freeez' came out it was the "in" sort of thing and now we're doing the "in" sort of thing again.'

Having decided that they wanted to work with Arthur Baker, Freeez made a loose arrangement with the producer and subsequently turned up at Baker's New York studio with a far clearer idea of what they wanted to achieve than New Order had been able to manage. 'We went there with about fifteen songs which we thought were pretty good and just needed knocking into shape,' bass-player Peter Maas explained to *Record Mirror* in October, 'Arthur didn't much care for them, though, so we started writing new stuff with him and ended up throwing the first lot out.' 'When we got there Arthur made us go out and buy a radio to listen to all the black and R&B stations,' added Maas's bandmate, vocalist John Rocca in the same interview. 'We had to learn the sound by listening to BLS, Kiss FM, KTU, stations like that as well as going to the clubs.'

Released in June, 'I.O.U.' entered the Top 40 of the UK singles chart at twenty-three a fortnight after release, launched by a positive response from radio and some encouraging reviews in the music press. '[One of] the best, the boldest and the brassiest electrofunk filaments to short the circuit since 'Looking For the Perfect Beat',' enthused the *NME*'s David Dorrell. 'Freeez find themselves and their fairly average North London soft shoe shuffle transported from these redundant shores to the enclaves of Baker's megamix utopia.' Wham! reviewed the single for *Smash Hits* the following week, and while George Michael was already familiar with the track from hearing it in clubs, and was disappointed by the power of the single when played over a domestic stereo system, Andrew Ridgeley was cautiously enthusiastic. 'A bit sparse. The production sounds rather amateurish but at least the chorus has a good melody,' Ridgeley mused. 'I quite like it.' 'I.O.U.' climbed the charts steadily and a month later peaked at number two, a position it held for three successive weeks, each time held off the top spot by Paul Young's 'Wherever I Lay My Hat (That's My Home)'.

Despite the length of its chart tenure, and its number two chart placing, 'I.O.U.' was neither Arthur Baker's most successful production of 1983, nor the most influential record he was involved in that year. New Edition had scored a number one hit in the UK singles chart earlier in the year with their single 'Candy Girl', which had been produced for the band by Arthur Baker and Maurice Starr of US electro act the Jonzun Crew. An album, *Candy Girl*, also produced by Baker and Starr, failed to chart in the UK and two further singles – 'Popcorn Love' and 'Is This The End' – peaked at forty-three and eighty-three in August and October, respectively.

Meanwhile Baker's most influential and critically acclaimed project of 1983 was arguably Afrika Bambaataa & The Soulsonic Force's follow-up to the previous year's 'Planet Rock'. Released in the UK in February after making considerable waves as a US import, 'Looking For The Perfect Beat' received enthusiastic reviews from the UK music press. 'Bambaataa's musical mayhem is enough to wrench anybody out of bed... As with 'Planet Rock', Bambaataa and Arthur Baker team up to turn out another superior snippet of computerised insanity,' enthused the *NME*'s Lloyd Bradley. 'Without the shock value of its predecessor 'Looking' at first feels simpler, and true, the basic beat is more immediate. Even if the perfect beat remains hidden, you're left with the most enduring and interesting electronic funk around.' 'Looking For The Perfect Beat' was Single of the Week in *Sounds*, where journalist Johnny Waller described the release as 'Scratch-disco-mixing with A-bombs for percussion! It's Grandmaster Flash meets ABC through Marvin Gaye, into one huuuuuuge, tantalising soul-scorching dance-floor jerker.' Despite the enthusiasm of the press, 'Looking For The Perfect Beat' spent just five weeks in the UK singles chart in February and March, peaking at a lowly eighty-six, although the track's influence would endure for decades to come.

In a way the failure of 'Looking For The Perfect Beat' to become a significant mainstream hit worked in its favour, and in the favour of the new underground scene which was springing up to celebrate a new wave of dance sounds, by retaining a crucial level of credibility. Quick to recognise the potential of this new audience was young music industry executive Morgan Khan, who had cut his teeth in the market by licensing and championing American dance records, The Sugarhill Gang's 'Rapper's Delight' among them, for UK release and distribution. By the end of 1982, having fallen out with his previous employer, Pye Records, Khan decided it was time to strike out on his own and founded his own label, Streetwave.

In January 1983 *Smash Hits* announced the first releases from Khan's new label: "Street Sounds' is a bright idea for disco music fans. Every month, in between seven and ten 12″ versions of the latest dance tracks will be put together on a compilation C60 cassette which can also be bought as an LP,' explained the report, which went on to add, 'The first 'Street Sounds' was released in December, including recent hits by Grandmaster Flash and Raw Silk, and number two will be out towards the end of this month on the Streetwave label.' The first *Street Sounds* album featured eight tracks, including Grandmaster Flash & The Furious Five's 'The Message', a special extended version of Raw Silk's recent Top 20 disco hit 'Do It To The Music', a ten-and-a-half-minute version of Peech Boys 'Don't Make Me Wait' and an Arthur Baker production of Northend's 'Tee's Happy'. *Street Sounds 2* followed in February and included an eleven-and-a-half-minute special extended mix of Whodini's 'Magic's Wand', Melle Mel & Duke Bootee's 'Message II' and another Arthur Baker production, Nairobi's 'Soul Makossa', across its eight tracks.

Although the initial reaction to the series was slow, Khan started to TV advertise the *Street Sounds* albums, which was enough for them to start selling in healthy quantities. 'Album one suddenly went silver, the next one silver too, because we captured a mood. It wasn't just the records. It was a mood of a nation that was playing catch-up to what was going on in the States,' Khan told the Red Bull Music Academy later. 'The funny thing was our albums started shipping back to the States and selling more than the original twelve-inch singles. What we always tried to do with *Street Sounds* was see what the next trend was going to be.' As the compilations began to gain an increasing foothold in the market, the media began to latch on to the series. 'What you are offered for your £3.99 is eight full length mixes of all out guaranteed quality soul, most released between one and two months before the compilation itself,' enthused the *NME* of the series in March.

Recognising that the *Street Sounds* compilations were too general for those purchasers with more niche musical tastes, Morgan Khan's next move was to launch a second series of albums, *Street Sounds Electro*, alongside the original series. Released at beginning of October the first *Street Sounds Electro* compilation contained eight tracks, among them extended versions of The Packman's 'I'm The Packman', Newcleus's 'Jam On Revenge (The Wikki-Wikki Song)' and West Street Mob's 'Break Dance – Electric Boogie'. *Street Sounds Electro* entered the UK album chart at a peak position of number eighteen, remaining in the chart for seven weeks and earning an enthusiastic review from *Record Mirror*: "Electro 1' sums up the energy and vitality that good disco should be all about; the sheer abandon that embodies the perfect hedonistic dancefloor experience,' enthused Betty Page. 'A wicked collection for making a complete, joyful idiot of yourself to.'

In addition to their success with *Street Sounds Electro*, the Streetwave label placed five of their first seven *Street Sounds* compilations inside the Top 40 of the UK albums chart over the course of the year, adding up to a total of forty-four weeks of chart activity in 1983. *Sounds'* Chris Roberts interviewed Morgan Khan about Streetwave's success in 1984 and asked him what, exactly, the term 'electro' meant? 'Basically, it's synthesised, wholly electronic, very percussive, high energy music with a certain uptempo beat and the right dance quality,' was Khan's quick response. 'In their own way, people like Kraftwerk have been doing it for years, but when records like Tyrone Brunson's 'The Smurf' and 'Play At Your Own Risk' by Planet Patrol came along, no one could believe what they were hearing! There are two types of electro artist,' Khan continued. 'There's the artist of yesteryear who always cuts what's happening – if it's funk they'll cut funk, soul – soul, electro – electro; the prime case being Herbie Hancock with his *Future Shock* album and 'Rockit'.'

Released in August 1983, *Future Shock* was the latest project from American musician Herbie Hancock. Hancock, best known as a virtuoso jazz player, had previously been a pioneer of what had become known as jazz fusion, a genre which combined jazz sounds with musical structures taken from the world of rock and pop, before scoring two jazz-disco hits – 'I Thought It Was You' and 'You Bet Your Love' – in 1978 and 1979, respectively. By 1983 Hancock was looking for a new direction. 'I got turned on to new wave groups like Talking Heads, Duran Duran, Simple Minds, by a friend of mine. So I had him make a tape for me of all kinds of new stuff,' Hancock told *The Face* in September 1983, recalling how one track in particular had caught his attention, Malcolm McLaren's 'Buffalo Gals': 'When I heard that I couldn't believe it, I said "What is this guy doing?" I'd never heard scratching before, I thought it was so clever, and I didn't even know what it was.' (By coincidence Hancock had found himself working in the same studio complex as Simple Minds in the summer of 1982, which led to Hancock playing a synthesiser solo on the track 'Hunter And The Hunted', which subsequently appeared on 1982's *New Gold Dream (81-82-83-84)* album.)

Future Shock reached number twenty-seven in the UK albums chart for Herbie Hancock at the end of August, equalling the chart position of his previously most successful UK album release, 1978's *Sunlight*. While *Future Shock* picked up some encouraging reviews from the music press – 'On this album, he concentrates on aligning his craft with the current disco techniques and gets more mileage out of it in six tracks than some of his hipper brethren will manage in six albums,' wrote *Sounds'* Hugh Fielder at the beginning of September – the success of the project fell squarely at the feet of the extraordinary single that had preceded the album: 'Rockit'. 'It is absolutely not an easy option to make pop records. You can't just say I think I'll write a hit...' Hancock told *The Face*. 'You have to learn the language and it is definitely not an easy language to learn.'

'Rockit' was released in July as a regular seven-inch single and as an extended 'Stretched' twelve-inch remix, both featuring the scratch skills of Afrika Bambaataa collaborator and DJ at New York's Roxy Club, Grandmixer D.ST. 'I definitely think we influenced each other – the scratching is a major part of 'Rockit', working with a jazz artist like that is a big step for hip-hop. That record has crossed over all the charts, black and white,' D.ST told *Record Mirror*'s Graham K. Smith of the collaboration the following year. 'Rockit' was a major hit for Herbie Hancock in the UK, where the single spent two consecutive weeks at number eight in August as part of a three-month run in the charts, and in the USA, where it topped the *Billboard* Hot Dance Club Play chart and earned Hancock the 1984 Grammy award for Best R&B Instrumental Performance.

Such was the impact of 'Rockit' that Herbie Hancock was not only invited to perform the track at the 1984 Grammy Awards ceremony, where he turned in a slick performance of the song, supported by Grandmixer D.ST, a full band of musicians, and an extraordinary cast of breakdancing robots, but was also asked to reprise the performance the following year. The continuing impact of electronic music in the USA subsequently saw the 1985 Grammy Awards featuring a synthesiser medley in the form of an electronic supergroup which included not only Herbie Hancock and 'Rockit', but also Thomas Dolby, Howard Jones and Stevie Wonder, who contributed extracts from 'She Blinded Me With Science', 'What Is Love?' and 'Go Home', respectively. 'At the end we did a rather overblown combination of 'God Save The Queen' and 'America The Beautiful', accompanied by the Grammy's orchestra. I was dressed like Beethoven, and conducted with a baton in manic style,' Thomas

Dolby would recall in his memoir *The Speed of Sound*. 'People seemed to like it well enough,' Dolby added modestly, 'and for Howard and me it was very flattering to be sharing the stage with two living legends in front of millions of people.'

But in 1983, two years before pulling on a Beethoven wig and conducting superstars at the Grammy Awards, Thomas Dolby was having a year mostly out of the spotlight, although not entirely by choice. In June a reissued release of 'She Blinded Me With Science' once again failed to duplicate its American success in Britain and peaked at a lowly fifty-six in the UK singles chart in July, Dolby's only chart action of the year. But later in the year a second, more curious release appeared which stemmed from Thomas Dolby's fascination with dance music: 'Get Out Of My Mix', credited to Dolby's Cube. "Europa And The Pirate Twins' and 'She Blinded Me With Science' mixed into a strange dance record,' reported the *NME*'s news page in November. 'The flip side ['Get On Out Of My Mix'] is an a capella version of the a-side – which can be synchronised up to, and overlaid on, any 115 BPM drum track.' 'An electro mega mix for the hip hop contortionists,' marvelled *Record Mirror* in their review of the single the same week. Unfortunately, as innovative as the release undoubtedly was, 'Get Out Of My Mix' was not a hit.

Released at the same time as 'Get Out Of My Mix', and worth a mention because it featured production and co-writing credits from both Thomas Dolby and Conny Plank, was November's Whodini album *Whodini*, which came out alongside a flurry of interviews with the US duo as well as some unusually positive reviews. 'Jalil Hutchins and Ecstasy manage to weave their way through waves of electro rhythms with the ease of a jaywalker in a London rush hour,' wrote Simon Hills in a four-out-of-five-star review for *Melody Maker*. 'Thumbs up to anyone who can sustain an album's worth of material of such high quality as this.' Hills also identified Whodini's collaboration with Thomas Dolby, 'Magic's Wand', as the album's strongest track 'by far', while also complimenting Conny Plank's production work: 'There's no escaping it, when you mix Whodini and producer Conny Plank together, you'd feel happy locked in a safe for 40 minutes with the product.' 'He's the most innovative guy I've ever met,' enthused Whodini's Jalil of Plank in an interview for *Record Mirror* at the end of November. 'We wanted to get into computer sounds so we figured, why not do it with the guy who actually started it?'

Although he still had moments of magic ahead of him, and despite his up-to-the-minute hip-hop dabbling, in the bright, brittle pop environment of 1983. Conny Plank was already yesterday's electronic music producer. By 1983, following his success as an artist in Buggles, Trevor Horn had stepped up to become the new producer of the moment, having delivered a dazzling run of irresistible pop hits from the likes of Dollar, ABC, Spandau Ballet and Malcolm McLaren since the start of the decade. Paul Morley was dispatched to interview Horn for the *NME* in June 1982 and, despite some residual awkwardness remaining from a previous interview where Morley had described Horn as 'a dustbin man of pop', the pair got on well and each identified something interesting in what the other was doing. 'While Trevor Horn was in Buggles I interviewed him for *NME* and slagged him off something rotten. Trevor said afterwards that the interview really made him think about what he was doing,' Morley recalled to writer Kim Fenton later. 'When producing Malcolm McLaren and ABC, I interviewed him again, this time to say I liked what he was doing. Then I decided to leave *NME*. I was at my wits' end deciding what to do when he rang me and suggested we should set up a record label. I thought great, the possibilities are endless.'

With Trevor Horn's wife, Jill Sinclair, looking after the business side of things, the trio, led by Morley's lofty conceptualising, set about designing a record label. 'Zang Tumb Tuum,' wrote *No.1* magazine of the label name in October 1983, pondering whether that might be a Zulu battle cry or a small Australasian mammal before revealing, 'Guess what, it's a brand new record company.' Zang Tumb Tuum, frequently abbreviated to ZTT, actually came from an Italian Futurist poem, written by Filippo Tommaso Marinetti and admired by Morley, in which the sound of the words echoed the sound of machine guns firing. 'Two bands who will shortly be appearing on ZTT are Liverpool's Frankie Goes To Hollywood, and Düsseldorf's Propaganda,' continued *No.1*. 'But the first release is the curious Art Of Noise's 'Into Battle' single.' 'I went back to the *Thames and Hudson Guide to Futurism* for the band's name,' Morley confessed to *The Guardian* later. '*The Art of Noises* was a 1913 manifesto about musical aesthetics, we performed an edit and named the group the Art Of Noise.'

An EP rather than a traditional single, *Into Battle With The Art Of Noise* was released on twelve-inch vinyl at the end of September 1983. Containing nine tracks, only two of which – 'Beat Box' and 'Moments In Love' – were full-length pieces, *Into Battle* came out to a mixture of confusion, bafflement and admiration on the part of the music press and the listening public alike. *Sounds*' Dave Henderson was an immediate convert: 'A magnificent collection of noise, sound, speech, anything you can imagine in fact, which has been pilfered, in part, from other records. Not ripped off, merely borrowed and reworked into the structure of something new.' 'An extremely odd 12-inch collection of different electronic rhythms and textures,' was the verdict of *Record Mirror*'s dance music page, 'all very experimental but pretty well essential for any truly serious scratch mixers.' 'More men (and women?) bashing bits of metal and such like,' was Steve Sutherland's dismissal of *Into Battle* in *Melody Maker*, while on their singles review page *Record Mirror*'s Simon Hills described the release as 'A crashing electro beat number that sounds like cars crashing into each other to the rhythm of a metronome,' and added, 'it just reeks of hipper than thou pomposity.'

While Thomas Dolby created 'Get Out Of My Mix' from parts of his tracks 'Europa And The Pirate Twins' and 'She Blinded Me With Science' as a way of becoming familiar with his recently acquired Fairlight CMI, Trevor Horn had been engaged in a similar project of his own. 'If you want an example of a record from that time that uses a sampler then without a doubt it would have to be Art Of Noise,' Vince Clarke says today. 'That was all Fairlight. Trevor Horn used one a lot. I had one too. I think Peter Gabriel had the first one in the country and it was his cousin who sold them over here. I was a working-class kid who'd come into a bit of money and they were so posh, and they had this amazing showroom in London and you'd go there and they'd give you coffee and everything, and they'd tell you about all the amazing things the Fairlight could do so I bought one. That was the most expensive cup of coffee I ever bought.' 'The Art of Noise came together during the time when McLaren wasn't in the studio for the recording of *Duck Rock*,' reported *Melody Maker*'s Lynden Barber in an interview with Paul Morley the following year. 'Horn, Fairlight operator [J. J.] Jeczalik, engineer [Gary] Langan and classically trained musician [Anne] Dudley would mess around in the studio, come up with odd combinations of sound.'

Into Battle With The Art Of Noise wasn't a commercial hit upon its initial release, although both its main tracks – 'Beatbox' and 'Moments In Love' – would later appear in the lower reaches of the UK singles chart in reissued editions in their own right, but as an introductory salvo it summed up the launch of ZTT perfectly. '*Into Battle With The Art Of Noise* was our opening statement of intent, the first sign of how we were going to ignore the set limits of industry organisation and imagination drawn up by the titanic terrifying record industry,' Paul Morley explained to the *NME* in February 1984, the same week that the EP topped the *Billboard* Dance Chart, fuelled by America's enthusiasm for its cutting-edge hip-hop beats, despite the unconventional nature of the band and the release. 'We didn't think about what a pop group is supposed to be because to do that is to die, we didn't think about what dance music is supposed to do, or how muzak type theories have unexplained attractions,' Paul Morley told the *NME*'s Chris Bohn shortly after the release of *Into Battle*. 'And we used the most up-to-date technology not to calculate perfect pop but to harness the sounds of our time, to explore and gamble in an old fashioned adventurer's type of way.'

In an echo of The Human League's practice of colour-coding their singles to reflect the music they contained, *Into Battle* was conceived as the first in ZTT's 'Incidental Series', which the *NME*'s Chris Bohn would helpfully describe as a 'series of shocks to the nervous system calculated to jar bodies out of disco straitjackets and expose them to the cold, bracing blast of the winter that must precede spring'. While the 'Incidental Series' would be used to denote ZTT's more experimental and eclectic releases, a second category, the label's 'Bold Action Series', would contain more commercial pop-orientated material. ZTT's second release fell firmly into the second category: Frankie Goes To Hollywood's debut single, 'Relax'.

Frankie Goes To Hollywood had previously been making small waves in the music press over the course of 1983 and writer David Dorrell in particular had been an early champion of the band, whom he introduced to the readers of the *NME* in February. 'The basic Frankie Goes To Hollywood – Holly (vocals), Mark (bass), Brian (guitar) and Ped (drums) – came about six months ago. The second frontman, Paul, joined a while later from a local group, the Spitfire Boys,' Dorrell reported. 'On stage (as in real life) the band are a leather-bound bordello of punk funk; whipping up a scorching, sleazy beat while Paul and Holly shed layer upon layer of black skin and sweat: all much to the frenzied appreciation of their burgeoning "chain gang" fans.' 'It's nightlife, subculture and sexuality all rolled into one,' added the band's Holly Johnson. 'I think that's a good phrase for it.'

Released at the end of October, Frankie Goes To Hollywood's debut single, 'Relax', was accompanied by a series of ZTT advertisements in the music press, their stylish minimal designs belying the S&M imagery, the sleeve's provocative sloganeering and the single's initial seven-inch and twelve-inch delights: 'The Nineteen Inches – Excess As A Sign Of Pleasure,' purred the headline. A more straightforward proposition than The Art Of Noise, 'Relax' was generally well received by the music press. 'Horn's production is magnificent; I can see what ZTT are getting at with Frankie,' nodded Dave McCullough in *Sounds*. 'Basically a chant over the rhythmic vibration of the very latest digital kitchen sinks,' reported the *NME*'s Charles Shaar Murray more doubtfully. ''Relax' is the subject of an ad campaign which suggests that one requires 19 inches to comprehend the music fully. Having only been issued with seven, I eventually made do with about three.' 'Naughty lyrics that will shock the powers that be at BBC. Which is a shame as this Trevor Horn-produced powerhouse dance record screams out to be heard,' enthused Mark Steels in *Smash Hits*. 'In the sterile, germ-free world of disco this is one contagious disease which should be caught.'

'It's like these untamed creatures meet Trevor Horn and his stamp is all over it. Because it was our first single, and there's no ready made market, we just had to have as much fun we could when we were making it,' Frankie Goes To Hollywood's Holly Johnson told Gavin Martin in a cover feature for Paul Morley's former employer, the *NME*, at the beginning of November. 'We used to know Paul Morley when he was in Manchester and he was working for the *NME*,' Johnson added mischievously. 'We used to hate him to be quite honest, he was like this div from Manchester.' But it was the suitably sleazy and decadent video that ZTT had commissioned to accompany the release of 'Relax' which was the subject of most of the discussion in Frankie Goes To Hollywood's early interviews, where the band's lyrical and visual themes were frequently compared to those previously explored by Soft Cell. 'It's interesting drawing a comparison with the Soft Cell thing,' Holly Johnson told Martin. 'Where they pantomimed it we're going to do it for real,' he declared, 'I don't think we're like them.' 'In the video we tell Frankie's tale. Frankie is on the street and is lured into this Roman den, showing the seedy side of life, and he goes to the bar and doesn't salute Nero, so Nero sentences him to the lions, yet what happens is he finds the tiger really cute and starts hugging him,' Johnson explained in an interview with *Record Mirror*. 'Soft Cell are sleaze and seedy cabaret, we have stories to tell, they're just funny,' Johnson added in response to another question about Frankie Goes To Hollywood's parallels with Soft Cell.

Transformed from rock to electronic by the guiding hand of Trevor Horn, 'Relax' charted at seventy-seven in the UK singles chart and took a further eight weeks of slow advances to finally break into the Top 40 in the first new chart of 1984. A week later, with the band's debut *Top of the Pops* appearance under their belts, radio airplay was finally starting to pick up, which put 'Relax' in front of Radio 1 DJ Mike Read, who expressed his distaste for both the single's sleeve and for its lyrics. Read subsequently refused to play the single and the BBC rallied around their presenter and extended the ban across the network. Instead of killing the single, the furore created by the BBC's ban was enough to propel 'Relax' to the top of the charts, a position it held for five consecutive weeks at the end of January and for all of February. 'Relax' remained in the UK singles chart for two weeks shy of an entire year, and even returned to the Top 10 in June, where it spent a further nine consecutive weeks, including two weeks at number two and four weeks at number three. 'Relax' was not only the best-selling UK single of 1984 but to date remains the seventh best-selling UK single of all time, providing Frankie Goes To Hollywood with the first of three consecutive number one singles in 1984, the others being 'Two Tribes' and 'The Power Of Love', earning the band and ZTT combined sales of approaching two million singles.

As 'Relax' climbed the UK singles chart in November and December of 1983, Trevor Horn was enjoying simultaneous success with Yes whose *90125* album, which Horn had produced, peaked at number sixteen in the UK albums chart, while the first single from the album, 'Owner Of A Lonely Heart', scored Yes their biggest hit single since 1977. 'Three years since their last album and two and a half years after their apparent break-up, former members of Yes are currently in the studio recording a new album,' *Melody Maker* had announced in June, further adding that the band's Chris Squire, Alan White and Trevor Rabin had recently been joined by original Yes singer Jon Anderson in the studio, where the band were working on an album with the working title 'Cinema'. By the time of the album's release in November the album had been rechristened *90125*, named after the release's catalogue number, and entered the UK albums chart at its peak of sixteen, remaining on the chart for a further three months.

The idea of bringing in Trevor Horn to produce *90125* didn't come out the blue. Yes had parted company with both vocalist Jon Anderson and keyboard virtuoso Rick Wakeman following the band's 1978 *Tormato* album project and, by good fortune, found themselves working in an adjacent rooms to Buggles at London's Townhouse Studios. Yes were in need of a singer, a keyboard player and some songs, and Buggles could supply all three. An exploratory collaboration between the two acts was successful and Geoff Downes and Trevor Horn were invited to join Yes for their 1980 album *Drama* and the band's subsequent American and UK tours. 'Me and Geoff Downes joined in June and by August we were doing Madison Square Garden in front of twenty-odd thousand people,' Horn told the *NME* in 1982. 'It was insanity.'

Although Yes fizzled out after the *Drama* tour, in 1982 Chris Squire and Alan White started working on new material under the name Cinema and attempted to recruit Trevor Horn to join them. 'I offered him the job of singing in Cinema,' Chris Squire recalled later. 'But Trevor was really making a name for himself at the time as a producer – he'd already had success with ABC and Dollar – so he didn't want to give up this new career and join a band. However, Trevor did agree to produce our album, and I was delighted to have him on board.' The unexpected return of Jon Anderson as frontman meant that Cinema could return to calling themselves Yes, and the new line-up returned to the public eye. 'It would be a shame if we were written off as a has-been band,' Anderson told *Smash Hits* at the end of November. 'We've grown up with and pushed the current electronic boom and now we want to give off some vibe of the modern musical age.'

The contemporary commercial and electronic sound which Trevor Horn's production had brought to *90125* came as shock to the music press, who had long since dismissed Yes as prime exponents of the self-indulgent excesses which came to characterise progressive rock. 'A crisp, delicious and thoroughly satisfying morsel, which, in its 12″ version, becomes a veritable feast,' enthused *Smash Hits*' Mark Steels, reviewing 'Owner Of A Lonely Heart' in October. 'Putting on some looser trousers has done Jon Anderson's voice a power of good. That, and some producer called Trevor Horn.' 'I was going to do a quick hatchet job and bury them in the ground, but instead I had to leave my shovel in the shed,' confessed Robin Smith in *Record Mirror*. 'On '90125' they've recaptured the techno rock trophy. Big and hard hitting, they've built new empires under the guiding hand of Trevor Horn.'

Having come out as fans of electronic music as early as 1980 when they had shared the *The Old Grey Whistle Test* stage with OMD, American rock act ZZ Top also delivered their most commercial and most overtly electronic album in 1983, a record which would be the biggest success of their long and illustrious career. *Eliminator* was inspired in part by ZZ Top frontman Billy Gibbons' longstanding interest in electronic music and fascination with the precision offered by the latest electronic technology. 'The crack in the code was the fact that the drum machine introduced for the first time to the listening ear close-to-perfect time, which had been the aspiration of musicians since the invention of the metronome,' Gibbons told the *Financial Times*' Michael Hann in 2012. And it was the music of the new generation of electronic artists, OMD and Depeche Mode in particular, which had given Gibbons a glimpse of what he might achieve if he was to combine ZZ Top's bluesy rock'n'roll with the precision beats and limitless potential of the latest electronic technology.

Eliminator was recorded in 1982 and released in 1983, when it spent just four weeks on the UK albums chart, peaking at number sixty-seven, but the combination of American success and a string of electro-tinged hit singles – 'Gimme All Your Lovin'', 'Sharp Dressed Man' and 'Legs', each accompanied by suitably glossy, high-tech videos – meant that the album eventually hit a chart peak of number three in January 1985 as part of 139 weeks on the album charts, representing around one million album sales in the UK alone. 'Yes, they did influence ZZ Top,' Gibbons declared when asked about the particular influence of Depeche Mode in a syndicated interview in 2021. 'The success of *Eliminator* remains a solid statement to the time. It still comes out as based in the blues but with some refreshing touches.'

BLANCMANGE STARTED 1983 ON a high with their 1982 single 'Living On The Ceiling' in no apparent hurry to leave the Top 40. 'It meant a lot to me when the record got into the Top 40, then it went to number seven and it wasn't quite real,' Arthur admitted in a *Record Mirror* front cover feature on the duo in January. But the success of 'Living On The Ceiling' came with its own challenges. 'Having a hit for the first time is a dream come true in one sense but on the other hand it's more important for us right now to make sure we've got something to back it up,' the frontman told *Flexipop* around the same time.

At the beginning of February, as 'Living On The Ceiling' finally left the UK singles chart, Blancmange announced that their new single would be a re-recorded version of the track 'Waves', from their *Happy Families* album, later that month. 'It's my favourite song,' Neil Arthur confessed to *Record Mirror*. 'Another hit. Obviously these men are on a winning streak, and here they make no bones about deploying their electro-suss to sly emotional effect,' observed *Melody Maker*. 'Full blown orchestral epic that eases nicely from sweet understatement to the sound of sea, synth and practically everything bar the kitchen sink. A very cleverly crafted record and a very big hit,' predicted *Record Mirror*'s Jim Reid. 'A ballad!' exclaimed Dave Henderson in *Sounds*. 'A dangerous escapade indeed, but this romantic opus is so well written that I wouldn't be surprised if it turned up on the next Frank Sinatra LP.'

'Waves' scored Blancmange another hit and spent two weeks at a peak position of nineteen in the UK singles chart in March as part of seven weeks in the Top 40. But while 'Waves' helped to support the ongoing and steady success of their *Happy Families* album, Blancmange were ready to switch their attention to new material, and in April they announced that a new single, 'Blind Vision', the first from their forthcoming second album, would be released at the end of the month. Recorded in New York with producer John Luongo – the same John Luongo whose remix of Visage's 'Night Train' for the American market had caused Midge Ure so much distress the previous year – the single would, the announcement promised, feature additional guitar work courtesy of David Rhodes, plus a brass section, strings and a backing vocalist.

The music press was cautiously encouraging about 'Blind Vision' upon its release at the end of April. Least convinced was the *NME*'s Don Watson who wrote, 'More evidence that electro-pop has bopped itself into a corner. Does the synthesiser inevitably erode articulacy to the extent that songwriters who have come in close proximity end up with only a handful of mundane trigger words to scatter across the endless blimping?' 'Moody and (surprise, surprise) more shouted than sung,' noted John Shearlaw in *Record Mirror*. 'A boinging bass and the odd brass trip keep the pressure on and that's just as well.' 'This is perhaps the tightest fist Blancmange have ever held up under your nose, but they seem to have lost some of the eccentricity which made 'Ceiling' so off the wall,' added *Melody Maker*.

'Blind Vision' earned Blancmange a performance on an expanded edition of *Top of the Pops* to celebrate the show's 1,000th episode, which broadcast on May 5th and featured the latest hits alongside vintage performances pulled from the show's illustrious history. As a consequence, Blancmange not only joined their 1983 peers, including The Human League and Heaven 17, on the show, but they also appeared alongside archive footage of The Beatles, David Bowie, The Rolling Stones and The Supremes, among others. The *Top of the Pops* appearance came after 'Blind Vision' entered the UK singles chart at twenty-eight, the first of eight weeks in the chart which included a peak position of ten a fortnight later, and earned Blancmange a *Top of the Pops* showing of the 'Blind Vision' video.

'It's now got to the stage where a single like 'Blind Vision' goes in at twenty-eight and up to twelve in two weeks. It suddenly makes me think why has it done that, what is it about that record, and I start to analyse everything,' Stephen Luscombe confessed to *Record Mirror*'s Betty Page at the end of May. 'In a way that is a danger, you start getting paranoid, and wonder if you can do another one.' But in general Blancmange managed to remain upbeat as they set about recording their second album, *Mange Tout*, in New York with John Luongo. 'He's virtually one of the group now and tells the most fantastic jokes,' Neil Arthur told *Smash Hits* in November when the band announced the release of their next single 'That's Love, That It Is', 'usually when we finish recording we sit around in his hotel room, telling stupid jokes all night.'

'That's Love, That It Is' was released on November 18th and Blancmange set about reintroducing themselves after a relatively long time out of the spotlight. 'I remember listening to [John Luongo's] mix and wondering if it was really us,' Neil Arthur marvelled in a *Smash Hits* interview in the middle of November. 'Did you notice how long it is?' Arthur asked of the single. 'Four minutes and twenty seconds. Nobody does. We didn't realise ourselves until we'd done it, but it's great because you can't edit it, so we'll get four minutes on the radio every time anybody plays it.' Unfortunately radio didn't really get behind 'That's Love, That It Is', and while the single attracted some encouraging reviews – 'Certainly their most affecting single yet and one that functions with a stirring, diamond hard precision,' wrote Paolo Hewitt in the *NME*, adding, 'Blancmange have produced genuinely stirring music here' – it subsequently stalled at thirty-three in the UK singles chart in December, although it did remain in the charts for eight weeks, in part due to the additional release of a John Luongo remix of the track at the start of the month.

In February Virgin Records put out what they claimed was the UK's first video single, a three-track release from The Human League which featured the videos for 'Mirror Man', 'Love Action' and 'Don't You Want Me', available in both VHS and Betamax for a recommended price of £10.99. The week following the announcement, Virgin also announced that The Human League would be one of the first acts to be released on the music industry's newest music format, the compact disc. 'The Human League's 'Dare' album will soon be only 4.7 inches wide,' enthused *Record Mirror* of the news. 'It plays on a new type of stereo which uses a minute laser instead of a normal stylus. Its advantages are not only its size, but you can finger and even step on the record without damaging quality as it's read by light not contact, and the makers claim that the sound quality is far superior to normal albums.' *Dare* was scheduled to be one of Virgin's first ever CD releases in March, part of an initial set of releases alongside OMD's *Architecture And Morality* and key backlist albums from Culture Club, Mike Oldfield and Phil Collins. At the same time the label announced that a second batch of Virgin CDs – including

Simple Minds' *New Gold Dream (81-82-83-84)* and Heaven 17's forthcoming album *The Luxury Gap* – was also scheduled for release shortly after the first titles hits the streets.

In fact the announcement of the CD format of *The Luxury Gap* was the first mention of the title of the band's second album to appear anywhere, and may not have even been confirmed at that point. At the end of February, *Smash Hits*, in an update on Heaven 17's plans for 1983, reported, 'Heaven 17, who never quite achieved the great things expected of them in 1982, intend to make amends in March with the release of a new LP. We don't know what it's going to be called but we do know that they've dispensed with the one-time working title of 'Ashes And Diamonds'.' It wasn't until the start of April that Virgin Records formally announced that Heaven 17's new album would be called *The Luxury Gap* and was scheduled for release at the end of the same month, preceded by a brand new single in early April.

That single, 'Temptation', earned Heaven 17 their first ever Top 40 hit in April when it hit thirty-one in the UK singles chart a fortnight after release, securing the band their first *Top of the Pops* appearance since 'Play To Win' – alongside Blancmange on the show's celebratory 1,000th double-edition, which was also simultaneously broadcast on Radio 1 – despite a largely tepid reception from the music press. 'The boys from the BEF seem hell-bent on making brilliant disco records. Unfortunately this isn't one of them,' wrote Dave Rimmer in *Smash Hits*. 'They've got all the right ideas, but seem to get them in the wrong order.' 'Heaven 17 seek to emulate the grace and glory of classic black soul music, and end up with a sorry non-song pastiche that's all production and no passion,' echoed Garry Bushell in *Sounds*. Fortunately not all the critics took such a dim view of the single. "'Temptation' throbs and explodes with exhilarating ferocity, with guest singer Karol Kenyon [sic] wailing furiously above the 17 production machine at full tilt to deliver the coup de grace,' reported *Melody Maker*'s Colin Irwin. 'A ripping yarn delivered with power, stealth and knock-you-on-the-head production,' enthused *Record Mirror*'s Robin Smith. 'Heaven 17's first real monster and the single that realises their full potential. The Human League should be worried.'

The Human League were worried. Not about Heaven 17 specifically, but about pretty much everything. Having released just one new single, 'Mirror Man', over the course of 1982, by the end of that year The Human League were under pressure to deliver a new album. 'We're supposed to have an LP written by Christmas,' Phil Oakey had told Paul Morley in an in-depth interview for the *NME*, conducted in December 1982 and published in January 1983. 'We've done three songs after all this time, largely because of a lyric hold up. I feel that I can't write lyrics any more,' Oakey admitted, adding, 'It's more likely this time round to be an improved version of the ideas on *Dare*: a proper production, proper songs, and a proper group playing rather than a few people working computers.'

Despite The Human League's apparent crisis of confidence, the week following the release of Heaven 17's 'Temptation' they announced that they were ready to follow 1982's 'Mirror Man' with a new single of their own: '(Keep Feeling) Fascination'. Utilising their previous practice of colour-coding their singles to reflect the sound of the music they contained, The Human League deemed '(Keep Feeling) Fascination' to be red to reflect its dance content.

Released in the middle of April, '(Keep Feeling) Fascination' received a largely enthusiastic reception from the music press. *Sounds'* Geoff Barton admitted being initially sceptical about the single's chances of success but then declared '(Keep Feeling) Fascination' a 'strong enough song to transcend the fickle faith of short-memoried pop consumers', continuing, "Fascination' has the ability to stamp its identity on the feeblest of brains by virtue of its immediately, magnificently memorable chorus lines and delightful male/female vocal interplay.' 'They've got impeccable taste but beneath there's neither the zest, obsessiveness or magic that goes with being a major pop force,' mused Gavin Martin in the *NME*. 'The more I listen to this the more its, er, eclectic patchwork of golden moments tears apart leaving spaces in-between that are blank, unloved and unloveable.' *Melody Maker* agreed: 'The single is a pleasure, sure, but it's an uneasy one,' noted Mark Brennan. 'I wonder how long the League themselves can keep feeling fascination if they don't heed their other advice of "looking, learning, moving on".'

'(Keep Feeling) Fascination' entered the UK singles chart at number sixteen after one week of sales and the band appeared on *Top of the Pops* in the same week that Heaven 17 were performing 'Temptation' on the show. The Human League's single jumped to three the following week before peaking at number two in the middle of May, where it was held off the top spot by Spandau Ballet's 'True'. For the video to accompany the release of '(Keep Feeling) Fascination' The Human League reunited with filmmaker Steve Barron, who had previously made the videos for 'Love Action' and 'Don't You Want Me', and who had recently delivered the video for 'Billie Jean' for

Michael Jackson. In the video, the camera zooms in on an orange dot on a map of London only to find that the dot is painted on the landscape and also includes an orange-painted house and car. Accessing the house through an open window, the camera enters an entirely grey-painted room containing the six members of The Human League, all wearing black, engaged in a performance of '(Keep Feeling) Fascination'.

Melody Maker subsequently declared the '(Keep Feeling) Fascination' video the second best of the year (after This Mortal Coil's 'Song To The Siren') in a special feature in December. "Fascination' achieves what all other clips can only dream of, being simultaneously clever, stylish, danceable and too confident for words. In fact, this video is so seamlessly well done that it's almost easy to pass by,' enthused the report. 'This promo is a joy because the art direction is nothing short of superb. Check out the sheer glamour of the colours – black clothes and red lips in a totally pale room – and understand that true genius lies in simplicity… Plus, anyone who tints the entire corner of a street and remembers to paint the light bulb deserves to collaborate on such a killer tune.'

'The aim of the video,' Phil Oakey told *Smash Hits* in June, 'is to show that we're a group who play music together… This should help us in America where they believe we are a manufactured item mainly because we've never been live on TV there.' The Human League's preoccupation with how they might be perceived in America came on the back of the band's massive success with 'Don't You Want Me' and the subsequent failure of their follow-up single, 'Love Action'. Although *Dare* had been a huge record for them, the band's US record label, A&M, chose not to release 'Mirror Man' as a single without a forthcoming album to link it to, but they did add the track to a five-track 'mini-album', alongside '(Keep Feeling) Fascination'. The strategy worked and the EP, entitled *Fascination*, scored The Human League their second US hit when it topped the *Billboard* Hot Dance Music/Club Play chart and reached number eight on the main *Billboard* Hot 100 singles chart in July.

'The Human League must be a very, very arty object,' Phil Oakey told Paul Morley at the start of the year. 'What we're trying to do with The Human League is make it look… adult for a start. That was one of the first decisions we made, we do not go onto children's television, we will not talk to children's magazines. Which looks really hard, but in the end it works the opposite way, 'cos there are no kids out there who want to be treated like kids.' But following '(Keep Feeling) Fascination' The Human League were starting to feel increasingly out of step with the times, and Oakey was already second-guessing their earlier uncompromising stance. 'I'm pretty worried at the moment though, that all this stuff might be working for people like Duran Duran. The same as Spandau Ballet, they're doing all the things that we said we'll last longer by avoiding – and we did it because we thought we were being clever,' Oakey admitted to *Sounds'* Tony Mitchell in June.

Combined with enthusiastic radio support for 'Temptation', and a less stringent promotional policy to that of The Human League, Heaven 17's *Top of the Pops* performance was enough to move the single up to number fourteen on its way to five weeks in the Top 10, where it replaced '(Keep Feeling) Fascination)' at number two and, in an echo of The Human League's experience, was also kept from the top of the charts by Spandau Ballet's 'True'. 'Temptation' spent an impressive thirteen weeks in the UK singles chart, earning Heaven 17 their first silver single award for sales in excess of 200,000 copies. The single was also Heaven 17's first hit in the USA, where it reached thirty-four on *Billboard*'s Dance Club Songs chart. 'I think our sound is very acceptable to their market,' Martyn Ware told *Sounds* when asked about the band's US success. 'Although we don't sound black we have a great understanding for it and a genuine appreciation of it, and have done for some time.'

Inevitably Heaven 17 were also asked about The Human League as they set about promoting 'Temptation' and *The Luxury Gap*. What did the trio think of '(Keep Feeling) Fascination', *Record Mirror*'s Jim Reid asked the band in a cover feature at the end of April? 'I like the chorus but that's about all,' was Glenn Gregory's immediate response. 'The only way it hangs on in there is because it's got a good chorus.' 'I think it is really strangely tacky for them,' added Ian Marsh. "Cos Philip was going on so much about control and how he wouldn't let things out. And it's so obviously not quite finished.' Marsh's assessment of '(Keep Feeling) Fascination' wasn't far off the mark, and *Smash Hits* subsequently reported that the single had taken eight months to complete and had gone through ten different mixes, causing some 'ferocious battles' within the band in the process. 'It's a constant struggle to keep going,' Oakey had admitted to Paul Morley at the beginning of the year. 'It's a constant struggle to keep working with the same people you've been working with when they haven't got your brain, they've got a different brain.'

'(Keep Feeling) Fascination' would be The Human League's only new release of 1983 and represented the end of another chapter in the band's history as, shortly after finishing work on the single, they also parted company with producer Martin Rushent. 'Martin Rushent has "resigned" and is replaced by Chris Thomas,' announced *Smash Hits* in April, citing familiarity as the reason for the split: 'The problem was that the band got to know Martin too well and they would spend more time enjoying themselves than grafting in the studio.' 'Martin didn't feel altogether confident with some of the new material we were coming up with, and eventually he resigned,' The Human League's Ian Burden explained to *Electronics & Music Maker* magazine later, 'though I must stress there was no animosity between us. He taught us an awful lot about recording synthesisers, how to use Microcomposers and that sort of thing, for which we're obviously very grateful.'

'It was almost like a reverse situation between me and Phil,' Martin Rushent told writer Simon Reynolds in an interview for the latter's *Totally Wired*. 'Now Phil wanted it to be poppy and I wanted it to be edgy. I thought that we had made the pop statement; now we want to break down a few more barriers and progress and take our audience with us.' But the problems ran deeper than just musical direction, as Rushent admitted in the same interview: 'Everybody wanted to write songs by that point because they all realised you could make a lot more money if you wrote the song. Some of them just didn't write, period, and yet they expected to have a song on the album… it drove me up the fucking wall. I just wanted to follow the same modus operandi that created *Dare*. Why change a winning formula, a winning team, by suddenly including people who weren't involved before?'

Propelled by the success of 'Temptation', Heaven 17's second album, *The Luxury Gap*, came out in May and entered the UK albums chart at a peak position of number four, remaining in the Top 10 for six consecutive weeks, earning the band a gold album for sales of 100,000 copies by the end of May on its way to platinum status early the following year. Jim Reid awarded *The Luxury Gap* four out of a possible five stars and did his best to turn in a positive review. 'Though the ideas are strong, the execution often does little justice to the imagination that fed it. Heaven 17's music could (and can) be a sensuous thing; a heady mixture of dance floor awareness and high tech intelligence,' Reid mused. 'Unfortunately too often there is a cold, antiseptic feel to Heaven 17's music. And that's a real pity, for Heaven 17 have it in them to be one of the most powerful groups of their age.' 'While most of today's synth merchants have found success by re-working old pop ideas for new-fangled instrumentals, Heaven 17 have always looked forward rather than back. Respect them for it,' wrote *Smash Hits*' Dave Rimmer in an eight-and-a-half-star review, although, in an echo of Jim Reid's his positivity also faltered slightly by the end: 'These nine tracks of mainly disco-directed electronics are by turns entertaining, irritating, danceable, thoughtful and downright daft. A little cluttered, and no absolute winners, but a fine album overall.'

'We actually decided to avoid using synth clichés on the album because it was getting so ubiquitous, and used an orchestra instead to see what it was like with instruments for a change,' Martyn Ware told *Sounds* at the end of April. How was the experience of working with an orchestra, wondered writer Carole Linfield in the same interview? 'Bloody terrible! Union problems. Every time we were just getting on with something they'd fuck off for a tea break!' exclaimed Glenn Gregory, adding, with considerable understatement, 'If you're not used to working like that it's a bit hard.' In a cover feature for *Record Mirror* in support of *The Luxury Gap* the following week, journalist Jim Reid was curious to find out if Heaven 17 considered themselves to be technicians or musicians? 'A bit of both,' replied Martyn Ware. 'Ian's more technician than musician. I'm more musician than technician. Glenn? I give up!'

Heaven 17's next release was another single from *The Luxury Gap*, 'Come Live With Me', in June. 'Despite the last hit, despite all the talk, here at last is the single that proves that Glenn and the boys aren't really in the big League at all,' rued *Record Mirror*. 'It's a fine idea (as usual) but one that gets lost entirely with some incredibly clumsy phrasing and unnecessary frippery.' 'They can't blind us to the fact that this is Not Up To Standard,' added *Sounds*' Robbi Millar. 'I reckon Heaven 17 have gone off the boil, musically speaking.' Wham! – evidently not huge fans of Heaven 17 – were given the task of reviewing 'Come Live With Me' for *Smash Hits*. 'Some people said that Carol Kenyon's singing was the only reason that 'Temptation' got to number two,' observed George Michael. 'I would agree with them. This is not as original and it's really a return to the "clever" Heaven 17.' 'Even more of a dirge than 'Temptation',' added Andrew Ridgeley. 'They've definitely gone downhill since *Penthouse And Pavement*.' Which left just *Melody Maker* to file a more positive take on the single: 'How could they ever follow 'Temptation' with anything better?' asked their review. 'They haven't, but this song is still sublime.'

The public response to 'Come Live With Me' was similar to *Melody Maker*'s, and although the single failed to match the heights of 'Temptation' it nevertheless peaked at number five at the end of July as part of five weeks in the Top 10 and eleven weeks in the UK singles chart. And as 'Come Live With Me' dropped out of the chart at the beginning of September it was immediately replaced by Heaven 17's next single, 'Crushed By The Wheels Of Industry', which *Record Mirror* made their Record of the Week. 'Thankfully Heaven 17 have finally clicked and make dance records that you can actually dance to,' enthused Mike Gardner. 'Now their stylish sound is pure nourishment for the feet, as well as for the head and heart.' *Sounds*' Tom Hibbert was also impressed: 'Highly entertaining pop funk with sardonic "woo-woos" and a cynical jab at society in general.'

Twisted Sister frontman Dee Snider was reviewing the singles for *Melody Maker* the week that 'Crushed By The Wheels Of Industry' was released: 'It's very hip, very modern, very now. It's a very now looking cover, it's very in. It's Bowie. It's Roxy. It's Motown. It's Stax. I dunno… at least heavy metal is proud enough to admit that it's all the same old shit re-hashed. These people are actually trying to convince me that it's something new and original and different. It isn't.' 'Crushed By The Wheels Of Industry' spent seven weeks in the UK singles chart, which included two consecutive weeks at a peak position of seventeen in the second half of September 1983.

Heaven 17 finished their year on a high with an appearance on the prestigious Christmas Day edition of *Top of the Pops*, and while The Human League were conspicuous by their absence, Glenn Gregory, Ian Marsh, and Martyn Ware performed 'Temptation' alongside an illustrious selection of their 1983 peers, which included the Eurythmics performing 'Sweet Dreams (Are Made Of This)' and Freeez performing 'I.O.U.', alongside an airing of the video for Duran Duran's 'Is There Something I Should Know?' and The Flying Pickets' performance of the current number one, their cover of Yazoo's 'Only You'. A second festive special, broadcast on December 29th, added performances of 'True' by Spandau Ballet and 'New Song' from Howard Jones to illustrate just how far electronic music, and the original electronic music pioneers, had insinuated their way into the mainstream and into the public consciousness over the course of 1983.

By coincidence, the first *Top of the Pops* of 1984 was another special edition, this time dedicated to celebrating the show's 20th anniversary with an expanded edition which presented current hits – including Frankie Goes To Hollywood making their *Top of the Pops* debut with 'Relax' – alongside some of the show's finest moments from the previous two decades, an eclectic selection which presented archive footage of Gary Numan performing 'Cars' and Soft

Cell performing 'Tainted Love', alongside archive performances from Procol Harum, Engelbert Humperdinck, Cliff Richard and The Beatles.

As Frankie Goes To Hollywood's star ascended, Soft Cell's faltered. In August 1983, in response to a vicious assessment of *Torment And Toreros*, the latest album from his side project Marc & The Mambas, Soft Cell's Marc Almond had issued a press release announcing his retirement from recording. 'Finding myself increasingly confused and unhappy within the music business, I no longer wish to continue on the recording side of the music scene, whatever that may be and whoever I may be,' Almond began, adding unequivocally, 'I no longer wish to sing on records, in fact I no longer wish to sing. I don't want to be involved in any more interviews.' By the time the statement had been distributed to the media and was ready to go to press, a further statement from Marc Almond's representatives put the situation into better perspective. 'Fresh indications suggest, however, that Marc might have acted rashly in posting the letter,' reported the *NME*. 'Some Bizzare report he is feeling much happier and has decided to go ahead with the recording of Soft Cell's next single and third LP in September.'

'I do tend to make overdramatic statements, like I never want to be involved in music again,' Almond admitted in an interview with the *NME* later. 'Immediately after I said it I saw myself as a bit of a defeatist, which is not my thing, really. I want to be a fighter, I don't want to give up.' Subsequently Soft Cell released their new single in September as planned, and the release saw the band back in the Top 20 of the UK singles chart for the first time since the release of 'What' a year earlier when 'Soul Inside' peaked at number sixteen and spent a month in the Top 40. The *NME*'s Richard Cook liked the single – "Soul Inside' is a mad tumult of disco melodies and rich keyboard underlay crowned by a tempestuous vocal' – but *Sounds*' Garry Bushell did not. 'On the evidence of 'Soul Inside' Almond's search for a tune is still unsuccessful. He couldn't write a decent song if he was stranded on Fantasy Island,' sniped Bushell. 'But at least this makes a change from his usual dragging banal drone, being an uptempo banal drone.'

In December, following a successful tour of the USA, Soft Cell announced that they would play three farewell shows at London's Hammersmith Palais in January. 'We haven't any plans to bring out another single. The album will be released in the new year and that will be the last thing Soft Cell will bring out,' Marc Almond told *Record Mirror* at the end of the month. 'I think we achieved a certain subversiveness in the charts and brought back the sort of over dramatic ballad like 'Say Hello, Wave Goodbye'. I hear a lot of other things now and think "oh yeah, we did that two years ago".' *This Last Night In Sodom*, which would be Soft Cell's last album for almost twenty years, was released in March 1984 and peaked at a respectable number twelve on the UK albums chart.

As Soft Cell bowed out gracefully, their manager and label head, Stevo Pearce, turned his attentions back to the latest signing to his Some Bizzare label, Cabaret Voltaire, who he had signed in May and had subsequently licensed to Virgin Records for a reported £135,000 advance plus Richard Branson's tie, a water bed, a CD player, three suitcases and a bubble car. As the various contracts were finalised, Cabaret Voltaire announced that their first single under the new deal would be 'Just Fascination' – which featured additional synthesiser work from new label-mate, Soft Cell's Dave Ball – to be followed by an album entitled *The Crack Down* [sic]. 'Just Fascination' was released as a seven-inch single at the start of July alongside a twelve-inch single where an extended mix of 'Just Fascination' appeared on the B-side while the A-side featured an extended mix of the album's title track 'Crackdown'.

Although Cabaret Voltaire had released an album a year since 1979 and had enjoyed independent chart success (1981's *Red Mecca* and 1982's *2x45* had both topped the independent albums chart, and *2x45* had actually scraped into the UK albums chart at ninety-eight for a single week), none of their single or album releases to date had crossed into the mainstream. But with major label Virgin Records behind the new album project, all eyes were on Cabaret Voltaire, who were under suspicion of selling out. 'Cabaret Voltaire's first big money venture brings in star NY producer John Luongo to help them break their increasingly restrictive mould,' the *NME*'s Chris Bohn wrote in his review of 'Just Fascination' at the end of June. 'Sensibly he has done little to disturb the pulsating fear at the heart of the CV art. On the contrary he highlights it by cutting away all extraneous noises, clipping the sound back to brute sensual rhythms sparsely coloured by spindly guitar and punctuated with terse organ phrases.' *Sounds* were similarly impressed and made 'Just Fascination' their 'Modern Single of the Week' (alongside Elvis Costello, whose 'Everyday I Write The Book' was made 'Traditional Single of the Week'), Hugh Fielder calling the release a 'Forceful and determined start to the Cabs' career with Some Bizzare. Their austere approach has been nudged into a more commercial path by American producer John Luongo but he never loses sight of the essence of the group or the song.'

Cabaret Voltaire, now slimmed down to Richard H. Kirk and Stephen Mallinder following the amicable departure of fellow founding member Chris Watson, embarked on a series of interviews to promote the single, and their forthcoming album *The Crackdown*. Naturally the question they were asked repeatedly was why they had made the move to Virgin Records. 'We wanted to try another formula, just change things around and see what the end result was, instead of carrying on releasing another album that we'd do in isolation and release on Rough Trade again,' Stephen Mallinder told *Melody Maker*'s Lynden Barber. 'That seemed like a formula that we'd tried and tested and we thought it was getting a bit safe.' 'We've never really been champions of the independent label thing, it was more of a case of sticking out for control over what you're doing,' added Richard H. Kirk. 'With the new set-up we've got total control over everything that's released and everything we do.'

The media were also curious about Cabaret Voltaire's new commercial sound. 'It's certainly more "accessible" and if we can utilise the things available to us now, we're certainly going to cut across more barriers than, say, the last couple of records have done. We've made sure we steered clear of that notion that if something is more commercial or accessible then those terms are synonymous with "bland",' Mallinder admitted in a cover story for the *NME*. 'We're very self-conscious about that — we've tried to make sure that what we've done has maintained the energy and aggression and atmosphere of what we did before.' 'We've just cleaned up the dirt a bit, that's all. The dirt is still there, it's just that you can hear it better,' he joked in an interview for *Flexipop*. 'We still play out of tune and out of time.' 'Just Fascination' became Cabaret Voltaire's first mainstream singles chart entry when it spent one week in the UK singles charts at ninety-six.

Three weeks after 'Just Fascination''s foray into the singles chart, Cabaret Voltaire's newly released fifth album, *The Crackdown*, entered the UK albums chart at thirty-one and spent four weeks on the chart in total. *The Crackdown* was also rapturously reviewed by the music press. 'Forget that old, grey image — these new-age Cabs have no stigma attached. In fact, they're right in there with the front runners, surfacing with an entirely satisfying slice of metallic electropunk-phunk,' declared *Record Mirror*'s Betty Page in a five-out-of-five review. *Sounds*' Dave Henderson also awarded *The Crackdown* five out of five. 'The jigsaw is carefully pieced together and the result is an album that will be influential in years to come and, hopefully, enlarged on with their next release,' reported Henderson, declaring, 'Their integrity is still intact.' In the

NME, Paul Du Noyer agreed: 'While 'The Crackdown' is in no way a betrayal of the group's long-standing virtues – they've refined them, not abandoned them – the record's an essential progression which should render them accessible to a huge new audience. If, as the signs suggest, Cabaret Voltaire's new music earns them a rightful spot in the commercial sun, then the charts will be a richer and more real place for their presence.'

ULTRAVOX CONTINUED TO WORK their 1982 album *Quartet* in 1983 and released two further singles from the album in the spring. 'Visions Of Blue' came out at the beginning of March, accompanied by another round of withering reviews. 'I blew the dust off the stylus, changed the turntable speed and got the bloke in from next door to check my wiring,' reported *Smash Hits*' David Hepworth. 'But no use. This still sounded awfully dirge-like.' 'I don't know what it's going to sound like on the radio but on the office hifi it sounds like 100 synthesisers fighting in vain to be heard against the QE2 foghorn,' added Gavin Martin in the *NME*. Only *Record Mirror*'s Robin Smith had anything positive to report. 'I've been unmercifully unkind to Ultravox in the past, but I always liked 'Vienna' and this has the same ring of confidence and enterprising style,' Smith declared. 'All is forgiven, this should be huge.'

'Visions In Blue' peaked at number fifteen in the UK singles charts at the end of March after a *Top of the Pops* showing of Chris Cross and Midge Ure's video to accompany the single – actually an edited version of the video after the original cut caused a frisson of controversy when it was revealed that it contained scenes which *Record Mirror* gleefully described as 'two naked girls soaping each other down in a bath and a sweet young thing slipping out of her military uniform during a ballroom scene'. Anticipating that the 'Visions In Blue' video would raise some eyebrows at the BBC, Ultravox had made two versions of the video, and were immediately able to provided *Top of the Pops* with a family-friendly edit. 'I certainly wouldn't say that it's pornographic or even blue. We filmed it in tasteful soft focus like one of those David Hamilton pictures, so I can't really see that the film is going to offend anybody,' Chris Cross told *Record Mirror*'s Robin Smith with a dignity which slipped a little as he described some of the further challenges he and Ure faced when making the video: 'When you're directing two attractive naked girls, you don't shout, "Cor, they've got nice tits", you act professionally. If you didn't then you'd be a panting mess on the floor.'

The final single to be taken from *Quartet* was 'We Came To Dance' in May. 'Leagues ahead of much of the puerile electro bop-bop that's around at the moment,' reported *Smash Hits*' Mark Steels in an unusually enthusiastic review. 'This is surprisingly vigorous and unpompous for Ultravox,' reported *Sounds*' Tony Mitchell, who also went on to declare 'We Came To Dance' 'The first Ultravox single I've actually liked.' Elsewhere in the music press it was business as usual: 'Ultravox have "expired" stamped all over them, from their weak-kneed vocals to their gutlessly twittering synths and wholly pitiful sense of what makes a song,' sniffed *Melody Maker*'s Adam Sweeting. 'Imagine running through quick-setting concrete while wearing a suit of armour and you have a very fair assessment of this record.' 'Pompous mid-tempo meandering that will probably limp into a chart position somewhere before simpering off after a week or two,' added *Record Mirror*'s Simon Hills, not incorrectly. Nevertheless 'We Came To Dance' spent five weeks in the Top 40 of the UK singles chart, during which time it peaked at eighteen in the middle of June.

Before turning their collective attention to the next Ultravox album, the band's Warren Cann and Midge Ure each announced side projects to be released in the interim. Since 1980 Warren Cann had been collaborating with composer Hans Zimmer on a project they called Helden, and by March 1983 the duo were ready to release their first album, *Spies*. 'Gaping jaws and stiff necks were the order of the evening for the unveiling of Helden – alias Ultravox drummer Warren Cann and synthesiser professor Hans Zimmer – last week,' enthused *Sounds*. 'The location was London's Planetarium and the discomfort was caused by trying to follow some bewitching laser patterns around the star-covered dome. Unfortunately the music didn't have as much flair, sticking to ponderous electronic pomp more reminiscent of the Seventies than the Eighties.' Despite the high-profile launch, *Spies* was still unreleased in June, when *Smash Hits* caught up with Ultravox and asked Cann about the status of the project: 'We've had real trouble getting a deal for *Spies*,' Cann admitted. 'Nobody has turned us down because they didn't like it – they just don't know how to handle it.' The Helden project was subsequently sidelined as Cann refocused on Ultravox and Zimmer became an increasingly in-demand composer of film music. To date, *Spies* remains unreleased.

In the spring of 1983, at around the same time as Warren Cann's ill-fated Helden launch, Midge Ure and Japan bassist Mick Karn announced a collaboration of their own, which resulted in the release of a June single, 'After A Fashion', the first release on Ure's own label, Musicfest. 'Committed music makers they may be,' noted *Record Mirror*'s Paul Sexton the same week, 'but when all's said this still remains pretentious piffle and the title seems to sum them up.' Over at *Melody Maker*, Steve Sutherland agreed, describing the single as 'more pompous pontification about nothing that matters. For all its reptilian, fake East European ambience, it's a needless, humourless, motiveless supersession involving two chaps who obviously deem their art seriously above all these sorts of things.'

Mick Karn and Midge Ure promoted the single with some good-natured interviews which promised that more material from the collaboration was to be recorded and released. 'We'll do some more recordings, definitely,' Ure stated in *Record Mirror* in July, to which Karn added, 'Working with Midge is like a break, really. I find it enjoyable and much lighter in terms of responsibility, and he probably feels the same. It's like a breath of fresh air.' But would the collaboration go the same way as Visage, *Smash Hits*' Mark Steels asked Ure at the end of June? 'No, never. Mick's different, a very talented guy, and there's no question of a fight for control as we've both got very similar ideas.' However, despite a big-budget video – filmed in Egypt and featuring Hazel O'Connor as its leading lady – 'After A Fashion' spent just two weeks in the Top 40 of the UK singles chart, both weeks at a peak chart position of thirty-nine at the end of July.

Released at the same time as 'After A Fashion' was David Sylvian's own first single release since Japan's split, and while promoting 'Forbidden Colours', a new collaboration with Ryuichi Sakamoto, it was inevitable that Sylvian would be asked his opinion of 'After A Fashion'. 'I like it, I really like the instrumentation,' the singer admitted to Radio 1's Richard Skinner. 'I'm not an Ultravox fan, to be honest. I don't listen to Ultravox and therefore I'm quite surprised that I like it, because it does seem to lean more on that side for me.'

'Forbidden Colours' was an instrumental track that Ryuichi Sakamoto had composed for the soundtrack to the film *Merry Christmas Mr Lawrence* – starring Sakamoto himself alongside David Bowie – which Sakamoto had sent to David Sylvian at the end of 1982 in the hope that Sylvian might add some lyrics. Sylvian, who was experiencing a creative block following the demise of Japan, did so and the collaborative version was released at the end of June. Although the single was a commercial hit, spending two months in the UK singles chart and peaking at sixteen at the end of July, the press response to the single was largely muted. Wham! were cautious in their review of 'Forbidden Colours' for *Smash Hits*. 'Very much a film theme rather than a song,' noted George Michael. 'It would probably be better as an instrumental. I quite enjoyed it.' 'Pleasant enough background music,' nodded Andrew Ridgeley. Richard Cook, reviewing the single for the *NME*, was the most positive: 'Although the stately, poised orchestration is down to Sakamoto's music Sylvian's voice discovers a tenderness to overlay the appropriately brusque and courtly theme. No matter how careful stylised, Sylvian's work has a caress of faith about it that is hard to dispel.'

In his interview with Richard Skinner, David Sylvian was also asked about Japan's swansong release *Oil On Canvas*, a live album recorded in London at the end of 1982 which had entered the UK album charts at number five in June and spent a further eight weeks in the Top 40. 'In a way *Oil On Canvas* had to be done because we had to produce a live album. Virgin were going to put one out anyway beforehand, a live album of past recorded things, but I said no, I'd much rather do it from this tour and take complete control of it and do it in the best way possible,' Sylvian explained, adding, 'Live albums aren't that important, they are documentation at best – and really that's all it can be sold as, as a documentation of the live shows.' In his review of the release, *Melody Maker*'s Steve Sutherland agreed: "Oil On Canvas' is the sound of saving face while reluctantly celebrating the face, an unloved task lovingly performed; a dignified, unsentimental farewell.' 'It's not intended to make any converts, thank God, but it'll surely make a sad but satisfying memorial for the ever present ranks of devotees, like me,' wrote Betty Page in her review of *Oil On Canvas* for *Record Mirror*.

While Ultravox would spend much of the rest of 1983 working on their next album, *Lament*, which would be released in April 1984, the band did take a leaf out of Japan's book by releasing a live mini-album of their own at the end of 1983 in the wake of their lavish *Quartet* tour. *Monument – The Soundtrack* featured six tracks: the title track, which had previously been released as the B-side to Ultravox's 1982 single 'Hymn', and five live tracks – 'Reap The Wild Wind', 'The Voice', 'Vienna', 'Mine For Life' and 'Hymn' – all recorded at London's Hammersmith Odeon in December 1982. *Monument – The Soundtrack* peaked at number nine in the UK albums chart at the end of October and remained in the charts until the end of 1983, selling over 100,000 albums in the process. A live video, *Monument*, for which *Monument – The Soundtrack* was the soundtrack, came out at the same time. 'Ultravox, for all the technical wizardry, are also one of the best live bands around,' proclaimed an unusually supportive *Record Mirror* of the video. '"Monument" captures this about as well as any recorded set I've seen.'

In March, Gary Numan, Ultravox's most famous fan, announced that he was in the Channel Islands working on material for a new album, but had remained determined to return to live performance. 'There will be a new album and when it's launched he will be doing something live,' a spokesman declared. The announcement was followed in April with the news that former Be-Bop Deluxe frontman Bill Nelson was in the frame to produce the new Numan album and that a forty-date UK tour was being planned to start in September. 'After the Wembley dates I got so sick of the slagging that I decided to give it a break. Now I want to get out and play a proper tour with experience behind me,' Numan explained of his decision.

Record Mirror's Simon Hills visited Numan in the Channel Islands for an interview in April and found the singer in good spirits. Talking about the plan to play more concerts after bowing out of live work with such finality in 1981, this was a more mature and confident Gary Numan: 'At the end I just thought what an unpleasant business this is. With experience and age you know how to deal with it, but I was very young. I hadn't had the years on the road that everyone else had.' The same spirit of independence had also carried into the songwriting for the new album: 'Record company people try and push you into making each song sell more than the last,' Numan explained, 'but that's the wrong way to talk to a bloke who writes songs. It's wrong to make him think about what he should be writing instead of what he wants to write.'

Numan announced the first of his 1983 tour dates in June. 'We're told that his new show, named 'Warriors', will be as spectacular as the 'Touring Principle' and 'Teletour' concert tours – and he'll be backed by original group members Chris Payne, Ced Sharpley and Russell Bell,' reported the *NME*, alongside news of twenty-one UK concerts, ahead of a further fourteen announced the following week. 'Warriors' was subsequently confirmed as the title of the new Gary Numan single and album. 'I wanted to come out fighting, to be more positive. A lot of the records in the charts are very pure and very sweet, but I find them unchallenging,' Numan told *Record Mirror*'s Robin Smith later in the year. 'I think you should use synths like a steamroller, they should be big and powerful to get your heart thumping. The Human League do it very well. The feel and power of instruments has always fascinated me.'

The release of his 'Warriors' single in August also provided Gary Numan fans with a first glimpse at the singer's latest image. Inspired by Mel Gibson's costumes in the post-apocalyptic *Mad Max* films, Numan's latest look paired blonde hair with black leather and motorcycle boots. The styling for the new project immediately raised some eyebrows across the reviews of 'Warriors': 'Now [Gary Numan] thinks he's some futuristic Mad Max-orientated street "warrior". Dear oh dear!' twittered *Smash Hits'* Tom Hibbert. 'At least his records remain the same.' 'You may laugh at the sight of Gaz, all dressed up in his Mad Max swag to promote his 'Warriors' image. But the music, you may depend upon it, will wipe the smile straight off your face,' reported Paul Du Noyer in the *NME*. 'Tedious nonsense. With knobs on.' And Twisted Sister's Dee Snider pulled no punches in his review of 'Warriors' for *Melody Maker*: 'Gary Numan! I see you're making a comeback! Didn't we bury you deep enough?' 'Warriors' nevertheless entered the UK singles chart at thirty at the start of September and climbed ten places to a peak position of twenty the following week after an appearance on the ever-supportive *Top of the Pops*.

'I know the new album's going to get slagged off, but now the jibes won't sting. There are probably journalists out there who can't wait to review it so they can carve it up, but I don't care any more,' Numan told *Melody Maker*'s Helen Fitzgerald before the release of the *Warriors* album in September. In the case of *Smash Hits*, Numan's prediction was correct, Tim de Lisle awarding the album just two out of ten and writing, 'This is about as much fun as watching an Open University programme. The words are meaningless, the rhythms plod, the vocals grate. The odd chord change or keyboard phrase hints at talent but Gary has stood still for four years and in pop music you can't do that.' But *Warriors* also attracted more considered, if not exactly enthusiastic, notices from *Record Mirror* and *Melody Maker*: "Warriors' is about the most bearable Numan record I've heard. It's well played, sweetly produced, and at times, Dick Morrissey's sax is quite lovely,' admitted the former's Jim Reid.

'All this should give Numan a base to work on, but unfortunately his song writing is colourless, his singing whiney and his lyrics just plain embarrassing.' "Warriors' suffers from Numan's critical identity crisis: should he step boldly into a new arena and disown the past, or should he reassemble old components in a frantic attempt at mass deception?' asked Helen Fitzgerald in the latter. 'Despite a few well orchestrated stabs at camouflaging old methods with a new funky jazz overlay, the absurd mixture of sterile frigidity and bubbling funk overtones can't quite be reconciled.' *Warriors* charted at number twelve towards the end of September before dropping out of the Top 40 a fortnight later, and out of the charts entirely after just six weeks.

Despite the confident swagger of the Gary Numan who appeared on stage at forty shows across the UK in September, October and November – including three nights at London's Hammersmith Odeon and a further two at the capital's Dominion Theatre – behind the scenes the *Warriors* project had proved challenging at best. The recording sessions with Bill Nelson were fraught – something *Sounds* had reported on their gossip page earlier in the year, revealing, 'Rumour has it that the mild mannered and talented Nelson was on the point of walking out of the sessions more than once, over attitudes from the Numan camp which are not normally encountered outside the schoolroom' – to the extent that Nelson requested that his production credit be removed from the final album, while Numan's relationship with WEA, who financed, marketed and distributed his releases for Beggars Banquet, hit a new low after changes in the label's personnel left him unsupported despite previous assertions to the contrary. 'When the new people came in, I was as far from a priority act as it was possible to be. I felt as though they'd cut me down at the knees,' Numan wrote in *Praying to the Aliens* later, 'it was the last time I got excited about a promise in the music business.'

Given everything that was going on, it was hardly a surprise when the second and final single from *Warriors*, 'Sister Surprise', spent just three weeks in the UK singles chart in October, where it peaked at thirty-two despite another *Top of the Pops* appearance. 'A crummy cousin to 'Sister Midnight'. Cold,' wrote the *NME*'s Barney Hoskyns. 'This is the usual electro-jerk disfiguration, a very poor approximation of Bowie's gloomy teutonic escapades. Terminally embarrassing,' added an underwhelmed Allan Jones in *Melody Maker*.

As *Warriors* descended the UK albums charts, John Foxx's third album, *The Golden Section*, entered at its chart peak position of twenty-seven at the beginning of October. 'It was a definite decision to go back to pop music, because there's a big trend at the moment where everyone is using American soul as their vocabulary for writing songs and that produces some interesting things – but I wanted to use a vocabulary that was English,' Foxx told *Sounds'* Johnny Waller in response to a question about the apparently psychedelic influences on the first single from the album, 'Endlessly', which had reached an unpromising sixty-six in the UK singles chart in July. 'That Beatles era is tremendously unfashionable now, but if you listen to 'Strawberry Fields', they were using electronic techniques of reverse tapes that were very fresh and innovative,' Foxx explained. 'There's no nostalgia involved, it's the excitement in the records because they used to go into the studio and perform – which is slightly different to the way people record now.'

Reviews of *The Golden Section* were mixed. 'It should have been called 'The Strawberry Section',' scoffed *Record Mirror*'s Sharon Machola, awarding the album one-and-a-half marks out of five and continuing, 'From the opening track, 'Wild Love', you've let yourself in for an hour of the modern surf sound alias the Beatles' 'Strawberry Fields' harmonies, which get really irritating by side two.' *Smash Hits*' Jo-Anne Smith was significantly more positive and marked *The Golden Section* eight and a half out of ten, declaring, 'The onetime Ultravox singer's third LP retains that vital spark that made the first synthesiser music so exciting. The songs are poppy without being trite and are delivered with real warmth and passion.' A review which perfectly matched the vision for his music that Foxx had expressed to *Sounds'* Johnny Waller in July, when he had offered the music of Kraftwerk as a tangible influence, explaining, 'It sounded so new and the thinking behind what they did was immaculate and beautifully considered and I wanted to use what they'd done in the context of English pop.'

Meanwhile Kraftwerk, who – with the exception of a 1982 reissue of their 'Showroom Dummies' single – had been quiet since their 1981 *Computer World* project, and their UK number one with 'The Model', were also reported to be preparing new material for release in 1983. 'It was confirmed this week that Kraftwerk will be playing some UK concerts in the early spring,' the *NME* had announced at the start of February. 'They're being set up for late March and early April, and details are expected shortly. The visit will coincide with the release by EMI of their new studio album titled 'Technopop', their first since 'Computer World' was issued in 1981.'

March and April came and went with no further word from Kraftwerk with regards to a new album or to any plans the band might have to play live, and it wasn't until July that the band finally broke their silence with the announcement that they had recorded the official theme music for French TV's coverage of the forthcoming Tour De France, and that a single of the same name was to be released later in the month. 'There's still no hint of their new album coming out for some time,' *Record Mirror* added. 'Kraftwerk have taken time off from their Dusseldorf studios to watch the Tour De France, leaving the last touches to the LP still to be completed. There are plans to go out on the road when the album finally comes out, hopefully in the autumn.'

'Kraftwerk begin their next phase with an interesting, if not innovative, single which still manages to outshine the painful predictability of the Depeche Modes of this world,' reported Dave Henderson in his review of 'Tour De France' for *Sounds* at the end of July. 'It's mindless pop, without doubt, that will be repeated yet again next year. The secret is that the chemistry is constant and pleasing to the ear.' 'Sung in French, Kraftwerk seem to find an almost military sense of purpose and unity in the event – stern and relentless in their evocation,' mused Colin Irwin in *Melody Maker*, while the *NME*'s Gavin Martin turned in the most positive review of all when he described 'Tour De France' as 'A breathtaking and unsurpassable arrangement of savage electro-dynamics.'

The single entered the UK singles chart at forty-one in the first week of August after a single week of sales and spent the next month climbing slowly but steadily to its chart peak of twenty-two by the end of the month, as part of an eight week run in the charts. A new version of 'Tour De France', this time remixed by François Kevorkian, was released the following year and spent almost three months in the UK singles chart, where it peaked at twenty-four. 'Tour De France' performed better in the USA, however, reaching number four on *Billboard*'s Dance Club Songs, and being used in the soundtrack to the 1984 breakdance film *Breakin'*. Kraftwerk's much-anticipated new album wouldn't appear until the end of 1986, by which time its name had changed from *Techno Pop* to *Electric Cafe* and 'Tour De France' had been dropped from the album tracklisting.

Another European band enjoyed their first commercial success in the UK in 1983 when the *You Gotta Say Yes To Another Excess* album provided Yello with their first UK album chart position in May. Although the album – their third – only spent two weeks in the chart, peaking at sixty-five, the critical reception to the record was extraordinary. 'This almost unclassifiable Swiss group make playful use of danceable rhythms, deep voices, jerky electronics and anything else that comes to hand,' enthused Dave Rimmer in *Smash Hits*. 'They'd be easy to dismiss as a bunch of loonies but, although weird, repeated listenings reveal this to be a rewardingly daft collection.' 'Their sound is like their vision: one where funny peculiar blends with funny ha-ha, and where we're left none the wiser but all the more disturbed,' added *Melody Maker*'s Mark Brennan with enthusiasm. 'In a word: brilliant. In two: brilliantly subversive.' *Record Mirror* awarded *You Gotta Say Yes To Another Excess* a maximum five stars: 'There are people using the new music technology and there are people being used by the new music technology. Yello are using these new gadgets, and to great effect,' declared Jim Reid. 'This album is quite simply the most adventurous I've heard all year. Yello shed the constraints of the modern frigidity and create a music whose boundaries are those of the imagination, not the studio.'

Chris Burkham interviewed Yello – Boris Blank, Dieter Meier and Carlos Perón – for *Sounds* and opened his piece by describing the trio as 'a pinprick in the party balloon of pomposity'. 'I hope that there is a lot of joy, and a lot of fun in Yello, because we are having fun doing it,' Meier confirmed. 'For us each piece is more or less like a movie, almost. And the musical element, the singing and everything is quite different from piece to piece, but it always, I hope, has the same spirit in it.' Nor did Yello consider themselves musicians. 'We started as sound makers, we never played instruments. We recorded on cassettes using beer cans as drums, making sound pictures that were very rhythmically oriented,' Meier explained to *Record Mirror*'s Betty Page a few weeks later. 'We work together in a special way, creating things on tape, keeping that unique moment of something found. A painter doesn't rehearse a painting.'

A single, 'I Love You', followed the release of the album at the end of May and remained in the UK singles chart for seven weeks, slowly climbing to a chart peak of forty-one at the start of July on the back of a novel format courtesy of their label, Stiff: 'Yello are to bring out the first-ever 3D picture disc this week. It is a one-sided record called 'I Love You' and is issued with free 3D specs,' *Record Mirror* announced at the end of June. 'I Love You' received an enthusiastic response. 'A lovely slice of thoroughly modern music. Modern in that it allies the newest techniques with a sensibility that rides the bumps and bruises of the eighties,' wrote Jim Reid at the end of May. 'If this gets on the radio the autobahns of the western world will be transfigured into a network of neon and chrome,' declared Richard Cook in the *NME*. But not everyone was as enthusiastic. Paul Strange declared himself unimpressed by the extravagant praise that Yello had received at the hands of his peers and used his *Melody Maker* review of the single to redress the balance: "I Love You' shows [Yello] in their true light – minimalist dickheads with little talent, but capable of fooling the majority with booming beat and a dubious buzz.'

REACTION

1984–1993

'Well I don't think you can talk about electronic music as distinct from pop music any more, because pop music is electronic.'

Phil Oakey, *Sounds*, June 26th, 1982

AT THE END OF 1983 the American music media began reporting on the extraordinary success that British acts were enjoying in the USA. At the end of November 1983, *Rolling Stone* put Boy George on their cover under the headline 'England Swings – Great Britain Invades America's Music and Style. Again', while in the accompanying feature writer Parke Puterbaugh declared, 'A revolution in sound and style – lying somewhere between artful ingenuity and pure pop fun – has taken root in this country over the past year and a half. Much like the first great explosion of pop culture upon mass consciousness, which commenced with the Beatles' arrival in America in February 1964, the primary impetus for all this has been emanating from the far side of the Atlantic.' Puterbaugh further reported that over the course of 1983 a staggering 30 per cent of US record sales were by British artists, a sensation which had symbolically peaked in July 1983 when a staggering eighteen of America's Top 40 singles were of British origin, beating the previous record for such a feat, which had been set in 1965 by the 'British Invasion' groups including The Beatles, The Dave Clark Five, Herman's Hermits and The Swinging Blue Jeans.

Attempting to uncover the reasons behind the phenomena, Puterbaugh noted the importance of the 'fascinating new music' being made by the new wave of electronic acts. The success of M's 'Pop Muzik', The Human League's 'Don't You Want Me' and Soft Cell's 'Tainted Love' were all offered as specific examples of electronic music's creeping hold on the US charts, as were the emerging success stories of acts including Eurythmics, Depeche Mode and Ultravox. As diverse as the spectrum of British music undoubtedly was, Puterbaugh also identified a shared belief in the importance of image and presentation which played to the strengths of another cornerstone of this success story: MTV.

'Who could have guessed that the public would raptly enjoy listening to music through the low-fi speaker of a TV set while watching musicians cavort in awkwardly literal video stagings of a song's narrative?' marvelled Puterbaugh, evidently puzzled by the appeal of MTV, but nevertheless conceding, 'The British won out here, hands down. Next to the prosaic, foursquare appearance of the American bands, such acts as Duran Duran seemed like caviar. MTV opened up a whole new world that could not be fully apprehended over the radio. The visual angle played to the arty conceits of Britain's young style barons, suggesting something more exotic than the viewer was likely to find in the old hometown. The big Duran Duran hits, 'Girls on Film' and 'Hungry like the Wolf', were MTV favorites three months before radio began to pick up on them.'

The success of MTV also impacted on the formats of American radio stations. 'I think the kids who watched it felt that there was something more than what they were being spoon-fed on local radio stations,' Polygram Records' Head of A&R, Jerry Jaffe, told Puterbaugh in the *Rolling Stone* piece. 'Radio stations, for the first time, were getting requests for songs they were not playing.' Jaffe also made an important point about the division between the approach of the British acts and their American contemporaries: 'Nine out of ten bands you see in America are an amalgam of what they've heard on AOR radio. The motivation for American kids is, "We want to be the next Van Halen and get rich."' 'Breaking America was what everyone wanted to do,' British journalist Dave Rimmer echoed in his 1985 book *Like Punk Never*

Happened. 'Not just for the money, though that was most of it, but also because if you made it in America then you *made* it.'

Another British band to enjoy US success in the second half of the eighties was Pet Shop Boys, who released their debut single in 1984. Pet Shop Boys was the creation of former *Smash Hits* journalist Neil Tennant – 'I think my enduring contribution to *Smash Hits* was that I was the first person to call Billy Idol "Sir William Idol",' Tennant told the magazine in 1985, adding, 'Oh, and might I add that my other big contribution was "purlease"?' – and architect Chris Lowe. 'We met in an electrical shop on the King's Road. I was getting a plug for my synthesiser, Chris was buying something and we started talking and Chris came back to my flat to look at my synthesiser,' Tennant told *Smash Hits*' Chris Heath in 1986. 'After that we became friends and started writing songs together. No one will believe that a) we met like that and b) we got the name the Pet Shop Boys from some friends who worked in a pet shop – people think it means something rude. But both stories are true.'

By the end of 1993 Pet Shop Boys had placed five studio albums in the Top 3 of the UK albums chart – *Please* (1986) reached number three, *Actually* (1987), *Introspective* (1988) and *Behaviour* (1990) all reached number two, and *Very* (1993) topped the charts – as well as a spin-off remix album, *Disco*, which reached number fifteen in 1986, and a compilation album, *Discography*, which reached number three in November 1991. Over the same period the band also scored four number one singles with their 1985 debut 'West End Girls', 1987's 'It's A Sin' and 'Always On My Mind', and 1988's 'Heart', part of a run of twenty-one hit singles between 1986 and 1993.

While the fact that Pet Shop Boys were gay was something of an open secret – it wasn't until 1994, in an interview with *Attitude* magazine, that Neil Tennant publicly acknowledged his homosexuality – Erasure's Andy Bell was less coy. 'I didn't want there to be any doubt in anyone's mind as to who I was,' he acknowledges today, while admitting that the revelation also allowed him to develop an exaggerated theatrical persona which he could use to disguise his underlying shyness. Erasure formed in 1985 when Bell responded to a *Melody Maker* advert placed by Vince Clarke, who was looking for a singer for a new project. 'What I was looking for was someone young, enthusiastic with the kind of attitude I like,' Clarke told *Melody Maker*'s Helen Fitzgerald in April 1985. 'I took out an ad in *Melody Maker*. I had about eighty replies, auditioned forty of them – a mammoth task – and chose a guy called Andy Bell who I think is quite brilliant.'

Given that both acts were electronic duos and both were experiencing huge success at the same time, it was inevitable that parallels would be constantly drawn between Pet Shop Boys and Erasure, although both acts remained – and still remain – sanguine about any perceived rivalry. But success wasn't as immediate for Erasure as it had been for Pet Shop Boys. The first three Erasure singles – 'Who Needs Love Like That', 'Heavenly Action' and 'Oh L'Amour' – all failed to break into the Top 40, and it wasn't until the release of 'Sometimes' in October 1986 that Clarke and Bell enjoyed their first hit when the single reached number two in the UK singles chart in December, only held off the top spot by Europe's rock anthem 'The Final Countdown'.

Although Erasure's debut album, *Wonderland*, peaked at an unpromising seventy-one in the middle of 1986, Andy Bell and Vince Clarke remained philosophical about their situation, and set about further honing their craft. 'It does take a long time [to form a partnership] because when you write with someone you're kind of exposing yourself because you put yourself in the position where you're up for criticism from the other person,' Clarke would say of his emerging creative relationship with Bell later. 'Not that Andy is ever going to say to me "That's shit" or vice versa, but we now have an understanding such that if one of us isn't one hundred percent behind the idea then the idea gets dropped. I think that's the key to our relationship and our longevity.'

Following the success of 'Sometimes', Erasure's commercial floodgates opened and their second album, *The Circus*, reached number six in the UK albums chart. Erasure subsequently enjoyed a run of sixteen Top 20 hits, six of which reached the Top 5, before finally topping the UK singles chart for five weeks in 1992 with their four-track *Abba-Esque* EP. Erasure's first hits compilation, *Pop! The First 20 Hits*, followed later the same year and earned the band a triple platinum album in the process, scoring the duo their fourth number one album in a row following *The Innocents* (1988), *Wild!* (1989) and *Chorus* (1991), and securing Erasure's place in electronic pop history.

Erasure's rise to prominence came alongside another pop duo, The Communards, who would enjoy a 1986 number one with their version of Harold Melvin & The Blue Notes' 'Don't Leave Me This Way' which topped the UK singles chart for four successive weeks in September and October and sold around half a million copies. The Communards – Jimmy Somerville (also variously known as Jimmi or Jimi) on vocals and Richard Coles on keyboards – followed a similar format to both Erasure and the Pet Shop Boys, and to Soft

Cell before them, in that they presented their singer as the focus of the band while the keyboard player was content to remain in the background. Less overtly electronic than their peers – Coles was actually a classically trained pianist and multi-instrumentalist – The Communards released nine singles, all of which made it into the Top 30, and two studio albums: *Communards*, which made number seven in the UK albums chart in 1987, and *Red*, which peaked at four the following year.

Jimmy Somerville and Richard Coles met on the London gay scene and worked together as participants in a documentary film, *Framed Youth: The Revenge of the Teenage Perverts*, produced by the London Lesbian and Gay Youth Video Project in 1983. Somerville also met Steve Bronski and Larry Steinbachek at the shoot, and the trio formed Bronski Beat. 'The idea was never "Let's have a band." It was just "Let's do some music together." It was only the opportunity to perform that turned us into a band,' Steinbachek told *Spin*'s Barney Hoskyns in 1985, by which time the trio had four hit singles and a hit album under their belts. 'I just did it because I wasn't doing anything else,' added Somerville. 'I'd never wanted to be in a band and I'd never wanted to sing. I was just unemployed and it was something to do in my spare time.'

Emerging in the wake of Frankie Goes To Hollywood, Bronski Beat, who made no effort to hide or blur their homosexuality, quickly found themselves frustrated when much of the focus that came their way was directed towards their sexuality rather then their politics or their music. 'Gay has become trendy in a horrible way,' Somerville told *Melody Maker*'s Helen Fitzgerald in 1984. 'The first question people ask us is what do we think of Boy George – that infuriates me. We get categorised along with Frankie just because we're another pop band, but we're not just another pop band. We each have different reasons for doing what we're doing. My reasons for doing this at the moment are purely political, Larry is doing it because he wants to be a producer, and Steve just likes playing music.'

Fitzgerald's interview came in the wake of the staggering success of Bronski Beat's debut single, 'Smalltown Boy', which spent three months in the UK singles chart, peaking at number three in June 1984 and spending three weeks inside the Top 10. A second single, 'Why?', reached number six in October in advance of the release of Bronski Beat's debut album, *The Age Of Consent*, the same month. *The Age Of Consent* spent two weeks at a peak position of number four before spending a further fifty weeks in the UK albums chart, during which time it achieved platinum sales, assisted by a third single, a cover of

George and Ira Gershwin's 'Ain't Necessarily So' – complete with a clarinet part played by Richard Coles – which reached number sixteen in January 1985. By the time of the release of the fourth and final single from *The Age Of Consent* – a medley of the Donna Summer classics 'Love To Love You Baby' and 'I Feel Love', and John Leyton's 'Johnny Remember Me', which the band performed with Marc Almond on guest vocals and which spent two weeks at number three in the UK singles chart in June – the trio was starting to fracture under the pressure of their success and of Jimmy Somerville's restlessness within the confines of the group.

In the spring of 1985 Somerville announced he'd left Bronski Beat and was launching a new project, The Committee – later to be changed to The Communards so as not to antagonise an existing band working under the name The Committee – with Richard Coles. 'Jimmi's decision to leave was brought on by his reluctance to accept the pressures of the business of success, and felt that the business was taking over from the sheer fun of singing,' reported a spokesman for Bronski Beat's record label. Steinbachek and Bronski put out

Bronski Beat & Marc Almond, 1985.

a statement of their own, saying, 'There are no hard feelings between us and Jimmi and we both wish him the best of luck in his future project.'

In an interview with the *NME*'s Paolo Hewitt in May, Somerville cited two main reasons for his decision: a failure to deal with the demands put on a successful group; and his bandmates' increasing reluctance to engage in direct political activity, a result of what Somerville perceived as apathy on the part of Bronski and Steinbachek. 'I just realised that I would much rather work with someone who I knew for a long time, especially politically,' Somerville continued. 'We're [Somerville and Coles] both involved in Gays Support The Miners and things like that, and he's much more politically involved than Larry and Steve were… I really enjoy the stuff we do,' Somerville added, 'it's really good work… I just hope it goes well but I won't see it as the end of the world if it doesn't.' A year later The Communards found themselves with 1986's best-selling UK single for 'Don't Leave Me This Way', which was also a significant American success for the duo when it topped the *Billboard* Dance Club Songs chart the same year.

In 1990, Factory Records founder Tony Wilson was invited to conceive and host a panel session at the New Music Seminar in New York. In true renegade fashion Wilson devised an event under the title 'Wake Up America, You're Dead!' and invited a selection of interested parties to join him on stage for a vigorous discussion about the state of the music industry. 'What people in America don't seem to know,' Wilson began, 'is that the music which has come out of Chicago and Detroit in the last ten years has so changed British pop music – not only dance music but also rock music – that now if you're a British rock group and you cannot play rock music in the style to which you can dance and with the rhythms that have come out of America but that have been ignored here, then you aren't a rock group that matters. You're dead.' That the session subsequently collapsed in shambles comes as no surprise when you consider that Wilson's panelists included comedian Keith Allen – introduced as 'Dr Keith Allen of the Post-Freudian Therapy Centre in Geneva' – who made it his sole responsibility to seize every opportunity to taunt the New Music Seminar audience, but Wilson had a point.

The music coming out of Chicago and Detroit that Tony Wilson was referring to was house and techno, interrelated dance genres born from the city's underground dance clubs and exported to the UK and the rest of the world with palpable effect throughout the eighties and beyond. Two of the movers and shakers from that world, Derrick May and Marshall Jefferson –

producers, label heads and artists in their own right – had been recruited to Wilson's New Music Seminar panel in recognition of their contributions to what had been a seismic shift in dance music. Wilson provided his audience with a potted history of the new dance scene, and of the cast of characters that populated it, a story which began with Frankie Knuckles.

Although he had been born in New York and had honed his considerable skills as a DJ there, in 1977 Frankie Knuckles was invited to play a run of DJ dates at Chicago club the Warehouse. The Warehouse had previously run a series of parties in warehouse spaces across Chicago, hence its name, but now the club had its own permanent premises and Knuckles was invited to launch the new venue. Having played a fortnight of inaugural shows, and with nothing waiting for him back in New York, Knuckles was invited to remain in Chicago and become a partner in the Warehouse, which he did. 'I figured, "What the hell?" and that move was probably the best thing that ever happened to me,' Knuckles admitted to writer Sheryl Garratt later.

Frankie Knuckles started his tenure at the Warehouse playing sets which largely reflected the disco boom which was successful at the time, but with an additional intellectual rigour that made the Warehouse an immediate success. But as time went on, and disco fell out of favour, Knuckles found himself having to resort to more innovative techniques to keep ahead of the curve and retain the loyalty of his audience. 'By '81 when they had declared that disco is dead, all the record labels were getting rid of their dance departments, or their disco departments, so there was no more uptempo dance records, everything was downtempo,' Knuckles later recalled in Bill Brewster and Frank Broughton's book *Last Night a DJ Changed My Life*. 'That's when I realised I had to start changing certain things in order to keep feeding my dance floor.'

Knuckles' solution was to start making his own dance mixes as a way of refreshing classic songs and giving them a new and contemporary lease of life. The DJ started assembling his reworkings by hand using a reel-to-reel tape recorder and, although similar tactics were also being employed to rescue dance floors in New York and elsewhere, the effect on Chicago was seismic. 'They went for it immediately,' Knuckles recalled in an interview for the Red Bull Music Academy in 2018. 'They would rush to the record stores the next day looking for that particular version and never find it. It used to drive the record stores crazy.'

At the end of 1984 Knuckles left the Warehouse and set up a new club, the Power Plant. Knuckles' decision was initially a blow to the Warehouse management, but the timing was fortuitous as the lease on their original premises expired shortly after Knuckles' departure, which allowed the club to quietly relocate and then reopen as the Music Box with a dynamic new DJ in place in an attempt to win back their old audience. Originally from Chicago, the new DJ, Ron Hardy, had spent the previous few years honing his DJ craft in Los Angeles and the impact of his return to his hometown cannot be underestimated. While Hardy lacked Knuckles' technical finesse and attention to detail, he was young, exciting and enthusiastic and performed with a kind of reckless, infectious enthusiasm that made his DJ sets a thing of legend. 'Ron Hardy was the greatest DJ that ever lived,' Marshall Jefferson told *i-D* magazine in 1995. 'It took a really special DJ to make people forget about Frankie, but Ron Hardy tore up shit so tough that the Power Plant gave up Saturdays and only opened on Fridays. They were competitive. Like two gunslingers.'

In addition to expanding, adapting and changing disco tracks to better suit his new playlists, and in an echo of the early electro experimentation that Afrika Bambaataa was exploring in New York, Frankie Knuckles began to move away from the disco format which had underpinned his early sets at the Warehouse in favour of adding tracks from across the musical spectrum: Philadelphia soul music sitting alongside tracks from Kraftwerk, Yello and Giorgio Moroder. Frankie Knuckles' transition to the Power Plant also saw the DJ introduce a drum machine into his DJ sets. 'I would use it live in the club,' Knuckles told Frank Broughton later, 'I would program different patterns into it throughout the week, and then use it throughout the course of a night, running it live, depending on the song and playing it underneath, or using it to segue between something.'

Ron Hardy followed suit, as did a group of virtuoso DJs who called themselves the Hot Mix 5 – Farley 'Jackmaster' Funk, Kenny 'Jammin' Jason, Mickey 'Mixin' Oliver, Ralphi Rosario and Scott 'Smokin' Seals – who launched a show on Chicago radio station WBMX to showcase their skills. 'We started experimenting, playing with drum machines,' Farley 'Jackmaster' Funk explained in Sheryl Garratt's book *Adventures in Wonderland*. 'In the early days, a kick drum and the electric tom-toms of the 808 was enough to make people dance without even putting any music to it. So a lot of stuff was just beat tracks in the beginning. Then we came to steal everybody's bass lines. See, all we ever did was regurgitate disco again by just stealing everybody's music. Because all the original house stuff that came out was somebody else's bass line.' Such was the popularity of the sets that after each broadcast

Chicago record shops would put up a list of the tracks the DJs had recently played so as not to have to deal with individual questions from customers keen to get their hands on the records.

The resultant sets, with their extended mixes, new edits, DJ sleight of hand, and additional drum machine rhythms became the template for what would quickly become known locally as house music. Although the term also had earlier street connotations in Chicago – 'For a long time the word "house" referred not to a particular style of music so much as to an attitude,' wrote Brewster and Broughton in *Last Night a DJ Saved My Life*, continuing, 'If a song was "house" it was music from a cool club, it was underground, it was something you'd never hear on the radio' – house music is generally acknowledged to be named after Frankie Knuckles' club – after Chicago record shops' practice of assigning the tunes Knuckles played to a section dedicated to 'Warehouse Music' or just 'House Music'.

So striking and new were the sounds that Knuckles, Hardy and the Hot Mix 5 were cooking up in their musical laboratories that it was inevitable that a new wave of musical artists should start to absorb those influences and use them as a template in the creation of a brand new music. Popular wisdom states that Jamie Principle's 'Your Love' was the first house record to be recorded; Frankie Knuckles had played it from tape as a mainstay of his sets for a year or so before it was finally pressed and released as a record, by which time Jesse Saunders' similarly groundbreaking 1984 single 'On And On' was already out.

With their newly pressed records in their hands, this new generation of artists needed to get their music heard, and the Chicago clubs became their testing ground. Frankie Knuckles was the target of choice for acts whose sound was smoother and more polished, while Ron Hardy was more likely to put his support behind more left field and experimental releases. 'I used to take my tapes down to Frankie. That's how you got your score, that's how you found out if that song was gonna make it or not; by giving it to Knuckles and, if the people screamed – I guess it was the energy of the club he worked in, the power of that system – if you got that crowd going it gave you a feeling like there was no stopping you,' Steve 'Silk' Hurley told the *NME*'s Simon Witter in 1987.

DJ Pierre, Earl 'Spanky' Smith Jr and Herbert Jackson approached Ron Hardy with a tape of a track entitled 'In Your Mind', which the trio had recorded under the name Phuture. 'We thought about all the DJs in Chicago that might be open to it and we could only come up with one, and that was Ron Hardy. He was the guy we listened to, we knew he played a lot of different sounds,' DJ Pierre told *The Fader* later. 'So we took it to Ron, and Ron said he liked it and then, as the story goes, he dropped it four times. The first two times, people were like "What the heck is this?" The third time people were like, "Okay, this sounds alright, I guess." Then the fourth time, people went crazy. So he literally broke the record. He could have played it twice and been like, forget it, these people don't get it. But he got it, and he had the vision that it was something.'

'In Your Mind' became a word of mouth success, with people talking about 'Ron Hardy's Acid Track' after the DJ's repeated plays at the Music Box, so Pierre, Smith Jr and Jackson retitled the song 'Acid Trax' and in 1987 signed it to Chicago label Trax, where producer Marshall Jefferson turned it into the first Phuture single. 'I thought it was fucking brilliant. Everyone thought I was nuts, but every time my friends said something was whack, I'd go ahead with it,' Jefferson told Sheryl Garratt in *Adventures in Wonderland*. By pushing the Roland TB-303 bass synthesiser to its limits – 'The resonant filter knobs were designed to be turned slightly to alter the tone of the bass. However if you twisted them rapidly in away they were never intended to be abused, the oddest squelching sound came out' Garratt explained – Phuture had unwittingly invented house's first sub-genre: acid house.

In the UK the acid house baton was picked up by an unlikely collaboration between Genesis P-Orridge's post-Throbbing Gristle project Psychic TV and The Grid, who featured Soft Cell's Dave Ball alongside producer Richard Norris. The collaboration resulted in a compilation album, *Jack The Tab – Acid Tablets Volume One*, which appeared to feature tracks from a range of artists – including Psychic TV, King Tubby and Godstar – although all the tracks were actually the work of Ball, P-Orridge and Norris. 'We thought, let's make the British equivalent of what we thought it should be: psychedelic dance music using and abusing technology to the fullest effect,' Dave Ball told writer Kris Needs later. 'The only space left that allowed for experimentation was the, ironically, once really conservative area of dance music,' P-Orridge told *Offbeat* in 1988.

'These compilations ushered in the British acid sound, a swampy, woozy reconciliation of Electric Ladyland with 'Autobahn' and dub reggae, enlivened by backwards drum fills, wolf howls, a looped phrase sung by the Hindu singer Najma, and snatches of '50s juvenile delinquent movies,' recalled writer Mark Dery in a retrospective piece on the scene for *Keyboard* magazine in 1992, in which he also considered that P-Orridge's interpretation of the term 'acid' house may have been at odds with that of the vehemently anti-drug stance of Phuture. 'Acid house came about in 1988 as a result of Throbbing Gristle member Genesis P-Orridge's felicitous misunderstanding of the house term, "acid," as in Phuture's 1987 single 'Acid Tracks', on the Chicago-based Trax label,' Dery wrote. 'To P-Orridge, a techno-pagan whose private pantheon is peopled with dandies and debauchees from Aleister Crowley to Brian Jones, "acid" conjured visions of paradise regained with the aid of confetti-sized squares of blotter paper.' Either way, Ball, P-Orridge and Norris's sonic experimentation, in all the guises they adopted for the *Jack The Tab* compilation, were among the first British acid house recordings, and although their success was strictly underground, the releases nevertheless fed into Britain's burgeoning dance culture.

As the new sounds coming out of Chicago became increasingly accepted, the movement itself began to fragment into sub-genres as the original innovators and new generations explored new directions. 'Well, the groove now is much more hypnotic,' Frankie Knuckles told the *NME*'s Simon Witter in 1987, explaining the direction his own music had taken, 'it has a very sexual feel, and the music is a lot more full-bodied, there's more to the production. The kids here call it "deep house", songs that are more serious in the lyrics, and have more music going on.' Knuckles also declared that the next chapter in the house music story was being written in Detroit, three hundred miles away from Chicago: 'Derrick May is the biggest thing this summer by far,' Knuckles enthused. 'His sound takes house to a new level, real energetic and spacey. It'll make any dance floor move.'

Derrick May was, alongside Juan Atkins and Kevin Saunderson, one of a trio of young musical pioneers emerging from Detroit who initiated a second seismic dance music revolution of their own. Fascinated by electronic music technology, Juan Atkins started spending more and more of his time in music shops, trying out the keyboards and saving up for his own equipment. Although he was familiar with some of the possibilities of electronic music through hearing Donna Summer's work with Giorgio Moroder, it was hearing Kraftwerk for the first time which provided the young Atkins with his Damascene moment. 'I just froze in my tracks,' Atkins told Sheryl Garratt later. 'Everything was so clean and precise, so robotic. That's what blew me away.' Atkins, in turn, shared his discovery with his friend Derrick May:

'[Atkins] brought the records around to my house,' May told *Melody Maker*'s Dave Simpson in 1992. 'I'd never heard them before in my life, man, and as soon as I heard them they were an automatic influence to me… Kraftwerk was always very culty, but it was very Detroit too because of the industry in Detroit, and because of the mentality. That music automatically appeals to the people like a tribal calling,' May continued. 'The music, man, it sounded like somebody making music with hammers and nails.'

The source of Atkins' introduction to Kraftwerk was a Detroit radio DJ who called himself The Electrifying Mojo and broadcast an extraordinary and eclectic playlist of songs on Detroit radio station WGPR. 'He was an underground cult hero,' Atkins told the Red Bull Music Academy later. 'We would listen to him religiously every night.' Mojo played music from artists across the musical spectrum and as well as being known as an important early champion of both Prince and The B-52's, his shows would frequently contain tracks from the likes of Kraftwerk, The Human League, Yazoo, Gary Numan and Depeche Mode.

Juan Atkins was the first of the trio to start making music of his own, and the influence of the European electronic artists played by The Electrifying Mojo all fed into his musical vision. By 1981 Atkins was ready to release his first record, 'Alleys Of Your Mind', which he had created with Richard Davies, also known as 3070. Released under the name Cybotron, one of the first people to hear the finished track was The Electrifying Mojo himself, who started to play 'Alleys Of Your Mind' on his show. 'Mojo was a fantastic visionary,' DJ Carl Craig told the Red Bull Music Academy later. 'He had a spiritual intergalactic quality to him. Mojo was playing music from around the world that was so impactful, not commercially but spiritually and creatively.'

With the support of The Electrifying Mojo, and with one foot in the world of electro – popularised by Afrika Bambaataa and his New York peers – and the other foot in the Detroit future, 'Alleys Of Your Mind' sold an estimated 15,000 copies in Detroit, and is now widely held to be the first tangible step away from the Chicago house sound and towards what would become Detroit techno. 'Chicago was an influence, but the sound they were creating was different,' Atkins explained in Sheryl Garratt's book *Adventures in Wonderland*. 'Detroit's music was more about alienation and a yearning to overcome. Techno had no soul.' Over the next few years Atkins and Davies put out further slices of proto-techno – including the groundbreaking 1983 single

'Clear' – before Atkins left Cybotron following disagreements with Davies over musical direction.

Atkins' first project after leaving Cybotron was a collaboration with Derrick May on the track 'Let's Go', which the duo put out under the name Xray as the first release on May's Transmat label in 1986. The second Transmat release was a Derrick May track called 'Nude Photo', which followed in 1987 under the name Rhythim Is Rhythim, widely considered the first techno release, although that wasn't a name yet associated with the emerging movement. A second Rhythim Is Rhythim single, 'Strings Of Life', followed later the same year, a curiosity which lacked a traditional bass line and was built from samples taken from recordings of orchestras. 'I want my music to sound like machines talking to each other. I don't want it to sound like a "real" band. I want it to sound like a technician made it. That's what I am: a technician with human feelings,' May told Sheryl Garratt later.

Given the European influences which fed into those early releases it's understandable that the UK was one of the first markets to embrace the new Detroit sound. Virgin Records commissioned a compilation album and Neil Rushton travelled to Detroit on behalf of the label to license tracks in collaboration with his US contact, Derrick May. Two journalists, *The Face*'s Stuart Cosgrove and the *NME*'s John McCready, joined the trip to report on the new Detroit scene, and it was while Cosgrove was interviewing Juan Atkins for his piece that the movement was dubbed 'techno' for the first time in print: 'Within the last five years or so, the Detroit underground has been experimenting with technology, stretching it rather than simply using it. As the price of sequencers and synthesisers has dropped, so the experimentation has become more intense. Basically we're tired of hearing about being in love or falling out, tired of the R&B system, so a new progressive sound has emerged,' Atkins told Cosgrove. 'We call it techno.' 'Juan threw the term "techno" in our face,' Derrick May told Kris Needs in an interview for *Black Echoes* later. 'When I'd first done 'Nude Photo', I said, "I'm not calling my shit techno; that's garbage, man." As far as I was concerned techno was considered hip-hop and I didn't want to be lumped in with hip-hop. Juan did it in an interview with *The Face* when Stuart Cosgrove said he need a name for the music and the whole concept. Juan stood up and said, "techno!" Voila!'

So perfectly did the new name fit the Detroit sound that the Virgin compilation, initially compiled under the working title *The House Sound Of Detroit*, was retitled *Techno! The New Dance Sound Of Detroit* and was released in

Juan Atkins, 1990.

1988 featuring tracks from Juan Atkins, Derrick May and Kevin Saunderson alongside the great and the good from contemporary Detroit's underground scene assembled by Derrick May. *Techno! The New Dance Sound Of Detroit* was almost released as an eleven-track album, as Rushton and May struggled to find a twelfth track to complete it, until Kevin Saunderson – who already had one track, 'Electronic Dance', on the compilation under the name KS Experience – presented a last-minute selection of tracks which included one, 'Big Fun', which he'd recorded with vocalist Paris Grey under the name Inner City. While *Techno! The New Dance Sound Of Detroit* failed to translate into significant sales for Virgin, it was when they released 'Big Fun' as a single in 1988 that they suddenly found themselves with a commercial hit on their hands. The single spent fourteen weeks in the UK singles chart, where it peaked at number eight at the end of September.

Inner City followed 'Big Fun' with 'Good Life' at the end of 1988 and scored an even bigger hit when the single spent a fortnight at a peak UK singles chart position of four in January 1989, selling in excess of 200,000 singles in the process. Inner City's hastily assembled debut album, *Paradise*, followed in May 1989 and entered the UK albums chart at a peak position of number three, a position it held for a fortnight on its way to spending six months in the charts and earning Saunderson and Grey a platinum album for 300,000 records sold.

At the same time, ZTT declared their interest in signing up Atkins, May and Saunderson together as a kind of techno supergroup under the name Intellex, and while Inner City's success subsequently ruled out Saunderson's involvement, the idea of Atkins and May working together in such a way got as far as contracts being drawn up for signature. 'We started discussions with ZTT,' Neil Rushton, acting on behalf of the US acts, told Dan Sicko in the latter's book *Techno Rebels: The Renegades of Electronic Funk*, 'they wanted to join in on techno and had this really dreadful idea that they would be the black Pet Shop Boys. I said "Oh shit, that's not what we want is it?" But Derrick said, "No, it'll be great!"' Despite his initial enthusiasm for the project, May subsequently decided that he was not prepared to appear on *Top of the Pops*, should an appearance be required, and the deal subsequently collapsed.

But Inner City weren't the first house act to enjoy success in the UK. The new dance revolution's shift into the UK mainstream was propelled in part by the unlikely hand of former Spandau Ballet producer, Landscape's Richard

Burgess. Burgess had been recruited to produce three tracks for emerging US artist Colonel Abrams' debut album, including what would become the latter's biggest hit, 'Trapped'. 'Trapped' was a monster hit for Abrams, spending three consecutive weeks at a peak position of number three in the UK singles chart in October and November 1985, part of an enviable twenty-four-week chart run and UK sales in excess of 400,000 copies.

For house purists, 'Trapped' was no more than a diluted interpretation of the Chicago sound, but to the uninitiated it was the first taste of a bright, new, dance-orientated sound which was quickly picked up by a rush of artists entering the same space in the hope of similar success. For many the first UK hit which truly represented the Chicago sound was Farley 'Jackmaster' Funk's 'Love Can't Turn Around', which came out on the DJ International label the following summer and scored the scene a Top 10 hit at the end of September 1986. Steve 'Silk' Hurley would have to wait another few months before scoring house's first number one single, 'Jack Your Body', which spent a fortnight at the top of the charts in January 1987.

But house had never been about commercial success and the scramble of new artists wanting to jump onto the bandwagon was anathema to the original spirit of the movement, as Frankie Knuckles told the *NME*'s Simon Witter in August: 'Too many [of the new artists] are trying to sound like Colonel Abrams, selling out for major deals. House represents basement music, club music, and if they forget that and go soft, kids will think that's what house is about. We're diehards. I'll sign to a major label, but only if they let me do what I want. Kissing ass is definitely out of the question.'

The commercial success of house and techno was enough for critics and social commentators to look more closely at the roots of the new sounds coming out of Detroit and Chicago. Much was made of the new movement's unlikely debt to European electronic pop, and for Depeche Mode the reappraisal presented an opportunity to position themselves as something other than unfashionable pop puppets. In 1989, as house and techno started to dominate the UK charts, *The Face* sent Depeche Mode to the USA to meet some of the architects of the original Detroit sound. Depeche Mode, it has to be said, were mostly bemused by their status as techno pioneers. 'When rave culture started, a lot of techno musicians cited Depeche Mode as big influences,' Daniel Miller told *Uncut* magazine's Stephen Dalton later. 'They didn't quite understand that initially. I understood it completely, but they didn't really like the music very much. They were partiers but not ravers.'

'In America, they are spoken about in the same reverential tones as New Order and even Kraftwerk. Frankie Knuckles won't deny owning a well-worn copy of 'Just Can't Get Enough' and Todd Terry will talk about them as his favourite dance group,' wrote John McCready in his feature for *The Face*. 'In America, Depeche Mode are a phenomenon, a white English 'pop' group respected on the black club scene in New York, Chicago and Detroit.' Depeche Mode spent an evening visiting the Detroit clubs with Derrick May, although it wasn't quite the kind of night out they were used to, as Andy Fletcher confessed to *Uncut* later: 'In those days, that scene was orange juice and no drugs. We just wanted a beer. It was frustrating.'

'They have dance in their blood,' Derrick May told John McCready over the course of the night. 'Aligning them with Nitzer Ebb, New Order, DAF, Yello and the rest of the European rhythm invaders, Derrick believes that Depeche Mode were an important part of the club collision that evolved as Chicago house,' McCready reported. 'The Detroit Techno sound was created on a musical diet of Clinton and European rhythm-based tracks like Depeche's classic 'People Are People'. This intercontinental collision at the heart of Chicago house, Techno and Todd Terry's New York sample sound is the key to the future of contemporary American dance music.'

'We can't create dance music, and I don't think we've ever really tried,' Depeche Mode's Martin Gore admitted to McCready in the same piece. 'We honestly wouldn't know where to start.' Dave Gahan was equally bewildered by Depeche Mode's unexpected role in the development of techno, but was happy to accept the accolades. 'I can feel the excitement of it,' Gahan admitted to McCready. 'In a way it's confirmed that what we are doing has been right all along. House seems to me the most important musical development of the eighties, in that it's combined dance and the electronic sound. What Derrick is doing looks to the future.'

By the time of their trip to Detroit, Depeche Mode had released a further three albums – *Some Great Reward*, *Black Celebration* and *Music For The Masses*, all of which made the Top 10 in the UK albums chart – since 1983's *Construction Time Again*. Looking back on that album in an interview with *Melody Maker*'s Jon Wilde in 1990, Gahan described *Construction Time Again* as 'a massive changing-point for us, both musically and lyrically.' The album represented the band's first step towards a more confident and self-assured Depeche Mode, or perhaps more correctly the first step away from the old Depeche Mode. 'We faced the problem that other people wouldn't allow us to grow up and develop. We came out in 1981 wearing these stupid clothes and found ourselves grouped with bands like Duran and Spandau,' Gahan continued. 'We just classed ourselves as a pop band.'

But in America, Depeche Mode were viewed rather differently. 'People Are People' was the band's first major hit in the USA when it reached number thirteen on the *Billboard* Hot 100 chart in August 1985, which meant that for many American fans their first view of Depeche Mode came through the 'People Are People' video, which featured the band dressed in uniform black while they pulled levers, bashed metal and posed on a warship, the performance intercut with vintage war footage of soldiers marching, parachutes ascending and descending, guns firing and scenes of the 'People Are People' single being pressed and manufactured. Gone were the sensible shirts and the mismatching outfits in favour of a more powerful, more purposeful, and altogether more sophisticated image than the one Depeche Mode had previously presented in the UK.

So successful was Depeche Mode's reinvention that by the end of the decade the band had become an unlikely stadium act in the USA, a fact they illustrated to great effect with the release of a double live album and concert film, *101*, in March 1989. Recorded on the previous year's *Music For The Masses* tour at the band's 101st and final show of the tour at the Rose Bowl in Pasadena, California – with OMD, Wire and Thomas Dolby in support – in front of a reported audience of 72,000 fans, *101* reached number five in the UK albums chart and, alongside the acclaim heading Depeche Mode's way from Detroit's techno community, was an important piece of propaganda in repositioning Depeche Mode as a successful, credible band in the eyes of the media.

As Depeche Mode took the *Music For The Masses* tour around the world in 1987 and 1988 they also introduced their young audience to a selection of carefully chosen support acts, among them Front 242 and Nitzer Ebb. Front 242 were the support act for the mainland European dates at the end of 1987, Nitzer Ebb for the tour's second run of European shows the following year. Both bands fell into another electronic music category, one which is almost too broad to be particularly useful, but which was very influential nonetheless: industrial music, a term invented to denote an extreme crossover between rock and electronic music.

The idea of classifying music as 'industrial' is generally acknowledged as originating with Throbbing Gristle and their American friend and co-

collaborator Monte Cazazza, with whom they coined the slogan 'Industrial Music for Industrial People' as a banner for music released on their Industrial Records label. The popular interpretation of 'industrial music' actually covers a vast spectrum of sounds and artistic approaches, from the electronic innovation of Cabaret Voltaire to the sonic experimentation and metallic collisions of Einstürzende Neubauten.

'Einstürzende Neubauten have long since dissolved borderlines between art and daily toil. For them, the act of creation is physically and emotionally draining work, the tools for which are a pneumatic drill, Black & Decker, bits of girder, tangled strands of steel, lead mallets, crowbars, old radios, bass and guitars,' reported the *NME*'s Chris Bohn when dispatched to Germany to report on the band in 1983. In fact it was Einstürzende Neubauten – the name translates from German as 'Collapsing New Buildings' – who were the first industrial act to pique the interest of Depeche Mode, as Martin Gore would tell the *NME*'s Don Watson in 1984: 'I was at their ICA date, when they did the Metal Concerto, and the power and the excitement of it was brilliant. What we're doing, though, is using the ideas in a different context, in the context of pop.'

While Depeche Mode were a long way from being architects of industrial music, their appropriation of industrial and metallic sampled sound in their work from 1983's *Construction Time Again* onwards went a long way towards introducing an entirely new audience to industrial concepts. 'We kinda subtly corrupt the world,' Gore told *Record Mirror*'s Andy Strickland in 1986, 'basically if you call yourself a pop band you can get away with anything.'

Influenced to make music by both Depeche Mode and Einstürzende Neubauten was US musician Trent Reznor, who in 1988 left Exotic Birds – the Cleveland, Ohio band he'd joined in 1985 and with whom he'd played support to artists including the Eurythmics – in favour of reinventing himself as Nine Inch Nails and releasing his debut album, *Pretty Hate Machine*, in 1989. 'I was hearing bands that were using electronics, and they didn't sound like Howard Jones or Re-Flex. They had all this fucking aggression and tension that the hardest of heavy metal or punk had. But they were using tools I understood,' Reznor told *Spin*'s Eric Weisbard later. 'And it seemed more interesting, because this music couldn't have been made five years ago, let alone twenty. It was based on tools that were now.'

In interviews Reznor admitted to being uncomfortable with the term 'industrial', particularly when it was applied to his own music, and tried to distance himself from the categorisation. 'What was originally called industrial music was about twenty years ago, Throbbing Gristle and Test Dept,' Reznor told *Axcess* magazine later. 'We have very little to do with it other than there is noise in my music and there is noise in theirs. I'm working in the context of a pop song structure whereas those bands didn't.' In an echo of Depeche Mode, Reznor's pop sensibility crossed *Pretty Hate Machine* into a far more commercial arena than most of Nine Inch Nails' peers, and the album has since racked up over ten million sales worldwide. 'I wanted to make Test Dept music, but a lifetime of growing up with AM radio pop and the idea of choruses, verses and hooks being instilled in me meant I couldn't help but think in terms of pop,' Reznor told The Quietus in 2014. 'I was intrigued by the idea of bringing in noise and using samples and found sounds, but through the blender and my style of writing, pop songs started coming out.'

Nine Inch Nails' position at the vanguard of the electronic rock scene also gave Trent Reznor the chance to acknowledge his influences in a very public way, allowing his audience to follow the threads that led to the launch of the project. In addition to acknowledging his debt to industrial pioneers Throbbing Gristle, Test Dept and Einstürzende Neubauten – Reznor later signed Einstürzende Neubauten to his Nothing Records label, and also invited Throbbing Gristle's Genesis P-Orridge to remix Nine Inch Nails' 'While I'm Still Here', and Peter 'Sleazy' Christopherson to collaborate on a variety of Nine Inch Nails remixes and film projects – Reznor was unabashed in citing the influence of newer acts, including Ministry, Skinny Puppy and Front 242, each of which was instrumental in taking the industrial electronic template and reshaping it for their own needs.

Of the three, Ministry was the act that aligned most closely with the idea of 'industrial' music as rock combined with electronics, and would also become the most successful of the three bands, with two US gold albums and one US platinum album – for *The Land of Rape And Honey*, *The Mind Is A Terrible Thing To Taste* and *Psalm 69*, respectively – to their name. Formed by Al Jourgensen in 1981, Ministry was originally an electro-pop act – in fact in Ministry's first interview for *Melody Maker* in 1982, Jourgensen waxed lyrical about both Simple Minds and Japan: 'I think Jim Kerr and David Sylvian are brilliant,' he told Adam Sweeting, 'absolute geniuses' – and over the course of 1982 played support to both Depeche Mode and A Flock Of Seagulls.

Distancing himself from the inconsequential pop of Ministry's 1983 debut album *With Sympathy* – which Jourgensen blamed on record company interference and his own inexperience of how to handle the music industry – the frontman became more interested in making his music tougher and more muscular. Ministry's sound quickly moved away from their early pop direction and, by the time they released their second album, *Twitch*, in 1986, the band had started to absorb the influence of acts including Cabaret Voltaire, Skinny Puppy and Front 242, as they adopted the tougher industrial trajectory that would come to define them.

Walking a similar path from pop to industrial rock, Skinny Puppy was born out of Canadian new wave band Images In Vogue, whose percussionist, Kevin Crompton, started working under that name as a side project with vocalist Kevin Ogilvie, a collaboration which allowed the duo to explore their mutual interest in the darker sonic possibilities suggested by Throbbing Gristle, Thomas Leer, Robert Rental and Cabaret Voltaire. After recording two albums with Images In Vogue, and playing support tours with both Duran Duran and Depeche Mode, Crompton left that band in 1985. Crompton and Ogilvie reinvented themselves as cEvin Key and Nivek Ogre, respectively, added Bill Leeb (who would later form Front Line Assembly) to the line-up and made Skinny Puppy their full-time concern.

Known for the precision of their beats, the harshness of their vocals and for their use of samples of movie dialogue, Skinny Puppy's modest commercial success belies their influence. Trent Reznor admits that the early Nine Inch Nails song 'Down In It' was heavily influenced by Skinny Puppy's 'Dig It', and Ministry's Al Jourgensen was such a fan that he produced and played on Skinny Puppy's 1989 album *Rabies*. Other fans include Moby, Tool and Marilyn Manson, the latter of whom is thought to have been inspired in his elaborate stagecraft by the theatrical presentation of Skinny Puppy's live show, which included fake blood, mock hangings and simulated vivisection. 'We started as a reaction to every other electronic band doing nothing on stage but having a keyboard player – now reduced to a laptop – and a person singing,' Ogre said later. 'I wanted to do something different. I started off quite primitive in the sense of trying to find things that would shock people.'

Similarly disconnected from the core music business axis of London, New York and Los Angeles were Front 242, who hailed from Brussels, Belgium. Echoing Kraftwerk's intent to create a new music, free of Anglo-American influence, Front 242 set out on a similar creative journey and chose to use electronics more through circumstance than by choice, as the band's Patrick Codenys explained to the Red Bull Music Academy later: 'If you live in

London and you need a drummer to start a band, you have twenty people ringing at your door if you put an announcement in the paper. In Belgium… No drummer? OK, I'll take a rhythm box. No bass player? OK, I'll take one synth to do the bass line.'

Taking inspiration from Throbbing Gristle and Cabaret Voltaire, Front 242 was formed by in 1981 by Daniel Bressanutti, who released the band's debut single before recruiting Codenys and Jean-Luc De Meyer, who had been working on electronic music together as Underviewer since 1978, to the band. Front 242 released their debut album, *Geography*, in 1982. 'When we first started the situation was very frustrating,' Bressanutti told *Option*'s David Shirley in 1993. 'Everywhere you went, it was always the same; it was never what you wanted to hear. We thought that maybe we could use synthesisers to make music that we wanted ourselves.' Front 242 started playing live the following year and recruited Richard Jonckheere, known as Richard 23, as a dynamic live frontman to bring energy to their presentation. 'The last thing we wanted was the kind of cool, disinterested image that you have in a lot of electronic bands, with a bunch of guys just standing behind keyboards,' Patrick Codenys told Shirley in the same feature. 'We've worked really hard to bring energy and excitement to our live performances.'

Front 242 took their live show to the USA for the first time in 1984 when, in support of their second album, *No Comment*, they opened for Ministry, their first step towards the critical and commercial success they would later enjoy in America. That success started with 1988's *Front By Front* album, from which Front 242 released the single 'Headhunter', which peaked at number thirteen on the *Billboard* Dance Chart. Popular myth states that the video for 'Headhunter', a black-and-white film from Anton Corbijn – which features the band in various industrial settings, dressed in black and sporting their trademark dark glasses – is full of visual references to eggs after Corbijn misheard the song title and instead drew up a storyboard to accompany a single called 'Egghunter'.

Although they conducted their business with intellectual rigour, Front 242 never lost sight of the fact that they were essentially a dance band: 'We've always talked about it,' Richard 23 told *Rif Raf* magazine's Alain Benisty. 'This movement [dance music] was considered as the poor relation of music. Anyone making dance had no future, no horizon, which was false. To my mind, it is the musical genre the closest to people. From the beginning, it is not a music you listen to at home, it is the music of your most intense moments.

When you go out, when you dance, you're generally at your highest.' As a result, Front 242 took a keen interest in what was happening in music at the time, particularly in the eclectic selection of acts which were at the vanguard of the next electronic generation.

Towards the end of 1987, UK proto-shoegazers AR Kane decided they wanted to make a dance record. Recently signed to 4AD Records the duo – Alex Ayuli and Rudy Tambala, who recruited Russell Smith to work on the record with them – were matched with the label's Colourbox – Martyn and Steve Young – with a view to working on a dance-orientated collaboration together. 'Originally we were trying to do a totally new thing,' Ayuli told *Sounds*' Robin Gibson in September 1987. 'But for some reason, after talking and throwing things around, we realised it just wasn't gonna work out... square pegs and round holes. Colourbox's approach is very methodical, almost tutored. Ours goes on gut reaction, and noise.' Instead the two acts decided to each record a track and then turn their work over to the other for extra input. 'There wasn't much of a collaboration going on, really. We let 'em get on with their side, and they stuck a guitar track on ours...' admitted Martyn Young.

The two tracks – Colourbox's 'Pump Up The Volume' and AR Kane's 'Anitina' – were then mixed by DJs C.J. Mackintosh and Dave Dorrell and put on either side of a double A-side single which was released under the name M/A/R/R/S – Martyn, Alex, Rudi, Russell, Steve – at the end of August. Three weeks later the single – propelled by 'Pump Up The Volume', which was also released as a remix – was in the Top 10 of the UK singles chart, where it spent six weeks, including two weeks at number one at the start of October. At M/A/R/R/S's chart peak, the production team Stock Aitken Waterman took out an injunction against the record for its unauthorised use of a sample of their hit 'Roadblock'. In fact 'Pump Up The Volume' was almost entirely constructed from samples from other records, including material from Afrika Bambaataa, James Brown, Public Enemy, Kool & The Gang and D.ST. The injunction and subsequent legal wrangling also had the effect of putting sampling firmly in the eyes of the mainstream. 'In the music industry, ethics and aesthetics become blurred very quickly,' wrote Jon Savage in a piece for the *Observer* at the time. 'The difficulty is how to judge whether sampling is used creatively, which, although potentially important in law, is very much a matter of personal interpretation.'

'You can't be Luddite about it,' Stock Aitken Waterman's Pete Waterman told *Q* magazine later the same year. 'You can't stop people sampling on bass and snare drum. But if you steal lines or musical phrases, that's the integrity of the performance. The limits should be defined. The BPI have to put up a code of practice and enforce it.' M/A/R/R/S's Martyn Young was also at pains to defend the true nature of his band's work, as he explained to the *NME*'s Sean O'Hagan in November 1987: 'A lot of what people think is actually sampled on 'Pump Up The Volume' is really CJ scratching. Scratching is actually more creative than sampling. With sampling you are basically limited to a staccato effect whereas a good scratcher can really mess things up.'

In his *Observer* piece, Jon Savage also referred to another act battling with the legal implications of sampling, The Justified Ancients Of Mu Mu, whose recent album *1987 (What The Fuck Is Going On?)* had been withdrawn after ABBA objected to an unauthorised sample of their hit 'Dancing Queen'. *Sounds* sat down with The Justified Ancients Of Mu Mu's Rockman Rock and King Boy D (later revealed to be Jimmy Cauty and Bill Drummond) and found the duo unrepentant. 'It doesn't bother us,' declared Cauty. 'Their records are still there, it's not as if we're taking anything away, just borrowing and making things bigger. If you're creative you aren't going to stop working just because there is a law against what you're doing.' 'It's like saying Andy Warhol just stole other people's graphics, which he didn't,' added Drummond. 'He took other people's images and re-cycled them and re-used them. That doesn't mean he's robbed them and left them with nothing. We're just doing musically what he did with Campbell's soup cans and pictures of Marilyn Monroe.'

In the same way that affordable synthesisers had put musical tools in the hands of aspiring musicians in the wake of punk, the affordable sampler – an entry-level model could be purchased for just a couple of hundred pounds at the end of the eighties – had a similarly empowering effect on a new generation of musicians and DJs. In February 1988, Bomb The Bass, a studio collaboration led by Tim Simenon with the assistance of Pascal Gabriel, had a major hit for Mute Records' dance offshoot Rhythm King with 'Beat Dis', which followed the same sample-heavy template as 'Pump Up The Volume'. 'I got into splicing tape and became fascinated by chopping things up and putting samples into a different order,' Simenon told *The Guardian* in 2021. 'I was eighteen years old and completely naive. Royalties didn't cross my mind.' 'The first cheap sampler had come out a month before, which was revolutionary because you could completely rearrange a record at whim,' Gabriel added in the same piece. 'Multi-tracks had been a real pain in the arse and took forever but this way was really quick.' 'Beat Dis' spent two weeks at a peak position of number two in the UK singles chart at the end of February and the beginning of March 1988, only kept from the top spot by Kylie Minogue's 'I Should Be So Lucky'.

Sharing the Top 10 with 'Beat Dis' was 'Doctorin' The House' from Coldcut – Matt Black and Jonathan More – who were also unashamed advocates of sampling. 'It's like the whole history of recorded sound is waiting there for us to murder,' Black had told the *NME* the previous November. 'And I can't wait to get my hands on Jonathan's weird records and make them make the sound that I want.' Having released 'Say Kids, What Time Is It?' as a limited-edition single for clubs at the start of 1987, and having enjoyed their first success as remixers of Eric B. & Rakim's 'Paid In Full' later the same year, 'Doctorin' The House' saw Coldcut recruit previously unknown singer Yazz for their first full release under the Coldcut name. 'Doctorin' The House' spent nine weeks in the UK singles chart in the spring of 1988, including a month in the Top 10 and a week at its chart peak of number six. The single would be Coldcut's biggest chart success, and Yazz would go on to score one of the year's biggest singles with the Coldcut-produced 'The Only Way Is Up', which stayed in the charts for four months and spent five weeks at number one in August 1988, selling around half a million records in the process.

In March 1988, a fortnight after 'Beat Dis' left the UK singles chart, the Rhythm King label's next single, also made in collaboration with Pascal Gabriel, was released. S-Express's 'Theme From S-Express' went on to spend over three months in the charts, including six weeks in the Top 10 and two weeks at number one. The work of London DJ Mark Moore, 'Theme From S-Express' was careful to obscure its sources: 'I can't say exactly what's in it. I'd be arrested! No, not really. It's 100 per cent original. We wrote and played everything ourselves… we're signed to a proper label and we have to uphold the law,' Moore told *Melody Maker*'s Push in April, although he couldn't resist adding, 'There are loads of excellent ideas which the law simply won't permit.'

Excellent ideas which the law simply won't permit was very much at the heart of the next project from Jimmy Cauty and Bill Drummond, who in 1988 had dropped the name The Justified Ancients Of Mu Mu in favour of calling themselves The Timelords and releasing a novelty single, 'Doctorin' The Tardis', predominantly built on samples from the theme music to *Doctor Who*, The Sweet's 'Block Buster' and Gary Glitter's 'Rock And Roll (Part Two)'.

'Doctorin' The Tardis' was a number one hit for The Timelords – Lord Rock and Time Boy (Cauty and Drummond) alongside Ford Timelord, a 1968 Ford Galaxie American police car which was allegedly the brains behind the project – in June. 'They asked me for permission on behalf of the car, Ford Timelord, who had this idea for what turned out to be 'Doctorin' The Tardis'. I of course agreed immediately,' Gary Glitter told the *NME*'s Jack Barron in June. 'When we bought the car everything seemed to be normal,' Cauty added helpfully, 'but then things started to get a bit out of hand.'

Drummond and Cauty's subsequent singles would be released over the course of the next two years under the name The KLF, who went on to have another number one single with '3 A.M. Eternal'; two number two singles with 'Last Train To Trancentral' and 'Justified And Ancient'; and a number five single with 'What Time Is Love?' before the end of 1991, in the process positioning themselves as true musical mavericks. 'A lot of the time people see us as a couple of scamsters, I'm sure,' Drummond told *The Face* later the same year. 'Sometimes I wish we were. Life might be easier. Then we wouldn't be in the studio every day of the week worrying about edits and the like.'

It was Bomb The Bass's Tim Simenon who, in putting a smiley face image on the sleeve of the 'Beat Dis' single, sparked the imagination of an entire new generation of clubbers when the logo was adopted as the symbol of UK dance music's newest sensation, initially dubbed acid house but quickly extended to rave. Inspired by the use of the smiley symbol in his favourite comic book series, *Watchmen*, Simenon was nonplussed about his unwitting contribution to the scene and, in an interview with *Melody Maker*'s Everett True at the end of 1988, admitted, 'I used it simply because I liked the comic.' Simenon was much more enthusiastic about the new rave music, however. 'It's the music of the future,' he declared in the same interview. 'It's got off to a bad start because of the name, but once all the furore dies away and the media find something else to crucify, the music will progress, digging deep underground. This is what's going on now, and this is how I want my music to sound – futuristic, electronic.'

'The official line is this. Yes, there are some drugs involved but not as much as you'd like to think,' wrote Paolo Hewitt in a feature on the dance scene for the *NME* in October. 'Instead why don't you concentrate on the good things. The new music, the attitude, the fact that we now have a movement as big as punk on our hands.' 'Acid is going underground,' DJ Paul Oakenfold predicted in the same feature. 'It's got to go that way because of all the fuss.

The media are out to kill it.' 'We are now witnessing the acid movement breaking out of London and becoming fashionable, and it's right across the country, hence the smiley badge and T-shirt craze,' added D Mob's Danny D, whose anthemic 'We Call It Acieed' peaked at number three in the UK singles chart the same month. 'Personally, I would give it six months to a year. Let's not forget, though, that the acid movement has brought thousands of people back into the clubs. It's pumped a new energy into the dance movement. All kinds of people are going along now to find out what it's about.'

And all kinds of people were. As a measure of how far from the underground acid house actually was, by September 1988 *The Sun* was cheerfully peddling smiley T-shirts under the headline 'It's Groovy And It's Cool – It's Our Acid House T-Shirt' and D Mob's 'We Call It Acieed' had been introduced on *Top of the Pops* by relentlessly mainstream Radio 1 DJ Steve Wright, resplendent in his own smiley T-shirt. 'Out of all the options open to British youth, acid house had proved to be the most attractive,' wrote the *NME*'s Paolo Hewitt in a second piece at the end of the year. 'For the musicians involved, acid house is a case of "can you steal it?", for the club goer it is "can you feel it?". And the answer on both counts is a resounding "yes!"'

When it came, towards the end of October, the backlash against rave culture was swift and uncompromising. '*The Sun* kicked off such an anti-acid fuss that Burton's decided it would no longer stock smiley-adorned garments, the Mecca group banned raves from its venues and acid hits like D Mob's 'We Call It Acieed' and Jolly Roger's 'Acid Man' were excluded from coverage on *Top of the Pops*,' wrote the *NME*'s Andy Crysell in a retrospective piece on the rave scene in 1998. 'Consequently, 1989 was the year acid house went ballistic, with raves attracting upwards of 10,000 punters; who'd buy tickets from agents listed on the mammoth-sized flyers, phone an 0898 number or tune into pirate radio stations like Centre Force to find the location of the bash, then head off in expansive convoys, dodging the police in the hope they'd eventually make it to the field where DJs like Carl Cox and Judge Jules were holding court on massive stages.'

As rave exploded and the mainstream press went into overdrive in their condemnation of the scene, more and more clubbers signed up to take part in what became dubbed 'The Second Summer of Love'. The police, charged with stopping the movement, were fighting a losing battle as a new network of organisers and promoters put on in excess of 200 events a week around the UK. The sudden proliferation of parties and raves also had the effect of forcing the events to be more competitive as they wrestled for the patronage of the public, and as a result the events increased in size and scale. 'It was no longer good enough to proclaim on the garish flyers for your bash that you had a 20K sound system and ten DJs playing. Now you had to promise a 75K system, at least 30 DJs and five live acts – whether it was true or not,' declared Andy Crysell in his *NME* retrospective.

Stepping up to satiate the rave scene's new appetite for acts which were able to bring elements of live performance to events in addition to DJ sets were a disparate selection of acts – 808 State, Adamski, The Shamen, Black Box and Orbital among them – each joining the circus from different directions. Prior to embracing the rave scene, Scottish indie band The Shamen had been exploring psychedelic rock before embracing the possibilities of dance music. 'We decided that the real excitement was happening in the dance sphere, using new technology,' the band's Colin Angus told *Q* magazine in 1990, 'and the origin for bands doing that kind of stuff wasn't new then – it had come from the Gang Of Four, New Order and Cabaret Voltaire. What we were trying to do wasn't radical in this respect; what was radical was trying to put upfront heavy rhythm tracks with well-composed, melodic pieces.'

'The first gig we did was in the summer of '89 and it was obvious from the start that people were into the idea of seeing live techno,' recalled Orbital's Paul Hartnoll in Crysell's *NME* piece. 'They were crowding round the front of the stage and were genuinely interested in seeing what we were doing. And the DJs never seemed jealous because they knew we were limited to what we'd produced, whereas they could come screaming back in with a fantastic Todd Terry or whoever.' '[We were] making music before the term house was around,' Hartnoll told the *NME*'s Stephen Dalton in a similar conversation in 1992. 'We were listening to New Order and Divine, a lot of Hi-NRG, Cabaret Voltaire, Kraftwerk. We were just lucky, the sort of thing we were doing became popular.' 'We're not musicians onstage; we're sort of arrangers and conductors,' Hartnoll explained to *The Boston Globe*'s Jim Sullivan later. 'We have all our sequencers primed and ready to go, but we decide what to play as we're going along. We feed off the audience. We sit there with basic sequences and throw things in and out willy-nilly, as we fancy.'

Underworld had enjoyed a tiny piece of chart success as a band called Freur, whose 'Doot-Doot' single had reached number fifty-nine in the UK singles chart in April 1983, catching the attention of Heaven 17's Martyn Ware, who nominated them as 1983's Best Group and Most Promising Act

For 1984 in *Smash Hits*' festive edition at the end of 1983. Freur disbanded in 1986 and the band's Karl Hyde and Rick Smith subsequently formed Underworld, who disbanded briefly in 1990 after releasing two pop-funk albums, at which point they embarked on a brief sabbatical before recruiting DJ Darren Emerson and returning to music in 1991. 'We had a sense, even before the old Underworld had finished, that acid house was happening,' Smith told *The Guardian*'s David Bennun when asked about the recruitment of Emerson in a retrospective on the band in 1999. 'We tried a couple of experiments, but we weren't part of that culture. It was so bogus, it was never going to work. We were taking a karaoke approach.' The combination of Hyde and Smith's electronic rock background and Emerson's experiences as a hip-hop and house DJ made them perfect for the rave scene, and Underworld started building a live reputation, performing at rock venues, festivals and dance clubs.

In Essex another band was taking a similar route. The Prodigy was originally adopted as a DJ name by teenage electro fan Liam Howlett. 'Like Grandmaster Flash had a grand name, larging himself up with his name. When I first thought of the name, obviously I didn't consider it could be four people,' Howlett told *Rolling Stone* in 1997. 'It was just me, faceless, in my bedroom, writing music: the prodigy.' The Prodigy expanded into a group after Keith Flint and Leeroy Thornhill offered to perform as dancers to accompany Howlett's DJ sets, and the trio then expanded further to include the MC talents of Keith Palmer, who called himself Maxim Reality. 'All we wanted to do when we started off was play the clubs we were going to as ravers,' Howlett admitted in Ben Thompson's book *Seven Years of Plenty*. The Prodigy did exactly that and in doing so built up enough of a buzz that Howlett was quickly signed by XL Recordings, who put out the band's debut release, the *What Evil Lurks* EP, in February 1991, followed by a single, 'Charly', in August.

Propelled by the enthusiasm of the burgeoning rave scene, 'Charly' entered the UK singles chart at number nine at the end of August and spent six weeks in the Top 10, including two consecutive weeks at number three in September. The Prodigy's next single, 'Everybody In The Place', reached number two in January 1992, and the band scored four further hit singles and a Top 20 album, *Experience*, by the end of 1993, by which time Howlett realised that something had to change. 'When I wrote 'Charly' I thought it was a mad underground tune. Soon as it got in the charts I began to think

"Oh f---",' Howlett told the *NME* in December 1992. 'It wasn't the direction I wanted The Prodigy to go in. I haven't written another record like it – it's something you can only do one of.'

The Prodigy reinvented themselves again and again, effortlessly blurring the boundaries between genres and styles. 'We've always been a band, I believe, that has kind of stolen and thieved elements we like out of cultures we've dipped out feet into,' Liam Howlett told PopMatters. 'We came from the dance culture originally, but when that disappeared, we just kept on stealing bits we liked out of it and re-presenting them in different ways. And then we stole bits out of the punk culture that we liked, without trying to be too obvious, to make them into something new. I think we'll just carry on stealing things as we go along. You know, that's just what we do.'

'The question is where does electronic music begin or end?' muses Daniel Miller today as he looks back over the forty-five years since releasing 'T.V.O.D.' as The Normal in 1978. 'All music is electronic music now, or it uses electronic devices, even traditional rock bands are processing their sounds.' 'I would agree with that. With all the sampling it's a bit of a con,' pondered Vince Clarke when asked the same question. 'I can't play trumpet but on a keyboard I can make a trumpet sound,' he added after a moment's thought: 'I suppose electronic music is a bit of a con really.'

FURTHER READING

Listening To The Music The Machines Make was inspired by my reading of previous titles which broadly covered the same period of music history: the late seventies and early eighties which was not only a dizzyingly exciting chapter in the history of popular music, but also coincided with the period when my personal taste in music was being shaped and formed. While reading around the subjects covered here it occurred to me that, although there are titles available which tell some of the individual stories of the artists and releases which shaped the same period of time, there wasn't one book which brought all of those things together and laid them over each other to present everything as a single story.

At the same time I began to realise that, perhaps inevitably given that decades have passed since the original events took place, recent accounts of the same period are sometimes misremembered or misrepresented, and sometimes history has been entirely rewritten to better fit the narrative. For that reason, wherever possible, I made the decision to go back to the original sources whenever I could and to that end I spent many days at the British Library where I immersed the music, style and cultural press of the late seventies and early eighties to collect the thousands of individual reports, features, interviews and reviews which form the backbone of this book. Thank you to the writers of those original pieces which appeared in editions of *The Face*, *Flexipop*, *i-D*, *Melody Maker*, *New Sounds New Styles*, the *NME*, *Record Mirror*, *Smash Hits*, *Sounds*, *ZigZag* and beyond between 1978 and 1983.

Many of the key characters in this story have gone on to write their own career-spanning autobiographies which inevitably include chapters and sections that focus on the same period and events covered in this book. New Order and Joy Division are best represented in this category with one memoir from Bernard Sumner (*Chapter & Verse*, Bantam, 2014) and two each from Peter Hook (*Unknown Pleasures*, Simon & Schuster, 2012 and *Substance*, Simon & Schuster, 2016) and Stephen Morris (*Record Play Pause*, Constable, 2019 and *Fast Forward*, Constable, 2020). There are three memoirs from Spandau Ballet: Martin Kemp's *True* (Orion, 2000), Tony Hadley's *To Cut A Long Story*

Short (Sidgwick & Jackson, 2004) and Gary Kemp's *I Know This Much* (Fourth Estate, 2009), and there are two each from Duran Duran - Andy Taylor's *Wild Boy* (Orion, 2008) and John Taylor's *In The Pleasure Groove* (Sphere, 2012) - and Gary Numan - *Praying To The Aliens* (Andre Deutsch, 1997) and *R(evolution)* (Constable, 2020). There are also interesting and useful autobiographies from Steve Strange (*Blitzed!*, Orion, 2002), Midge Ure (*If I Was*, Virgin, 2004), Boy George (*Take It Like A Man*, Sidgwick & Jackson, 1995), Marc Almond (*Tainted Life*, Sidgwick & Jackson, 1999), Dave Stewart (*Sweet Dreams Are Made Of This*, New American Library, 2016) and Thomas Dolby (*The Speed Of Sound*, Icon, 2017).

The genres covered in the first part of the book - exploring the musical influences that helped to shape the synth pop pioneers - are also reasonably well covered but key titles would include Jon Savage's *England's Dreaming* (Faber & Faber) covering punk rock; Barney Hoskyns' *Glam!* (Faber & Faber, 1998), Dave Thompson's *Children Of The Revolution* (Cherry Red, 2010), Simon Reynolds' *Shock And Awe* (Faber & Faber, 2016) and Alwyn Turner's *Dandies In The Underworld* (V&A, 2013) on glam rock; Peter Shapiro's revised *Turn The Beat Around* (Faber & Faber, 2009), Daryl Easlea's *Everybody Dance* (Helter Skelter, 2004), Dave Thompson's *I Feel Love* (Backbeat Books, 2021) and Nile Rodgers' *Le Freak* (Sphere, 2011) covering disco; and Julian Cope's *Krautrocksampler* (Head Heritage, 1995), Rudi Esch's Electri_city (Omnibus, 2016), and David Stubbs' *Future Days* (Faber & Faber, 2014) on Krautrock.

There are a multitude of titles covering the career and influence of David Bowie but I found David Buckley's *Strange Fascination* (Virgin, 1999) Dylan Jones' *When Ziggy Played Guitar* (Preface, 2012) particularly useful within the scope of this book. David Buckley's *Publikation* (Omnibus, 2012) was equally informative on the subject of Kraftwerk, as were Wolfgang Flür's *I Was A Robot* (Omnibus, 2017) and Pascal Bussy's *Kraftwerk: Man, Machine and Music* (SAF, 1995). Jon Savage's *This Searing Light, The Sun And Everything Else* (Faber & Faber, 2019) provides vivid insight into the career of Joy Division, while Dave Thompson's *True Faith* (Helter Skelter, 2005) and Mick Middles' *Factory - The Story Of A Record Label* (Virgin, 1996) were both useful references for all things Joy Division and New Order.

Mike Humphreys & Johnny Waller's official OMD biography *Messages* (Sidgwick & Jackson, 1987) is well worth hunting out, as is Richard Houghton's more recent official biography of the band, *Pretending To See The Future* (This Day In Music, 2019). Soft Cell's official biography, *Soft Cell*, by

Simon Tebbutt (Sidgwick & Jackson, 1984) and Gary Numan's first official biography, *Gary Numan* by Ray Coleman (Sidgwick & Jackson, 1982) were also useful, as were Steve Malins' *Duran Duran: Notorious* (Andre Deutsch, 2006) and *Depeche Mode: A Biography* (Cooper Square Press, 2001). Simon Spence's *Just Can't Get Enough* (Jawbone, 2011) also provides an insight into the formation and early career of Depeche Mode. The first five years of The Human League are well documented in Peter Nash's *Perfect Pop: The Human League* (Star, 1982) and Alaska Ross's *The Story Of A Band Called The Human League* (Proteus, 1982)

Some of the ideas explored in the second part of the book, charting the development of electronic pop music between 1978 and 1983, are also documented, notably Dave Rimmer's *The Look* (Omnibus, 2003) and *Like Punk Never Happened* (Faber & Faber, 1986) which cover the New Romantics and the New Pop respectively; Graham Smith's *We Can Be Heroes* (Unbound, 2012) which looks at London's clubland in the latter part of the seventies and into the early eighties; and Simon Reynolds' *Rip It Up And Start Again* (Faber & Faber, 2005), and its companion volume *Totally Wired* (Faber & Faber, 2009), which examine the same era and more broadly explore the foundations of the various musical genres and sub-genres of that time.

The final part of the book, which looks at some of the directions electronic pop music took in the decade after 1983 was informed by Bill Brewster & Frank Broughton's *Last Night A DJ Saved My Life* (Headline, 2000); Matthew Collin's *Altered State* (Serpent's Tail, 1997) and *Rave On* (Serpent's Tail, 2018); Sheryl Garratt's Adventures In Wonderland (Headline, 1999). *The Face* magazine's *Nightfever* (Boxtree, 1997) and *Keyboard* magazine's *The Evolution of Electronic Dance Music* (Backbeat, 2011), each provide very different stories of electronic and dance music through collected features collated from those respective journals. Dan Sicko's *Techno Rebels: The Renegades Of Electronic Funk* (Billboard, 1999) and S. Alexander Reed's *Assimilate: A Critical History Of Industrial Music* (Oxford University Press, 2013) provided useful insights into the various industrial genres.

Broader in their scope, but valuable nonetheless, I can also recommend Dylan Jones' *Sweet Dreams* (Faber & Faber, 2020), Lori Majewski & Jonathan Bernstein's *Mad World* (Abrams Image, 2014) and David Stubbs *Mars By 1980 - The Story of Electronic Music* (Faber & Faber, 2018). Theo Cateforis' *Are We Not New Wave? Modern Pop At The Turn Of The 1980s* (University of Michigan Press, 2011) provided a thoughtful and immaculately researched insight into the American perspective of the same period covered by *Listening To The Music*

The Machines Make. Equally impressive was Jaki Florek and Paul Whelan's oral history *Liverpool Eric's: All The Best Clubs Are Downstairs, Everybody Knows That* (Feedback, 2009).

For consistency chart dates and positions are taken from the Official Charts website, but Tony Jasper's *The Top Twenty Book* (Javelin, 1986) and Barry Lazell's guide to the independent charts, *Indie Hits 1980 - 1989* (Cherry Red, 1997), were also invaluable reference sources. For the same reason of consistency all *Top Of The Pops* dates and statistics are taken from the unofficial but exhaustive *Top Of The Pops* Archive website, but additional insights into the history of *Top Of The Pops* comes from Steve Blacknell's *The Story Of Top Of The Pops* (PSL, 1985) and Ian Gittins' *Top Of The Pops: Mishaps, Miming and Music* (BBC Books, 2007).

Thank you to the teams at *Electronic Sound* and *Classic Pop* magazines for creating such compelling recent archives of writing on electronic music across the genres, and for revisiting some of the events and releases covered in *Listening To The Music The Machines Make* with such rigour and respect. Your efforts were invaluable in the writing of this book.

The task of assimilating all this information and assembling it into the book you are now holding in your hands was entirely mine and, despite the best efforts of everyone who helped and advised me along the way, I also take responsibility for any errors or misinterpretations which may have crept into the story. I hope there aren't too many of those but if you find one then please let me know via the Listening to the Music the Machines Make companion website – inventingelectronicpop.com – in case I'm able to update the text in time for future editions, and thank you to Chi Ming Lai for doing just that for this paperback edition.

PICTURE CREDITS

INDEX